Constitutional Powers of Florida's State and Local Governments

by

Patrick John McGinley

of the Florida Bar and District of Columbia Bar

ISBN: 978-1-5136-5908-4

Printed in the United States of America.

Distributed by IngramSpark, a U.S. subsidiary of Ingram Content Group.

DEDICATION

To my wife Bernadette,
To our children Patrick and Madeleine,
To the Blessed Virgin Mary, Mother of God,
but above all,
To our Lord and Savior, Jesus Christ.

OTHER BOOKS BY THIS AUTHOR

FLORIDA ELEMENTS OF AN ACTION

FLORIDA MUNICIPAL LAW AND PRACTICE

FLORIDA WORKERS' COMPENSATION

FLORIDA INSURANCE LAW (with co-authors)

INTERPRETING FLORIDA'S CONSTITUTION

ANALYZING FLORIDA'S CONSTITUTION (forthcoming May 2020)

Table of Contents

Chapter One

Federalism and Subnational Governments

A. Why Do States Have Constitutions?

If you are familiar with the U.S. Constitution, then you know it to be the supreme law of the land. You know it to be applicable everywhere in the United States of America: throughout all 50 states, all sixteen territories, and the District of Columbia. You know it to be an adequate source of authority for striking down unconstitutional legislation or government action. With the U.S. Constitution being so broadly applicable and powerful, why do states have their own constitutions?

The historian could answer that states had constitutions before the enactment of the U.S. Constitution. Historians tell us that the similarities between some language in the U.S. Constitution and some language in the constitutions of the original thirteen colonies is because the federal constitution was inspired by the colonies' constitutions. The historian could also answer that before the U.S. Supreme Court's incorporation doctrine made the U.S. Constitution's Bill of Rights applicable to the states, state constitutions were the primary source of individual rights. The historian's answers tell us how state constitutions arose and what purpose they served in the past. The historian's answers do not tell us why state constitutions persist in the modern era.

The pragmatist could answer that states have constitutions as an organic source of law for establishing state and local governments. Indeed, the source and structure of any given state's legislative, executive, and judicial branches of state government is found in its state constitution. The pragmatist's answer describes a role that state constitutions play in our federal republic. The pragmatist's answer does not tell us why states desire a separate constitution to address issues that could be addressed uniformly in the federal constitution or in federal laws.

Perhaps the truest answer why state constitutions exist in the modern era is the human need for subsidiarity. Subsidiarity, as described by Saint Pope John Paul II's 1991 encyclical *Centesimus Annus*, means that:

> a community of a higher order should not interfere in the internal life of a community of a lower order, depriving the latter of its functions, but rather should support it in case of need and help to coordinate its activity with the activities of the rest of society, always with a view to the common good.

Stated somewhat differently, subsidiarity means that local problems sometimes require local solutions. Subsidiarity rejects the notion that all problem-solving power should be vested only with the highest sovereign or federal authority. Subsidiarity respects the proper role in problem solving by states, counties and cities, and where appropriate, by non-governmental organizations, private industry, religious institutions, corporations, charities and families. Elements of subsidiarity may be present in governmental structures, such as its explicit reference in Article 5 of the Treaty on European Union. Although the word subsidiarity may not appear as explicitly in the text of any U.S. state's constitution, state constitutions serve the purposes of subsidiarity when they empower state and local governments to solve state and local problems. People of good will crave a voice in solving the issues facing their communities and they deserve to be heard. Subsidiary brings government's problem-solving power closer to the people and increases their opportunity to be heard.

One benefit of subsidiarity in the context of subnational constitutional law is the ability to experiment on a regional level with new or expanded rights for the region's citizens. What if a given state wanted to experiment with granting its citizens not less but more rights than those provided by the U.S. Constitution? It is not difficult to imagine the benefits of allowing states to do so. "It is one of the happy incidents of the federal system that a single courageous state may, if its citizens choose, serve as a laboratory; and try novel social and economic experiments without risk to the rest of the country." *New State Ice Co. v. Liebmann*, 285 U.S. 262, 311 (1932) (Brandeis, J., dissenting). The existence of the national constitution would guarantee that the region's citizens do not have less rights than the nation, even while the subnational constitution experiments with granting greater rights to the citizens of that region. Commentators call this concept the "laboratory of democracy."

This concept of a "laboratory of democracy" contemplates that a state constitution can be a source for state-by-state expansion of fundamental rights and constitutional protection while federal law serves as a "floor" below which no state may sink. A given state's citizens continue to benefit from the full panoply of federal rights, while also benefitting from their own state's experiments in granting even greater rights.

Florida's Supreme Court fully embraced this concept in decisions such as *State v. Horwitz*, 191 So. 3d 429 (Fla. 2016). Donna Horowitz's silence was used against her by the prosecution, which the trial court agreed it could do under the U.S. Constitution as interpreted by *Miranda v. Arizona*, 384 U.S. 436 (1966) and its progeny. The U.S. Constitution was inadequate to protect Donna Horowitz. Could Florida's Constitution provide greater protection?

STATE

V.

HORWITZ

Supreme Court of Florida, 2016

191 So. 3d 429

... The issue before the Court is whether, under article I, section 9 of the Florida Constitution ... the State is precluded from using a defendant's pre-arrest, pre-*Miranda* silence as substantive evidence of guilt when the defendant does not testify at trial. The State asserts that a defendant's silence occurring prior to his or her arrest is admissible [under the U.S. Constitution as interpreted by *Miranda v. Arizona*, 384 U.S. 436 (1966) and its progeny which holds that] the privilege against self-incrimination does not apply outside of the context of arrest or custodial interrogation, unless the defendant has expressly invoked the privilege against self-incrimination.... Horwitz counters that the Florida Constitution is more protective of the privilege against self-incrimination than its federal counterpart....

In addressing the contours of the restrictions on the State's use of a defendant's pre-arrest, pre-*Miranda* silence, we begin with the Florida Constitution's more protective privilege against self-incrimination as compared to its federal counterpart….

I. Florida's Constitutional Privilege Against Self–incrimination

… The pertinent provision of the Florida Constitution provides that "No person shall ... be compelled in any criminal matter to be a witness against oneself." Art. I, § 9, Fla. Const. This constitutional right has been referred to interchangeably as the "right to remain silent" and the "privilege against self-incrimination."

Florida's privilege against self-incrimination is fundamental; it is part of the Florida Constitution's Declaration of Rights, "a series of rights so basic that the framers of our Constitution accorded them a place of special privilege." *Traylor v. State,* 596 So. 2d 957, 963 (Fla.1992); art. I, Fla. Const. As this Court explained…:

> …These rights [enumerated in the Declaration of Rights] curtail and restrain the power of the State. It is more important to preserve them, even though at times a guilty man may go free, than it is to obtain a conviction by ignoring or violating them. The end does not justify the means. Might is not always right. Under our system of constitutional government, the State should not set the example of violating fundamental rights guaranteed by the Constitution to all citizens in order to obtain a conviction.

Bizzell v. State, 71 So. 2d 735, 738 (Fla.1954). Thus, even here — especially here — where the rights of those suspected of wrongdoing are concerned, the framers drew a bright line and said to government, "Thus far shalt thou come, but no farther."...

… Unless the Florida Constitution specifies otherwise, this Court, as the ultimate arbiter of the meaning and extent of the safeguards and fundamental rights provided by the Florida Constitution, may interpret those rights as providing greater protections than those in the United States Constitution. *State v. Kelly,* 999 So. 2d 1029, 1042 (Fla.2008). Put simply, the United States Constitution generally sets the "floor"—not the "ceiling"—of personal rights and freedoms that must be afforded to a defendant by Florida law. *Id.* As we explained in *Kelly,* "we have the duty to *independently* examine and determine questions of state law so long as we do not run afoul of federal constitutional protections or the provisions of the Florida Constitution that require us to apply federal law in state-law contexts." 999 So. 2d at 1043 (emphasis in original). Our Court reemphasized what we previously stated in *Traylor:* "[w]hen called upon to decide matters of fundamental rights, Florida's state courts are bound under federalist principles to give primacy to our state Constitution and to give independent legal import to every phrase and clause contained therein." *Id.* at 1044 (quoting *Traylor,* 596 So. 2d at 962–63).

As this Court held in *Traylor,* the privilege against self-incrimination, as one of our Constitution's fundamental rights, must be—and has long been—broadly construed. 596 So. 2d at 965 (citing *Ex parte Senior,* 37 Fla. 1, 19 So. 652, 654 (1896)). Indeed, as this Court has since reemphasized, the privilege against self-incrimination provided in the Florida Constitution offers *more* protection than the right provided in the Fifth Amendment to the United States Constitution. *Rigterink v. State,* 66 So. 3d 866, 888 (Fla.2011).

This Court's interpretation of the state constitutional privilege against self-incrimination as providing more protection than its federal counterpart was applied to a defendant's post-arrest, pre-*Miranda* silence in *Hoggins,* 718 So. 2d 761. In that case, we held that the State's use of this post-arrest, pre-*Miranda* silence to impeach the defendant's trial testimony violated Florida's constitutional privilege against self-incrimination, even though such impeachment evidence is not barred by the Fifth Amendment. *Id.* at 765, 769–72. In other words, we interpreted the Florida constitutional right as providing more "rigorous constraints on the use of" a defendant's post-arrest, pre-*Miranda* silence than what is permissible under the Federal Constitution. *Id.* at 768. In *Hoggins,* we expressly departed from the United States Supreme Court's decision in *Fletcher v. Weir,* 455 U.S. 603, 606, 102 S.Ct. 1309, 71

L.Ed.2d 490 (1982), which held that the federal constitution did not preclude states from using a defendant's post-arrest, pre-*Miranda* silence for impeachment purposes. *Id.* at 769.

In *Hoggins,* after an armed robbery of a convenience store, the perpetrator "absconded with the cash register drawer and a cigar box containing lottery tickets." *Id.* at 762. The defendant was spotted riding a bicycle while carrying the missing items. *Id.* The defendant testified at trial, claiming that his bicycle had been stolen and that he had witnessed someone run into his apartment complex and hide something, which he later discovered was the drawer and cigar box. *Id.* at 763. The prosecutor cross-examined the defendant, asking whether the defendant had previously provided that explanation after his arrest, and the defendant admitted that he had not. *Id.* The prosecutor also relied on this "silence" in closing arguments, pointing out that the defendant did not tell the same version of events to the police on the night of his arrest that he provided in his testimony at trial. *Id.* at 764.

We reached a different conclusion in *Hoggins* than the Supreme Court on the issue of post-arrest, pre-*Miranda* silence for two reasons: (1) "unlike the United States Supreme Court, Florida courts have recognized that the defendant does not waive his or her right to silence at the time of arrest by taking the stand in his or her own defense," and (2) "[w]hile the absence of *Miranda* warnings may prevent a federal due process violation from occurring where the defendant's post-arrest silence is used for impeachment purposes, the same is not true of the defendant's right to remain silent. The absence of such warnings does not add to or detract from an individual's right to remain silent." *Id.* at 769–70….

[So] in *Hoggins,* this Court concluded that "the use of a defendant's silence at the time of arrest violates article I, section 9 of Florida's Constitution regardless of whether *Miranda* warnings have been given," ….

The defendant should not be compelled to make the choice between testifying—with the possibility that his or her earlier silence might be used to impeach him or her—and not testifying—thereby, under the State's view, allowing the State to use the defendant's earlier silence as substantive evidence of the defendant's guilt. Our analysis is entirely consistent and directly flows from our decision in Hoggins, as well as our consistent commitment to providing greater protection to a defendant's privilege against self-incrimination guaranteed by the Florida Constitution....

For all these reasons, we conclude that a defendant's privilege against self-incrimination guaranteed under article I, section 9 of the Florida Constitution is violated when his or her pre-arrest, pre-Miranda silence is used against the defendant at trial as substantive evidence of the defendant's consciousness of guilt....

It is so ordered.

B. Florida's Constitution as a Restriction Upon Legislative Power

Florida's sovereignty gives it an inherent power called the "police power." Florida's Constitution is not a grant of the police power, but may be a limitation upon it.

This truth is often expressed by this phrase: "a state constitution is not a grant of power, but a limitation upon power." It is far too easy to misinterpret this phrase. Many a course on state constitutional law, and many a book about Florida's Constitution, begins with a bold proclamation akin to the following:

> The basic consideration in any course dealing with the constitutional law of a state is the fact that although the governmental power of the United States flows either directly or impliedly from its Constitution, the governmental power of a state does not flow from its constitution. The source of a state's governmental power is, rather, inherent. The state's constitution is, therefore, essentially a limitation on that inherent power.

The quote above is from John F. Cooper, Tichia A. Dunham, Carlos L. Woody, *Florida Constitutional Law: Cases and Materials* (5th ed. Carolina Academic Press 2013). Words of similar import may be found in nearly every text regarding nearly any state's constitution. These words are not erroneous, but are widely misunderstood. The misunderstanding is in reaching the conclusion that state constitutions only limit powers and do not grant any powers. To the contrary, as a source of organic law, a state's constitution grants a plethora of powers, such as the power to create a court system, or powers of individual liberties and civil rights. So it is a misunderstanding to conclude that state constitutions never grant a power. To reach a proper understanding, it is important to note that a state's constitution is a limitation upon *legislative* power.

Some but not all court opinions are careful to include the word *legislative* when explaining the concept of a state constitution as a limitation upon power. For example, *Chiles v. Phelps*, 714 So. 2d 453 (Fla. 1998) holds:

> This decision is guided, in part, by the nature of our state constitution. We have noted that:
>
> > The Constitution of this state is not a grant of power to the Legislature, but a limitation only upon legislative power, and unless legislation be clearly contrary to some express or necessarily implied prohibition found in the Constitution, the courts are without authority to declare legislative Acts invalid. The Legislature may exercise any lawmaking power that is not forbidden by organic law.
>
> *Savage v. Board of Public Instruction*, 101 Fla. 1362, 1369, 133 So. 341, 344 (1931) (citing *State v. [Bryan]*, 50 Fla. 293, 39 So. 929 (1905); *Jordan v. Duval County*, 68 Fla. 48, 66 So. 298 (1914); and *Stone v. State*, 71 Fla. 514, 71 So. 634 (1916)). The legislature's power is inherent, though it may be limited by the constitution. Thus, the legislature "looks to the Constitution for limitations on its power and if not found to exist its discretion reasonably exercised is the sole brake on the enactment of legislation." *State v. Board of Pub. Instruction*, 126 Fla. 142, 151, 170 So. 602, 606 (1936).

Id. at 458.

The proposition that "[t]he Constitution of this state is not a grant of power to the Legislature, but a limitation only upon legislative power" means that the Legislature has general legislative or policy-making power except as those powers are specifically limited by the constitution. *Chiles v. Phelps*, 714 So. 2d 453, 458 (Fla. 1998). That is because "[t]he legislature's power is inherent, though it may be limited by the constitution." *Id.* For this reason, "[t]he legislative branch looks to the Constitution not for sources of power but for limitations upon power." *State ex rel. Green v. Pearson*, 153 Fla. 314, 14 So. 2d 565, 567 (1943)

Do not misinterpret these words to mean that state actors other than Florida's Legislature have an inherent power to act. Despite this inherent power of Florida's Legislature to enact laws in ways and on topics not forbidden by federal law or Florida's Constitution, it and all other state actors still must obey the rule of law.

You know this to be true based upon your own personal experience interacting with the State of Florida. Consider these two examples.

Do its officers and officials have inherent power over you, or only that power given to them by the rule of law? Consider this hypothetical. What if you were to meet a Florida State Trooper who believes correctly that his government agency needs funding and that you have plenty of money in your pocket. Surely that Trooper has the right to urge his state legislative representatives to pass a law providing additional funding to his agency. But does that Trooper have the inherent authority to take your money from your pocket and give it to his agency? Of course not. The rule of law, and due process of law, exist to protect us from such invasions of our freedom and confiscations of our wealth.

Likewise, if a county believes your home is the perfect location for a new ballpark, the county's legislative body may follow the rule of law and begin the procedures for eminent domain. But may the county simply bring its wrecking ball and start knocking down your house? Of course not. Laws exist granting counties the right of eminent domain, but due process of law requires that the stated formalities occur, and the rule of law requires appropriate burdens of proof to be met.

As these two examples illustrate, when a Florida county wants to take away your land, or a Florida official wants to take away your money, such actions do not occur due to some kind of an inherent power vested with all parts of Florida's government. Instead, the rule of law applies and requires there must there be a legal basis for Florida's government to do such things, and due process of law requires certain minimum formalities.

Is this merely a modern view? As to what our founding fathers may have thought, consider the following excerpt from an article in the New York University 2003 Annual Survey of American Law and its Symposium on State Constitutional Law.

RESTORATION OF LIMITED STATE CONSTITUTIONAL GOVERNMENT:

A DISSENTER'S VIEW

By Richard B. Sanders and Barbara Mahoney

59 N.Y.U. Ann. Surv. Am. L. 269

The prevailing view of courts and scholars alike is that because the federal government is a government of limited and enumerated powers, state governments have plenary powers subject only to those restrictions set forth in the federal and state constitutions. This presumption gives rise to a theory of constitutional interpretation vesting virtually unlimited power in the state government, subject only to constitutional limitations expressly stated. Yet, virtually every state in the Union has a constitutional provision memorializing the fact that "all just authority in the institutions of political society is derived from the people, and established with their consent."

We posit here the unorthodox view that the people have retained all powers of government except those expressly relinquished by the ratification of their respective state and federal constitutions. As set forth below, state constitutions prescribe the nature and limits of the people's consent to be governed. They are contracts between the people and their state government, delegating limited authority to exercise certain powers not otherwise retained by the people. To the extent a state government exercises its power to undertake activities beyond those necessary to protect and maintain individual rights, courts must look for specific manifestations of the people's consent that evidence constitutional grants of that authority. But, where a legislature acts without express or necessarily implied authorization of the constitution, it exceeds its authority--even if there is no constitutional provision barring such actions. . . .

I. Presumption of Inherent State Powers

The proposition that the Federal Constitution created a federal government of delegated and limited powers is well-established and generally accepted. But after acknowledging that truth, many courts and scholars jump to the opposite conclusion about state constitutions. . . . Unfortunately this oft-repeated proposition is seldom if ever justified by reasoned analysis. At times, some scholars have augmented it with the corresponding idea that all powers reserved to the people are vested in the legislature.

Yet, this idea is equally unsubstantiated and historically suspect. Indeed, Federalist Number 48 warns: “It will not be denied that power is of an encroaching nature and that it ought to be effectually restrained from passing the limits assigned to it.” Similarly, Hamilton warned: “Nothing is more common than for a free people, in times of heat and violence, to gratify momentary passions, by letting into the government principles and precedents which afterwards prove fatal to themselves.” Why would the people who were so protective of their liberty confer upon their own state government the virtually unlimited power of the British Parliament? Given the preoccupation with the corruptive influence of power in the eighteenth and nineteenth centuries, when most of our state constitutions were drafted, is it not more likely the powers conferred upon the state were few and surrendered reluctantly?

The only authority that appears to support the presumption of plenary state power can be found in Federalist Number 45, and even there the text may be misinterpreted. Madison states:

> The powers delegated by the proposed Constitution to the federal government are few and defined. Those which are to remain in the State governments are numerous and indefinite. . . . The powers reserved to the several States will extend to all the objects which, in the ordinary course of affairs, concern the lives, liberties, and properties of the people, and the internal order, improvement, and prosperity of the State.

This statement might be construed to reflect the presumption of plenary state power. But, the Federalist papers address the relationship of the states to the federal government, not the relationship of the people to their respective state. Federalist Number 45 merely describes the powers the people may confer upon their state legislatures; it does not delineate powers inherent to state governments. Nor does it dispel the basic notion that "[e]very American legislature is the creature of the constitution, and strictly subordinate to it."

Nevertheless, the presumption that state governments have inherent powers underlies judicial interpretation of state constitutions. State courts interpreting their own constitutions routinely place the burden to prove legislative action unconstitutional on the challenger. Moreover, state courts typically will uphold legislative action unless the challenger can point to a state constitutional provision prohibiting the exercise of such powers.

However, this presumption of state plenary power does not accord with the political atmosphere of the American Revolution and the constitutional conventions of the original states. Akhil Reed Amar explains that the Colonial leaders were unwilling to accept the idea of authority vested in the British Parliament, and from there a distinctive idea of American sovereignty emerged.

Whereas the British adhered to the view that their sovereignty resided "in the indivisible entity consisting of King, Lords, and Commons" whose power was necessarily boundless, the colonists "came to define the British Constitution not merely as the structure and arrangement of governmental institutions, but also as a set of substantive legal principles limiting the legitimate exercise of government power."

The colonial experience under corporate charters prepared the ground for revolutionary ideas. "By the eve of the Revolution the charters that the crown had granted to many of the colonies in the previous century had come to be seen as just so many miniature magna cartas." The corporate charters provided for the establishment of a colonial government consistent with the terms expressed in the charter by circumscribing the rights and privileges to which the colonists were entitled and limiting the powers of the crown. For example, the Virginia Charter of 1606 provided for a council with plenary governmental powers beyond the requirements of the English Privy Council. But it also guaranteed the colonists would "HAVE and enjoy all Liberties, Franchises, and Immunities . . . to all Intents and Purposes, as if they had been abiding and born, within this our Realm of England, or any other of our said Dominions." Even the Charter for the Province of Pennsylvania of 1681, which granted William Penn "absolute" authority to establish a code of laws, a judiciary, and a means of enforcement, required "[t]hat the said Lawes bee consonant to reason, and bee not repugnant or contrarie, but as neare as conveniently may bee agreeable to the Lawes and Statutes, and rights of this Our Kingdome of England."

Over time the colonial charter experience resulted in a radical redefinition of governmental sovereignty whereby the people retained their sovereignty except to the extent they delegated the powers of governing to their federal, state, or local governments. This development informed American Revolutionaries, and most of the original state constitutions of the former colonies specifically provide that "all political power is vested in and derived from the people only."

Most of the later-joining states obtained statehood through a federal enabling act. Every congressional enabling act since 1864 requires the state to ratify a state constitution not "repugnant to . . . the principles of the Declaration of Independence." In pertinent part, the Declaration provides:

> We hold these truths to be self-evident, that all men are created equal, that they are endowed by their Creator with certain unalienable Rights, that among these are Life, Liberty, and the pursuit of Happiness. That to secure these rights Governments are instituted among Men, deriving their just powers from the consent of the governed . . . .

The Declaration articulates the first premise of American government, that sovereignty resides in the people and governments obtain the powers to govern by the consent of the people. Thus, the power of government extends only insofar as it is delegated by the consent of the governed. This principle was adopted, for example, in the Washington Constitution, which provides a specific provision ensuring consent of the governed.

Against this historical backdrop and in the face of express state constitutional provisions advocating a government of limited powers, it is simply unfathomable that courts and scholars persist in the naked presumption of plenary state power.

II. Limitations on State Police Power

The Founders adopted John Locke's view of a limited government, the essential function of which was to preserve life, liberty, and property. They rejected the more expansive view of the inherent powers of government, which Blackstone would later describe as "the due regulation and domestic order of the kingdom, whereby the individuals of the state, like members of a well-governed family, are bound to conform their general behaviour to the rules of propriety, good neighbourhood, and good manners; and to be decent, industrious, and inoffensive in their respective stations." Early on the Supreme Court recognized the limited nature of the state's police power:

> The people of the United States erected their Constitutions, or forms of government, to establish justice, to promote the general welfare, to secure the blessings of liberty; and to protect their persons and property from violence. The purposes for which men enter into society will determine the nature and terms of the social compact; and as they are the foundation of the legislative power, they will decide what are the proper objects of it: The nature, and ends of legislative power will limit the exercise of it. . . . An ACT of the Legislature (for I cannot call it a law) contrary to the great first principles of the social compact, cannot be considered a rightful exercise of legislative authority. The obligation of a law in governments established on express compact, and on republican principles, must be determined by the nature of the power, on which it is founded. . . . To maintain that our Federal, or State, Legislature possesses such powers, if they had not been expressly restrained; would, in my opinion, be a political heresy, altogether inadmissible in our free republican governments.

The Lockean essential function of government, sometimes described as the police power, is, therefore, to protect our lives, liberty, and property from transgressions by our neighbors. If a government is to do more, the evidence of delegation of that authority should reside in a specific provision of the constitution. State constitutions contain many such provisions. For example, the Washington Constitution authorizes the legislature to establish educational institutions "for the blind, deaf, or otherwise disabled." However, the rule should remain that, absent express delegation of constitutional authority, the people have reserved to themselves all else.

But even the police power, understood in this narrow sense of preventing serious harm to individuals in violation of their legal entitlements, does not authorize the state to encroach upon rights guaranteed in the state declaration of rights.

This intention is evident in the text of many of the declared rights, which prescribe the limits within which the right may be exercised free of interference. For example, Washington's Religious Freedom Clause provides in relevant part:

> Absolute freedom of conscience in all matters of religious sentiment, belief and worship, shall be guaranteed to every individual, and no one shall be molested or disturbed in person or property on account of religion; but the liberty of conscience hereby secured shall not be so construed as to excuse acts of licentiousness or justify practices inconsistent with the peace and safety of the state.

Similarly, Washington's Right of Petition and Free Assemblage Clause provides: "The right of petition and of the people peaceably to assemble for the common good shall never be abridged." The only exception to "absolute freedom" of religion is express, i.e., "acts of licentiousness or . . . practices inconsistent with the peace and safety of the state"; nor may the right to petition or assemble be limited unless it poses a serious risk of violence or other harm.

As originally expressed by Alexander Hamilton when advocating adoption of the Federal Constitution absent a national Bill of Rights, a bill of rights serves only one function: "to delineate exceptions to otherwise legitimate exercises of governmental powers." In the view of the founders, the very purpose of a declaration of rights is to except from the reach of government any power to abridge the rights secured thereby. If the rights guaranteed by a declaration of rights are not exceptions to governmental power, including otherwise legitimate exercises of the police power, then those rights are illusory because the government has no authority to exceed its legitimate functions in any case.

But how has this principle been applied to state constitutional provisions? Several states have subjected their constitutions' unconditional guarantee of the right to bear arms to the state's police power. A recent decision of the Washington Supreme Court held even the free exercise of religion may be subject to zoning regulations enacted pursuant to the state's police power. What is next? Privacy? Press? Speech? Assembly? Can it not be argued that these are also at the mercy of the state--a power that some argue only ends where the declaration of rights begins, but now predominates over even that?

CONCLUSION

The practice of interpreting state constitutions as granting the state legislature plenary power except where such power has been expressly limited by the constitution presumes that state governments have inherent powers, that sovereignty resides with the servant rather than the popular masters. However, this presumption contradicts the basic premise of American government that all power resides in the people except as it has been delegated to the government. Because courts have uniformly and uncritically adopted this presumption, they have interpreted state constitutions contrary to the clear meaning of the text and allowed an unwarranted expansion of state power that threatens individual rights. Once this presumption is debunked, a defensible theory of constitutional interpretation emerges that embodies that principle of limited government expressed by the people who ratified their state constitutions....

Notes and Questions to Consider:

1. Can Florida's inherent police power justify violating the U.S. Constitution?

2. Does Florida's inherent police power empower the government of the State of Florida to ignore or disobey federal laws?

3. Florida case law precedent identifies three "first principles" of state constitutional jurisprudence. First, the people are the ultimate sovereign. Second, unlike the federal constitution, our state constitution is a limitation upon the power of government rather than a grant of that power, which means that the Legislature has general and inherent legislative or policy-making power. Third, because general legislative or policy-making power is vested in the legislature, the power of judicial review over legislative enactments is strictly limited. To what extent to these "first principles" help you to understand better the concept that Florida's Constitution is a restriction upon power not a grant of power?

Chapter Two

Government Transparency and Accountability

A. Florida's Sunshine Laws

A series of amendments to Florida's Constitution require transparency and accountability – or "sunshine" if you will – in the operations of Florida's state and local governments. These amendments, combined with some Florida Statutes applying the concepts found in these constitutional amendments, commonly are called Florida's Sunshine Law. Florida's Supreme Court notes that Florida's "Sunshine Law was enacted in the public interest to protect the public from 'closed door' politics and, as such, the law must be broadly construed to effect its remedial and protective purpose." *Wood v. Marston*, 442 So. 2d 934, 938 (Fla. 1983).

Public records, open meetings, and public accountability were not always the norm in the state of Florida. Perhaps this is best illustrated by the group of Florida state senators in the 1950s known as the Pork Chop Gang. They were a group of North Florida Democrats who dominated the Florida State Senate due to a late-19th century apportionment rule that gave disproportionate voting power to rural districts. They were known to meet on the Isola River at lobbyist Rayburn Horn's fish camp to play poker and drink whiskey. During legislative sessions, the Pork Chop Gang lived and plotted together at Tallahassee's Cherokee Hotel, Floridan Hotel, and The Duval Hotel. Although Florida law did not make this behavior illegal at that time, this behavior came under increasing criticism from then-Governor LeRoy Collins and newspapermen like then-Editor of the Tampa Tribune James Clendinen. *See* Patrick John McGinley, FLORIDA MUNICIPAL LAW AND PRACTICE § 10:2 (2017-18 ed.).

Part of the criticism was that decisions about legislative actions and laws were being made at these informal gatherings. When the Pork Chop Gang lived and plotted together as to how to cast their block of legislative votes, the public could not attend. No notes were kept. No dissenting voices were heard. The public could not participate in any meaningful way. The Pork Chop Gang's legislative power block was inaccessible and largely unaccountable.

In 1967, the Florida Legislature took a step forward toward government transparency and accountability by revising and somewhat strengthening Florida's Sunshine Laws, which at the time were statutes only and were not self-executing constitutional amendments. For this reason and others, the 1967 legislation had its limits. It did not apply to Florida's legislative or judicial branches of state government. It applied only to Florida's executive branch and to local governments, including counties, municipalities, and districts. In 1978, the Constitution Revision Commission proposed elevating these laws to constitutional status and applying them to records and meetings of the Legislature. That proposal was not adopted. *Id.* at § 10:2.

Then in November 1990, an amendment to Florida's Constitution added Article III, §4 bringing accountability, open government, and sunshine to the Florida Legislature. It provides, in relevant part, that:

> (e) The rules of procedure of each house shall provide that all legislative committee and subcommittee meetings of each house, and joint conference committee meetings, shall be open and noticed to the public. The rules of procedure of each house shall further provide that all prearranged gatherings, between more than two members of the legislature, or between the governor, the president of the senate, or the speaker of the house of representatives, the purpose of which is to agree upon formal legislative action that will be taken at a subsequent time, or at which formal legislative action is taken, regarding pending legislation or amendments, shall be reasonably open to the public. All open meetings shall be subject to order and decorum. This section shall be implemented and defined by the rules of each house, and such rules shall control admission to the floor of each legislative

> chamber and may, where reasonably necessary for security purposes or to protect a witness appearing before a committee, provide for the closure of committee meetings. Each house shall be the sole judge for the interpretation, implementation, and enforcement of this section.

The plain language of this subsection (e) requires that all legislative committee and subcommittee meetings be open to the public. Outside of these legislative meetings, all prearranged gatherings with more than two legislators must be open to the public also. Likewise, meetings between the Governor, the President of the Senate, or the Speaker of the House of Representatives for the purpose of agreeing upon formal legislative action fall under the definition of "public meetings." The definition of "formal legislative action" was not provided in the Constitution but was left to legislative rule. The amendment leaves each house of the Legislature as the "sole judge for the interpretation, implementation, and enforcement" of this section. As such, the Legislature is insulated from any judicial enforcement of this section. *Id.* at § 10:2.

In November 1992, an amendment to Florida's Constitution took a giant leap forward toward greater accountability, open government, and sunshine. Florida's Constitution was amended to add Article I section 24 that brought requirements of transparency and public access to all branches of Florida government. In relevant part, those 1992 amendments to Article I section 24 provide:

> (a) Every person has the right to inspect or copy any public record made or received in connection with the official business of any public body, officer, or employee of the state, or persons acting on their behalf, except with respect to records exempted pursuant to this section or specifically made confidential by this Constitution. This section specifically includes the legislative, executive, and judicial branches of government and each agency or department created thereunder; counties, municipalities, and districts; and each constitutional officer, board, and commission, or entity created pursuant to law or this Constitution.

(b) All meetings of any collegial public body of the executive branch of state government or of any collegial public body of a county, municipality, school district, or special district, at which official acts are to be taken or at which public business of such body is to be transacted or discussed, shall be open and noticed to the public and meetings of the legislature shall be open and noticed as provided in Article III, Section 4(e), except with respect to meetings exempted pursuant to this section or specifically closed by this Constitution.

(c) This section shall be self-executing. The legislature, however, may provide by general law passed by a two-thirds vote of each house for the exemption of records from the requirements of subsection (a) and the exemption of meetings from the requirements of subsection (b), provided that such law shall state with specificity the public necessity justifying the exemption and shall be no broader than necessary to accomplish the stated purpose of the law. The legislature shall enact laws governing the enforcement of this section, including the maintenance, control, destruction, disposal, and disposition of records made public by this section, except that each house of the legislature may adopt rules governing the enforcement of this section in relation to records of the legislative branch. Laws enacted pursuant to this subsection shall contain only exemptions from the requirements of subsections (a) or (b) and provisions governing the enforcement of this section, and shall relate to one subject.

(d) All laws that are in effect on July 1, 1993 that limit public access to records or meetings shall remain in force, and such laws apply to records of the legislative and judicial branches, until they are repealed. Rules of court that are in effect on the date of adoption of this section that limit access to records shall remain in effect until they are repealed.

Note how these amendments impose transparency, open meetings and public records requirements upon virtually all branches of Florida's state government, all Florida local governments, and all Florida officers, agencies, boards, and employees. FLORIDA MUNICIPAL LAW AND PRACTICE describes the effect of these amendments as follows:

> Subsection (a) ensures the right of public access to any public record not exempted in the manner set out in the amendment, made or received in connection with the official business of any public body, officer, or employee of the state, or persons acting on their behalf.
>
> Subsection (b) requires that all meetings of any collegial public body of the executive branch or collegial bodies of local governments, at which official acts are to be taken or at which the business of the entity is to be transacted or discussed, must be open and noticed to the public. On the contrary, legislative meetings are open and noticed as provided in Article III, section 4(e), which operates quite differently. As to the executive branch and local government collegial bodies, any gathering of two or more members to discuss a matter that may foreseeably come before that body is considered a public meeting and must be noticed and open. On the other hand, Article III, section 4(e) requires that only legislative committees, subcommittees, and conference committees must be open and noticed.
>
> Subsection (c) grants the Legislature the power to enact general laws governing the enforcement of this section and to enact exemptions to the requirements for public access. Any law creating an exemption: (1) must state with specificity the public necessity justifying the exemption; (2) may be no broader than necessary to accomplish the stated purpose of the exemption; and (3) may contain no other subject except exemptions and provisions governing the enforcement of this section and must relate to a single subject.

See Patrick John McGinley, FLORIDA MUNICIPAL LAW AND PRACTICE § 10:2 (2017-18 ed.). "These constitutional amendments give great strength to Florida's Sunshine Law." *Id.*

Supplementing these amendments to Florida's Constitution, Florida Statutes section 268.011 add additional requirements of transparency, accountability and openness. In relevant part, Florida Statutes section 268.011 provides:

> (1) All meetings of any board or commission of any state agency or authority or of any agency or authority of any county, municipal corporation, or political subdivision, except as otherwise provided in the Constitution, at which official acts are to be taken are declared to be public meetings open to the public at all times, and no resolution, rule, or formal action shall be considered binding except as taken or made at such meeting. The board or commission must provide reasonable notice of all such meetings.
>
> (2) The minutes of a meeting of any such board or commission of any such state agency or authority shall be promptly recorded, and such records shall be open to public inspection. The circuit courts of this state shall have jurisdiction to issue injunctions to enforce the purposes of this section upon application by any citizen of this state.
>
> (3)
>
> (a) Any public officer who violates any provision of this section is guilty of a noncriminal infraction, punishable by fine not exceeding $500.
>
> (b) Any person who is a member of a board or commission or of any state agency or authority of any county, municipal corporation, or political subdivision who knowingly violates the provisions of this section by attending a meeting not held in accordance with the provisions hereof is guilty of a misdemeanor of the second degree, punishable as provided in s. 775.082 or s. 775.083.
>
> (c) Conduct which occurs outside the state which would constitute a knowing violation of this section is a misdemeanor of the second degree, punishable as provided in s. 775.082 or s. 775.083.
>
> (4) Whenever an action has been filed against any board or

commission of any state agency or authority or any agency or authority of any county, municipal corporation, or political subdivision to enforce the provisions of this section or to invalidate the actions of any such board, commission, agency, or authority, which action was taken in violation of this section, and the court determines that the defendant or defendants to such action acted in violation of this section, the court shall assess a reasonable attorney's fee against such agency, and may assess a reasonable attorney's fee against the individual filing such an action if the court finds it was filed in bad faith or was frivolous. Any fees so assessed may be assessed against the individual member or members of such board or commission; provided, that in any case where the board or commission seeks the advice of its attorney and such advice is followed, no such fees shall be assessed against the individual member or members of the board or commission. However, this subsection shall not apply to a state attorney or his or her duly authorized assistants or any officer charged with enforcing the provisions of this section.

(5) Whenever any board or commission of any state agency or authority or any agency or authority of any county, municipal corporation, or political subdivision appeals any court order which has found said board, commission, agency, or authority to have violated this section, and such order is affirmed, the court shall assess a reasonable attorney's fee for the appeal against such board, commission, agency, or authority. Any fees so assessed may be assessed against the individual member or members of such board or commission; provided, that in any case where the board or commission seeks the advice of its attorney and such advice is followed, no such fees shall be assessed against the individual member or members of the board or commission.

(6) All persons subject to subsection (1) are prohibited from holding meetings at any facility or location which discriminates on the basis of sex, age, race, creed, color, origin, or economic status or which operates in such a manner as to unreasonably restrict public ac-

cess to such a facility.

(7) Whenever any member of any board or commission of any state agency or authority or any agency or authority of any county, municipal corporation, or political subdivision is charged with a violation of this section and is subsequently acquitted, the board or commission is authorized to reimburse said member for any portion of his or her reasonable attorney's fees.

(8) Notwithstanding the provisions of subsection (1), any board or commission of any state agency or authority or any agency or authority of any county, municipal corporation, or political subdivision, and the chief administrative or executive officer of the governmental entity, may meet in private with the entity's attorney to discuss pending litigation to which the entity is presently a party before a court or administrative agency, provided that the following conditions are met:

(a) The entity's attorney shall advise the entity at a public meeting that he or she desires advice concerning the litigation.

(b) The subject matter of the meeting shall be confined to settlement negotiations or strategy sessions related to litigation expenditures.

(c) The entire session shall be recorded by a certified court reporter. The reporter shall record the times of commencement and termination of the session, all discussion and proceedings, the names of all persons present at any time, and the names of all persons speaking. No portion of the session shall be off the record. The court reporter's notes shall be fully transcribed and filed with the entity's clerk within a reasonable time after the meeting.

(d) The entity shall give reasonable public notice of the time and date of the attorney-client session and the names of persons who will be attending the session. The session shall commence at an open meeting at which the persons chairing the meeting shall announce the commencement and estimated length of the attorney-client session and the names of the persons attending. At the conclusion of the attorney-client session, the meeting shall be reopened, and the person chairing the meeting shall announce the termination of the session.

(e) The transcript shall be made part of the public record upon conclusion of the litigation.

As a reading of this statute and the prior constitutional amendments show, "there are three basic requirements of Florida's Sunshine Law: (1) meetings of public boards or commissions must be open to the public; (2) reasonable notice of such meetings must be given; and (3) minutes of the meetings must be taken and promptly recorded." Patrick John McGinley, FLORIDA MUNICIPAL LAW AND PRACTICE § 10:2 (2017-18 ed.).

B. Scoope of Florida's Sunshine Laws and "Public Records"

To whom does Florida's Sunshine Laws apply, and what exactly is a "public record" under that law? To answer these questions, keep in mind that Florida's Sunshine Law, "having been enacted for the public benefit, should be interpreted most favorably to the public." *Canney v. Board of Public Instruction of Alachua Cty.*, 278 So. 2d 260 (Fla. 1973). Florida's Sunshine Law "must be broadly construed to [advance] its remedial and protective purpose." *Wood v. Marston*, 442 So. 2d 934 (Fla. 1983). Importantly, Florida's Sunshine Law "should be construed so as to frustrate all evasive devices." *Palm Beach v. Gradison* 296 So. 2d 473 (Fla. 1974).

Perhaps the answers to these questions are best illustrated by Florida's First District Court of Appeal's 2009 decision in *National Collegiate Athletic Association v. Associated Press*, 18 So. 3d 1201 (Fla. 1st DCA 2009), review denied, 37 So. 3d 848 (2010).

NATIONAL COLLEGIATE ATHLETIC ASSOCIATION

v.

ASSOCIATED PRESS

First District Court of Appeal of Florida, 2009

18 So. 3d 1201

The National Collegiate Athletic Association (NCAA) appeals a final judgment requiring it to disclose certain documents under Florida's Sunshine Law to The Associated Press and other news organizations. We find no error in the decision by the trial court. Accordingly, we affirm.

Records created and maintained by the NCAA are not generally subject to public disclosure. However, the documents at issue in this case were examined by lawyers for a public agency, Florida State University, and used in the course of the agency's business. Because the documents were received in connection with the transaction of official business by an agency, they are public records. The NCAA has failed to show that an exception applies under state or federal law, and thus the records must be disclosed.

I.

The events leading to the present controversy began when the University became aware of allegations that a learning specialist and an academic tutor had provided improper assistance to a number of students, some of whom were participating in athletic programs. The University engaged the services of a private firm to conduct an internal investigation on its behalf. After the completion of a comprehensive self-investigation of academic misconduct, the University reported its findings to the NCAA.

Several months later, the NCAA issued a notice of allegations to the University. The effect of the notice was to formally initiate a disciplinary proceeding regarding the misconduct the University had previously reported to the NCAA. The University submitted a response to the allegations, and the case was called up for a hearing before the NCAA's Committee on Infractions. The transcript of the hearing before the committee has not been made public.

Thereafter, the NCAA's Committee on Infractions issued an infractions report. It imposed penalties against the University for the academic misconduct, including an order that certain athletic victories be vacated. The report was provided to the University in paper form, and, after the names of the students had been redacted, the report was made public.

The University then retained the GrayRobinson law firm to file an appeal to the NCAA from the penalties imposed by the committee. Because the work of the committee was done in private, the lawyers had to make an arrangement with the NCAA to obtain access to the records relevant to the enforcement proceeding. The arrangement was as follows. The NCAA put images of the transcript of the October 28, 2008 hearing and other records on a secure Internet website. Lawyers for GrayRobinson signed a confidentiality agreement with the NCAA promising not to disclose any information they obtained from the website. The NCAA then gave the lawyers a password they could use to obtain the information from the website.

This is the system the NCAA uses with all of its member institutions as part of an effort to go "paperless." She referred to the secure website as the "custodial website." Authorized representatives of member institutions could go to the website to obtain access to information they needed to resolve their disputes with the NCAA, and, at the same time, the NCAA could avoid public disclosure of confidential sources of information used in its investigations.

After they had signed the confidentiality agreement, the lawyers at GrayRobinson examined the transcript of the hearing before the Committee on Infractions. The lawyers then used the information in the transcript to prepare the University's appeal to the NCAA. They filed the initial brief on behalf of the University, and the Committee on Infractions filed a written response. The response was submitted to the NCAA as a part of the appeal. It was considered to be the property of the NCAA and it was not disclosed to the public.

The Associated Press sought disclosure of documents in the NCAA disciplinary proceeding and appeal and, when the request was denied, they filed suit under Florida's Sunshine Law against the NCAA, Florida State University, its President, and the GrayRobinson law firm.

The public records case was tried before the court. Two documents were at issue in the litigation: the transcript of the hearing before the NCAA Committee on Infractions and the Committee's response to the University's appeal. The plaintiffs argued that both documents were "public records" under Florida's Sunshine Law. The NCAA argued that the documents were not public records.

The trial court concluded that the transcript and response were public records because they were received by an agency of the state government. The court ordered the immediate disclosure of the transcript and response, but the NCAA appealed to this court, and the judgment by the trial court was stayed pending the disposition of the appeal.

II.

The issues presented in this appeal are governed by the organic law of the state. The Florida Constitution creates a broad right to inspect the records of any state or local governmental body. Article I, section 24(a) of the Florida Constitution grants "[e]very person ... the right to inspect or copy any public record made or received in connection with the official business of any public body, officer or employee of the state, or persons acting on their behalf." The right to inspect a public record in Florida is not one that is merely established by legislation, it is a right demanded by the people.

Article I, section 24(c) of the Florida Constitution provides that the right to inspect public records shall be "self-executing." Legislation is not required to implement the right, but section 24(c) expressly grants authority to the Florida Legislature to "enact laws governing the enforcement of this section." The rights created by the constitution may be enforced under the procedures in the public records law, Chapter 119, Florida Statutes. The opening sentence of the law declares that "[i]t is the policy in this state that all state, county and municipal records are open for personal inspection and copying by any person" and that "[p]roviding access to public records is a duty of each agency."

Florida courts construe the public records law liberally in favor of the state's policy of open government. If there is any doubt about the application of the law in a particular case, the doubt is resolved in favor of disclosing the documents.

a.

With these principles in mind, we address whether the transcript and response are public records. We begin by observing that the public records law is not limited to paper documents but that it applies, as well, to documents that exist only in digital form. Florida's Sunshine Law makes it clear that the public records law applies to documents maintained on a computer in the same way that it would apply to those kept in a file cabinet. This section notes the increased dependency on computerized records and it directs that "each agency must provide reasonable access to records electronically maintained." It goes on to conclude that the automation of public records "must not erode the right of access to those records."

To determine whether a particular document qualifies as a public record the court must look first to the definition given in the law itself. Section 119.011(12) defines the term "public record" as:

> all documents, papers, letters, maps, books, tapes, photographs, films, sound records, data processing software, or other material, regardless of the physical form, characteristic or means of transmission, made or received pursuant to law or ordinance in connection with the transaction of official business.

By this definition, a document may qualify as a public record under the statute if it was prepared by a private party, so long as it was "received" by a government agent and used in the transaction of public business.

The Florida Supreme Court provided additional guidance to the lower courts in *Shevin v. Byron, Harless, Schaffer, Reid & Associates, Inc.*, 379 So. 2d 633 (Fla.1980). In that case, the court defined the term "record" as used in section 119.011(12) as "any material prepared in connection with official agency business which is intended to perpetuate, communicate, or formalize knowledge of some type." *Shevin*, 379 So. 2d at 640. This definition was intended "to give content to the public records law" by attributing a meaning to the term "record" that is "consistent with common understanding of the term." *Shevin* at 640.

Based on these authorities, we conclude that the transcript and response are public records. Although these documents were prepared and maintained by a private organization, they were "received" by agents of a public agency and used in connection with public business. The purpose of the transcript was to perpetuate the information presented to the infractions committee, in the event the parties wished to appeal the sanction imposed by the committee. The response was designed to communicate information to the body that would hear the appeal within the NCAA.

The term "received" in section 119.011(12) refers not only to a situation in which a public agent takes physical delivery of a document, but also to one in which a public agent examines a document residing on a remote computer. If that were not the case, a party could easily circumvent the public records laws. The appeal by the University is a matter of public concern. It is not transformed into a private matter merely because the documents the University lawyers used to prepare the appeal reside on a computer owned by a private organization. The definition of a public record does not turn on the sender's method of transmission.

Our conclusion that the transcript and response became public records when they were examined by state lawyers and used for a public purpose is supported by the decision of the Second District Court of Appeal in *Times Publishing Co. v. City of St. Petersburg*, 558 So. 2d 487 (Fla. 2d DCA 1990).

That case involved negotiations between the Chicago White Sox and the City of St. Petersburg for the use of the Suncoast Dome. The documents pertaining to the negotiations were prepared and maintained exclusively by the White Sox, but they were examined by agents for the City under a confidentiality agreement. The court held that the documents were subject to disclosure under the public records law because they were examined by agents for the City and used in the course of its business.

These principles apply with equal force here. It is true, as the NCAA points out, that the documents at issue in *Times Publishing* were modified at the request of the City, but that is a distinction without a difference. A document that is used in the course of public business is a public record under the definition in section 119.011(12) if it was made by a public official or if was received by the official. If it was received, that is enough. It is not necessary to also show that it was made, partly made, or modified in some way by the official.

We would be more inclined to accept the NCAA's argument that viewing is not the equivalent of receiving if the documents at issue had not been directly related to the work these lawyers were doing for the state. If the GrayRobinson lawyers had used their password to look at the disciplinary records of a student athlete from a private school in New York, the NCAA would have a good argument that the record did not become public merely because it was "viewed" by someone who happened to work for the State of Florida. The point overlooked in the NCAA's argument, however, is that the records in this case were examined and used for an official state purpose.

The GrayRobinson lawyers signed a confidentiality agreement with the NCAA, but that has no impact on our decision that the transcript and response are public records. A public record cannot be transformed into a private record merely because an agent of the government has promised that it will be kept private. Nor is it material that the NCAA had an expectation that the documents would remain private. As we explained in *Sepro Corp. v. Florida Department of Environmental Protection*, 839 So. 2d 781, 784 (Fla. 1st DCA 2003), "[A] private party cannot render public records exempt from disclosure merely by designating information it furnishes a governmental agency confidential." The right to examine these records is a right belonging to the public; it cannot be bargained away by a representative of the government.

In limited but well-defined circumstances, a record created and maintained by a private organization can be subject to disclosure as a public record on an agency theory. For example, if a private entity is acting on behalf of the state or local government and creates a document that reflects the business of the governmental entity, the document can become a public record. In *News and Sun–Sentinel Co. v. Schwab, Twitty & Hanser Architectural Group, Inc.*, 596 So. 2d 1029 (Fla.1992), the supreme court set out a nine-factor test to determine whether records held by a private party must be disclosed under the public record act on the theory that the private party is acting on behalf of the government.

The critical question in this line of cases is whether the private party is a "private agency, person, partnership, corporation or business entity acting on behalf of [a] public agency " that has therefore become an "agency," as defined in section 119.011(2) Florida Statutes. The common feature of all of the cases in this line of authority is that they all involve efforts to determine whether a private entity has assumed the role of the government. Typically, the private entity has a contract with the government and performs a public function in the course of its duties under the contract. The private entity is acting not as a business adversary to the government but as a surrogate for the government.

The issue in the present case is much less complicated. The transcript and response are public records because they were received by agents of the state and used in the course of the state's business. We need not apply the nine-factor test in *Schwab* to come to this conclusion. Nor is it necessary to decide whether the NCAA became a public "agency" in its own right under section 119.011(2) by stepping into the shoes of the University and assuming a public duty of the University. The documents at issue in this case became public records by a much more direct route: they were received by agents of the University and used in connection with the University's business. The legal status of these records is no different than it would be if they had been prepared by the University's lawyers and if the only existing copies were in the NCAA's possession.

The enforcement of the public records law is also relatively straightforward in a situation like this. Section 119.07(1)(a), Florida Statutes states that "every person who has custody of a public record shall permit the record to be inspected and copied by any person desiring to do so ...." The plain meaning of this statute is that the public records law can be enforced against any person who has custody of public records, whether that person is employed by the public agency creating or receiving the records or not. It makes no difference that the records in question are in the hands of a private party. If they are public records, they are subject to compelled disclosure under the law.

b.

We come now to the final argument on appeal, that the public records law is unconstitutional as applied under the facts of this case. The NCAA contends that the law as applied here violates its rights under the dormant Commerce Clause and under the First Amendment right to freedom of association. These arguments lack merit.

The Commerce Clause states: "The Congress shall have Power ... To regulate Commerce ... among the several States...." U.S. Const., Art. I, § 8, cl. 3. The United States Supreme Court has recognized that this affirmative grant of authority to Congress also encompasses an implicit or "dormant" limitation on the authority of the States to enact legislation affecting interstate commerce. See *Hughes v. Oklahoma*, 441 U.S. 322, 326 (1979). The United States Supreme Court has adopted a two-tiered test to determine whether a state law violates the dormant Commerce Clause. If a statute "directly regulates or discriminates against interstate commerce, or [if] its effect is to favor in-state economic interests over out-of-state interests," the court may declare it unconstitutional as applied, without further inquiry. *Brown–Forman Distillers, Inc. v. New York State Liquor Authority*, 476 U.S. 573,

578–79 (1986). However, if the statute regulates evenhandedly and if it has only an indirect effect on interstate commerce, the court must determine whether the state's interest is legitimate and, if so, whether the burden on interstate commerce exceeds the local benefits.

The public records law does not attempt to regulate or discriminate against interstate commerce. It does not deal with the subject of commerce at all. Nor does the application of the law in this case favor in-state economic interests over out-of-state interests. The law would apply in the same way we have applied it here if a private Florida corporation doing business entirely within the borders of the state had provided information to a public official and if the information had then been used in connection with public business.

We are not persuaded that the Public Records law has an indirect effect on interstate commerce, but even if some effect had been established, we could not say that the law violates the dormant Commerce Clause. The Public Records law implements a right guaranteed to members of the public under the Florida Constitution and it therefore promotes a state interest of the highest order. The negligible impact the law might have on interstate commerce clearly does not outweigh the goal of ensuring open government.

The NCAA relies on *NCAA v. Miller*, 10 F.3d 633 (9th Cir.1993), and *NCAA v. Roberts*, 1994 WL 750585 (N.D.Fla.1994), in support of its dormant Commerce Clause argument, but these cases are distinguishable. Both involve state statutes purporting to regulate disciplinary proceedings by college athletic associations. In contrast, the public records law is a law of general application; it does not single out athletic associations.

The NCAA's claim that the application of the Florida public records law would impair its ability to function also assumes that the law imposes a burden that would not be imposed in other states. That is not the case. Many other states also define a public record broadly to include records that are connected with the business of the government yet are not in the hands of a public agent. Some statutes are like the one in Florida, in that they refer to documents that were made or "received" by a public agent in connection with public business. Others are even broader, in that they refer to documents that were "used" by a public agent in the course of public business. We do not suggest that the analysis would be precisely the same in every state, but merely that Florida law is not so distinctive that it would force the NCAA to change the way it does business. This case arose in Florida, but it is likely that the NCAA would be dealing with the same issue had it arisen most anywhere in the United States.

The argument that the application of the Florida public records law violates the NCAA's right to freedom of association under the First Amendment is also unavailing. We acknowledge that the NCAA is a private voluntary organization and that it enjoys the freedom of association guaranteed by the First Amendment, but the NCAA has not shown that the application of the Florida public records law impairs that right. The application of the Florida public records law could not, by any stretch of the imagination, require the NCAA to admit or reject certain institutions. Nor does it require the NCAA to reject the values it wishes to express. The law may prevent the NCAA from conducting secret proceedings against a public school in this state, but that does not impair the NCAA's freedom of expression or its freedom of association.

III.

In summary, we hold that the application of the Florida public records law does not violate any constitutional right under the facts of this case, that the transcript of the hearing before the Committee on Infractions and the Committee's response are public records, and that these documents are not exempt from disclosure under state or federal law. For these reasons, we affirm the judgment of the trial court and order the disclosure of the transcript, and the response in its original form.

Affirmed.

Notes and Questions to Consider:

1. The holding in *NCAA v. Associated Press* does not mean that

the records of all private corporations and nongovernmental entities are made public by Florida's Sunshine Law. Sunshine applies to Florida's state and local governments and agencies, but generally does not apply to private entities. The exception is when the private entity steps into the shoes of the government and assumes the duty to provide a governmental service. This can occur, for example, when the private entity has a contract with the government and performs a public function in the course of its duties under the contract. The nine-factor *Schwab* test, named after the Florida Supreme Court decision in *News and Sun–Sentinel Co. v. Schwab, Twitty & Hanser Architectural Group, Inc.*, 596 So. 2d 1029 (Fla. 1992), determines whether the private entity's actions are sufficient to make its records public under Florida's Sunshine Law. The critical question answered by the nine-factor *Schwab* test is whether the private party is a "private agency, person, partnership, corporation or business entity acting on behalf of a public agency " that has therefore become an "agency," as defined in section 119.011(2) Florida Statutes. The nine-factor *Schwab* test is satisfied only in these limited but well-defined circumstances. How is it beneficial that Florida's Sunshine Law is not generally applicable to private entities?

2. What if the *Schwab* test did not exist and the records in possession of private entities were never subject to public inspection under Florida's Sunshine Law. How would that contradict the purposes of Florida's Sunshine Law? How would that thwart the goal that Florida's Sunshine Law "should be construed so as to frustrate all evasive devices?"

3. Note that *NCAA v. Associated Press* did not need to enumerate and apply the nine-factor *Schwab* test. The court found it unnecessary to decide whether the NCAA was acting on behalf of a public agency as required by *Schwab*. Instead, the court found that the state (specifically, the Florida State University) acted on its own. Specifically, the lawyers of GrayRobinson, acting for their state client, the University, examined the NCAA's records in order to defend the state. That means the records were received by agents of the state and used in the course of the state's business. This is enough to qualify those particular records of the NCAA as public records under Florida's Sunshine Law. Does that mean that every one of the NCAA's

records must now be open to inspection by the public?

4. Were you surprised by the holding that the Florida State University was a "public agency" subject to the requirements of Florida's Sunshine Law? Case law precedent interprets "public agency" quite expansively, as seen from this condensed version of the list of public entities appearing in Patrick John McGinley, FLORIDA ELEMENTS OF AN ACTION § 2101:1 (2019-2020 edition):

> every board of commission of the state, or of any county or political subdivision; boards created by interlocal agreement; the State Fair Authority; school advisory councils; committees to help screen public job applicants; a mayor's group of concerned citizens advising on legislation; a liaison between a mayor's office and a Chamber of Commerce; the postelection transition team of a newly elected official; private organizations that were created by a public entity to serve it; entities assisting the Florida Department of Corrections with its corrections work programs....

Id. How does an expansive definition of "public agency" help advance the purposes of Florida's Sunshine Law?

5. Did you notice that the public agency need not have actual possession of the document for it to become subject to public disclosure under Florida's Sunshine Law? Instead, *NCAA v. Associated Press* held it was enough that the public agency (or, more precisely, the lawyers representing the public agency) used and examined the document in the course of the state's business. Does this make it difficult for public agencies to keep track of what documents are public documents?

6. Were you surprised that the public agency need not create the document in order for it to become subject to public disclosure under Florida's Sunshine Law? Perhaps many people are, because most public websites and letters sent by public agencies warn the public that any correspondence

or email sent to the public agency becomes a public record under Florida's Sunshine Law.

C. Sunshine Law Exceptions and Exclusions

Fans of Florida's Sunshine Law allege that "Florida's Sunshine Law has long been lauded as one of the best in the nation." *See, e.g.,* John Cooper, *Sending the Wrong Message: Technology, Sunshine Law, and the Public Record in Florida*, 39 Stetson L. Rev. 411 (Winter 2010). If this is true, then perhaps it is because "Florida's Sunshine Law has fewer exemptions than most other states' open meetings statutes." Sandra F. Chase and Christina Locke, *The Government-in-the-Sunshine Law Then and Now: Model for Implementing New Technologies Consistent with Florida's Position as a Leader in Open Government*, 35 Fla. St. U. L. Rev. 245 (Winter 2008).

The applicability of Florida's Sunshine Law and the restrictions it imposes are interpreted broadly, whereas the few exceptions to Florida's Sunshine Law are interpreted narrowly. One might say that "coverage is expressed generally; exemptions are identified explicitly." *Wood v. Marston*, 442 So. 2d 934, 938 (Fla. 1983). Perhaps these words from Florida's Supreme Court say it best: "The principle to be followed is very simple: When in doubt, the members of any board, agency, authority or commission should follow the open-meeting policy of the State." *Town of Palm Beach v. Gradison*, 296 So. 2d 473, 477 (Fla.1974).

Florida's Constitution empowers the Florida Legislature to enact exceptions to public access, but any such exception is facially unconstitutional unless it (1) specifies the public necessity for the exception, (2) is not broader than necessary to accomplish the stated necessity; and (3) does not contain any other subject matter other than the exceptions and their enforcement.

Unless the Florida Legislature enacts such an exception, then in general, only two limited exceptions exist: the "use-of-staff" exception, and the "fact-finding" exception. Both exemptions are narrow in scope and ultimately turn on whether there was actual or apparent decision-making authority, as explained in this excerpt from FLORIDA MUNICIPAL LAW AND PRACTICE:

The "use-of-staff" exception can be said to be the broader of the two exceptions because it is available to any governmental group or entity. Its purpose is to allow government officials to have clerical assistants who ultimately bear no responsibility or authority of their own, but who help the government official carry out his or her responsibility and authority. As a general rule, government officials may call upon staff members for factual information and advice without being subject to the Sunshine Law's requirements. Also, a Sunshine violation does not occur when a governmental executive uses staff for a fact-finding and advisory function in fulfilling his or her duties. This exception to the Sunshine Law only applies to staff meetings that are informal, where the discussions were "merely informational," where none of the staff members attending the meetings had any decision-making authority during the meetings, and where no formal action was taken or possibly could have been taken at the meetings. However, if one or more of the staff committee members are delegated any decision-making authority, then the committee as a whole loses its exemption from the Sunshine Law because it stands in the shoes of such public officials from whom the authority was delegated. Stated somewhat differently, if a staff committee has been delegated any decision-making authority in addition to mere fact-finding or information-gathering, then the Sunshine Law applies to the committee. Thus, it is the nature of the act performed by the staff committee, and not the makeup of the committee or the proximity of the act to the final decision, that determines whether a committee composed of staff is subject to the Sunshine Law. For this reason, the use-of-staff exception may never apply when the government official and the staff he consulted made joint decisions. Likewise, the use-of-staff exception may never apply when the government official has delegated part of his or her decision-making authority to a staff member.

The very limited "fact-finding" exception applies only to advisory committees. Such a committee (by whatever name they may be called by the board or entity that created it) is exempt from Florida's Sunshine Law only if the committee has been delegated mere "infor-

> mation-gathering or fact-finding authority" by its board and does not have any "decision-making authority" whatsoever. Where the committee has been delegated decision-making authority, the committee's meetings must be open to public scrutiny, regardless of the review procedures eventually used by the traditional governmental body. The question of decision-making authority is broadly answered to find such authority for Sunshine Law purposes even when the authority is limited to giving nonbinding advice to the entity who has sole decision-making power. Only when a group, on behalf of a public entity, functions solely as a fact finder or information gatherer with no decision-making authority or decision-recommending role can that group be considered exempt from Florida's Sunshine Law.
>
> For this reason, the "fact-finding exception" is further restricted to be available only to the appointing entity's qualifying fact-finding committee and never to the appointing entity itself. This is true even when the appointing board steps down from its decision-making role to embark on a purely fact-finding mission because despite this stated restriction, the board nevertheless remains the ultimate decision-making governmental authority. Note that the requirement that certain board meetings must be open to the public does not imply that the board could meet privately to discuss other matters.

Patrick John McGinley, FLORIDA MUNICIPAL LAW AND PRACTICE § 10:3 (2018-19 ed.) (internal footnotes and quotation marks omitted).

Concerns for equity or fairness will not justify a judicially-created exception to Florida's Sunshine Law, as is illustrated by *Neu v. Miami Herald Publishing Co.*, 462 So. 2d 821 (Fla. 1985). In *Neu*, Florida's then-existing version of the Sunshine Law conflicted with the Florida Evidence Code, Florida's attorney-client privilege, and the Rules Regulating The Florida Bar. The facts of *Neu* involved a governmental entity that was a party to a lawsuit. Sometimes, state and local governments get sued. What if a government entity subject to the open government requirements of Florida's Sunshine Laws wants to meet with its defense attorneys in private to discuss the litigation and its potential settlement? What if the defending governmental unit wants to hear its defense attorney's opinion as to the likelihood of winning the case and the attorney's opinion as to the proper settlement amount? Should such a meeting be open to the public so that the newspaper can report about such opinions -- and the plaintiff can learn about them, too? *Neu v. Miami Herald* discusses the application of Florida's Sunshine Laws to such a situation at a time before the Florida Legislature amended the Sunshine Law to provide for private meetings.

NEU

V.

MIAMI HERALD PUBLISHING COMPANY

Supreme Court of Florida, 1985

462 So. 2d 821

The state attorney and the Miami Herald sought a declaratory judgment that a proposed meeting between the city council and its attorney to discuss pending litigation was subject to the open meeting provisions of the Sunshine Law, section 286.011, Florida Statutes (1981). Relying on *Bassett v. Braddock*, 262 So. 2d 425 (Fla. 1972), the trial court concluded that the proposed meeting was neither official nor formal action under section 286.011 and, thus, there was no requirement that the meeting be open to the public. On appeal, the district court reversed [and] distinguished *Bassett* on the basis that it dealt with a different question arising under a constitutional exception to the Sunshine Law. The district court also rejected the argument that the attorney-client privilege provisions of the Florida Evidence Code granted an exception for closed meetings because, in the court's view, section 286.011(1) limited exceptions to the Sunshine Law to those created by the constitution. Because of the continuing significance of the issue, the court certified the following question of great public importance:

> Whether the Sunshine Law applies to meetings between a City Council and the City Attorney held for the purpose of discussing the set-

tlement of pending litigation to which the city is a party.

We answer the question affirmatively and approve the decision of the district court.

Before turning to the dispositive questions, we dispose of two peripheral questions which have been raised. First, the city council devised a procedure whereby representatives of the press and the state attorney, among others, were to be admitted to the meeting and a record maintained which would later be released to the public. The representatives attending the meeting would be pledged to respect the confidentiality of the cases discussed in the meeting until the cases had been resolved. Whatever merits there may be in this procedural attempt to compromise the competing values between open meetings and private discussion with an attorney, the procedure has no legal impact. Under the Sunshine Law, a meeting is either fully open or fully closed; there are no intermediate categories.

Second, the district court opinion suggests that in enacting the Sunshine Law the legislature, by the use of the words "except as otherwise provided in the constitution," established a requirement that future legislatures could not establish statutory exceptions to the open meeting requirements of the Sunshine Law. This is, of course, incorrect. A legislature may not bind the hands of future legislatures by prohibiting amendments to statutory law.

Turning now to the dispositive questions, the trial court concluded, and petitioners urge, that our decision in *Bassett* creates an exception to the Sunshine Law permitting governmental bodies to meet privately with their attorneys to discuss pending litigation. In *Bassett,* we held that an attorney representing a governmental body could meet privately with employee representatives to negotiate a collective bargaining agreement, and that the governmental body could meet privately with its attorney representative to instruct and consult on the negotiations. We agree that much of our rationale in *Bassett* would appear to support the proposition that private consultations are permitted with attorneys representing governmental bodies in pending litigation. Indeed, we went so far as to comment that "where the negotiator is an *attorney* that certainly he is entitled to consult with the Board on matters regarding preliminary advices." *Bassett*, 262 So. 2d at 428 (emphasis in original). Despite the broadness of such language, our decision was restricted to and rested on what we saw to be a constitutional exception to the Sunshine Law, to wit: the Article I, section 6 right of public employees to bargain collectively.

Petitioners urge that opening up the consultation of the governmental body with its attorney to its adversary in pending litigation gives the adversary an unfair advantage which can be used to secure unmerited or excessive judgments or settlements against the public. There is a good deal of wisdom in petitioners' argument but, as will be made clear below, we have no constitutional or statutory authority to create an exception to the Sunshine Law for governmental bodies to meet privately with their attorneys to discuss pending litigation.

Petitioners next urge that [the] attorney/client privilege [allows] governmental bodies [to] meet privately with their attorneys. Although we agree that the legislature has the authority to exempt such meetings from the Sunshine Law, we do not agree that it has done so. [The attorney-client privilege as codified in Florida Statutes] Section 90.502(1)(c) provides that "[a] communication between lawyer and client is 'confidential' if it is not intended to be disclosed to third persons ...." The Law Revision Council Note to section (1), Florida Statutes Annotated 90.502 (1979), comments that "[w]hen the communication is made in public ... the intent to keep the communication confidential is lacking and the privilege cannot be claimed." The Sunshine Law explicitly provides for public meetings; communications at such public meetings are not confidential and no attorney/client privilege can arise therefrom. In construing legislation, courts should not assume that the legislature acted pointlessly. *Sharer v. Hotel Corp. of America*, 144 So. 2d 813, 817 (Fla. 1962).

Petitioners next urge, alternatively, that reading section 286.011 to deny them a right to private meetings with their attorney places section 286.011 in conflict with Florida Bar Code of Professional Responsibility [the predecessor to the Rules Regulating The Florida Bar], and infringes on the constitutional authority of this Court under Article V, section 15, Florida Constitution to regulate the practice of law. Petitioners cite *Times Pub. Co. v. Williams*, 222 So. 2d 470 (Fla. 2d DCA 1969), in support. We disagree and disapprove that portion of *Times Publishing Co.* which holds that the legislature is without authority to regulate the relationship of public bodies with their attorneys. We note first that Disciplinary Rule 4-101 and Ethical Consideration 4-2 both provide that an attorney may divulge communications with his client when required by law. Further, as we noted above, there are no confidential communications to protect when the communications occur in a public meeting. Finally, the attorney/client privilege belongs to the client, not the attorney. The legislature has plenary constitutional authority to regulate the activities of political subdivisions and can require, as it has done in section 286.011, that meetings be open to the public. The attorney's right to invoke the attorney/client privilege is derivative of the client's right to that privilege. Under the circumstances, it would truly be a case of the tail wagging the dog to hold that an attorney, or this Court, could require closed meetings of public bodies, contrary to statutory law, based on the Code of Professional Responsibility.

Petitioners also urge that they have a due process right under the fourteenth amendment to the United States Constitution to privately consult with their attorney. We will not make any sweeping pronouncements on the distinction between due process rights of governmental entities and private persons. It is enough to say that the legislature has the power to require open meetings and that petitioners' argument has been rejected by the United States Supreme Court. *Williams v. Mayor and City Council of Baltimore*, 289 U.S. 36 (1933).

One can argue and reargue whether the broad reading of the Sunshine Law is politically wise. We have no interest in nor responsibility for debating political questions. As we said in *Wait v. Florida Power & Light Co.*, 372 So. 2d 420, 424 (Fla. 1979):

> This argument should be addressed to the legislature. Courts deal with the construction and constitutionality of legislative determinations,

not their wisdom. In this case, we are confined to a determination of the legislature's intent.

The certified question is answered in the affirmative and the decision of the district court approved.

It is so ordered.

Notes and Questions to Consider:

1. Sometimes the requirements of Florida's Sunshine Law may conflict with other laws, such as in *Neu v. Miami Herald* where the open meetings requirements of the Sunshine Law conflicted with the Florida Evidence Code, the attorney-client privilege, and the Rules Regulating The Florida Bar. Generally speaking, when such a conflict exists, does Florida's Sunshine Law prevail?

2. The holding of *Neu v. Miami Herald* constitutes an unequitable result from the perspective of the governmental entity that is the defendant in the lawsuit. The advice from its attorney about that suit will be made public. Newspapers and others may spread that information far and wide. The opposing counsels in the suit, and their clients, may learn what advice the defendant's lawyers gave the governmental defendant. On the other hand, the governmental defendant does not learn what advice the opposing counsels are giving to the opposing party. Are such inequities sufficient to permit a judicially-created exception to Florida Sunshine Law?

3. *Neu v. Miami Herald* interpreted the 1985 version of Florida's Sunshine Law which had not yet been amended to provide a procedure for government officials to meet privately with defense attorneys. In the first of the two "peripheral questions" addressed near the beginning of *Neu*, the court considers and rejects the city council's makeshift solution for complying with Florida's Sunshine Law yet preserving the attorney-client privilege. Why did the court find this makeshift solution impermissible?

4. *Neu* ends with the admonition that the question of whether Florida's Sunshine Law was politically wise is one for the legislature not the courts. Did the legislature act? As discussed in Part A of this chapter, the current version of Florida's Sunshine Law contains an exception intended to preserve the attorney-client privilege in situations similar to *Neu v. Miami Herald.* Florida Statutes section 286.011(8) provides in relevant part that the governmental entity may meet in private with the entity's attorney to discuss pending litigation provided that the following conditions are met:

> (a) The entity's attorney requests it.
>
> (b) The discussion is confined to settlement or litigation expenditures.
>
> (c) The discussion recorded by a certified court reporter who records the start and stop time, all discussions, the names of all persons present and all persons speaking. No portion of the session shall be off the record. The court reporter's notes shall be fully transcribed and filed with the entity's clerk within a reasonable time after the meeting.
>
> (d) The entity gives reasonable public notice of the time and date of the attorney-client session and the names of persons who will be attending. The session shall commence at an open meeting at which the persons chairing the meeting shall announce the commencement and estimated length of the attorney-client session and the names of the persons attending. At the conclusion of the attorney-client session, the meeting shall be reopened, and the person chairing the meeting shall announce the termination of the session.
>
> (e) The transcript shall be made part of the public record upon conclusion of the litigation.

D. Audio or Video Recording by the Public

Clearly, a record of government gatherings or meeting is contemplated by the Florida Sunshine Law's requirement that the government make "minutes" of the meeting, promptly record them into the public record, and make that public record open to public inspection. But "minutes" are not a verbatim transcript, and "minutes" do not record every single word or action.

What if the news media, or even just a citizen, wants to make a complete audio or video recording of a gathering or meeting of government officials? Some people do not wish to be recorded. Some people act awkwardly once they know they are being recorded. The effect of Florida's Sunshine Law upon the ability to record what is said and observed at government gatherings and meetings is illustrated by the following case of *Pinellas County Sch. Bd. v. Suncam, Inc.*, 829 So. 2d 989 (Fla. 2d DCA 2002).

PINELLAS COUNTY SCHOOL BOARD

V.

SUNCAM, INC.

Florida's Second District Court of Appeal, 2002

829 So. 2d 989

The Pinellas County School Board appeals from a final judgment which determined that the board had committed a violation of the Florida Sunshine Law, section 286.011, Florida Statutes (2001). We affirm.

The facts are not in dispute. The Pinellas County School Board scheduled a public meeting of the Special Services Selection Committee for the purpose of evaluating applications of general contractors for the remodeling, renovation, and new construction of Gibbs High School in Pinellas County. It is agreed that the board complied with all other requirements of the Florida Sunshine Law, section 286.011, Florida Statutes (2001), with the exception of denying the request of Suncam, Inc. to videotape the proceedings.

The asserted justification for denial by the board was that participants in the meeting would not act normally while being videotaped and that this would impair the work of the committee. It is agreed that the videotaping itself would be unobtrusive. It is also agreed that although the board vacillated on whether to allow videotaping, in the final analysis, videotaping was permitted solely at the discretion of the board through its superintendent. The ultimate issue for our determination is whether the board retains unfettered authority to deny videotaping of its otherwise public meeting. We answer the question in the negative, but limit our response to the sufficiency of the board's stated reason for not allowing videotaping in this instance.

The Sunshine Law was enacted to protect the public from "closed door" politics. See *Wood v. Marston*, 442 So. 2d 934, 938 (Fla.1983). As a result, the law "must be broadly construed to effect its remedial and protective purpose." *Id.* "The breadth of such right is virtually unfettered...." *Lorei v. Smith*, 464 So. 2d 1330, 1332 (Fla. 2d DCA 1985). In *Hough v. Stembridge*, 278 So. 2d 288, 289 (Fla. 3d DCA 1973), the Third District held that violation of the Sunshine Law can occur where a state agency meets and violates the "statute's spirit, intent, and purpose." Thus, although the statute does not explicitly provide for the video recording of public meetings, the refusal to allow such recording certainly violates the "statute's spirit, intent, and purpose."

This specific issue was addressed by the attorney general several years ago. Op. Att'y. Gen. Fla. 91–28 (1991). See *Beverly v. Div. of Beverage of Dep't of Bus. Regulation*, 282 So. 2d 657 (Fla. 1st DCA 1973) (holding that opinions of Florida's Attorney General are entitled to great weight in construing the law of the state, but are not binding on Florida's District Courts of Appeal). The attorney general stated: "A municipality may not prohibit a citizen from video taping the meetings of the city council through the use of nondisruptive video recording devices." The attorney general concluded its opinion with the following statement:

> In previously considering a similar issue, this office stated that a rule which prohibits the use of all tape recorders, including silent taping devices that are neither distracting nor disruptive, was in conflict with

> the public policy of the state as interpreted under Florida Statutes section 286.011. While a public board may adopt reasonable rules and policies to ensure the orderly conduct of its public meeting and to require orderly behavior on the part of those attending, rules prohibiting the use of silent or nondisruptive tape recording devices would appear to be unreasonable and arbitrary and, therefore, invalid.
>
> Moreover, the Legislature in Florida Statutes section 934.02(1) appears to implicitly recognize the public's right to silently record public meetings. Chapter 934, the Security of Communications Law, regulates the interception of oral communication. Section 934.02(2), however, defines "oral communication" as specifically excluding "public oral communication uttered at a public meeting."

Op. Att'y. Gen. Fla. 91–28 (footnotes omitted).

We determine that the board was in violation of the Florida Sunshine Law in the instant case and, therefore, affirm the final judgment.

Affirmed and remanded for proceedings pursuant to this opinion.

Notes and Questions to Consider:

1. Nowadays, it seems like everyone has a phone in their pocket or bag, and those phones can be used to make audio or video recordings. Does Florida's Sunshine Law entitle Floridians to use their phones to make an audio or video recording of Florida government gatherings or meetings? Can people record the government gathering surreptitiously? In addressing these questions, FLORIDA MUNICIPAL LAW AND PRACTICE summarizes Florida case law precedent as follows:

> Regarding the public's available means for making a record of or recording a municipal meeting, the municipality or its board may adopt reasonable rules and policies which ensure the orderly conduct of a public meeting and require orderly behavior on the part of those persons attending that meeting.

> Despite this power, it may not ban the use of nondisruptive recording devices. Therefore, the public may record the meeting using any nondisruptive means, including secret or covert methods of an audio or video recording.

Patrick John McGinley, FLORIDA MUNICIPAL LAW AND PRACTICE § 10:7 (2019-2020 ed.) (footnotes omitted).

2. How does permitting the audio and video recording of government gatherings or meetings promote the Florida Sunshine Law's goals of transparency and accountability?

3. By permitting surreptitious audio or video recordings, does the Florida Sunshine Law discourage -- or to borrow a phrase from federal First Amendment jurisprudence, have a "chilling effect" upon -- public debate or free speech at government meetings?

4. What if some people who attend public meetings wish to make a statement to the government "off the record." How can this be achieved in compliance with Florida's Sunshine Law?

E. Notice Requirements

One requirement of Florida's Sunshine Law is for the government to provide "due public notice" of all government gatherings or meetings. What exactly does that require? Consider the following Opinion of the Florida Attorney General.

FLORIDA ATTORNEY GENERAL ADVISORY OPINION

NUMBER: AGO 73-170

Date: May 17, 1973

Re: Sunshine Law—Meaning of Term "Due Public Notice"

To: Jack Faircloth, Clerk, Circuit Court, Bonifay

Prepared by: Henry George White, Assistant Attorney General

Question:

What is the meaning of the term "due public notice" in s. 125.001, Florida Statutes, as that term relates to the provisions of the Florida Sunshine Law?

Summary:

The meaning of the term "due public notice" is variable, depending on the facts of each situation. The purpose of notice is to apprise individuals or the public generally of the pendency of matters which may affect their personal or property rights and afford them the opportunity to appear and present their views. The nature of the proceeding at which these rights are to be affected, the nature of the rights themselves, the applicable statutory provisions, and other surrounding circumstances will influence the notice requirements of each case. But in every case the notice must reasonably convey all the information required in that situation and it must afford a reasonable time for interested persons to make an appearance if they wish.

Discussion:

The Government in the Sunshine Law is a policy declaration by the legislature that all meetings of public bodies at which official acts are to be taken shall be open to the public. Implicit in this policy is the requirement that the public have notice of such meetings. While the Sunshine Law does not expressly mention notice, the cases construing it do speak of the public's right "to be present and to be heard," *Board of Public Instruction of Broward County v. Doran,* 224 So. 2d 693 (Fla. 1969), and the right of "public scrutiny and participation," *City of Miami Beach v. Berns*, 245 So. 2d 38 (Fla. 1971). It is axiomatic that the right "to be present and to heard" has little meaning or value unless the public is informed that particular matters are pending and can choose whether or not to attend and participate in a meeting. An understanding of the purpose of notice assists in the formulation of a functional definition of that term.

There is no precise definition of or formula for due notice which is applicable to every situation. Due notice is a relative term, the meaning and sufficiency of which can be ascertained only in reference to the particular facts and circumstances upon which it bears. Notice which is adequate under normal conditions may be impractical or impossible in emergency situations. So the purpose behind the requirement of notice, the events about which notice is given, and the nature of the rights affected will determine what is required in each case.

I have previously stated in AGO 071-32 that any meeting which is subject to the provisions of the Sunshine Law must be preceded by:

> "a reasonable and ample period of notice to the public and representatives of the press so that they may attend the meeting if they wish. Both the period of notice of the meeting and the method of promulgating the notice to the public must be performed in strict accordance with legislative requirements when these requirements exist; where there is no legislative prescription, then the serving of notice and the promulgation of the notice must be given in a reasonable manner calculated to timely inform the public."

Accord: Attorney General Opinions 071-346 and 072-400.

As noted above, Florida's Sunshine Law requires "due public notice" of regular or special meetings of the board of county commissioners, but the type or period of notice required in this situation is not covered by the statute. As the statute does not identify the prerequisites for adequate notice, the criteria outlined above will come into play. Thus, even though Florida Statutes section 125.66(2) requires at least fifteen days' notice of an intention to enact a county ordinance, and prescribes the manner in which the notice of intention must be given, such notice will not satisfy the requirements of Florida's Sunshine Law unless there is proper notice of the time and place of the meeting at which such action is to be taken by the board of county commissioners. Similarly, Florida Statutes section 125.66(3) allows a waiver of the notice requirements by a four-fifths vote of the county commissioners declaring that an emergency exists and that the immediate enactment of an ordinance is necessary. Nevertheless, this section, read with Florida's Sunshine Laws, contemplates that due notice of the time and place of the regular or special meeting at which the emergency enactment is acted upon will have been given.

In sum: In every situation in which some type of notice is required, the content of the notice and the method of promulgating it will be influenced by applicable statutory requirements and by what the particular circumstances may fairly and reasonable dictate or require. If the purpose for notice is kept in mind, together with the character of the event about which notice is to be given and the nature of the rights to be affected, the essential requirements for notice in that situation will suggest themselves. Good faith adherence to those guidelines will assure that the notice requirements of each situation will be satisfied.

Notes and Questions to Consider:

1. The opinion above is not a court opinion. It is an Opinion of the Attorney General of the State of Florida. Article IV of Florida's Constitution authorizes Florida's Attorney General to issue formal legal opinions at the request of such public officials on questions relating to the application of state law. The opinion was issued to the inquiring Florida Clerk of the Circuit Court, who may be an elected public official under Article VIII, section 1(d) of Florida's Constitution. Then, in accordance with Florida's Sunshine Law, the opinion became public. What precedential value do these Attorney General Opinions hold? *Browning v. Fla. Prosecuting Attorneys Ass'n, Inc.*, 56 So. 3d 873 (Fla. 1st DCA 2011) states that "Attorney General opinions are not binding on Florida courts and can be rejected. However, this court has previously held Attorney General opinions are entitled to great weight in construing the law of this State. Furthermore, the fact that two different Attorney Generals have reached the same conclusion with respect to the exact issue now before us lends considerable persuasive influence to their opinions and weighs heavily in favor of our conclusion herein." Id. at 878 n.2 (internal citations and quotes omitted).

2. The concept of procedural Due Process of Law, as embodied in the Fifth and Fourteenth Amendments to the U.S. Constitution, imposes upon state governments, at a minimum, the requirements of providing adequate notice and an opportunity to be heard. In light of these minimum federal requirements, are the notice requirements of Florida's Sunshine Law superfluous, or does Florida's Sunshine Law increase these federal minimums?

3. This Attorney General Opinion number AGO 73-170 concludes by stating: "If the purpose for notice is kept in mind, together with the character of the event about which notice is to be given and the nature of the rights to be affected, the essential requirements for notice in that situation will suggest themselves." To what extent is this an actionable, bright-line rule? FLORIDA MUNICIPAL LAW AND PRACTICE attempts to answer that question as follows:

> Florida's Sunshine Law does not state with specificity what is required in order for the public to have received a timely and proper notice of a hearing. Florida courts have so far declined to create a bright-line rule or an explicit time period for providing notice, but instead hold only that "reasonable notice" of a public meeting is mandatory. Like any legal standard based upon the notion of reasonableness, the actions necessary depend upon the circumstances. For example, the court found that a six-days' notice of a city commission meeting did not violate Florida's Sunshine Law. Likewise, the court found that a three-days' notice constituted reasonable notice of a meeting of the city of Perry's City Council where it considered renovating and upgrading certain aspects of its utility system. A three-days' notice was again found reasonable when notice of a city's special meeting held on Monday, September 15 was posted at city hall and faxed to the media on Friday, September 12. However, a 90-minutes' notice of a city commission's special meeting was once found inadequate.
>
> Clearly, the meaning of "reasonable notice" will vary depending on the fact situation, but the purpose of requiring "reasonable notice" is to apprise the public of the pendency of matters that might af-

> fect their rights, afford them the opportunity to appear and present their views, and afford them a reasonable time to attend the meeting if they wish. Perhaps, with this purpose in mind, a reasonable notice may be devised based upon the circumstances presented.

Patrick John McGinley, FLORIDA MUNICIPAL LAW AND PRACTICE § 10:4 (2017-18 ed.).

4. Do the notice requirements imposed by Florida's Sunshine Laws entitle the government to receive notice from the Floridian of the fact that the Floridian will make an audio or video recording of a government gathering or meeting?

It was once said, and is oft repeated, that "life is what happens to us while we are busy making other plans." Allen Saunders, READER'S DIGEST MAGAZINE, Jan. 1957. Can an unforeseen event, or even a perceived emergency, justify the government's omission of the usual advance notice of a public meeting? Consider the decision of Florida's First District Court of Appeal in *Rhea v. City of Gainesville*, 574 So. 2d 221 (Fla. 1st DCA 1991).

RHEA

v.

CITY OF GAINESVILLE

First District Court of Appeal of Florida, 1991

574 So. 2d 221

Appellant, Darnell Rhea, appeals the trial court's dismissal with prejudice of his amended complaint. We reverse.

The record indicates that, on February 20, 1990, the mayor of Gainesville called a special meeting of the Gainesville City Commission. The meeting was held that afternoon at 3:00 p.m. The minutes of the 3:00 p.m.

meeting indicate that all members of the local news media were contacted regarding the special meeting no later than 1:35 p.m. that day. The purpose of the meeting was to respond to the upcoming appointment by the Alachua County legislative delegation of a committee to study the operation of Gainesville Regional Utilities. At the meeting, discussion was had and a motion was passed authorizing the mayor to write to the delegation conveying the Commission's position on the issue and offering the Commission's support.

On March 9, 1990, appellant (a resident of Alachua County) filed a complaint against the City purporting to allege that the February 20, 1990 meeting had been held without proper notice to the public, and was therefore in violation of the "Sunshine Law" (section 286.011, Florida Statutes). The City filed a motion to dismiss for failure to state a cause of action, and the motion was granted with leave to amend. On May 4, 1990, appellant filed an amended complaint requesting the court find that the meeting violated the notice requirement, that it void all formal action taken at the meeting, and that it award appellant costs pursuant to section 286.011(4). The City again moved to dismiss for failure to allege facts establishing a violation of section 286.011 and, on June 12, 1990, the court dismissed the amended complaint with prejudice, finding "the acts complained of by the plaintiff are not formal actions contemplated within the provisions of Florida Statute 286.011."

Although the statute does not contain a specific notice requirement, it has been held that "reasonable notice" of a public meeting is mandatory in order for the meeting to be public in essence. In *Yarbrough v. Young*, 462 So. 2d 515 (Fla. 1st DCA 1985), this court found that three days' notice of a meeting constituted reasonable notice. In a 1973 attorney general's opinion, it was stated that the meaning of the term "due public notice" would vary depending on the fact situation, but that its purpose was to apprise the public of the pendency of matters that might affect their rights, afford them the opportunity to appear and present their views, and afford them a reasonable time to make an appearance if they wished. Op. Atty. Gen., 73-170, May 17, 1973.

The Florida Supreme Court held that the Sunshine Law covers "any gathering of the members where the members deal with some matter on which foreseeable action will be taken by the board." *Board of Public Instruction of Broward County v. Doran*, 224 So. 2d 693, 698 (Fla. 1969). Further, the Second District has held that "[e]very step in the decision-making process, including the decision itself, is a necessary preliminary to formal action. It follows that each such step constitutes an 'official act,' an indispensable requisite to 'formal action,' within the meaning of the act." *Times Pub. Co. v. Williams*, 222 So. 2d 470, 473 (Fla. 2d DCA 1969).

Under the above authorities, we find appellant's amended complaint to have stated a sufficient cause of action under section 286.011, by making a prima facie showing that the Commission held a public meeting at which official acts or formal action took place, without providing reasonable notice to the public. We therefore reverse the dismissal of the amended complaint, and remand for further proceedings.

F. Public Meetings

Florida's Supreme Court holds: "A secret meeting occurs when public officials meet at a time and place to avoid being seen or heard by the public." *City of Miami Beach v. Berns*, 245 So. 2d 38, 41 (Fla. 1971). Perhaps for this reason, Florida's Supreme Court interprets Florida's Sunshine Law to impose restrictions upon the location of public meetings held by state or municipal governmental entities.

In the private sector, employers and other entities sometimes hold off-site workshops, company outings that involve both work and entertainment, and the like. In the public sector, does Florida's Sunshine Law allow such activities? This is the question raised in the case of *Rhea v. School Board of Alachua County*, 636 So. 2d 1383 (Fla. 1st DCA 1994) which proposes a "balancing of interests" test.

RHEA

V.

SCHOOL BOARD OF ALACHUA COUNTY

First District Court of Appeal of Florida, 1994.

636 So. 2d 1383

Darnell Rhea (Rhea) appeals a summary judgment entered in favor of the Alachua County School Board (Board). The trial court found that the Board's workshop held in Orlando, Florida, on December 3, 1991, did not violate section 286.011, Florida Statutes (1991), commonly known as the "Government in the Sunshine Law." We reverse.

The Board announced, during its regular November meeting, that it intended to conduct a workshop for Board members in Orlando on December 3, 1991, to take advantage of the fact that all the members already would be in Orlando to attend the semi-annual convention of the Florida School Boards Association. The Board also advertised the meeting by placing a detailed notice in the *Gainesville Sun* newspaper on November 26, 1991, stating that the meeting was "a public workshop to which all persons are invited." The Board met on the evening of December 3, 1991, as planned, at the Twin Towers Hotel in Orlando.

Rhea filed a complaint on May 29, 1992, seeking injunctive and declaratory relief against the Board, alleging that the Board violated section 286.011 in holding a Board meeting in a place located outside the geographical boundaries of the Board's district, that is, Alachua County, and more than 100 miles from Gainesville, the Board's headquarters.

Both parties moved for summary judgment. Rhea's affidavit stated that he would have attended the meeting but for the fact it was held outside Alachua County, over 100 miles from him. The Board attached a copy of the minutes of the workshop and two affidavits in support of its motion. One affidavit was from a Board member, who stated that the Orlando workshop was open to the public at all times, that is, the meeting was held in a public meeting room, the room had sufficient space for those in attendance, and the meeting was properly noticed. The second affidavit was from the Board's attorney, who stated that the workshop occurred in a hotel public meeting room, the door to which was left open throughout the session. Moreover, the hotel's staff was advised to direct anyone who inquired about the meeting to the appropriate location.

The Board properly concedes that the school board workshop held in Orlando was a "public meeting" for purposes of the Sunshine Law. The Board, however, denies that any violation of that law took place. Section 286.011(1) provides in relevant part:

> All meetings of any board ... at which official acts are to be taken are declared public meetings *open to the public* at all times, and no resolution, rule, or formal action shall be considered binding except as taken or made at such meeting.

(Emphasis added.) The mere fact that a meeting is held in a public room does not make it public within the meaning of the Sunshine Law. For a meeting to be "public," it is essential that the public be given advance notice and a reasonable opportunity to attend.

Adequacy of notice is not an issue in this case. Rhea challenges instead the scope of the word "public," as contemplated by the Sunshine Law. Rhea contends "public" refers to the constituency of the public entity that is convening. The "public" for the Alachua County School Board, therefore, would be members of Alachua County, as opposed to members of Orange County or the Florida public at large. Rhea argues that by meeting outside Alachua County, at a hotel more than 100 miles from its headquarters, the Board denied reasonable access to its public.

Section 286.011 does not define the word "public." Applying the plain and ordinary meaning of the word to the instant case, the relevant "public," the community that would be affected by the Board's official actions, is Alachua County. The Alachua County school board represents the entire county, and the relevant community is Alachua County. Thus, whether the Orlando Board workshop was sufficiently "open to the public" depends on whether Alachua County residents had a "reasonable opportunity" to attend the meeting.

Rhea urges this court to fashion an absolute rule which would prohibit any Board workshop from being held under any circumstances at a site more than 100 miles from the usual meeting place. We can envision circumstances which would warrant the conduct of a workshop beyond the county boundaries and perhaps even more than 100 miles from the usual meeting place. Thus, we decline to adopt a bright line test which would resolve every dispute on this issue. Rather, we hold that a balancing of interests test is the most appropriate method by which to determine which interest predominates in a given case. The interests of the public in having a reasonable opportunity to attend a Board workshop must be balanced against the Board's need to conduct a workshop at a site beyond the county boundaries. A significant and obvious factor to be considered in the weighing process is the extent of the distance from the usual meeting place to the out-of-county workshop, an issue which both parties to this cause addressed extensively. We conclude that the greater the distance, the heavier the burden is upon the Board to demonstrate a need for the alternate site. It follows that the shorter the distance, the lighter the burden is upon the Board to justify the out-of-county site.

Another factor to be considered is any good faith action by the Board to minimize the expense and inconvenience of the public in attending an out-of-county workshop. For example, an offer by the Board to provide transportation for the public at the Board's expense, would serve to mitigate the disadvantage to the public, thus enhancing the weight of the Board's position in the matter.

We would ordinarily expect a Board workshop to be held within the county boundaries for reasons of sound logic and common sense. However, when a perceived need to do otherwise arises, the Board must apply the balancing of interests test.

The foregoing factors are not intended to be all-inclusive. Any consideration of the balancing process must focus upon the issue of whether the Board's need for a workshop at a particular geographical site is outweighed by the resulting barriers which tend to prevent public attendance. Thus, any factor or circumstance which impacts thereon must be considered on a case-by-case basis.

When applying this balancing test to the circumstances of the instant case, we conclude that the Board's workshop held at a hotel in Orlando, Florida, on December 3, 1991, did not afford the citizens of Alachua County a reasonable opportunity to attend. There was nothing peculiar about the Orlando site, that is, there was nothing physically located there, nor any activity taking place, which necessitated the Board's observation or discussion at that particular location. The only reason for holding the workshop in Orlando was because the Board members were already assembled at the same hotel for a semi-annual meeting of the Florida School Boards Association. The only advantage to the Board was the elimination of travel time and expense ordinarily incurred by Board members and staff in making the usual trip from home or office to the regular meeting site in Gainesville on an alternate date. We consider this to be an insignificant advantage. When compared to the disadvantages visited upon the public in terms of additional time and expense of travel, we conclude that the balancing process weighs heavily in favor of a finding that the public was denied a reasonable opportunity to attend the workshop. While the failure of the Board to mitigate any of the barriers would ordinarily be significant, the need for the workshop in Orlando was such that we do not believe that even significant mitigation could have overcome the minimal need for the workshop at that site.

We accordingly REVERSE and REMAND for consistent proceedings.

Notes and Questions to Consider:

1. In *Rhea v. School Board of Alachua County*, the School Board's Orlando meeting was open to the public. So why did the court hold that it violated Florida's Sunshine public meeting requirement?

2. When we examined the Florida Sunshine Law's notice requirements in the subsection of this text above, we questioned whether those

requirements created an actionable, bright-line rule. Can the same criticism be raised as to these requirements about the location of meetings?

3. Does the location of the meeting violate Florida's Sunshine Law if the room is too small for the number of people who choose to attend? Citing to an unpublished opinion from Florida's Fifth District Court of Appeal, FLORIDA MUNICIPAL LAW AND PRACTICE opines that:

> The public entity violates the Sunshine Law if it does not provide ample space for the meeting. This does not mean that the room hosting the meeting must be large enough for an unexpected crowd, but that reasonable access be granted to all regardless of the size of the crowd. For example, in the case of a Water Management District meeting which drew an overflow crowd, the district did not violate the Sunshine Law even though not all members of the public were able to enter the meeting room. The district board was holding its meeting at the board's usual meeting place and therefore had not moved the meeting to inconvenience the crowd. Once noting the size of the turnout, the district chose its largest available room. Also, the district board set up a computer with external speakers so that those who were not able to enter the meeting room could view and hear the proceedings. These types of accommodations yield compliance with the Sunshine Law even when the size of the room exceeds the size of the crowd attending.

Patrick John McGinley, FLORIDA MUNICIPAL LAW AND PRACTICE § 10:5 (2017-18 ed.).

4. Does the location of the meeting violate Florida's Sunshine Law if it is hard to hear the speakers? Consider this advice from the Florida Attorney General's Office as published in the 2012 version of their GOVERNMENT IN THE SUNSHINE MANUAL:

> A violation of the Sunshine Law may occur if, during a recess of a public meeting, board members discuss issues before the board in a manner not generally audible to the public attending the meeting. Although such a meeting is not clandestine, it nonetheless violates the

> letter and spirit of the law. *Rackleff v. Bishop*, No. 89-235 (Fla. 2d Cir. Ct. March 5, 1990). And see Opinion of the Florida Attorney General number AGO 71-159, stating that discussions of public business which are audible only to "a select few" who are at the table with the board members may violate the "openness" requirement of the law.

Office of Fla. Atty. Gen., GOVERNMENT IN THE SUNSHINE MANUAL Vol. 34 (2012 Electronic Edition).

5. Florida's Supreme Court describes the Florida Sunshine Law's right of the public to attend government meetings as an "inalienable" right. *Board of Public Instruction of Broward County v. Doran*, 224 So. 2d 693 (Fla. 1969). Does the balance-of-interests tests in *Rhea v. School Board of Alachua County* adequately protect a right so cherished as to be declared inalienable?

6. Florida experiences hurricanes and other dangerous weather conditions on a recurring basis. Under Florida's Sunshine Law as interpreted by *Rhea v. School Board of Alachua County*, to what extent would the weather be a permissible factor in setting the location of a government meeting? How would it affect the balance of interests?

G. Sunshine Law Remedies

Did you notice a strange thing in common between the last two cases we read? Compare the name of the appellant in the case appearing immediately above with the name of the appellant in the case immediately preceding it. See how the later case is called *Rhea v. School Board of Alachua County*, 636 So. 2d 1383 (Fla. 1st DCA 1994)? And the former case is called in *Rhea v. City of Gainesville*, 574 So. 2d 221 (Fla. 1st DCA 1991)? See how both cases begin with *Rhea*? That is because, in both cases, the appellant is one and the same: Mr. Darnell Rhea.

It appears that Mr. Darnell Rhea is no stranger to the courtrooms of Florida. Assuming WestLaw is correct, then other reported decisions appear also to involve Mr. Darnell Rhea, perhaps including *Rhea v. Dist. Bd. of Trustees of Santa Fe Coll.*, 109 So. 3d 851 (Fla. 1st DCA 2013); *Rhea v. Bradford County Prop. Appraiser*, 106 So. 3d 933 (Fla. 1st DCA 2013); *Grover v. Bradford County Sheriff's Office*, 90 So. 3d 277 (Fla. 1st DCA 2012) (listing "Darnell Rhea" as a co-appellant); *Hess v. Sch. Bd. of Alachua County*, 704 So. 2d 523 (Fla. 1st DCA 1997) (listing "Darnell Rhea" as a co-appellant); and *Sch. Bd. of Alachua County v. Rhea*, 661 So. 2d 331, 332 (Fla. 1st DCA 1995) (a subsequent appeal from an order addressing attorney fees entered after remand from 636 So. 2d 1383). It may be a coincidence of similar-sounding names, or perhaps each Darnell Rhea is one and the same. If so, then more than one of Mr. Rhea's cases involved Florida's Sunshine Law, and more than one of Mr. Rhea's cases involved Mr. Rhea having lawyers who represented him.

How can one Floridian afford to bring so much litigation under Florida's Sunshine Law? Perhaps Mr. Rhea found pro bono lawyers who, like Mr. Rhea, appear to be dedicated to the public interest and are staunch defenders of Florida's Constitution.

But it is at least theoretically possible that Mr. Rhea's lawyers were not intending to work for free, and possible that an economic incentive might be present for Mr. Rhea's lawyers. Consider the following remedies, sanctions and damage awards that may be available upon a successful litigation under Florida's Sunshine Law:

- Entry of a declaratory judgment holding the action taken in violation of Florida's Sunshine Law to be null, void and unenforceable
- A noncriminal infraction, punishable by a fine not exceeding $500 (awardable against any public officer)
- A second degree misdemeanor for knowingly attending a meeting held in violation of the Sunshine Law (awardable against any person who is a member of a board or commission or of any state agency or authority of any county, municipal corporation, or political subdivision)

- A second degree misdemeanor for conduct occurring outside the state that would constitute a knowing violation of Florida's Sunshine Law
- Reasonable attorney fees against the guilty agency
- Reasonable attorney fees against the guilty individuals (i.e., against the individual member or members of such board or commission; provided, that in any case where the board or commission seeks the advice of its attorney and such advice is followed, no such fees shall be assessed against the individual member or members of the board or commission. However, this subsection shall not apply to a state attorney or his or her duly authorized assistants or any officer charged with enforcing the provisions of this section)
- Taxable costs of the litigation (awardable against the nonprevailing party or parties)

Note that these remedies enumerated above can involve attorney fee awards. The entitlement to attorney fees under Florida's Sunshine Law is usually a "one-way street," so-to-speak, in that the court must award fees against the government if the Floridian prevails, but the court must not award fees against the Floridian unless the court finds that action was filed in bad faith or was frivolous.

Notes and Questions to Consider:

1. Do the potential attorney fee awards available under Florida's Sunshine Law improperly incentivize the filing and pursuit of litigation? Or do they merely reimburse victims of violations of Florida's Constitution?

2. If you are a Florida attorney, and your potential new client is the victim of a violation of Florida's Sunshine Law, could you represent her on a contingency fee basis? Would you?

H. Inadvertent or Unplanned Gatherings

Even an inadvertent meeting or unforeseen gathering of public officials is subject to the requirements of Florida's Sunshine Law if government business reasonably could be discussed or is discussed. The meeting or gathering might have been intended for another purpose, but nevertheless, can be subject to Florida's Sunshine Law. For example, consider the mediation that occurred under a federal court rule requiring privacy and confidentiality at issue in the case of *Brown v. Denton*, 152 So. 3d 8 (Fla. 1st DCA 2014).

BROWN

V.

DENTON

First District Court of Appeal of Florida, 2014.

152 So. 3d 8

In this consolidated appeal, the appellants, Mayor Alvin Brown (the Mayor), the City of Jacksonville (the City), and the Jacksonville Police and Fire Pension Fund Board of Trustees (the Board), appeal an order granting summary final judgment in favor of the appellee, Frank Denton (Denton). Finding no grounds for reversible error, we affirm.

In February 2013, Randall Wyse, who was employed as the fire district chief and who also served as the Chief Negotiator for the Firefighters' Union—the Jacksonville Association of Fire Fighters Local 122, IAFF (JAFF)—along with several other plaintiffs, filed suit against the City and the Board in the United States District Court for the Middle District of Florida. In March 2013, the City, the Board, and the plaintiffs voluntarily sought mediation in the federal case. For the next few months, several closed-door mediation sessions were held at a stipulated mediator's office in Gainesville, Florida. Although not parties to the federal litigation, the JAFF and the Fraternal Order of Police Lodge 5–30 (FOP and, collectively with JAFF, the Unions) attended the mediation sessions. No party informed the federal court that the negotiations would entail collective bargaining or that the provisions of the Florida Statutes and Constitution may require such collective bargaining to be conducted in public. There was no public notice of the mediation sessions nor was any transcript made of the proceedings.

The end result of the private mediation sessions was a Mediation Settlement Agreement (MSA), which, on its face, changed the specific, defined pension benefits of City employees in the Unions. The signatories to the MSA included: the Mayor's Chief of Staff, General Counsel for the City, Wyse (who signed "individually" and also as the President/Chief Negotiator of JAFF), the Executive Director of the Pension Fund, legal counsel for the Pension Fund, legal counsel for the Unions, and the President/Chief Negotiator of FOP as well as the remaining federal plaintiffs. The parties were to use their best efforts to obtain approval from their respected officials necessary for implementation of the MSA. It was also undisputed that the parties intended to seek further mediation if the MSA were not adopted.

In May 2013, the Mayor held a press conference announcing an agreement on retirement reform with the Unions. An ordinance was subsequently introduced to the City Council seeking approval of the MSA. In July 2013, the City Council voted down the proposed ordinance and, therefore, decided not to adopt the MSA.

In August 2013, Denton, an editor of the Florida Times–Union newspaper in Jacksonville, filed a verified amended complaint for declaratory and injunctive relief in circuit court against the Mayor, in his official capacity, the City, and the Board. The complaint alleged that the closed-door mediation sessions constituted collective bargaining negotiations that, under section 447.605(2), Florida Statutes (2013), were conducted in violation of Florida's Sunshine Law as codified in section 286.011, Florida Statutes (2013). The complaint sought a declaration that the MSA was void ab initio and that a Sunshine Law violation occurred and would continue to occur were the mediation sessions allowed to continue. Finally, the complaint sought an injunction prohibiting the defendants from adopting, performing, or implementing the MSA and from engaging in future mediation.

Following motions for summary judgment on the issues, on December 31, 2013, the circuit court entered an order granting summary final judgment in favor of Denton. The circuit court found that it had jurisdiction to determine whether collective bargaining had been held in compliance with the Sunshine Law and to enjoin further violations. The circuit court found that in negotiating the MSA, the City and the Board made changes to the terms of the employee pension benefits, which were a mandatory subject of collective bargaining, and, absent a clear waiver, were required to be conducted in the sunshine. The circuit court found that the Board acted as the Unions' representative and bargaining agent in the negotiations or the Unions themselves participated to some degree in negotiating the MSA. As such, the circuit court held that the federal mediation sessions violated the Sunshine Law, voided the MSA *ab initio*, and enjoined "the parties from conducting further proceedings entailing collective bargaining of the police officer and firefighter pension funds in private outside of the sunshine." The circuit court further held,

The Local Rules for the Middle District of Florida require that mediations be privileged. Given the parameters of the Sunshine Law and its place within the Florida Constitution, however, it is appropriate that the parties be ordered to inform a federal court that they are obligated to comply with Florida's Sunshine Law requirements and further ordered to take all reasonable steps to seek a waiver of the local federal rules in order to comply with this Court's judgment, the Constitution of the State of Florida, and applicable Florida laws mandating Government in the Sunshine. If, after fully complying with this Court's judgment, the parties nevertheless are ordered by the federal court to conduct mediations in private, the Supremacy Clause of the United States Constitution requires that the parties comply with the federal court's order.

The appellants then individually initiated appeals, between them challenging the circuit court's jurisdiction, its determination that collective bargaining occurred, its determination that the entities present at the mediation sessions had the ability to collectively bargain pension benefits, and its determination that the Board acted as the Unions' bargaining agent. They also argued that the circuit court's order violated the rule of confidentiality of mediation sessions, principles of comity, and the Supremacy Clause. We are not persuaded that any of these issues require reversing Judge Wallace's well-reasoned and sound order.

The Sunshine Law provides a right of access to government. See Art. 1, § 24, Fla. Const.; § 286.011, Fla. Stat. (2013). It was enacted in the public interest to protect the public from "closed door" politics. See *Pinellas Cnty. Sch. Bd. v. Suncam, Inc.*, 829 So. 2d 989, 990 (Fla. 2d DCA 2002) (citing *Wood v. Marston*, 442 So. 2d 934, 938 (Fla.1983)). The Sunshine Law is to be liberally construed to give effect to its public purpose, and exemptions should be narrowly construed. See *Bd. of Pub. Instruction of Broward Cnty. v. Doran*, 224 So. 2d 693, 699 (Fla.1969). In addition, it should be construed so as to frustrate all evasive devices. See *City of Miami Beach v. Berns*, 245 So. 2d 38, 41 (Fla.1971).

Chapter 447, Part II, Florida Statutes (PERA), governs collective bargaining of public employees. Section 447.605(2), Florida Statutes (2013), provides:

> The collective bargaining negotiations between a chief executive officer, or his or her representative, and a bargaining agent shall be in compliance with the provisions of Florida Statutes section 286.011.

Thus, once the collective bargaining process begins, whenever one side or any of its representatives at any time meets with the other side or any of its representatives to discuss anything relevant to the terms and conditions of the employer-employee relationship, such a meeting is subject to the Sunshine Law. *City of Fort Myers v. News–Press Publ'g Co., Inc.*, 514 So. 2d 408, 412 (Fla. 2d DCA 1987).

The matters here were presented to the circuit court in the context of violations of the Sunshine Law. Considering and determining Sunshine Law violations are within the circuit court's purview. See § 286.011(2), Fla. Stat. (2013) (vesting jurisdiction to enforce the public meeting requirements in the circuit courts). While the circuit court made some determinations regarding collective bargaining, those determinations were not dispositive of any issues particularly relating to the collective bargaining process itself so as to fall under PERC's exclusive jurisdiction. Rather, they constituted necessary threshold determinations in the context of whether the mediation sessions triggered application of the Sunshine Law. Cf. *Miami Ass'n of Firefighters Local 587 v. City of Miami*, 87 So. 3d 93 (Fla. 3d DCA 2012) (finding that the union was required to exhaust its administrative remedies with PERC before seeking relief in circuit court where the claims against the City raised violations of both chapter 447, Florida Statutes, and the Sunshine Law).

The circuit court found that the Board acted as the Unions' bargaining agent in the mediation sessions, which, in the context of the Sunshine Law, was a proper finding. The circuit court focused on the fact that section 447.605(2) requires collective bargaining to be conducted in the sunshine when negotiations involve a "bargaining agent." Considering the definition of bargaining agent in section 447.203(12), Florida Statutes (2013), the circuit court found that it included more than just PERC-certified bargaining agents as it also included the certified entities' "representative." Thus, the fact that the Board had not been formally designated as the Unions' bargaining agent did not necessarily mean that it did not function as a representative of the Unions so as to qualify as a "bargaining agent" for purposes of Sunshine Law application.

With regard to whether collective bargaining occurred during the mediation sessions, the circuit court found that the parties negotiated pension benefits, an undisputed mandatory subject of collective bargaining. The circuit court appropriately considered the parties that went in to the closed-door mediation sessions and the end product, which by its terms made changes to employee pension benefits. As further evidence of the changes made by the MSA, the circuit court recognized that the Mayor held a press conference announcing an agreement on retirement reform with the Unions. The fact that the MSA was tentative and conditioned upon further approval does not cure any prior Sunshine Law violation as the purpose of the Sunshine Law is to "prevent at nonpublic meetings the crystallization of secret decisions to a point just short of ceremonial acceptance." *Zorc v. City of Vero Beach*, 722

So. 2d 891, 896 (Fla. 4th DCA 1998) (citing *Town of Palm Beach v. Gradison*, 296 So. 2d 473, 477 (Fla.1974)). The circuit court's findings with regard to the parties as well as the nature of the mediation sessions were supported by the record such that they should not be disturbed on appeal.

With regard to the remedy ordered, the circuit court took appropriate care in recognizing the federal court's supremacy and the limited scope of the Sunshine Law issue before it. The circuit court narrowly crafted its remedy to respect the interplay between Sunshine Law principals and federal mediation.

We affirm the order on appeal under the broad public policy of Florida's Sunshine Law. We cannot condone hiding behind federal mediation, whether intentionally or unintentionally, in an effort to thwart the requirements of the Sunshine Law. Caution should be taken to comply with the Sunshine Law, and compliance should be the default rather than the exception. See *Gradison*, 296 So. 2d at 477 ("The principle to be followed is very simple: When in doubt, the members of any board, agency, authority or commission should follow the open-meeting policy of the State."). By holding closed-door negotiations that resulted in changes to public employee's pension benefits, the appellants ignored an important party who also had the right to be in the room—the public.

AFFIRMED.

Notes and Questions to Consider:

1. In *Brown v. Denton*, the settlement agreement reached at the mediation was tentative and subject to further approval. So why did the court find a violation of Florida's Sunshine Law?

2. In discussing the significance of *Brown v. Denton*, an article in the Stetson Law Review cites to my book, FLORIDA ELEMENTS OF AN ACTION, and opines:

> *Brown* explains that Florida's Sunshine Law requiring open meetings applies even in federal litigation. Thus, when agents collective-

> ly bargain during mediations in federal litigation, parties must inform the federal court of Sunshine Law obligations and obtain a waiver of local federal rules to comply. This case asserts the importance of transparency in negotiations, whether in state or federal court.

Kayli Keough, *Public Records & Meetings*, 44 Stetson L. Rev. 683, 694 (2015) (citing Patrick John McGinley, FLORIDA ELEMENTS OF AN ACTION, 21 Fla. Prac. § 2101:1 (2014-2015 ed.)). Do you agree or disagree with the opinion quoted above from this Stetson Law Review article?

Chapter Three

Local Government

A. Why Local Governments Exist

Floridians have more than just a federal and a state government. FLORIDA MUNICIPAL LAW AND PRACTICE describes the situation as follows:

> A Floridian may fall under the jurisdiction of more sovereigns than just the United States and Florida. Inside Florida's 1,350 miles of coastline lies 65,755 square miles of counties, cities, municipalities, and unincorporated areas. There are 67 counties in Florida, but some reports show only 66 because of Duval County, which is consolidated with the City of Jacksonville. There are 379 cities in Florida (out of 411) that report regularly to the Florida Department of Revenue. There are other incorporated municipalities.
>
> The authority of the state of Florida geographically overlaps the authority of Florida's counties, cities, municipalities, and unincorporated areas. The authority of other municipal governments also overlaps. All of Florida's potable water resources, and designated activities of persons and companies that affect those resources, are regulated by five regional water authorities that geographically overlap with and cross the borders of Florida's counties, cities, and municipalities. Various utility commissions regulate various persons, counties, cities, and municipalities within the concern of the commissions' activities in providing utilities. The Florida Legislature, from time to time, has created various compacts and empowered the agencies governing those compacts to impose fees and otherwise exercise jurisdiction over Floridians and their counties, cities, municipalities, and unincorporated areas.

Patrick John McGinley, FLORIDA MUNICIPAL LAW AND PRACTICE § 10:2 (2017-18 ed.).

Is there an advantage to having local governments? Proponents of local governments argue:

- that local governments are more responsive to the specific needs of unique communities and that local institutions can provide better and increased services. Neighborhood-level governments can tailor their policies and allocate resources more efficiently than can larger governments. They also provide increased opportunities for political participation and thus offer venues for individual engagement in collective governance, which is a positive good for the individual and for the wider political community. Indeed, neighborhoods may be our most central and resilient sites for civic involvement, the best loci of community and fellowship that we have in an increasingly fractured metropolitan area and an increasingly globalized society.

Richard C. Schragger, *The Limits of Localism*, 100 Mich. L. Rev. 371, 381–82 (2001).

Proponents suggest that the "idea that localization of government begets more responsive and effective government is deeply ingrained in the American ethos. This idea stems from a Jeffersonian notion that local government is an effective way to ensure citizen participation in government." Russel M. Lazega & Charles R. Fletcher, *The Politics of Municipal Incorporation in South Florida*, 12 J. Land Use & Envtl. L. 215, 225–27 (1997). The theory is that "citizens are more apt to participate in smaller, more localized government because they are more likely to believe that their participation counts. This … restores decision-making power to the community." *Id.*

In addition to efficiency and greater civic involvement, proponents suggest that "[l]ocalization of government also provides more basic benefits. Citizens are closer to their local officials.… [L]ocalization restores control of government to people who are both familiar to and familiar with the community." *Id.*

Localization might even help thwart partisanship. "There's no Democratic or Republican way to fix a pothole, pick up garbage, respond to a 911 call or build parks for our children." Florida League of Cities, *Home Rule Handbook* (2018).

Notes and Questions to Consider:

1. Do you agree with these arguments in favor of localism? How would you make the argument against localism?

2. Image a Floridian, living in the Orange County city of Winter Park, who has a concern about a problem occurring in her own backyard. Would it be easier for her voice to be heard if the decisionmaker was in Washington D.C.? In Tallahassee? In Orange County? In Winter Park?

B. State's Power to Create Local Governments

Considering the supremacy of the federal Constitution, what rights do states hold to create and regulate local governments such as counties, cities, towns, and similar municipal corporations? The U.S. Constitution is silent about the powers related to local governments. As can be seen in the following excerpt from the 1907 decision of the U.S. Supreme Court in *Hunter v. City of Pittsburgh,* 207 U.S. 161 (1907), the creation and regulation of local government is a matter of state not federal law.

HUNTER

V.

CITY OF PITTSBURGH

Supreme Court of the United States, 1907

207 U.S. 161, 28 S. Ct. 40, 52 L. Ed. 151

The plaintiffs in error seek a reversal of the judgment of the Supreme Court of Pennsylvania, which affirmed a decree of a lower court, directing the consolidation of the cities of Pittsburgh and Allegheny. This decree was entered by authority of an act of the General Assembly of that State. The act authorized the consolidation of two cities.

We have nothing to do with the policy, wisdom, justice or fairness of the act under consideration; those questions are for the consideration of those to whom the State has entrusted its legislative power, and their determination of them is not subject to review or criticism by this court. We have nothing to do with the interpretation of the constitution of the State and the conformity of the enactment of the Assembly to that constitution; those questions are for the consideration of the courts of the State, and their decision of them is final.

This court has many times had occasion to consider and decide the nature of municipal corporations, their rights and duties, and the rights of their citizens and creditors. It would be unnecessary and unprofitable to analyze these decisions or quote from the opinions rendered. We think the following principles have been established by them and have become settled doctrines of this court, to be acted upon wherever they are applicable. Municipal corporations are political subdivisions of the State, created as convenient agencies for exercising such of the governmental powers of the State as may be entrusted to them. For the purpose of executing these powers properly and efficiently they usually are given the power to acquire, hold, and manage personal and real property. The number, nature and duration of the powers conferred upon these corporations and the territory over which they shall be exercised rests in the absolute discretion of the State. Neither their charters, nor any law conferring governmental powers, or vesting in them property to be used for governmental purposes, or authorizing them to hold or manage such property, or exempting them from taxation upon it, constitutes a contract with the State within the meaning of the Federal Constitution.

The State, therefore, at its pleasure may modify or withdraw all such powers, may take without compensation such property, hold it itself, or vest it in other agencies, expand or contract the territorial area, unite the whole or a part of it with another municipality, repeal the charter and destroy the corporation. All this may be done, conditionally or unconditionally, with or without the consent of the citizens, or even against their protest. In all these respects the State is supreme, and its legislative body, conforming its action to the state constitution, may do as it will, unrestrained by any provision of the Constitution of the United States.

Although the inhabitants and property owners may by such changes suffer inconvenience, and their property may be lessened in value by the burden of increased taxation, or for any other reason, they have no right by contract or otherwise in the unaltered or continued existence of the corporation or its powers, and there is nothing in the Federal Constitution which protects them from these injurious consequences. The power is in the State and those who legislate for the State are alone responsible for any unjust or oppressive exercise of it.

For these reasons we are without jurisdiction to consider it, and neither express nor intimate any opinion upon it.

The judgment is: Affirmed.

Notes and Questions to Consider:

1. *Hunter* discusses "municipal corporations." What are they? Florida's Supreme Court once held that:

> a municipal corporation is an instrumentality of the state established for the more convenient administration of local government. It is possessed of certain governmental powers which it may exercise only in

> the manner prescribed in the law by which it is created. These powers are generally vested in a city council or other such governing body chosen by the electors who act for the municipality.

Turk v. Richard, 47 So. 2d 543, 543–44 (Fla. 1950). Under Article VIII of Florida's Constitution, Florida's municipal corporations take one of two forms: counties or municipalities. The sole exception is Miami-Dade County, which takes both forms because Article VIII Sections 6(e) and 6(f) of Florida's Constitution provides that "the Metropolitan Government of Dade County" may exercise "all the powers conferred now or hereafter by general law upon municipalities" and Miami-Dade's charter does so.

2. How do counties differ from municipalities in Florida? Article VIII of Florida's Constitution provides that counties include charter counties and non-charter counties, the difference being whether the county operates under a county charter. All land in Florida falls within one and just one county. Within a county's borders, various municipalities may exist. Municipalities include cities, towns and villages. Not all land falls within a municipality. Land that does not is called an unincorporated area. All of the geography of a municipality must exist within the borders of a single county, and a municipality's borders may not exceed the borders of that county. For this reason, all of Florida's municipalities are geographically smaller than their county of residence with one exception. The City of Jacksonville's borders are coterminous with the borders of Duval County, making that city and county the same size.

3. What powers can local governments wield? In *Hunter v. Douglas,* the U.S. Supreme Court holds that "[m]unicipal corporations are ... given the power to acquire, hold, and manage personal and real property. The powers conferred upon these corporations ... rests in the absolute discretion of the state .... Neither their charters, nor any law conferring [their] governmental powers ... [is controlled by] the Federal Constitution ...." *Id.* at 178. For this reason, a state "at its pleasure, may modify or withdraw all such powers .... In all these respects the state is supreme, and its legislative body, conforming its action to the state Constitution, may do as it will, unrestrained

by any provision of the Constitution of the United States." *Id.* at 178. This means that states like Florida can determine the rules under which local governments are created, the powers they exercise, and their relationships to the other local governments in the state. Is this a good result?

4. Imagine the people of the State of Florida amend Florida's Constitution, and pursuant to that amendment, the Legislature of the State of Florida passes a law dissolving Florida's current counties, dividing the state into new counties, and distributing the assets of the former counties to the new counties. What rights would the old counties hold under *Hunter v. City of Pittsburg* to challenge this as a violation of federal constitutional rights?

5. Imagine a group of neighbors would like their neighborhood to be its own city, but the state of Florida will not allow it. What federal constitutional rights, if any, might be violated?

C. Home Rule

"Home Rule" describes the concept that Florida's charter counties, cities, towns and villages have governmental, corporate and proprietary powers unless expressly prohibited by federal law, Florida's Constitution or the Florida Legislature. Home Rule is the source of authority to provide municipal services, perform municipal functions, own municipal property and enact municipal laws unless provided otherwise by law. *See, e.g.*, Judge James R. Wolf and Sarah Harley Bolinder, *The Effectiveness of Home Rule: A Preemption and Conflict Analysis*, Florida Bar Journal 92-94 (June 2009).

Commentators suggest that "[t]here is perhaps no term in the literature of political science or law which is more susceptible to misconception and a variety of meaning than 'home rule.'" Hugh Spitzer, *"Home Rule" vs. "Dillon's Rule" for Washington Cities*, 38 Seattle U.L. Rev. 809, 820 (2015). The Florida League of Cities, in their *Home Rule Handbook,* acknowledges that the public does not always fully understand the meaning of Home Rule and appears to try to simplify its meaning as follows:

> The people of Florida overwhelmingly support Home Rule. The term, however, is not recognized by all. It is our job to explain it in a simple way.... *Home Rule is the flexibility to address unique local needs with local solutions....*
>
> When it comes to local issues like tree trimming, vacation rentals, neighborhood safety, road improvements or even urban chickens, we turn to our city leaders. Why? Because Miami is not Mount Dora. Tampa is not Titusville. Local leaders are more connected to our needs and better reflect our values than state politicians.

Florida League of Cities, *Home Rule Handbook* (2018) (emphasis in original).

Home Rule delegates sufficient police powers to local governments to allow them to pass local laws (which, in Florida and elsewhere, are called ordinances and resolutions). Without Home Rule or some other form of delegation of the state's police power, a Florida county or municipality would need the Florida Legislature to pass a special law applicable to the county or municipality. Home Rule empowers the county or municipality to make that law itself.

1. Home Rule versus Dillon's Rule

Historically, Florida and the majority of U.S. states did not provide their municipal corporations with Home Rule power. The prevailing rule was Dillon's Rule where "powers not granted a municipality by the legislature were deemed to be reserved to the legislature. This reservation of authority was known as 'Dillon's Rule' [because it refers to the works of law professor and Iowa Judge] John F. Dillon, THE LAW OF MUNICIPAL CORPORATIONS § 55 (1st ed. 1872)." *City of Boca Raton v. State*, 595 So. 2d 25, 27 (Fla. 1992).

The difference between Home Rule and Dillon's Rule is that the former means a municipal corporation can enact a local law unless forbidden, and the latter means a municipal corporation cannot enact a local law unless permitted. The result is that Dillon's Rule defines the powers of local governments more narrowly than Home Rule:

> Municipal home rule provisions provide more autonomy to local governments, which was not traditionally granted under "Dillon's Rule." In *City of Clinton v. Cedar Rapids & M.R.R. Co.*, [24 Iowa 455 (1868), overruled by *Berent v. City of Iowa City*, 738 N.W.2d 193 (Iowa 2007),] Judge John Dillon created what would be known as "Dillon's Rule" by recognizing state control over municipal government, except as limited by the state or federal constitution. According to Dillon's Rule, a municipality may only act in accordance with the powers granted to it by the state. The United States Supreme Court in *Hunter v. City of Pittsburgh* later adopted Dillon's Rule, and as a result, local governments across the United States were denied what they considered to be the inherent right of self-government.
>
> Dillon's Rule ultimately created undue state interference and left local governments without power in municipal affairs. As a result, many municipalities sought to reclaim their autonomy from the states. Municipalities did so by lobbying for the enactment of home rule provisions, which would allow them greater self-governance.

Jarit C. Polley, *Uncertainty for the Energy Industry: A Fractured Look at Home Rule*, 34 Energy L.J. 261, 267–68 (2013).

Today, there are as many as forty-eight states that grant Home Rule powers to their municipal corporations. Richard Briffault & Laurie Reynolds, STATE AND LOCAL GOVERNMENT LAW 268 (6th ed. 2004). Florida is among them, having added Home Rule to Florida's 1968 Constitution and to various Florida Statutes thereafter.

2. Limits Upon Home Rule

Florida's Home Rule does not include fiscal home rule. Florida's Constitution reserves all taxing authority for the Florida Legislature. Home

Rule contains the power to enact a valid special assessment or fee, but not a tax.

Florida's Home Rule does not preempt the U.S. Constitution or Florida's Constitution. Stated somewhat differently, Florida's Home Rule is an insufficient basis to uphold an unconstitutional local law or unconstitutional local government action. "A Florida municipality may not make any law on a matter preempted to the state or county government by the Florida Constitution, by general law, or pursuant to a county charter. Patrick John McGinley, FLORIDA MUNICIPAL LAW AND PRACTICE § 10:3 (2017-18 ed.).

Home Rule power does not preempt general or special laws of the Florida Legislature. "A municipal corporation derives not only its existence but its power from the Legislature." *Brooks v. Watchtower Bible & Tract Soc. of Florida, Inc.*, 706 So. 2d 85, 87 (Fla. 4th DCA 1998). The Legislature has not given Florida's municipal corporations the power to contradict the Legislature. Home Rule gives Florida's counties broad power to govern "to the extent not inconsistent with general or special law." *See* Fla. Stat. § 125.01(1). Home Rule gives Florida's municipalities broad power to govern "except when expressly prohibited by law." *See* Fla. Stat. § 125.01(1). So regardless of whether the Florida municipal corporation is a county, city, town or village, its laws may not be inconsistent with the Florida Statutes. "Generally speaking, local ordinances are consistent with general or special law unless state preemption precludes a local government from exercising authority in a particular area or unless state legislation may override local action because that action expressly conflicts with the state legislation." Patrick John McGinley, FLORIDA MUNICIPAL LAW AND PRACTICE § 10:3 (2017-18 ed.).

3. "Constitutional Home Rule" and "Statutory Home Rule"

Home Rule power is extended to all of Florida's counties, and to all of its incorporated cities, towns and villages. But what is the source of that home rule power? Does it flow directly from a self-executing provision in Florida's Constitution, which is what scholars call a "Constitutional Home

Rule?" Does it flow from a state statute, which is what scholars call a "Statutory Home Rule?" Scholars explain that:

> Municipal home rule states can be divided into three varieties: two types of constitutional home rule states, and statutory home rule states. The two types of constitutional home rule states are the following: states that follow the *imperium in imperio* model, which grants full police power over municipal issues and immunity from state legislative interference; and states that follow the legislative model, which grants municipalities power to legislate, subject to restriction by state legislation.

Jarit C. Polley, *Uncertainty for the Energy Industry: A Fractured Look at Home Rule*, 34 Energy L.J. 261, 268 (2013). Florida's counties benefit from what scholars call a "Statutory Home Rule." Florida's incorporated cities, towns and villages benefit from it also, but in addition, benefit from a "Constitutional Home Rule." The following paragraphs explain why.

The Home Rule power of cities, towns and villages appears in the plain language of the text of Florida's Constitution. Article VIII, section 2 is titled Municipalities and has a subsection labeled "powers" that reads: "Municipalities shall have governmental, corporate and proprietary powers to enable them to conduct municipal government, perform municipal functions and render municipal services, and may exercise any power for municipal purposes except as otherwise provided by law." This phrase provides incorporated cities, towns and villages with Home Rule, but omits counties.

The Home Rule power of counties is not so plain in the text of Florida's Constitution. Article VIII, Section 1 is titled Counties. But section does not have a subsection labeled "powers." Article VIII, Section 6(e) preserves the Home Rule status of four Florida counties that were granted Home Rule by the Constitution of 1885, but does not provide a means of Home Rule for Florida's other 63 counties. Also, Florida's Constitution does not contain a sentence for counties similar to the one empowering municipalities to "exercise any power for municipal purposes except as otherwise provided by law."

It seems one must look beyond the plain text of Florida's Constitution to find a source of Home Rule power for at least 63 of Florida's 67 counties.

For these counties, one source of Home Rule power is the Municipal Home Rule Powers Act. It contains, at Florida Statutes section 166.021, a subsection labeled "powers." It says that "[t]he provisions of this section shall be so construed as to secure for municipalities the broad exercise of home rule powers granted by the constitution." It adds virtually the same sentence found in Article VIII's section on Municipalities when it says "municipalities shall have the governmental, corporate, and proprietary powers to enable them to conduct municipal government, perform municipal functions, and render municipal services, and may exercise any power for municipal purposes, except when expressly prohibited by law." Oddly, it does not define the word "municipalities." But it contains this important definition: "'municipal purpose' means any activity or power which may be exercised by the state or its political subdivisions." With this expansive definition of "municipal purpose," Home Rule power exists.

Another source of Home Rule for counties is the enactment of a charter that imbues the county with Home Rule power. This assumes that the county charter can be interpreted properly to say that the county has Home Rule power. It also assumes that the county has a charter. Florida's Constitution in Article VIII section 1 contemplates the continued existence of non-charter counties.

Perhaps the most direct source of Home Rule power is Florida Statutes section 125.01. This statute grants counties "the power to carry on county government[] . . . [t]o the extent not inconsistent with general or special law." This statute enumerates a long list of county powers, and then states that the "power to carry on county government ... is not restricted to" the enumerated subjects. This statute provides that the "provisions of this section shall be liberally construed in order to effectively carry out the purpose of this section and to secure for the counties the broad exercise of home rule powers authorized by the State Constitution." Most importantly for non-charter counties, this statute is interpreted to grant Home Rule power to all counties with or without a charter. As Florida's First District Court of Appeal held:

> The Florida Supreme Court has commented on the broad scope of home-rule authority conferred upon non-charter counties in no less than three opinions: *Taylor v. Lee County*, 498 So. 2d 424 (Fla.1986); *Speer v. Olson*, 367 So. 2d 207 (Fla.1979); and *State v. Orange County*, 281 So. 2d 310 (Fla.1973). As the court recognized in *Speer*, 367 So. 2d at 211:
>
> > The first sentence of Section 125.01(1), Florida Statutes, (1975), grants to the governing body of a county the full power to carry on county government. Unless the Legislature has pre-empted a particular subject relating to county government by either general or special law, the county governing body, by reason of this sentence, has full authority to act through the exercise of home rule power.
>
> Thus, the specific powers enumerated under section 125.01 are not all-inclusive, and a non-charter county's authority comprises that which is reasonably implied or incidental to carrying out its enumerated powers. The only limitation on a county's implied power to act occurs if there is a general or special law clearly inconsistent with the powers delegated.

Santa Rosa County v. Gulf Power Co., 635 So. 2d 96, 99 (Fla. 1st DCA 1994), cause dismissed sub nom. *Escambia River Elec. Co-op., Inc. v. Santa Rosa County*, 641 So. 2d 1345 (Fla. 1994).

In conclusion, Florida's counties, as well as its incorporated cities, towns and villages, derive their Home Rule power from Florida's Constitution, from the Municipal Home Rule Powers Act codified at Florida Statutes chapter 166, from the laws empowering county governments codified at Florida Statutes section 125.01, and from the laws empowering municipalities codified at Florida Statutes section 166.012. For cities, towns and villages, the statutes serve to strengthen an existing Home Rule power found in the text of Florida's Constitution. For counties, and for noncharter counties in particular, the statutes serve as the source of their Home Rule power.

D. Charter Counties

Article VIII of Florida's Constitution provides for the creation of counties, county charters, and county governance when it states, in relevant part:

> **Section 1. Counties.**
> (a) POLITICAL SUBDIVISIONS. The state shall be divided by law into political subdivisions called counties. Counties may be created, abolished or changed by law, with provision for payment or apportionment of the public debt.
> (b) COUNTY FUNDS. The care, custody and method of disbursing county funds shall be provided by general law.
> (c) GOVERNMENT. Pursuant to general or special law, a county government may be established by charter which shall be adopted, amended or repealed only upon vote of the electors of the county in a special election called for that purpose.
> (d) COUNTY OFFICERS. There shall be elected by the electors of each county, for terms of four years, a sheriff, a tax collector, a property appraiser, a supervisor of elections, and a clerk of the circuit court; except, when provided by county charter or special law approved by vote of the electors of the county, any county officer may be chosen in another manner therein specified, or any county office may be abolished when all the duties of the office prescribed by general law are transferred to another office. When not otherwise provided by county charter or special law approved by vote of the electors, the clerk of the circuit court shall be ex officio clerk of the board of county commissioners, auditor, recorder and custodian of all county funds.

> (e) COMMISSIONERS. Except when otherwise provided by county charter, the governing body of each county shall be a board of county commissioners composed of five or seven members serving staggered terms of four years. After each decennial census the board of county commissioners shall divide the county into districts of contiguous territory as nearly equal in population as practicable. One commissioner residing in each district shall be elected as provided by law.
> (f) NON-CHARTER GOVERNMENT. Counties not operating under county charters shall have such power of self-government as is provided by general or special law. The board of county commissioners of a county not operating under a charter may enact, in a manner prescribed by general law, county ordinances not inconsistent with general or special law, but an ordinance in conflict with a municipal ordinance shall not be effective within the municipality to the extent of such conflict.
> (g) CHARTER GOVERNMENT. Counties operating under county charters shall have all powers of local self-government not inconsistent with general law, or with special law approved by vote of the electors. The governing body of a county operating under a charter may enact county ordinances not inconsistent with general law. The charter shall provide which shall prevail in the event of conflict between county and municipal ordinances.

Technically, a county's charter is not the county's "constitution." But it is helpful to note the similarities between a constitution and a county charter so as to better understand the workings of a charter. Like a constitution, a county charter may possess a unique set of laws different from neighboring territories. The county charter, like a constitution, forms the legal foundation of the county's local system of government. Florida's Supreme Court once held that "the word 'charter,' when used in connection with a municipal corporation, is defined as follows: 'The charter, as it is called, consists of the creative act and all laws in force relating to the [municipal] corporation, whether in defining its powers or regulating their mode of exercise." *City of St. Petersburg v. English*, 45 So. 483, 487 (Fla. 1907). This definition from Florida's Supreme Court has much in common with a constitution.

A county may, but is not required, to have a charter. As of June 2019, the website of the Florida Association of Counties reports that, "[t]o date, there are 20 charter counties in Florida. Collectively these counties are home to more than 75 percent of Florida's residents." https://www.fl-counties.com/charter-county-information (visited June 7, 2019).

Article VIII Section 1 of Florida's Constitution provides that "[c]ounties not operating under county charters shall have such power of self-government as is provided by [the applicable law]" and that "[c]ounties operating under county charters shall have all powers of local self-government not inconsistent with [the applicable law]...."

One advantage of a charter is that it structures the county's government as specified in that county's charter. This is an advantage because representatives of that county's electorate draft the charter and a majority of that county's electorate must vote affirmatively as part of enacting the charter. This may result in a unique charter for that county, whereas non-charter county governments are all uniform. This may also result in a charter handcrafted by the residents to meet the specific local needs of those residents. Perhaps most advantageously, it empowers the electorate of the county to change the structure of county government more flexibly because the county's electorate remains free to enact changes and amendments to the county's charter. In a non-charter county, the structure of the county government is specified in Florida's Constitution and the Municipal Home Rule Powers Act. So the structure of a non-charter county can only be changed by amending Florida's Constitution or the Florida Statutes, and thus, by amending every non-charter county's charter in the same way.

The website of the Florida Association of Counties summarizes more differences between Florida's charter and non-charter counties as follows. In non-charter counties, state Statutes do not provide for initiative or referendum, or recall of county officers. But a county charter may provide for initiative, referendum and recall at the county level. In non-charter counties, the

Florida Statutes do not require an Administrative Code. But a county charter can require an Administrative Code detailing all regulations, policies and procedures. A non-charter county cannot levy a utility tax in the unincorporated area. But a county charter can provide that a "municipal utility tax" is levied in the unincorporated area.

Yet perhaps the most critical difference between charter and non-charter counties is the charter county's greater ability to preempt municipalities when passing local laws. In a noncharter county, in the event of a conflict between a county ordinance and a municipal ordinance, the noncharter county's ordinance shall not be effective within the municipality to the extent of such conflict. *Santa Rosa County v. Gulf Power Corp.*, 635 So. 2d 96 (Fla. 1st DCA 1994). This topic is the subject of further discussion in this text in the chapter titled Legislative Power and its subsection titled Lawmaking and Its Limits.

What are the limits of a noncharter county's power that a charter might fix? Consider, for example, the following case of *Gretna Racing, LLC v. Florida Department of Business and Professional Regulation*, 225 So. 3d 759 (Fla. 2017).

GRETNA RACING, LLC

V.

FLORIDA DEPARTMENT OF BUSINESS AND PROFESSIONAL REGULATION

Supreme Court of Florida, 2017

225 So. 3d 759

"Shall slot machines be approved for use at the pari-mutuel [horse track] facility in Gretna, F[lorida]?" This is the question presented by the Gadsden County Commission to the county's voters in a ballot question. And it is the question we now must decide. A majority of the voters answered the question in the affirmative, but the Division of Pari–Mutuel Wagering subsequently denied a slot machine permit to Gretna Racing, LLC. The First District upheld the Division's denial of the permit and certified a question of great public importance, which establishes our jurisdiction. *See* art. V, § 3(b)(4), Fla. Const. Gretna Racing contends that the Division was required to issue the permit once the voters had answered the ballot question in the affirmative. Based on the provisions of chapter 551, Florida Statutes (2013), governing slot machines and the law establishing the powers of non-charter counties, we conclude that the Division's denial of the slot machine permit sought by Gretna Racing was correct because submission of the ballot question to the voters was not legally authorized....

To explain our decision on this point, we turn first to the text of the constitutional provision and the general statutory provisions relied on by Gretna Racing.

Article VIII, section 1(f) of the Florida Constitution provides:

> NON–CHARTER GOVERNMENT. Counties not operating under county charters shall have such power of self-government as is provided by general or special law. The board of county commissioners of a county not operating under a charter may enact, in a manner prescribed by general law, county ordinances not inconsistent with general or special law ....

Art. VIII, § 1(f), Fla. Const.

As the text specifies, the powers granted to non-charter counties are "such power[s] of self-government as [are] provided by general or special law." *Id.* The general law relied on by Gretna Racing is section 125.01(1), Florida Statutes (2013), which provides broadly that "[t]he legislative and governing body of a county shall have the power to carry on county government." The statute goes on to provide that the power to carry on county government, "[t]o the extent not inconsistent with general or special law, ... includes, but is not restricted to, the power to" do certain enumerated things. § 125.01(1), Fla. Stat. (2013). Among those enumerated things is the power specified in subsection (1)(y) to conduct a "straw ballot." § 125.01(1)(y), Fla. Stat. (2013). But none of the enumerated powers relate to slot machine gaming. Nor is a general power to conduct binding referenda among the enumerated powers.

Of course, the absence of a relevant enumerated power is not dispositive. In addition to the provision in section 125.01(1) that the "power to carry on county government ... is not restricted to" the enumerated subjects, section 125.01(3)(a) provides that the enumeration of powers will "not be deemed exclusive or restrictive, but shall be deemed to incorporate all implied powers necessary or incident to carrying out such powers enumerated, including, specifically, authority to employ personnel, expend funds, enter into contractual obligations, and purchase or lease and sell or exchange real or personal property." Further, section 125.01(3)(b) contains a rule of liberal construction: "The provisions of this section shall be liberally construed in order to effectively carry out the purpose of this section and to secure for the counties the broad exercise of home rule powers authorized by the State Constitution." Which brings us back to the constitutional specification of "such power of self-government as is provided by general or special law," art. VIII, § 1(f), Fla. Const., and the general law provision of the "power to carry on county government" in a way that is "not inconsistent with general or special law," § 125.01(1), Fla. Stat. (2013).

Based on the analysis we employ to resolve this case, we reframe the certified question as follows:

> Is a referendum conducted by a non-charter county concerning approval of slot machine licenses at pari-mutuel facilities authorized by the general powers conferred on non-charter counties by article VIII, section 1(f) of the Florida Constitution and section 125.01(1), Florida Statutes (2013)?

An affirmative answer to this question could only be given if we conclude that conducting such a referendum regarding the issuance of slot machine licenses by the Division is inherent in the "power to conduct county government."...

In support of its position on this point, Gretna Racing relies on two decisions upholding the authority of a county to conduct a referendum—*Speer v. Olson*, 367 So. 2d 207 (Fla. 1978), which approved the issuance of bonds authorized by a referendum for the expansion of sewer and water systems, and *Watt v. Firestone*, 491 So. 2d 592 (Fla. 1st DCA 1986), which rejected a challenge to a ballot initiative for a constitutional amendment authorizing casino gambling in certain areas if approved in an initiative referendum by county voters. An examination of these cases shows that they do not support Gretna Racing's argument. In both cases, the authorization to conduct a referendum did not stem from the general home rule power conferred by section 125.01(1). Instead, the authority to conduct the referendum in each of the two cases was based on specific constitutional or statutory authority to act on a subject that required approval by referendum. Here, in contrast, there is no specific constitutional or statutory authority for Gadsden County to act on the subject of slot machine gaming.

In *Speer*, Pasco County had "enacted an ordinance creating a Municipal Service Taxing Unit ... composed of the entire unincorporated area of the county." *Speer*, 367 So. 2d at 208. The county had "called a special election by the residents of the Unit for the purpose of securing their approval for the issuance of ... general obligation bonds by the Unit." *Id.* The purpose of the issuance of the bonds was "for the expansion of sewer and water systems." *Id.* In rejecting the claim that the referendum was unauthorized, we referred to the enumerated power provided in section 125.01(1)(k), Florida Statutes, to "[p]rovide and regulate waste and sewage collection and disposal, water supply, and conservation programs." *Speer*, 367 So. 2d at 208–09. We also referred to the power in section 125.01(1)(q) to create municipal service taxing units for various purposes including "water" and "waste and sewage collection and disposal," which includes "the authorization for all counties to levy additional taxes, within the limits fixed for municipal purposes, within such municipal service taxing units under the authority of the second sentence of Article VII, Section 9(b) of the State Constitution." *Speer*, 367 So. 2d at 209. …

Watt addressed removal from the ballot of a proposed constitutional amendment providing for casino gambling if approved by initiative referendum of county voters. Removal was sought on the ground that the proposed amendment violated due process because of "the alleged lack of authority, by statute or ordinance, for many of Florida's counties to conduct initiative referenda." *Watt*, 491 So. 2d at 593. The challengers thus contended that "many Floridians would be unable to implement casino gambling in their own counties because an initiative referendum on the subject could not be held." *Id.*

The First District in *Watt* rejected this argument, reasoning as follows:

> Charter counties have the authority to conduct such referenda under Article VIII, section 1(g) of the Florida Constitution and non-charter counties have similar power under Article VIII, section 1(f) of the state constitution and section 125.01 of the Florida Statutes. Even if some counties do not have currently valid ordinances to spell out the specifics of holding a referendum, we hardly find this to be grounds for invalidating a proposed constitutional amendment. If the proposal is approved and the governing body of a county fails to provide for referenda, an aggrieved citizen could seek redress in the courts.

Id.

We reject the suggestion that *Watt* supports a broad home rule authority to conduct binding referenda on any and every subject. *Watt*'s discussion of the legal powers of counties cannot be divorced from the authorization of initiative referenda in the proposed constitutional amendment. *Watt* simply holds that if a constitutional provision authorizes initiative referenda in certain counties then those counties will—under the general authority to exercise the power of self-government—have the power to establish the mechanism necessary to implement the constitutional provision. As in *Speer*, the authority to conduct a binding referendum was predicated on a constitutional provision empowering counties to conduct referenda on a particular subject.

Here, no relevant analogous constitutional authority exists regarding the subject of slot machine gaming. As the Division points out, in Florida gambling is generally illegal. Section 849.08, Florida Statutes (2013), provides that "game[s] of chance" are illegal. But certain forms of gambling are legal. *See, e.g.*, ch. 550, Fla. Stat. (2013) (the "Florida Pari-mutuel Wagering Act"). And although slot machines and slot machine gaming are specifically outlawed under section 849.15(1), Florida Statutes (2013), in sweeping terms, slot machine gaming is permitted under tight restrictions as laid out by the Legislature in chapter 551. Nothing in chapter 551, however, grants any authority to regulate slot machine gaming to any county. The only role that counties play regarding slot machine gaming is conducting referenda when authorized by law....

... The First District thus was correct in upholding the Division's decision to deny the license sought by Gretna Racing. So we approve the result reached by the First District....

It is so ordered.

Notes and Questions to Consider:

1. The particular local option at issue in *Gretna Racing v. DBPR* did not prove to be popular with Floridians. Today, it is no longer available due to an amendment to Florida's Constitution enacted in 2018.

2. What power did the noncharter county lack that resulted in its inability to hold a valid referendum?

E. Right of Local Governments to Provide Utilities and Services

Of course, one role of local government is to provide services to Floridians. Is this the local government's right, or is it a privilege? Consider the case of *City of Winter Park v. S. States Utilities, Inc.*, 540 So. 2d 178 (Fla. 5th DCA 1989):

CITY OF WINTER PARK

v.

SOUTHERN STATES UTILITIES, INC.

Fifth District Court of Appeal of Florida, 1989

540 So. 2d 178

Appellant, City of Winter Park, enacted, pursuant to section 180.02(3), Florida Statutes, an ordinance extending its corporate power over its municipal sewer service zone outside its corporate limits so as to require property owners outside the city but within such service zone to connect to the city's sewer system when it became available. Appellee Southern States Utility, Inc., a non-governmental utility company (public service corporation) with a certificate issued by the Florida Public Service Commission (PSC) pursuant to section 367.031, Florida Statutes, authorizing it to provide sewer service, entered into a contract with appellee landowners to supply sewer service to a tract of land lying within a portion of the area embraced within the city's ordinance where the city does not presently have sewer service capability.

The city filed this action against the utility company and the landowners alleging that the utility company was providing sewer service to the landowners within the city's exclusive sewer service zone and that the city would have capacity to serve the land owners' property by a date about 17 months in the future from the date the action was originally filed. The complaint prayed for a declaratory judgment to the effect that the landowners would be required to disconnect from the utility company's sewer system and connect with the city's sewer system when the city could provide sewer service.

The trial court held that the city under its ordinance could compel the landowners to connect with its sewer system only if the city sewer treatment capacity was available at the time it was needed by the landowners and found that there was no material issue as to the fact that the city did not have the present ability to provide sewer service to the landowners' property and that, accordingly, the utility company was free to contract to provide sewer service to the landowners' property without intervention [interference] from the city. Although not affirmatively expressed, the effect of the trial court's denial of the city's prayer for a declaratory judgment that the landowners would be required to disconnect from the utility company's sewer system and connect with the city's sewer system when it became available and entry of summary judgment against the city was that the landowners would not be required to terminate their sewer service contract with the utility company and connect to the city's sewer system if and when it became available to the landowners' property. The city appeals.

Interestingly, this litigation is somewhat of a shadow of a prior litigation as to the same issue between the same parties that came about as follows: earlier, the utility company applied to the Public Service Commission to amend its certificate of public necessity to provide sewer service to the property now in question and other property. The city objected. The PSC, by order numbered 18525, and dated December 9, 1987 (87 FPSC 12:125), found that the city had more demand for sewer service than it had capacity and that while the city expected to be able to provide sewer service at some time in the future, the city would not execute a commitment to provide sewer service and desired to place those needing service on a list to wait until the city could provide service while the utility company had existing unused sewer treatment capacity and was willing and able to serve the public. As to the city's claim to the exclusive right to serve the property in question under its municipal service zone, the commission noted that it is not bound by the city's ordinance extending its corporate power beyond its city limits, nor by a local comprehensive plan enacted under section 163.3161, Florida Statutes, stating that the test was who was in the best position to provide the needed sewer service which the commission found to be the utility company rather than the city. The commission expressly declined the city's request that the utility company's certificate for authority to serve this area be issued subject to the condition requiring disconnection when the city became able to supply sewer service, noting that the commission had no jurisdiction over the city sewer system.[1] The city appealed the Public Service Commission's order to the First District Court of Appeal which affirmed. *See City of Winter Park v. Southern States Utilities,* 530 So. 2d 310 (Fla. 1st DCA 1988).

We agree with the Public Service Commission and the trial court. All corporations which voluntarily undertake to engage in performing a service of a public nature whether a governmental agency, such as a municipality, or a private corporation, assume an obligation implied by law to render, for reasonable compensation and without discrimination and to all of the public in the area sought to be served, a service reasonably adequate to meet the just requirements of those sought to be served.

A city cannot undertake to extend its service franchise beyond an area it is able to serve and thereby prevent the public from being served by anyone else. The public is entitled to be served and served by the entity best able to serve it. In this case, the utility company is able to provide the public with the service that the city is unable to provide. The city has no legal right to prevent the utility company from serving the consuming public and no right to require the public to disconnect from the utility company that can now serve it and connect with the city's sewer system if and when the city gets around to meeting its duty to provide the service that it has undertaken to provide.

AFFIRMED.

Note and Question to Consider:

1. Was the City of Winter Park's desire to be the utilities provider unreasonable in your opinion? Consider MCQUILLIN's summary of the majority rule in other jurisdictions:

> In most jurisdictions a municipality may contract to furnish a supply from its plant, for use outside the city, where not prohibited by statute or charter provision, and where the supply is sufficient to furnish the residents all that is necessary for their use. This may include the pow-

> er to furnish a supply to another municipality or to a state institution, or to customers in a housing development, or to residents within the service area of an incorporated water and sewer authority contiguous to but lying outside the municipal limits.... Further, a municipality may extend its own services to municipal-owned facilities located outside its territorial limits, even though these facilities may have already been supplied through a private company. According to some authorities this power is implied. The power to so imply may exist despite the apparent failure of the city to indicate it was ready, willing and able to provide for new customers, at least where the extension of the service is a reasonable move in terms of possible future annexation and the policy of favoring inter local service agreements.

12 McQuillin Mun. Corp. § 35:36 (3d ed.).

F. Right of Local Governments to Deny Utilities and Services

Can a local government use its position as the provider of services to gain concessions from those who wish to receive services? This was the main issue Florida's Supreme Court addressed in *Allen's Creek Properties, Inc. v. City of Clearwater*, 679 So. 2d 1172 (Fla. 1996).

Allen's Creek Properties, Inc.

v.

City of Clearwater

Supreme Court of Florida, 1996

679 So. 2d 1172

We have for review *City of Clearwater v. Allen's Creek Properties, Inc.*, 658 So. 2d 539 (Fla. 2d DCA 1995), wherein the district court, by separate order, certified the following question to be of great public importance:

> *May a municipality refuse to provide sewer service, or condition the provision of sewer service on annexation, as to nonresidents located within its exclusive sewer service territory established pursuant to inter–local agreements with neighboring municipal sewer service providers?*

Id. at 543. We have jurisdiction. Art. V, § 3(b)(4), Fla. Const. We answer the question in the affirmative based upon the general rule that a municipality has no duty to supply services to areas outside its boundaries. *See Allstate Insurance Co. v. City of Boca Raton,* 387 So. 2d 478 (Fla. 4th DCA 1980); C.C. Marvel, Annotation, *Right to Compel Municipality to Extend its Water System,* 48 A.L.R. 1222, 1230 (1956). Allen's Creek Properties (Allen's Creek) contends that the facts in this case establish an exception to this general rule and that consequently, Clearwater's refusal to provide services to unincorporated property located within its service area was improper. For the reasons expressed below, we disagree.

Allen's Creek owns a parcel of land located in the unincorporated area of Pinellas County immediately adjacent to Clearwater's city limits. In September 1990, Allen's Creek submitted to Pinellas County a site plan for the development of this parcel. Pinellas County officials directed Allen's Creek to apply to Clearwater for sewer services because the parcel was located within Clearwater's sanitary sewer service district.

Upon receiving the request for sewer services, Clearwater officials informed Allen's Creek that, pursuant to City of Clearwater, Florida, Ordinance 68–97 (August 5, 1968), the developer would have to consent to annexation before receiving sewer services. Allen's Creek refused to allow the City to annex the property and filed suit for declaratory and other relief.

The trial court held that Clearwater, through the Central Pinellas County 201 Facilities Plan (the 201 Plan) and its interlocal agreement with the City of Largo, had assumed an obligation to provide sewer service in its designated service area. That service area included the land owned by Allen's Creek. Further, the trial court concluded that the record did not present a rational basis to require annexation as a condition to service.

Clearwater appealed the trial court's decision, and the district court reversed. *Allen's Creek,* 658 So. 2d at 542. The district court examined each of the documents on which the trial court based its decision. The first document, the 201 Plan, was devised pursuant to the Federal Water Pollution Control Act of 1972, Pub.L. No. 92–500, § 2, 86 Stat. 816....

Clearwater, along with the several other entities, participated in the development of a 201 Plan for its geographic area. The Plan delineated service areas for Clearwater as well as the other local entities involved in developing the Plan. ...

The district court also examined the interlocal agreement that the City of Clearwater and the City of Largo entered pursuant to section 163.01, Florida Statutes (1983). The agreement designated service areas for the City of Clearwater and the City of Largo consistent with the service areas designated for those cities in the 201 Plan. With respect to these service areas the agreement provides: "The parties shall have the exclusive right to provide wholesale and retail sanitary sewer service within the area allocated to such part and further agree not to compete with each other as to the provision of such sewer service outside their designated area."

... Allen's Creek maintains that this case establishes an exception to the general rule that a municipality cannot be compelled to supply services to areas outside its municipal boundaries. We recognize that exceptions to this general rule do exist. For example, a municipality may be required to extend its services if it has agreed to do so by contract. A contract may require the municipality to serve only a particular entity outside its municipal boundaries. Such a contract does not necessarily require the municipality to serve other similarly situated entities. On the other hand, a contract may require the municipality to service an entire area outside its limits. In such cases the municipality will be required to serve all the public in that area at the lowest possible cost with the most efficiency as demonstrated by the decision in *City of Clearwater v. Metco Development Corp.,* 519 So. 2d 23 (Fla. 2d DCA 1987), *review denied,* 525 So. 2d 876 (Fla.1988).

In *Metco,* the developer owned unincorporated property located in

Clearwater's water service area. 519 So. 2d at 24. The City was already serving the northern portion of the developer's property but refused to serve the southern portion unless the developer agreed to annexation. *Id.* The court determined that the City by contractually agreeing to serve the entire water service area, which included the developer's land, became obligated to do so. *Id.* at 24–25. A contract like that relied on by the court in *Metco* does not exist in the instant case. This exception is therefore inapplicable.

Some jurisdictions recognize another exception to the general rule for those municipalities that through their conduct hold themselves out as public utilities. According to the jurisdictions that recognize this exception, a municipality that holds itself out as a public utility for a particular area outside its city limits has a duty to supply everyone in that area. Allen's Creek contends that Clearwater held itself out as a public utility by entering an interlocal agreement that designated certain unincorporated areas as a part of its service area and by supplying sewer services to certain nonresidents. Accordingly, Allen's Creek contends that Clearwater has a legal obligation to provide sewer service to nonresidents located within its service area.

We agree that through its conduct a municipality may assume the legal duty to provide reasonably adequate services for reasonable compensation to all of the public in an unincorporated area. See *City of Winter Park v. Southern States Utilities, Inc.*, 540 So. 2d 178, 180 (Fla. 5th DCA 1989) (city's passage of ordinance requiring property owners outside the city but within a zone designated by the ordinance to connect to the city's sewer service when available was conduct sufficient to bring into effect law applicable to public utilities). We add however that the conduct must expressly manifest the municipality's desire or intent to assume that duty. A municipality's decision to provide service without restriction in an area outside its boundaries would meet this requirement. The 201 Plan and interlocal agreement relied on here do not. Like the plan in *Allstate*, nothing in either the Plan or agreement affirmatively states that Clearwater will provide services to the unincorporated area. … Providing service outside its boundaries in only limited situations, as Clearwater has done here, does not amount to an affirmative expression of intent to serve all in the area. Clearwater therefore has not accepted a duty to provide services to the unincorporated land located in its service area.

Because Clearwater has no duty to provide services to the unincorporated land within its service area, we conclude that the City may condition upon annexation the landowner's receipt of sewer services. That condition however must be applied consistently, and a reasonable justification for the condition must exist. *See Sebring Utilities Comm'n. v. Home Savings Ass'n. of Florida,* 508 So. 2d 26, 28 (Fla. 2d DCA) ("Courts will not interfere with a municipal utility's exercise of its authority as long as the municipality does not arbitrarily discriminate between its customers and can present reasonable justifications for its actions."), *review denied,* 515 So. 2d 230 (Fla. 1987). We find that Clearwater's condition of annexation meets both these requirements. The annexation policy is applied to the entire unincorporated area with only specific limited exceptions....

Accordingly, we approve the decision of the district court. We find that the agreements entered by Clearwater in this case did not affirmatively express the City's intent to supply sewer service to the unincorporated portion of its sewer service area. Nor did Clearwater engage in any other conduct that expressed the intent to serve this area. The general rule thus still applies to this case and requires us to answer the certified question in the affirmative.

It is so ordered.

Note and Question to Consider:

1. The slang phrase "up a creek without a paddle" (and its four-letter variants) describes being in an awkward or unpleasant predicament without a ready means of resolution. In a Florida Bar Journal article titled *Up* Allen's Creek *Without a Paddle: Can Cities Leverage Utility Service for Annexation?*, the author describes *Allen's Creek* as follows:

> Cities should beware because even 20 years after it was decided, *Allen's Creek Properties, Inc. v. City of Clearwater*, 679 So. 2d 11

> 72 (Fla. 1996), continues to raise questions about the legality of municipalities compelling county property owners to annex into a city to obtain that city's utilities. Hailed as a victory for cities, the Florida Supreme Court decision held that cities can require landowners in unincorporated areas to execute "voluntary" annexation petitions in return for access to city utilities. But the decision brings up many troubling issues familiar to those in local government, such as judicial interference in the operation of local government, cities' ability to control growth on their borders through annexation, and the right to leverage annexation for utilities.
>
> Cities are often looking to expand their boundaries because annexation results in increased revenue and lower tax rates in the future. Specifically, annexation helps spread the costs of constructing and operating municipal utility systems to all customers, not just city residents. Although hardly perfect, tending to create pockets of incorporated areas, by mandating annexation petitions from county property owners for utility service, a city addresses the public policy concern of county residents on cities' borders reaping the benefits of city life tax-free.
>
> The Florida Supreme Court recognized that annexation solves the widespread problem of county residents enjoying urban city life, including city utilities, without paying city taxes and fees….

Catherine D. Reischmann, *Up* Allen's Creek *Without A Paddle: Can Cities Leverage Utility Service for Annexation?,* Fla. B.J., July/August 2016, at 60 (footnotes omitted). Do you agree that *Allen's Creek* creates an appropriate solution to these problems?

2. So the rule of *Allen's* Creek is that a Florida local government is not obliged to provide utility services, even within its exclusive area. But what are the exceptions to the rule? Consider the following case of *Corrections Corp. of Am., Inc. v. City of Pembroke Pines*, 230 So. 3d 477 (Fla. 4th DCA 2017), *review denied*, SC17-2117, 2018 WL 1057372 (Fla. Feb. 27, 2018).

CORRECTIONS CORPORATION OF AMERICA, INC.

V.

CITY OF PEMBROKE PINES

Fourth District Court of Appeal of Florida, 2017

230 So. 3d 477

Corrections Corporation of America ("CCA") appeals a trial court order—sounding in declaratory relief—holding that the City of Pembroke Pines did not have a duty to provide water and sewer services to CCA's property site, as well as a final order dismissing CCA's counterclaims. Because we find that Pembroke Pines affirmatively expressed its intention to assume such a duty, we reverse the order....

Background

CCA sought sewer and water services from Pembroke Pines for its property located in the Town of Southwest Ranches but adjacent to Pembroke Pines ("the CCA site"). Pembroke Pines operates potable water and sewer systems that service properties within its boundaries, as well as some properties outside of those boundaries. Those services provided outside of the boundaries extend to a limited number of residential and commercial properties. Southwest Ranches does not have potable water or sewer systems to service its residents, and Pembroke Pines is the only provider in the area. The CCA site is surrounded by four other properties, all of which are, or were at one time, serviced by Pembroke Pines' water or sewer systems (or both). Only one of these properties is actually located within the boundaries of Pembroke Pines. At all times relevant to this dispute, Pembroke Pines admitted that it had the capacity and infrastructure in place to provide water and sewer services to the CCA site through its systems that abut the site.

In 2005, CCA and Southwest Ranches entered into an agreement concerning the development of a correctional facility on the CCA site. The agreement provided that "all required water, sewer and other utility services are available" at the CCA site. CCA was advised that while a water and sewer agreement with Pembroke Pines would be required, it was unclear whether the Pembroke Pines City Commission would grant those services. However, later in 2005, Southwest Ranches entered into an interlocal agreement with Pembroke Pines regarding local roadways and other matters ("Roadways ILA"), in which Pembroke Pines agreed not to interfere with the development or operation of CCA's jail facility:

> *Jail Facility:* [Pembroke Pines] shall not interfere with [CCA's], or its successors or assigns, development and/or operation of the jail facility, or with [Southwest Ranches]'s Agreement with [CCA] concerning development of same.

In 2011, Immigration and Customs Enforcement ("ICE") tentatively selected the CCA site to build a new detention facility. A few days later, Pembroke Pines and Southwest Ranches entered into another interlocal agreement concerning emergency medical and fire services (the "EMS ILA") that provided in pertinent part:

> *Jail Facility:* [Pembroke Pines] acknowledges that it has sufficient capacity to deliver emergency medical protection and fire prevention services to [Southwest Ranches]'s future 2,500 bed detention/corrections facility, located on property currently owned by [CCA]. [Pembroke Pines] agrees to timely provide Broward County, upon request, any documentation that Broward County may require to acknowledge that Pembroke Pines has the capacity, ability, and the willingness to service this facility under the terms and conditions contained herein.... Further, [Pembroke Pines] agrees that it has sufficient capacity to provide water and sewer service to [Southwest Ranches]'s future 2,500 bed detention/corrections facility (approximately 500,000 gross square feet of floor area), *and that it will expeditiously approve a water/waste water utility agreement to provide such service, at* [*Pembroke Pines*]*'s then prevailing rate, in accordance with state law* ([Pembroke Pines]'s rate + surcharge).

(Emphasis added). In a special meeting on June 27, 2011, the Pembroke Pines City Commission voted on and approved the EMS ILA in Resolution No. 3312.

Some five months later, in December 2011, the City Commission passed yet another affirmative motion, that one being "to approve direction that, should CCA come forward with a request for Pembroke Pines to provide them water and sewer service, that the water and sewer agreement stipulate that it would be for not more than 1,500 beds based on the Engineer's report" (the "December 2011 Motion"). CCA then submitted to Pembroke Pines a proposed Water and Sewer Installation and Service Agreement (the "W & S Agreement") for a 1,500–bed facility....

...In an abrupt departure from the numerous manifestations of intent expressed by the Pembroke Pines City Commission over the previous six years, the City Commission did not vote on the W & S Agreement and quite to the contrary, formally adopted a resolution *expressing its opposition* to erecting the ICE detention center on the CCA site. In a later meeting, the City Commission voted to both terminate the EMS ILA and, because it was "in doubt as to its rights and obligations," and to direct the city attorney to seek declaratory relief.

In its action for declaratory judgment, Pembroke Pines sought a ruling that it was not required to provide CCA with water and sewer services.... Following trial, the court entered an order determining that Pembroke Pines did not, in fact, have a duty to provide water and sewer services to CCA.

Analysis

On appeal, CCA argues that Pembroke Pines assumed a legally enforceable duty to provide the CCA site with those services by expressly manifesting a desire or intent to provide the services. CCA maintains the evidence at trial established that the ongoing conduct of Pembroke Pines created a duty to provide utilities. As such, the trial court's rulings concerned a question of fact that "must be sustained if supported by competent substantial evidence." *Bellino v. W & W Lumber & Bldg. Supplies, Inc.*, 902 So. 2d 829, 832 (Fla. 4th DCA 2005) (quoting *State v. Glatzmayer*, 789 So. 2d 297, 301 n.7 (Fla. 2001)). We agree with CCA.

As a general rule, "a municipality has no duty to supply services to areas outside its boundries." *Allen's Creek Props., Inc. v. City of Clearwater*, 679 So. 2d 1172, 1174 (Fla. 1996). In *Allen's Creek*, the Florida Supreme Court recognized exceptions to this general rule where (1) a municipality has agreed to extend its services by contract, and (2) where a municipality has assumed a duty to provide such services through its conduct. *Id.* at 1175–76. With regard to the conduct exception, the court explained:

> According to the jurisdictions that recognize this exception, a municipality that holds itself out as a public utility for a particular area outside its city limits has a duty to supply everyone in that area....
>
> We agree that through its conduct a municipality may assume the legal duty to provide reasonably adequate services for reasonable compensation to all of the public in an unincorporated area. *See City of Winter Park v. Southern States Utilities, Inc.*, 540 So. 2d 178, 180 (Fla. 5th DCA 1989) (city's passage of ordinance requiring property owners outside the city but within a zone designated by the ordinance to connect to the city's sewer service when available was conduct sufficient to bring into effect law applicable to public utilities). We add however that *the conduct must expressly manifest the municipality's desire or intent to assume that duty*. A municipality's decision to provide service without restriction in an area outside its boundaries would meet this requirement.

Id. at 1176 (emphasis added).

Allen's Creek presents a scenario somewhat similar to the one at hand. There, Allen's Creek owned a parcel of land located in the unincorporated area of Pinellas County, but adjacent to Clearwater. *Id.* at 1174. When Allen's Creek submitted a site development plan to Pinellas County, Pinellas officials directed Allen's Creek to Clearwater for sewer services because the parcel was located within Clearwater's sanitary sewer service district. *Id.* Clearwater informed Allen's Creek that it would have to consent to annexation before receiving sewer services. *Id.* Allen's Creek declined and filed suit for declaratory judgment. *Id.*

On appeal to the Florida Supreme Court, Allen's Creek argued that the conduct exception to the general rule applied, as Clearwater had assumed an obligation to provide sewer service in its designated service area through the Central Pinellas County 201 Facilities Plan ("201 Plan") and its interlocal agreement with the City of Largo. *Id.* at 1175–76. The interlocal agreement between Clearwater and the City of Largo designated service areas and stated, "The parties shall have the exclusive right to provide wholesale and retail sanitary sewer service within the area allocated to such part and further agree not to compete with each other as to the provision of such sewer service outside their designated area." *Id.* at 1175.

The 201 Plan was created in connection with the Federal Water Pollution Control Act of 1972, the goal of which was "to eliminate the discharge of pollutants into navigable waters by 1985," and a provision of which was federal "funding for the research and development of wastewater treatment management plans." *Id.* at 1174. Within the 201 Plan, "service areas" were designated "to determine the scope of facilities needed in the future." *Id.* Allen's Creek's property was within Clearwater's service area as designated by the plan. *Id.* Clearwater approved the 201 Plan by local resolution in 1978, but the EPA rejected it, so the plan was never implemented and Clearwater proceeded with development of alternative methods for wastewater disposal. *Id.*

The supreme court declined to extend the conduct exception to Allen's Creek, reasoning:

> *[N]othing in either the Plan or agreement affirmatively states that Clearwater will provide services to the unincorporated area.* Nor do these agreements preclude those located outside Clearwater's city limits but within its service area from seeking services from an alternative source....

> ...We find that the agreements entered by Clearwater in this case did not affirmatively express the City's intent to supply sewer service to the unincorporated portion of its sewer service area. Nor did Clearwater engage in any other conduct that expressed the intent to serve this area.

Id. at 1176–77 (emphasis added). The court concluded that Clearwater's annexation requirements were therefore permissible, so long as the requirements were reasonably justified and consistently applied. *Id.*

While similar to the facts of the instant case, *Allen's Creek* is somewhat distinguishable. There, the 201 Plan and interlocal agreement on which Allen's Creek relied were in place before it requested service from the city. As an apparent consequence, the court looked to the agreements at issue for "affirmative[ ] state[ments] that Clearwater will provide services to the unincorporated area." *Id.* at 1176. In other words, the court reviewed the documents for expressions of Clearwater's intent to provide utility services to anyone located within the specific, unincorporated service area. *Id.*

Here, on the other hand, CCA relies on documents *specifically addressing* the CCA site. Applying *Allen's Creek* to the agreements at hand, we find direct expressions of intent to provide services to the area at issue in the EMS ILA:

> *Jail Facility:* ... [Pembroke Pines] agrees to timely provide Broward County, upon request, any documentation that Broward County may require to acknowledge that Pembroke Pines has the capacity, ability, and the willingness to service this facility .... Further, [Pembroke Pines] agrees that it has sufficient capacity to provide water and sewer service to [Southwest Ranches]'s future 2,500 bed detention/corrections facility (approximately 500,000 gross square feet of floor area), *and that it will expeditiously approve a water/waste water utility agreement to provide such service, at [Pembroke Pines]'s then prevailing rate, in accordance with state law* ([Pembroke Pines]'s rate + surcharge).

(Emphasis added). By including a statement that it would "approve a water/waste water agreement to provide such service," Pembroke Pines affirmatively and expressly manifested its desire and intent to assume that duty.

Further, although they may not constitute *affirmative* expressions of intent to provide water and sewer service, other actions of the City of Pembroke Pines indicated its willingness to provide services to the CCA site. Pembroke Pines provided these services to all surrounding sites. Also, knowing that it was the only water and sewer service provider in the area, Pembroke Pines agreed in the Roadways ILA that it "shall not interfere with [CCA's] ... development and/or *operation* of the jail facility." Finally, Pembroke Pines indicated its willingness to provide these services by the City Commission's passage of the December 2011 motion to direct CCA to limit its request for water and sewer services to a 1,500–bed facility....

Consequently, we find that the conduct exception to the general rule that a municipality has no duty to supply services to areas outside its boundaries applies in the instant case. We reverse the trial court's determination to the contrary.

Reversed and remanded for further proceedings.

Notes and Questions to Consider:

1. What are the exceptions to the rule of *Allen's Creek* as identified in this case?

2. Are these exceptions enough to provide justice when equity requires it?

Chapter Four

Legislative Power

A. Purpose of the State Legislature

What is the purpose of Florida's Legislature? Consider the opinions expressed in this excerpt from Daniel Webster & Donald L. Bell, *First Principles for Constitution Revision*, 22 Nova L. Rev. 391 (1997):

> *The Legislative Branch*
>
> John Locke saw the establishment of legislative power as the first and foremost of all positive laws. He called the law-making function the "supreme power of the commonwealth" because it is the responsibility of the legislative branch to make laws that will govern all, including the executive and the judiciary. Accordingly, he believed that some sharp controls on the legislative power were necessary. The first of these controls is, of course, the people themselves, who protect against the rise of tyranny through their ability to remove legislators from office by the power of their votes. A second control on the Legislature is the fact that the lawmaking power is never concentrated in the hands of a single person or of a small group of people. In Florida, the constitution divides the Legislature between two separate houses--the House of Representatives, with one-hundred and twenty members, and the Senate, with forty members. Both houses must agree, by a majority vote of its respective members, before a law can be created, amended, or repealed. Still a third control on the Legislature, suggested by Locke and applied successfully in Florida, is the part-time Legislature. Locke correctly noted that there is not a constant need for new laws. Accordingly, it is best that legislators meet on a part-time basis and then return home to live under the laws they have created. Finally, the Legislature is controlled by the executive veto power. Any law created by the Flor-

ida Legislature is subject to veto by the Governor.

Florida's Constitution also has a significant set of rules that the Legislature must follow in creating laws, including restrictions on the kinds of laws it can make. The Florida Constitution may be considered superior to some others, in part, because of these rules. For example, the "single subject rules" found in the Florida Constitution have caused our state to develop a body of statutory law and an appropriations process that are far more clear and well-reasoned than those produced under the Federal Constitution. The great significance of these seemingly modest provisions lies in the fact that they are the only constraints, outside the Federal Constitution, on the Legislature's ability to make any laws it chooses. The people can only be secure in granting the Legislature such broad power to make laws, so long as there is a guiding foundation of moral law contained in the constitution, to which all other law is subservient.

One would also hope that in making legislative decisions, the Legislature would avoid creating laws that are sharply opposed to natural human interests or behaviors. ...Adam Smith once said:

> [Man] seems to imagine that he can arrange the different members of the great society with as much ease as the hand arranges the pieces upon a chessboard; he does not consider that the pieces upon the chessboard have no other principle of motion than that which the hand impresses upon them; but that, in the great chessboard of human society, every single piece has a principle of motion of its own, altogether different from that which the Legislature may wish to impress upon it. If those two principles coincide and act in the same direction, the game of human society will go on easily and harmoniously, and is very likely to be happy and successful. If they are opposite or different, the game will go on miserably, and the society must be at all times in the highest degree of disorder.

Where the law allows them to do so, bureaucrats and other authorities will impose unreasonable expectations on an unwilling populace. This is one of the principle reasons why our foundational legal document should be applied to limit the exercise of legislative power by executive branch officials.

Notes and Questions to Consider:

1. In the discussion of Florida's legislative branch in the article quoted above, the authors opine that "our foundational legal document should be applied to limit the exercise of legislative power by executive branch officials." Years after this article appeared, Florida's Supreme Court did what the article suggested. In *Bush v. Schiavo*, 885 So. 2d 321 (Fla. 2004), Florida's Supreme Court held:

> In addition to concluding that the Act is unconstitutional as applied in this case because it encroaches on the power of the judicial branch, we further conclude that the Act is unconstitutional on its face because it delegates legislative power to the Governor. The Legislature is permitted to transfer subordinate functions "to permit administration of legislative policy by an agency with the expertise and flexibility to deal with complex and fluid conditions." *Microtel, Inc. v. Fla. Public Serv. Comm'n*, 464 So. 2d 1189, 1191 (Fla. 1985). However, under article II, section 3 of the constitution the Legislature "may not delegate the power to enact a law or the right to exercise unrestricted discretion in applying the law." *Sims v. State*, 754 So. 2d 657, 668 (Fla. 2000). This prohibition, known as the nondelegation doctrine, requires that "fundamental and primary policy decisions ... be made by members of the legislature who are elected to perform those tasks, and [that the] administration of legislative programs must be pursuant to some minimal standards and guidelines ascertainable by reference to the enactment establishing the program." *Askew v. Cross Key Waterways*, 372 So. 2d 913, 925 (Fla. 1978); see also *Avatar Dev. Corp. v. State*, 723 So. 2d 199, 202 (Fla. 1998) (citing *Askew* with approval). In other words, statutes granting power to the executive branch "must clearly announce adequate standards to guide ... in the execution of the powers delegated. The statute must so clearly define the power delegated that the [executive] is precluded from acting through whim, showing favoritism, or exercising unbridled discretion."

Lewis v. Bank of Pasco County, 346 So. 2d 53, 55–56 (Fla. 1976). The requirement that the Legislature provide sufficient guidelines also ensures the availability of meaningful judicial review:

> In the final analysis it is the courts, upon a challenge to the exercise or nonexercise of administrative action, which must determine whether the administrative agency has performed consistently with the mandate of the legislature. When legislation is so lacking in guidelines that neither the agency nor the courts can determine whether the agency is carrying out the intent of the legislature in its conduct, then, in fact, the agency becomes the lawgiver rather than the administrator of the law.

Askew, 372 So. 2d at 918–19.

We have recognized that the "specificity of the guidelines [set forth in the legislation] will depend on the complexity of the subject and the 'degree of difficulty involved in articulating finite standards.' " *Brown v. Apalachee Regional Planning Council*, 560 So. 2d 782, 784 (Fla. 1990) (quoting *Askew*, 372 So. 2d at 918). However, we have also made clear that "[e]ven where a general approach would be more practical than a detailed scheme of legislation, enactments may not be drafted in terms so general and unrestrictive that administrators are left without standards for the guidance of their official acts." *State Dep't of Citrus v. Griffin*, 239 So. 2d 577, 581 (Fla. 1970).

Id. at 332–33 (Fla. 2004).

2. Florida's Supreme Court once held: "Generally speaking, legislative action results in the formulation of a general rule of policy, whereas judicial action results in the application of a general rule of policy." *Bd. of County Com'rs of Brevard County v. Snyder*, 627 So. 2d 469, 474 (Fla. 1993). Can you think of some instances where government action might blur the lines between legislative action and judicial action?

B. Florida Entities Authorized to Make Laws

As seen in previous chapters, Florida's sovereignty gives it an inherent power called the police power. Florida's Constitution is not a grant of the police power, but may be a limitation upon it. The police power enables Florida to pass laws. Florida's Constitution limits the state's lawmaking power to the Florida Legislature and, through Constitutional Home Rule, to Florida's incorporated cities, towns and villages. The Florida Legislature, through Statutory Home Rule, delegates its Constitutional Home Rule to noncharter counties as well as to charter counties, cities, towns and villages.

Therefore, Florida's lawmaking power is not limited to Florida's Legislature. Instead, Florida's Constitution grants the power to make Florida laws to the Florida Legislature and Florida's municipal corporations (charter counties, noncharter counties, cities, towns and villages).

The Florida Legislature's lawmaking authority is the result of Florida's Constitution vesting the state's sovereign police power directly in its legislature. Specifically, Florida's Constitution provides at Article III, Section 1: "The legislative power of the state shall be vested in a legislature of the State of Florida, consisting of a senate composed of one senator elected from each senatorial district and a house of representatives composed of one member elected from each representative district." A law made by the Florida Legislature is called an "act." Collectively, acts are called the Florida Statutes or the Laws of Florida.

Local laws made by municipal corporations, typically, are named either ordinances or resolutions. Regarding counties, Florida's charter counties and noncharter counties have the same lawmaking authority but obtain it differently. Florida's Constitution contemplates a county having a governing body, enacting ordinances, legislating on topics that might also be addressed by the Florida Legislature or a municipality, recording such laws, and naming punishments applicable to those who violate the law. This is because Article VIII of Florida's Constitution provides:

> (f) NON-CHARTER GOVERNMENT. Counties not operating under county charters shall have such power of self-government *as is provided by [the applicable law]....*

> (g) CHARTER GOVERNMENT. Counties operating under county charters shall have all powers of local self-government *not inconsistent with [the applicable law]....*

Id. at subsections (f) and (g) (emphasis added). The emphasized language illustrates that charter counties can enact an ordinance or resolution unless a law forbids it, whereas noncharter counties can enact an ordinance or resolution if a law permits it. This would be a meaningful difference but for Florida's Municipal Home Rule Powers Act codified at Florida Statutes chapter 166 and the Florida Supreme Court's expansive reading of that statutory Home Rule power. Because binding precedent of Florida's Supreme Court interprets the Municipal Home Rule Powers Act to give noncharter counties the same, broad Home Rule power as charter counties, the relevant inquiry as to any county becomes whether the exercised power of local self-government is "not inconsistent with" the applicable law.

Regarding municipalities, Florida's Constitution provides: "Municipalities shall have governmental, corporate and proprietary powers to enable them to conduct municipal government, perform municipal functions and render municipal services, and may exercise any power for municipal purposes *except as otherwise provided by law*." Art. VIII, §2, Fla. Const. (emphasis added). The emphasized language means that the relevant inquiry as to any city's, town's or village's law becomes whether the exercised power is "not inconsistent with" the applicable law. This makes the inquiry the same as counties.

C. How a Bill Becomes Law in Florida's Legislature

During a session of the Florida Legislature, new Florida laws may be enacted. The process begins with the drafting of the proposed law, which is called a bill. Anyone can draft a bill, and it if it not drafted by the House or Senate's Bill Drafting Service, then the service will review it for style. All bills contain, at a minimum, a short one-paragraph description of the bill called its "title," an enacting clause, and an effective date.

A bill can originate in either chamber: Florida's Senate or Florida's

House of Representatives. Under House rules, each House member is given six bill slots. Senate rules do not impose such a limit on the number of bills that a senator may file.

Bills are filed with the Secretary of the Florida Senate or the Clerk of the House of Representatives. Preferably, when a bill is filed with one chamber (the chamber of origination), a companion bill is filed with the other. A bill is considered a companion bill if it is similar to, and addresses the same issues as, a bill on file with the other chamber. The secretary or clerk files the bill, prints it, and numbers it. Florida Senate bill numbers begin with the letters SB and are even numbers. House bills begin with HB and are odd numbers.

At any time after a bill is filed, it may "die" for that legislative session, which means it will no longer be considered. In a typical legislative session, many bills die at various stages during the following process.

Before a bill can be passed by a chamber, it must be "read" by that chamber three times, unless this rule is waived by a two-thirds vote. On each reading, it shall be read by title only, unless one-third of the members present desire it to be read in full. The first reading is by publication in the chamber's Journal of the bill's title, the bill's number, and the name of the senator or representative that is the bill's sponsor.

After the bill's first reading, it either dies or is assigned to one or more committees or subcommittees by the Speaker of the House or the President of the Senate. The membership of these committees and subcommittees consists of representatives in the House or senators in the Senate. Committees are named for and focused upon to particular topics such as appropriations, commerce, education, finance and tax, government accountability, health and human services, rules, ways and means, and judiciary. The committee's role is to analyze bills, to conduct hearings to obtain information about the subject of the bill, and if desired, to vote on the bill. All committee and subcommittee meetings must be open and noticed to the public.

After the committee or committees of reference receives the referral of the bill, it will die if the committees' chairpersons do not include it on their committee's agenda. After a bill is debated and possibly amended at these committees, the chairs may call it up for a vote if the bill did not die during debate. Bills voted favorably are placed on the chamber's Calendar, making the bill available for a Second Reading.

The Rules and Calendar Committee decides which bills from the Calendar die and which get heard "on the floor" (meaning read by and possibly debated by the full chamber). Rules and Calendar does so by created a recommended Special Order Calendar of bills, and the chamber votes on each Special Order Calendar prior to the chamber hearing those bills on the floor. After a bill has been introduced and read on the Special Order Calendar, then the chamber considers debating the bill, amending the bill, or allowing the bill to die. Bills that do not die are reported by the committee to the chamber with the result of the committee's vote. This constitutes the Second Reading of the bill.

The Third Reading occurs on a subsequent legislative day. Amendments are still permitted at this stage, but only on a two-thirds vote. Debate may occur. The bill's sponsor makes a closing statement. Then the chamber votes, and the bill either passes or dies.

Bills that pass the chamber of origin go to the other chamber with a "message." The process differs slightly depending on whether the other chamber is the House or the Senate, but generally speaking, the other chamber can kill the bill or refer it to one or more committees where it might be debated or amended or killed. Bills making it out of committee may be defeated or passed by on the floor of the chamber with or without amendments. If passed, the bill returns to its chamber of origin.

If the passed bill returns to its chamber of origin without amendments, it is enrolled then sent to the Governor for consideration. If there were amendments, the chamber of origin must consider passage of those amendments because amendments require approval by both chambers. Both the House and Senate must pass identical bills for the bill to become a law. Therefore, amendments can kill the bill if rejected by the chamber of origin.

Back-and-forth negotiations between the House and Senate occur, usually informally, but sometimes via a Conference Committee comprised of Representatives and Senators that is open and noticed to the public. If successful, the amended bill is enrolled and sent to the Governor.

The Governor can sign the bill into law, allow the bill to become law without signing it, or veto the bill. A two-thirds vote of the Legislature is required to override a veto. A bill becomes law if too much time passes without the Governor's signature or veto. The Governor has 7 days to sign if the Legislature remains in session, or 15 days if the Legislature adjourns "sine die."

A bill that the Florida Legislature enacts into law is called an Act. It is printed in the Laws of Florida and codified in the Florida Statutes. If the Legislature overrode a Governor's veto to make the bill a law, then it takes effect on the 60th day after adjournment sine die of the session in which the veto is overridden, on a later date stated in the law, or on a date fixed by a resolution passed by both the Florida House of Representative and the Florida Senate. If the law passed without a veto, then the law takes effect on the date stated in the law, or if not stated, then on the 60th day after adjournment sine die of the session of the Legislature in which the law was enacted.

Notes and Questions to Consider:

1. Although much of the legislative lawmaking procedures of Florida's Legislature as summarized above are the result of a requirement found in Florida's Constitution, some are the result of rulemaking by Florida's Legislature. In your opinion, would Floridians be better served by a more simplified procedure?

2. Back in 1970, a proposal to amend Florida's Constitution to create a unicameral legislature existed, but that proposal failed to qualify to appear on the ballot. See *Adams v. Gunter*, 238 So. 2d 824 (Fla. 1970). If ever such a proposal were on the ballot, how would you vote, and why?

D. Lawmaking and its Limits

Now we identify limitations upon the power of lawmaking in Florida. Almost invariably, past Florida Constitutional Law questions on the Florida Bar Exam raised one or more issues about lawmaking and its limits.

In making any list of the limits upon state lawmaking, we would be remiss not to reiterate that a Florida law may not violate the U.S. Constitution or Florida's Constitution. A statute that is inconsistent with either constitution is invalid and legally ineffective. These constitutions provide substantive matters that make a law invalid, such as a violation of one of the rights in the Declaration of Rights in Florida's Constitution or the Bill of Rights in the U.S. Constitution. These were the topics of prior chapters of this text.

Here, we examine technical or procedural flaws in Florida lawmaking that render laws invalid. These flaws are fatal, and result in the law being facially unconstitutional, regardless of the substantive matter addressed in that lawmaking. For the lawmaker, these are pitfalls to be avoided. For the litigant fighting to strike down a law as unconstitutional on its face, the following are the arrows in the quiver.

1. Valid Exercise of the State's Police Power

For the Florida Legislature, Florida's Counties, and Florida's incorporated cities, towns and villages, their power to make laws is a result of the state's police power. So any law, to be valid, must be a valid exercise of the state's police power.

To be a valid exercise of the state's police power, a Florida law must be for a public purpose and it must be enacted to protect the health, safety, and welfare of the people. This is the most basic test of the constitutionality of any Florida law. Any law that is not for a public purpose, or was not enacted to protect the health, safety and welfare of the people, is void and unconstitutional as an improper exercise of the state's police power.

As to whether a law serves a public purpose, Florida's courts grant broad discretion to the decision of the lawmaking body. "The Legislature is vested with wide discretion to determine the public interest and the measures necessary for its achievement." *Fraternal Order of Police, Metro. Dade County, Lodge No. 6 v. Dep't of State*, 392 So. 2d 1296, 1302 (Fla. 1980). Florida's Supreme Court holds:

> The fact that the legislature may not have chosen the best possible means to eradicate the evils perceived is of no consequence to the courts provided that the means selected are not wholly unrelated to achievement of the legislative purpose. A more rigorous inquiry would amount to a determination of the wisdom of the legislation . . . would usurp the legislative prerogative to establish policy.

Id. at 1302. So the test for whether a law serves a "public purpose" is not a rigorous inquiry but instead is a deferential one.

As a special application of the requirement of a "public purpose," as applied to lawmaking by Florida's counties, cities, towns and villages, the law is invalid if not done for a "municipal purpose." In most instances, this is a requirement without bite, because Florida's Municipal Home Rule Powers Act as codified in Florida Statutes chapter 166 defines "municipal purpose" so broadly. There, a municipal purpose is "means any activity or power which may be exercised by the state or its political subdivisions." This broad definition of "municipal purpose" is a full delegation and extension of the state's sovereign police power to municipalities because the Municipal Home Rule Powers Act states that:

> The provisions of this section shall be so construed as to secure for municipalities the broad exercise of home rule powers granted by the constitution. It is the further intent of the Legislature to extend to municipalities the exercise of powers for municipal governmental, corporate, or proprietary purposes not expressly prohibited by the constitution, general or special law, or county charter and to remove any limitations, judicially imposed or otherwise, on the exercise of home rule powers other than those so expressly prohibited.

Id. at section 166.021(4), Fla. Stat.

Why does the law establish that a state has an inherent police power, and why does that police power have its limits? The answer lies in the freedom of the individual, and in society's limited need for the subordination of individual freedom to the common welfare. As noted by the United States Supreme Court in its 1905 decision in *Jacobson v. Massachusetts*, 197 U.S. 11 (1905) the state's limited right to subordinate individual freedom is known as its "police power." As noted by the Florida Supreme Court in its 1986 case of *State v. Saiez*, 489 So. 2d 1125 (Fla. 1986), the Florida Legislature implements the state's "police power" when it enacts statutes for the protection of the public health, safety, welfare, or morals. Relevant portions of both cases appear below.

JACOBSON

V.

MASSACHUSETTS

Supreme Court of the United States, 1905

197 U.S. 11, 25 S. Ct. 358, 49 L. Ed. 643

… The authority of the state to enact [a] statute is to be referred to what is commonly called the police power — a power which the state did not surrender when becoming a member of the Union under the Constitution. Although this court has refrained from any attempt to define the limits of that power, yet it has distinctly recognized the authority of a state to enact quarantine laws and 'health laws of every description;' indeed, all laws that relate to matters completely within its territory and which do not by their necessary operation affect the people of other states. According to settled principles, the police power of a state must be held to embrace, at least, such reasonable regulations established directly by legislative enactment as will protect the public health and the public safety.… It is equally true that the state may invest local bodies called into existence for purposes of local administration with authority in some appropriate way to safeguard the public health and the public safety. The mode or manner in which those results are to be accomplished is within the discretion of the state, subject, of course, so far as Federal power is concerned, only to the condition that no rule prescribed by a state, nor any regulation adopted by a local governmental agency acting under the sanction of state legislation, shall contravene the Constitution of the United States, nor infringe any right granted or secured by that instrument. A local enactment or regulation, even if based on the acknowledged police powers of a state, must always yield in case of conflict with the exercise by the general government of any power it possesses under the Constitution, or with any right which that instrument gives or secures….

… But the liberty secured by the Constitution of the United States to every person within its jurisdiction does not import an absolute right in each person to be, at all times and in all circumstances, wholly freed from restraint. There are manifold restraints to which every person is necessarily subject for the common good. On any other basis organized society could not exist with safety to its members. Society based on the rule that each one is a law unto himself would soon be confronted with disorder and anarchy. Real liberty for all could not exist under the operation of a principle which recognizes the right of each individual person to use his own, whether in respect of his person or his property, regardless of the injury that may be done to others. This court has more than once recognized it as a fundamental principle that 'persons and property are subjected to all kinds of restraints and burdens in order to secure the general comfort, health, and prosperity of the state; of the perfect right of the legislature to do which no question ever was, or upon acknowledged general principles ever can be, made, so far as natural persons are concerned.' ...The possession and enjoyment of all rights are subject to such reasonable conditions as may be deemed by the governing authority of the country essential to the safety, health, peace, good order, and morals of the community. Even liberty itself, the greatest of all rights, is not unrestricted license to act according to one's own will. It is only freedom from restraint under conditions essential to the equal enjoyment of the same right by others. It is, then, liberty regulated by law….

STATE

V.

SAIEZ

Supreme Court of Florida, 1986

489 So. 2d 1125

. . . The [Florida L]egislature enacts penal statutes ... under the state's "police power" which derives from the state's sovereign right to enact laws for the protection of its citizens. See *Carroll v. State*, 361 So. 2d 144, 146 (Fla. 1978). Such power, however, is not boundless and is confined to those acts which may be reasonably construed as expedient for protection of the public health, safety, welfare, or morals. *Hamilton v. State*, 366 So. 2d 8, 10 (Fla. 1978); *Newman v. Carson*, 280 So. 2d 426, 428 (Fla. 1973). The due process clauses of our federal and state constitutions do not prevent the legitimate interference with individual rights under the police power, but do place limits on such interference. *State v. Leone*, 118 So. 2d 781, 784 (Fla. 1960). See also *Coca-Cola Co., Food Division v. State, Department of Citrus*, 406 So. 2d 1079, 1084-85 (Fla. 1981), appeal dismissed sub nom. *Kraft, Inc. v. Florida Department of Citrus*, 456 U.S. 1002 (1982).... See also *Foster v. State*, 286 So. 2d 549, 551 (Fla. 1973) ("[i]t would be an unconstitutional act — in excess of the State's police power — to criminalize the simple possession of a screwdriver")....

So long as the legislative activity does not encroach upon constitutional guarantees, or run afoul of federal statutory law, a state has a broad scope of discretion in which to regulate the conduct of its citizens.... It need only be shown that the challenged legislative activity is not arbitrary or unreasonable.... Courts will not be concerned with whether the particular legislation in question is the most prudent choice, or is a perfect panacea, to cure the ill or achieve the interest intended.... If there is a legitimate state interest which the legislation aims to effect, and if the legislation is a reasonably related means to achieve the intended end, it will be upheld.... Nevertheless, despite a state's wide discretion, and the cautious restraint of the courts, there remain basic restrictions and limits on a state's legislative power to intrude upon individual rights, liberties, and conduct. To exceed those bounds without rational justification is to collide with the Due Process Clause.... Such an exercise of the police power is unwarranted under the circumstances and violates the due process clauses of our federal and state constitutions.

Notes and Questions to Consider:

1. In the context of state constitutional law, what is the definition of a state's "police power?" When may a state exercise it?

2. What are the limits of a sovereign state's police power? In addressing this question near height of the U.S. Supreme Court's use (or some might say, abuse) of that power, author Ray A. Brown, in his 1927 article "Due Process of Law, Police Power, and the Supreme Court" appearing in the Harvard Law Review at 40 Harv. L. Rev. 943, cites us to these opinions of the Supreme Court of the United States: *Otis v. Parker*, 187 U.S. 606, 608 (1903) ("It is true, no doubt, that neither a state legislature nor a state constitution can interfere arbitrarily with private business or transactions, and the mere fact that an enactment purports to be for the protection of public safety, health or morals, is not conclusive upon the courts."); *Eubank v. City of Richmond*, 226 U.S. 137, 143 (1912) (holding that the police power necessarily "has its limits and must stop when it encounters the prohibitions of the [U.S.] Constitution."); *Atlantic Coast Line R. R. v. City of Goldsboro*, 232 U.S. 548, 559 (1914) ("If ... there is wanton or arbitrary interference with private rights, the question arises whether the lawmaking body has exceeded the legitimate bounds of the police power."); *Buchanan v. Warley*, 245 U.S. 60, 74 (1917) ("It is equally well established that the police power, broad as it is, cannot justify the passage of a law or ordinance which runs counter to the limitations of the Federal Constitution.") *Truax v. Corrigan*, 257 U.S. 312, 329 (1921) ("... the legislative power of a State can only be exerted in subordination to the fundamental principles of right and justice which the guaranty of due process in the Fourteenth Amendment is intended to preserve.") For an egregious example of a misapplication of the federal police power, and its use as an excuse for a lack of judicial restraint, see the infamous case of *Lochner v. New York,* 198 U.S. 45, 25 S. Ct. 539, 49 L. Ed. 937

(1905), overruled in part by *Day-Brite Lighting Inc. v. State of Mo.*, 342 U.S. 421, 72 S. Ct. 405, 96 L. Ed. 469 (1952), and overruled in part by *Ferguson v. Skrupa*, 372 U.S. 726, 83 S. Ct. 1028, 10 L. Ed. 2d 93 (1963), and abrogated by *W. Coast Hotel Co. v. Parrish*, 300 U.S. 379, 57 S. Ct. 578, 81 L. Ed. 703 (1937).

2. Proper Subject Matter

Despite the state's inherent police power, lawmaking is limited to a proper subject matter. For the Florida Legislature, lawmaking is proper on any subject matter that is not preempted by federal law and not forbidden by the U.S. Constitution or Florida's Constitution. A bill on any topic may originate in either chamber: the Florida Senate or the Florida House of Representatives. This differs from the U.S. Congress, where tax and appropriations bills must originate in the U.S. House of Representatives.

Florida's counties, cities, towns and villages may enact legislation on any subject matter on which the Florida Legislature may act, if done for a municipal purpose, except (1) annexation, merger, or exercise of extraterritorial power; (2) any subject expressly preempted by the U.S. Constitution, Florida's Constitution or general law; (3) any subject expressly prohibited by Florida's Constitution; and (4) any subject preempted to a county pursuant to a Supremacy Clause enacted in a County Charter.

The first restriction is because the language of Florida's Constitution, such as Article VIII Section 2 where it restricts such action to the Florida Legislature by stating: "Municipal annexation of unincorporated territory, merger of municipalities, and exercise of extra-territorial powers by municipalities shall be as provided by general or special law." Note that an exception exists regarding the lack of extra-territorial power of a local government: the Florida Legislature can pass a general or special law granting extraterritorial power. For example, Florida Statutes section 180.02 empowers a municipality to enact "an ordinance extending its corporate power over its municipal sewer service zone outside its corporate limits so as to require property owners outside the city but within such service zone to connect to the city's sewer system when it became available." *City of Winter Park v. S. States Utilities, Inc.*, 540 So. 2d 178, 179 (Fla. 5th DCA 1989).

The second and third restrictions are because Home Rule is a lesser power than a constitution or a statute. Stated somewhat differently, a local government, even with its Home Rule power, cannot make legal what a constitution or a statute has made illegal.

The fourth restriction is because Article VIII Section 1 provides: "The governing body of a county operating under a charter may enact county ordinances not inconsistent with general law. The charter shall provide which shall prevail in the event of conflict between county and municipal ordinances."

Note that the result of these restrictions upon counties, cities, towns and villages is that they can enact ordinances on the exact same topics as one another and as the Florida Legislature. The mere fact that the Florida Legislature or a local government enact a law on a particular topic does not preclude another county, city, town or village from legislating on that same topic. This is true even if one is within the territorial jurisdiction of another.

With all these legislating bodies free to enact laws on many of the same topics at the same time and over the same territory, it is possible that a law of the Florida Legislature might preempt, either expressly or impliedly, a local government law on that same subject. It is possible that a Supremacy Clause in a county's charter might preempt a law of a city, town or village located within that county. These and other topics of preemption are discussed later in this chapter.

3. "Be It Enacted" or "Be It Resolved"

Article III of Florida's Constitution, which discusses the Florida Legislature, states:

> SECTION 6. Laws.—... The enacting clause of every law shall read: "Be It Enacted by the Legislature of the State of Florida:".

Therefore, in order to be validly enacted, all laws of the Florida Legislature must begin with this phrase: "Be It Enacted by the Legislature of the State of Florida." A law is invalid, and unconstitutional on its face, if the bill passed into law by the Florida Legislature did not begin with this phrase.

A resolution does not begin with the phrase "Be It Enacted" but instead begins with this phrase: "Be It Resolved." Not just the Florida Legislature, but also Florida's local governments, are empowered to enact a resolution.

4. Resolution Made When Ordinance or Statute was Required

A resolution is not always enough. If Florida's Legislature enacts a resolution when an act (a statute) was required -- or if a Florida city, town or village enacts a resolution when an ordinance is required -- then the resolution is ineffective, facially unconstitutional, and unenforceable.

The difference between the two depends on administration and permanency. Resolutions are sufficient for ceremonial or nonbinding purposes. Likewise, resolutions are sufficient for a matter that is purely administrative in nature, or if not permanent.

To be valid, any local law intended to be permanent must be passed as an ordinance, not a resolution, unless it is a matter of administration or administrative business. Florida Statutes chapter 166 defines "ordinance" to be "an official legislative action of a governing body, which action is a regulation of a general and permanent nature and enforceable as a local law." It defines "resolution" to be "an expression of a governing body concerning matters of administration, an expression of a temporary character, or a provision for the disposition of a particular item of the administrative business of the governing body."

This point is well illustrated by *White v. Town of Inglis*, 988 So. 2d 163 (Fla. 2008).

WHITE

v.

TOWN OF INGLIS

First District Court of Appeal of Florida, 2008

988 So. 2d 163

Michael A. White appeals a final summary judgment entered in favor of the Town of Inglis, Florida, appellee, in his action challenging the Town's adoption of Resolution Number R14–05 (R14–05) which prohibits White's access to a street from his commercial property adjoining that street. We hold that R14–05 constitutes an "ordinance" as defined in [Florida's Municipal Home Rule Powers Act] and, because the Town adopted this ordinance without complying with the ten-day notice requirement in [Florida's Municipal Home Rule Powers Act], we hold the ordinance void. Accordingly, we reverse and remand for further proceedings.

White owns two contiguous lots in the Town of Inglis which front on Highway U.S. 19 and operates a used car business on the lots. Palm Point Drive is a residential street located immediately to the north of and adjacent to White's commercial property. On October 20, 2005, the Inglis Town Commission held a workshop meeting at which the subject of closing off commercial access to Palm Point Drive was discussed. White was present at the meeting. He states in his affidavit included in the record that he "had informally heard that the Town, was considering the construction of a fence along the road which might affect my access." According to the affidavit of Town Clerk Sally McCranie, those at the meeting were advised that a special meeting would be held on October 31, 2005, to consider a resolution to close commercial access to Palm Point Drive.

On October 31, 2005, the Town enacted R14–05 as a "resolution." R14–05 makes it unlawful for a person to drive from commercial properties onto Palm Point Drive. A fence has now been constructed along the drive blocking view of White's property and any access to Palm Point Drive from the property.

> [Florida's Municipal Home Rule Powers Act] defines "ordinance" as "an official legislative action of a governing body, which action is a regulation of a general and permanent nature and enforceable as a local law." [Florida's Municipal Home Rule Powers Act] defines "resolution" to mean "an expression of a governing body concerning matters of administration, an expression of a temporary character, or a provision for the disposition of a particular item of the administrative business of the governing body." "A resolution cannot be substituted for and have the force and effect of an ordinance, nor can a resolution supply initial authority which is required to be vested by ordinance." *Wallace v. Leahy,* 496 So. 2d 970, 971 (Fla. 3d DCA 1986) (citing *Brown v. City of St. Petersburg,* 111 Fla. 718, 153 So. 140 (1933); and *Carlton v. Jones,* 117 Fla. 622, 158 So. 170 (1934) ("An act which is required to be accomplished by ordinance may not be accomplished by resolution.")).
>
> It is clear that the action by the Town is . . . neither a matter of administration for the Town nor an expression of a temporary character. Because the Town enacted R14–05 without following the requirements of [Florida's Municipal Home Rule Powers Act], the ordinance is void. *Ellison v. City of Fort Lauderdale,* 183 So. 2d 193 (Fla.1966); *Healthsouth Doctors' Hosp. v. Hartnett,* 622 So. 2d 146 (Fla. 3d DCA 1993); *see also Carlton v. Jones,* 158 So. at 171 (recognizing that when an ordinance is not published according to law it is "invalid and of no effect"); *Webb v. Town Council of Town of Hilliard,* 766 So. 2d 1241 (Fla. 1st DCA 2000). Because we hold the ordinance void, it is not necessary to reach the other issues raised on appeal.
>
> REVERSED and REMANDED for proceedings consistent with this opinion.

5. Procedural Requirements

Florida's Constitution at Article III provides certain procedures that the Florida Legislature must use when enacting laws. Different procedures apply to the Florida Legislature than apply to Florida's counties, cities, towns and villages.

Generally speaking, due to the doctrine of the separation of powers, issues unaddressed by Florida's Constitution as to how the Florida Legislature conducts its business and fulfills its legislative function are issues to be decided solely by the Florida Legislature itself. For this reason, the Florida Legislature's procedural requirements are governed by the rules of the House and Senate.

As to local lawmaking bodies, Florida Statutes section 125.66 provides the minimum procedural requirements for counties to enact, and Florida's Home Rule Powers Act at Florida Statutes section 166.041 provides nearly identical minimum requirements for cities, towns and villages. The following minimum requirements may be strengthened but not reduced by an ordinance or a county charter. A notice of intent to enact the ordinance must be published in a newspaper of general circulation at least 10 days prior to enactment. The required format of, and statements in, the notice appears as a form in the Florida Statutes. An exception to the 10-day notice requirement may be made in an emergency. But a four-fifths vote of the legislating body must find that such an emergency exists warranting short notice. An emergency is not sufficient grounds for short notice when enacting a change to a zoning map. A 5 year statute of limitations applies to an action or defense arising out of the failure to meet these procedural requirements. *See* Patrick John McGinley, FLORIDA MUNICIPAL LAW AND PRACTICE § 3:4 (2017-2018 edition).

6. Single Subject Rule

Together, Florida's Constitution and Florida's Municipal Home Rule Powers Act require that each statute, ordinance or resolution "shall embrace but one subject and matters properly connected therewith." For example, Article III of Florida's Constitution contains these two clauses:

> SECTION 6. Laws.—Every law shall embrace but one subject and matter properly connected therewith,

> SECTION 12. Appropriation bills.—Laws making appropriations for salaries of public officers and other current expenses of the state shall contain provisions on no other subject.

Therefore, every law enacted by the Legislature, a county, a city, a town or a village may cover only one subject. This "Single Subject Rule" is interpreted by Florida's Supreme Court to contain three requirements. First, each law must embrace only one subject. Second, the law may include any matter that is properly connected with the subject. The third requirement, related to the first, is that the subject shall be briefly expressed in the title. The three requirements are given a liberal not strict interpretation because any doubt is resolved in favor of finding that the Single Subject Rule is not violated.

Florida Municipal Law and Practice identifies the following public policy reasons behind the Single Subject Rule:

> Two major considerations underlie the Single Subject Rule. The first is the need to prevent a legislative practice sometimes called "logrolling." Logrolling is when a legislature or lawmaking body includes in a single act some desirable or important matters together with some undesirable or unimportant matters. The result is that, order to enact into law the desirable matter, the bill must be passed in its entirely including the unwanted portion. Logrolling may have adverse affects upon the legislative process. Good bills can be held hostage by those who add undesirable or unimportant matters to the bill. The relative negotiating strengths of the proponents and opponents of a bill can be affected. Logrolling also severely limits if not destroys the veto power of the Governor or chief executive, and thereby negates one of the intended checks on the authority of the legislature.
>
> The second consideration behind the Single Subject Rule is to ensure the integrity of the legislative process in substantive lawmaking. The Florida Constitution demands that each bill dealing with substantive matters be scrutinized separately. Putting provisions on different substantive topics into a single bill could hinder the ability to

fully debate some of the topics. Bills should not be cluttered with extraneous matters which might cloud the legislative mind when it should be focused solely upon the one substantive matter addressed in the bill. Legislatures and lawmaking bodies include, by necessity, large numbers of elected members representing even larger numbers of individuals from diverse locations and backgrounds with diverse concerns. All want their ideas considered and their concerns heard. Under these conditions, debating a single subject is difficult enough.

Commentators suggest that the general disposition of Florida's courts is to avoid interpreting the Single Subject Rule in such a way so as to strike down otherwise valid laws as unconstitutional by use of a construction whose strictness is unnecessary to the accomplishment of the beneficial purposes for which the law has been adopted. Sometimes a broadly phrased title for the act will justify covering various subjects in that act. A statute will not be unconstitutional for embracing more than one subject if the title is sufficiently broad to connect it with the general subject matter of the enactment.

Likewise, laws containing provisions that are corollaries to the act's main purpose do not violate the Single Subject Rule. For example, a statute designed to confer exclusive jurisdiction on a court of record does not violate the Single Subject Rule when it contains a provision abolishing the court previously holding that jurisdiction.

Patrick John McGinley, FLORIDA MUNICIPAL LAW AND PRACTICE (2017-2018 edition). A fine illustration of Florida's use of its Single Subject Rule appears in *Franklin v. State*, 887 So. 2d 1063 (Fla. 2004).

FRANKLIN

V.

STATE

Supreme Court of Florida, 2004

887 So. 2d 1063

The issue in this case is the constitutionality of ... the "Three-Strike Violent Felony Offender Act." The specific constitutional question presented is whether the fourteen provisions of the Act "embrace but one subject and matter properly connected therewith" as mandated by article III, section 6 of the Florida Constitution, the single subject clause. We ... conclude that the Act does not violate the single subject clause of the Florida Constitution.

I. Summary of [the "Three Strikes Act"]

... [The "Three Strikes Act"] is identified at the beginning of its full title as "an act relating to sentencing." The remainder of the full title sets forth the statutory provisions .... A lengthy preamble, consisting of twenty-one "Whereas" clauses, follows the full title. The Act contains fourteen separate sections, twelve of which are substantive. . . . [O]nly two of the Act's twelve substantive sections relate specifically to the "Three-Strike" violent felony provisions .... However, three of the other sections, sections 2, 4, and 5, establish harsher sentences for violent and repeat offenders.

Four of the remaining sections involve substantive criminal offenses ....

Finally, [the "Three Strikes Act"] contains two administrative provisions. Section 11 requires the clerk of the court to transmit to the appropriate United States immigration officer records pertaining to aliens who are convicted of or who enter a plea to any crime. Section 12 requires the Governor to publish the penalties contained in the Act.

II. Facts and Procedural Background

Franklin was convicted of armed robbery and resisting arrest based on acts that occurred after the effective date of [the "Three Strikes Act"]. He received a sentence of forty years in prison as a habitual felony offender, pursuant to [a law that] had been amended by [the "Three Strikes Act"]. Franklin's prior criminal history consisted of one felony conviction (possession of cocaine) and one felony for which adjudication of guilt was withheld (burglary of a dwelling). Prior to [the "Three Strikes Act"], an offense for which adjudication of guilt had been withheld would not have qualified as a predicate for habitual offender ....

Franklin appealed [to Florida's Third District Court of Appeal]. While his appeal was pending, [Florida's] Second District held in *Taylor v. State*, 818 So. 2d 544 (Fla. 2d DCA 2002), that [the "Three Strikes Act"] violated the single subject requirement of article III, section 6. In [Franklin's appeal] the Third District held that [the "Three Strikes Act"] did not violate the constitutional requirement of a single subject. The Third District also certified conflict with *Taylor*. . . .

...As the [conflicting] cases from the district courts illustrate, the methods for determining both the single subject of an act and those matters that are properly connected to that subject vary. We take this opportunity to review our jurisprudence in this area of the law and clarify the single subject analysis.

IV. Single Subject Rule Analysis

A. Applicable Law

1. The Purpose of the Single Subject Clause

Currently, forty-three states have some form of single subject clause applicable to legislation contained in their state constitutions. In Florida, the single subject clause has been part of our state constitution since 1868 ... and is presently set forth [as follows]:

> Every law shall embrace but one subject and matter properly connected therewith, and the subject shall be briefly expressed in the title.

Art. III, § 6, Fla. Const.

Thus, the single subject clause contains three requirements. First, each law shall "embrace" only "one subject." Second, the law may include any matter that is "properly connected" with the subject. The third requirement, related to the first, is that the subject shall be "briefly expressed in the title." ...[T]he purposes of the single subject provision [are]: (1) to prevent hodgepodge or "log rolling" legislation, i.e. putting two unrelated matters in one act; (2) to prevent surprise or fraud by means of provisions in bills of which the title gave no intimation, and which might therefore be overlooked and carelessly and unintentionally adopted; and (3) to fairly apprise the people of the subjects of legislation that are being considered, in order that they may have opportunity of being heard thereon.

In *Colonial Inv. Co. v. Nolan*, 100 Fla. 1349, 131 So. 178 (1930), this Court explained the historical backdrop for the constitutional mandate:

> It had become quite common for legislative bodies to embrace in the same bill incongruous matters having no relation to each other, or to the subject specified in the title[. B]y [these] means, measures were often adopted without attracting attention. And frequently such distinct subjects, affecting diverse interests, were combined in order to unite members who favored either in support of all. And the failure to indicate in the title the object of the bill often resulted in members voting ignorantly for measures which they would not knowingly have approved. And not only were the members thus misled, but the public also; and legislative provisions were sometimes pushed through which would have been made odious by popular discussion and remonstrance if their pendency had been seasonably demonstrated by the title of the bill.

Id. at 179. In fact, as we observed in *State v. Bryan*, 50 Fla. 293, 39 So. 929 (1905),

> [n]early all the states having Constitutions of recent adoption have incorporated therein provisions in nearly identical language, and their courts agree as to the purpose of such provisions. They also agree that the provision refers to the subject-matter of the legislation, and not to a single purpose or end sought to be accomplished. Its purpose was to avoid the confusion incident to the evil which had grown out of 'omnibus' legislation.

Id. at 961 (quoting *Gibson v. State*, 16 Fla. 291, 299, 1877 WL 2625 (1877)).

Extant in our constitution since 1868, the single subject clause is a direct expression of the people's intent to provide a limitation on the Legislature's power to enact laws. The judiciary's obligation is to apply the constitutional limitation to legislation that violates the constitution. See generally *Sebring Airport Authority v. McIntyre*, 783 So. 2d 238, 244 n.5 (Fla. 2001) ("To the judges belongs the power of expounding the laws; and although in the discharge of that duty they may render a law inoperative by declaring it unconstitutional, it does not arise from any supremacy which the judiciary possesses over the Legislature, but from the supremacy of the Constitution over both.") …

2. Standard of Review

When courts are called upon to assess legislation for compliance with article III, section 6, the standard of review is highly deferential. "[T]he general disposition of the courts [is] to construe the constitutional provision liberally, rather than to embarrass legislation by a construction whose strictness is unnecessary to the accomplishment of the beneficial purposes for which it has been adopted." … [T]o overcome the presumption in favor of constitutionality, the single subject violation must occur beyond a reasonable doubt ….

3. Defining the Single Subject

The key to determining whether a legislative enactment violates the single subject clause of the Florida Constitution is the method by which the court defines the "single subject" of the legislation and the analysis employed to determine matters "properly connected therewith." …

In determining the single subject, we start with the basic principle that "the subject is the one that is expressed in the title of the act." …. Indeed, the constitutional provision requires that the subject be briefly expressed in the title.

For purposes of single subject analysis, every law published in the

Laws of Florida has both a short title, i.e. "An act relating to ...," and a full title, which begins with the chapter law number and ends with "providing an effective date," and encompasses the short title. ...

This Court has adhered to the presumption that an act complies with article III, section 6, even when the full title of an act is lengthy .... [T]he precise language of the constitution itself mandates that the single subject be "briefly expressed in the title." Although the full title may be as lengthy as the Legislature chooses, the actual expression of the single subject within the full title must be briefly stated. Therefore ... the single subject of an act is derived from the short title, i.e., the language immediately following the customary phrase "an act relating to" and preceding the indexing of the act's provisions. In so doing, we specifically note that although many acts may contain a citation name by which either the entire act or portions of it may be identified, the citation name is not synonymous with the single subject.

This relatively simple method for defining the one subject of an act is supported by our precedent. Indeed, we have consistently stated that only the subject, not matters connected to the subject, must be expressed in the title .... In order to comply with the requirement that the subject of a law be briefly expressed in the title, the title need not be an index of all the features of the legislation. In other words, it is not constitutionally necessary to index the provisions contained in the body of the act in the title .... However, the full title nonetheless must be "so worded as not to mislead a person of average intelligence as to the scope of the enactment and [be] sufficient to put that person on notice and cause him to inquire into the body of the statute itself."

Our determination that the single subject of an act can be found in the short title is subject to the following caveat: the title of an act may be general, "so long as it is not made a cover to legislation incongruous in itself." In other words, the short title of the legislation cannot be so broad as to purportedly cover unrelated topics, and thus provide no real guidance as to what the body of the act contains. Indeed, allowing an overly broad short title to become the single subject runs the risk of permitting logrolling and hodgepodge or omnibus legislation .... [I]f the Legislature's short title is suspect for being overly broad, a court should look to the remainder of the act and the history of the legislative process to determine if the act actually contains a single subject or violates the constitution by encompassing more than one subject.

Ordinarily, determining the single subject of an act by reference to the short title will be a straightforward process. The more difficult analysis is whether the various provisions are "properly connected" to the single subject. We now turn to the analysis to be used when evaluating the "properly connected" question.

4. Properly Connected

As stated above, the second requirement of the single subject clause in article III, section 6 mandates that all provisions in the body of the act be "properly connected" to the single subject....

A review of our jurisprudence reveals that we have defined a "proper" connection in various ways. We have described a proper connection as one that is "natural or logical." .... We have stated that whether a connection is proper will depend on "common sense .... We have also stated that if the provision is "necessary" to the subject, "fairly and naturally germane" to the subject, or promotes the purposes of the legislation as set forth in the subject, the provision may be regarded as properly connected. As we explained in surveying the law to date as of 1957,

> if a matter is germane to or reasonably connected with the expressed title of the act, it may be incorporated within the act without being in violation of [the single subject provision] of our constitution. Provisions which are necessary incidents to, or tend to make effective or promote the object and purpose of the legislation included in the subject expressed in the title of the act may be regarded as matters properly connected with the subject thereof .... In determining if matters are properly connected with the subject, the test is whether such provisions are fairly and naturally germane to the subject of the act, or are such as are necessary incidents to or tend to make effective or promote the objects and purposes of legislation included in the sub-

ject.

Canova, 94 So. 2d at 184 (citations omitted).

More recently, we explained that a connection between the subject and the provision is proper if a "reasonable explanation" exists as to why the Legislature chose to join the provision to the legislative act ....

After reviewing these various methods of defining a "proper connection," we take this opportunity to set forth the correct test to be applied when determining whether a connection between a provision in the act and the act's subject is "proper" within the meaning of the single subject clause: A connection between a provision and the subject is proper (1) if the connection is natural or logical, or (2) if there is a reasonable explanation for how the provision is (a) necessary to the subject or (b) tends to make effective or promote the objects and purposes of legislation included in the subject.

In setting forth this test, we clarify that there is a difference between the subject of the act that is briefly stated in the title and the object of the act. Simply stated, "The subject is the matter to which an act relates; the object, the purpose to be accomplished." ... In this regard, we caution that the "accomplishment of several 'purposes' may be logically embraced in one 'subject' so long as all such purposes are germane to ... the expressed general subject." ... The term 'subject' is broader than the word 'object,' as one subject may contain many objects." ... The purposes of an act may be instructive in determining whether there is a reasonable explanation for the inclusion of a specific provision in the chapter law. However, the purposes of an act cannot be used to either define or expand the single subject. The single subject clause contained in article III, section 6 "refers to the subject-matter of the legislation, and not to a single purpose or end sought to be accomplished." ...

... [I]n determining whether a reasonable explanation exists for the connection between a specific provision and the single subject, the court may consider the citation name, the full title, the preamble, and the provisions in the body of the act .... However, if, after examining the act in its entirety, we cannot discern a "reasonable explanation" for the inclusion of a seemingly disparate provision, we will look to the history of the legislative process to determine how the challenged provision was added to the act. In other words, this Court has looked to the legislative history of the enactment to buttress our conclusion that the provision is not properly connected ….

… [P]articular combinations of various statutory provisions may not be properly connected. To date, this Court has regarded two such combinations with caution: substantive changes to the criminal law that are contained in acts that do not predominately address the substantive criminal law, and chapter laws that combine civil and criminal provisions. However, other improperly combined provisions may run afoul of the single subject clause as well. For example, we recently found that a provision concerning the assignment of bad check debts to a private debt collector had "no natural or logical connection" to an act's subject, which was driver's licenses, operation of motor vehicles, and vehicle registrations.

There is no bright line rule this Court can create to determine whether a connection is proper—that is, whether the connection is natural or logical, or if a reasonable explanation exists for how the provision is necessary to the subject or tends to make effective or promote the objects and purposes of legislation included in the subject. Nonetheless, we examine [the "Three Strikes Act"] against the backdrop of this jurisprudence.

B. [the "Three Strikes Act"]

… [O]ur resolution of this case flows from our highly deferential standard of review in this area of the law—that every reasonable doubt should be resolved in favor of a law's constitutionality ….

The short title of [the "Three Strikes Act"] is "An act relating to sentencing." The citation name is the "Three-Strike Violent Felony Offender Act." The full title is lengthy, running two pages and almost one thousand words. As we have explained, the constitution requires that the subject be briefly expressly in the title and we give considerable deference to the Legislature's selection of the title. Based on our determination that ordinarily the subject will be found in the short title, we conclude that the subject [the

"Three Strikes Act"] is sentencing ....

We now turn to the controverted issue of whether sections 11 and 13 [of the "Three Strikes Act"] are properly connected to sentencing. The Second District in *Taylor* determined that sections 11 and 13 lack a proper connection. The test we utilize is whether there is a natural or logical connection to sentencing, or whether a reasonable explanation exists for how these provisions are either necessary to sentencing or tend to make effective or promote the purposes of the sentencing legislation ....

We first address section 11, which provides that the clerk of the court shall furnish to the INS officers the charging document, judgment, and sentence "in every case in which an alien is convicted of a felony or misdemeanor or enters a plea of guilty or nolo contendre to any felony or misdemeanor charge." Under the language of the provision, this shall be done after the alien offender's sentencing proceeding.

We conclude that there is a natural or logical and thus proper connection between the requirements of section 11 that sentences of non-citizen offenders be provided to INS and the Act's subject of sentencing, in that section 11 is a post-sentencing measure. Our conclusion that the connection is proper is buttressed by the fact that in requiring the transmission of sentences to the INS, section 11 also promotes the Act's purpose of protecting the public from persons sentenced as serious or repeat violent offenders .... [S]ection 11 aids in the removal of violent alien offenders from the country after sentence completion. ... Thus, there is also a reasonable explanation why the Legislature would include a provision that facilitates the removal of non-citizens who are serious or repeat violent offenders after sentence completion in an Act whose subject is sentencing and whose purposes include the use of sentencing to protect the public from this class of criminals.

In reaching this conclusion, we are not persuaded by Franklin's argument that the fact that the section applies to all persons who receive a criminal sentence, whether felony or misdemeanor, violent or nonviolent, first offense or fiftieth, renders this provision in violation of article III, section 6. The inquiry is not whether the section solely relates to the purpose of protecting the public from violent and repeat offenders, but rather whether the section is properly connected to the single subject of sentencing. Accordingly, the inclusion of section 11 does not result in a violation of the single subject clause of article III, section 6.

We next turn to section 13, which expands the substantive crime of burglary to specifically add “railroad vehicle” to the definition of conveyance. The Second District found the relationship between the substantive crime of burglary and sentencing too “tenuous, so dependent on the happenstance of individual cases, that it simply cannot be characterized as natural or logical.” *Taylor*, 818 So. 2d at 549. In contrast, the Third and Fourth Districts determined that including section 13 does not violate the single subject clause because the section expands the definition of the crime of armed burglary, which is an offense included in section 775.084, the habitual offender sentencing statute. See *Franklin*, 836 So. 2d at 1113–1114; *Hernandez-Molina*, 860 So. 2d at 490.

We agree with the Third and Fourth Districts. The proper connection between the expanded definition of burglary and sentencing is found in the fact that armed burglary is one of the qualifying offenses for a harsher sentence in the Act. In broadening the definition of conveyance in section 810.11, Florida Statutes, which previously encompassed a “railroad car” but not a “railroad vehicle,” the Legislature ensured that a serious crime against a person inside a railroad vehicle (to wit, a locomotive) will be punished accordingly. See *Hernandez-Molina*, 860 So. 2d at 490.28 Thus, there is a proper connection to sentencing in that section 13 makes effective one of the purposes included within the subject—imposing harsher sentences on violent offenders. Considering that the purpose of the Act is to protect the public from serious and repeat violent offenders, a reasonable explanation exists for including this substantive section within an Act whose subject is sentencing.

In determining that section 13 did not relate to sentencing and therefore violates article III, section 6, the Second District in Taylor and Judge Cope in his dissenting opinion in Franklin relied, in part, on the fact that section 13 substantively amended the criminal law. See *Taylor*, 818 So. 2d at

549; *Franklin*, 836 So. 2d at 1120 (Cope, J., dissenting). However, we do not consider this fact to be determinative in this case.

In contrast to other acts that we found in violation of the single subject rule because they combined the creation of new crimes with other disparate provisions, in this case, section 13 is one of four sections of the Act that relate to and amend the substantive criminal law. We note that section 7 creates a new category of offender, a repeat sexual batterer; section 8 adds references to the new statute defining "repeat sexual batterer" to the sexual battery statute, section 794.011, wherein "sexual battery" is defined; and section 9 modifies the drug trafficking statute to allow prosecution on the basis of the number of cannabis plants which a person possesses, sells, or delivers, and modifies the weight benchmarks for prosecution. Therefore, similar to section 13, sections 7 and 9 amend substantive crimes. We note that both the Taylor court and Judge Cope in his dissent determined that section 9 was logically related to sentencing because the modified crime was punishable by a mandatory minimum term created by the Act. See *Taylor*, 818 So. 2d at 549; *Franklin*, 836 So. 2d at 1120 (Cope, J., dissenting). The same is true of the new "repeat sexual batterer" offense classification created in section 7.

This reasoning is equally applicable to section 13. Although not every person charged under the modification to the burglary statute contained in section 13 will be subject to a mandatory minimum sentence, the fact remains that armed burglary, which is an aggravated form of the crime modified by section 13, is subject to an enhanced sentence under this Act. Therefore, as with sections 7 and 9, there is a proper connection between section 13 and the single subject of sentencing.

For the reasons stated above, we conclude that sections 11 and 13 are properly connected to the single subject of sentencing. [The "Three Strikes Act"] does not violate the single subject clause of article III, section 6 of the Florida Constitution. Accordingly, we approve the Third District's decision in *Franklin*, which is before us for review. We also approve the Fourth District's decision in *Hernandez-Molina* and disapprove the Second District's decision in *Taylor*.

It is so ordered.

Notes and Questions to Consider:

1. Two considerations addressed by the Single Subject Rule are "logrolling" and legislative integrity. Is this a difference between Florida's Legislature and the U.S. Congress? As a famous example, consider Congress's 2010 passage of the Patient Protection and Affordable Care Act, colloquially known as Obamacare. The U.S. Supreme Court noted that the Affordable Care Act contained many topics unrelated to the subject of affordable health care:

> The ACA is over 900 pages long. Its regulations include requirements ranging from a break time and secluded place at work for nursing mothers, ... to displays of nutritional content at chain restaurants.... The Act raises billions of dollars in taxes and fees, including exactions imposed on high-income taxpayers ... and tanning booths.... It spends government money on, among other things, the study of how to spend less government money.... And it includes a number of provisions that provide benefits to the State of a particular legislator....
>
> Such provisions validate the Senate Majority Leader's statement, "I don't know if there is a senator that doesn't have something in this bill that was important to them.... [And] if they don't have something in it important to them, then it doesn't speak well of them.["]... (quoting Sen. Reid). Often, a minor provision will be the price paid for support of a major provision....
>
> ...[T]he ACA ... includes not only many provisions that are ancillary to its central provisions but also many that are entirely unrelated—hitched on because it was a quick way to get them passed despite opposition, or because their proponents could exact their enactment as the quid pro quo for their needed support. ...[W]e are confronted with ... a so-called "Christmas tree," a law to which many nongermane ornaments

> have been attached.... We have no reliable basis for knowing which pieces of the Act would have passed on their own.

Nat'l Fed'n of Indep. Bus. v. Sebelius, 567 U.S. 519, 704 (2012). If the U.S. Constitution had a Single Subject Rule like Florida's Constitution, would federal laws like Obamacare have the characteristics described by the U.S. Supreme Court? Is that good or bad?

2. Exceptions to the Single Subject Rule include corollaries and a well-drafted title. To what extent to the exceptions eliminate the rule?

3. Are there "suspect classes," so-to-speak, in the jurisprudence of the Single Subject Rule? Consider this statement from the *Taylor* opinion above: "Particular combinations of various statutory provisions may not be properly connected. To date, this Court has regarded two such combinations with caution: substantive changes to the criminal law that are contained in acts that do not predominately address the substantive criminal law, and chapter[s] that combine civil and criminal provisions."

7. Amending Existing Laws

Once the Florida Legislature or the legislative body of a county, city, town or village enact a law, can that law be changed later? Yes, but special requirements apply, such as this one from Article III of Florida's Constitution:

> SECTION 6. Laws.—... No law shall be revised or amended by reference to its title only. Laws to revise or amend shall set out in full the revised or amended act, section, subsection or paragraph of a subsection.

Although this requirement appears in the article of Florida's Constitution discussing Florida's Legislature, it also applies to lawmaking by Florida's counties, cities, towns and villages as explained in FLORIDA MUNICIPAL LAW AND PRACTICE:

> The Florida Constitution says that a law may not be amended

> solely by reference to its title. This requires that any law amending an existing law must set out in full the complete text of the newly-amended law as it will read after amendment. It is not enough to simply state what is amended. Instead, the old law with its new amendments incorporated into it must be printed out in its entirety. If a statutory enactment is complete and intelligible in itself, without the necessity of referring to the books to relate it to an amended statute in order to ascertain the meaning of an amendment, then the section of the Constitution concerning the amendment of a law is satisfied; but if the amendatory enactment is not a complete, coherent, and intelligible act, or if it necessitates separate research and analysis of the statute which is being amended, it does not meet the requirements of the constitutional provision.
>
> Because of this state constitutional requirement, neither a state statute nor a local ordinance is effectively amended or revised simply by reference to its title. Instead, laws or ordinances intended to revise or amend are only effective when they set out in full the revised or amended act, section, subsection, or paragraph of a subsection.
>
> For this reason, it is invalid to reenact a law simply by passing an amendment that does nothing more than state that the soon-to-expire law's expiration clause is stricken. For example, an amendment to reenact a law is invalid where a section of an original act provided for the expiration of the act by a certain date . . . and an amendatory act simply stated that such section "is amended to read: 'The provisions of this act shall be in full force and effect until terminated by law.'"
>
> This applies to all laws or ordinances that assume, in terms, to revise, alter, or amend some prior act or section thereof.

Patrick John McGinley, FLORIDA MUNICIPAL LAW AND PRACTICE § 3:6 (2017-2018 ed.). What if a bill is intended to create a new law that does not amend an old law but instead replaces it in its entirety? That was the question addressed in the following century-old Florida lawyer applicant case called

In re: De Woody, 113 So. 677, 678–80 (Fla. 1927). At this point in Florida's history, Florida's Constitution was not an impediment to the legislative branch enacting laws regulating the admission of lawyers to the Florida Bar. We examine this case today for the procedure not the substance of the law-making. Putting aside the substance of the law at issue in *In re De Woody*, this case remains instructive on the issue of what procedure is required when a new law replaces an old law.

IN RE:

DE WOODY

Supreme Court of Florida, 1927

113 So. 677

Charles F. De Woody moves for his admission to the bar. [He was denied admission by] the State Board of Law Examiners, [which] provides, amongst other things, for the method of examination and admission to the bar of applicants.

The movant contends that [the statute creating the Board of Law Examiners is] inoperative, because it violates … article 3, section 16, of [Florida's] Constitution, that 'no law shall be amended or revised by reference to its title only, but in such case the act, as revised, or section, as amended, shall be reenacted and published at length,' was not observed in the passage of [the statute creating the Board of Law Examiners.]

… [The movant is correct that the statute creating the Board of Law Examiners] contains no express repealing clause, nor does it in terms undertake to amend any other statute, though its provisions may be in conflict with certain prior statutes, thereby, and to the extent of the manifest inconsistency or repugnancy, effecting the repeal by implication of such prior statutes.

This court has previously held that:

> It was never intended by the Constitution that every law which

> would affect some previous statute of varied provisions on the same subject should set out the statute, or statutes, so affected at full length.
>
> The constitutional provision forbidding the amendment or revision of a law by reference to its title only, and requiring the act as revised, or section as amended, to be re-enacted and published at length, does not apply to amendments or repeals of statutes that are affected by implication, but applies only to laws that assume in terms to revise, alter, or amend some particular prior act or section of an act.

Van Pelt v. Hilliard, 78 So. 693 (1918).

… The Legislature is presumed to have known what the existing law was when [the statute creating the Board of Law Examiners] was enacted. It is also presumed to have known what the effect of the enactment … would be upon the existing statutes on the subject. The journals of the House and Senate disclose that [the statute creating the Board of Law Examiners] was carefully considered by committees composed of members of the bar. …

None of the objections here urged by the movant to the constitutional validity of [the statute creating the Board of Law Examiners] are well taken. The motion must be and is hereby denied.

Notes and Questions to Consider:

1. Does *In re: De Woody* mean that a Florida lawmaking body need not underline the text in a bill that is new language, and need not ~~strike through~~ the text that is to be deleted from an existing law? Consider the following from SUTHERLAND STATUTORY CONSTRUCTION:

> To enforce the constitutional limitation that no act shall be amended by reference to its title only, but the act as amended shall be set out and published at length, courts have upheld legislation and avoided classifying an act as an amendment wherever possible. In litigation, the issue of compliance with the constitutional provision gen-

> erally arises where a statute does not purport to amend any prior act, since the legislature usually complies with the limitation when a statute purports to amend a prior statute. To sustain legislation, courts have tested the amendatory character of an act by its form. Thus, if an act does not purport to amend a prior act, either directly or by inserting or striking words, it is not an amendatory act within the constitutional limitation...
>
> Also as a result of this policy to uphold legislation, several classes of statutes that do not purport to amend but which in fact change the law are recognized by courts and held not to be amendments within the constitutional limitations. An implied amendment, an act complete within itself, an implied repeal, an express repeal, a supplementary act, and an act adopting the provisions of another statute by reference are not treated as amendments within the constitutional limitations.

Amendment of an Act by Reference to Its Title—Acts Amendatory in Form, 1A SUTHERLAND STATUTORY CONSTRUCTION § 22:17 (7th ed.).

2. Are "reference statutes" permitted under Florida's Constitution? Stated somewhat differently, can a new Florida law adopt by reference the terms or procedures of an existing law without copying-and-pasting the existing law into the text of the new law? Consider the following from Florida Jurisprudence:

> Enactments that refer to other statutes and make them applicable to the subject of the new legislation are called "reference statutes." ...A statute incorporating the provisions of other statutes by reference and adoption thereby avoids encumbering the statute books with unnecessary repetition. Such a procedure is not improper. A code or compilation of laws need not be set out in the statute adopting it....
>
> Where a statute adopts a part of, or all of, another statute by a specific and descriptive reference thereto, the effect is the same as if the provisions adopted were written into the adopting statute.

Reference Statutes, 48A Fla. Jur 2d Statutes § 11 (Mar. 2019 update).

8. Title Requirements

Florida's Constitution, at Article III, requires the following:

> SECTION 6. Laws.—[For e]very law … the subject shall be briefly expressed in the title.

In addition to this phrase in Florida's Constitution, Florida's Municipal Home Rule Powers Act contain identical requirements for Florida's counties, cities, towns and villages. *See* Florida Statutes section 166.041. Together, these requirements mean that "for each and every law—including every local ordinance or resolution – Art. III, § 6, Fla. Const. requires that the subject of the law, ordinance, or resolution must be clearly stated in the title." Patrick John McGinley, FLORIDA MUNICIPAL LAW AND PRACTICE § 3:7 (2017-2018 ed.). Stated somewhat differently, the act, "ordinance or resolution may include every matter germane, incidental, or subsidiary to, and not inconsistent with or foreign to, the general subject of the law as expressed in its title." *Id.*

What is the "title" of a law? It is not the "citation name," which is the short name given by a law for use in citing to that law. For example, Florida Statutes chapter 166 tells us that "[t]his chapter shall be known and may be cited as the 'Municipal Home Rule Powers Act'" but that phrase is its citation name and is not its title. Florida's Supreme Court, in *Franklin v. State*, 887 So. 2d 1063 (Fla. 2004), tells us exactly what is meant by the "title" and makes the following observations regarding the Florida Legislature's use of titles:

> [E]very law published in the Laws of Florida has both a short title, i.e. "An act relating to ...," and a full title, which begins with the chapter law number and ends with "providing an effective date," and encompasses the short title. *Cf. State v. Kaufman,* 430 So. 2d 904, 907 (Fla.1983). "[F]ormerly the title of an act was not considered a part of

> it and, anciently, acts had no title prefixed at all ....[" *State ex rel. Flink v.*] *Canova,* 94 So. 2d [181,] 183–84 [(Fla. 1957)]. ...
>
> Over the years, full titles have varied in length, some being relatively brief and others spanning pages.... Although article III, section 6 [of Florida's Constitution] imposes the restriction that the subject be "briefly expressed in the title," we have remained deferential to the Legislature's choice to craft a title to an act with few words or many. Indeed, we noted as early as 1905 that although a lengthy full title may be "unduly drawn out ..., cumbersome, and awkwardly worded," its length alone will not invalidate an act.... As noted above, in recent years full titles have consistently begun with the phrase "an act relating to" and ended with "providing an effective date."

Franklin v. State, 887 So. 2d 1063, 1074–75 (Fla. 2004).

Notes and Questions to Consider:

1. Do prior topics previously discussed in this text contribute to the fact that the Florida Legislature uses such lengthy, detailed titles when such verbosity is not constitutionally required? For instance, recall our discussion of the how Florida's Legislature enacts a bill into a law. Recall that the constitutionally required First Reading of a bill is accomplished by publication of the bill's title in the chamber's Journal. Does this help explain why, "[d]espite the Single Subject Rule discussed above, a statute will not be unconstitutional for embracing more than one subject if the title is sufficiently broad to connect it with the general subject matter of the enactment?" Patrick John McGinley, FLORIDA MUNICIPAL LAW AND PRACTICE § 3:7 (2017-2018 ed.).

2. Lengthy titles may be the norm but a short title is not necessarily unconstitutional. Case law precedent holds that "the title need not contain a detailed explanation of every provision found in that title's law. So long

as the matters addressed in the act are fairly related to the subject described in the title, the title is constitutionally sufficient." Patrick John McGinley, FLORIDA MUNICIPAL LAW AND PRACTICE § 3:7 (2017-2018 ed.).

9. Zoning Laws

Florida's Supreme Court holds that "[z]oning is a legislative function which reposes ultimately in the governing authority of a municipality." *Gulf & E. Dev. Corp. v. City of Fort Lauderdale*, 354 So. 2d 57, 59 (Fla. 1978). Therefore, in Florida, zoning laws are the province of counties, cities, towns and villages but not the Florida Legislature. Any zoning law enacted by Florida's Legislature would be invalid.

As to the validity of local zoning laws, both the U.S. Supreme Court and Florida's Supreme Court adopted a highly deferential standard of judicial review early in the history of local zoning. The U.S. Supreme Court held in *Village of Euclid, Ohio v. Ambler Realty Co.*, 272 U.S. 365, 388 (1926), that "[i]f the validity of the legislative classification for zoning purposes be fairly debatable, the legislative judgment must be allowed to control." Florida's Supreme Court adopted this same "fairly debatable" rule of law in *City of Miami Beach v. Ocean & Inland Co.*, 3 So. 2d 364 (1941). But see *Bd. of County Com'rs of Brevard County v. Snyder*, 627 So. 2d 469, 471 (Fla. 1993) (granting less deference to requests for rezoning).

Despite the deference to zoning laws granted by federal and Florida constitutional law, Florida's Growth Management Act requires local governments to enact a Comprehensive Plan. So local lawmaking is invalid if inconsistent with that Comprehensive Plan. Each county, city, town or village must create then gain the approval of the Florida Department of Community Affairs for a Comprehensive Plan that includes "principles, guidelines, and standards for the orderly and balanced future economic, social, physical, environmental, and fiscal development" of the local government's jurisdictional area. At the minimum, the local plan must include elements covering future land use; capital improvements generally; sanitary sewer, solid waste, drainage, potable water, and natural ground water aquifer protection specifically; conservation; recreation and open space; housing; traffic circulation; intergovernmental coordination; coastal management (for local government in the coastal zone); and mass transit (for local jurisdictions with 50,000 or more people). *See* Florida Statutes section 163.3177. In summary, a "comprehensive plan is intended to provide for the future use of land, which contemplates [achieving] a gradual and ordered growth." *Bd. of County Com'rs of Brevard County v. Snyder*, 627 So. 2d 469, 475 (Fla. 1993). The Comprehensive Plan results in a "zoning map."

Proposed ordinances changing the zoning map and affecting a parcel or parcels of land less than 10 acres in size require individualized notice before enactment. "A failure to strictly comply with the following notice requirements will invalidate the local zoning ordinance." Patrick John McGinley, FLORIDA MUNICIPAL LAW AND PRACTICE § 3:8 (2017-2018 ed.) The clerk of the governing body must notify by mail each real property owner whose land is affected and whose address is known by reference to the latest ad valorem tax records. That notice must be given at least 30 days prior to the public hearing. *See* Florida Statutes sections 125.66 and 166.041. This results in an increased requirement for notice before enactment of such a zoning map change as compared to the enactment of other laws or ordinances that do not require such individualized notice.

Not every law that affects land is a zoning ordinance. Consider the facts and holding of *City of Sarasota v. 35 S. Lemon, Inc.,* 722 So. 2d 268 (Fla. 2d DCA 1998).

CITY OF SARASOTA

V.

35 SOUTH LEMON, INC.

Second District Court of Appeal of Florida, 1998

722 So. 2d 268

The City of Sarasota (the City) appeals the partial final summary judgment in favor of 35 S. Lemon, Inc.... The trial court determined that the City's Permitting Ordinance and Noise Ordinance were not enacted properly because the ordinances regulated land development and were subject to review by the City's local planning agency. We conclude that the Noise Ordinance regulates conduct and is not subject to review by the City's local planning agency; therefore, we reverse the partial final summary judgment.

In 1997, the City adopted the Noise Ordinance by amending chapter 20 of its City Code. This amendment affected the appellees because their restaurant and nightclub were zoned C–CBD.

The City also enacted the Permitting Ordinance on the same day as the Noise Ordinance.... These code changes adversely affected the music provided by the appellees at their restaurant and nightclub.

Both the Noise Ordinance and the Permitting Ordinance were adopted pursuant to the procedures set forth in [Florida's Municipal Home Rule Powers Act codified at] section 166.041(3)(a), Florida Statutes (1995). After the ordinances were adopted, the appellees were cited with several violations of the Noise Ordinance. The ... trial court granted partial summary judgment finding that the Noise Ordinance was void because it was not reviewed by the City's local planning agency [which must review all zoning ordinances].... The partial summary judgment further enjoined the City from enforcing the Noise Ordinance.

In the order, the trial court sets forth the definition of "land development regulation" as defined in section 163.3164(23), Florida Statutes (1995), and emphasized that portion of the statute which provides that a land development regulation includes "the making of any material change in the use of or appearance of any structure or land." The court then cited this court's opinion in *Lee County v. Lippi,* 693 So. 2d 686 (Fla. 2d DCA 1997), in support for finding that the Noise Ordinance was a land development regulation subject to review by the planning agency. We conclude that the trial court incorrectly applied *Lippi* to the facts in this case.

In *Lippi,* this court was asked to determine whether two ordinances were properly enacted under similar facts to this case. The first ordinance prohibited the use of water craft within a certain area of the shoreline. The second ordinance regulated the location for personal water craft rentals. This court determined that the first ordinance was "patently a regulatory ordinance, not subject to the review requirements" of the statute. *See id.* at 689. This court then determined that the second ordinance regulating the placement of rental businesses, which required some businesses to close and relocate, sufficiently impacted a previously permitted land use and should have been reviewed by the local planning agency. *See id.*

If the Noise Ordinance is a land development regulation within the meaning of section 163.3164(23), Florida Statutes (1995), then the ordinance was improperly enacted because the City failed to submit the proposed ordinance for review by the planning agency. If the ordinance is an attempt to regulate conduct, it is exempt from this review process. Here, the appellees' business is still able to operate according to its previous use. It simply has to comply with the noise level requirements. This case is more concerned with regulating conduct rather than with regulating land development. *See T.J.R. Holding Co., Inc. v. Alachua County,* 617 So. 2d 798 (Fla. 1st DCA 1993) (ordinance which prohibited nudity and sexual conduct, or simulated sexual conduct, within establishments serving alcoholic beverages, was not a land-use regulation).

We conclude that the Noise Ordinance is a regulatory ordinance which is not subject to the review requirements of chapter 163. Accordingly, we reverse the trial court's partial summary judgment and remand this case to the trial court to resolve other matters still pending in this case.

Notes and Questions to Consider:

1. This case was not the end of the City of Sarasota's attempts to regulate amplified music. "Again, in 2000, the city imposed an absolute ban on amplified noise within certain zoning districts during specified hours of the day and night. Luckily for the city, the court struck down this ordinance, finding that the First Amendment prohibits cities from completely banning amplified music." Ashley Suarez, *The Great Mash-Up Debate: A Holistic Approach to Controlling Noise Pollution in Florida's Downtown Districts*, 14 Ave Maria L. Rev. 222, 230–31 (2016).

2. A Florida City Commission enacts an ordinance prohibiting new building construction in the Central Business District to 2 stories high or less. Was it required to provide individualized notice by mail to all landowners 30 days prior to enacting this ordinance?

3. A Florida City Commission enacts an ordinance prohibiting nudity within establishments in the Central Business District that sell or serve alcohol. Was it required to provide individualized notice by mail to all landowners 30 days prior?

10. Inconsistency Between State and Local Law

Recall the potential for overlap in the eligible subject matter for lawmaking by the Florida Legislature and local legislatures. Florida's Legislature, its counties, its cities, its towns and its villages can enact ordinances on many of the exact same topics as one another. This is true even if one is within the territorial jurisdiction of another. With more than one legislating body enacting laws on many of the same topics at the same time and over the same territory, inconsistencies may arise.

Perhaps in order to address this problem of inconsistency, Florida's Municipal Home Rule Powers Act gives counties and municipalities broad power to govern "to the extent *not inconsistent* with general or special law." So a Florida county, city, town or village would need a source of legislative power other than the Municipal Home Rule Powers Act in order to enact a law that is inconsistent. An inconsistent law would fall unless something other than the Municipal Home Rule Powers Act enables such a law. But when is a local law inconsistent?

Generally speaking, inconsistency occurs in one of two ways: via preemption or via conflict of law. Florida's Supreme Court explains these two ways as follows:

> First, a county [or other municipal corporation] cannot legislate in a field if the subject area has been preempted to the State. *See City of Hollywood v. Mulligan*, 934 So. 2d 1238, 1243 (Fla. 2006). "Preemption essentially takes a topic or a field in which local government

> might otherwise establish appropriate local laws and reserves that topic for regulation exclusively by the legislature." *Id.* (quoting *Phantom of Clearwater[, Inc. v. Pinellas County]*, 894 So. 2d [1011] , 1018 [(Fla. 2d DCA 2005)]). Second, in a field where both the State and local government can legislate concurrently, a county [or other municipal corporation] cannot enact an ordinance that directly conflicts with a state statute.

Orange County v. Singh, SC18-79, 2019 WL 1716301, at *5 (Fla. Apr. 18, 2019). Let us first discuss inconsistency via a conflict of law, and then inconsistency via other types of preemption.

a. Inconsistency Via Conflict of Law

This type of inconsistency exists when the law impermissibly conflicts with a higher sovereign's law. Florida's Supreme Court explains that:

> There is conflict between a local ordinance and a state statute when the local ordinance cannot coexist with the state statute. *See City of Hollywood*, 934 So. 2d at 1246; *see also State ex rel. Dade County v. Brautigam*, 224 So. 2d 688, 692 (Fla. 1969) (explaining that "inconsistent" as used in article VIII, section 6(f) of the Florida Constitution "means contradictory in the sense of legislative provisions which cannot coexist"). Stated otherwise, "[t]he test for conflict is whether 'in order to comply with one provision, a violation of the other is required.'" *Browning v. Sarasota Alliance for Fair Elections, Inc.*, 968 So. 2d 637, 649 (Fla. 2d DCA 2007) ….

Orange County v. Singh, SC18-79, 2019 WL 1716301, at *6 (Fla. Apr. 18, 2019). Although this quote from Florida's Supreme Court addresses specifically a conflict of laws between the state and a county, the same rule of law applies to a conflict between a county and another municipal corporation such as a city, town or village. As FLORIDA MUNICIPAL LAW explains:

> County and municipal ordinances are inferior to laws of the state and must not conflict with any controlling provision of a state statute. A local government ordinance must not specifically conflict

with a state statute. Similarly, a municipal ordinance may not conflict with a county ordinance if the county has reserved such power to itself. As discussed earlier, the Florida Constitution permits Florida's counties to be chartered or nonchartered. A county's enactment of a charter creates situations where charter county laws prevail over conflicting municipal laws. They prevail whenever the charter county law is a regulatory ordinance. They also prevail on other topics whenever the "supremacy clause" in the charter of the charter county states so.

Conflicts of law can arise under Florida's governmental structure of overlapping sovereigns of state, county, and municipal government. Yet, two or more laws addressing the same subject or behavior need not be found to be conflicting. Divergent local and state legislation may coexist without conflict. The mere fact that local and state laws address the same or similar subject matter does not mandate a finding of conflict.

The Supreme Court of Florida holds that the test to determine whether there is such a conflict is whether one must violate one provision in order to comply with the other….

… A municipality cannot forbid what the Florida Legislature has expressly licensed, authorized, or required. A municipality cannot authorize what the Florida Legislature has expressly forbidden. A municipality may provide a penalty less severe than that imposed by a state statute for the same offense or violation.

Patrick John McGinley, Florida Municipal Law and Practice §3:11 (2017-2018 ed.).

b. Inconsistency Via Preemption

This type of inconsistency exists when a lawmaking body with the power to preempt others from legislating on a particular subject, topic or field of law exercises that power expressly or impliedly by enacting a law that preempts the field. FLORIDA MUNICIPAL LAW AND PRACTICE reminds us that a Florida city, town or village "may not make any law on a matter preempted to the state or county government by the Florida Constitution, by general law, or pursuant to a county charter" and also reminds us that "a county may not make any law on a matter preempted to the state." Patrick John McGinley, FLORIDA MUNICIPAL LAW AND PRACTICE § 3:10 (2017-2018 ed.). The reason for this is that "[p]reemption is a matter of consistency. If the state preempts by creating a legislative scheme, then the various local governments must not add their own legislation in that area because to do so would render local laws inconsistent with the State Constitution or a state statute."

(1). Preemption of Local Law by State Law

The mere fact that a state law and a local law address the same topic does not mean that the state law preempts. Some Florida Statutes contemplate the enactment of local ordinances to supplement or fulfill the intent of the statute. Other Florida Statutes address the particular subject, topic or field of law but do not fully preempt the field. One must analyze the legislation to determine whether it preempts.

In any instance of potential preemption, one must look for express preemption or implied preemption. Commentators suggest that "cases in which the courts have found express state preemption are rare." *See* Judge James R. Wolf and Sarah Harley Bolinder, *The Effectiveness of Home Rule: A Preemption and Conflict Analysis*, Florida Bar Journal, June 2009 at 92. "Implied preemption" occurs if a legislative scheme is so pervasive that it occupies the entire field, creating a danger of a conflict between local and state laws, as illustrated by the 1991 decision of the Supreme Court of Florida in *Florida Power Corp. v. Seminole County,* 635 So. 2d 96 (Fla. 1st DCA 1994), cause dismissed, 641 So. 2d 1345 (Fla. 1994).

Express preemption arises out of statements appearing in the plain text of the law that preempts. The specificity of the language needed for express preemption can be described as follows. "Express pre-emption requires a specific statement; the pre-emption cannot be made by implication nor by inference." *Board of Trustees of City of Dunedin Mun. Firefighters Retirement System v. Dulje*, 453 So. 2d 177, 178 (Fla. 2d DCA 1984). Therefore, express preemption exists when one or more statements in a law do more than imply an intent to preempt the field. "An 'express' reference is one which is distinctly stated and not left to inference." *Edwards v. State*, 422 So. 2d 84, 85 (Fla. 2d DCA 1982). Although the preemption must be "specific," "not made by implication," and "distinctly stated" in order to be an express preemption, nevertheless, "[t]he preemption need not be explicit so long as it is clear that the legislature has clearly preempted local regulation of the subject." *Tribune Co. v. Cannella*, 458 So. 2d 1075 (Fla. 1984). What is required is that the express preemption "be accomplished by clear language stating that intent." *Phantom of Clearwater, Inc. v. Pinellas County*, 894 So. 2d 1011, 1018 (Fla. 2d DCA 2005).

FLORIDA MUNICIPAL LAW AND PRACTICE tells us that:

> One might think, and indeed one Florida court held, that "[i]n cases where the Legislature expressly or specifically preempts an area, there is no problem with ascertaining what the Legislature intended." Yet, things are not always that simple. As commentators have noted:
>
> Even in cases of express preemption, it is unlikely that a specific portion of a state statute expressly declaring preemption will directly address the exact action contemplated by the local government. It is more likely that the state statute will demonstrate an intent to occupy a field of regulation. The court must then examine whether the local government action is within the scope of the preemption.

Patrick John McGinley, FLORIDA MUNICIPAL LAW AND PRACTICE § 3:10 (2017-2018 ed.).

(2). Preemption of Local Law by Another Local Law

The mere fact that a county law and the law of a municipality located within that county (city, town, or village) address the same topic does not mean that the county law preempts. Such a case of potential preemption cannot be decided merely on the basis that one type of local government "stands higher than a municipality upon the ladder of governmental hierarchy…."

City of Temple Terrace v. Hillsborough Ass'n for Retarded Citizens, Inc., 322 So. 2d 571, 577 (Fla. 2d DCA 1975), aff'd, 332 So. 2d 610 (Fla. 1976). If preemption exists, then sometimes the county preempts the city, town or village; but sometimes the city, town or village prempts the county. Florida Municipal Law explains:

> Recall that under the Florida Constitution, Florida's counties may be chartered or nonchartered. A county's enactment of a charter may be a means by which the county broadens its preemption power over municipalities. This is true because, although state law may continue to prevail over conflicting county laws regardless of whether the county has a charter, charter county laws can prevail over conflicting municipal laws. They prevail whenever the charter county law is a regulatory ordinance. They also prevail on other topics whenever the "supremacy clause" in the charter of the charter county states so. For noncharter counties, county laws do not prevail over conflicting municipal laws.

Patrick John McGinley, FLORIDA MUNICIPAL LAW AND PRACTICE § 3:10 (2017-2018 ed). FLORIDA JURISPRUDENCE 2D expresses the same idea as follows:

> The charter of a county must provide which will prevail in the event of conflict between county and municipal ordinances. With respect to noncharter counties, a county ordinance that conflicts with a municipal ordinance is not effective within the municipality to the extent of the conflict. A county ordinance need not yield in incorporated areas of the county when it is not identical in scope to a city ordinance; thus, a county ordinance prohibiting seminude entertainment where alcoholic beverages were served, regardless of whether the entertainers were topless or bottomless, was not in conflict with a city ordinance prohibiting only topless entertainment.
>
> Where a county ordinance is adopted under a constitutional amendment and home rule charter of government, it supersedes municipal charters and ordinances when in conflict with them except

where the charter specifically provides otherwise.

12A Fla. Jur 2d Counties, Etc. § 229.

11. General Laws, Special Laws, and General Laws of Local Application

Florida's Legislature may make general laws or special laws. A special law applies to particular persons or things; a general law relates to subjects, persons, or things as a class. *Lawnwood Med. Ctr., Inc. v. Seeger*, 990 So. 2d 503, 509 (Fla. 2008). Another name for a special law is a "general law of local application." Florida's Supreme Court tells us that "[a] general law of local application is a law that uses a classification scheme based on population or some other criterion so that its application is restricted to particular localities." *City of Miami Beach v. Frankel*, 363 So. 2d 555, 558 (Fla. 1978). So a "general law of local application," and a "special law," are one and the same.

Special laws have valid purposes. For example, once the electors of a county hold a referendum that approves their county charter, Florida's Legislature may pass a special law enacting that county's charter. That charter then becomes the charter for that particular county, but not for any other county. In this way, special laws empower local governments to have unique charters. This is just one example of the Florida Legislature's permissible use of a special law.

Special laws have restrictions as to their procedure for enactment and as to their permissible topics. Florida's Constitution contains an individualized notice requirement, so that those affected by the special law either are given notice in advance of its enactment or are empowered to hold a referendum before the special law becomes effective. *See* Art. III, sec. 10, Fla. Const. Florida's Constitution contains an itemized list of topics for which special laws are impermissible. *See* Art. III, sec. 11, Fla. Const. The relevant language reads:

> ARTICLE III, SECTION 10. *Special laws.*—No special law

shall be passed unless notice of intention to seek enactment thereof has been published in the manner provided by general law. Such notice shall not be necessary when the law, except the provision for referendum, is conditioned to become effective only upon approval by vote of the electors of the area affected.

ARTICLE III, SECTION 11. *Prohibited special laws.—*

(a) There shall be no special law or general law of local application pertaining to:

(1) election, jurisdiction or duties of officers, except officers of municipalities, chartered counties, special districts or local governmental agencies;

(2) assessment or collection of taxes for state or county purposes, including extension of time therefor, relief of tax officers from due performance of their duties, and relief of their sureties from liability;

(3) rules of evidence in any court;

(4) punishment for crime;

(5) petit juries, including compensation of jurors, except establishment of jury commissions;

(6) change of civil or criminal venue;

(7) conditions precedent to bringing any civil or criminal proceedings, or limitations of time therefor;

(8) refund of money legally paid or remission of fines, penalties or forfeitures;

(9) creation, enforcement, extension or impairment of liens based on private contracts, or fixing of interest rates on private contracts;

(10) disposal of public property, including any interest therein, for private purposes;

(11) vacation of roads;

(12) private incorporation or grant of privilege to a private corporation;

(13) effectuation of invalid deeds, wills or other instruments, or change in the law of descent;

(14) change of name of any person;

(15) divorce;

(16) legitimation or adoption of persons;

(17) relief of minors from legal disabilities;

(18) transfer of any property interest of persons under legal disabilities or of estates of decedents;

(19) hunting or fresh water fishing;

(20) regulation of occupations which are regulated by a state agency; or

(21) any subject when prohibited by general law passed by a three-fifths vote of the membership of each house. Such law may be amended or repealed by like vote.

(b) In the enactment of general laws on other subjects, political subdivisions or other governmental entities may be classified only on a basis reasonably related to the subject of the law.

The difference between a general law and a special law is illustrated by Florida's Supreme Court's decision in *License Acquisitions, LLC v. Debary Real Estate Holdings, LLC*, 155 So. 3d 1137 (Fla. 2014).

LICENSE ACQUISITIONS, LLC

v.

DEBARY REAL ESTATE HOLDINGS, LLC

Supreme Court of Florida, 2014

155 So. 3d 1137

LABARGA, C.J.

This case is before the Court on appeal from a decision of the First District Court of Appeal … which held section 550.054(14)(a), Florida Statutes (2010), to be an invalid special law. This Court has jurisdiction of the appeal under article V, section 3(b)(1) of the Florida Constitution. For the following reasons, we reverse the First District and hold that section 550.054(14)(a) is a valid general law.

FACTS

…[T]he First District's per curiam decision declar[ed] section 550.054(14)(a) to be invalid as a special law enacted without either providing advance notice of intent to enact the law or conditioning the law's effectiveness upon a referendum of the electors of the areas affected in violation of article III, section 10, of the Florida Constitution….

[S]ection 550.054(14) provides as follows:

> (14)(a) Any holder of a permit to conduct jai alai may apply to the division [of pari-mutuel wagering] to convert such permit to a permit to conduct greyhound racing in lieu of jai alai if:
>
> 1. Such permit is located in a county in which the division has issued only two pari-mutuel permits pursuant to this section;
>
> 2. Such permit was not previously converted from any other class of permit; and

> 3. The holder of the permit has not conducted jai alai games during a period of 10 years immediately preceding his or her application for conversion under this subsection.
>
> (b) The [Division of Business and Professional Regulation, or DBPR], upon application from the holder of a jai alai permit meeting all conditions of this section, shall convert the permit and shall issue to the permitholder a permit to conduct greyhound racing....

§ 550.054(14), Florida Statutes (2010).

West Volusia Racing, Inc. (West Volusia Racing), and License Acquisitions, LLC (License Acquisitions), applied for the conversion of their jai alai permits under section 550.054(14)(a) on the day section 550.054 became effective. Approximately three weeks later, the DBPR granted the applications. Shortly thereafter, Debary Real Estate Holdings, LLC (Debary), instituted a declaratory judgment action alleging in pertinent part that section 550.054(14) is an unconstitutional special law—a law designed to operate upon particular persons or things, or one that purports to operate upon classified persons or things when classification is not permissible or the classification adopted is illegal—enacted without notice or conditioning the law's effectiveness upon a referendum. The appellants argued that the statute is a general law—a law that operates uniformly within a permissible classification and is not subject to the notice or referendum requirements of article III, section 10, of the Florida Constitution. Specifically, Debary alleged that section 550.054(14)(a) 1. was only applicable to two jai alai permits and that the classification adopted was not rationally related to the purpose of the statute because the statute would never be capable of application to additional parties. Therefore, according to Debary, the classification adopted was illegal....

...At the time of the statute's enactment, there were twenty-one total section 550.054 permits existing in nine counties in Florida, eleven of which were jai alai permits. West Volusia Racing and License Acquisitions held jai alai permits that were eligible for conversion at the time of the statute's enactment because the permits were dormant for ten years and were located in counties where the DBPR had issued exactly two [pari-mutuel] permits....

Thus, the appellees contended that the statute was invalid as a special law enacted under the guise of a general law....

ANALYSIS

Special Law v. General Law

"A law that operates universally throughout the state, uniformly upon subjects as they may exist throughout the state, or uniformly within a permissible classification is a general law." *[Department of Business Regulation v.] Classic Mile, Inc.,* 541 So. 2d [1155,] 1157 [(Fla. 1989)]. A special law is one designed to operate upon particular persons or things, or one that purports to operate upon classified persons or things when classification is not permissible or the classification adopted is illegal; a local law is one relating to, or designed to operate only in, a specifically indicated part of the State, or one that purports to operate within a classified territory when classification is not permissible or the classification is illegal. *Id.* Article III, section 10, of the Florida Constitution prohibits the Legislature from passing a special law without either providing advance notice of intent to enact the law or conditioning the law's effectiveness upon a referendum of the electors of the areas affected. A special law, however, is not converted into a general law by the Legislature's treating it and passing it as a general law. *Id....*

A statutory classification scheme must bear a reasonable relationship to the purpose of the statute in order for the statute to constitute a valid general law. *Id....* Statutes that employ arbitrary classification schemes are not valid as general laws. *Id.* A statute is invalid if " 'the descriptive technique is employed merely for identification rather than classification.' " *Id....* Ultimately, the criterion that determines if a reasonable relationship exists between the classification adopted and the purpose of the statute is whether the classification is potentially open to additional parties. *Id....; see also Ocala Breeders' Sales Co., Inc. v. Fla. Gaming Ctrs., Inc.,* 731 So. 2d 21, 25 (Fla. 1st DCA 1999) ("If it is possible in the future for others to meet the criteria set forth in the statute, then it is a general law and not a special law."). A classification scheme is not considered closed "merely because it is unlikely that it will include anyone else." *Fla. Dep't of Bus. & Prof'l Regulation v.*

Gulfstream Park Racing Ass'n, Inc., 967 So. 2d 802, 808–09 (Fla. 2007). However, a classification scheme is not considered open "merely because there is a theoretical possibility that some day it might include someone else. That approach would undermine the constitutional requirements for the adoption of special laws.... *[T]he proper standard is whether there is a reasonable possibility that the class will include others.*" *Id.* at 809.

The parties do not dispute that the Legislature did not provide notice of its intent to enact the statute or condition its effectiveness on a referendum of the electors of the areas affected. Thus, the issue on appeal to this Court is whether section 550.054(14)(a) is unconstitutional as a special law passed under the guise of a general law. The question of whether a law is a special or general law is a legal question subject to de novo review. *Gulfstream Park Racing,* 967 So. 2d at 806…. "Although our review is de novo, statutes come clothed with a presumption of constitutionality and must be construed whenever possible to effect a constitutional outcome." *Lewis v. Leon Cnty.,* 73 So. 3d 151, 153 (Fla. 2011). "To overcome the presumption, the invalidity must appear beyond reasonable doubt, for it must be assumed the [L]egislature intended to enact a valid law." *Id.*…

The … statute when enacted and at the time of the trial court proceedings only applied to License Acquisitions and West Volusia Racing. The [parties disagree as to] whether there is a reasonable possibility that the class is open to additional parties….

[In determining whether the statute creates a reasonable possibility that the class is open to additional parties in the future, t]he Court is obligated to accord legislative acts a presumption of constitutionality and to construe challenged legislation to effect a constitutional outcome whenever reasonably possible…. "[E]ven where the statute is reasonably susceptible of two interpretations, one of which would render it invalid and the other valid, we must adopt the constitutional construction." ... *Miami Dolphins, Ltd. v. Metro. Dade Cnty.,* 394 So. 2d 981, 988 (Fla.1981) ("Given that an interpretation upholding the constitutionality of the act is available to this Court, it must adopt that construction.")….

The appellants [allege the statute offers the following constitutional construction. The appellants] claim that adoption of their suggested interpretations would result in a class open for conversion to all of the remaining permits except one—thus a total of ten of the eleven existing permits at the time of the statute's enactment—without a change in the law. Indeed, review of the record demonstrates that Hillsborough County had three total section 550.054 permits, one of which was a dormant jai alai permit; Gadsden County had a dormant jai alai permit, but it previously converted and could never be eligible; Miami–Dade County and Broward County both had two active jai alai permits, and five total section 550.054 permits; St. Lucie County had one active jai alai permit and no other section 550.054 permits; Hamilton County had one active jai alai permit and no other section 550.054 permits; Marion County had one active jai alai permit and no other section 550.054 permits; and two other counties, possibly Bay County and Dixie County, did not presently have any 550.054 permits and could legally acquire a permit without violating the mileage restrictions in section 550.054(2) noted above. Thus, only one current jai alai permit holder would be ineligible, and two counties without a present jai alai permit holder could conceivably join the class. Accordingly, the class is open to additional parties pursuant to this construction of the statute, which renders the statute a valid general law. *See Classic Mile,* 541 So. 2d at 1157 ("A statutory classification scheme must bear a reasonable relationship to the purpose of the statute in order for the statute to constitute a valid general law.")....

This case, when considered in light of our precedent, supports our conclusion that this statute is a valid general law pursuant to this construction of the statute. In *Sanford–Orlando Kennel Club,* this Court considered whether a statute that permitted the conversion of any harness racing track to dog racing was an unconstitutional special law. 434 So. 2d at 880–81. Pursuant to the statute, a harness racing track could be converted to a dog racing track if that track earned a certain amount of average daily income over a period of years and generated a certain amount of tax revenue for the state. *Id.* at 880. Although the statute's classification scheme only applied to the two then-existing permits, the Court held that the classification scheme was a general law. The Court noted that "[a] general law operates uniformly, not because it operates upon every person in the state, but because every person brought under the law is affected by it in a uniform fashion. Uniformity of treatment within the class is not dependent upon the number of persons in the class." *Id.* at 881. Further, the Court reasoned that the controlling point in evaluating the statute's constitutionality was that "even though this class did in fact apply to only one track, it is open and has the potential of applying to other tracks." *Id.* at 882.

In *Biscayne Kennel Club, Inc. v. Fla. State Racing Comm'n,* 165 So. 2d 762 (Fla.1964), this Court considered the constitutionality of a statute that provided "for the transfer, under certain conditions, of existing racing permits to allow establishment of harness racing operations in counties which have by previous referendum for two years approved the operation of race track pari-mutuel pools, excluding those having more than one horse track permit or one with an average daily pari-mutuel pool less than a specified minimum." *Id.* at 763–64. The Court upheld the classification because a number of Florida counties could, by future referendum, acquire racing establishments and have "not more than one horse track with a daily pool above the minimum set." *Id.* at 764.

Other cases from this Court holding a statute unconstitutional largely involved classification schemes that were clearly applicable to only one individual, entity, or geographic area. *See, e.g., Gulfstream Park,* 967 So. 2d at 809 (addressing a statute that prohibited thoroughbred permit holders from engaging in intertrack wagering in "any area of the state where there are three or more horserace permitholders within 25 miles of each other," and holding that it was unconstitutional because there was no reasonable possibility that these conditions would ever exist in another part of the state); *City of Miami v. McGrath,* 824 So. 2d 143, 146, 151 (Fla. 2002) (addressing a statute which authorized only municipalities with populations of more than 300,000 on a date certain to impose a parking tax, and holding that the statute was a special law because its express terms limited its application and excluded any other municipalities from joining the class in the future); *Classic Mile,* 541 So. 2d at 1158–59 (declaring statute unconstitutional because conditions only applied to Marion County, could never apply to others, and the appellants made no attempt to demonstrate a reasonable relationship between the classification and the subject of the statute); *W. Flagler Kennel Club,* 153 So. 2d at 8 (holding the statute applicable only to Broward County and noting that the appellants failed to attempt to demonstrate a reasonable relationship between the classification and the subject of the statute). It is also noted that in *Gulfstream Park,* this Court held that "a statute that appears to apply to one ... area at the time of enactment may still be considered a general law if it could be applied to other ... areas in the future." 967 So. 2d at 808. As discussed above, although section 550.054(14)(a) applied to two permits at the time of enactment, it could be applied to other permits in the future.

... Accordingly, we agree with the appellants' interpretation of the statute because it is a fair construction of the statute that is consistent with legislative intent and results in a determination that the statute is a valid general law.

CONCLUSION

Based on the foregoing, we reverse the First District's decision holding section 550.054(14)(a) unconstitutional and ... we hold that section 550.054(14)(a) is a valid general law....

It is so ordered.

Notes and Questions to Consider:

1. In in *License Acquisitions v. Debary Real Estate Holdings*, the court heard two plausible interpretations of the relevant statute. It chose one interpretation over the other so that the statute could be upheld as constitutional. Was this the proper result?

2. On November 6, 2018, Floridians enacted the following amendment to Florida's Constitution:

> *Prohibition on racing of and wagering on greyhounds or other dogs.*- The humane treatment of animals is a fundamental value of the peo-

> ple of the State of Florida. After December 31, 2020, a person authorized to conduct gaming or pari-mutuel operations may not race greyhounds or any member of the *Canis Familiaris* subspecies in connection with any wager for money or any other thing of value in this state, and persons in this state may not wager money or any other thing of value on the outcome of a live dog race occurring in this state. The failure to conduct greyhound racing or wagering on greyhound racing after December 31, 2018, does not constitute grounds to revoke or deny renewal of other related gaming licenses held by a person who is a licensed greyhound permitholder on January 1, 2018, and does not affect the eligibility of such permitholder, or such permitholder's facility, to conduct other pari-mutuel activities authorized by general law. By general law, the legislature shall specify civil or criminal penalties for violations of this section and for activities that aid or abet violations of this section.

Art. X, § 32, Fla. Const.

E. Quasi-Legislative Power

Article IV of Florida's Constitution requires that "the laws be faithfully executed" by the Executive Branch. Can it essentially make law by enacting administrative rules?

Florida's Administrative Procedures Act (APA), which is codified at Florida Statutes chapter 120, empowers or requires every "agency" -- a term that is broadly defined by the APA -- to engage in "rulemaking." "Rulemaking is a quasi-legislative function, as opposed to an adjudicative proceeding." *Booker Creek Preservation, Inc. v. Southwest Florida Water Management District*, 534 So. 2d 419, 422 (Fla. 5th DCA 1988). The APA defines a "rule" as follows:

> "Rule" means each agency statement of general applicability that implements, interprets, or prescribes law or policy or describes the procedure or practice requirements of an agency and includes any form which imposes any requirement or solicits any information not specif-

> ically required by statute or by an existing rule. The term also includes the amendment or repeal of a rule....

§ 120.52(15), Fla. Stat. (2003). Stated somewhat differently, "rules" are "statement[s] of general applicability that implement[ ], interpret[ ], or prescribe[ ] law or policy or describe[ ] the procedure or practice requirements of an agency." § 120.52(16), Fla. Stat. (2010). Accordingly, "[w]hen an agency promulgates a rule having the force of law, it acts in place of the legislature." *Whiley v. Scott,* 79 So. 3d 702, 710 (Fla. 2011) Florida's Supreme Court acknowledges that agency rulemaking pursuant to this statutory authority constitutes the performance of a quasi-legislative function. *Id.* (citing *General Telephone Co. of Fla. v. Fla. Public Service Comm'n*, 446 So. 2d 1063, 1066 (Fla. 1984)).

Florida's Supreme Court observes that "[r]ulemaking is a derivative of lawmaking. An agency is empowered to adopt rules if two requirements are satisfied. First, there must be a statutory grant of rulemaking authority, and second, there must be a specific law to be implemented." *Id.* at 710. Under the APA, an agency lacks the power to create standard practices and procedures without first having a statute enabling it to do so, then writing down the practice, publishing it, getting public input, and allowing the public to challenge the practice or procedure -- all before adopting the practice. By so doing, Floridians have a weapon against "red tape."

For example, if a Floridian is stymied by an agency practice that has not been promulgated as a rule, the affected Floridian can file a "rule challenge" which is a quasi-judicial administrative law action arising out of the APA.

The rule challenge is not filed in a court or law but instead is filed with the Florida Division of Administrative Hearings. The burden is upon the affected Floridian to prove that the agency has adopted a standard practice that was not promulgated as a rule as required under the APA.

The relief available to a successful challenger can include compelling the agency to engage in rulemaking or in declaring the agency's practice inapplicable to the challenger.

Notes and Questions to Consider:

1. The courts give greater deference to quasi-legislative actions than to quasi-judicial actions. "The scope of review of the quasi-legislative function of rulemaking is more limited than that with respect to quasi-judicial action…." *Brewster Phosphates v. State, Dept. of Envtl. Regulation*, 444 So. 2d 483, 486 (Fla. 1st DCA 1984). Why, in your opinion, would such deference be warranted?

2. Why might a successful challenger in a rule challenge under Florida's Administrative Procedures Act want to compel the agency to engage in rulemaking?

Chapter Five

Executive Power

A. Florida's Executive Branch

Perhaps Florida's executive branch is best described as the branch that executes, or carries out, the requirements of the law. Its role under Florida's Constitution is described in this excerpt from Daniel Webster & Donald L. Bell, *First Principles for Constitution Revision*, 22 Nova L. Rev. 391 (1997):

> *The Executive Branch*
>
> The executive branch is responsible for executing the laws the legislative branch creates. While there is, as Locke suggested, an area of executive "prerogative" that arises from the Legislature's inability to foresee all circumstances in which immediate action might be required, the executive risks being discredited whenever it acts without explicit legislative authorization. Consequently, it is constrained to act only in those ways unlikely to create public controversy.
>
> In establishing the executive branch of government, the Florida Constitution goes further than most other constitutions to protect the public from tyranny by assigning certain duties and responsibilities to particular officers and agencies of the government. Unlike the constitutions of some other states, the Florida Constitution does not vest all executive power in the state's Governor. It establishes the Governor as the state's chief executive officer, but then proceeds to divide the executive power among a wide range of other executive officers and agencies.
>
> Florida's Constitution … has an elected Cabinet…. Not unexpectedly, it has been a source of vexation to many governors, including the current one, that the Office of Governor must share its power

with members of the cabinet who may be political opponents. However, establishing some competition at the highest levels of executive decision making sometimes causes an extraordinary level of inquiry and public debate to surround those decisions.

In those areas of policy that require them to work with the cabinet, Florida's governors are undoubtedly more restrained and less capricious in making decisions. This provides some worthwhile protection for the people....

The division of executive and legislative branch power does not stop with the cabinet. The Florida Constitution creates a multitude of constitutional agencies, offices, and commissions. These offices and agencies vary in the extent to which they are subject to the Governor's power and some agencies even have a measure of independence from legislative oversight. These additional distributions of power were intended to protect the people from tyranny. However, where any of these offices is not subject to an adequate system of checks and balances, they can become tyrannies within their area of authority....

Notes and Questions to Consider:

1. Where is the line between executing the law and creating the law?

2. In the discussion of Florida's executive branch in the excerpt above, the authors refer to Florida's elected Cabinet. In the next subsection of this chapter, we consider this fact more closely.

B. Elected Cabinet

Unlike the federal Constitution where the President's cabinet are appointed by the President and confirmed by the U.S. Senate, Florida's Cabinet is elected by the people. Article IV of Florida's Constitution provides:

SECTION 4. *Cabinet.*—

(a) There shall be a cabinet composed of an attorney general, a chief financial officer, and a commissioner of agriculture. In addition to the powers and duties specified herein, they shall exercise such powers and perform such duties as may be prescribed by law. In the event of a tie vote of the governor and cabinet, the side on which the governor voted shall be deemed to prevail.

(b) The attorney general shall be the chief state legal officer. There is created in the office of the attorney general the position of statewide prosecutor. The statewide prosecutor shall have concurrent jurisdiction with the state attorneys to prosecute violations of criminal laws occurring or having occurred, in two or more judicial circuits as part of a related transaction, or when any such offense is affecting or has affected two or more judicial circuits as provided by general law. The statewide prosecutor shall be appointed by the attorney general from not less than three persons nominated by the judicial nominating commission for the supreme court, or as otherwise provided by general law.

(c) The chief financial officer shall serve as the chief fiscal officer of the state, and shall settle and approve accounts against the state, and shall keep all state funds and securities.

(d) The commissioner of agriculture shall have supervision of matters pertaining to agriculture except as otherwise provided by law.

(e) The governor as chair, the chief financial officer, and the attorney general shall constitute the state board of administration, which shall succeed to all the power, control, and authority of the state board of administration established pursuant to Article IX, Section 16 of the Constitution of 1885, and which shall continue as a body at least for the life of Article XII, Section 9(c).

(f) The governor as chair, the chief financial officer, the attorney general, and the commissioner of agriculture shall constitute the trustees of the internal improvement trust fund and the land acquisition trust fund as provided by law.

(g) The governor as chair, the chief financial officer, the attorney general, and the commissioner of agriculture shall constitute the agency head of the Department of Law Enforcement.

Notes and Questions to Consider:

1. Can an elected cabinet create controversy within the executive branch? Consider this commentary from the *West Virginia Law Review*:

> In forty-three states, including West Virginia [and Florida], the executive department operates under the supervision of an elected Governor and elected executive department officers. The holders of these constitutional executive department offices may be members of differing political parties.... Even if all executive officers are members of the same political party, because each is an independently elected executive officer, each may possess significantly different perspectives as to desirable policies under prevailing law. Each officer may have different views on the proper operation of their offices in relation to other components of the executive, legislative and judicial departments. In addition, in a divided executive department, the elected executive officers may assume differing positions regarding issues of policy which arise in the administration of various state statutes.

Patrick C. McGinley, *Separation of Powers, State Constitutions & the Attorney General: Who Represents the State?,* 99 W. Va. L. Rev. 721, 722 (1997).

2. Although Florida's Governor's cabinet is composed of separately-elected officials, Florida's Lieutenant Governor is elected on the same ticket as the Governor. The people elect their Governor and Lieutenant Governor, and elect the other members of the cabinet, "each for a term of four years beginning on the first Tuesday after the first Monday in January of the succeeding year. In primary elections, candidates for the office of governor may choose to run without a lieutenant governor candidate. In the general election, all candidates for the offices of governor and lieutenant governor shall form joint candidacies in a manner prescribed by law so that each voter shall cast a single vote for a candidate for governor and a candidate for lieutenant governor running together." Art. IV, sec. 5, Fla. Const.

3. Florida's Constitution imposes qualifications upon those who would run for Governor or Lieutenant Governor: "When elected, the governor, lieutenant governor and each cabinet member must be an elector not less than thirty years of age who has resided in the state for the preceding seven years." Art. IV, sec. 5, Fla. Const.

4. Also, term limits are imposed as follows: "No person who has, or but for resignation would have, served as governor or acting governor for more than six years in two consecutive terms shall be elected governor for the succeeding term." Art. IV, sec. 5, Fla. Const.

C. Enumerated Powers of the Governor

Article IV of Florida's Constitution provides:

SECTION 1. Governor.—

(a) The supreme executive power shall be vested in a governor, who shall be commander-in-chief of all military forces of the state not in active service of the United States. The governor shall take care that the laws be faithfully executed, commission all officers of the state and counties, and transact all necessary business with the officers of government. The governor may require information in writing from all executive or administrative state, county or municipal officers upon any subject relating to the duties of their respective offices. The governor shall be the chief administrative officer of the state responsible for the planning and budgeting for the state.

(b) The governor may initiate judicial proceedings in the name of the state against any executive or administrative state, county or municipal officer to enforce compliance with any duty or restrain any unauthorized act.

(c) The governor may request in writing the opinion of the justices of the supreme court as to the interpretation of any portion of this constitution upon any question affecting the governor's executive powers and duties. The justices shall, subject to their rules of procedure, permit interested persons to be heard on the questions presented and shall render their written opinion not earlier than ten days from the filing and docketing of the request, unless in their judgment the delay would cause public injury.

(d) The governor shall have power to call out the militia to preserve the public peace, execute the laws of the state, suppress insurrection, or repel invasion.

(e) The governor shall by message at least once in each regular session inform the legislature concerning the condition of the state, propose such reorganization of the executive department as will promote efficiency and economy, and recommend measures in the public interest.

(f) When not otherwise provided for in this constitution, the governor shall fill by appointment any vacancy in state or county office for the remainder of the term of an appointive office, and for the remainder of the term of an elective office if less than twenty-eight months, otherwise until the first Tuesday after the first Monday following the next general election.

SECTION 2. *Lieutenant governor.*—There shall be a lieutenant governor, who shall perform such duties pertaining to the office of governor as shall be assigned by the governor, except when otherwise provided by law, and such other duties as may be prescribed by law.

SECTION 3. *Succession to office of governor; acting governor.*—

(a) Upon vacancy in the office of governor, the lieutenant governor shall become governor. Further succession to the office of governor shall be prescribed by law. A successor shall serve for the remainder of the term.

(b) Upon impeachment of the governor and until completion of trial thereof, or during the governor's physical or mental incapacity, the lieutenant governor shall act as governor. Further succession as acting governor shall be prescribed by law. Incapacity to serve as governor may be determined by the supreme court upon due notice after docketing of a written suggestion thereof by three cabinet members, and in such case restoration of capacity shall be similarly determined after docketing of written suggestion thereof by the governor, the legislature or three cabinet members. Incapacity to serve as governor may also be established by certificate filed with the custodian of state records by the governor declaring incapacity for physical reasons to serve as governor, and in such case restoration of capacity shall be similarly established.

. . .

SECTION 8. *Clemency.—*

(a) Except in cases of treason and in cases where impeachment results in conviction, the governor may, by executive order filed with the custodian of state records, suspend collection of fines and forfeitures, grant reprieves not exceeding sixty days and, with the approval of two members of the cabinet, grant full or conditional pardons, restore civil rights, commute punishment, and remit fines and forfeitures for offenses.

(b) In cases of treason the governor may grant reprieves until adjournment of the regular session of the legislature convening next after the conviction, at which session the legislature may grant a pardon or further reprieve; otherwise the sentence shall be executed.

(c) There may be created by law a parole and probation commission with power to supervise persons on probation and to grant paroles or conditional releases to persons under sentences for crime. The qualifications, method of selection and terms, not to exceed six years, of members of the commission shall be prescribed by law.

Notes and Questions to Consider:

1. Note that, as an exception to the "case and controversy" requirements of Florida law, Florida's Constitution empowers Florida's Governor to seek an advisory opinion from Florida's Supreme Court "as to the interpretation of any portion of this constitution upon any question affecting the governor's executive powers and duties." See art. IV, sec. 1(c), Fla. Const. The same exception is extended to Florida's Attorney General for the purpose of requesting a ruling from Florida's Supreme Court as to the validity of any initiative petition seeking to amend Florida's Constitution under the procedures of Section 3 of Article XI of Florida's Constitution. See art. IV, section 10, Fla. Const. Was it wise to except these officers from the case and controversy requirement for these purposes?

2. Note that "the governor shall fill by appointment any vacancy

in state or county office for the remainder of the term of an appointive office, and for the remainder of the term of an elective office if less than twenty-eight months…." Art. IV, sec. 1(f), Fla. Const. For this reason, when a Florida court judge dies, resigns or otherwise leaves before finishing enough of the term of office, the Governor appoints a replacement to finish the term from the list of names provided by the Judicial Nominating Commission. Florida Jurisprudence 2d describes the process as follows:

> The Governor is required to fill each vacancy in a judicial office by appointment for a term specified by statute. The Governor is to select from among no less than three nor more than six persons nominated by the appropriate judicial nominating commission. Similarly, the Governor shall fill each vacancy on a circuit court or on a county court, wherein the judges are elected by a majority vote of the electors, by appointment for a specific term. The Governor is to select from among no less than three nor more than six persons nominated by the appropriate judicial nominating commission. An election shall be held to fill that judicial office for the term of the office beginning at the end of the appointed term.
>
> The Florida Constitution requires that a judge's former seat be filled via gubernatorial appointment rather than the election process where filling the seat with an elected judge would mean that the office would remain vacant for an extended time.
>
> The nominations by the appropriate judicial nominating commission must be made within 30 days from the occurrence of a vacancy unless the period is extended by the Governor for a time not to exceed 30 days. The Governor is required to make an appointment to fill the vacancy within 60 days after the nominations have been certified to him or her. The legal duty imposed on the Governor by these provisions is enforceable by mandamus. The Governor is without authority under the constitution to reject the certified list of the Judicial Nominating Commission and request that a new list be certified.

13 Fla. Jur 2d Courts and Judges § 295 (2018).

3. Note that Florida's Lieutenant Governor's powers are not

enumerated but instead are "shall be assigned by the governor, except when otherwise provided by law, and such other duties as may be prescribed by law." Art. IV, sec. 2, Fla. Const. Like the Vice President under the federal constitution, the Lieutenant Governor becomes Governor upon the death or disability of the Governor. See art. IV, sec. 3(a) – (b), Fla. Const.

D. Faithful Execution of the Laws

Article IV, section 1(a), of Florida's Constitution, states in pertinent part that Florida's "governor shall take care that the laws be faithfully executed…." For further power to faithfully execute the laws, Article IV, section 7, of Florida's Constitution provides that Florida's "governor may suspend from office any state officer not subject to impeachment ... for malfeasance, misfeasance, neglect of duty, drunkenness, incompetence, permanent inability to perform official duties, or commission of a felony."

Without running afoul of Florida's Constitution, can the laws of the State of Florida grant Florida's Governor the power to assure the faithful execution of the laws by taking an action less than removing a state officer from office? Consider the case of *Ayala v. Scott*, 224 So. 3d 755, 761 (Fla. 2017).

AYALA

V.

SCOTT

Supreme Court of Florida, 2017

224 So. 3d 755

Aramis Donell Ayala, State Attorney for Florida's Ninth Judicial Circuit, petitions this Court for a writ of quo warranto, challenging Governor Rick Scott's authority under section 27.14(1), Florida Statutes (2016), to reassign the prosecution of death-penalty eligible cases in the Ninth Circuit to Brad King, State Attorney for Florida's Fifth Judicial Circuit. We have jurisdiction. See article V, § 3(b)(8), Fla. Const. For the reasons below, we deny Ayala's petition.

Background

At a March 15, 2017, press conference, Ayala announced that she "will not be seeking [the] death penalty in the cases handled in [her] office." Several times during the same press conference, Ayala reiterated her intent to implement a blanket "policy" of not seeking the death penalty in any eligible case because, in her view, pursuing death sentences "is not in the best interest of th[e] community or in the best interest of justice," even where an individual case "absolutely deserve[s] [the] death penalty."

In response to Ayala's announcement, Governor Rick Scott issued a series of executive orders reassigning the prosecution of death-penalty eligible cases pending in the Ninth Circuit to King. In support of these orders, the Governor cited his duty as Florida's chief executive officer under article IV, section 1(a), of the Florida Constitution to "take care that the laws be faithfully executed" and his authority under section 27.14(1), Florida Statutes, to assign state attorneys to other circuits "if, for any ... good and sufficient reason, the Governor determines that the ends of justice would be best served." The reassignment orders do not direct King to pursue the death penalty in any particular case, and in a statement filed in this Court, King has sworn that the Governor made no attempt to influence his decision as to whether the circumstances of any of the reassigned cases warrant pursuing the death penalty.

After unsuccessfully seeking a stay of the reassignment orders in the Ninth Circuit, Ayala filed this petition for a writ of quo warranto challenging the Governor's authority to reassign the cases at issue to King. The record reflects that Ayala and her office have abided by the lower courts' denial of her motion and fully cooperated with King.

Analysis

Ayala argues that the Governor exceeded his authority under section 27.14 by reassigning death-penalty eligible cases in the Ninth Circuit to King over her objection because article V, section 17, of the Florida Constitution makes Ayala "the prosecuting officer of all trial courts in [the Ninth] [C]ircuit." While quo warranto is the proper vehicle to challenge the Governor's authority to reassign these cases to King, see *Fla. House of Representa-*

tives v. Crist, 999 So. 2d 601, 607 (Fla. 2008), Ayala is not entitled to relief because the Governor did not exceed his authority on the facts of this case.

As Florida's chief executive officer, the Governor is vested with the "supreme executive power" and is charged with the duty to "take care that the laws be faithfully executed." Art. IV, § 1(a), Fla. Const. Florida law facilitates the Governor's discharge of this duty, among other ways, through state attorney assignments. Specifically, section 27.14(1), the constitutionality of which Ayala concedes, provides:

> If any state attorney is disqualified to represent the state in any investigation, case, or matter pending in the courts of his or her circuit or *if, for any other good and sufficient reason, the Governor determines that the ends of justice would be best served, the Governor may, by executive order filed with the Department of State,* either order an exchange of circuits or of courts between such state attorney and any other state attorney or *order an assignment of any state attorney to discharge the duties of the state attorney with respect to one or more specified investigations, cases, or matters, specified in general in the executive order of the Governor*. Any exchange or assignment of any state attorney to a particular circuit shall expire 12 months after the date of issuance, unless an extension is approved by order of the Supreme Court upon application of the Governor showing good and sufficient cause to extend such exchange or assignment.

§ 27.14(1), Fla. Stat. (2016) (emphasis added).

This Court has previously recognized that the Governor has broad authority to assign state attorneys to other circuits pursuant to section 27.14:

> It is the duty of the Governor under Fla. Const. F.S.A., art. IV, § 1(a) in the exercise of his executive power to "take care that the laws be faithfully executed." The exercise of this power and the performance of this duty are clearly essential to the orderly conduct of government and the execution of the laws of this State. An executive order assigning a state attorney is exclusively within the orbit of authority of the Chief Executive when exercised within the bounds of the stat-

> ute. See *Kirk v. Baker*, 224 So. 2d 311 (Fla. 1969). The Governor is given broad authority to fulfill his duty in taking "care that the laws be faithfully executed," and he should be required to do no more than make a general recitation as to his reasons for assigning a state attorney to another circuit.

Finch v. Fitzpatrick, 254 So. 2d 203, 204–05 (Fla. 1971); see also *Austin v. State ex rel. Christian*, 310 So. 2d 289, 293 (Fla. 1975) ("The statutes authorizing assignments of state attorneys should be broadly and liberally construed so as to complement and implement the duty of the Governor under the Constitution of the State of Florida to 'take care that the laws be faithfully executed.' " (quoting art. IV, § 1(a), Fla. Const.)).

Accordingly, this Court reviews challenges to the Governor's exercise of his "broad discretion in determining 'good and sufficient reason' for assigning a state attorney to another circuit," *Finch*, 254 So. 2d at 205, similar to the way in which it reviews exercises of discretion by the lower courts. Compare *Johns v. State*, 197 So. 791, 796 (1940) ("If the Governor should abuse [the assignment] power, by arbitrarily and without any reason whatsoever [for] making such an assignment, it might be that his action could be inquired into by writ of quo warranto ...."); with *McFadden v. State*, 177 So. 3d 562, 567 (Fla. 2015) ("Discretion is abused only when the trial court's decision is 'arbitrary, fanciful, or unreasonable.' " (quoting *Gonzalez v. State*, 990 So. 2d 1017, 1033 (Fla. 2008))).

Applying this well-established standard of review to the facts of this case, the executive orders reassigning the death-penalty eligible cases in the Ninth Circuit to King fall well "within the bounds" of the Governor's "broad authority." *Finch*, 254 So. 2d at 204–05. Far from being unreasoned or arbitrary, as required by section 27.14(1), the reassignments are predicated upon "good and sufficient reason," namely Ayala's blanket refusal to pursue the death penalty in any case despite Florida law establishing the death penalty as an appropriate sentence under certain circumstances. See generally § 921.141, Fla. Stat. (2017).

Notwithstanding the Governor's compliance with all of the requirements of section 27.14(1), however, Ayala and her amici urge this Court to invalidate the reassignment orders by viewing this case as a power struggle over prosecutorial discretion. We decline the invitation because by effectively banning the death penalty in the Ninth Circuit—as opposed to making case-specific determinations as to whether the facts of each death-penalty eligible case justify seeking the death penalty—Ayala has exercised no discretion at all. As New York's high court cogently explained, "adopting a 'blanket policy' " against the imposition of the death penalty is "in effect refusing to exercise discretion" and tantamount to a "functional[ ] veto" of state law authorizing prosecutors to pursue the death penalty in appropriate cases. *Johnson v. Pataki*, 91 N.Y.2d 214, 668 N.Y.S.2d 978, 691 N.E.2d 1002, 1007 (1997).

Although *Johnson* applied New York law, the standards to which this Court holds its own judicial officers establish that Ayala's actions have the same impact under Florida law. For example, our trial judges may not "*refuse* to exercise discretion" or "rely on an inflexible rule for a decision that the law places in the judge's discretion." *Barrow v. State*, 27 So. 3d 211, 218 (Fla. 4th DCA 2010), approved, 91 So. 3d 826 (Fla. 2012). Instead, exercising discretion demands an individualized determination "exercised according to the exigency of the case, upon a consideration of the attending circumstances." *Barber v. State*, 5 Fla. 199, 206 (Fla. 1853) (Thompson, J., concurring).

Thus, under Florida law, Ayala's blanket refusal to seek the death penalty in any eligible case, including a case that "absolutely deserve[s] [the] death penalty" does not reflect an exercise of prosecutorial discretion; it embodies, at best, a misunderstanding of Florida law. Cf. *Doe v. State*, 499 So. 2d 13, 14 (Fla. 3d DCA 1986) (holding "the trial court failed to exercise its independent sentencing discretion" in light of its erroneous view of the law); see also *Taylor v. State*, 38 So. 380, 383 (1905) (recognizing that "a failure of the state's interests" occurs where "the regular state attorney is unwilling or refuses to act").

Moreover, while Ayala's blanket prohibition against the death penalty provided the Governor with "good and sufficient reason" to reassign the cases at issue to King, also important to our holding is that the Governor did not attempt to decide which cases are deserving of the death penalty. The Governor's orders do not direct King to seek the death penalty in any of the reassigned cases, and King has sworn that the Governor has not attempted to interfere with his determination as to whether to pursue the death penalty in any case. Rather, consistent with the Governor's constitutional duty, effectuated pursuant to his statutory assignment authority, the executive orders ensure the faithful execution of Florida law by guaranteeing that the death penalty—while never mandatory—remains an option in the death-penalty eligible cases in the Ninth Circuit, but leaving it up to King, as the assigned state attorney, to determine whether to seek the death penalty on a case-by-case basis.

On these facts, the Governor has not abused his broad discretion in reassigning the cases at issue to King.

Conclusion

The executive orders reassigning death-penalty eligible cases in the Ninth Circuit to King do not exceed the Governor's authority on the facts of this case. Therefore, we deny Ayala's petition.

It is so ordered.

Notes and Questions to Consider:

1. Did the court in *Ayala v. Scott* overlook a separation of powers issue? A footnote, omitted from the opinion as transcribed above, suggests the issue was considered but rejected as follows. The court noted that, in *Fulk v. State*, 417 So. 2d 1121 (Fla. 5th DCA 1982), Florida's Fifth District Court of Appeal holds that "[a]lthough state attorneys, like all attorneys, are officers of the court, the execution of criminal statutes by enforcement, including prosecution, is an executive function of government. The state attorney, when acting as a prosecuting officer under Article V, section 17, of the Florida Constitution and under chapter 27 of the Florida Statutes, is performing an executive function and not a judicial function." *Id.* at 1126 (Cowart, J., concurring specially) (footnote omitted). Therefore, according to the

footnote in *Ayala v. Scott*, the holding of *Fulk v. State* explains why the facts of *Ayala v. Scott* did not raise an issue regarding the separation of powers. Instead, Florida's Supreme Court viewed this case as raising the issue of the scope of Florida's executive power. A dissenting opinion disagreed. Do you agree?

2. In light of *Ayala v. Scott*, what is a Florida elected official, who hold the power of discretion as part of their elected powers, supposed to do when faced with a law that the elected official finds morally repugnant?

3. *Ayala v. Scott* involved an elected prosecutor's discomfort with the death penalty. Florida law grants a prosecutor the discretion to seek the death penalty for crimes of first degree murder, felony murder, capital drug trafficking, and capital sexual battery. The laws of many nations forbid the use of a death penalty, and the beliefs of many faiths are troubled by the use of the death penalty. For example, the Catechism of the Catholic Church states that "[t]he traditional teaching of the Church does not exclude, presupposing full ascertainment of the identity and responsibility of the offender, recourse to the death penalty, when this is the only practicable way to defend the lives of human beings effectively against the aggressor." *Id.* at para. 2267. Stated somewhat differently, "[w]hile the Catholic Church does not condemn the death penalty as intrinsically evil … because of the Church's high value of human life, the circumstances under which the death penalty is morally acceptable are rare." Bill Piatt, CATHOLIC LEGAL PERSPECTIVES 185 (2d ed. 2015). What are your personal beliefs about the death penalty?

E. Quasi-Executive Power

"While the general executive power of the state is vested in the executive branch, and chiefly in the Governor, the Legislature [or the state constitution itself] may delegate ministerial or quasi-executive powers…." Jack K. Levin, 8 MICH. PL. & PR. § 60:20 (2d ed., Mar. 2019 update).

One example of quasi-executive power delegated by Florida's Constitution is the discretionary power of prosecutors, as held by *Valdes v. State*, 728 So. 2d 736 (Fla. 1999):

VALDES

v.

STATE

Supreme Court of Florida, 1999

728 So. 2d 736

Frank Valdes appeals the trial court's summary denial of his motion for postconviction relief, filed pursuant to Florida Rule of Criminal Procedure 3.850....

Valdes was found guilty and sentenced to death for the 1987 murder of a corrections officer.... The murder occurred during an aborted attempt by Valdes and his accomplice to assist a friend in escaping police custody. The Court unanimously affirmed the conviction and sentence on appeal....

[The motion for post-conviction relief] stated one claim, as follows:

> The Defendant's rights ... have been denied to him by and through the Florida Supreme Court's effectuation of an unauthorized amendment to the Judiciary article of Florida's Constitution--delegating away its prosecutorial arm (i.e., State Attorneys) to the Executive branch--resulting in the Defendant's wrongful prosecution, convictions, and sentences, which rights arise directly and/or are guaranteed against invasion by ... the Florida Constitution....

[T]he merits of this claim ... [are] fatally flawed in an important respect. Article V, section 17, *specifically provides* that state attorneys are the prosecuting officers of all trials in each circuit. This Court has long held that as the prosecuting officer, the state attorney has "complete discretion" in the decision to charge and prosecute, *Cleveland v. State,* 417 So. 2d 653, 654 (Fla. 1982), and the judiciary cannot interfere with this "discretionary executive function." *State v. Bloom,* 497 So. 2d 2, 3 (Fla.1986).

As this Court explained in *The Office of the State Attorney v. Parrotino,* 628 So. 2d 1097, 1099 (Fla. 1993), state attorneys fulfill a unique role, which is both quasi-judicial and quasi-executive. This unique role is due to the tradition of their exclusive discretion in prosecution, combined with their status as officers of the court. The office of state attorney thus "shares some attributes of the executive" by virtue of its power as the prosecuting authority to determine whom and how to prosecute, as well as some attributes of the judicial branch, such as judicial immunity. *Id.* at 1099 n. 2. Nothing about the *placement* of the constitutional provision in article V providing for the creation of the state attorneys undermines these long-held principles….

Based on the foregoing, the trial court's summary denial of Valdes' petition is affirmed….

Notes and Questions to Consider:

1. *Valdes v. State* holds that "[n]othing about the *placement* of the constitutional provision in article V providing for the creation of the state attorneys undermines these long-held principles." So the placement argument was a losing argument, but was it a frivolous argument? Consider the fact that Florida's Constitution addresses executive powers in Article IV, but creates state attorneys in Article V with its creation of Florida's judicial branch.

2. "Regardless of the method of review, the court exercises a more limited review of quasi-executive or quasi-legislative action than of quasi-judicial action." *Broward County v. Admin. Comm'n*, 321 So. 2d 605, 610 (Fla. 1st DCA 1975). In your opinion, why would it be appropriate to show such deference to quasi-executive action?

Chapter Six

Judicial Power

A. Florida's Judicial Branch

The role of the judicial branch of Florida's state government is described in this excerpt from Daniel Webster & Donald L. Bell, *First Principles for Constitution Revision*, 22 Nova L. Rev. 391 (1997):

> *The Judicial Branch*
>
> Even when ruled by a king, "[b]etwixt subject and subject. . . there must be measures, laws, and judges. . . ." The third branch of government, the judiciary, which has been called the least dangerous branch, was developed in society to substitute for two powers that people had in nature. The first is the power to do whatever one sees fit to assure self preservation. The second is the power to punish those who attempt to infringe the right of self preservation. Upon joining society, a person gives up both of these rights, but in exchange receives the support of the civil authorities to accomplish these matters on his behalf.
>
> In western society, these objectives are accomplished through the law of torts, the criminal law, and the laws of free economy that allow parties to apportion rights, duties, and privileges amongst themselves with the support of the government. If these remedies ceased to be available the people would resort to self-help, as if in nature. Furthermore, since as Locke noted, "[t]he great end of men's entering into society being the enjoyment of their properties in peace and safety. . ." there would be no reason for people to continue under the laws of a society if these interests were not protected.
>
> Article V of the Florida Constitution establishes a system of courts and judges consistent with the fundamental purpose of the ju-

diciary by establishing that all judicial officers of the state shall be "conservators of the peace." As Tocqueville explained:

> The great end of justice is to substitute the notion of right or that of violence. . . . The moral force which courts of justice possess renders the use of physical force very rare and is frequently substituted for it; but if force proves to be indispensable, its power is doubled by its association with the idea of law.

Thus, the principal function of the judiciary is public and private dispute resolution. The courts have the power under article V to review the constitutionality of legislative acts. But, like the other branches of government, the courts are confined to the exercise of those powers assigned to them under the constitution. The courts must take care that, in rendering their opinions, they do not go beyond the Legislature's intent, thereby creating new laws of their own. Similarly, it is beyond the power of the courts to execute the laws.

Florida's judicial officers have enormous independence. Appellate judges, including the Justices of the Supreme Court of Florida, do not stand for popular election as do the officers of the executive and legislative branches. Instead, they are initially appointed and must stand for a merit retention election every six years thereafter. If a majority of the electors casting ballots do not vote for retention, the Governor must appoint a replacement. The practical effect of merit retention elections has been to give judges permanent tenure, subject only to the requirement that they retire at age seventy [which requirement was amended in 2018 to age 75]. Because this is the case, some have expressed concern that Florida's judges are too far removed from the public will.

Judges, like all other public officers, derive their power from the people. If the judiciary is not subject to adequate checks and balances, judges, like other public officers, can exert tyrannical power over the people. Unlike officers of the executive and legislative branches who are directly responsible to a majority of the voters,

> judges should be free from day-to-day political pressures. One of the principal functions of the courts is to protect political minorities from "the tyranny of the majority." However, the judiciary should not be so far removed from public control that judges can afford to consistently ignore the public will.... When considering revisions that would affect the judiciary, one point deserves consideration. It is clear that the Florida Constitution contains some provisions that lend themselves to expansive judicial interpretation. Our judiciary would be more restrained if we had a more restrained constitution. Thus, [we] should consider making changes that move the constitution in a direction more conducive to judicial restraint.

Notes and Questions to Consider:

1. In the discussion of Florida's judicial branch in the excerpt above, the authors note that "Article V of the Florida Constitution establishes a system of courts and judges." Why would Florida need to create, maintain and fund a system of courts and judges when the U.S. Constitution already creates a federal one?

2. The discussion above ends with the authors' opinion that: "Our judiciary would be more restrained if we had a more restrained constitution. Thus, [we] should consider making changes [to Florida's Constitution] that move [it] in a direction more conducive to judicial restraint." Do you agree?

B. Florida's State Court System

Just as Article III of the U.S. Constitution creates a federal court system, Article V of Florida's Constitution creates Florida's system of state courts. In relevant part, Article V provides:

SECTION 1. Courts.—The judicial power shall be vested in a supreme court, district courts of appeal, circuit courts and county courts. No other courts may be established by the state, any political subdivision or any municipality. The legislature shall, by general law, divide the state into appellate court districts and judicial circuits following county lines. Commissions established by law, or administrative officers or bodies may be granted quasi-judicial power in matters connected with the functions of their offices. The legislature may establish by general law a civil traffic hearing officer system for the purpose of hearing civil traffic infractions. The legislature may, by general law, authorize a military court-martial to be conducted by military judges of the Florida National Guard, with direct appeal of a decision to the District Court of Appeal, First District.

SECTION 2. Administration; practice and procedure.— . . .The supreme court shall adopt rules for the practice and procedure in all courts including the time for seeking appellate review, the administrative supervision of all courts, the transfer to the court having jurisdiction of any proceeding when the jurisdiction of another court has been improvidently invoked, and a requirement that no cause shall be dismissed because an improper remedy has been sought….

SECTION 3. Supreme court.—

(a) ORGANIZATION.—The supreme court shall consist of seven justices. Of the seven justices, each appellate district shall have at least one justice elected or appointed from the district to the supreme court who is a resident of the district at the time of the original appointment or election. Five justices shall constitute a quorum. The concurrence of four justices shall be necessary to a decision. When recusals for cause would prohibit the court from convening because of the requirements of this section, judges assigned to temporary duty may be substituted for justices.

(b) JURISDICTION.—The supreme court:

> (1) Shall hear appeals from final judgments of trial courts imposing the death penalty and from decisions of district courts of appeal declaring invalid a state statute or a provision of the state constitution.
>
> (2) When provided by general law, shall hear appeals from final judgments entered in proceedings for the validation of bonds or certificates of indebtedness and shall review action of statewide agencies relating to rates or service of utilities providing electric, gas, or telephone service.

(3) May review any decision of a district court of appeal that expressly declares valid a state statute, or that expressly construes a provision of the state or federal constitution, or that expressly affects a class of constitutional or state officers, or that expressly and directly conflicts with a decision of another district court of appeal or of the supreme court on the same question of law.

(4) May review any decision of a district court of appeal that passes upon a question certified by it to be of great public importance, or that is certified by it to be in direct conflict with a decision of another district court of appeal.

(5) May review any order or judgment of a trial court certified by the district court of appeal in which an appeal is pending to be of great public importance, or to have a great effect on the proper administration of justice throughout the state, and certified to require immediate resolution by the supreme court.

(6) May review a question of law certified by the Supreme Court of the United States or a United States Court of Appeals which is determinative of the cause and for which there is no controlling precedent of the supreme court of Florida.

(7) May issue writs of prohibition to courts and all writs necessary to the complete exercise of its jurisdiction.

(8) May issue writs of mandamus and quo warranto to state officers and state agencies.

(9) May, or any justice may, issue writs of habeas corpus returnable before the supreme court or any justice, a district court of appeal or any judge thereof, or any circuit judge.

(10) Shall, when requested by the attorney general pursuant to the provisions of Section 10 of Article IV, render an advisory opinion of the justices, addressing issues as provided by general law....

SECTION 4. District courts of appeal.—

(a) ORGANIZATION.—There shall be a district court of appeal serving each appellate district. Each district court of appeal shall consist of at least three judges. Three judges shall consider each case and the concurrence of two shall be necessary to a decision.

(b) JURISDICTION.—

(1) District courts of appeal shall have jurisdiction to hear appeals, that may be taken as a matter of right, from final judgments or orders of trial courts, including those entered on review of administrative action, not directly appealable to the supreme court or a circuit court. They may review interlocutory orders in such cases to the extent provided by rules adopted by the supreme court.

(2) District courts of appeal shall have the power of direct review of administrative action, as prescribed by general law.

(3) A district court of appeal or any judge thereof may issue writs of habeas corpus returnable before the court or any judge thereof or before any circuit judge within the territorial jurisdiction of the court. A district court of appeal may issue writs of mandamus, certiorari, prohibition, quo warranto, and other writs necessary to the complete exercise of its jurisdiction. To the extent necessary to dispose of all issues in a cause properly before it, a district court of appeal may exercise any of the appellate jurisdiction of the circuit courts....

SECTION 5. Circuit courts.—

(a) ORGANIZATION.—There shall be a circuit court serving each judicial circuit.

(b) JURISDICTION.—The circuit courts shall have original jurisdiction not vested in the county courts, and jurisdiction of appeals when provided by general law. They shall have the power to issue writs of mandamus, quo warranto, certiorari, prohibition and habeas corpus, and all writs necessary or proper to the complete exercise of their jurisdiction. Jurisdiction of the circuit court shall be uniform throughout the state. They shall have the power of direct review of administrative action prescribed by general law.

SECTION 6. County courts.—

(a) ORGANIZATION.—There shall be a county court in each county. There shall be one or more judges for each county court as prescribed by general law.

(b) JURISDICTION.—The county courts shall exercise the jurisdiction prescribed by general law. Such jurisdiction shall be uniform throughout the state….

…

SECTION 8. Eligibility.—No person shall be eligible for office of justice or judge of any court unless the person is an elector of the state and resides in the territorial jurisdiction of the court. No justice or judge shall serve after attaining the age of seventy years except upon temporary assignment or to complete a term, one-half of which has been served. No person is eligible for the office of justice of the supreme court or judge of a district court of appeal unless the person is, and has been for the preceding ten years, a member of the bar of Florida. No person is eligible for the office of circuit judge unless the person is, and has been for the preceding five years, a member of the bar of Florida….

…

SECTION 10. Retention; election and terms.—

(a) Any justice or judge may qualify for retention by a vote of the electors in the general election next preceding the expiration of the justice's or judge's term in the manner prescribed by law. If a justice or judge is ineligible or fails to qualify for retention, a vacancy shall exist in that office upon the expiration of the term being served by the justice or judge. When a justice or judge so qualifies, the ballot shall read substantially as follows: "Shall Justice (or Judge) (name of justice or judge) of the (name of the court) be retained in office?" If a majority of the qualified electors voting within the territorial jurisdiction of the court vote to retain, the justice or judge shall be retained for a term of six years….

SECTION 11. Vacancies.—

(a) Whenever a vacancy occurs in a judicial office to which election for retention applies, the governor shall fill the vacancy….

SECTION 12. Discipline; removal and retirement.— …

(1) There shall be a judicial qualifications commission vested with jurisdiction to investigate and recommend to the Supreme Court of Florida the removal from office of any justice or judge whose conduct, during term of office … demonstrates a present unfitness to hold office, and to investigate and recommend the discipline of a justice or judge whose conduct, during term of office … warrants such discipline. For purposes of this section, discipline is defined as any or all of the following: reprimand, fine, suspension with or without pay, or lawyer discipline….

SECTION 13. Prohibited activities.—All justices and judges shall devote full time to their judicial duties. They shall not engage in the practice of law or hold office in any political party….

SECTION 14. Funding.—

(a) All justices and judges shall be compensated only by state salaries fixed by general law….

(b) All funding for the offices of the clerks of the circuit and county courts performing court-related functions, [with certain enumerated exceptions], shall be provided by adequate and appropriate filing fees for judicial proceedings and service charges and costs for performing court-related functions as required by general law. Selected salaries, costs, and expenses of the state courts system may be funded from appropriate filing fees for judicial proceedings and service charges and costs for performing court-related functions, as provided by general law….

(c) No county or municipality, except as provided in this subsection, shall be required to provide any funding for the state courts system, state attorneys' offices, public defenders' offices, court-appointed counsel or the offices of the clerks of the circuit and county courts performing court-related functions. Counties shall be required to fund the cost of communications services, existing radio systems, existing multi-agency criminal justice information systems, and the cost of construction or lease, maintenance, utilities, and security of facilities for the trial courts, public defenders' offices, state attorneys' offices, and the offices of the clerks of the circuit and county courts performing court-related functions. Counties shall also pay reasonable and necessary salaries, costs, and expenses of the state courts system to meet local requirements as determined by general law.

Notes and Questions to Consider:

1. Currently, Florida's 67 counties are divided into twenty judicial circuits, each of which consists of at least a single county and some of which as many as six counties. No county falls within more than one judicial circuit. The five judicial circuits are all within one of five territorial District Courts of Appeal. The geographic jurisdiction of Florida's five District Courts of Appeal are:

First DCA: 1st, 2nd, 3rd, 8th and 14th Circuit Courts (as well as statewide jurisdiction over orders of the Florida Division of Administrative Hearings Offices of the Judges of Compensation Claims, which is the administrative agency that adjudicates claims of injured workers seeking benefits from employers under Florida's Workers' Compensation Law)

Second DCA: 6th, 10th, 12th, 13th and 20th Circuit Courts

Third DCA: 11th and 16th Circuit Courts

Fourth DCA: 15th, 17th and 19th Circuit Courts

Fifth DCA: 5th, 7th, 9th and 18th Circuit Courts.

The First DCA is in Tallahassee. The Second DCA is the only Florida district court of appeal that operates on from two fixed locations: Lakeland and Tampa. The Third DCA is in Miami. The Fourth DCA is in West Palm Beach. The Fifth DCA is in Daytona Beach. Florida's Supreme Court is at 500 S. Duval St., Tallahassee, FL 32399.

2. Note how Florida's court system is funded. Does this seem adequate? What can Florida's court system do if funding proves inadequate in any given year?

3. Note further that each court in Florida's court system is given

authority to issue certain "writs." Those are discussed in greater detail later in this chapter.

C. Jurisdiction of Florida's Courts

The Florida Statutes provide the following jurisdiction of Florida's county courts as of May 24, 2019:

> Florida Statutes section 34.01. *Jurisdiction of county court.--*
>
> (1) County courts shall have original jurisdiction:
>
> (a) In all misdemeanor cases not cognizable by the circuit courts.;
>
> (b) Of all violations of municipal and county ordinances.;
>
> (c) Of all actions at law, except those within the exclusive jurisdiction of the circuit courts, in which the matter in controversy does not exceed, exclusive of interest, costs, and attorney fees:
>
> 1. If filed on or before December 31, 2019, the sum of $15,000.
>
> 2. If filed on or after January 1, 2020, the sum of $30,000.
>
> 3. If filed on or after January 1, 2023, the sum of $50,000.
>
> (d) Of disputes occurring in the homeowners' associations as described in s. 720.311(2)(a), which shall be concurrent with jurisdiction of the circuit courts....

The Florida Statutes provide the following appellate jurisdiction of Florida's circuit courts as of May 24, 2019:

> Florida Statutes section 26.012. *Jurisdiction of circuit court.--*
>
> (1) Circuit courts shall have jurisdiction of appeals from county courts except:
>
> (a) Appeals of county court orders or judgments where the amount in controversy is greater than $15,000. This paragraph is repealed on January 1, 2023.

(b) Appeals of county court orders or judgments declaring invalid a state statute or a provision of the State Constitution.

(c) Orders or judgments of a county court which are certified by the county court to the district court of appeal to be of great public importance and which are accepted by the district court of appeal for review.

Circuit courts shall have jurisdiction of appeals from final administrative orders of local government code enforcement boards....

Notes to Consider:

1. The statutes quoted above implement Article V Section 5 of Florida's Constitution (providing that Florida's "circuit courts shall have original jurisdiction not vested in the county courts, and jurisdiction of appeals when provided by general law") and Article V Section 6 (providing that Florida's "county courts shall exercise the jurisdiction prescribed by general law.").

2. The statutes quoted above reflect amendments made in June 2019 expanding the amount-in-controversy jurisdiction of Florida's county courts and the appellate jurisdiction of Florida's circuit courts. House Bill 337, which is the bill that was signed into law, provides that "[t]he amendments to the jurisdiction of a court made by this act shall apply with respect to the date of filing the cause of action, regardless of when the cause of action accrued." See section 32 of 2019 Fla. Sess. Law Serv. Ch. 2019-58 (C.S.C.S.H.B. 337).

D. Extraordinary Writs

Article V of the Constitution of the State of Florida empowers all Florida state courts except County Courts to issue certain "writs." What is a writ, and how is it used? The February 2006 issue of the Florida Bar Journal provides this introduction to writ practice in Florida:

Under Florida law, unless an order completely disposes of judicial labor on a claim or falls within the narrow, enumerated categories of appealable nonfinal orders, a litigant must wait until a case is over before obtaining the right to appeal. In some circumstances, however, certain orders subject a litigant to irreparable harm and require immediate review. Perhaps a trial court has ordered immediate disclosure of materials protected by attorney-client or trade secret privileges, or denied a motion to dismiss a premature claim for punitive damages or a motion to disqualify. In such instances, and others, a litigant may be able to obtain immediate review and issuance of a common law writ, which is ingrained in our common law tradition and has evolved with our judicial framework. Understanding the general principles governing common law writs provides a litigant with unique tools that are both practical and extraordinary.

Original Proceedings Described in Rule 9.100

Florida Rule of Appellate Procedure 9.100 describes the courts' original jurisdiction to issue common law writs. The rule identifies writs of mandamus, prohibition, quo warranto, certiorari, habeas corpus, and all writs necessary to the complete exercise of the courts' jurisdiction. Each of these writs warrants individual discussion, but certain general principles are universally applicable. An original writ proceeding is initiated by filing a petition directly within the appellate forum, with the appropriate filing fee, rather than by filing a notice of appeal in the lower tribunal. Fla. R. App. P. 9.100(b). In many cases, this shortens the time frame for preparing necessary materials for seeking review because certain extraordinary writ petitions must be filed within 30 days following rendition of the challenged order. Because the clerk does not transmit a record in writ proceedings, parties wishing to include record materials must file an appendix with the petition. Fla. R. App. P. 9.100(i) & 9.220.

Unlike an appellate proceeding, the party seeking a writ is identified as the petitioner and all other parties as respondents. Fla. R. App. P. 9.100(b). Neither the trial court nor other decision-making body should be named as a respondent. Fla. R. App. P. 9.100(c)(4). Furthermore, a respondent should not respond to an original writ petition unless the court issues an order to show cause or otherwise requires a response.

> Fla. R. App. P. 9.100(e)(3) & (h). Once a response is served, the petitioner has 20 days to serve a reply and supplemental appendix, if any. Fla. R. App. P. 9.100(k). An original petition dispenses with many of the stylistic requirements for an appellate brief, such as tables of contents and authorities; however, a petitioner and respondent must adhere to the font, page size, and page limit requirements and provide certificates of service and typeface compliance. Fla. R. App. P. 9.100(1).4

Jack R. Reiter, *Common Law Writs - from the Practical to the Extraordinary*, Fla. B.J., February 2006, at 32.

This introduction outlines the pleading requirements for each of the various writs. But the substantive elements of each writ are different, and its use is also different. Therefore, we examine each in turn with excerpts from FLORIDA ELEMENTS OF AN ACTION (with internal footnotes and citations omitted).

1. Writ of Mandamus

Elements of the Prima Facie Case for a Writ of Mandamus

from FLORIDA ELEMENTS OF AN ACTION

by Patrick John McGinley

21 Fla. Prac. § 1701:1

© 2017 by Thomson Reuters

> A petition for writ of mandamus is an action seeking to remedy a government's failure to do something it is supposed to do. Mandamus is a proceeding to enforce a clear legal right to the performance of a clear legal duty.
>
> . . . If granted, a writ of mandamus is an enforceable command from a court directed to the government or a representative of the government (such as an inferior court, public officer or governmental entity) requiring it to perform an act that it has a legal duty to perform because of its official position. Therefore, a mandamus action is a means by which to seek a court order commanding a government official to do something he is legally obliged to do.

The six required elements for a writ of mandamus are:

(1) the petitioner has a clear and certain legal right

(2) to the performance of a particular duty

(3) by a government or a representative of the government

(4) whose performance of that duty is ministerial and not discretionary,

(5) who has failed to perform despite an adequate request, and

(6) who has left the petitioner with no other legal method for obtaining relief.

Id. at § 1701:1.

2. Writ of Prohibition

Elements of the Prima Facie Case for a Writ of Prohibition

from FLORIDA ELEMENTS OF AN ACTION

by Patrick John McGinley

21 Fla. Prac. § 1702:1

© 2017 by Thomson Reuters

A writ of prohibition is an original action filed with an appellate court seeking a discretionary remedy to prevent a lower court or tribunal from improperly exercising its judicial power. "Prohibition" is that process by which a superior court exercises its discretion to prevent an inferior court (or tribunal possessing judicial or quasi-judicial powers) from exceeding its jurisdiction in matters over which it has cognizance or usurping matters not within its jurisdiction to hear or determine.

. . . If granted, a writ of prohibition is an enforceable command from a court directed to the lower court or tribunal preventing it from performing certain acts. Therefore, a prohibition action is a means by which to seek a greater court's order preventing a lesser tribunal from doing something it should be forbidden to do.

The five required elements for a writ of prohibition are:

(1) an inferior court or quasi-judicial tribunal

(2) will make but has not yet made

(3) an unauthorized use of its judicial or quasi-judicial power

(4) that will cause the petitioner a harm for which there is no other appropriate and adequate remedy, and therefore,

(5) the reviewing court should exercise its discretion to stop this harm from happening.

Id. at § 1702:1 (footnotes omitted).

3. Writ of Quo Warranto

Elements of the Prima Facie Case for a Writ of Quo Warranto

from FLORIDA ELEMENTS OF AN ACTION

by Patrick John McGinley

21 Fla. Prac. § 1703:1

© 2017 by Thomson Reuters

A petition for writ of quo warranto is an action to challenge "the exercise of some right or privilege, the peculiar powers of which are derived from the state." Statutes exist empowering the Florida Attorney General to bring petitions for writ of quo warranto, but the right to bring such a petition is not the Attorney General's alone. Quo warranto proceedings seek the enforcement of a public right, so "the people" are the real party to the action and the person bringing suit "need not show that he has any real or personal interest in it." Also, the person bringing the petition for quo warranto need not show he suffers any harm. Thus, actions in the nature of quo warranto to question the authority for the exercise of rights, privileges, and powers derived from the state can be brought by any person. A statutory exception exists for a quo warranto action challenging an election or a right to hold office arising from that election, for the person making such a quo warranto challenge must be either the Florida Attorney General or, if that attorney refuses to bring the suit, then it must be a person claiming the right to hold that office….

> ...The four elements of an action for quo warranto are:
>
> (1) A Florida official, government agency or other alleged recipient of a power or right that is derived from the State of Florida
>
> (2) has or will exercise that power
>
> (3) but such use is or will be legally improper
>
> (4) and therefore, the court should exercise its discretion to grant this discretionary writ.

Id. at § 1703:1 (footnotes omitted).

The use of, and a limitation upon, Florida's writ of quo warranto is illustrated by the following case of *League of Women Voters of Fla. v. Scott*, 232 So. 3d 264 (Fla. 2017). A special interest group petitioned for a writ of quo warranto against then-Governor Rick Scott to prohibit him from filling three upcoming judicial vacancies on Florida's Supreme Court. The factual basis was because Governor Scott's term concludes at the end of the day on the first Monday in January, which is the same day that the Justices' terms end. Governor Scott intended to make the appointments on his last day. The special interest group sought to stop him.

LEAGUE OF WOMEN VOTERS OF FLORIDA

V.

SCOTT

Supreme Court of Florida, 2017

232 So. 3d 264

This case is before the Court on the petition of the League of Women Voters of Florida (the League) for a writ of quo warranto. Because the issue presented is not ripe for consideration, we dismiss the petition.

The League asks this Court to issue a writ of quo warranto against Governor Rick Scott prohibiting him from "filling any judicial vacancies on Florida's appellate courts that occur due to terms expiring in January 2019." The League's basis for filing the petition is Governor Scott's December 2016 announcement of intent to appoint the replacements for three justices of this Court. However, use of the writ to address prospective conduct is not appropriate.

Quo warranto is used "to determine whether a state officer or agency has improperly exercised a power or right derived from the State," *Fla. House of Representatives v. Crist*, 999 So. 2d 601, 607 (Fla. 2008), and the history of the extraordinary writ reflects that petitions for relief in quo warranto are properly filed only after a public official has acted. In *Swoope v. City of New Smyrna*, 98 Fla. 1082, 125 So. 371 (1929), we explained that a challenge to an individual's exercise of official authority

> will not be determined by bill in chancery, such a case being regarded as appropriately falling within the jurisdiction of the common law courts by proceedings in quo warranto. And since this remedy is applicable the moment an office or franchise is usurped, an injunction will not lie to prevent the usurpation, even though the respondent has not yet entered upon the office or assumed to exercise its functions. In such case the party aggrieved should wait until an actual usurpation has occurred, and then seek his remedy in quo warranto.

Id. at 372. A party must wait until a government official has acted before seeking relief pursuant to quo warranto because a threatened exercise of power which is allegedly outside of that public official's authority may not ultimately occur. To address whether quo warranto relief is warranted under such premature circumstances would amount to an impermissible advisory opinion based upon hypothetical facts.

We previously considered whether issuance of the writ was appropriate in situations where the state officer or agency had already acted. For example, in *Whiley v. Scott*, 79 So. 3d 702, 705 (Fla. 2011), we reviewed a completed action, in that the challenged executive order had already been issued. The same is true of *State ex rel. Butterworth v. Kenny*, 714 So. 2d 404, 406 (Fla. 1998), receded from on other grounds by *Darling v. State*, 45 So. 3d 444 (Fla. 2010), where we considered the authority of the Office of the Capital Collateral Regional Counsel for the Northern and Southern Regions to represent death row inmates in civil rights actions. Most recently, in

Ayala v. Scott, 224 So .3d 755, 756–57 (Fla. 2017), we held that quo warranto was an appropriate vehicle for the state attorney for the Ninth Judicial Circuit to challenge a series of executive orders that reassigned the prosecution of a number of pending death-penalty eligible cases to the state attorney of another judicial circuit.

Although Governor Scott announced his intent to appoint the replacements for three justices of this Court, clearly no appointments have been made. To use quo warranto to review an action which is merely contemplated but not consummated, as in the present case, would require this Court to depart from the historical application of the writ. This we decline to do. Until some action is taken by the Governor, the matter the League seeks to have resolved is not ripe, and this Court lacks jurisdiction to determine whether quo warranto relief is warranted.

Based upon the foregoing, the petition is hereby dismissed.

LABARGA, C.J., and CANADY, POLSTON, and LAWSON, JJ., concur.

QUINCE, J., concurring in result only.

While I agree with the majority's conclusion that the "issue presented is not ripe for consideration," majority op. at 264, I also agree with Justice Lewis that this Court could properly review a petition for quo warranto prior to the actual appointment of a new justice. I write separately to clarify what I believe to be an improper focus in both opinions and to highlight the concessions made by Governor Scott's counsel during oral argument regarding the Governor's authority to make these appointments.

The majority currently states:

> Although Governor Scott announced his intent to appoint the replacements for three justices to this Court, clearly no appointments have been made. To use quo warranto to review an action which is merely contemplated but not consummated, as in the present case, would require this Court to depart from the historical application of the writ. This we decline to do. Until some action is taken by the Governor, the matter the League seeks to have resolved is not ripe, and this Court lacks jurisdiction to determine whether quo warranto

relief is warranted.

Majority op. at 266 (emphasis added). First, the majority implies that the action would not be ripe until the Governor makes an appointment ("clearly, no appointments have been made ... merely contemplated but not consummated"). However, the majority then appears to suggest that only "some action" would be necessary for this Court to consider the Governor's authority to make said action. Majority op. at 266. This inconsistent language creates unnecessary confusion about when a future petition for quo warranto would be ripe for this Court's consideration. This confusion is compounded by Justice Lewis' dissent, which also focuses on the presumption that the issue may only become ripe once the Governor has made an appointment. See Dissenting op. at 269 ("The majority's statement today that the appointment must be consummated before quo warranto applies ....").

Furthermore, the majority ignores that we have previously granted a petition for a writ of quo warranto challenging the Governor's authority to endeavor to fill a judicial vacancy. *Lerman v. Scott*, No. SC16-783, 2016 WL 3127708 (Fla. Jun. 3, 2016). In *Lerman*, the petitioners sought the writ of quo warranto "to show by what authority [Governor Scott] has endeavored to fill a vacancy, created by the Resign to Run statute, in the office of county court judge, in Group 11 of the Fifteenth Judicial Circuit, through an appointment." Petition at 1, 2016 WL 2760518, *Lerman v. Scott*, No. SC16–783. We granted the writ in *Lerman* because Governor Scott acted by requesting the Judicial Nominating Commission to provide a list of names for his consideration to make an appointment. *Lerman*, 2016 WL 3127708, at *1 ("The Governor shall not utilize the Fifteenth Judicial Circuit Judicial Nominating Commission to perform any functions related to nominating candidates for this judicial office."). Thus, unlike the dissent's characterization of *Lerman*, we were not merely responding to an announced intention, dissenting op. at 268-69, but did find an action short of an actual appointment by which the petitioner could question the Governor's authority. Under this Court's precedent, we have the authority to act prior to the Governor's making an appointment that is contrary to law.

On the merits of the instant petition, at oral argument in this Court,

Governor Scott's counsel conceded that "the Governor's term concludes at the end of the day on [the first] Monday" in January, "the same day that the Justices' terms end." The Governor's counsel further conceded that if the justices do not leave before the end of their terms and "if the new governor's term has begun, then the new governor would have the authority to make the appointment." This position is the same as that taken by the majority of Florida voters in 2014 in response to a proposed constitutional amendment which would have required the Governor "to prospectively fill vacancies in a judicial office."

The Governor's concession reflects Florida law. Under the Florida Constitution, when a vacancy occurs in a judicial office to which election for retention applies, "the governor shall fill the vacancy by appointing for a term ending on the first Tuesday after the first Monday in January of the year following the next general election." Art. V, § 11(a), Fla. Const. However, a vacancy exists only "upon the expiration of the term being served by the justice." Art. V, § 10(a), Fla. Const. We have explained that this provision "expressly provides that a vacancy in a merit retention judicial office does not occur until the end of the judge or justice's term." *Advisory Op. to Governor re Judicial Vacancy Due to Mandatory Retirement*, 940 So. 2d 1090, 1091 (Fla. 2006) (emphasis added).

Moreover, under article IV, section 5(a), of the Florida Constitution, a governor's term does not begin until "the first Tuesday after the first Monday in January" of the year following the general election. As noted in an appendix to the instant petition filed in this Court, Governors Bush, Crist, and Scott all took the oath of office well before the first Tuesday after the first Monday in January so as to assume gubernatorial duties immediately on the first day of their respective terms. See App. to Pet'rs' Reply at 2–4.

Although not before us, the Governor also conceded that a declaratory action would be appropriate to challenge his endeavor to replace the retiring justices. I agree. Moreover, while I agree with the majority that it is not appropriate for us to rule on the petition at this time, I do not agree that it would only become appropriate to do so after Governor Scott has consummated an appointment. Furthermore, the concession made by the Governor during oral argument effectively answers the question raised in the petition.

PARIENTE, J., concurs.

LEWIS, J., dissenting.

It is most unfortunate that the majority finds it necessary to summarily dismiss this common law action to protect our State from blatantly unconstitutional actions for reasons other than a proper analysis of the law and do so directly contrary to the application of quo warranto in this judicial appointment context in 2016 in Lerman v. Scott, No. SC16-783, 2016 WL 3127708 *1 (Fla. June 3, 2016), in which the entire Court either concurred or concurred in result. It is even more regrettable and distressing that future Floridians have lost the ability to protect themselves and society from clearly unconstitutional action. The Florida Constitution requires devoted protection and the Florida citizens deserve better. Contrary to Florida law and the general common law, the majority has now announced that the challenged conduct must have already produced a constitutional crisis and calamitous result before illegal acts of government officials are subject to quo warranto review or relief. Florida law has generally recognized that quo warranto is available to prevent significant impacts on the operation of government, *Whiley v. Scott*, 79 So. 3d 702, 708 (Fla. 2011), but the majority now negates that common sense, reasonable, and logical analysis to require that illegal and unconstitutional conduct which produces disarray must have already occurred to allow judicial action. While writs of quo warranto may be applied to acts of state officials that have already been committed, the writ is not foreclosed as an avenue of relief for threatened and imminent future actions of state officials, based on the clear Florida law.

As recently as the summer of 2016, this Court granted a petition for writ of quo warranto in response to an announced intention by a Governor to appoint (not having already appointed) a judicial officer to fill a position vacated by a judge seeking higher office. *Lerman*, 2016 WL 3127708, at *1. County Court Judge Johnson resigned pursuant to the Resign to Run statute and *Lerman* submitted the necessary paperwork to become a candidate for the judicial position previously held by Judge Johnson. Governor Scott, as he has done here, announced that he was going to make an appointment to the position held by Judge Johnson. Lerman filed a petition for writ of quo warranto in this Court to prevent Governor Scott from appointing or attempting to appoint a person to the position previously held by Judge Johnson contrary to law. This Court granted the petition for quo warranto and ordered the position filled by election. *Id.* This Court further ordered that any functions related to the future appointment of candidates for this position terminate. *Id.* The majority's statement today that the appointment must be "consummated" before quo warranto applies is simply incorrect, contrary to common sense, and, in my view, dangerous. Majority op. at 266.

Under the majority view, elected politicians can announce their intentions and plan to engage in all types of illegal and harmful conduct but no relief is available until the illegal and harmful act has already inflicted its damage. Magnificent trees cut, pristine waters fouled, and unthinkable harm inflicted upon our citizens, which may not be prevented when the actor plans and even announces his intentions. Today, we have a new test. The writ is only available when the illegal act is taken and harm is actually inflicted—at times even irreparable harm.

The majority simply ignores that the Supreme Court of Vermont has recently granted a petition for writ of quo warranto under virtually identical circumstances as we face here. *Turner v. Shumlin*, 163 A.3d 1173 (Vt. 2017). In Vermont, the former Governor announced his intention to appoint the replacement for a current Supreme Court Justice who decided not to seek retention for another term. *Id.* at 1176. The Justice's term would not expire until after the current Governor's term had expired. *Id.* The same argument was made in Vermont as is advanced by the majority here that the court could not act until an illegal appointment was actually made. *Id.* at 1177. In rejecting the principle announced by the majority here, the Supreme Court of Vermont recognized that the circumstances were not conjectural, hypothetical, or abstract. *Id.* The announced intentions were concrete and unequivocal. *Id.* Understanding that there is a fundamental interest in ensuring that the constitutional process is sound, the court held that the Governor could not constitutionally appoint the Justice in question's replacement. *Id.* at 1188. We must all heed the closing words from the Vermont Supreme Court:

> We reach our decision having in mind the overarching principles of our democracy: the integrity of our governing institutions and the people's confidence in them.

Id.

Today, the majority opinion has chosen to cherrypick only certain rules with regard to writs of quo warranto, while ignoring the clear precedent from Florida and other jurisdictions that have emphasized the notion that the writ can be appropriate in cases of threatened or attempted action by a state official. *State ex rel. Bruce v. Kiesling*, 632 So. 2d 601, 603 (Fla. 1994) ("[W]e note that the common law remedy of quo warranto is employed either to determine the right of an individual to hold public office or to challenge a public officer's attempt to exercise some right or privilege derived from the State."); *State ex rel. Ervin v. Jacksonville Expressway Auth.*, 139 So. 2d 135, 137 (Fla. 1962) ("It is a proper function of the Attorney General, in the interest of the public, to test the exercise, or threatened exercise, of power by such a corporate state agency through the process of a quo warranto proceeding."); *Adm'r, Retreat Hosp. v. Johnson*, 660 So. 2d 333, 339 (Fla. 4th DCA 1995) ("The remedy of quo warranto is designed to challenge a public officer's attempt to exercise some right or privilege derived from the state.").

Notes and Questions to Consider:

1. The majority rules that a writ of quo warranto is not available until after the respondent acts. The respondent's stated intention to act is insufficient. What are the advantages and disadvantages to this rule?

2. The facts of this case involved an incumbent chief executive, his desire to fill a supreme court seat, and an attempt to keep the seat open until the incumbent was replaced by his successor. Are not those the same facts that fairly recently occurred on the national stage? In March 2016, outgoing U.S. President Barak Obama nominated federal appellate Judge Merrick Garland to fill a vacant seat on the U.S. Supreme Court, but the U.S. Senate, lead by majority leader Mitch McConnell, successfully prevented Judge Garland's appointment and kept the seat open for the incoming Presi-

dent to fill. Would the result had been the same if this played out in Florida instead of the national stage?

3. Three of the justices deciding this case are the justices that the Governor intends to replace. Although technically this may not have caused a conflict of interest, did it not place the Governor and his counsel in an awkward position? Does it impact your answer to know that Governor Scott campaigned on a platform of promising to appoint more conservative judges and the three outgoing justices are often considered to be more liberal judges? If you were the Governor's attorney, would you have discussed the possibility of filing a motion to recuse or disqualify the personally affected justices?

4. Under Florida's Constitution, when does a vacancy occurs in a judicial office to which election for retention applies? For the answer, see the fifth or sixth paragraph of Justice Quince's concurring opinion above.

5. Under Florida's Constitution, when does a newly-elected Florida Governor's term begin? For the answer, see the next-to-last paragraph of Justice Quince's concurring opinion.

6. Justice Quince's concurring opinion cites to *Advisory Opinion to Governor re Judicial Vacancy Due to Mandatory Retirement*, 940 So. 2d 1090, 1091 (Fla. 2006). Under what circumstances can Florida's Supreme Court issue an advisory opinion?

7. Justice Quince writes: "the Governor also conceded that a declaratory action would be appropriate to challenge his endeavor to replace the retiring justices. I agree." Why do you think the League of Women Voters filed a Petition for Writ of Quo Warranto, the proper place for which was Florida's Supreme Court, instead of filing a Complaint for Declaratory Judgment, the proper place for which was Florida's Circuit Court for the Second Judicial Circuit in and for Leon County, Florida?

8. Judge Quince's concurrence, and the second paragraph of Justice Lewis' dissent, reference "the Resign to Run statute." This refers to Florida Statutes section 99.012, an enabling statute for the sentence in the Florida Constitution's Article II, Section 5 that reads:

> No person shall hold at the same time more than one office under the government of the state and the counties and municipalities therein, except that a notary public or military officer may hold another office, and any officer may be a member of a constitution revision commission, taxation and budget reform commission, constitutional convention, or statutory body having only advisory powers.

Id. at clause 2. Section 99.012, as amended in 2018, provides in relevant part:

> "Officer" means a person, whether elected or appointed, who has the authority to exercise the sovereign power of the state pertaining to an office recognized under the State Constitution or laws of the state. . . . No officer may qualify as a candidate for another state, district, county, or municipal public office if the terms or any part thereof run concurrently with each other without resigning from the office he or she presently holds. . . . The resignation is irrevocable. . . . The written resignation must be submitted at least 10 days prior to the first day of qualifying for the office he or she intends to seek. . . . The resignation must be effective no later than the earlier of the following dates: 1. The date the officer would take office, if elected; or 2.The date the officer's successor is required to take office.

Id. at subsection (1). The 2018 amendment extended these requirements to certain officers becoming candidates for one of various federal offices.

4. Constitutional Writ (the "All Writs" Power)

Elements of the Prima Facie Case for a Constitutional Writ (An "All Writs" Claim)

from FLORIDA ELEMENTS OF AN ACTION

by Patrick John McGinley

21 Fla. Prac. § 1704:1

Events transpiring now or in the future may sometimes affect a court's jurisdiction. Florida law provides a limited means to proactively thwart such events. A Petition for Constitutional Writ is an original action filed to preserve a court's jurisdiction that has already been invoked or to protect a court's jurisdiction that likely will be invoked in the future. It is often called an "all writs" action due to the language appearing in the enabling article of the Florida Constitution (granting courts the power to issue "all writs necessary" to preserve their jurisdiction). This doctrine of "all writs" is not an independent basis for a court's jurisdiction, but rather, its use is restricted to preserving jurisdiction that exists now or is likely to exist in the future. Therefore, "[i]n practice, stay of lower court proceedings is the most common occasion for invoking the all writs power."

The elements of an action for a Constitutional Writ under the "all writs necessary" clauses of Article V of the Florida Constitution are:

(1) The court has jurisdiction now, or is likely to have such jurisdiction in the future;

(2) Events are transpiring that are a threat to that jurisdiction; and

(3) The court should exercise its discretionary authority to protect its jurisdiction.

Id. at § 1704:1 (footnotes omitted).

5. Writ of Certiorari

Elements of the Prima Facie Case for a Writ of Certiorari

from FLORIDA ELEMENTS OF AN ACTION

by Patrick John McGinley

21 Fla. Prac. § 1705:1

Certiorari is a "special mechanism" by which a superior court under quite limited circumstances can review either a quasi-judicial act, or review the progress of a pending judicial case, so that the higher court can be made fully aware of the "events below and evaluate the proceedings for regularity." In Florida state courts, a Petition for Writ of Certiorari has three potential uses: to appeal from certain orders that are not eligible for an appeal under the Florida Rules of Appellate Procedure; to appeal from the outcome of a prior Petition for Writ of Certiorari; or to seek review of certain quasi-judicial actions of local government entities or state agencies over whom the Florida Administrative Procedure Act does not apply when appellate jurisdiction for such entities is not otherwise conferred by law. All three uses bear the name Certiorari, are often called "cert," and can properly be referred to by the name Common Law Certiorari. Yet the three uses are different enough in kind and in legal standards to warrant proposing three different names: Certiorari from Interlocutory Orders (a type of First-Tier Certiorari), Certiorari from Quasi-Judicial Acts (another type of First-Tier Certiorari), and Second-Tier Certiorari (a type of Certiorari review of a prior Certiorari proceeding). Before we discuss each separately, we first identify the source of authority for certiorari review, and then discuss some criteria common to each of the three types of certiorari.

Source of Authority

The Supreme Court of the State of Florida does not have authority under the Constitution of the State of Florida to grant or deny petitions for writs of certiorari. Florida's Circuit Courts are granted such authority under Article V Section 5, and Florida's District Courts of Appeal are granted such authority under Article V Section 4 of the state Constitution. The omission of the Supreme Court of Florida from having the authority to grant certiorari review is the result of a 1980 amendment to the Florida Constitution that achieved its intent to remove the Florida Supreme Court's certiorari jurisdiction.

Jurisdiction

Regarding the authority of a District Court of Appeal to grant a petition for writ of certiorari, the Constitution of the State of Florida provides, in relevant part:

> Art. V, § 4. District Courts of Appeal …
>
> (b) (3) … may issue writs of mandamus, certiorari, prohibition, quo warranto and other writs necessary to the complete exercise of its jurisdiction.

Regarding the authority of a Circuit Court to grant a petition for writ of certiorari, the Constitution of the State of Florida provides, in relevant part:

> Art. V, § 5. Circuit Courts …
>
> (b)… have … power to issue writs of mandamus, quo warranto, certiorari, prohibition … and other writs necessary to the complete exercise of its jurisdiction.

Venue

Although both a circuit court and a district court of appeal may have constitutional jurisdiction, the proper venue for filing the Petition for Writ of Certiorari is the circuit court if the case or controversy at issue did not occur in circuit court. For example, the circuit court with geographic jurisdiction over the intended recipient of the writ of certiorari is the proper venue if the case or controversy at issue occurred in County Court, before a local government entity, or before a state agency. The circuit court routinely assigns such petitions to its appellate division. Of course, if the case or controversy from which certiorari is sought occurred in the state circuit court, then the District Court of Appeal with geographic jurisdiction over that circuit is the proper venue for filing the Petition for Writ of Certiorari. Perhaps this language from a 1966 decision of Florida's Second District Court of Appeal best describes venue for extraordinary writs such as certiorari:

> The jurisdiction to issue such writs initially follows the route of direct appellate jurisdiction …. The jurisdiction of this court to issue such writs might at first blush be construed to be without limitation or restriction, but we do not so conclude …. The provisions of the constitution granting this court jurisdiction to issue such writs must be construed to mean that such jurisdiction is limited to those causes in which a direct appeal to this court would be allowed as a matter of right at a later stage of the proceedings below. Any other interpretation would permit a picking and choosing of courts by litigants and the usurpation by one court of the jurisdiction of another, thereby disrupting the carefully laid pattern of ap-

pellate jurisdiction set forth in the constitution. We, therefore, hold that jurisdiction of this court to issue writs of mandamus, certiorari, prohibition and quo warranto, insofar as they apply to a court exercising the judicial power of the state, is limited to those causes then pending in which this court has direct appellate jurisdiction.

Certiorari from Interlocutory Orders

In this type of first-tier certiorari review, a Petition for Writ of Certiorari may be used to review certain types of judicial orders that are not otherwise subject to review at this time via an immediate appeal. Such a judicial order may be called "interlocutory" because it is not a final decree, does not prevent the underlying litigation from continuing, allows the trial court to maintain control of and jurisdiction over the underlying suit, and is entered prior to a final judgment. The Florida Rules of Appellate Procedure lists those final and non-final orders from which an appeal may be taken immediately, and most if not all interlocutory orders are absent from that list. For such an order, certiorari may be an option, and if so, an independent review of that order may occur in the appellate court while the underlying lawsuit remains pending in the trial court.

"Very few categories of non-final orders qualify for the use of this extraordinary writ" of Certiorari from an Interlocutory Order. "Whether the appellate court will entertain the petition [for Certiorari from an Interlocutory Order] depends not only on the seriousness of the error in the lower tribunal, but also on the need for immediate relief." For this reason, the petitioner bears the burden to prove the following three elements:

(1) a departure from the essential requirements of the law,

(2) resulting in material injury for the remainder of the case

(3) that cannot be corrected on post-judgment appeal.

This is the customary order for listing the three elements, but they are listed in reverse order because "[t]he last two elements are jurisdictional and must be analyzed before the court may even consider the first element."

The last two elements require that "the appellate court must focus on the threshold jurisdictional question: whether there is a material injury that cannot be corrected on appeal, otherwise termed as irreparable harm." It is a waste of appellate judicial resources for the appellate court to take certiorari jurisdiction when an adequate remedy exists upon plenary appeal. Thus, these two elements require a showing that there is no adequate remedy on appeal. For example, "[a]n order of abatement is properly reviewable by writ of certiorari, because there is no adequate remedy for the delay caused by abatement after final judgment."

But "[i]f the harm caused by an erroneous order can be corrected by an award of damages or if it can be redressed on appeal from the final order in some other way, the reviewing court will likely decline to review the order by certiorari. The fact that the aggrieved party will be forced to spend time and money on a trial that is claimed to be unnecessary is not regarded as an irreparable injury." Thus, "[t]he expenditure of time and money to litigate a case that would be dismissed if the petition were granted is not an irreparable injury."

Pre-trial discovery orders are frequent fodder for attempts at this type of first-tier certiorari review. "For a denial of discovery to constitute material, irreparable harm, thus conferring certiorari jurisdiction, the denial must 'effectively eviscerate[ ] a party's claim, defense, or counterclaim.'" Such an evisceration would mean that there would be no adequate appellate remedy because "there is no practical way to determine after judgment how the requested discovery would have affected the outcome of the proceedings." On the other hand, an order erroneously granting impermissible discovery constitutes irreparable harm only when it is "one that would let the 'cat out of the bag' and provide the opponent material that could be used by an unscrupulous litigant to injure another person." For this reason, "[o]rders improperly requiring the disclosure of trade secrets or other proprietary information often create irreparable harm and are thus appropriate for certiorari review.". . .

Once certiorari jurisdiction exists because the petitioner showed the presence of an irreparable harm, then—and only then—the court must determine whether the petitioner meets his burden under the first element of showing that the order "departed from the essential requirements of law—something that is more than just a legal error." "[A] petitioner can demonstrate a departure from the essential requirements of the law by showing 'that the trial court made an error so serious that it amounts to a miscarriage of justice.'" This means that the reviewing court "should not be as concerned with the mere existence of legal error as much as with the seriousness of the error." Adequate notice of the proceedings, and an appropriate opportunity to be heard, are certainly among the essential requirements of law. Thus, "Certiorari is often the proper remedy to challenge a pretrial order that has the effect of denying a party a procedural right" that may result in denying the petitioner her constitutional right to due process of law in the proceedings below. For example, the Florida Supreme Court finds that Florida Statutes section 768.72 (1995) "creates a substantive legal right not to be subjected to a punitive damages claim and ensuing financial worth discovery until the trial court makes a determination that there is a reasonable evidentiary basis for recovery of punitive damages." Therefore, the Florida Supreme Court "concluded that certiorari jurisdiction is appropriate to review whether a trial judge has conformed with the procedural requirements of section 768.72 but not so broad as to encompass review of the sufficiency of the evidence when the trial judge has followed the procedural requirements of section 768.72."

The essential requirements of law expand further than such procedural due process concerns, but quite limitedly. For example, when "the trial court reached the right result, albeit for the wrong reasons, the [court] did not depart from the essential requirements of law." For there to be a departure from the essential requirements of substantive law, the law must be settled and clear in that area. "[T]he clearly established law which if violated by an inferior court authorizes a [reviewing] court of appeal to grant certiorari review, can derive from a variety of legal sources including case law dealing with the same issue, an interpretation or application of a statute, a procedural rule, or a constitutional provision." For example, the failure to conduct an in-camera inspection of the discovery materials a party asserts are protected by the work-product privilege constitutes a departure from the essential requirements of law subject to certiorari relief. Likewise, it is a departure from the essential requirements of the law applicable to dependency proceedings when the trial court entered an order that relieved the father from complying with the tasks enumerated in an earlier case plan approved by the court, when a recent recurrence of violence in the presence of the child contradicted the claim that the father no longer needed the services in the case plan, nothing in the record supported the elimination of any of the services or the amendment of the case plan, and the elimination of the tasks and services comprising the plan exposed the child to more of the same harm that prompted the filing of the dependency petition. Other examples of departures from the essential requirements of law include granting an order of abatement that effectively amounts to a dismissal of the plaintiff's complaint, ordering a non-resident defendant to appear in the state for an independent medical examination to determine his capacity to testify and ordering juror interviews without determining whether any information elicited through those interviews will entitle the moving party to a new trial.

Yet the petitioner's success in obtaining jurisdiction and proving a departure from the essential requirements of law might not result in his success in obtaining certiorari. The reviewing "court may refuse to grant a petition for common-law certiorari even though there may have been a departure from the essential requirements of law." "It is this discretion which is the essential distinction between review by appeal and review by common-law certiorari." The writ is discretionary.

Certiorari from Quasi-Judicial Acts

In this type of first-tier certiorari review, a Petition for Writ of Certiorari may be used to seek review of certain quasi-judicial actions of local government entities or agencies over whom the Florida Administrative Procedure Act does not apply when appellate jurisdiction over such entities is not otherwise conferred by law. "Although termed 'certiorari' review, review at this level is not discretionary but rather is a matter of right and is akin in many respects to a plenary appeal." So a significant difference between this type of first-tier certiorari review and Certiorari from Interlocutory Orders is that this type of first-tier review gives the petitioner an absolute right to be heard on the merits of his certiorari claim.

But this type of certiorari is limited to quasi-judicial acts. Local government entities or agencies perform functions that may be legislative, quasi-legislative, quasi-executive, or quasi-judicial. "It is the character of the hearing that determines whether or not board action is legislative or quasi-judicial.... Generally speaking, legislative action results in the formulation of a general rule of policy, whereas judicial action results in the application of a general rule of policy." Stated somewhat differently, a "judicial or quasi judicial act determines the rules of law applicable, and the rights affected by them, in relation to past transactions. On the other hand, a quasi-legislative or administrative order prescribes what the rule of requirement of administratively determined duty shall be with respect to transactions to be executed in the future, in order that same shall be considered lawful. But even so, quasi legislative and quasi executive orders, after they have already been entered, may have a quasi judicial attribute if capable of being arrived at and provided by law to be declared by the administrative agency only after express statutory notice, hearing, and consideration of evidence to be adduced as a basis for the making thereof." This means that an action is quasi-judicial when a local government entity or an agency "exercised a statutory power given it to make a decision having a judicial character or attribute and consequent upon some notice or hearing provided to be had before it as a condition for the rendition of the particular decision made. Unless, therefore, a particular decision complained of can be said to have a judicial quality or attribute sufficient to stamp it as a quasi judicial, as distinguished from a quasi legislative or quasi executive commission function, certiorari, which is a remedy limited solely to judicial or quasi judicial determinations, will not lie." In Florida, "[i]t is not within the power of the Legislature to change the nature of a judicial function by merely creating another agency to participate in its performance." So, like local government entities, Florida state agencies commit quasi-judicial acts when their behavior meets these definitions of quasi-judicial.

With regard to such quasi-judicial acts, certiorari provides two levels of review. "Once the local agency has ruled … the parties may seek review in the court system, twice. First, a party may seek certiorari review in circuit court, i.e., 'first-tier' certiorari review. Although termed 'certiorari' review, review at this level is not discretionary but rather is a matter of right and is akin in many respects to a plenary appeal…. Next, a party may seek certiorari review of the circuit court decision in the district court, i.e., 'second-tier' certiorari review. Review at this level is circumscribed and is similar in scope to true common law certiorari review."

In the initial (or first-tier) certiorari review from such a quasi-judicial local act, the circuit court applies the following legal standard when determining whether to quash the local act:

(1) whether procedural due process is accorded,

(2) whether the essential requirements of the law have been observed, and

(3) whether the administrative findings and judgment are supported by competent, substantial evidence."

Note that, unlike any other type of certiorari review, this first-tier certiorari review of a quasi-judicial local act examines whether competent, substantial evidence supports the quasi-judicial findings and judgment. Also note that, unlike all other attempts at certiorari review, the petitioner is entitled to such review "as of right," meaning this instance of certiorari review is not a discretionary act for the reviewing court but instead more closely resembles a plenary appeal where the reviewing court is obliged to grant relief upon a proper showing of entitlement to relief.

Regarding the first and second elements of first-tier certiorari from a quasi-judicial act, they are interpreted consistently with the similarly-phrased requirements for first-tier certiorari from an interlocutory order

> discussed above. Regarding the third element, "[c]ompetent substantial evidence is tantamount to legally sufficient evidence." When answering the inquiry as to whether there is competent substantial evidence, "[t]he circuit court's task is to review the record for evidence that supports the agency's decision, not that which rebuts it."
>
> *Second-Tier Certiorari*
>
> After either type of first-tier certiorari, be it a certiorari from an interlocutory order or a certiorari from a quasi-judicial local act, any further appellate review is also via a Petition for Writ of Certiorari. This is because Article V of the Florida Constitution grants Florida's District Courts of Appeal "jurisdiction to hear appeals, that may be taken as a matter of right, from final judgments or orders" yet an opinion issued as to whether to grant or deny a writ of certiorari does not meet the technical definition of either a "judgment" or an "order." So the appellate court's review of the grant or denial of certiorari is itself via certiorari, and thus, it is often called Second-Tier Certiorari.
>
> "Second-tier certiorari review is not a matter of right and … second-tier review is so extraordinarily limited." The decision as to whether to grant any type of relief upon second-tier certiorari is purely at the discretion of the district court of appeal reviewing the case, and "[t]he district courts should use this discretion cautiously so as to avert the possibility of common-law certiorari being used as a vehicle to obtain a second appeal."
>
> On second-tier certiorari review, "appellate courts must exercise caution not to expand certiorari jurisdiction to review the correctness of the circuit court's decision." This is because "the departure from the essential requirements of law necessary for the issuance of a writ of certiorari is something more than a simple legal error." Second-tier certiorari is appropriate "only when there has been a violation of a clearly established principle of law resulting in a miscarriage of justice."

Id. at § 1705:1 (footnotes omitted).

The limited review provided by a second-tier certiorari is represented well by the facts and holding of *Futch v. Florida Dept. of Highway Safety & Motor Vehicles*, 189 So. 3d 131 (Fla. 2016).

FUTCH

V.

FLORIDA DEPT. OF HIGHWAY SAFETY & MOTOR VEHICLES

Supreme Court of the State of Florida, 2016

189 So. 3d 131

Nils Futch seeks review of the decision of the Fifth District Court of Appeal in *Futch v. Department of Highway Safety & Motor Vehicles*, 142 So. 3d 910 (Fla. 5th DCA 2014), on the ground that it expressly and directly conflicts with two decisions of the Second District Court of Appeal in *Department of Highway Safety & Motor Vehicles v. Robinson*, 93 So. 3d 1090 (Fla. 2d DCA 2012), and *McLaughlin v. Department of Highway Safety & Motor Vehicles*, 128 So. 3d 815 (Fla. 2d DCA 2012), and a decision of the First District Court of Appeal in *Department of Highway Safety & Motor Vehicles v. Edenfield*, 58 So. 3d 904 (Fla. 1st DCA 2011), on a question of law. We have jurisdiction. See art. V, § 3(b)(3), Fla. Const. Because the Fifth District inappropriately granted certiorari review, we quash the district court's decision and remand for reinstatement of the circuit court's decision.

During a traffic stop, Futch allegedly refused to submit to a blood-alcohol test. The Department of Highway Safety and Motor Vehicles ("DHSMV") suspended Futch's driver license for one year, effective March 15, 2013. Futch sought review of the driver license suspension. See §§ 322.2615, 322.64, Fla. Stat. (2012). During the administrative review, the hearing officer refused to permit Futch's counsel to ask more than two questions of Futch's expert witness. The hearing officer subsequently upheld the suspension. On certiorari review of the administrative decision, the circuit court found that the hearing officer's actions denied Futch due process, and invalidated the suspension. *Futch v. Dep't of Highway Safety & Motor Vehs.*, 21 Fla. L. Weekly Supp. 16, 18 (Fla. 7th Cir.Ct. Sept. 3, 2013). On second-tier certiorari review of the circuit court's decision, the Fifth District agreed with the circuit court that the hearing officer violated Futch's due process by refusing to allow his expert to testify. See *Futch*, 142 So. 3d at 915. However, the Fifth District held that the circuit court was required to remand the case back to DHSMV for another administrative hearing, and "that the circuit court misapplied the law when it directed DHSMV to set aside the suspension and reinstate Futch's driver's license." Id. at 916.

"Appellate courts must exercise caution not to expand certiorari jurisdiction to review the correctness of the circuit court's decision." *Nader v. Dep't of Highway Safety & Motor Vehs.*, 87 So. 3d 712, 723 (Fla. 2012); see also *Haines City Cmty. Dev. v. Heggs*, 658 So. 2d 523, 526 (Fla. 1995). "The departure from the essential requirements of law necessary for the issuance of a writ of certiorari is something more than a simple legal error." *Allstate Ins. Co. v. Kaklamanos*, 843 So. 2d 885, 889 (Fla.2003). Certiorari is appropriate "only when there has been a violation of a clearly established principle of law resulting in a miscarriage of justice." *Id.*

Here, the Fifth District inappropriately exercised its certiorari jurisdiction to review the circuit court order. We reassert that "second-tier certiorari should not be used simply to grant a second appeal; rather, it should be reserved for those situations when there has been a violation of a clearly established principle of law resulting in a miscarriage of justice." *Nader*, 87 So. 3d at 717; see also *Kaklamanos*, 843 So. 2d at 889. There was no miscarriage of justice here. Accordingly, because the Fifth District was without jurisdiction, we quash the decision below and remand for reinstatement of the circuit court's decision.

It is so ordered.

LABARGA, C.J., and PARIENTE, LEWIS, and QUINCE, JJ., concur.

CANADY, J., dissents with an opinion, in which POLSTON, J., concurs.

CANADY, J., dissenting.

Although I acknowledge that the Fifth District did not state that the granting of second-tier certiorari relief requires a showing that the circuit court violated a clearly established principle of law resulting in a miscarriage of justice, I nevertheless would approve the result reached by the district court.

On second-tier certiorari review, the district court must consider "whether the circuit court afforded procedural due process and whether the circuit court applied the correct law.... [T]hese two components are merely expressions of ways in which the circuit court decision may have departed from the essential requirements of the law." *Haines City Cmty. Dev. v. Heggs*, 658 So. 2d 523, 530 (Fla.1995). A district court may only exercise its discretion to grant second-tier certiorari relief when the circuit court "has violated a clearly established principle of law resulting in a miscarriage of justice." *Custer Med. Ctr. v. United Auto. Ins. Co.*, 62 So. 3d 1086, 1092 (Fla.2010).

When a circuit court reviewing an administrative order determines that certiorari relief is warranted, the court has only one option—namely, to "quash the order reviewed." *Broward Cty. v. G.B.V. Int'l, Ltd.*, 787 So. 2d 838, 844 (Fla. 2001). And when an order is quashed on certiorari review, "it leaves the subject matter, that is, the controversy pending before the tribunal, commission, or administrative authority, as if no order or judgment had been entered. " *G.B.V.*, 787 So. 2d at 844. The law is clearly established that "the reviewing court has no power when exercising its jurisdiction in certiorari to enter a judgment on the merits of the controversy under consideration, nor to direct the tribunal, commission, or administrative authority to enter any particular order or judgment." Id. Consistent with these principles of law, the Fifth District "ha[s] consistently held that when a circuit court quashes a hearing officer's order on due process grounds, the matter is to be remanded to the hearing officer for further proceedings." *Futch*, 142 So. 3d at 915.

In this case, the Fifth District correctly recognized that this clearly established principle of law required the circuit court to remand the case for another administrative hearing. See, e.g., *G.B.V.*, 787 So. 2d at 844. Accordingly, because the circuit court invalidated the suspension of Futch's driver license—without the authority to do so—instead of quashing the order and remanding the case, the circuit court disregarded this Court's precedent and the Fifth District's precedent requiring that the matter be remanded for further proceedings. In doing so, the circuit court violated a clearly established principle of law.

Although the Fifth District did not expressly hold that the circuit court's violation of this clearly established principle of law resulted in a miscarriage of justice, I would conclude that the circuit court's error resulted in a miscarriage of justice that is "sufficiently egregious or fundamental to merit the extra review and safeguard provided by certiorari." *Heggs*, 658 So. 2d at 531. Specifically, the circuit court's error denied DHSMV the opportunity for the suspension of Futch's driver license to be properly considered by the hearing officer on the merits. The circuit court's error also resulted in a miscarriage of justice because it has precedential value in the Seventh Judicial Circuit, could affect many other administrative proceedings in that circuit, and substantially deprives DHSMV of its opportunity to sustain driver license suspensions in that circuit. Moreover, in holding that "no miscarriage of justice" occurred under the facts of this case, the majority has arguably created a scenario immune from second-tier certiorari review in which any circuit court in the State of Florida can invalidate any administrative driver license suspension on the sole basis that an evidentiary error violates due process. Majority op. at 132.

The circuit court not only transgressed the limitations on the authority of a court granting first-tier certiorari relief but also violated a cardinal rule of the appellate process. When an error made in a ruling on an evidentiary question is identified in a review proceeding, the result is not an automatic victory for the party aggrieved by the error. It is an "elementary" principle of the appellate process that "where findings are infirm because of an erroneous view of the law, a remand is the proper course unless the record permits only one resolution of the factual issue." *Pullman–Standard v. Swint*, 456 U.S. 273, 292 (1982). Indeed, no principle of the appellate process is more firmly-fixed and well-understood. The majority's conclusory decision contravening this principle holds the potential for much mischief.

In sum, the Fifth District was justified in granting certiorari relief because the circuit court violated a clearly established principle of law resulting in a miscarriage of justice. I dissent.

POLSTON, J., concurs.

6. Writ of Habeas Corpus

Florida's Constitution provides that "[t]he writ of habeas corpus shall be grantable of right, freely and without cost. It shall be returnable without delay, and shall never be suspended unless, in case of rebellion or invasion, suspension is essential to the public safety." Art. I, § 13, Fla. Const.

Florida's Supreme Court, in an opinion quoting heavily from Florida's First District Court of Appeal, provides a detailed recitation of the history and use of the "Great Writ," the Writ of Habeas Corpus, in *Henry v. Santana*, 62 So. 2d 1122 (Fla. 2011).

HENRY

V.

SANTANA

Supreme Court of Florida, 2011

62 So. 3d 1122

This case is before the Court for review of the decision of the First District Court of Appeal in *Santana v. Henry,* 12 So. 3d 843 (Fla. 1st DCA 2009). The district court certified that its decision is in direct conflict with the decision of the Third District Court of Appeal in *Pope v. State,* 898 So. 2d 253 (Fla. 3d DCA 2005). We have jurisdiction. *See* art. V, § 3(b)(4), Fla. Const.

The issue presented is whether a court may sua sponte dismiss a petition for a writ of habeas corpus, in which a prisoner is seeking immediate release, based upon the petitioner's failure to allege exhaustion of administrative remedies. As further explained below, we hold that such a petition may not be dismissed on such grounds where the issue of the petitioner's failure to exhaust administrative remedies has not been raised by the parties.

Facts and Procedural Background

On June 24, 2008, Santana, an inmate, filed a pro se petition for writ of habeas corpus in the circuit court in Jackson County, alleging that he was entitled to immediate release. He filed the petition against Mark Henry, warden of the facility in Jackson County where he was housed. Santana's claim concerned the sentences that were imposed on October 4, 2007, following his violation of probation (VOP). The relevant facts are set forth in the district court opinion below:

> Runner O. Santana appeals the dismissal of his petition for writ of habeas corpus alleging "that he is entitled to immediate release when properly credited with time served" and requesting "issuance of an Order com[m]anding the Florida Department of Corrections ... to immediately release" him. Without prior notice to the parties or input from them, the trial court summarily dismissed the petition. It reasoned, in part, that Mr. Santana failed to exhaust administrative remedies, although the Department of Corrections (DOC) never raised this below....
>
> The petition below alleges that, after his probation (in three separate cases) was revoked, Mr. Santana was sentenced anew on October 4, 2007, receiving three concurrent prison sentences. In case No. 95–CF–4926, the petition alleges, he was sentenced to six years in prison with credit for 2,023 days, to be followed by two years' probation; in case No. 96–CF–9601 to 60.75 months with credit for 831 days; and in case No. 96–CF–10668 to six years with credit for 1682 days. In addition, against each sentence, the petition alleges, he was awarded "credit for time served at the State Hospital," and a separate credit for 142 days for time spent in jail before the revocation hearing....
>
> Attached to the petition are the sentencing documents, as well as a transcript of the sentencing hearing.

Santana v. Henry, 12 So. 3d 843, 844–45 (Fla. 1st DCA 2009) (footnotes omitted).

The district court framed the issue before it narrowly, as follows:

> At issue is whether the habeas court properly dismissed the petition on its own motion without hearing from the authorities alleged to hold the petitioner unlawfully. We are not concerned here with mere conditions of confinement, or gain-time calculations not affecting DOC's current right to hold the petitioner, or anything less than a state prisoner's alleged right to immediate release from custody.

Id. at 845–46 (citations omitted). The district court then addressed the traditional role of the writ of habeas corpus versus the role of the doctrine of exhaustion of administrative remedies and held that the trial court erred in dismissing Santana's habeas petition on the basis of a technicality not raised by the parties—i.e., Santana's failure to allege that he had exhausted his administrative remedies:

> In any event, we hold the trial court erred by dismissing Mr. Santana's petition for writ of habeas corpus on the basis of a technicality—an assumed pleading defect—that was not raised by the parties. It is not clear DOC would have defended in this fashion, left to its own devices. "A trial judge may not sua sponte dismiss an action based on affirmative defenses not raised by proper pleadings." *Liton Lighting v. Platinum Television Group, Inc.,* 2 So. 3d 366, 367 (Fla. 4th DCA 2008).

Santana, 12 So. 3d at 847–48 (citations omitted). The district court ruled as follows:

> Mindful that the "writ of habeas corpus is the fundamental instrument for safeguarding individual freedom against arbitrary and lawless state action," *Harris v. Nelson,* 394 U.S. 286, 290–91 (1969), we reverse and remand with directions that the trial court issue an order to show cause to the Department of Corrections before proceeding further.

Santana, 12 So. 3d at 844–45 (citations omitted). The district court certified conflict with *Pope v. State,* 898 So. 2d 253 (Fla. 3d DCA 2005).[1] DOC sought review in this Court, which was granted.

Analysis

The writ of habeas corpus, or the Great Writ, is a high prerogative writ and, when properly issued, supersedes all other writs. *State ex rel. Perky v. Browne,* 142 So. 247, 248 (1932). The writ, which literally means "that you have the body," is a writ of inquiry and has traditionally been used to compel the custodian of the prisoner to bring the body of the prisoner into court so that the legality of the detention might be tested. This Court in *State ex rel. Deeb v. Fabisinski,* 152 So. 207 (1933), addressed the deep roots of the writ in Anglo–American jurisprudence:

> The great writ, known commonly by the name of "habeas corpus," was a high prerogative writ known to the common law, the object of which was the liberation of those who were imprisoned without sufficient cause. *See Ex parte Watkins,* 3 Pet. (U.S.) 193, 7 L.Ed. 650 [(1830)].
>
> It is a writ of inquiry upon matters of which the state itself is concerned in aid of right and liberty....
>
> The name of the writ is "habeas corpus ad subjiciendum et recipiendum." It is not an action or suit, but is a summary remedy open to the person detained. It is civil rather than criminal in nature and is a legal and not equitable remedy. *See Ex parte Watkins, supra; Ex parte Bollman,* 4 Cranch (U.S.) 75, 2 L.Ed. 554 [(1807)].
>
> ... [W]hile the writ had been in use in England from remote antiquity, it was often assailed by kings who sought tyrannical power and the benefits of the writ were in a great degree eluded by time-serving judges who assumed a discretionary power in awarding or refusing it and were disposed to support royal and ministerial usurpations. Owing to such abuses, the writ became powerless to release persons imprisoned without any cause assigned. In the fight by the people against the abuses of the writ, petitions of rights were submitted to the king, and during the reign of Charles I, A.D. 1641, provisions were enacted intended to make the writ effectual. These activities were, however, in vain. At last, in 1679, the Statute 31 Chas. II, chap. 2, was enacted. That act is known as the [H]abeas [C]orpus [A]ct. That act has been substantially incorporated in-

to the jurisprudence of every state in the Union and the right to it secured by their Constitutions. The Constitution of the United States provides that the privilege of the writ of habeas corpus shall not be suspended except in certain circumstances. Article 1, § 9, par. 2, U.S. Const.

....

The great writ of habeas corpus is the one mentioned in Magna Charta in the year 1215; the writ which alone was the subject of the acts of 16 Chas. I and 31 Chas. II. It was the writ referred to in the Declaration of Independence and secured to the people of this country by the Constitution of the United States and the Constitutions of the different states.

Fabisinski, 152 So. at 209–10. This Court subsequently in *Allison v. Baker,* 11 So. 2d 578 (1943), reiterated the basic purpose of the writ:

> The writ of habeas corpus is a high prerogative writ of ancient origin designed to obtain immediate relief from unlawful imprisonment without sufficient legal reasons. Essentially, it is a writ of inquiry and is issued to test the reasons or grounds of restraint and detention. The writ is venerated by all free and liberty loving people and recognized as a fundamental guaranty and protection of their right of liberty.

Id. at 579.

Given the basic purpose and fundamental importance of the writ, this Court has long recognized the necessity of informality and tolerance with regard to the pleading requirements for the writ:

> The writ of habeas corpus is a writ of right. It is sometimes issued upon very informal application. *Ex parte Pells,* 9 So. 833 [(1891)]. Neither the right to the writ nor the right to be discharged from custody in a proper case is made to depend upon meticulous observance of the rules of pleading. The purpose of bringing the petitioner before the court is to inquire into the legality of his detention, and if during the proceedings it appears formally or informally to the court's satisfaction that the person

> is unlawfully deprived of his liberty and is illegally detained in custody against his will he will be discharged.

Ex parte Amos, 112 So. 289, 291–92 (1927). This Court has emphasized this need for informality repeatedly:

> [H]istorically, habeas corpus is a high prerogative writ. It is as old as the common law itself and is an integral part of our own democratic process. The procedure for the granting of this particular writ is not to be circumscribed by hard and fast rules or technicalities which often accompany our consideration of other processes. If it appears to a court of competent jurisdiction that a man is being illegally restrained of his liberty, it is the responsibility of the court to brush aside formal technicalities and issue such appropriate orders as will do justice. In habeas corpus the niceties of the procedure are not anywhere near as important as the determination of the ultimate question as to the legality of the restraint.

Anglin v. Mayo, 88 So. 2d 918, 919–20 (Fla.1956). This Court has gone so far as to rule that "[n]o formal application for habeas corpus is required." *Martin v. State,* 166 So. 467, 467 (1936).

The gravamen of the issue before the Court is whether the writ of habeas corpus should be encumbered by a pleading requirement regarding the exhaustion of administrative remedies in those cases where an inmate is seeking immediate release. DOC contends that unless the inmate first exhausts administrative remedies, he or she will be unable to file an informed petition because the petition will be based on mere speculation concerning the inmate's term of imprisonment and release date. DOC also contends that if the inmate fails to exhaust administrative remedies, the courts too will be operating in the dark in the same respect. DOC contends that the district court's ruling below will encourage inmates to file free habeas petitions instead of utilizing the Department's internal grievance procedure. In brief, it appears that DOC, for its own purposes, would prefer to respond to such inmate inquiries via its own internal grievance procedure rather than respond to orders to show cause issued by the courts. In light of the above authorities, however, it appears that DOC's proposed pleading requirement is antithetical to the basic purpose and fundamental importance of the writ.

In the decision under review, the district court addressed at length the traditional role of the writ of habeas corpus in relation to the doctrine of exhaustion of remedies:

> "The writ of habeas corpus is a high prerogative writ of ancient origin designed to obtain immediate relief from unlawful imprisonment without sufficient legal reasons. Essentially, it is a writ of inquiry and is issued to test the reasons or grounds of restraint and detention. The writ is venerated by all free and liberty loving people and recognized as a fundamental guaranty and protection of their right of liberty." *Allison v. Baker,* 11 So. 2d 578, 579 (1943). "The great writ has its origins in antiquity and its parameters have been shaped by suffering and deprivation. It is more than a privilege with which free men are endowed by constitutional mandate; it is a writ of ancient right." *Jamason v. State,* 447 So. 2d 892, 894 (Fla. 4th DCA 1983). "[H]istorically, habeas corpus is a high prerogative writ. It is as old as the common law itself and is an integral part of our own democratic process." *Anglin v. Mayo,* 88 So. 2d 918, 919 (Fla. 1956).
>
> By comparison, judicial abstention in favor of exhaustion of administrative remedies is a relatively recent invention. The doctrine of exhaustion of remedies counsels against judicial intervention in the decision-making function of the executive branch in certain circumstances. Whether to require exhaustion of administrative remedies is a question of judicial "policy rather than power." *Gulf Pines Mem'l Park, Inc. v. Oaklawn Mem'l Park, Inc.,* 361 So. 2d 695, 699 (Fla. 1978). *See also State, Dep't of Revenue v. Brock,* 576 So. 2d 848, 850 (Fla. 1st DCA 1991) ("[T]he doctrine requiring the exhaustion of administrative remedies is not jurisdictional. The exhaustion requirement is a court-created prudential doctrine; it is a matter of policy, not of power." (citations omitted)).
>
> Notions of administrative autonomy have been thought to require that agencies be given the opportunity to discover and correct their own

errors, even after a case has reached the courts for judicial review of agency action. In some contexts, judicial restraint may be necessary "to support the integrity of the administrative process and to allow the executive branch to carry out its responsibilities as a co-equal branch of government." [*Key Haven Associated Enters., Inc. v. Bd. of Trs. of the Internal Improvement Trust Fund,* 427 So. 2d 153, 157 (Fla.1982)]. When an agency has discretion to exercise, it should of course be allowed to make discretionary decisions. If a party succeeds in vindicating its rights in the administrative process, thus obviating the need for judicial intervention, judicial resources are conserved; and immediate judicial access can weaken the effectiveness of an agency by encouraging people to ignore its procedures.

But the rationales for requiring exhaustion of administrative remedies diminish and disappear where an executive branch agency has little or no discretion to exercise and little or no expertise to bring to bear. The Department of Corrections does have discretion in deciding, for example, the conditions of confinement, and does have its own procedures on this subject deserving of judicial deference. On the other hand, the DOC has no discretion about which prisoners to release upon expiration of their sentences. Sentencing is a power, obligation, and prerogative of the courts, not the DOC.

....

... While the general rule is that exhaustion of administrative remedies is an affirmative defense, *see* Sylvia H. Walbolt, Matthew J. Conigliaro & J. Andrew Meyer, *Florida Civil Practice Before Trial,* § 25.34 at 25–30 (7th ed. 2004) ("Affirmative defenses to extraordinary writs include impossibility or lack of power to perform, laches, unclean hands, absence of parties whose substantial rights would be affected, illegality of purpose, detriment to the public interest, mootness, and failure to exhaust administrative remedies. *See* FLORIDA APPELLATE PRACTICE § 20.38 (Fla. Bar CLE 5th ed. 2003)"), moreover, in the prisoner habeas context, it has been held that certain petitions must allege exhaustion of administrative remedies in order to be facially suffi-

> cient. But none of the cases to which our attention has been drawn has laid down such a pleading requirement for petitions for writ of habeas corpus alleging entitlement to immediate release. The petitioners in [the other cases] sought relief from conditions of confinement or restoration of forfeited gain time, not immediate release from the DOC's custody.

Santana, 12 So. 3d at 846–47 (citations omitted).

The district court held that the trial court erred in dismissing Santana's habeas petition based on a technicality not raised by the parties, and the court then noted the following:

> The general rule that pleadings ought not be dismissed on grounds no party urges has special force when the pleading is a petition for writ of habeas corpus. "The scope and flexibility of the writ—its capacity to reach all manner of illegal detention—its ability to cut through barriers of form and procedural mazes—have always been emphasized and jealously guarded by courts and lawmakers. The very nature of the writ demands that it be administered with the initiative and flexibility essential to insure that miscarriages of justice within its reach are surfaced and corrected." *Harris v. Nelson,* 394 U.S. 286, 291 (1969). When a petition for writ of habeas corpus alleging that the petitioner is entitled to immediate release sets out plausible reasons and a specific factual basis in some detail, the custodian should be required to respond to the petition.

Santana, 12 So. 3d at 848 (citations omitted).

The district court added as a postscript the following passage explaining its ruling further:

> If in this case the petition had not been summarily denied and the trial court had instead ordered the DOC to show cause why Mr. Santana's petition should not be granted, the DOC might have resisted by moving to dismiss on exhaustion of administrative remedies grounds or for failure to allege exhaustion but it might also have decided that the petition was meritorious and released the petitioner. "The procedure for the granting of this particular writ [i.e., habeas corpus] is not to be

> circumscribed by hard and fast rules or technicalities which often accompany our consideration of other processes. If it appears to a court of competent jurisdiction that a man is being illegally restrained of his liberty, it is the responsibility of the court to brush aside formal technicalities and issue such appropriate orders as will do justice. In habeas corpus the niceties of the procedure are not anywhere near as important as the determination of the ultimate question as to the legality of the restraint." *Anglin,* 88 So. 2d at 919–20.

Santana, 12 So. 3d at 848 (brackets in original).

In light of the constitutional and statutory authorities and precedent from this Court noted above, we conclude that the district court below ruled correctly, and we hold that a petition for a writ of habeas corpus, in which a prisoner is seeking immediate release, may not be dismissed based upon the petitioner's failure to allege exhaustion of administrative remedies where such failure has not been raised by the parties.

Conclusion

Based on the above, we approve the First District Court of Appeal's decision below and disapprove the Third District Court of Appeal's decision in *Pope v. State,* 898 So. 2d 253 (Fla. 3d DCA 2005), to the extent it is inconsistent with this opinion.

It is so ordered.

Notes and Questions to Consider:

1. Although Florida's Constitution grants more than one court the authority to consider a Petition for Writ of Habeas Corpus, this does not mean that a prisoner may file for Habeas Corpus in each of these courts addressing the one same incarceration. In *Florida Parole & Prob. Comm'n v. Baker*, 346 So. 2d 640 (Fla. 2d DCA 1977), a prisoner filed but did not win a Petition for Writ of Habeas Corpus before Florida's Second District Court of Appeal. So the prisoner filed another Petition for Writ of Habeas Corpus, this

time with the circuit court. He won. The state appealed to Florida's Second District Court of Appeal, and they reversed, holding:

> The circuit, district and supreme courts have concurrent jurisdiction in habeas corpus. It is well established that a petitioner may not have three direct, repetitious applications for habeas corpus available to him upon the same subject matter. The two petitions both involve the same subject matter and, in fact, the petition filed in the circuit court was filed prior to this court's denial of appellee's petition for rehearing.
>
> For the reasons stated above we hold that the defense of res judicata is established on this record.
>
> The order appealed granting the writ of habeas corpus and ordering appellee released is hereby reversed and the cause remanded.

Id. at 641.

2. Florida Rule of Criminal Procedure 3.850(m) assists prisoners in determining the proper court for filing a Petition for Writ of Habeas Corpus. That rule provides:

> *Habeas Corpus*. An application for writ of habeas corpus on behalf of a prisoner who is authorized to apply for relief by motion pursuant to this rule shall not be entertained if it appears that the applicant has failed to apply for relief, by motion, to the court that sentenced the applicant or that the court has denied the applicant relief, unless it also appears that the remedy by motion is inadequate or ineffective to test the legality of the applicant's detention.

E. Quasi-Judicial Power

Does Florida's Constitution restrict judicial power solely to Florida's judiciary? To answer this question, first consider Article V of Florida's Constitution where it states:

> SECTION 1. *Courts.* -- [J]udicial power shall be vested in a Sup. Ct., [DCA's], circuit courts and county courts. No other courts may be established by the state, any political subdivision or any municipality....

Commissions established by law, or administrative officers or bodies may be granted quasi-judicial power in matters connected with the functions of their offices.

As the italicized language reveals, judicial power can be extended to other branches of government to use in matters connected with the functions of their offices. When judicial power is authorized, but is used by an entity other than Florida's judiciary, we call that use "quasi-judicial."

Therefore, by use of quasi-judicial powers, an administrative officer or body can hear a Floridian's complaint, consider the sworn testimony of the complainant and other witnesses, allow for cross-examination, accept documents into evidence, and issue an individualized ruling based upon the testimony and evidence, all without violating Florida's separation of powers.

Note and Question to Consider:

1. Of all the quasi-powers, quasi-judicial power is according the least deference by Florida's Courts. "Regardless of the method of review, the court exercises a more limited review of quasi-executive or quasi-legislative action than of quasi-judicial action." *Broward County v. Admin. Comm'n*, 321 So. 2d 605, 610 (Fla. 1st DCA 1975). In your opinion, why would this be appropriate?

Chapter Seven

Separation of Powers

A. Three Branches of State Government

In Florida's Constitution as in the U.S. Constitution, government consists of three branches: an executive, a legislative, and a judicial. Article II of Florida's Constitution provides:

> *SECTION 3. Branches of government.*—The powers of the state government shall be divided into legislative, executive and judicial branches. No person belonging to one branch shall exercise any powers appertaining to either of the other branches unless expressly provided herein.

This language is an explicit requirement for a separation of powers, unlike the U.S. Constitution, where such a separation is implicit.

Why separate powers in this way? One purpose for Florida's separation of powers is summarized and criticized in this excerpt from Daniel Webster & Donald L. Bell, *First Principles for Constitution Revision*, 22 Nova L. Rev. 391 (1997):

PROTECTING AGAINST TYRANNY:

THE SEPARATION OF POWERS

"In framing a government which is to be administered by men over men, the great difficulty lies in this: You must first enable the government to control the governed; and in the next place oblige it to control itself." The Federalist No. 51 at 322 (James Madison) (Clinton Rossiter ed., 1961). Tyranny arises most easily when all power is concentrated in the hands of a single person or in the hands of just a few. A constitution that divides power in numerous ways and in numerous directions will best serve the constitutional function of protecting against tyranny. Accordingly, the Florida Constitution, the United States Constitution, and the constitutions of the remaining forty-nine states divide government into three branches: the legislative, the executive, and the judiciary.

Dividing government powers on paper, however, does no good, if the divisions are not respected in practice. The federal government and the states vary in the extent to which they allow one branch of government to engage in the essential functions of another. About his vision for the federal system, Madison commented:

> In the compound republic of America, the power surrendered by the people is first divided between two distinct governments, and then the portion allotted to each subdivided among distinct and separate departments. Hence a double security arises to the rights of the people. The different governments will control each other, at the same time that each will be controlled by itself.

Thus, the framers of the Federal Constitution intended to create a system incorporating strong divisions of power. However, through judicial acquiescence and the constant pressure the branches of government exert on each other those divisions have largely given way.

The Florida Constitution, unlike its federal counterpart, contains an explicit separation of powers requirement. The purpose of this provision was to limit the extent to which any branch of government may perform functions assigned by the constitution to another branch. Florida courts have indicated that Florida's separation of powers requirement is stronger than the federal requirement because it is explicit.

Under Florida's doctrine against encroachment, no branch of government may encroach on the powers delegated to another branch by the constitution. For example, the Legislature cannot reserve to itself the right to execute the laws it creates because the power to execute the laws is reserved to the executive branch. Similarly, an officer of the executive branch cannot engage in lawmaking--a function that, because of its supreme nature, is reserved exclusively to the legislative branch adjudicate the rights or claims of an individual, a function reserved to the judicial branch.

A concordant policy, the doctrine of non-delegation, was intended to prevent the Legislature from delegating its lawmaking power to either of the other two branches of government. While it could, and should, be given stronger effect, the courts have at least found that the doctrine forbids the Legislature from delegating its core functions without any guidance or limits as to how those functions are to be exercised. The doctrine against encroachment and the doctrine of non-delegation are valuable policies derived from hundreds of years of wisdom. …[T]hese doctrines can provide the people with a high level of protection against tyranny…).

Notes and Questions to Consider:

1. Florida's Supreme Court holds: "We must zealously guard America's traditional separation of powers in the legislative, executive and judicial bodies of government; for that time tested formula will fail if each does not 'check and balance' the other." *Municipal Court, City of Fort Lauderdale v. Patrick*, 254 So. 2d 193, 194 (Fla. 1971). In the context of the separation of powers among the legislative, executive and judicial branches, what is meant by "checks and balances."

2. Florida's Supreme Court, in *Bush v. Schiavo*, 885 So. 2d 321 (Fla. 2004), observed that Florida case law precedent:

> "has traditionally applied a strict separation of powers doctrine," *State v. Cotton*, 769 So. 2d 345, 353 (Fla. 2000), and has explained that this doctrine "encompasses two fundamental prohibitions. The first is that no branch may encroach upon the powers of another. The second is that no branch may delegate to another branch its constitutionally assigned power." *Chiles v. Children A, B, C, D, E, & F*, 589 So. 2d 260, 264 (Fla. 1991).

Id. at 329 (citation omitted). Florida case law is replete with examples of laws or actions of government that Florida's courts held constitutionally infirm because one branch encroached upon the power of another. *See* John F. Cooper, Tishia A. Dunham and Carlos L. Woody, *Florida Constitutional Law: Cases and Materials* (Carolina Academic Press 5th ed. 2013) (citing *Florida House of Representatives v. Crist*, 999 So. 2d 601 (Fla. 2008) as an example of encroachment by Florida's executive upon the legislative; *Office of the State Attorney for the Eleventh Judicial Circuit v. Polites*, 904 So. 2d 527 (Fla. 3d DCA 2005) as an example of encroachment by Florida's judicial upon the executive; *Jones v. Chiles*, 638 So. 2d 48 (Fla. 1994) as an example of encroachment by Florida's legislative upon the executive; *McNeil v. Canty*, 12 So. 3d 215 (Fla. 2009) as an example of encroachment by Florida's executive upon the judicial; and *Bush v. Schiavo*, 885 So. 2d 321 (Fla. 2004) as an example of encroachment by Florida's legislative upon the judicial).

3. As noted in this text in its separate chapters addressing executive power, judicial power, and legislative power, Florida's Constitution, in a proper circumstance, allows for the use of quasi-executive, quasi-judicial, or quasi-legislative power. Despite these allowances, violations of the separation of powers can occur. The following case law provides some examples.

B. Dissention Among the Branches

Florida House of Representatives v. Crist, 999 So. 2d 601 (Fla. 2008) is a story of dissention between and among Florida's branches of government. The story begins with a federal law empowering Native American tribes to negotiate a compact with a state. Florida's Legislature's only response to the tribe was inaction. Florida's Governor acted when Florida's Legislature would not act, and when he did, Florida's Legislature complained to Florida's judicial branch that the Governor's actions were improper. As we follow this story, the opinion illustrates several concepts important to Florida's separation of powers.

FLORIDA HOUSE OF REPRESENTATIVES

V.

CRIST

Supreme Court of Florida, 2008

999 So. 2d 601

CANTERO, J.

After almost sixteen years of sporadic negotiations with four governors, in November 2007 the Seminole Indian Tribe of Florida signed a gambling "compact" (a contract between two sovereigns) with Florida Governor Charles Crist. The compact significantly expands casino gambling, also known as "gaming," on tribal lands. For example, it permits card games such as blackjack and baccarat that are otherwise prohibited by law. In return, the compact promises substantial remuneration to the State.

The Florida Legislature did not authorize the Governor to negotiate the compact before it was signed and has not ratified it since. To the contrary, shortly after the compact was signed, the Florida House of Representatives and its Speaker, Marco Rubio, filed in this Court a petition for a writ of quo warranto disputing the Governor's authority to bind the State to the compact. We have exercised our discretion to consider such petitions, *see* art. V, § 3(b)(8), Fla. Const., and now grant it on narrow grounds. We hold that the Governor does not have the constitutional authority to bind the State to a gaming compact that clearly departs from the State's public policy by legalizing types of gaming that are illegal everywhere else in the state.

In the remainder of this opinion, we describe the history of Indian gaming compacts in general and the negotiations leading up to the compact at issue. We then explain our jurisdiction to consider the petition. Finally, we discuss the applicable constitutional provisions, statutes, and cases governing our decision.

I. THE FACTUAL AND LEGAL BACKGROUND

We analyze the compact in the context of the federal regulations authorizing it as well as the background of the negotiations in this case. We first review the statutory foundation for the compact: the Indian Gaming Regulatory Act, 25 U.S.C. §§ 2701–2721 (2000) (IGRA). Next, we detail the history of the Tribe's attempts to negotiate a compact with the State. Finally, we explain the compact's relevant terms.

A. IGRA

Indian tribes are independent sovereigns. The Indian Commerce Clause of the United States Constitution grants only Congress the power to override their sovereignty on Indian lands. U.S. Const., art. I, § 8, cl. 3 ("The Congress shall have Power ... [t]o regulate Commerce with ... the Indian Tribes."); *see also California v. Cabazon Band of Mission Indians,* 480 U.S. 202, 207, 107 S.Ct. 1083, 94 L.Ed.2d 244 (1987) (noting that tribal sovereignty is subordinate only to the federal government). Before IGRA, states had no role in regulating Indian gaming. *See Cabazon,* 480 U.S. at 202, 107 S.Ct. 1083.

Congress enacted IGRA in 1988. Among other things, the statute provides "a statutory basis for the operation of gaming by Indian tribes as a means of promoting tribal economic development, self-sufficiency, and strong tribal governments." 25 U.S.C. § 2702(1). IGRA divides gaming into three classes: Class I includes "social games solely for prizes of minimal value." *Id.* § 2703(6). Class II includes "the game of chance commonly known as bingo" and "non-banked" card games—that is, games in which participants play against only each other; the host facility (the "house") has no stake in the outcome. *Id.* § 2703(7). Class III—the only type relevant here—comprises all other types of gaming, including slot machines, pari-mutuel wagering (such as horse and greyhound racing), lotteries, and "banked" card games—such as baccarat, blackjack (twenty-one), and *chemin de fer*—in which participants play against the house. *Id.* § 2703(6)-(8).

IGRA permits Class III gaming on tribal lands, but only in limited circumstances. It is lawful *only* if it is (1) authorized by tribal ordinance, (2) "located in a State that permits such gaming for any purpose by any person, organization, or entity," and (3) "conducted in accordance with a Tribal–State compact entered into by the Indian tribe and the State ... *that is in effect.*" *Id.* § 2710(d)(1) (emphasis added).

IGRA provides for tribes to negotiate compacts with their host states. Upon a tribe's request, a state "*shall* negotiate with the Indian tribe in good faith to enter into such a compact." *Id.* § 2710(d)(3)(A) (emphasis added). If the parties successfully negotiate a compact and the Secretary of the Department of the Interior (Department) approves it, the compact takes effect "when notice of approval by the Secretary" is published in the Federal Register. *Id.* § 2710(d)(3)(B), (8).

If negotiations fail, IGRA allows a tribe to sue the state in federal court. If the state continues to refuse consent, the Secretary may "prescribe ... procedures" permitting Class III gaming. *See id.* § 2710(d)(7)(B)(vii). The United States Supreme Court has held, however—in a case involving the Seminole Tribe's attempts to offer Class III gaming in Florida—that IGRA did not abrogate the states' Eleventh Amendment immunity. *See Seminole Tribe of Fla. v. Florida,* 517 U.S. 44, 47, 116 S.Ct. 1114, 134 L.Ed.2d 252 (1996). Therefore, states need not consent to such lawsuits. The Department later created an alternative procedure under which, when a tribe cannot negotiate a compact and a state asserts immunity, the Secretary may prescribe Class III gaming. *See* Class III Gaming Procedures, 64 Fed.Reg. 17535–02 (Apr. 12, 1999) (codified at 25 C.F.R. pt. 291 (2007)). At least one federal court, however, has held that the Secretary lacked authority to promulgate such regulations. *See Texas v. United States,* 497 F.3d 491, 493 (5th Cir.2007), *petition for cert. filed sub nom. Kickapoo Traditional Tribe of Texas v. Texas,* 76 U.S.L.W. 3471 (U.S. Feb. 25, 2008) (No. 07–1109). Therefore, their validity remains questionable.

B. The Negotiations Between the Tribe and the State

With this statutory framework in mind, we briefly describe the protracted history of the Seminole Tribe's efforts to negotiate a compact for conducting Class III gaming in Florida. These negotiations spanned sixteen years and four different governors.

The Seminole Indian Tribe is a federally recognized Indian tribe whose reservations and trust lands are located in the State. The Tribe currently operates Class II gaming facilities, offering low stakes poker games and electronically aided bingo games. The Tribe first sought a compact allowing it to offer Class III gaming in 1991. That January, the Tribe and Governor Lawton Chiles began negotiations, but they ultimately proved fruitless. That same year, the Tribe filed suit in federal court alleging that the State had failed to negotiate in good faith. As noted earlier, the Supreme Court ultimately ruled that the State could assert immunity, and it did. *See Seminole Tribe,* 517 U.S. at 47, *aff'g Seminole Tribe of Fla. v. Fla.,* 11 F.3d 1016 (11th Cir.1994).

Over the next several years, the Tribe repeatedly petitioned the Department to establish Class III gaming procedures. In 1999, the Department did so. It found the Tribe eligible for the procedures and called an informal conference, which was held in Tallahassee that December. At the State's suggestion, however, the Tribe agreed to suspend the conference, though only temporarily. In January 2001, the Secretary issued a twenty-page decision allowing the Tribe to offer a wide range of Class III games. When the State requested clarification, however, the Secretary withdrew the decision. The delay continued. Finally, five years later—in May 2006—the Department reconvened the conference in Hollywood, Florida, and in September of that year warned that if the Tribe and the State did not execute a compact within 60 days, the Department would issue Class III gaming procedures. Despite the parties' failure to negotiate a compact, however, the Department never issued procedures.

Apparently exasperated with the slow progress of the procedures, in March 2007 the Tribe sued the Department in federal court. *See Seminole Tribe of Fla. v. United States,* No. 07–60317–CIV, 2007 WL 5077484 (S.D. Fla. filed Mar. 6, 2007). The Department then urged Governor Crist to negotiate a compact, warning that if a compact was not signed by November 15, 2007, the Department would finally issue procedures. Under the proposed procedures, the State would not receive any revenue and would have no control over the Tribe's gaming operations. The Tribe would be authorized to operate slot machines and "card games," defined as "a game or series of games of poker (other than Class II games) which are played in a *nonbanking* manner." (Emphasis added.) Notably, the alternative procedures would *not* have permitted the Tribe to operate banked card games such as blackjack.

On November 14—the day before the deadline—the Governor agreed to a compact with the Tribe (Compact). Five days later, the House and its

Speaker, Marco Rubio, filed this petition disputing the Governor's authority to bind the State to the Compact without legislative authorization or ratification. We allowed the Tribe to join the action as a respondent.

On January 7, 2008, upon publication of the Secretary's approval, the Compact went into effect. *See* Notice of Deemed Approved Tribal–State Class III Gaming Compact, 73 Fed.Reg. 1229 (Jan. 7, 2008). The parties agree, however, that the Secretary's approval does not render the petition moot.

C. The Compact

The Compact recites that the Governor "has the authority to act for the State with respect to the negotiation and execution of this Compact." It covers a period of twenty-five years and allows the Tribe to offer specified Class III gaming at seven casinos in the State. It establishes the terms, rights, and responsibilities of the parties regarding such gaming. We discuss only its more relevant provisions.

The Compact authorizes the Tribe to conduct "covered gaming," which includes several types of Class III gaming: slot machines; any banking or banked card game, including baccarat, blackjack (twenty-one), and *chemin de fer;* high stakes poker games; games and devices authorized for the state lottery; and any new game authorized by Florida law. The Compact expressly does *not* authorize roulette- or craps-style games. The gaming is limited to seven casinos on tribal lands in six areas of the state: Okeechobee, Coconut Creek, Hollywood (two), Clewiston, Immokalee, and Tampa. Compact pt. IV.B., at 7–8.

The Compact grants the Tribe the exclusive right to conduct certain types of gaming. That is, the Tribe may conduct some Class III gaming, such as banked card games, that is prohibited under state law. Based on that "partial but substantial exclusivity," the Tribe must pay the State a share of the gaming revenue. That share is based in part on amounts that increase at specified thresholds: when the Compact becomes effective, the State receives $50 million. Over the first twenty-four months of operation, it will receive another $175 million. Thereafter, for the third twelve months of operation the State will receive $150 million, and for each twelve-month cycle after that, a minimum of $100 million. If the State breaches the exclusivity provision, however—by legalizing any Class III gaming currently prohibited under state law—the Tribe may cease its payments. The Compact (attached as an appendix to this opinion) is thirty-seven pages long and contains several other provisions we need not detail here.

II. JURISDICTION

Before discussing the issue presented, we first address our jurisdiction. The House and Speaker Rubio have filed in this Court a petition for writ of quo warranto. The Governor contends that this Court lacks jurisdiction because the House does not seek either to remove him from office or to enjoin the future exercise of his authority. We conclude, however, that these are not the only grounds for issuing such a writ.

The Florida Constitution authorizes this Court to issue writs of quo warranto to "state officers and state agencies." Art. V, § 3(b)(8), Fla. Const. The term "quo warranto" means "by what authority." This writ historically has been used to determine whether a state officer or agency has improperly exercised a power or right derived from the State. *See Martinez v. Martinez,* 545 So. 2d 1338, 1339 (Fla. 1989); *see also* art. V, § 3(b)(8), Fla. Const. Here, the Governor is a state officer. The House challenges the Governor's authority to unilaterally execute the Compact on the State's behalf.

The Governor argues that because he already has signed the Compact, quo warranto relief is inappropriate. But the writ is not so limited. In fact, petitions for the writ historically have been filed *after* a public official has acted. *See, e.g., Chiles v. Phelps,* 714 So. 2d 453, 455 (Fla. 1998) (holding that the Legislature and its officers exceeded their authority in overriding the Governor's veto); *State ex rel. Butterworth v. Kenny,* 714 So. 2d 404, 406 (Fla. 1998) (issuing the writ after the Capital Collateral Regional Counsel had filed a federal civil rights suit, concluding that it had no authority to file it). The Governor's execution of the Compact does not defeat our jurisdiction.

The concurring-in-result-only opinion expresses concern that by considering a more narrow issue than the Governor's authority to execute IGRA compacts in general—that is, whether the Governor has the authority to bind the State to a compact that violates Florida law—we are expanding our quo warranto jurisdiction to include issues normally reserved for declaratory judgment actions. In prior quo warranto cases, however, we have considered separation-of-powers arguments normally reviewed in the context of declaratory judgments, such as whether the Governor's action has usurped the Legislature's power, "where the functions of government would be adversely affected absent an immediate determination by this Court." *Phelps,* 714 So. 2d at 457; *see also Martinez,* 545 So. 2d at 1339 (holding quo warranto appropriate to test the governor's power to call special sessions); *Orange County v. City of Orlando,* 327 So. 2d 7 (Fla. 1976) (holding that the legality of city's actions regarding annexation ordinances can be inquired into through quo warranto).

In this case, the Secretary has approved the Compact and, absent an immediate judicial resolution, it will be given effect. In fact, according to news reports, the Tribe already has begun offering blackjack and other games at the Seminole Hard Rock Hotel and Casino. *See* Amy Driscoll, "Casino Gambling: Amid glitz, blackjack's in the cards," The Miami Herald, June 23, 2008, at B1. Thus, if indeed the Governor has exceeded his constitutional authority, a compact that violates Florida law will, nevertheless, become effective in seven casinos located on tribal lands located in the state. As in *Phelps,* therefore, the importance and immediacy of the issue justifies our deciding this matter now rather than transferring it for resolution in a declaratory judgment action.

III. DISCUSSION OF LAW

We now discuss the law that applies to this inter-branch dispute. In deciding whether the Governor or the Legislature has the authority to execute a compact, we first define a "compact" and its historical use in Florida. We then discuss how other jurisdictions have resolved this issue. Next, we review the relevant provisions of our own constitution. Finally, we explain our conclusion that the Governor lacked authority under our state's constitution to execute the Compact because it changes the state's public policy as expressed in the criminal law and therefore infringes on the Legislature's powers.

A. Compacts and their Use in Florida

A compact is essentially a contract between two sovereigns. *Texas v. New Mexico,* 482 U.S. 124, 128 (1987); *see Black's Law Dictionary* 298 (8th ed.1999) (defining a compact as "[a]n agreement or covenant between two or more parties, esp[ecially] between governments or states"). The United States Supreme Court has described compacts as "a supple device for dealing with interests confined within a region." *State ex rel. Dyer v. Sims,* 341 U.S. 22, 27 (1951). The United States Constitution provides that "[n]o State shall, without the Consent of Congress ... enter into any Agreement or Compact with another State, or with a foreign Power." U.S. Const, art. I, § 10. IGRA establishes the consent of Congress to execute gaming compacts, but requires federal approval before they become effective. *See* 25 U.S.C. § 2710(d)(8).

Like many states, Florida has executed compacts on a range of subjects, including environmental control, water rights, energy, and education—more than thirty in all. The vast majority were executed with other states. In most cases, the Legislature enacted a law. *See, e.g.,* § 372.831, Fla. Stat. (2007) ("The Wildlife Violator Compact is created and entered into with all other jurisdictions legally joining therein in the form substantially as follows[.]"); § 257.28 (Interstate Library Compact); § 252.921 (Emergency Management Assistance Compact); § 322.44 (Driver License Compact). In others, the Legislature authorized the Governor to execute a compact in the form provided in a statute. *See, e.g.,* § 370.19, Fla. Stat. (2007) ("The Governor of this state is hereby authorized and directed to execute a compact on behalf of the State of Florida with any one or more of [the following states] ... legally joining therein in the form substantially as follows [.]"); § 370.20 (containing the same authorization and establishing the terms for the Gulf States Marine Fisheries Compact); § 403.60 (using the same authorization language for the Interstate Environmental Control Compact, establishing its terms, and "signi[ying] in advance" the Legislature's "approval and ratification of such compact"). In a few—including a compact among the State, the Tribe, and the South Florida Water Management District regulating water use on Tribal lands—the Legislature by statute approved and ratified the compact. § 285.165, Fla. Stat. (2007). Thus, by tradition at least, it is the Legislature that has consistently either exercised itself or expressly authorized the exercise of the power to bind the State to compacts. We have found no instance in which the governor has signed a compact without legislative involvement.

Although tradition bears some relevance, it does not resolve the question of which branch actually has the constitutional authority to execute compacts in general and gaming compacts in particular. As explained above, the Compact here governs Class III gaming on certain tribal lands in Florida. The issue is whether, regardless of whether the Governor bucked tradition, he had constitutional authority to execute the Compact without the Legislature's prior authorization or, at least, subsequent ratification.

B. How Other Courts Have Answered the Question

Although Florida has not addressed a governor's authority to bind a state to an IGRA compact, other states have....

In all these cases, to determine which branch had the authority to bind the state to the compact, courts analyzed the nature and effect of the IGRA compact at issue and compared it to the powers the state constitution delegated to the respective branches. The courts found the compacts within the legislative power because they created or assigned new duties to agencies, conflicted with state law, changed state law, or restricted the legislature's power. Finally, recognizing that state legislative power is limited only by the state and federal constitutions, several courts have ascribed to the legislature, rather than the executive, any residual power on which the state constitutions were silent. *See Clark,* 904 P.2d at 25; *Pataki,* 766 N.Y.S.2d at 668 n. 11, 798 N.E.2d at 1061 n. 11. We now review our own state constitution in the context of IGRA's provisions and the Compact signed in this case.

C. Florida Constitutional Provisions

The House contends that several of the Compact's provisions encroach on the Legislature's law- and policy-making powers. To answer the question, we first review the separation-of-powers provisions of the Florida Constitution and our interpretations of it. We then discuss one specific provision on which the Governor relies: the "necessary business" clause.

1. The Florida Constitution's Delegation and Separation of Powers

The Florida Constitution generally specifies the relative powers of the three branches of government. Article II, section 3 provides innocuously that "[t]he powers of the state government shall be divided into legislative, executive and judicial branches. No person belonging to one branch shall exercise any powers appertaining to either of the other branches unless expressly provided herein." In construing our constitution, we have "traditionally applied a strict separation of powers doctrine." *Bush v. Schiavo,* 885 So. 2d 321, 329 (Fla. 2004) (quoting *State v. Cotton,* 769 So. 2d 345, 353 (Fla. 2000)).

These provisions are not specific, however. In fact, as we first noted 100 years ago, the state constitution does not exhaustively list each branch's powers. *State v. Atlantic Coast Line R.R. Co.,* 47 So. 969, 974 (1908). Both the Governor and the House concede that the state constitution does not expressly grant *either* branch the authority to execute compacts.

We must therefore expand our analysis beyond the plain language of the constitution. We have held that the powers of the respective branches "are those so defined ... or such as are inherent or so recognized by immemorial governmental usage, and which involve the exercise of primary and independent will, discretion, and judgment, subject not to the control of another department, but only to the limitations imposed by the state and federal Constitutions." *Id.* at 974. A branch has "the inherent right to accomplish all objects naturally within the orbit of that department, not expressly limited by the fact of the existence of a similar power elsewhere or the express limitations in the constitution." *Sun Ins. Office, Ltd. v. Clay,* 133 So. 2d 735, 742 (Fla. 1961) (quoting *In re Integration of Neb. State Bar Ass'n,* 275 N.W. 265,

266 (1937)). As we noted over seventy-five years ago, what determines whether a particular function is legislative, executive, or judicial "so that it may be exercised by appropriate officers of the proper department" is not "the name given to the function or to the officer who performs it" but the "essential nature and effect of the governmental function to be performed." *Florida Motor Lines v. Railroad Comm'rs,* 129 So. 876, 881 (1930).

The House argues that, precisely because the state constitution does not expressly grant the governor authority to execute compacts, such authority belongs to the Legislature. In other words, the "residual" power—that is, powers not specifically assigned to the governor—belongs to the Legislature. Albeit many years ago and under different circumstances, we have implied as much. *See State ex rel. Green v. Pearson,* 14 So. 2d 565, 567 (1943) ("The legislative branch looks to the Constitution not for sources of power but for limitations upon power. But if such limitations are not found to exist, its discretion reasonably exercised may not be disturbed by the judicial branch of the government."); *State ex rel. Cunningham v. Davis,* 166 So. 289, 297 (1936) ("The test of legislative power is constitutional restriction; what the people have not said in their organic law their representatives shall not do, they may do."). And, as we noted above, other state courts have ascribed to their legislatures any residual power on which the state constitutions were silent. *See Clark,* 904 P.2d at 25; *Pataki,* 766 N.Y.S.2d at 668, n. 11, 798 N.E.2d at 1061 n. 11.

We need not decide, however, whether the authority to bind the state to compacts always resides in the legislature. Although the line of demarcation is not always clear, we have noted that "the legislature's exclusive power encompasses questions of fundamental policy and the articulation of reasonably definite standards to be used in implementing those policies." *B.H. v. State,* 645 So. 2d 987, 993 (Fla. 1994); *see also Askew v. Cross Key Waterways,* 372 So. 2d 913, 925 (Fla. 1978) (stating that under the nondelegation doctrine, "fundamental and primary policy decisions shall be made by members of the legislature"). Therefore, even if the Governor has authority to execute compacts, its terms cannot contradict the state's public policy, as expressed in its laws.

2. IGRA and the "Necessary Business" Clause

The Governor argues that his authority to execute the Compact derives from article IV, section 1 of the Florida Constitution. That provision states in part that "[t]he governor shall take care that the laws be faithfully executed ... and transact all necessary business with the officers of government." Art. IV, § 1(a), Fla. Const. The Governor submits that the phrase "transact all necessary business with the officers of government" includes negotiating with the Tribe and that he cannot ignore the federal directive to "negotiate"; therefore, negotiating the Compact was "necessary business" under IGRA.

IGRA provides that a tribe seeking to offer Class III gaming must "request [that] the State ... enter into negotiations" for a compact and that the "State shall negotiate with the Indian tribe in good faith." 25 U.S.C. § 2710(d)(3)(A). The Governor is therefore correct that IGRA requires states to negotiate. As other courts have recognized, however, nowhere does IGRA equate "the state" with "the governor." *See Seminole Tribe,* 517 U.S. at 75 n. 17 (contrasting IGRA's "repeated[ ] refer[ences] exclusively to 'the State' " with other federal statutes directed at a state's governor and concluding that "the duty imposed by the Act ... is not of the sort likely to be performed by an individual state executive officer or even a group of officers"); *Seminole Tribe,* 11 F.3d at 1029 ("IGRA uniformly addresses itself to 'the State'; not once does it impose duties or responsibilities on a particular officer of the state (e.g., the governor, the legislature, etc.)."). In addition, when a state fails to negotiate, a tribe must sue the *state*, not the governor. *Seminole Tribe,* 517 U.S. at 74–75 (holding that Congress intended § 2710(d)(3) to be enforced against the state, not the governor); *Seminole Tribe,* 11 F.3d at 1029 ("[T]hese suits are not against officials in an attempt to force them to follow federal law.").

More importantly, a State's "duty to negotiate" under IGRA cannot be enforced. A state may avoid its duty, as Florida has effectively done, by asserting its immunity. *Seminole Tribe,* 517 U.S. at 47, 116 S.Ct. 1114. Therefore, although IGRA requires a state to negotiate, it does not impose any duty on a state's governor. Moreover, IGRA does not prescribe the terms of a compact, *see* 25 U.S.C. § 2710(d), and it does not confer on the governor the authority to bind the state to a compact or act in contravention to state law. In other words, IGRA does not grant a governor, or any state actor, any powers beyond those provided by the state's constitution and laws. *See Clark,* 904 P.2d at 26 ("We do not agree that Congress, in enacting the IGRA, sought to invest state governors with powers in excess of those that the governors possess under state law.").

We express no opinion on whether the "necessary business" clause may ever grant the governor authority to bind the State to an IGRA compact. We do conclude, however, that the clause does not authorize the governor to execute compacts contrary to the expressed public policy of the state or to create exceptions to the law. Nor does it change our conclusion that "the legislature's exclusive power encompasses questions of fundamental policy and the articulation of reasonably definite standards to be used in implementing those policies." *B.H.,* 645 So. 2d at 993.

We now discuss why, in authorizing conduct prohibited by state law, the Governor exceeded his authority.

D. The Compact Violates the Separation of Powers

The House claims that the Compact violates the separation of powers on a number of grounds. We find one of them dispositive. The Compact permits the Tribe to conduct certain Class III gaming that is prohibited under Florida law. Therefore, the Compact violates the state's public policy about the types of gambling that should be allowed. We hold that, whatever the Governor's authority to execute compacts, it does not extend so far. The Governor does not have authority to agree to legalize in some parts of the state, or for some persons, conduct that is otherwise illegal throughout the state.

We first discuss whether state laws in general, and gaming laws in particular, apply to Indian tribes. We next discuss Florida law on gaming. We then address the House's argument that IGRA prohibits compacts from expanding the gaming allowed under state law. Finally, we explain why the

Governor lacked authority to bind the State to a compact, such as this one, that contradicts state law.

1. State Gaming Laws Apply to the Tribe

Generally, state laws do not apply to tribal Indians on Indian reservations unless Congress so provides. *McClanahan v. State Tax Comm'n of Ariz.,* 411 U.S. 164, 170, 93 S.Ct. 1257, 36 L.Ed.2d 129 (1973). Therefore, the extent to which a state may enforce its criminal laws on tribal land depends on federal authorization. *See Seminole Tribe of Fla. v. Butterworth,* 658 F.2d 310, 312 (5th Cir.1981). Congress has, however, conferred on the states the authority to assume jurisdiction over crimes committed on tribal land, *see* Act of Aug. 15, 1953, Pub.L. No. 280 § 6, 67 Stat. 588, 590 (1953), and Florida has assumed such jurisdiction. *See* ch. 61–252, §§ 1–2, at 452–53, Laws of Fla. (codified at § 285.16, Fla. Stat. (2007)); *see also* § 285.16(2), Fla. Stat. (2007) ("The civil and criminal laws of Florida shall obtain on all Indian reservations in this state and shall be enforced in the same manner as elsewhere throughout the state."); Op. Att'y Gen. Fla. 94–45 (1994) (discussing the state's jurisdiction over Indian reservations). The state's law is therefore enforceable on tribal lands to the extent it does not conflict with federal law. *See* Op. Att'y Gen. Fla. 94–45 (1994); *see also Hall v. State,* 762 So. 2d 936, 936–38 (Fla. 2d DCA 2000) (holding that the circuit court had jurisdiction over a vehicular homicide on an Indian reservation); *State v. Billie,* 497 So. 2d 889, 892–95 (Fla. 2d DCA 1986) (holding that a Seminole Indian was properly charged under state criminal law with killing a Florida panther on tribal land). In regard to gambling in particular, federal law provides that, except as provided in a tribal-state compact, state gambling laws apply on tribal lands. *See* 18 U.S.C. § 1166(a) (2000).

Based on these state and federal provisions, what is legal in Florida is legal on tribal lands, and what is illegal in Florida is illegal there. Absent a compact, any gambling prohibited in the state is prohibited on tribal land.

2. Florida's Gaming Laws

It is undisputed that Florida permits limited forms of Class III gaming. The state's constitution authorizes the state lottery, which offers various Class III games, and now permits slot machines in Miami–Dade and Broward Counties. *See* art. X, §§ 7, 15, Fla. Const. For a long time, the State also has regulated pari-mutuel wagering—for example, on dog and horse racing. *See* ch. 550, Fla. Stat. (2007) (governing pari-mutuel wagering).

It is also undisputed, however, that the State prohibits all other types of Class III gaming, including lotteries not sponsored by the State and slot machines outside Miami–Dade and Broward Counties. Florida law distinguishes between nonbanked (Class II) card games and banked (Class III) card games. A "banking game" is one "in which the house is a participant in the game, taking on players, paying winners, and collecting from losers or in which the cardroom establishes a bank against which participants play." § 849.086(2)(b); *see* § 849.086(1), Fla. Stat. (deeming banked games to be "casino gaming"). Florida law authorizes cardrooms at pari-mutuel facilities for games of "poker or dominoes," but only if they are played "in a nonbanking manner." § 849.086(2), Fla. Stat.; *see* § 849.086(1)-(3). Florida law prohibits banked card games, however. *See* § 849.086(12)(a), (15)(a). Blackjack, baccarat, and *chemin de fer* are banked card games. They are therefore illegal in Florida.

3. Does IGRA Permit Compacts to Expand Gaming?

Contrary to Florida law, the Compact allows banked card games such as blackjack, baccarat, and *chemin de fer*. The House argues that the Compact therefore violates IGRA itself, which permits Class III gaming *only* if the state "permits such gaming for any purpose by any person, organization, or entity." 25 U.S.C. § 2710(d)(1). The Governor, on the other hand, contends that, once state law permits *any* Class III gaming, a compact may allow *all* Class III gaming.

The meaning of the phrase "permits such gaming" has been heavily litigated. The question is whether, when state law permits some Class III games to be played, a tribe must be permitted to conduct only those particular games or all Class III games. *See* Kathryn R.L. Rand, *Caught in the Middle: How*

State Politics, State Law, and State Courts Constrain Tribal Influence Over Indian Gaming, 90 Marq. L.Rev. 971, 983 (2007) (citing cases). The Secretary's interpretation of this provision supports the House's argument. *See* Class III Gaming Procedures, 63 Fed.Reg. 3289, 3293 (Jan. 22, 1998) (Proposed Rules) ("IGRA thus makes it unlawful for Tribes to operate particular Class III games that State law completely and affirmatively prohibits."). So do a majority of federal courts. *See, e.g., Rumsey Indian Rancheria of Wintun Indians v. Wilson,* 64 F.3d 1250, 1258 (9th Cir.1994)("[A] state need only allow Indian tribes to operate games that others can operate, but need not give tribes what others cannot have."); *see also Cheyenne River Sioux Tribe v. South Dakota,* 3 F.3d 273, 279 (8th Cir.1993) (stating that IGRA "does not require the state to negotiate with respect to forms of gaming it does not presently permit"); *but see Lac du Flambeau Band of Lake Superior Chippewa Indians v. Wisconsin,* 770 F.Supp. 480, 486 (W.D.Wis.1991) ("Congress did not intend the term 'permits such gaming' to limit the tribes to the specific types of gaming activity actually in operation in a state."). Our Attorney General has agreed with the majority interpretation. *See* Op. Att'y Gen. Fla. 2007–36 at 3 (2007) ("[I]n light of the greater weight of federal case law and the Department of the Interior's interpretation of IGRA, Class III gaming activities subject to mandatory negotiations between a state and an Indian tribe do not include those specifically prohibited by state law.").

Whether the Compact violates IGRA, however, is a question we need not and do not resolve. Given our narrow scope of review on a writ of quo warranto, the issue here is only whether the Florida Constitution grants the Governor the authority to unilaterally bind the State to a compact that violates public policy. We conclude that *even if* the Governor is correct that IGRA permits the expansion of gaming on tribal lands beyond what state law permits, such an agreement represents a significant change in Florida's public policy. It is therefore precisely the type of action particularly within the Legislature's power. We now discuss that issue.

4. The Compact Violates Florida's Public Policy on Gaming

Article II, section 3 of the Florida Constitution prohibits the executive branch from usurping the powers of another branch. Enacting laws—and especially criminal laws—is quintessentially a legislative function. *See State v. Barquet,* 262 So. 2d 431, 433 (Fla.1972) ("The lawmaking function is the chief legislative power."). By authorizing the Tribe to conduct "banked card games" that are illegal throughout Florida—and thus illegal for the Tribe—the Compact violates Florida law. *See Chiles v. Children A, B, C, D, E, & F,* 589 So. 2d 260, 264 (Fla.1991) ("This Court has repeatedly held that, under the doctrine of separation of powers, the legislature may not delegate the power to enact laws or to declare what the law shall be to any other branch."). The Governor's action therefore encroaches on the legislative function and was beyond his authority. Nor does it matter that the Compact is a contract between the State and the Tribe. Neither the Governor nor anyone else in the executive branch has the authority to execute a contract that violates state criminal law. *Cf. Local No. 234, United Assoc. of Journeymen & Apprentices of Plumbing & Pipefitting Industry v. Henley & Beckwith, Inc.,* 66 So. 2d 818, 821 (Fla.1953) ("[A]n agreement that is violative of a provision of a constitution or a valid statute, or an agreement which cannot be performed without violating such a constitutional or statutory provision, is illegal and void."); *City of Miami v. Benson,* 63 So. 2d 916, 923 (Fla.1953) ("The contract in question, that is, the acceptance by the City of the proposal made by its agent, employee or advisor, to purchase the bonds, is contrary to public policy and is, therefore, void.").

IV. CONCLUSION

We conclude that the Governor's execution of a compact authorizing types of gaming that are prohibited under Florida law violates the separation of powers. The Governor has no authority to change or amend state law. Such power falls exclusively to the Legislature. Therefore, we hold that the Governor lacked authority to bind the State to a compact that violates Florida law as this compact does. We need not resolve the broader issue of whether the Governor ever has the authority to execute compacts without either the

Legislature's prior authorization or, at least, its subsequent ratification. Because we believe the parties will fully comply with the dictates of this opinion, we grant the petition but withhold issuance of the writ.

It is so ordered.

Notes and Questions to Consider:

1. Which branch of Florida's government does *Florida House of Representatives v. Crist* hold to be the branch that determines the public policy of the State of Florida? What impact could this have on Florida's other two branches?

2. An extraordinary writ like a Writ of Quo Warranto is a discretionary remedy, and so, a party that proves its entitlement to such a writ may still be denied issuance of that writ by the court. Indeed, here in *Florida House of Representatives v. Crist*, Florida's Supreme Court found that the House of Representatives was entitled to such a writ yet the court withheld its issuance. In what way was this in deference to the separation of powers?

3. *Florida House of Representatives v. Crist* attempts to tackle some of the nuances of the sovereignty of Native Americans. Some commentators once said, "The nuances of tribal sovereign immunity … are recommended only for the brave." David Getches, Charles Wilkinson, Robert Williams, and Matthew Fletcher, CASES AND MATERIALS ON FEDERAL INDIAN LAW 315 (2d ed. 1986). One of the points raised was to classify the agreement between the governor and the tribe as a "compact." What is a compact?

4. The Federal Constitution states: "The Congress shall have Power . . . To regulate Commerce . . . with the Indian Tribes . . . ." Art. 1, §8, clause 3, U.S. Const. "This phrase . . . has been interpreted to mean that the states lack jurisdiction over Native American reservation activity until granted that authority by the federal government." Patrick John McGinley, FLORIDA MUNICIPAL LAW AND PRACTICE § 6:3 (2017-2018 ed.). Section 7 of former "Public Law 280 [formerly codified at 18 USC § 1162 and 28 USC § 1360] granted Florida and other states the right to assume criminal and civil

jurisdiction by legislative enactment . . . ." *Id.* Under that authority, Florida's Legislature enacted Florida Statutes section § 285.16 in 1961 and that law endures. It provides:

> *Civil and criminal jurisdiction; Indian reservation.—*
>
> *(1) The State of Florida hereby assumes jurisdiction over criminal offenses committed by or against Indians or other persons within Indian reservations and over civil causes of actions between Indians or other persons or to which Indians or other persons are parties rising within Indian reservations.*
>
> *(2) The civil and criminal laws of Florida shall obtain on all Indian reservations in this state and shall be enforced in the same manner as elsewhere throughout the state.*

§ 285.16, Fla. Stat. Was it wise and fair for Florida to erode Native American sovereignty in this way?

5. Florida Statutes section 285.16 attempts to draw a line between civil and criminal laws. Is the line always so bright? Consider *Bryan v. Itasca County*, 426 U.S. 373 (1976) (assuming to divide all laws into either criminal or civil) and *California v. Cabazon Band of Mission Indians*, 426 U.S. 373 (1987) (acknowledging the division attempted in *Bryan v. Itasca County* did not always work, and proposing instead a division between civil/regulatory versus criminal/prohibitory).

6. *Florida House of Representatives v. Crist* holds that, unless there is a tribal-state compact allowing gambling, any gambling prohibited in Florida is prohibited on tribal land. Likewise, *Crist* holds that the tribal-state gaming compact violated state law by authorizing the tribe to conduct "banked card games" that were illegal throughout Florida, and therefore, illegal for the tribe. In light of Florida Statutes section 285.16, could the court have ruled any other way?

7. *Florida House of Representatives v. Crist* holds that Florida's Supreme Court has quo warranto jurisdiction alleging a violation of the sepa-

ration of powers, and has that jurisdiction even after the act has occurred. This holding defeated the Governor's defense that the House could have acted sooner and failed to act in time. Is it necessary for one to wait and suffer the harm inflicted by a violation of the separation of powers before one may seek quo warranto relief? Consider this holding from footnote 1 of *League of Women Voters of Florida v. Scott*, 232 So. 3d 264 (Fla. 2017):

> We recognize that [*Florida House of Representatives v.*] *Crist* contained language suggesting the writ could be used to prohibit future conduct. *See, e.g.*, 999 So. 2d at 607 ("The Governor contends that this Court lacks jurisdiction because the House does not seek either to remove him from office or to enjoin the future exercise of his authority. We conclude, however, that these are not the only grounds for issuing such a writ."). However, the history of quo warranto as well as our precedent belie any suggestion to this effect. In *Crist*, we explained that "petitions for the writ historically have been filed *after* a public official has acted," and the disputed act had already occurred. *Id.* In that case, the Florida House of Representatives challenged the execution by Governor Charles Crist of a compact with the Seminole Indian Tribe of Florida....

Id. at 265 n.1.

8. Article IV, Section 1 of Florida's Constitution states that "[t]he supreme executive power shall be vested in a governor, who shall ... transact all necessary business with the officers of government." *Florida House of Representatives v. Crist* holds that this "necessary business" clause of Florida's Constitution does not authorize Florida's Governor to execute compacts contrary to the expressed public policy of the state or to create exceptions to state law. Does this make the authority of Florida's Governor different that the authority of a U.S. President? Consider, for example, the proposed "Development, Relief, and Education for Alien Minors" Act, or "DREAM" Act, that failed to pass in the U.S. Congress from 2009 through 2012. It would have prevented deportation of certain "Dreamers" and made them eligible for work permits. After Congress did not pass that law, the U.S.

President issued an executive branch memorandum on June 15, 2012. It deferred action on deportation of "Dreamers" and made them eligible for work permits. In a way, the presidential action implemented a public policy that the national legislature decided not to implement. Does Florida's Governor have a similar power to implement a public policy that Florida's Legislature decides not to implement, or would that be a violation of Florida's separation of powers? See *Florida House of Representatives v. Crist*, 999 So. 2d at 614-17 (holding that Florida's Governor lacked authority to bind Florida to a compact that departed from our state's public policy by legalizing types of gaming that were illegal everywhere else in the state).

C. Cooperation Among the Branches

Just as the tale of dissention among the branches in *Florida House of Representatives v. Crist* illustrated many lessons about Florida's separation of powers, so too can a tale of cooperation among the branches. This tale begins in 1976, when Florida's Legislature enacted the first codified rules of evidence for Florida's courts. Perhaps Florida's Supreme Court could have rejected Florida's Legislature's enactment of an evidence code for Florida's courts. Instead, Florida's Supreme Court held that "[r]ules of evidence may in some instances be substantive law and, therefore, the sole responsibility of the legislature. In other instances, evidentiary rules may be procedural and the responsibility of this Court." *In re Fla. Evidence Code*, 372 So. 2d 1369, 1369 (Fla. 1979). The court therefore chose to adopt the rules.

Over the next 37 years, Florida's judiciary continued to accept Florida's Legislature's occasional amendments to Florida's evidence code. That spirit of cooperation ended in the 2000's when an amendment to the evidence code by the Legislature was held to violate the constitutional right to confront one's accusers in a criminal case. Then, as explained in FLORIDA WORKERS' COMPENSATION:

> In 2013, the Florida Legislature modified the Florida Evidence Code at Florida Statutes section 90.702 "to adopt the standards for expert testimony in the courts of this state as provided in *Daubert v. Merrell Dow Pharmaceuticals, Inc.*, 509 U.S. 579 (1993), *General Electric*

> *Co. v. Joiner*, 522 U.S. 136 (1997), and *Kumho Tire Co., Ltd. v. Carmichael*, 526 U.S. 137 (1999), and to no longer apply the standard in *Frye v. United States*, 293 F. 1013 (D.C.Cir.1923)." *Frye* and *Daubert* are competing methods for a trial judge to determine the reliability of expert testimony before allowing it to be admitted into evidence. By amending section 90.702, the Legislature signaled its intent "to tighten the rules for admissibility of expert testimony."

Patrick John McGinley, FLORIDA WORKERS' COMPENSATION § 42:12 (2019 ed.).

With that background in mind, we pick up this story with the decision in *DeLisle v. Crane Co.,* 258 So. 3d 1219 (Fla. 2018). But *DeLisle* does not end our tale. A few months later, with three Florida Supreme Court justices having retired and three new appointees having taken their place, Florida's Supreme Court spoke again in *In re Amendments to Florida Evidence Code,* SC19-107, 2019 WL 2219714 (Fla. May 23, 2019). Below, we start with *DeLisle*, and finish with *In re Amendments*.

DELISLE

V.

CRANE CO.

Supreme Court of Florida, 2018

258 So. 3d 1219

… After developing mesothelioma, [a disease that can be caused by exposure to asbestos,] DeLisle filed a personal injury action against … Crane, Lorillard Tobacco Co., and Hollingsworth & Vose Co. ("H & V").

At trial, DeLisle presented evidence that he was exposed to asbestos fibers from sheet gaskets…. Crane, a valve and pump manufacturer, used "Cranite" sheet gaskets containing chrysotile asbestos fibers. DeLisle also testified that he smoked Original Kent cigarettes with asbestos-containing "Micronite" filters from 1952 to 1956. These cigarettes were produced by

Lorillard's predecessor, and the filters were supplied by a former subsidiary of H & V. The filters contained crocidolite asbestos….

The parties hotly disputed causation, and even DeLisle's own experts did not agree on which products produced sufficient exposure to asbestos to constitute a substantial contributing factor to DeLisle's disease….

Appellees challenged each expert's opinions under section 90.702, Florida Statutes, which adopted the *Daubert* test for expert testimony…. Following *Daubert* hearings, the trial court admitted each expert's testimony….

Following three days of deliberation, the jury awarded DeLisle $8 million in damages….

Crane appealed …

The Fourth District reviewed the admission of the testimony of the experts under *Daubert v. Merrell Dow Pharmaceuticals, Inc.*, 509 U.S. 579 (1993), and found that the trial court "failed to properly exercise its gatekeeping function…." The Fourth District reversed for a new trial…. DeLisle sought review by this Court, which was granted.

The Florida Legislature and the Florida Supreme Court have worked in tandem for nearly forty years to enact and maintain codified rules of evidence. This arrangement between the branches to avoid constitutional questions of separation of powers continued uninterrupted from the Evidence Code's inception until 2000. In the instant case, we are asked to determine whether chapter 2013-107, section 1, Laws of Florida, which revised section 90.702, Florida Statutes (2015), and which we previously declined to adopt, to the extent it was procedural, infringes on this Court's rulemaking authority. We find that it does. Therefore, we reverse the Fourth District and remand for reinstatement of the final judgment.

The Florida Legislature enacted the first codified rules of evidence in 1976…. In 1979, we adopted the Florida Evidence Code, to the extent that the code was procedural…. We recognized that "[r]ules of evidence may in some instances be substantive law and, therefore, the sole responsibility of the legislature. In other instances, evidentiary rules may be procedural and the responsibility of this Court."... We therefore chose to adopt the rules, "[t]o avoid multiple appeals and confusion in the operation of the courts caused by assertions that portions of the evidence code are procedural and, therefore, unconstitutional because they had not been adopted by this Court under its rule-making authority." *Id.* Since then, we have traditionally continued to adopt the code, to the extent it is procedural, to avoid the issue of whether the Evidence Code is substantive in nature and therefore within the province of the Legislature or procedural in nature and therefore within the province of this Court….

Until 2000, the working arrangement between the Legislature and the Florida Supreme Court remained intact. However, in *In re Amendments to the Florida Evidence Code*, 782 So. 2d 339 (Fla. 2000), this Court for the first time declined to adopt, to the extent they were procedural, amendments to section 90.803, Florida Statutes (1997). *Id.* (declining to adopt chapter 98-2, section 1, Laws of Florida, amending section 90.803(22), Florida Statutes, which allows the admission of former testimony although the declarant is available as a witness, in part because of concerns about its constitutionality). We then considered the constitutionality of the provision in *State v. Abreu*, 837 So. 2d 400 (Fla. 2003), determining that the revised statute was unconstitutional because it infringed on a defendant's right to confront witnesses. *Id.* at 406.

Since then, we have only rarely declined to adopt a statutory revision to the Evidence Code….

Generally, the Legislature has the power to enact substantive law while this Court has the power to enact procedural law. *See Allen v. Butterworth*, 756 So. 2d 52, 59 (Fla. 2000). Substantive law has been described as that which defines, creates, or regulates rights—"those existing for their own sake and constituting the normal legal order of society, i.e., the rights of life, liberty, property, and reputation." *In re Fla. Rules of Criminal Procedure*, 272 So. 2d 65, 65 (Fla. 1972) (Adkins, J., concurring). Procedural law, on the other hand, is the form, manner, or means by which substantive law is implemented. *Id.* at 66 (Adkins, J., concurring). Stated differently, procedural law "includes all rules governing the parties, their counsel and the Court throughout the progress of the case from the time of its initiation until final judgment and its execution." *Allen v. Butterworth*, 756 So. 2d 52, 60 (Fla. 2000).... "It is the method of conducting litigation involving rights and corresponding defenses." *Haven Federal Savings & Loan Ass'n v. Kirian*, 579 So. 2d 730, 732 (Fla. 1991) (citing *Skinner v. City of Eustis*, 147 Fla. 22, 2 So. 2d 116 (1941)).

The distinction between substantive and procedural law, however, is not always clear. For example, a law is considered to be substantive when it both creates and conditions a right. *See ... Jackson v. Fla. Dep't of Corr.*, 790 So. 2d 381, 383-84 (Fla. 2000) (holding that the Legislature could properly limit the right of indigents to proceed without payment of costs); *Caple v. Tuttle's Design-Build, Inc.*, 753 So. 2d 49, 54 (Fla. 2000) (holding that a statute creating the right to petition for mortgage payment receipts during foreclosure proceedings and establishing the grounds for granting such a petition was constitutional); *School Bd. of Broward Cty. v. Price*, 362 So. 2d 1337 (Fla. 1978) (holding that section 230.23(9)(d)(2), Florida Statutes (1977), set the bounds of a substantive right conditioned on a waiver and was therefore not an unconstitutional infringement of the Court's power to set procedural rules). However, when procedural aspects overwhelm substantive ones, the law may no longer be considered substantive....

Here, the Legislature sought to adopt *Daubert* and cease the application of *Frye* to expert testimony. In *Frye v. United States*, 293 F. 1013 (D.C. Cir. 1923), a short opinion, the Court of Appeals for the District of Columbia pronounced that ... "the thing from which the deduction is made must be sufficiently established to have gained general acceptance in the particular field in which it belongs." *Id.* This rule—that expert testimony should be deduced from generally accepted scientific principles—has been the standard in Florida cases and, today, we reaffirm that it is still the standard. *See, e.g., ... Bundy v. State*, 471 So. 2d 9, 13 (Fla. 1985) (describing the *Frye* test as one in which "the results of mechanical or scientific testing are not admissible unless the testing has developed or improved to the point where experts in the field widely share the view that the results are scientifically reliable as accurate").

[W]e formally adopted *Frye* … [in] *Stokes v. State*, 548 So. 2d 188, 195 (Fla. 1989) …. [where] we noted:

> [A] courtroom is not a laboratory, and as such it is not the place to conduct scientific experiments. If the scientific community considers a procedure or process unreliable for its own purposes, then the procedure must be considered less reliable for courtroom use.

Stokes, 548 So. 2d at 193-94. We note that we adopted the *Frye* test irrespective of the Evidence Code, which was in place at the time.

In *Hadden v. State*, 690 So. 2d 573 (Fla. 1997), we rejected the argument that the Legislature's enactment and this Court's subsequent adoption of the Evidence Code replaced the *Frye* standard with the balancing test that existed in the code….

After decades of the federal courts' applying *Frye*, Congress revised the Federal Rules of Evidence. The revision was addressed by the United States Supreme Court in 1993. In *Daubert v. Merrell Dow Pharmaceuticals*, 509 U.S. 579 (1993), the United States Supreme Court determined the appropriate standard for admitting expert scientific testimony in a federal trial. *Id.* at 582. The Supreme Court ultimately agreed … that *Frye* had been superseded by the adoption of the revised Federal Rules of Evidence. *Id.* at 587.

The Court explained its decision, stating, "[I]n order to qualify as 'scientific knowledge,' an inference or assertion must be derived by the scientific method." *Daubert*, 509 U.S. at 590. The inquiry derived from *Daubert* is a flexible one, as emphasized by the Supreme Court. *Id.* at 594. "The focus, of course, must be solely on principles and methodology, not on the conclusions that they generate." *Id.* at 595….

…In short, in *Daubert*, the United States Supreme Court found that otherwise probative and scientifically valid evidence was being excluded under the *Frye* standard and the change in rule 702 was necessary to permit additional relevant evidence to be considered even if it was based on scientific methods or principles that were not yet generally accepted.

Nevertheless, in *Brim v. State*, 695 So. 2d 268 (Fla. 1997), we unanimously emphasized that we continue to apply *Frye* .... We opined:

> Despite the federal adoption of a more lenient standard in *Daubert v. Merrell Dow Pharmaceuticals, Inc.*, 509 U.S. 579 (1993), we have maintained the higher standard of reliability as dictated by *Frye*....

Brim, 695 So. 2d at 271-72 (footnote omitted).

Following our repeated affirmations of the *Frye* rule, in 2013 the Legislature amended section 90.702 to incorporate *Daubert* in[to] the Florida Rules of Evidence. The amendment revised the statute to read as follows:

> 90.702 *Testimony by experts.*—If scientific, technical, or other specialized knowledge will assist the trier of fact in understanding the evidence or in determining a fact in issue, a witness qualified as an expert by knowledge, skill, experience, training, or education may testify about it in the form of an opinion or otherwise, if:
>
> (1) The testimony is based upon sufficient facts or data;
>
> (2) The testimony is the product of reliable principles and methods; and
>
> (3) The witness has applied the principles and methods reliably to the facts of the case.

§ 90.702, Fla. Stat. (as amended by ch. 2013-107, § 1, Laws of Fla.).

Article II, section 3 of the Florida Constitution prohibits one branch of government from exercising any of the powers of the other branches. Further, article V, section 2(a) provides this Court the exclusive authority to "adopt rules for the practice and procedure in all courts." Art. V, § 2(a), Fla. Const. The Legislature may only repeal the rules of this Court by "general law enacted by two-thirds vote of the membership of each house of the legislature." *Id*.... The vote here did not meet the requirement. The House passed the bill with a majority, 70 to 41 (or 58.3% of the membership). The Senate passed the bill with more than the necessary two-thirds vote, 30 to 9 (or 75% of the membership). *Id.*

We have previously found that the Legislature exceeded its authority in adopting statutes we found to infringe on the authority of this Court to determine matters of practice or procedure....

In *Jackson v. Florida Department of Corrections*, 790 So. 2d 381 (Fla. 2000), we explained that a statute can have both substantive provisions and procedural requirements and "[i]f the procedural requirements conflict with or interfere with the procedural mechanisms of the court system, they are unconstitutional under both a separation of powers analysis, and because [they intrude upon] the exclusive province of the Supreme Court pursuant to the rulemaking authority vested in it by the Florida Constitution." *Id.* at 384 (citing art. II, § 3, art. V, § 2, Fla. Const.; *State v. Garcia*, 229 So. 2d 236, 238 (Fla. 1969))....

In *State v. Raymond*, 906 So. 2d 1045 (Fla. 2005), we determined that section 907.041(4)(b), Florida Statutes (2000), providing that a person charged with a dangerous crime was prohibited from receiving a nonmonetary pretrial release, was purely procedural and, therefore, an unconstitutional violation of the separation of powers clause. "It is a well-established principle that a statute which purports to create or modify a procedural rule of court is constitutionally infirm." *Id.* at 1048.... Further, "where there is no substantive right conveyed by the statute, the procedural aspects are not incidental; accordingly, such a statute is unconstitutional." *Id.* at 1049....

Section 90.702, Florida Statutes, as amended in 2013, is not substantive. It does not create, define, or regulate a right. Indeed, while we have stated that the Florida Evidence Code contains both substantive and procedural rights, this statute is one that solely regulates the action of litigants in court proceedings. *See, e.g.*, *Glendening v. State*, 536 So. 2d 212, 215 (Fla. 1988) (determining that section 90.803(23), Florida Statutes (1985), concerning out-of-court statements, was procedural for the purposes of ex post facto analysis).

Our consideration of the constitutionality of the amendment does not end with our determination that the provision was procedural. For this Court to determine that the amendment is unconstitutional, it must also conflict with a rule of this Court. *See Haven Fed. Sav. & Loan Ass'n v. Kirian*, 579

So. 2d 730, 732–33 (Fla. 1991) ("Where this Court promulgates rules relating to the practice and procedure of all courts and a statute provides a contrary practice or procedure, the statute is unconstitutional to the extent of the conflict.").... A procedural rule of this Court may be pronounced in caselaw.... While the Legislature purports to have pronounced public policy in overturning *Marsh*, we hold that the rule announced in *Stokes* and reaffirmed in *Marsh* was a procedural rule of this Court that the Legislature could not repeal by simple majority.

The expert testimony in this case was properly admitted [under *Frye*] and should not have been excluded by the Fourth District....

For the foregoing reasons, we quash the Fourth District's decision. Furthermore, because the causation of mesothelioma is neither new nor novel, the trial court's acceptance of the expert testimony was proper. We therefore remand to the Fourth District with instructions to remand to the trial court to reinstate the final judgment....

It is so ordered.

As promised in the introductory paragraphs preceding *DeLisle*, our tale does not end with *DeLisle*. We pick up our tale just a few months later when Florida's Supreme Court decided *In re Amendments to Florida Evidence Code*, SC19-107, 2019 WL 2219714 (Fla. May 23, 2019):

IN RE:

AMENDMENTS TO FLORIDA EVIDENCE CODE

Supreme Court of Florida, 2019

278 So.3d 551

The Court, according to its exclusive rulemaking authority pursuant to article V, section 2(a) of the Florida Constitution, adopts chapter 2013-107, sections 1 and 2, Laws of Florida (*Daubert* amendments), which amended sections 90.702 (Testimony by experts) and 90.704 (Basis of opinion testimony by experts), Florida Statutes, of the Florida Evidence Code to replace the *Frye* standard for admitting certain expert testimony with the *Daubert* standard, the standard for expert testimony found in Federal Rule of Evidence 702.

In *In re Amendments to Florida Evidence Code*, 210 So. 3d 1231, 1239 (Fla. 2017), at the recommendation of The Florida Bar's Code and Rules of Evidence Committee (Committee), which occurred by a close vote of 16-14, the majority of this Court previously declined to adopt the *Daubert* amendments, to the extent that they are procedural, solely "due to the constitutional concerns raised" by the Committee members and commenters who opposed the amendments. Without now readdressing the correctness of this Court's ruling in *DeLisle v. Crane Co.*, 258 So. 3d 1219, 1221, 1229 (Fla. 2018), we note that the decision determined that section 90.702 of the Florida Evidence Code, as amended by section 1 of chapter 2013-107, is procedural in nature. *DeLisle* did not address the amendment to section 90.704 made by section 2 of chapter 2013-107. Therefore, the Court has not determined the extent to which that amendment may be procedural.

As noted by *In re Amendments to Florida Evidence Code*, 210 So. 3d at 1236-37, the *Daubert* amendments were considered by The Florida Bar's Code and Rules of Evidence Committee. The Committee provided majority and minority reports against and in favor of the Court's adoption of the *Daubert* amendments. The Board of Governors of The Florida Bar approved the Committee's recommendation, and extensive comments were received in response to the published recommendation. The Court held oral argument in the case. Because of the extensive briefing and arguments on this issue previously made to the Court, and mindful of the resources of parties, members of The Florida Bar, and the judiciary, we revisit the outcome of the recommendation on the *Daubert* amendments without requiring the process to be repeated.

We now recede from the Court's prior decision not to adopt the Legislature's *Daubert* amendments to the Evidence Code and to retain the *Frye* standard. As Justice Polston has explained, the "grave constitutional concerns" raised by those who oppose the amendments to the Code appear unfounded:

[T]he United States Supreme Court decided *Daubert v. Merrell Dow Pharmaceuticals, Inc.*, 509 U.S. 579 (1993), in 1993, and the standard has been routinely applied in federal courts ever since. The clear majority of state jurisdictions also adhere to the *Daubert* standard. *See* 1 *McCormick on Evidence* § 13 (7th ed. June 2016 Supp.). In fact, there are 36 states that have rejected *Frye* in favor of *Daubert* to some extent. *See* Charles Alan Wright & Victor Gold, 29 *Federal Practice and Procedure* § 6267, at 308-09 n.15 (2016). Has the entire federal court system for the last 23 years as well as 36 states denied parties' rights to a jury trial and access to courts? Do only Florida and a few other states have a constitutionally sound standard for the admissibility of expert testimony? Of course not.

As a note to the federal rule of evidence explains, "[a] review of the caselaw after *Daubert* shows that the rejection of expert testimony is the exception rather than the rule." Fed. R. Evid. 702 advisory committee's note to 2000 amendment. "*Daubert* did not work a 'sea-change over federal evidence law,' and 'the trial court's role as gatekeeper is not intended to serve as a replacement for the adversary system.' " *Id.*...

Furthermore, I know of no reported decisions that have held that the *Daubert* standard violates the constitutional guarantees of a jury trial and access to courts. To the contrary, there is case law holding that the *Daubert* standard does not violate the constitution. *See, e.g., Junk v. Terminix Int'l Co.*, 628 F.3d 439, 450 (8th Cir. 2010) (rejecting legal merit of the constitutional claim "that the district court violated [appellant's] Seventh Amendment right to a jury trial by improperly weighing evidence in the course of its *Daubert* rulings" and explaining that "Junk does not cite any case for the notion that a proper *Daubert* ruling violates a party's right to a jury trial"); *E.I. du Pont de Nemours & Co. v. Robinson*, 923 S.W.2d 549, 558 (Tex. 1995) (rejecting claim "that allowing the trial judge to assess the reliability of expert testimony violates [the parties'] federal and state constitutional rights to a jury trial by infringing upon the jury's inherent

> authority to assess the credibility of witnesses and the weight to be given their testimony"); *see also Gen. Elec. Co. v. Joiner*, 522 U.S. 136, 142-43, 118 S.Ct. 512, 139 L.Ed.2d 508 (1997) (rejecting "argument that because the granting of summary judgment in this case was 'outcome determinative,' it should have been subjected to a more searching standard of review" and explaining that, while "disputed issues of fact are resolved against the moving party[,] ... the question of admissibility of expert testimony is not such an issue of fact").
>
> Accordingly, the ... "grave constitutional concerns" regarding the *Daubert* standard are unfounded.

In re Amends. to Fla. Evidence Code, 210 So. 3d 1231, 1242-43 (Polston, J., concurring in part and dissenting in part). While we find Justice Polston's observations instructive in deciding to now adopt the Legislature's *Daubert* amendments, we do not decide, in this rules case, the constitutional or other substantive concerns that have been raised about the amendments. Those issues must be left for a proper case or controversy.

Additionally, as outlined in the Committee minority report, the *Daubert* amendments remedy deficiencies of the *Frye* standard. Whereas the *Frye* standard only applied to expert testimony based on new or novel scientific techniques and general acceptance, *Daubert* provides that "the trial judge must ensure that any and all scientific testimony or evidence admitted is not only relevant, but reliable." *Daubert*, 509 U.S. at 589 (holding that the Federal Rules of Evidence superseded *Frye*). Moreover, also as argued in the minority report, the *Daubert* amendments will create consistency between the state and federal courts with respect to the admissibility of expert testimony and will promote fairness and predictability in the legal system, as well as help lessen forum shopping.

Accordingly, in accordance with this Court's exclusive rule-making authority and longstanding practice of adopting provisions of the Florida Evidence Code as they are enacted or amended by the Legislature, we adopt the amendments to sections 90.702 and 90.704 of the Florida Evidence Code made by chapter 2013-107, sections 1 and 2. Effective immediately upon the release of this opinion, we adopt the amendments to section 90.702 as procedural rules of evidence and adopt the amendment to section 90.704 to the extent it is procedural.

It is so ordered.

Notes and Questions to Consider:

1. In *DeLisle*, Florida' Supreme Court declines to replace the *Frye* rule with *Daubert.* A few months later and with three retiring Supreme Court justices having been replaced with new justices, Florida's Supreme Court replaces *Frye* with *Daubert* in its *In re Amendments* decision. To what extent was the different outcome attributable to changed circumstances, and to what extent was it attributable to changed personnel?

2. Noting that Florida's Constitution makes judicial rulemaking the sole province of Florida's Supreme Court, is it wrong if a change in judicial rules is the result of a change of personnel on the state's supreme court?

Chapter Eight

Sovereign Immunity

A. Public Policy Behind Sovereign Immunity

One result of the separation of powers is the concept of sovereign immunity. Judicial relief can be denied in a suit against a governmental entity if the entity possesses sovereign immunity as to the claims in that suit. Florida's Supreme Court explains:

> Florida law has enunciated three policy considerations that underpin the doctrine of sovereign immunity. First is the preservation of the constitutional principle of separation of powers. *See Commercial Carrier Corp. v. Indian River County,* 371 So. 2d 1010, 1022 (Fla. 1979) (stating that "certain functions of coordinate branches of government may not be subjected to scrutiny by judge or jury as to the wisdom of their performance"). Second is the protection of the public treasury. *See Spangler v. Fla. State Tpk. Auth.,* 106 So. 2d 421, 424 (Fla. 1958) (explaining that "immunity of the sovereign is a part of the public policy of the state[, which] is enforced as a protection of the public against profligate encroachments on the public treasury"). Third is the maintenance of the orderly administration of government. *See State Rd. Dep't v. Tharp,* 1 So. 2d 868, 869 (Fla. 1941) ("If the State could be sued at the instance of every citizen, the public service would be disrupted and the administration of government would be bottlenecked.").

Am. Home Assur. Co. v. Nat'l R.R. Passenger Corp., 908 So. 2d 459, 471 (Fla. 2005).

B. Sovereign Immunity Defined

"Sovereign immunity, or crown immunity, is a legal doctrine by which the sovereign or state cannot commit a legal wrong and is immune from civil suit or criminal prosecution." Patrick John McGinley, FLORIDA MUNICIPAL LAW AND PRACTICE § 7:2 (2017-2018 ed.).

The Federalist Papers explain the basis of, and the argument in support for, sovereign immunity as follows:

> It is inherent in the nature of sovereignty not to be amenable to the suit of an individual without its consent. This is the general sense, and the general practice of mankind; and the exemption, as one of the attributes of sovereignty, is now enjoyed by the government of every State in the Union. Unless, therefore, there is a surrender of this immunity in the plan of the convention, it will remain with the States, and the danger intimated must be merely ideal. The circumstances which are necessary to produce an alienation of State sovereignty … flows from the obligations of good faith. The contracts between a nation and individuals are only binding on the conscience of the sovereign, and have no pretensions to a compulsive force. They confer no right of action, independent of the sovereign will. To what purpose would it be to authorize suits against States for the debts they owe? How could recoveries be enforced? It is evident, it could not be done without waging war against the contracting State; and to ascribe to the federal courts, by mere implication, and in destruction of a pre-existing right of the State governments, a power which would involve such a consequence, would be altogether forced and unwarrantable.

Id. (citing The Federalist No. 81, p. 487 (C. Rossiter ed. 1961) (A. Hamilton) (cited with approval in *Seminole Tribe of Florida v. Florida*, 517 U.S. 44 (1996)).

FLORIDA MUNICIPAL LAW AND PRACTICE describes two historical rules of sovereign immunity, and the current state of sovereign immunity, as follows:

> The doctrine of sovereign immunity comprises two distinct rules, which are not always separately recognized: font of law and font of justice. The one rule holds that the King or the Crown, as the font of law, is not bound by the law's provisions. The other provides that the King or the Crown, as the font of justice, is not subject to suit

in its own courts. The font of law rule puts the sovereign beyond the reach of its laws. The font of justice rule puts the sovereign beyond the jurisdiction of its courts.

The font of law implements the ancient maxim that "the King can do no wrong." Professor Jaffe has argued this expression "originally meant precisely the contrary to what it later came to mean," that is, "'it meant that the king must not, was not allowed, not entitled, to do wrong.'" In any event, and as either Presidents Nixon or Clinton might readily attest, it is clear that the idea of the sovereign and its minions being in this sense "above the law" has not survived in American law.

The font of justice implements the idea that the sovereign's courts are not to be used against the sovereign. It took its common-law form in the high Middle Ages. "At least as early as the 13th century, during the reign of Henry III (1216–1272), it was recognized that the king could not be sued in his own courts."… "By the time of Bracton (1268) it was settled doctrine that the King could not be sued *eo nomine* in his own courts." The significance of the font of justice doctrine in the nascent American law is less clear, however, than its early development and steady endurance in England might suggest. Some colonial governments might have enjoyed some such immunity. However, historians dispute the scope (and even the existence) of this governmental immunity in pre-Revolutionary America.

Whatever the scope of sovereign immunity might have been in the Colonies, however, or during the period of the Confederation, the proposal to establish a National Government under the Constitution drafted in 1787 presented a prospect unknown to the common law prior to the American experience: the States would become parts of a system in which sovereignty over even domestic matters would be divided or parceled out between the States and the Nation, the latter to be invested with its own judicial power and the right to prevail against the States whenever their respective substantive laws might be in conflict. With this prospect in mind, the drafters of the 1787 federal

Constitution had several options. The federal Constitution could have addressed state sovereign immunity by eliminating whatever sovereign immunity the States previously had, as to any matter subject to federal law or jurisdiction. It could have addressed state sovereign immunity by recognizing an analogue to the old immunity in the new context of federal jurisdiction, but subject to abrogation as to any matter within that jurisdiction. It could have enshrined a doctrine of inviolable state sovereign immunity in the text, thereby giving it constitutional protection in the new federal jurisdiction.

Yet, the 1787 draft, in fact, said nothing on the subject, and it was this very silence that occasioned some, though apparently not widespread, dispute among the framers and others over whether ratification of the Constitution would preclude a state sued in federal court from asserting sovereign immunity as it could have done on any matter of nonfederal law litigated in its own courts. As it has come down to us, the discussion gave no attention to congressional power under the proposed Article I but focused entirely on the limits of the judicial power provided in Article III. Likewise, although the jurisdictional bases together constituting the judicial power of the national courts under § 2 of Article III included questions arising under federal law and cases between states and individuals who are not citizens, it was only upon the latter citizen-state diversity provisions that preratification questions about state immunity from suit or liability centered.

This brings us to the notion of state sovereign immunity in its modern and present form. Presently, there is little to no notion of immunizing the font of law insofar as it is abhorrent to modern American notions of justice that any one or thing be held wholly beyond the fair reach of the rule of law. Yet, immunizing the font of law persists insofar as the sovereign when writing the law might write itself to be exempt from the full restrictions or penalties imposed by that law. When a bill as so written is passed into law by the people's legislators, the people's sovereign becomes exempt from that new law because the people have held their sovereign to be exempt from that law. Such font of law exemptions may be upheld, or may fall, depending upon

> whether a higher power or higher constitution might govern. Font of justice immunizations are even more common and perhaps more accepted by modernity. In the modern system of geographically overlapping state courts and federal courts, which in and of themselves may be overlapped by specialty courts or regulatory agencies of various subject matter jurisdictions, it, perhaps, seems less offensive to the modern ear to hear that a particular claim might be barred from adjudication in a particular court. For this reason or others, it seems more and more common for the people to accept a new law exempting their sovereign from the jurisdiction of a particular court or courts. Such a sovereign may find itself immunized completely, unless the sovereign itself agrees to hold the jurisdiction of another court to be even higher than the sovereign's domestic courts. American domestic sovereigns appear more diligent in immunizing themselves from foreign jurisdictions than some other modern nation-states. Treaties such as those creating the Court of Justice of the European Communities or creating the European Economic Union may be examples of foreign nation-states' greater willingness to yield sovereign immunity than is currently popular domestically.
>
> It has been said in some jurisdictions that the doctrine of governmental immunity from suit is currently in disfavor, that courts are disposed to hear an action against the state unless good reason stands in the way, and that the current trend of legislative policy and judicial thought is toward the abandonment of the doctrine of governmental immunity. Florida has not followed this view, and still generally follows the rule, under the law of sovereign immunity, that a suit may not be maintained against the state of Florida without its consent.

Id.

Notes and Questions to Consider:

1. Why in the modern era would a concept such as sovereign immunity still exist? Imagine that sovereign immunity did not exist, and a jury is so

offended by the action or inaction of the State of Florida that it awards damages against the state in the amount of twenty billion dollars. Where would the State of Florida obtain that money? What Florida bills and obligations would be unpaid in order to satisfy that judgment? What government services would Florida stop providing in order to satisfy that judgment? Does this scenario illustrate how it might be in the best interest of Floridians for the State of Florida to have sovereign immunity?

2. Certainly it is practical for the State of Florida to have sovereign immunity, but in your opinion, is it equitable? Imagine a plaintiff who is injured catastropically by the negligence of the State of Florida and for whom all experts agree has suffered economic damages in the form of wage loss and future medical care in the amount of $12,000,000. Imagine that Florida's sovereign immunity caps that damage award at $300,000. Does sovereign immunity create a fair result for such a plaintiff?

3. In the scenario from the last question, has sovereign immunity achieved its goal of protecting the public treasury in such an instance? After the plaintiff's $300,000 award is exhausted, will the plaintiff turn to public assistance to finance the balance of the plaintiff's future financial needs? Will this adversely affect the public treasury?

C. Sovereign Immunity as an Inherent Power

Florida's Constitution addresses sovereign immunity in its Article X where it states:

> SECTION 13. *Suits against the state.*-- Provision may be made by general law for bringing suit against the state as to all liabilities now existing or hereafter originating.

This section of "the Florida Constitution provides that the Legislature can abrogate the state's sovereign immunity." *Am. Home Assur. Co. v. Nat'l R.R. Passenger Corp.*, 908 So. 2d 459, 471 (Fla. 2005). Note that neither this section, nor any other section of Florida's Constitution, purports to create Florida's sovereign immunity. Instead, the authors of this section write from the perspective of Florida's sovereign immunity pre-existing Florida's Constitution. This section constitutes a potential waiver of that pre-existing sovereign immunity insofar as it authorizes Florida's Legislature to waive or not waive the state's sovereign immunity upon terms set by the Legislature. Only Florida's Legislature has authority to enact a general law that waives the state's sovereign immunity. *Id.* (citing *Manatee County v. Town of Longboat Key*, 365 So. 2d 143, 147 (Fla. 1978). "Further, any waiver of sovereign immunity must be clear and unequivocal." *Id.* (citing, inter alia, *Rabideau v. State*, 409 So. 2d 1045, 1046 (Fla. 1982). "[W]aivers of sovereign immunity … must [be] strictly construe[d] … [and] the waiver … will not be found as a product of inference or implication." *Id.* at 471–72. Stated somewhat differently, "sovereign immunity is the rule, rather than the exception" in Florida. *Pan–Am Tobacco Corp. v. Department of Corrections*, 471 So. 2d 4, 5 (Fla. 1984).

Florida's Supreme Court noted the following principles of sovereign immunity under Florida law:

> sovereign immunity applies to actions where the state is a party, unless the Legislature waives this immunity by general law; in the torts context, the Legislature has authorized a limited waiver of state sovereign immunity through [Florida Statutes] section 768.28; and in *Pan–Am Tobacco Corp. v. Department of Corrections*, 471 So. 2d 4, 5 (Fla. 1984), this Court held that these statutory limitations do not apply in actions brought against the state for breach of contract.

Am. Home Assur. Co. v. Nat'l R.R. Passenger Corp., 908 So. 2d 459, 467 (Fla. 2005).

From these principles, we can identify who is immune and from what they are immune. By "who," we mean the state, its counties, and its municipal corporations (meaning its cities, towns, and villages). By "what," we mean either a claim arising under state or federal law. Claims arising under state law would be claims created by a Florida Statute or the common law of the State of Florida. Claims arising under federal law would be claims created by the United States Code, the Code of Federal Regulations, or federal common law to the limited extent it still exists after *Erie v. Thompkins*, 304 U.S. 64 (1938) (holding that "federal common law exists only in such narrow areas as those concerned with the rights and obligations of the United States, interstate and international disputes implicating the conflicting rights of States or our relations with foreign nations, and admiralty cases.").

Seen from this perspective, Florida's sovereign immunity raises three separate issues: (1) Is the State of Florida or its counties or its municipal corporations immune from state law claims? (2) Is the State of Florida immune from a federal law claim? (3) Are Florida's counties, municipal corporations or entities they create immune from a federal law claim? We address each issue in turn.

a. Sovereign Immunity of the State, Counties or Municipal Corporations from State Law Claims

To answer this question, we must first answer it under the common law, and then acknowledge how the Florida Statutes alter the common law.

First, without regard to the statutory alterations of the common law, the general rule of common law sovereign immunity is that the immunity of the state is total, but the immunity of counties and municipal corporations is not. Under the common law before it is altered by statute, the State of Florida is immune, and counties are immune unless Florida's Legislature by general law provides otherwise, but municipal corporations (cities, towns and villages) are not immune. For example, common law sovereign immunity did not protect a municipal corporation conducting "proprietary functions" meaning functions that a private entity can perform, and that are not uniquely for the benefit of the general public, such as operating an automobile or machinery, hiring and supervising employees, commercial activities, or administering local and internal affairs within its territory.

This is the common law of statutory immunity, but it is altered by the Florida Statutes. Recall that Article X, Section 13 of Florida's Constitution provides that "[p]rovision may be made by general law for bringing suit against the state as to all liabilities now existing or hereafter originating." Florida's Legislature has made various provisions in the Florida Statutes that alter the common law of statutory immunity.

Perhaps the most noteworthy example is the statute applicable to tort claims arising out of state law. That statute is amended quite regularly, and as of 2018 reads in relevant part as follows:

> The state and its agencies and subdivisions shall be liable for tort claims . . . but liability shall not include punitive damages or [prejudgment] interest.... Neither the state nor its agencies or subdivisions shall be liable to pay a claim or a judgment by any one person which exceeds the sum of $200,000 or . . . when totaled with all other claims or judgments . . . exceeds the sum of $300,000. . . . [T]hat portion of the judgment that exceeds these amounts . . . may be paid in part or in whole only by further act of the Legislature. . . .
>
> No attorney may charge, demand, receive, or collect, for services rendered, fees in excess of 25 percent of any judgment or settlement....
>
> No officer, employee, or agent of the state or of any of its subdivisions shall be held personally liable in tort or named as a party ... unless such officer, employee, or agent acted in bad faith or with malicious purpose or in a manner exhibiting wanton and willful disregard of human rights, safety, or property.... The exclusive remedy for injury or damage suffered as a result of an act, event, or omission of an officer, employee, or agent of the state or any of its subdivisions or constitutional officers shall be by action against the governmental entity ... unless such act or omission was committed in bad faith or with malicious purpose or in a manner exhibiting wanton and willful disregard of human rights, safety, or property. The state or its subdivisions shall not be liable in tort for the acts or omissions of an officer, employee, or agent committed while acting outside the course and scope of her or his employment or committed in bad faith or with malicious purpose or in a manner exhibiting wanton and willful disregard of human rights, safety, or property.

§ 768.28, Fla. Stat. (2018).

In explaining how the common law of sovereign immunity operates considering Florida Statutes section 768.28, former Florida Supreme Court Justice Raoul Cantero wrote the following:

> I write to further explain the historical differences in our state constitution and our common law between the sovereign immunity of the state and that of municipalities. As I explain below, these common law differences dictate that the sovereign immunity of municipalities must be construed strictly, whereas the immunity of the state must be construed more broadly....
>
> [Florida's Municipal Home Rule Powers Act provides] broad powers conferred on municipalities to "exercise *any* power for municipal purposes, except when expressly prohibited by law." § 166.021(1), Fla. Stat. (1993) (emphasis added). [Therefore], unlike the effect of section 768.28 on the immunity of the state, the statute actually granted partial immunity to municipalities that did not previously exist. Because the immunity the statute grants municipalities is in derogation of the common law, it must be strictly construed.
>
> The state and municipalities differ in the degree of their historical sovereign immunity. Under the common law, the state's immunity was total. See *Cauley v. City of Jacksonville*, 403 So. 2d 379, 381 (Fla. 1981); *Spangler v. Fla. State Tpk. Auth.*, 106 So. 2d 421, 422 (Fla. 1958) (holding that the state and its agencies are immune from suit); *Smith v. City of Arcadia*, 2 So. 2d 725, 728 (Fla. 1941) ("The State cannot be sued ....") ...; *State Road Dep't of Fla. v. Tharp*, 1 So. 2d 868, 869 (Fla. 1941) ("[The] State cannot be sued without its consent. As to tort actions, the rule is universal and unqualified unless relaxed by the State...."). [Florida's] 1868 Constitution granted [Florida's] Legislature the power to waive it. See *id.* (citing art. IV, § 19, Fla. Const. (1868) (now art. X, § 13, Fla. Const.)). However, the Legislature declined to act until 1973, when it adopted section 768.28. See Ch. 73–313, Laws of Fla.
>
> In contrast to the state, municipalities never enjoyed total immunity from suit. See *Cauley*, 403 So. 2d at 381–83 (recognizing that

state sovereign immunity "remained in full force until section 768.28's enactment" while municipal sovereign immunity became subject to many exceptions before the waiver statute); *Woodford v. City of St. Petersburg*, 84 So. 2d 25, 26 (Fla. 1955) (holding that a municipality exercising a proprietary function is liable in the same manner as private corporations); *City of Tampa v. Easton*, 198 So. 753, 754 (Fla. 1940) ("Unlike a county, a municipality is not a subdivision of the State with subordinate attributes of sovereignty in the performance of governmental functions...."); *City of Tallahassee v. Fortune*, 3 Fla. 19 (1850) (distinguishing precedent from the United States and England and holding that an action for trespass may lie against a municipal corporation); see also *Cauley*, 403 So. 2d at 382–84 (outlining the development of municipal sovereign immunity law in Florida from *Fortune* through the enactment of section 768.28).

Before section 768.28, questions of whether municipal sovereign immunity applied were analyzed as follows:

> 1) as to those municipal activities which fall in the category of proprietary functions a municipality has the same tort liability as a private corporation;
>
> 2) as to those activities which fall in the category of governmental functions "... a municipality is liable in tort, under the doctrine of respondent [sic] superior, [...] only when such tort is committed against one with whom the agent or employee is in privity, or with whom he is dealing or is otherwise in contact in a direct transaction or confrontation."
>
> 3) as to those activities which fall in the category of judicial, quasi judicial, legislative, and quasi legislative functions, a municipality remains immune.

Cauley, 403 So. 2d at 383 (quoting *Gordon v. City of West Palm Beach*, 321 So. 2d 78, 80 (Fla. 4th DCA 1975)) (citations omitted); see also *Commercial Carrier Corp. v. Indian River County*, 371 So. 2d 1010, 1015 (Fla. 1979) (reviewing the history of municipal sovereign immunity and recognizing that before section 768.28 a municipality would be held liable for torts committed in the performance of proprietary acts).

Essentially, the state and its agencies, on the one hand, and municipalities, on the other, arrived at section 768.28 from opposite directions: the state from a status of near-total immunity; and municipalities from a status of near-nonexistent immunity. In fact, when the statute was first enacted, its effect on municipalities was unclear. In 1976, the Attorney General issued an opinion that "municipalities possessed no aspect of the state's sovereign immunity from tort liability upon which the waiver contained in section 768.28, and the limitations specified therein, could operate." Op. Att'y Gen. Fla. 76–41 (1976). In other words, the Attorney General opined that section 768.28, including its limitation on the amount of damages, did not apply to municipalities because they did not enjoy any immunity from tort suits that could be waived. The Legislature quickly amended section 768.28 by adding the following language in subsection 5: "The limitations of liability set forth in this subsection shall apply to the state and its agencies and subdivisions whether or not the state or its agencies or subdivisions possessed sovereign immunity prior to July 1, 1974." Ch. 77–86, § 1, Laws of Fla.

Section 768.28, therefore, affected the State and counties differently than it did municipalities. As to the State, the statute waived its sovereign immunity up to specified limits. As to municipalities, the statute granted them immunity from judgments above those limits.

Section 768.28 nullified the common law affecting both the state and municipalities, and therefore must be strictly construed. See *Carlile v. Game & Fresh Water Fish Comm'n*, 354 So. 2d 362, 364 (Fla. 1977). But it nullified the common law in different ways. As to the state and its agencies, the statute waives traditional immunity. As to municipalities, however, it grants partial immunity. Therefore, in construing the statute strictly, it must be construed in favor of granting immunity to the state, but against granting it to a municipality.

Am. Home Assur. Co. v. Nat'l R.R. Passenger Corp., 908 So. 2d 459, 477–78 (Fla. 2005) (Justice Cantero concurring).

This explains how sovereign immunity works for the state, its counties, and its municipal corporations (cities, towns and villages) regarding state law tort claims. What about state law breach of contract claims? That question is answered by *Pan-Am Tobacco Corp. v. Dep't of Corr.,* 471 So. 2d 4 (Fla. 1984):

PAN-AM TOBACCO CORP.

V.

DEPARTMENT OF CORRECTIONS

Supreme Court of Florida, 1984

471 So. 2d 4

… Pan-Am Tobacco Corp. entered into a written contract with the Department of Corrections. Pan-Am was to provide vending machines in six correctional facilities. The contract provided that Department of Corrections could cancel the contract for unsatisfactory performance by Pan-Am if it gave Pan-Am sixty days' written notice and thirty days within which to correct any deficiencies. Additionally, the contract provided for liquidated damages. Department of Corrections canceled the contract on thirty days' written notice, specifying no deficiencies in Pan-Am's performance and giving no time within which to correct any deficiencies. Pan-Am brought suit … and the First District Court of Appeal … certified as a matter of great public importance the following question:

> *When a state agency improperly rescinds an express executory contract with a private vendor who suffers a loss of profit as a consequence, may the state invoke sovereign immunity as a bar to an action on the breach of contract?*

… We answer the question in the negative....

In Florida, sovereign immunity is the rule, rather than the exception, as evidenced by article X, section 13 of the Florida Constitution: "Provision may be made by general law for bringing suit against the state as to all liabilities now existing or hereafter originating."

In section 768.28, Florida Statutes (1981), the legislature has explicitly waived sovereign immunity in tort. There is no analogous waiver in contract. Nonetheless, the legislature has, by general law, explicitly empowered various state agencies to enter into contracts. *See e.g.*, §§ 23.017, 153.62(11), 163.370, 230.22(4), 337.19(1), Fla. Stat. (1981). Additionally, it has authorized certain goals and activities which can only be achieved if state agencies have the power to contract for necessary goods and services. *See e.g.*, §§ 20.315, 945.215, Fla. Stat. (1981).

It is basic hornbook law that a contract which is not mutually enforceable is an illusory contract. *Howard Cole & Co. v. Williams,* 27 So. 2d 352 (1946). Where one party retains to itself the option of fulfilling or declining to fulfill its obligations under the contract, there is no valid contract and neither side may be bound....

Where the legislature has, by general law, authorized entities of the state to enter into contract or to undertake those activities which, as a matter of practicality, require entering into contract, the legislature has clearly intended that such contracts be valid and binding on both parties. As a matter of law, the state must be obligated to the private citizen or the legislative authorization for such action is void and meaningless. We therefore hold that where the state has entered into a contract fairly authorized by the powers granted by general law, the defense of sovereign immunity will not protect the state from action arising from the state's breach of that contract.

We recognize that in so holding we recede from a line of cases holding that the state may not be sued in contract without express consent to the suit. *See, e.g., Gay v. Southern Builders, Inc.,* 66 So. 2d 499 (Fla. 1953), *Bloxham v. Florida Central and Peninsular Railroad,* 17 So. 902 (Fla. 1895). Nonetheless, we note that this is not the first time this Court has looked to the legislative intent in general law to find a sovereign amenable to suit. *Manatee County v. Town of Longboat Key,* 365 So. 2d 143 (Fla. 1978) (where the legislature clearly intended the county to participate in resolution of taxation dispute and the county ignored its statutory duty, courts had jurisdiction to fashion a remedy in equity).

We would also emphasize that our holding here is applicable only to suits on express, written contracts into which the state agency has statutory authority to enter. Accordingly, the decision of the district court is quashed and this cause is remanded for further proceedings.

It is so ordered.

Notes and Questions to Consider:

1. How can the outcome of *Pan-Am v. Department of Corrections* be reconciled with these prior rulings from Florida's Supreme Court:

a. Any waiver of sovereign immunity "must be 'clear and unequivocal.'" *Arnold v. Shumpert*, 217 So. 2d 116, 120 (Fla. 1968)?

b. "The only way that the State can give its consent to be made a party defendant to a suit is by legislative act…" *Suits v. Hillsborough County*, 2 So. 2d 353, 357 (Fla. 1941)?

2. *Pan-Am v. Department of Corrections* holds that, "where the state has entered into a contract fairly authorized by the powers granted by general law, the defense of sovereign immunity will not protect the state from action arising from the state's breach of contract." What Florida Statute says so? Prior to the decision in *Pan-Am v. Department of Corrections*, what Florida case law precedent said so?

3. The holding of *Pan-Am v. Department of Corrections* explicitly overrules all contrary prior decisions, including one decided back in 1895. When the Department of Corrections breached the contract in the 1980's, did not they have a right to rely on case law precedent dating back more than 85 years?

4. After Florida's Supreme Court decided *Pan-Am v. Department of Corrections*, none of the parties sought review from the United States Supreme Court. Under the "adequate and independent" doctrine as interpret-

ed by *Michigan v. Long* and discussed in Chapter 1 of this text, would the U.S. Supreme Court have jurisdiction to review *Pan-Am v. Department of Corrections*?

2. Sovereign Immunity of the State from Federal Claims

The supremacy of federal law means that the sovereign immunity of the State of Florida from federal law claims depends on federal law. The Eleventh Amendment to the U.S. Constitution provides, in relevant part, that the "[j]udicial power of the United States shall not be construed to extend to any suit … against one of the United States by Citizens of another State, or by Citizens or Subjects of any Foreign State."

"Despite the limited categories of suits barred by the [Eleventh] Amendment's literal language, the [U.S.] Supreme Court has long interpreted the Amendment as expressive of the broader proposition that a state has immunity from suits brought by her own citizens as well as by those of another states." *Duncan v. University of Texas Health Science Center at Houston*, 469 Fed. Appx. 364, 366 (5th Cir. 2012). Therefore, as FLORIDA MUNICIPAL LAW AND PRACTICE explains, "[b]ecause Florida has sovereign immunity, the U.S. Congress cannot use its powers under Article I of the federal Constitution to subject Florida or any other state to suit in federal court without the state's consent." Patrick John McGinley, Florida Municipal Law and Practice § 7:3 (2018-2019 ed.). However, that treatise adds:

> Exceptions arise when the text of the federal Constitution allows the U.S. Congress to abrogate state sovereign immunity, and Congress passes a law that properly utilizes that power. For example, the bankruptcy clause of Article I of the U.S. Constitution was properly implemented by Congress to abrogate state sovereign immunity. As another example, the 14th Amendment to the federal Constitution gives Congress the power to abrogate state immunity from suit to the extent necessary to protect the civil rights granted by the Constitution. Therefore, conduct by persons acting under color of state law which violates 14th Amendment civil rights protected by 42 U.S.C. § 1983 cannot be immunized by state law.

Id. Note that 42 U.S.C. section 1983, which is part of the federal Civil Rights Act, provides in relevant part:

> Every person who, under color of any statute, ordinance, regulation, custom, or usage, of any State or Territory or the District of Columbia, subjects, or causes to be subjected, any citizen of the United States or other person within the jurisdiction thereof to the deprivation of any rights, privileges, or immunities secured by the Constitution and laws, shall be liable to the party injured in an action at law, suit in equity, or other proper proceeding for redress

Therefore, although it is true that a state like Florida cannot be sued in federal court on a federal claim without Florida's permission, that permission can be implied. By Florida signing the federal constitution, Florida implied its permission to be sued in federal court on a federal claim when the text of the federal Constitution empowers such a claim and an act of the U.S. Congress properly implements that power. See Patrick John McGinley, FLORIDA MUNICIPAL LAW AND PRACTICE § 7:3 (2018-2019 ed.). This is why the debtor's filing of a federal bankruptcy petition is sufficient to cause an automatic stay of a pending state lawsuit, and is why a state becomes liable for violating the civil rights of its citizens under the federal Civil Rights Act.

As for state officers and those individuals acting under color of state law, sovereign immunity does not prevent the issuance of injunctive relief against them and their behavior in violating a federal law or a federal constitutional right, as per the U.S. Supreme Court's 1908's decision in *Ex parte Young*, 209 U.S. 123 (1908). "The basic doctrine of *Ex parte Young* can be simply stated. A federal court is not barred by the Eleventh Amendment from enjoining state officers from acting unconstitutionally, either because their action is alleged to violate the Constitution directly or because it is contrary to a federal statute or regulation that is the supreme law of the land." Alan Wright, Arthur R. Miller, et al., 17A FED. PRAC. & PROC. JURIS. § 4232 (3d ed.) (April 2019 update). But just like states, state officers acting within their official capacity are immune from suits for damages in federal court without their consent. *See id.* at § 4232 n.2.

3. Sovereign Immunity of Counties and Municipal Corporations from Federal Claims

Do Florida's counties, cities, towns and villages enjoy sovereign immunity from federal law claims? "The Eleventh Amendment does not protect counties, cities, or other local governmental units so long as they are not the alter ego of the state ... and the *Young* rule is not needed to sue those governmental units or their officers." Alan Wright, Arthur R. Miller, et al., 17A FED. PRAC. & PROC. JURIS. § 4232 (3d ed.) (April 2019 update). To see this rule in action, consider *Town of Lake Clarke Shores v. Page,* 569 So. 2d 1256 (Fla. 1990).

TOWN OF LAKE CLARKE SHORES

V.

PAGE

Supreme Court of Florida, 1990

569 So. 2d 1256

...We review the opinion of the Fourth District Court of Appeal in *Page v. Valentine,* 552 So .2d 212 (Fla. 4th DCA 1989), in which we accepted jurisdiction based on conflict with *Howlett ex rel. Howlett v. Rose,* 537 So. 2d 706 (Fla. 2d DCA), *review denied,* 545 So. 2d 1367 (Fla.1989), *rev'd,* 496 U.S. 356 (1990). We have jurisdiction. Art. V, § 3(b)(3), Fla. Const.

The respondent, Alan Page, sued the petitioner, Town of Lake Clarke Shores (Town), under 42 U.S.C. § 1983.... In his complaint Page alleged that he was formerly a police officer with the Lake Clarke Shores Police Department. He claimed that his employment was terminated because Town officials were "discontented" by a letter published in The Palm Beach Post in which Page expressed his opinion about the effects of stress on police officers. The trial court dismissed the action against the Town holding that the court had no subject matter jurisdiction over § 1983 actions due to Florida's sovereign immunity doctrine. The Fourth District Court of Appeal reversed, relying on *City of Riviera Beach v. Langevin,* 522 So. 2d 857 (Fla. 4th DCA

1987), *review dismissed,* 536 So. 2d 243 (Fla. 1988), and *Southern Alliance Corp. v. City of Winter Haven,* 505 So. 2d 489 (Fla. 2d DCA 1987).

We agree with the court below that state trial courts do have subject matter jurisdiction over § 1983 actions against municipalities. The United States Supreme Court recently decided *Howlett ex rel. Howlett v. Rose,* 496 U.S. 356 (1990), reversing the very decision upon which the Town relies. In that case, the Supreme Court reaffirmed its ruling in *Will v. Michigan Department of State Police,* 491 U.S. 58 (1989), that "an entity with Eleventh Amendment immunity is not a 'person' within the meaning of § 1983." *Howlett,* 110 S.Ct. at 2437. Therefore, "the State and arms of the State, which have traditionally enjoyed Eleventh Amendment immunity, are not subject to suit under § 1983 in either federal court or state court." *Id.* However, the Court further stated that

> since the Court has held that municipal corporations and similar governmental entities are "persons," see *Monell v. New York City Dept. of Social Services,* 436 U.S. 658, 663 (1978); cf. *Will,* 491 U.S. at 58 n. 9; *Mt. Healthy City Board of Education v. Doyle,* 429 U.S. 274, 280–281 (1977), a state court entertaining a § 1983 action must adhere to that interpretation. "Municipal defenses—including an assertion of sovereign immunity—to a federal right of action are, of course, controlled by federal law." *Owen v. City of Independence,* 445 U.S. [622] at 647 n. 30 [(1980)]. "By including municipalities within the class of 'persons' subject to liability for violation of the Federal Constitution and laws, Congress—the supreme sovereign on matters of federal law—abolished whatever vestige of the State's sovereign immunity the municipality possessed." *Id.,* at 647–648 (footnote omitted).

Id.... The Supreme Court pointed out that the Second District Court of Appeal had erroneously extended this Court's decision in *Hill v. Department of Corrections,* 513 So. 2d 129 (Fla. 1987), *cert. denied,* 484 U.S. 106 (1988), *holding limited, Howlett ex rel. Howlett v. Rose,* 496 U.S. 356 (1990), which involved a state agency, to a suit against a municipality.

Therefore, we approve the opinion below and remand for further proceedings.

It is so ordered.

Note and Question to Consider:

1. This case explains that the federal Civil Rights Act makes "persons" liable for violations under federal law. That Act, instead of defining "persons" to include only natural persons, also includes a "municipality" within its definition of the word "persons." This lead Florida's Supreme Court in *Town of Lake Clarke Shores v. Page* to hold: "By including municipalities within the class of 'persons' subject to liability for violation of the Federal Constitution and laws, Congress—the supreme sovereign on matters of federal law—abolished whatever vestige of the State's sovereign immunity the municipality possessed." Why was a federal statutory definition enough to abrogate a state's inherent power of sovereign immunity?

Chapter Nine

Delegation of Government Powers

Florida's executive, legislative and judicial branches of government may delegate their power, but they may not abdicate their power. Any delegation of authority "requires an intelligible principle to be laid down for the guidance of an administrative official in the performance of his duties." *Phillips Petroleum Co. v. Anderson*, 74 So. 2d 544, 547 (Fla. 1954).

A. Delegation of Legislative Powers

In *Whiley v. Scott*, 79 So. 3d 702 (Fla. 2011), a citizen was successful in challenging Florida's Governor's authority to reign in agency rulemaking by proving his involvement in that rulemaking ran afoul of the proper delegation of legislative powers.

WHILEY

V.

SCOTT

Supreme Court of Florida, 2011

79 So. 3d 702

This case is before the Court on the petition of Rosalie Whiley for a writ of quo warranto seeking an order directing Respondent, the Honorable Rick Scott, Governor of the State of Florida, to demonstrate that he has not exceeded his authority.... In exercising our discretion to resolve this matter, we grant relief and specifically hold that the Governor impermissibly suspended agency rulemaking to the extent that Executive Orders 11–01 and 11–72 include a requirement that the Office of Fiscal Accountability and Regulatory Reform (OFARR) must first permit an agency to engage in the rulemaking which has been delegated by the Florida Legislature....

[I.] BACKGROUND

On January 4, 2011, Governor Scott issued "Executive Order Number 11–01 (Suspending Rulemaking and Establishing the Office of Fiscal Accountability and Regulatory Reform)," which created that office (OFARR) within the Executive Office of the Governor.2 OFARR is tasked with the goal of ensuring that agency-created rules do not hinder government performance and that they are fiscally responsible.... The Secretary of State was ordered not to publish any rulemaking notices in the Florida Administrative Weekly absent authorization from OFARR....

II. DISCUSSION

Our precise task in this case is to decide whether the Governor has overstepped his constitutional authority by issuing executive orders which contain certain limitations and suspensions upon agencies relating to their delegated legislative rulemaking authority...

[Florida's] Legislature has delegated specific responsibilities to agency heads, such as the authority to determine whether to go forward with proposing, amending, repealing, or adopting rules. See § 120.54(3)(a)(1), Fla. Stat. (2010).... This authority of the agency head cannot be delegated or transferred. See § 120.54(1)(k), Fla. Stat. (2010). Thus, rulemaking is a legislative function. See *Sims v. State*, 754 So. 2d 657, 668 (Fla. 2000) ("[T]he Legislature may 'enact a law, complete in itself, designed to accomplish a general public purpose, and may expressly authorize designated officials within definite valid limitations to provide rules and regulations for the complete operation and enforcement of the law within its expressed general purpose.' ") ...The Legislature delegates rulemaking authority to state agencies because they usually have expertise in a particular area for which they are charged with oversight.... Accordingly, the Legislature may specifically delegate, to some extent, its rulemaking authority to the executive branch "to permit administration of legislative policy by an agency with the expertise and flexibility needed to deal with complex and fluid conditions." *Microtel, Inc. v. Fla. Pub. Serv. Comm'n.*, 464 So. 2d 1189, 1191 (Fla.1985); see also § 120.536(1), Fla. Stat. (2010).

To determine whether the executive orders encroach upon the legislative delegations of rulemaking authority, the Court must first consider the established procedure for rulemaking. When adopting rules, the agencies must specifically conform to the rulemaking procedure enacted by the Legislature as the Florida Administrative Procedure Act in chapter 120, Florida Statutes....

The foregoing leads the Court to conclude that the Governor's executive orders at issue here, to the extent each suspends and terminates rulemaking by precluding notice publication and other compliance with Chapter 120 absent prior approval from OFARR—contrary to the Administrative Procedure Act—infringe upon the very process of rulemaking and encroach upon the Legislature's delegation of its rulemaking power as set forth in the Florida Statutes....

III. CONCLUSION

We distinguish between the Governor's constitutional authority with respect to the provisions of the executive orders pertaining to review and oversight of rulemaking within the executive agencies under his control, and the Legislature's lawmaking authority under article III, section 1 of the Florida Constitution. The Legislature retains the sole right to delegate rulemaking authority to agencies, and all provisions in both Executive Order 11–01 or 11–72 that operate to suspend rulemaking contrary to the APA constitute an encroachment upon a legislative function. We grant Whiley's petition but withhold issuance of the writ of quo warranto. We trust that any provision in Executive Order 11–72 suspending agency compliance with the APA, i.e., rulemaking, will not be enforced against an agency at this time, and until such time as the Florida Legislature may amend the APA or otherwise delegate such rulemaking authority to the Executive Office of the Governor.

It is so ordered.

B. Delegation of Judicial Powers

In *Pearce v. State,* 968 So. 2d 92 (Fla. 2d DCA 2007), Florida's Second District Court of Appeal agreed that a Florida Statute resulted in an improper delegation of judicial powers.

PEARCE

V.

STATE

Second District Court of Appeal of Florida, 2007

968 So. 2d 92

Kelvin Pearce challenges a restitution order imposed after he pleaded guilty to petit theft, a first-degree misdemeanor. § 812.014(2)(e), Fla. Stat. (2000). He argues-and the State concedes-that the trial court erred when it authorized Mr. Pearce's probation officer to establish a payment schedule for the restitution amount. We agree and reverse the restitution order in part with directions.

The Restitution Order & Subsequent Orders

At Mr. Pearce's April 26, 2006, sentencing and restitution hearing, the trial court withheld adjudication on the petit theft offense. The trial court imposed a sentence of twelve months' probation, and it ordered Mr. Pearce to pay $10,515 in restitution to the victim. Notably, the trial court delegated the matter of establishing a payment schedule to Mr. Pearce's probation officer. Mr. Pearce timely filed his notice of appeal.

On November 20, 2006, Mr. Pearce filed a motion to correct sentencing error under Florida Rule of Criminal Procedure 3.800(b)(2). Mr. Pearce did not contest the amount of the restitution award, but he argued that the trial court erred when it authorized his probation officer to determine a schedule for the restitution payments. The trial court agreed, and on January 25, 2007, it filed an order granting Mr. Pearce's motion and awarding him a new restitution hearing. On February 7, 2007, the circuit court set a restitution payment schedule at $250 per month. Finally, on April 12, 2007, the circuit court entered an order modifying the terms of Mr. Pearce's probation so that any restitution amount outstanding at the end of his one-year probationary term would be converted to a lien.

Analysis

As the State concedes, the trial court erred in its original restitution order when it delegated to Mr. Pearce's probation officer the authority for determining the restitution payment schedule. Florida courts have long held that the determination of a restitution payment schedule is a judicial responsibility that cannot be delegated. *Lewellen v. State,* 685 So. 2d 1367, 1368 (Fla. 2d DCA 1996); *Douglas v. State,* 664 So. 2d 1099, 1099 (Fla. 2d DCA 1995); *Guinn v. State,* 652 So. 2d 902, 902 (Fla. 2d DCA 1995); *Briggs v. State,* 647 So. 2d 182, 182 (Fla. 1st DCA 1994); *see also Thomas v. State,* 635 So. 2d 1009, 1010 (Fla. 1st DCA 1994) (finding error where the trial court revoked probation based on the defendant's failure "to follow a payment schedule established, not by the trial court, but by the probation officer"). In addition, while the trial court clearly intended to correct its error when it granted Mr. Pearce's rule 3.800(b)(2) motion, we note that sixty-six days had elapsed from November 20, 2006 (the day Mr. Pearce filed his motion) to January 25, 2007 (the day the order granting the motion was filed). Consequently, Mr. Pearce's motion was deemed denied by rule when the trial court failed to dispose of it within sixty days--i.e., by January 19, 2007. *See* Fla. R.Crim. P. 3.800(b)(1)(B). For these reasons, we affirm the restitution order to the extent that it established the restitution amount, but we reverse the restitution order to the extent that it delegated to the probation officer the determination of the payment schedule.

Because the circuit court did not file an order ruling on the motion within the sixty-day time period, its jurisdiction to correct the error terminated on January 19, 2007. Thus the January 25 order granting Mr. Pearce's motion, the February 7 order setting the restitution payment schedule at $250 per month, and the April 12 order converting all outstanding restitution amounts to a lien are nullities. *Whitmore v. State,* 910 So. 2d 308, 308 (Fla. 2d DCA 2005); *Sessions v. State,* 907 So. 2d 572, 573 (Fla. 1st DCA 2005). Accordingly, we vacate these orders.

Conclusion

To summarize, we affirm Mr. Pearce's judgment and sentence, and we affirm the portion of the restitution order that establishes the restitution amount. We reverse the restitution order to the extent that it delegates authority to Mr. Pearce's probation officer to determine the restitution payment schedule. We vacate the three orders entered after January 19, 2007, and we remand with directions to conduct a new restitution hearing to determine the appropriate method for Mr. Pearce to satisfy the remainder of his restitution obligation.

Affirmed in part, reversed in part, and remanded with directions.

Chapter Ten

Elections

A. Regulation of Elections

Article VI of Florida's Constitution discusses suffrage and elections. As to the regulation of Florida's elections, Article VI provides:

> SECTION 1. *Regulation of elections.*—All elections by the people shall be by direct and secret vote. General elections shall be determined by a plurality of votes cast. Registration and elections shall, and political party functions may, be regulated by law; however, the requirements for a candidate with no party affiliation or for a candidate of a minor party for placement of the candidate's name on the ballot shall be no greater than the requirements for a candidate of the party having the largest number of registered voters.

Is the election process of any state more infamous than Florida's? In *Bush v. Gore*, 531 U.S. 98 (2000), "[s]even Justices of the [Supreme] Court [of the United States] agree[d] that there are constitutional problems with" Florida's election system. *Id.* at 111. The U.S. Supreme Court held that in Florida, a simple recount "cannot be conducted in compliance with the requirements of equal protection and due process without substantial additional work." *Id.* at 110. The "additional work" omitted by Florida seemed to be quite basic regulatory tasks: "the adoption (after opportunity for argument) of adequate statewide standards for determining what is a legal vote, and practicable procedures to implement them, but also orderly judicial review of any disputed matters that might arise." *Id.* at 110.

More than a decade later, has Florida solved its infirmities in the regulation of its elections? Consider the case of *Orange County v. Singh*, 268 So. 3d 668 (Fla. 2019).

ORANGE COUNTY

v.

SINGH

Supreme Court of Florida, 2019

268 So. 3d 668

PER CURIAM.

Respondents' Joint Motion to Recall Mandate is hereby granted. The opinion of this Court dated January 4, 2019, is hereby withdrawn, and this opinion is substituted in its place. *See*§ 43.44, Fla. Stat. (2018) ("An appellate court may, as the circumstances and justice of the case may require, reconsider, revise, reform, or modify its own opinions and orders for the purpose of making the same accord with law and justice."); Fla. R. Jud. Admin. 2.205(b)(5). In light of the substituted opinion, we hereby deny Respondents' Joint Motion for Clarification.

We have for review the Fifth District Court of Appeal's decision in *Orange County v. Singh*, 230 So. 3d 639 (Fla. 5th DCA 2017), which affirmed a trial court judgment invalidating an Orange County ordinance. Because home-rule counties may not enact ordinances on subjects preempted to the State and inconsistent with general law, we approve the decision of the Fifth District.

I. Background

. . .

On August 19, 2014, the Orange County Board of Commissioners enacted an ordinance proposing an amendment to the Orange County Charter to provide for term limits and nonpartisan elections for six county constitutional officers—clerk of the circuit court, comptroller, property appraiser, sheriff, supervisor of elections, and tax collector. The ordinance provided for the following ballot question to be presented for further approval:

> CHARTER AMENDMENT PROVIDING FOR TERM LIMITS AND NON–PARTISAN ELECTIONS FOR COUNTY CONSTITUTIONAL OFFICERS
>
> For the purpose of establishing term limits and nonpartisan elections for the Orange County Clerk of the Circuit Court, Comptroller, Property Appraiser, Sheriff, Supervisor of Elections and Tax Collector, this amendment provides for county constitutional officers to be elected on a non-partisan basis and subject to term limits of four consecutive full 4–year terms.
>
> _____ Yes
>
> _____ No

The ballot question appeared on the November 4, 2014[,] ballot and was approved by the majority of Orange County voters. As a result, the relevant portions of section 703 of the Orange County Charter were amended (as indicated **in boldface type below**) to read:

> B. Except as may be specifically set forth in the Charter, the county officers referenced under Article VIII, Section 1(d) of the Florida Constitution and Chapter 72–461, Laws of Florida, shall not be governed by the Charter but instead governed by the Constitution and laws of the State of Florida. **The establishment of nonpartisan elections and term limits for county constitutional officers shall in no way affect or impugn their status as independent constitutional officers, and shall in no way imply any authority by the board whatsoever over such independent constitutional officers.**
>
> **C. Elections for all county constitutional offices shall be nonpartisan. No county constitutional office candidate shall be required to pay any party assessment or be required to state the party of which the candidate is a member. All county constitutional office**

candidates' names shall be placed on the ballot without reference to political party affiliation.

In the event that more than two (2) candidates have qualified for any single county constitutional office, an election shall be held at the time of the first primary election and, providing no candidate receives a majority of the votes cast, the two (2) candidates receiving the most votes shall be placed on the ballot for the general election.

D. Any county constitutional officer who has held the same county constitutional office for the preceding four (4) full consecutive terms is prohibited from appearing on the ballot for reelection to that office; provided, however, that the terms of office beginning before January 1, 2015 shall not be counted.

Prior to the November 4, 2014 election, three Orange County constitutional officers—the sheriff, property appraiser, and tax collector (collectively "Appellees")—filed a suit for declaratory and injunctive relief against Orange County, challenging the underlying county ordinance as well as the ballot title and summary. After the election, in ruling on competing summary judgment motions, the trial court upheld the portion of the charter amendment providing for term limits, but struck down that portion providing for nonpartisan elections. The trial court concluded that Orange County was prohibited from regulating nonpartisan elections for county constitutional officers because that subject matter was preempted to the Legislature.

. . .

On appeal, the Fifth District affirmed the trial court's judgment.... The Fifth District held that section 97.0115, Florida Statutes, expressly preempts the Orange County ordinance requiring nonpartisan elections for county constitutional officers. [*Singh*, 230 So. 3d] at 641-42. The Fifth District reasoned that the Legislature regulates elections generally through the Florida Election Code and "enacted section 97.0115, which expressly provides that all matters set forth in the Florida Election Code were preempted" to the Legislature. *Id.* at 642. The Fifth District further reasoned that chapter 105, Florida

Statutes, "set forth provisions and procedures specific to nonpartisan elections," and "chapter 105 did not authorize counties to hold nonpartisan elections for the county constitutional officers that are the subject of the charter amendment at issue." *Id.*

II. The Florida Election Code

Article VI, section 1 of the Florida Constitution provides that "[r]egistration and elections shall, and political party functions may, be regulated by law[.]" *See Grapeland Heights Civic Ass'n v. City of Miami*, 267 So. 2d 321, 324 (Fla. 1972) ("[I]t necessarily follows that 'law' *in our constitution* means an enactment by the State Legislature ...—not by a City Commission or any other political body."). The Legislature regulates elections through the Florida Election Code, which encompasses chapters 97-106, Florida Statutes (2018). Importantly, the Florida Election Code contains express language of preemption as section 97.0115 states that "[a]ll matters set forth in chapters 97-105 are preempted to the state, except as otherwise specifically authorized by state or federal law." The Florida Election Code further explains that the Secretary of State, as "the chief election officer of the state," is to "[o]btain and maintain uniformity in the interpretation and implementation of the election laws." § 97.012(1), Fla. Stat. (2018).

The Florida Election Code generally contemplates partisan elections. In other words, candidates nominated by political parties in the primary election are to appear on the general election ballot for most offices. *See* § 101.151(2)(c), Fla. Stat. (2018) ("Each nominee of a political party chosen in a primary shall appear on the general election ballot in the same numbered group or district as on the primary election ballot."). In fact, section 97.021(29) (emphasis added), defines a "[p]rimary election" as "an election held preceding the general election for the purpose of nominating a party nominee to be voted for in the general election to fill a national, state, *county*, or district office."

Specifically, section 100.051 provides that "[t]he supervisor of elections of each county shall print on ballots to be used in the county at the next general election the names of candidates who have been nominated by a political party and the candidates who have otherwise obtained a position on the general election ballot in compliance with the requirements of this code." In addition to the candidates nominated by political parties, no-party affiliation candidates, minor political party candidates, and spaces for write-in candidates may be listed on the general election ballot and may compete for the same offices as the major political party candidates in compliance with the Florida Election Code. § 99.0955, Fla. Stat. (2018); § 99.096, Fla. Stat. (2018); § 99.061(4)(b), Fla. Stat. (2018).

Regarding qualifying for nomination or election to county offices in particular, section 99.061(2) (emphasis added) provides that "each person seeking to qualify for nomination or election to a county office ... shall file his or her qualification papers with, and pay the qualifying fee, which shall consist of the filing fee and election assessment, *and party assessment*, if any has been levied, to, the supervisor of elections of the county, or shall qualify by the petition process pursuant to s. 99.095." The same subsection also states that "the supervisor of elections shall remit to the secretary of the state executive committee of *the political party to which the candidate belongs* the amount of the filing fee, two-thirds of which shall be used to promote *the candidacy of candidates for county offices* and the candidacy of members of the Legislature." *Id.* (emphasis added).

Regarding timing, section 100.031, Florida Statutes (2018), provides that "[a] general election shall be held in each county on the first Tuesday after the first Monday in November of each even-numbered year." Section 100.061, Florida Statutes (2018), states that "a primary election for nomination of candidates of political parties shall be held on the Tuesday 10 weeks prior to the general election." Further, section 100.041(1), Florida Statutes (2018) (emphasis added), lists the following offices, including several county constitutional offices, that are to be chosen at the general election after a primary election:

> State senators shall be elected for terms of 4 years, those from odd-numbered districts in each year the number of which is a multiple of 4 and those from even-numbered districts in each even-numbered year the

> number of which is not a multiple of 4. Members of the House of Representatives shall be elected for terms of 2 years in each even-numbered year. *In each county, a clerk of the circuit court, sheriff, superintendent of schools, property appraiser, and tax collector shall be chosen by the qualified electors at the general election in each year the number of which is a multiple of 4*. The Governor and the administrative officers of the executive branch of the state shall be elected for terms of 4 years in each even-numbered year the number of which is not a multiple of 4. The terms of state offices other than the terms of members of the Legislature shall begin on the first Tuesday after the first Monday in January after said election. The term of office of each member of the Legislature shall begin upon election.

See also § 98.015(1), Fla. Stat. (2018) ("A supervisor of elections shall be elected in each county at the general election in each year the number of which is a multiple of four for a 4-year term commencing on the first Tuesday after the first Monday in January succeeding his or her election.").

However, while the Florida Election Code contemplates elections for most offices to include candidates nominated by political parties, it also specifies that elections for certain offices must be nonpartisan. Pursuant to section 97.021(22), Florida Statutes (2018), "'Nonpartisan office' means an office for which a candidate is prohibited from campaigning or qualifying for election or retention in office based on party affiliation." Then, chapter 105, entitled "Nonpartisan Elections," provides that judicial officers and school board members are nonpartisan offices. Candidates for judicial offices (or those seeking retention) are "prohibited from campaigning or qualifying for such [offices] based on party affiliation." § 105.011(2), Fla. Stat. (2018). Furthermore, section 105.09(1), Florida Statutes (2018), states that "[n]o political party or partisan political organization shall endorse, support, or assist any candidate in a campaign for election to judicial office." Section 105.035(1), Florida Statutes (2018), also explains that "[a] person seeking to qualify for election to the office of circuit judge or county court judge or the office of school board member may qualify for election to such office by means of the petitioning process prescribed in this section." And section 105.041(3)-(4),

Florida Statutes (2018), states that "[n]o reference to political party affiliation shall appear on any ballot with respect to any nonpartisan office or candidate," while "[s]pace shall be made available on the general election ballot" for write-in candidates for circuit and county court judge as well as school board members.

Regarding timing of the nonpartisan elections, section 105.051(1)(b), Florida Statutes (2018), provides that elections for judicial officers and school board members are to be conducted during the primary election with the possibility of a run-off during the general election:

> If two or more candidates, neither of whom is a write-in candidate, qualify for such an office, the names of those candidates shall be placed on the ballot at the primary election. If any candidate for such office receives a majority of the votes cast for such office in the primary election, the name of the candidate who receives such majority shall not appear on any other ballot unless a write-in candidate has qualified for such office. An unopposed candidate shall be deemed to have voted for himself or herself at the general election. If no candidate for such office receives a majority of the votes cast for such office in the primary election, the names of the two candidates receiving the highest number of votes for such office shall be placed on the general election ballot. If more than two candidates receive an equal and highest number of votes, the name of each candidate receiving an equal and highest number of votes shall be placed on the general election ballot. In any contest in which there is a tie for second place and the candidate placing first did not receive a majority of the votes cast for such office, the name of the candidate placing first and the name of each candidate tying for second shall be placed on the general election ballot.

Additionally, the nonpartisan chapter of the Florida Election Code, chapter 105, specifies that the retention elections of appellate judges are to take place during the general election. § 105.051(2), Fla. Stat. (2018).

Notably, chapter 105 does not include any county constitutional officers as nonpartisan. The specific references to the county constitutional officers in the Florida Election Code are in its more general provisions in which candidates nominated by political parties may appear on the general ballot. Moreover, although the Florida Election Code expressly allows for municipal elections to vary from its requirements pursuant to an ordinance or charter so long as the variance does not conflict with "any provision in the Florida Election Code that expressly applies to municipalities," § 100.3605(1), Florida Statutes (2018), there is no similar allowance for county elections.

III. The Orange County Ordinance is Expressly Preempted and in Conflict

Orange County contends that the ordinance at issue in this case is not expressly preempted by or in conflict with the Florida Election Code. We disagree.

In *Phantom of Brevard, Inc. v. Brevard County*, 3 So. 3d 309, 314 (Fla. 2008), this Court explained the following standards regarding whether a county ordinance is preempted by or in conflict with a statute:

> Pursuant to our Constitution, chartered counties have broad powers of self-government. *See* art. VIII, § 1(g), Fla. Const. Indeed, under article VIII, section 1(g) of the Florida Constitution, chartered counties have the broad authority to "enact county ordinances not inconsistent with general law." *See also* David G. Tucker, *A Primer on Counties and Municipalities, Part I*, Fla. B.J., Mar. 2007, at 49. However, there are two ways that a county ordinance can be inconsistent with state law and therefore unconstitutional. First, a county cannot legislate in a field if the subject area has been preempted to the State. *See City of Hollywood v. Mulligan*, 934 So. 2d 1238, 1243 (Fla. 2006). "Preemption essentially takes a topic or a field in which local government might otherwise establish appropriate local laws and reserves that topic for regulation exclusively by the legislature." *Id.* (quoting *Phantom of Clearwater[, Inc. v. Pinellas County]*, 894 So. 2d [1011] , 1018 [(Fla. 2d DCA 2005)]). Second, in a field where both the State and local government can legislate concurrently, a county cannot enact an ordinance that directly conflicts with a state statute. *See Tallahassee Mem'l Reg'l Med. Ctr., Inc. v. Tallahassee Med. Ctr., Inc.*, 681 So. 2d 826, 831 (Fla. 1st DCA 1996).

> Local "ordinances are inferior to laws of the state and must not conflict with any controlling provision of a statute." *Thomas v. State*, 614 So. 2d 468, 470 (Fla. 1993); *Hillsborough County v. Fla. Rest. Ass'n*, 603 So. 2d 587, 591 (Fla. 2d DCA 1992) ("If [a county] has enacted such an inconsistent ordinance, the ordinance must be declared null and void."); *see also Rinzler v. Carson*, 262 So. 2d 661, 668 (Fla. 1972) ("A municipality cannot forbid what the legislature has expressly licensed, authorized or required, nor may it authorize what the legislature has expressly forbidden.").
>
> There is conflict between a local ordinance and a state statute when the local ordinance cannot coexist with the state statute. *See City of Hollywood*, 934 So. 2d at 1246; *see also State ex rel. Dade County v. Brautigam*, 224 So. 2d 688, 692 (Fla. 1969) (explaining that "inconsistent" as used in article VIII, section 6(f) of the Florida Constitution "means contradictory in the sense of legislative provisions which cannot coexist"). Stated otherwise, "[t]he test for conflict is whether 'in order to comply with one provision, a violation of the other is required.'" *Browning v. Sarasota Alliance for Fair Elections, Inc.*, 968 So. 2d 637, 649 (Fla. 2d DCA 2007) (quoting *Phantom of Clearwater*, 894 So. 2d at 1020), *review granted*, No. SC07-2074 (Fla. Nov. 29, 2007).

In this case, the Florida Election Code expressly preempts the Orange County ordinance requiring nonpartisan elections for its county constitutional officers. Section 97.0115 provides that "[a]ll matters set forth in chapters 97-105 are preempted to the state, except as otherwise specifically authorized by state or federal law." As explained above, the Florida Election Code contemplates partisan elections for most offices, and it does not specifically authorize otherwise for county constitutional officers. Furthermore, article VIII, section 1(d) of the Florida Constitution does not expressly label the election of county constitutional officers as "partisan" or "nonpartisan." Therefore, this constitutional provision is not an exception to the preemption language contained in section 97.0115.

The Florida Election Code contains detailed provisions specific to county constitutional officers and county elections, provisions that are within the portions of the code providing for partisan elections. Section 100.041 states that "[i]n each county, a clerk of the circuit court, sheriff, superintendent of schools, property appraiser, and tax collector shall be chosen by the qualified electors at the general election in each year the number of which is a multiple of 4." *See also* § 100.031, Fla. Stat. ("A general election shall be held in each county ... to choose a successor to each elective ... county ... officer ...."); § 98.015 (1), Fla. Stat. ("A supervisor of elections shall be elected in each county at the general election ..."). Further, section 100.051 expressly provides that candidates listed on the general election ballot are "candidates who have been nominated by a political party *and* the candidates who have otherwise obtained a position on the general election ballot in compliance with the requirements of this code." (Emphasis added.)

In contrast, the Orange County ordinance provides as follows:

> Elections for all county constitutional offices shall be non-partisan. No county constitutional office candidate shall be required to pay any party assessment or be required to state the party of which the candidate is a member. All county constitutional offices candidates' names shall be placed on the ballot without reference to party affiliation.

Singh, 230 So. 3d at 640-41 (quoting amended charter).

The portion of the ordinance that requires elections for county constitutional officers to be held during the primary election conflicts with section 100.041, which requires county constitutional officers to appear on the general election ballot. It also conflicts with section 98.015, Florida Statutes, which separately addresses the election of the supervisor of elections. *See* § 98.015, Fla. Stat. ("A supervisor of elections shall be elected in each county at the general election ...").

Even if the portion of the Orange County ordinance that requires such an election to be held during the primary election is severed, a glaring and unconstitutional conflict remains. The Orange County ordinance prohibits a candidate for county constitutional office from being referenced on the ballot by party or seeking nomination by a party during the primary election. However, the Florida Election Code expressly provides for nomination of candidates for county office by their respective political parties during the primary election. *See* § 99.061(2), Fla. Stat. (candidates for county offices may qualify for nomination or election by filing the qualifying papers and paying "the filing fee and election assessment, and party assessment"); § 97.021(29), Fla. Stat. (defining "[p]rimary election" as "an election held preceding the general election for the purpose of nominating a party nominee to be voted for in the general election to fill a national, state, county, or district office"); § 100.051, Fla. Stat. (explaining that candidates listed on the general election ballot include those "candidates who have been nominated by a political party"); *see also* § 100.031, Fla. Stat. ("A general election shall be held in each county ... to choose a successor to each elective ... county ... officer ...."); § 100.041(1), Fla. Stat. ("In each county, a clerk of the circuit court, sheriff, superintendent of schools, property appraiser, and tax collector shall be chosen by the qualified electors at the general election in each year the number of which is a multiple of 4."); § 98.015(1), Fla. Stat. ("A supervisor of elections shall be elected in each county at the general election ...."). Therefore, by banning a candidate for county constitutional office from running by party or seeking nomination by party, the ordinance directly conflicts with the Florida Election Code. And this Court has explained that a local government "cannot forbid what the legislature has expressly licensed, authorized or required." *Rinzler*, 262 So. 2d at 668.

Accordingly, because the Orange County ordinance prohibits candidates from running based on their party affiliation or seeking the nomination of their party during the primary election, which is expressly provided for in the Florida Election Code, the ordinance directly conflicts with the Florida Election Code. It also conflicts with the Florida Election Code's requirement that the candidates for county constitutional officers appear on the general election ballot.

IV. Conclusion

As explained above, the Florida Election Code expressly preempts the Orange County ordinance, an ordinance that is in direct conflict with the Florida Election Code regarding whether candidates nominated by major political parties in the primary election may appear on the general election ballot for county constitutional officers. Therefore, we approve the decision of the Fifth District, which held that the Florida Election Code preempts the Orange County ordinance requiring nonpartisan elections for county constitutional officers.

It is so ordered.

CANADY, C.J., and POLSTON, LAWSON, LAGOA, LUCK, and MUÑIZ, JJ., concur.

LABARGA, J., dissents with an opinion.

LABARGA, J., dissenting.

In *Orange County v. Singh*, —— So. 3d ——, 44 Fla. L. Weekly S102 (Fla. Jan. 4, 2019) (opinion withdrawn), this Court held that the Florida Election Code does not expressly preempt the home rule authority of Orange County to determine that its constitutional officers be elected in a general election without partisan affiliation. I concurred in that decision, and I continue to agree with the analysis and conclusion reached by the earlier majority. Accordingly, I dissent from the current majority's holding that the nonpartisan-election portion of the Orange County ordinance is preempted by the Florida Election Code and to the decision of the majority to recall the mandate issued in this case.

B. Electors and Disqualification

In Florida election law, an "elector" is someone who is eligible to vote in an election. See *Harris v. Baden*, 17 So. 2d 608 (Fla. 1944). A "disqualification" is something that makes someone ineligible to be an elector.

Article VI of Florida's Constitution says the following about electors and their potential disqualification.

> SECTION 2. *Electors.*—Every citizen of the United States who is at least eighteen years of age and who is a permanent resident of the state, if registered as provided by law, shall be an elector of the county where registered.
>
> SECTION 3. *Oath.*—Each eligible citizen upon registering shall subscribe the following: "I do solemnly swear (or affirm) that I will protect and defend the Constitution of the United States and the Constitution of the State of Florida, and that I am qualified to register as an elector under the Constitution and laws of the State of Florida."
>
> SECTION 4. *Disqualifications.*—
>
> (a) No person convicted of a felony, or adjudicated in this or any other state to be mentally incompetent, shall be qualified to vote or hold office until restoration of civil rights or removal of disability. Except as provided in subsection (b) of this section, any disqualification from voting arising from a felony conviction shall terminate and voting rights shall be restored upon completion of all terms of sentence including parole or probation.
>
> (b) No person convicted of murder or a felony sexual offense shall be qualified to vote until restoration of civil rights.
>
> (c) No person may appear on the ballot for re-election to any of the following offices:
>
> (1) Florida representative,
>
> (2) Florida senator,
>
> (3) Florida Lieutenant governor,
>
> (4) any office of the Florida cabinet,

(5) U.S. Representative from Florida, or

(6) U.S. Senator from Florida

if, by the end of the current term of office, the person will have served (or, but for resignation, would have served) in that office for eight consecutive years.

Notes and Question to Consider:

1. Note that the language in Florida's Constitution in Article VI Section 4 about term limits violates the U.S. Constitution as applied to candidates for the U.S. Congress. In *U.S. Term Limits, Inc. v. Thornton*, 514 U.S. 779 (1995), the U.S. Supreme Court considered a similar term limit appearing in the Arkansas Constitution. The court affirmed the Arkansas Supreme Court's ruling that the term limits imposed upon candidates for the United States Congress was a violation of the U.S. Constitution. Specifically, the court held that states cannot impose qualifications upon candidates for the U.S. Senate or U.S. House of Representatives in addition to those imposed by the U.S. Constitution. The Tenth Amendment to the U.S. Constitution did not reserve such power to the states. So how could Florida impose such term limits in a way that would not violate the U.S. Constitution?

2. Note that the language in Article VI Section 4 stating "any disqualification from voting arising from a felony conviction shall terminate and voting rights shall be restored upon completion of all terms of sentence including parole or probation," and the language surrounding it, were the result of Amendment 4 that passed in 2018.

C. Primary, General and Special Elections

Regarding primary, general, and special elections, Florida's Constitution's Article VI provides:

SECTION 5. *Primary, general, and special elections.—*

(a) A general election shall be held in each county on the first Tuesday after the first Monday in November of each even-numbered year to choose a successor to each elective state and county officer whose term will expire before the next general election and, except as provided herein, to fill each vacancy in elective office for the unexpired portion of the term. A general election may be suspended or delayed due to a state of emergency or impending emergency pursuant to general law. Special elections and referenda shall be held as provided by law.

(b) If all candidates for an office have the same party affiliation and the winner will have no opposition in the general election, all qualified electors, regardless of party affiliation, may vote in the primary elections for that office.

SECTION 6. *Municipal and district elections.*—Registration and elections in municipalities shall, and in other governmental entities created by statute may, be provided by law.

SECTION 7. *Campaign spending limits and funding of campaigns for elective state-wide office.*—It is the policy of this state to provide for state-wide elections in which all qualified candidates may compete effectively. A method of public financing for campaigns for state-wide office shall be established by law. Spending limits shall be established for such campaigns for candidates who use public funds in their campaigns. The legislature shall provide funding for this provision. General law implementing this paragraph shall be at least as protective of effective competition by a candidate who uses public funds as the general law in effect on January 1, 1998.

Chapter Eleven

Homestead

A. Introduction to Homestead

"Florida has been a popular choice to take up residency for many individuals because of the expansive creditor protection afforded by the homestead laws in this state. This expansive protection stems from the purpose of homestead: to preserve the family home." Joseph M. Percopo, *The Impact of Co-Ownership on Florida Homestead*, Fla. B.J., at 32, 34–35 (May 2012).

Florida's Constitution protects homestead property from a forced sale by most creditors under Article X, §4, which states in relevant part:

> (a) There shall be exempt from forced sale under process of any court, and no judgment, decree or execution shall be a lien thereon except for the payment of taxes and assessments thereon, obligations contracted for the purchase, improvement or repair thereof, or obligations contracted for house, filed or other labor performed on the realty, the following property owned by a natural person:
>
> (1) a homestead, if located outside the municipality, to the extent of one hundred sixty acres of contiguous land and improvements thereon, which shall not be reduced without the owner's consent by reason of subsequent inclusion in a municipality; or if located within a municipality, to the extent of one-half acre of contiguous land, upon which the exemption shall be limited to the residence of the owner or the owner's family.

But protection from creditors is not the only right provided for homesteads. The Constitution of the State of Florida protects a Floridian's homestead in three distinct ways:

> First, a clause…provides homesteads with [a partial] exemption from taxes. Second, the homestead provision protects the homestead from

> forced sale by [most] creditors. Third, the homestead provision delineates the restrictions a homestead owner faces when attempting to alienate or devise the homestead property....As a matter of public policy, the purpose of the homestead exemption is to promote the stability and welfare of the state by securing to the householder a home, so that the homeowner and his or her heirs may live beyond the reach of financial misfortune and the demands of creditors who have given credit under such law.

Snyder v. Davis, 699 So. 2d 999, 1002 (Fla. 1997).

Any "natural person" may benefit from Florida's Homestead protection from creditors. Even if, perhaps, the original intent of the homestead protection might have been to protect those dependents living in the homestead after the breadwinner's death, the current scope of Florida's homestead protection is far broader due to a constitutional amendment making it available to more than just the head of household. "The [1985] change in the constitutional language from 'a head of household' to 'a natural person' expanded the class of persons afforded constitutional homestead protections to include individuals who are single and those with no dependents." Alex Cuello, *The Long-Standing Concept of "Abandonment" of the Homestead Did Not Survive the 1985 Amendments to the Florida Constitution*, Fla. B.J., December 2012, at 37, 38.

B. Homestead Protection from Full Taxation

As to the exemption from taxes, Article V, section 6 of the Constitution of the State of Florida states in pertinent part:

> Every person who has the legal or equitable title to real estate and maintains thereon the permanent residence of the owner, or another legally or naturally dependent upon the owner, shall be exempt from taxation thereon, except assessments for special benefits, up to the assessed valuation of twenty-five thousand dollars and, for all levies other than school district levies, on the assessed valuation greater than fifty thousand dollars

> and up to seventy-five thousand dollars, upon establishment of right thereto in the manner prescribed by law.
>
> The real estate may be held by legal or equitable title, by the entireties, jointly, in common, as a condominium, or indirectly by stock ownership or membership representing the owner's or member's proprietary interest in a corporation owning a fee or a leasehold initially in excess of ninety-eight years.

Id. at section 6(a). As I described in my book *Florida Elements of an Action:*

> The plain language of article VII, section 6(a) provides that an owner of residential real estate in Florida is constitutionally entitled to an exemption from ad valorem taxation—more accurately, a reduction in the assessed value—under either of the following two separate and independent scenarios:
>
> > 1. Where the owner of the property is a permanent resident on the property,
> >
> > OR
> >
> > 2. Where someone legally or naturally dependent on the owner is a permanent resident on the subject property.
>
> Florida Statutes Section 196.012 defines "permanent residence" for purposes of this provision as follows:
>
> > "Permanent residence" means that place where a person has his or her true, fixed, and permanent home and principal establishment to which, whenever absent, he or she has the intention of returning. A person may have only one permanent residence at a time; and, once a permanent residence is established in a foreign state or country, it is presumed to continue until the person shows that a change has occurred.

Patrick John McGinley, *Elements of a Prima Facie Case for a Property Tax Exemption for a Common Homestead*, in FLORIDA ELEMENTS OF AN ACTION § 1901:1 (2017-2018 ed.) (footnotes omitted).

C. Homestead Exemption from Forced Sale: May Enure to Heirs

Turning next to the protection of homestead beyond issues of state government taxation, we turn to the seminal case of *Snyder v. Davis*, 699 So. 2d 999 (Fla. 1997) (with its footnotes omitted).

SNYDER

v.

DAVIS

Supreme Court of the State of Florida, 1997

699 So. 2d 999

We have for review the decision of the Second District Court of Appeal [where the] district court held that the testator could not both devise her homestead property to her granddaughter and preserve its exemption from creditors. The court found that while the homestead could be devised, the constitutional exemption from creditors would follow the homestead only if it were devised to the person or persons who would have actually taken the homestead had the testator died intestate. In this case the granddaughter would not have taken the homestead under the intestacy statutes because the testator's natural son was still alive at the death of the testator. See § 732.103, Fla. Stat. (1995). The court then certified the following question to be of great public importance:

> whether Article X, Section 4, of the Florida Constitution exempts from forced sale a devise of a homestead by a decedent not survived by a spouse or minor child to a lineal descendant who is not an heir under the definition in section 731.201(18), Florida Statutes (1993).

Id. at 1193. We have jurisdiction. Art. V, § 3(b)(4), Fla. Const.

For the reasons expressed, we answer the certified question in the affirmative and quash the district court's decision. We find that in these circumstances the word "heirs," when determining entitlement to the homestead protections against creditors, is not limited to only the person or persons who would actually take the homestead by law in intestacy on the death of the decedent. Instead, we hold that the constitution must be construed to mean that a testator, when drafting a will prior to death, may devise the homestead (if there is no surviving spouse or minor children) to any of that class of persons categorized in section 732.103 (the intestacy statute). To hold otherwise would mean that a testator, when making an effort to avoid intestacy by drafting a will, would have to guess who his or her actual heirs would be on the date of death in order to maintain the homestead's constitutional protections against creditors.

Facts

Betty Snyder died testate on February 15, 1995. In her will, she made the following dispositions:

> First, the expenses of my funeral, burial, or other disposition of my remains I may have directed, my just debts, and the costs of administering my estate shall be paid out of the residue of my estate.
>
> Second, I give, devise and make special provisions as follows:
>
> a. The sum of $3,000 to my son, MILO SNYDER, provided he survives me.
>
> b. The sum of $2,000 to my friends, JOE BEDRIN and BARBARA BEDRIN, or to the survivor of them.
>
> Third, I give and devise all the rest, residue, and remainder of my property of every kind and wherever situated, as follows: All to my granddaughter, KELLI SNYDER.
>
> Betty Snyder was not survived by a spouse. She was, however, survived by her only son, Milo Snyder and his only daughter, Kelli Snyder. Both Milo and Kelli are adults.

Kent W. Davis, the personal representative of Betty Snyder's estate, sought to sell the homestead property to satisfy creditors' claims, to fund specific bequests, and to pay the costs of administration. Kelli Snyder, the residuary beneficiary, asserted that the testator's homestead passed to her free of claims because she was protected by article X, section 4, of the Florida Constitution (the homestead provision). The homestead provision reads, in relevant part, as follows:

> (a) There shall be exempt from forced sale under process of any court, and no judgment, decree, or execution shall be a lien thereon, except for the payment of taxes and assessments thereon, obligations contracted for the purchase, improvement or repair thereof, or obligations contracted for house, field or other labor performed on the realty, the following property owned by a natural person:
>
> (1) a homestead....
>
> ....
>
> (b) These exemptions shall inure to the surviving spouse or heirs of the owner.

Art. X, § 4, Fla. Const. (emphasis added).

There is no dispute in this case that Betty Snyder's home was homestead property for the purpose of distribution or that said property was properly devised in the residuary clause of her will. The sole issue is whether Kelli Snyder, as the granddaughter, may be properly considered an heir under the homestead provision, qualifying her for protection from the forced sale of the homestead property when her father, the next-in-line heir under statutory intestate succession, is still living.

The personal representative argues that, had Betty Snyder died intestate, Kelli Snyder would not have qualified as an heir under the intestacy statute. He asserts that Milo Snyder, as the testator's son, would have been the sole taker of the homestead under the intestacy statute and, consequently, the homestead was not devised to an heir by Betty Snyder's will. Accordingly, he argues that the homestead property is not protected by the homestead provision and is subject to creditors' claims.

The trial judge disagreed with these assertions and found that the homestead provision protected the homestead from creditors in this case. The district court reversed, finding that because Milo Snyder would have been the sole heir had there been intestacy, Kelli Snyder is precluded from benefitting from the homestead provision's protections against creditors. In so finding, the district court explained its position as follows:

> Section 731.201(18) defines "heirs" as "those persons, including the surviving spouse, who are entitled under the statutes of intestate succession to the property of a decedent." While Kelli Snyder is a lineal descendant of her grandmother, the decedent's adult son, Milo Snyder, is the only member of the next generation of "lineal descendant." A reference to "heirs" is generally considered as referring to those who inherit under the laws of intestate succession. See, e.g., Arnold v. Wells, 100 Fla. 1470, 131 So. 400 (1930). If Betty Snyder had died intestate, Milo Snyder would have inherited everything as her "heir," i.e., next lineal descendant in line, and Kelli Snyder, under any construction of section 732.103, would have inherited nothing. This would be so because inheritance in Florida is "per stirpes." § 732.104, Fla. Stat. (1993). Because Milo Snyder survived, Kelli Snyder is not an intestate "heir" of her grandmother. Therefore, for purposes of the homestead exemption inuring to "the heir of the decedent," as defined by intestate succession, the exemption cannot inure to Kelli Snyder.

681 So. 2d at 1193. We granted review in order to answer the certified question…

The circumstances under which a homestead may be devised while still retaining its protections against creditors present a significant issue for both the legal profession and the public in general. All Floridians need to fully understand how their homestead property might be properly devised while still maintaining its protections against creditors (when there are no surviving spouses or minor children).

The Homestead Provision

The homestead provision has been characterized as "our legal chameleon." Our constitution protects Florida homesteads in three distinct ways.

First, a clause, separate and apart from the homestead provision applicable in this case, provides homesteads with an exemption from taxes. Second, the homestead provision protects the homestead from forced sale by creditors. Third, the homestead provision delineates the restrictions a homestead owner faces when attempting to alienate or devise the homestead property. This case involves the second and third protections described above.

Homestead law in the United States has evolved over time and it is strictly an American innovation. In Florida, moreover, our case law surrounding the homestead provision has its own contours and legal principles. As a result, it is not susceptible to comparisons with similar provisions in other jurisdictions. Importantly, our courts have emphasized that, in Florida, the homestead provision is in place to protect and preserve the interest of the family in the family home. We recently reaffirmed that general policy by stating:

> As a matter of public policy, the purpose of the homestead exemption is to promote the stability and welfare of the state by securing to the householder a home, so that the homeowner and his or her heirs may live beyond the reach of financial misfortune and the demands of creditors who have given credit under such law.

Public Health Trust v. Lopez, 531 So. 2d 946, 948 (Fla. 1988). Further, it is clear that the homestead provision is to be liberally construed in favor of maintaining the homestead property.... As a matter of policy as well as construction, our homestead protections have been interpreted broadly.

In addition, in 1984, the people further expanded homestead provision to substantially broaden the class of people eligible to take advantage of our homestead protections. While those protections had been previously limited to the "head of a family," they are now available to any "natural person." Compare art. X, § 4(a), Fla. Const.(1972) ("There shall be exempt from forced sale under process of any court ... the following property owned by the head of a family") with art. X, § 4(a), Fla. Const. ("There shall be exempt from forced sale under process of any court ... the following property owned by a natural person").

Finally, it is important to note that creditors are aware of the homestead provision and its inherent protections. As we discussed in Public Health Trust, we will not narrowly interpret the homestead provision simply because "financially independent heirs" may receive a windfall. 531 So. 2d at 950. There we wrote:

> The homestead protection has never been based on principles of equity… but always has been extended to the homesteader and, after his or her death, to the heirs whether the homestead was a twenty-two room mansion or a two-room hut and whether the heirs were rich or poor.

Id. Creditors have been on notice for many years that the plain language of the constitution protects homestead property from most creditors.

It is with these policy considerations in mind that we address the two major issues in this case.

Devisees of a Homestead May Be Entitled to the Homestead Provision's Protections Against Creditors

The first question we must resolve is whether the protection against creditors found in the homestead provision can be transferred, with a will, to a devisee. This Court has never addressed whether the term "heirs" in the homestead provision includes devisees.

Under the common law, an heir was a person designated to inherit in the event of intestacy at the death of the decedent. Now, however, "the term is frequently used in a popular sense to designate a successor to property either by will or by law." Black's Law Dictionary 724 (6th ed. 1990) ("Word 'heirs' is no longer limited to designated character of estate as at common law.") If we define the term "heirs" in the homestead provision by its strict common-law definition, the very act of devising the homestead would abolish the homestead protections against creditors. We refuse to construe the homestead provision in such a narrow way. In reaching this conclusion, we are persuaded by the reasoning of the Third District Court of Appeal, sitting en banc, in *Bartelt v. Bartelt*, 579 So. 2d 282 (Fla. 3d DCA 1991). That court addressed the situation in which the decedent, who died without a surviving spouse but with two surviving adult children, a son and a daughter, devised his homestead only to his son. There, the district court held that the homestead exemption passed to the devisee through the will even though the omitted child would have been entitled to an equal share of the homestead had the decedent died intestate. In so holding, the *Bartelt* court stated:

> When the decedent's homestead is devised to his son-a member of the class of persons who are the decedent's "heirs"-the constitutional exemption from forced sale by the decedent's creditors found in Article X, Section 4(b) of the Florida Constitution, inures to that son. The test is not how title was devolved, but rather to whom it passed....
>
> The personal representative argues that, although "heirs" may avail themselves of the constitutional protection from creditors, "devisees" may not. Section 731.201(18), Florida Statutes (1989), defines heirs or heirs at law as "those persons ... who are entitled under the statutes of intestate succession to the property of a decedent." Devisees are defined in section 731.201(9) as persons "designated in a will to receive a devise." According to the personal representative, a devisee cannot be an heir because a devisee takes by will and an heir takes only where there is no will. We disagree. Heirs, as defined in section 731.201(18), are simply those persons entitled to receive property under the laws of intestacy; the decedent's son, as his lineal descendant, is a member of that class. § 732.103(1), Fla. Stat. (1989). The class designated as "heirs" does not exclude those who, but for the decedent's foresight in executing a will, would have taken by the laws of intestate succession.... Article X, section 4 of the Florida Constitution defines the class of persons to whom the decedent's exemption from forced sale of homestead property inures; it does not mandate the technique by which the qualified person must receive title.

Id. at 283-84. An academic commentator on this subject writes approvingly of the result reached by that district court:

> This author supports the *Bartelt* decision. The constitutional exemption from forced sale by creditors, as found in article X, § 4(b) of the Florida Constitution, inures to the surviving spouse or heirs of the owner. *Bartelt* includes within the term "heirs" devisees who but for the will would have been heirs. It properly takes a broad gauged approach to the constitutional terminology. It places substance over form. The persons involved as takers are the same whether there is a will or there is not a will. The court points out that without such a determination, with respect to homestead,

> Florida residents would be discouraged from making wills and would be encouraged to let the property in issue pass by intestate succession. Such a result would be an anathema.

David T. Smith, FLORIDA PROBATE CODE MANUAL § 4.05, at 29-30 (1995).

We agree that, in cases in which there is no surviving spouse or minor children, the protections against creditors found in the homestead provision may inure to the benefit of the person to whom the homestead property is devised by will. As explained below, though, the class of persons to which such protections may be devised is limited.

The Class of Devisees to Which the Protections Against Creditors Found in the Homestead Provision May Be Devised

Having found that the protections against creditors found in the homestead provision may be devised by will, we now must define the scope of the class of persons to which those protections may be so devised. The *Davis* court and the *Walker* court present us with two alternatives. First, the *Davis* court defined the word "heirs" narrowly and found that, in order to preserve the protection against creditors, a devisee had to be entitled to inherit the homestead property under the intestacy statute. The *Walker* court applied a broader definition of the term "heirs." It held that the protections against creditors could be devised to any of the class of potential heirs under the intestacy statute. It found no occasion to require that a testator leave the homestead property to the actual person or persons who would have actually inherited under the intestacy statute. These two views of the term "heirs" can be characterized as the "entitlement definition" and the "class definition," respectively.

We are persuaded by the *Walker* court's view. In a situation almost identical to that in this Davis case, the First District Court held that a decedent's grandson was entitled to the homestead protection even though the grandson was not the closest consanguine heir. In doing so, the court found that any person categorized in the intestacy statute was an heir for the purpose of the homestead provision. In particular, it wrote:

> Article X, section 4(b) of the Florida Constitution provides that the exemptions and protections established for homestead property under article X, section 4(a) "shall inure to the surviving spouse or heirs of the owner." As this court explained in *State Department of Health and Rehabilitative Services v. Trammell*, 508 So. 2d 422 (Fla. 1st DCA 1987), the term "heir" under article X, section 4(b) means "those who may under the laws of the state inherit from the owner of the homestead." *Id.* at 423. Because Bavle, as the decedent's grandson, was a lineal descendent of the decedent, he is a member of the class of persons entitled to receive property under the laws of intestacy, see sections 732.103(1) and 732.401(1), Florida Statutes (1993), and accordingly, is an "heir" for the purposes of article X, section 4(b). A remainderman is entitled to claim a homestead exemption.

687 So. 2d at 1329.

The *Walker* court expressly rejected the holding of the *Davis* court. It wrote:

> We find the *Davis* opinion contrary to the purpose of the homestead exemption from forced sale. We start with the well-established principle that the laws regarding homestead exemption are to be liberally construed. *Jetton Lumber Co. v. Hall*, 67 Fla. 61, 64 So. 440 (1914); and In re Estate of Skuro, 467 So. 2d 1098 (Fla. 4th DCA 1985), aff'd, 487 So. 2d 1065 (Fla. 1986). Although the constitution is silent as to the intent of the drafters with respect to the rights of creditors of estates, we conclude that, as amended in 1984, article V, section 4(b), however, does reflect the intent that the exemption is to inure to whomever the homestead property passes.

Id. at 1330. The *Walker* court grounded its conclusion on the following policy consideration:

> It seems clear to us that the intent of the homestead exemption is to protect the decedent's homestead from the decedent's creditors for the benefit of the decedent's heirs. To deny the exemption for a homestead property simply because the person chosen by the decedent to receive the property under the will, even though that person is within the class of persons enti-

> tled to take under the laws of intestate succession, is not the closest consanguine heir, is contrary to that constitutional intent.

Id. at 1331.

The *Walker* court, it seems to us, announces the correct view of our homestead provision. Indeed, the approach used by the *Davis* court would force a testator to guess as to his or her survivors in order to successfully devise, by will, the homestead property with the protections against creditors intact. That reading of our constitution is, in our view, unreasonable. If a severe limitation is to be placed on the ability of Floridians to keep the homestead within the family, it should not be done by a narrow judicial construction of the homestead provision.

We are reinforced in our view when the ramifications of the alternative position are considered. Under the *Davis* court's reasoning, an attorney would be faced with giving the following illogical advice to a potential testator with no surviving spouse or minor children:

> You have two bad choices. You can devise your homestead to any person you choose. If you do, though, the homestead provision's protections against creditors will be inapplicable and your homestead may be subject to forced sale. On the other hand, you can guess as to which family members will survive you. After we have established the list of your guesses, I can tell you which of those family members would inherit under our intestacy statute. If you leave your homestead to those family members and they really do survive you, the homestead provision's protections against creditors will remain intact. If you guess incorrectly, though, the protections against creditors will be inapplicable. The point is this: If you want to ensure protection of the homestead property against creditors under our constitution, you have no choice as to which family member might best maintain your homestead property. The law requires that in order to utilize the homestead provision's protections against creditors, the homestead property must pass to the person or persons dictated by the intestacy statute.

Creating a system, by engaging a narrow judicial construction of the homestead provision, in which this type of advice must be given is unreasonable. Will-making, in these circumstances, becomes an act of prophecy. Clearly, as a policy matter, we should not be encouraging intestacy as a means of distributing one's property. In many instances where there is no surviving spouse or minor children, the homestead property is the most significant part of a testator's estate. If a testator loses control over the disposition of his or her homestead property, the need for a will is effectively eliminated. Such an approach takes away from the testator any ability to make a choice as to which family member will best preserve and maintain the family homestead. Instead, it promotes absolute adherence to the strict priorities found in the intestacy statute without paying any respect to the needs of individual testators and their families.

The whole purpose of the homestead provision is to protect and maintain the family homestead. The testator is likely in the best position to know which family member is most likely to need or to properly maintain the homestead. A plain reading of the homestead provision establishes that it only prohibits devising the homestead property when the testator is survived by a spouse or minor children. There is no prohibition against devising the homestead property to any of that class of persons who could potentially receive the homestead property under the intestacy statute. We must emphasize, however, that today's ruling does not authorize a testator to devise homestead property to any person not categorized by our intestacy statute with any expectation that the protections against creditors will survive such a devise. See *State Dep't of Health & Rehabilitative Servs. v. Trammell*, 508 So. 2d 422 (Fla. 1st DCA 1987) (holding that a devise of homestead to a good friend does not qualify for the homestead exemption).

Conclusion

We have consistently made it clear that the homestead provision must be given a broad and liberal construction. In the context of this case, we reject the narrow entitlement definition of the term "heirs" that includes only those people who would inherit under the intestacy statute at the death of the decedent. Instead, we hold that the homestead provision allows a testator with no surviving spouse or minor children to choose to devise, in a will, the homestead property, with its accompanying protection from creditors, to any family member within the class of persons categorized in our intestacy statute.

Accordingly, we answer the certified question in the affirmative, quash the decision of the district court in *Davis*, and approve the district court's opinion in *Walker*.

It is so ordered.

Notes and Questions to Consider:

1. Under the facts of *Snyder v. Davis*, Florida's Supreme Court notes that "[t]here is no dispute in this case that Betty Snyder's home was homestead property…". But what about cases where this is in dispute? For a homestead to exist, "[t]here are four basic requirements that must be satisfied: (1) The real property must be owned by a 'natural person;' (2) The person claiming the exemption must be a Florida resident who established that he or she made, or intended to make, the real property his or her 'permanent residence;' (3) The person claiming the exemption must establish that he or she is the 'owner' of the property; [and] (4) The property claimed as the homestead must satisfy the 'size and continguity' requirements of [Florida's C]onstitution." John F. Cooper, Tishia A. Dunham, and Carlos L. Woody, FLORIDA CONSTITUTIONAL LAW: CASES AND MATERIALS 696 (Carolina Academic Press 5th edition 2013).

2. The size and continguity requirements are in Article X, §4(a)(1) of Florida's Constitution: "if located outside the municipality, to the extent of one hundred sixty acres of contiguous land and improvements thereon, which shall not be reduced without the owner's consent by reason of subsequent inclusion in a municipality; or if located within a municipality, to the extent of one-half acre of contiguous land, upon which the exemption shall be limited to the residence of the owner or the owner's family."

3. As seen above, *Snyder v. Davis* holds that homestead protection is lost after the death of the homesteader unless his or her estate plan de-

vises the homestead solely to one or more of his or her family members who fall within the class of persons categorized in §732.103, Fla. Stat. (which is Florida's intestacy statute). Yet the intestacy statute lists a long and deep line of consanguinity. *Synder v. Davis* cites to *State Dep't of Health & Rehabilitative Servs. v. Trammell*, 508 So. 2d 422 (Fla. 1st DCA 1987) for the example "that a devise of homestead to a good friend does not qualify for the homestead exemption." In light of the depth and breadth of Florida's Intestacy Statutes, are there any other examples?

D. Homestead Exemption from Forced Sale: May Enure to Co-Owners

Although "ownership" is required before homestead rights attach, "[a]n individual need not hold legal or fee simple title to the property to meet this requirement . . . . Homestead status may be derived from any equitable or beneficiary interest in real property." John F. Cooper, Tishia A. Dunham, and Carlos L. Woody, FLORIDA CONSTITUTIONAL LAW: CASES AND MATERIALS 697 (Carolina Academic Press 5th edition 2013) (citing *Bessemer Props., Inc. v. Gamble*, 27 So. 2d 832 (Fla. 1946) and *Heiman v. Capital Bank*, 438 So. 2d 932 (Fla. 3d DCA 1983)).

What exactly does this mean? Consider the following excerpt from Joseph Percopo's famous article *The Impact of Co-Ownership on Florida Homestead*, Fla. B.J., May 2012, at 32, 35–38:

THE IMPACT OF CO-OWNERSHIP ON FLORIDA HOMESTEAD

By Joseph M. Percopo

The Florida Bar Journal, May 2012

© 2012 by The Florida Bar and Joseph M. Percopo

Creditor Protection

> [I]n order to qualify for the homestead creditor exemption, three conditions must be satisfied: 1) acreage limitations, 2) residency requirements, and 3) ownership requirements. Provided all three of these conditions are satisfied, creditors of the person claiming the homestead creditor exemption will not be able to force sale of or place a lien on the home-

stead property. This article now examines how co-ownership of property affects the homestead creditor protection.

• Tenants by the Entirety -- Only married couples can own property as tenants by the entirety, and there is a presumption that real property acquired during marriage is owned as such.... Provided either spouse qualifies for the homestead creditor exemption, the property will be afforded protection from either spouse's creditors. However, upon dissolution of marriage, unless the divorce decree makes one spouse a complete owner or provides terms granting one spouse exclusive possession of the home, the spouses become tenants in common subject to the rules discussed below.

• Tenants in Common and Joint Tenants with Right of Survivorship -- ... Unless specific language is used indicating “survivorship rights,” tenants in common is the default form of co-owned property in Florida....Co-ownership of property will not prevent an owner from claiming the homestead creditor exemption; however, the status of each co-owner impacts the level of creditor protection retained by the property. When all co-owners qualify for the homestead creditor exemption, the home will be exempt from forced sale and liens....When at least one co-owner does not qualify for the homestead creditor exemption, a potential problem exists. In *Tullis v. Tullis*, 360 So. 2d 375 (Fla. 1978), the Florida Supreme Court held that the Florida “constitutional provisions allow the partition and forced sale of homestead property upon suit by one of the owners of that property” provided it is to protect the owner's beneficial enjoyment. Thus, any of the co-owners of real property can force the property to be partitioned and sold. Therefore, if a co-owner does not qualify for the homestead creditor exemption, a creditor of that co-owner can acquire that interest and then force a sale. ...A chain is only as strong as its weakest link, and this holds true for property owned as tenants in common or as joint tenants with right of survivorship. Property will be completely shielded from creditors when all co-owners qualify for the homestead creditor exemption. However, if at least one co-owner does not qualify for the homestead creditor exemption, the property becomes subject to that co-owner's creditors. This is extremely important to understand when acquiring property with others. It is common to see family, especially parents and children, purchase property together or add each other to the title of property. Parents need to know that if they place a child's name on the deed and that property is not the child's homestead for creditor protection purposes, then that property is subject to the child's creditors. Additionally, children need to be aware that if their parents are on the title to their homestead (maybe they helped purchase the property many years ago), that property is subject to their parents' creditors (unless, of course, the parents are now living there, and it is their homestead for creditor protection purposes).

• Life Estates and Remainder Interests -- Individuals may also take title to property in a manner that divides ownership into present and future interests. Under this type of ownership, a person may take a life estate, which means he or she has a present possessory interest in the property and is entitled to all ordinary uses of the property until death. However, ordinary use does not permit a life tenant to do anything that injures the future interest in the property. Therefore, a life tenant cannot neglect the property allowing it to fall into disrepair or commit waste, such as consuming or exploiting the resources upon the property. The remainder (future) interest holder must approve any improvements to the property, and has the right to inspect the property for waste or damage. Upon the death of the life tenant, the life estate ends and the remainderman (person with the remainder interest) becomes the owner by operation of law.

To determine if and how the homestead creditor exemption applies to life estates and remainder interests, the following questions must be addressed: 1) whether individuals with fractional ownership in time can claim the homestead creditor exemption, and if so 2) which of the co-owners qualify for the homestead creditor exemption. …The Florida Supreme Court in *Aetna Ins. Co. v. Lagasse*, 223 So. 2d 727 (Fla. 1969), held that remainder interests, including vested remainders, were not able to qualify for the homestead creditor exemption, even if he or she lived on the property, because there was no "present right to possession." Thus, a life tenant can qualify for the homestead creditor exemption with a life estate, but the Florida Supreme Court has determined that a remainderman cannot qualify with a remainder interest.

When the life tenant qualifies for the homestead creditor exemption, the property is still protected from the life tenant's creditors, but it is not safe from the remainderman's creditors. ... Co-owners who share interests in time (life tenants and remainderman), unlike co-owners who share present interests, may not partition life estates. Therefore, a life tenant...could continue to reside on the property without worrying about the remaindermans' creditors being able to force sale of the property.

However, it is important to note that recently, two Florida bankruptcy cases held that a person with a vested remainder who lived on and made the property his or her residence could qualify for the homestead creditor exemption. Therefore, if a remainderman finds himself or herself in a Florida bankruptcy court, he or she has precedent to argue for the homestead creditor exemption. Of course, for Florida courts, the bankruptcy court decisions are merely persuasive and not binding; nevertheless, it does leave room for discussion on the subject.

Id. at 35-38 (footnotes omitted).

Notes and Questions to Consider:

1. Florida Statutes § 732.401 provides that a homestead jointly owned via "tenancy by the entireties" or via "joint tenancy with rights of survivorship" becomes solely owned by the surviving owner upon the co-owner's death, and does so free and clear of the deceased's debts and financial obligations. *See also* Fla. Stat. § 731.201.

2. The excerpt above ends with a discussion of bankruptcy court interpretations of these portions of the homestead law but states this caveat: "the bankruptcy court decisions are merely persuasive and not binding." How persuasive do you find the logic of the cited bankruptcy court decisions?

E. Homestead Restrictions Upon Devise and Inheritance

What is meant by Florida's Constitution's restriction upon the inheritance and devise of homestead property? It means three things.

First, it means that the deceased's will or revocable living trust or other estate planning documents do NOT void or avoid homestead protection when there is a surviving child or spouse of the deceased because it does not control the devise of the homestead when there are such survivors. §732.4015, Fla. Stat. (2017).

Second, it means the decedent's surviving spouse inherits – despite any will, trust or estate plan to the contrary – the surviving spouse's choice of a life estate or undivided ½ interest if deceased's child or children survive deceased (and they, per stirpes, hold a vested remainder), or, if the deceased's child or children did not survive the deceased, then the surviving spouse inherits the homestead in fee simple unless the surviving spouse waived that right.

Third, it means that if the decedent does not have a surviving spouse, but has one or more surviving children, then the surviving child or children inherit – despite any espite will/trust, surviving kid(s) inherit [if no surviving spouse] the homestead in fee simple as tenants in common. § 732.103(1), Fla. Stat. (2015).

For a more detailed understanding of these rules, let us again consider another excerpt from Joseph Percopo's famous article *The Impact of Co-Ownership on Florida Homestead*, Fla. B.J., May 2012, at 32, 35–38:

THE IMPACT OF CO-OWNERSHIP ON FLORIDA HOMESTEAD

By Joseph M. Percopo

The Florida Bar Journal, May 2012

Alienation, Devise, and Descent

Florida has certain restrictions on how homestead property may be alienated and devised, as well as rules dealing with improperly devised homestead upon the owner's death. Fla. Const. art. X, §4(c) provides that:

> (c) The homestead shall not be subject to devise if the owner is survived by spouse or minor child, except the homestead may be devised to the owner's spouse if there be no minor child. The owner of homestead real estate, joined by the spouse if married, may alienate the homestead by mortgage, sale or gift and, if married, may by deed transfer the title to an estate by the entirety with the spouse.

This provision is codified in [Florida Statutes] §732.4015(1), where it is similarly states that "the homestead shall not be subject to devise if the owner is survived by a spouse or a minor child or minor children, except that the homestead may be devised to the owner's spouse if there is no minor child or children." [Florida Statutes] §732.401(1) further states that "[i]f not devised as authorized by law and the constitution, the homestead shall descend in the same manner as other intestate property; but if the decedent is survived by a spouse and one or more descendants, the surviving spouse shall take a life estate in the homestead, with a vested remainder to the lineal descendants in being at the time of the decedent's death per stirpes."

However, the spouse may also make an election "to take an undivided one-half interest in the homestead as tenants in common, with the remaining one-half interest vesting in the decedent's descendants in being at the time of the decedent's death, per stirpes," instead of taking the life estate.

When an individual has no spouse or minor children, he or she is free to devise the homestead property anyway he or she pleases. Conversely, when an individual is survived either by a spouse or minor child(ren), then the property is not subject to devise and will pass as intestate property (meaning that the sole surviving spouse will become the sole owner if there are no descendants, or the surviving minor child(ren) will become the sole owner if there is no surviving spouse).

The rules concerning alienation, devise, and descent only apply to a co-owner if the property is the co-owners' homestead pursuant to Fla. Const. art. X, §4 ("transfer restricted homestead"); thus, any of the other co-owners who do not reside on the property are free to dispose of their property as they see fit. The article now examines how these rules apply to a co-owner of property where he or she owns transfer restricted homestead property.

• Alienation -- With regard to alienation of property, the Florida Constitution does not place any restrictions on alienation except that a married owner must have spousal consent to do so (despite whether the spouse has an ownership interest of his or her own in the property).

• Devise and Descent, Tenants by the Entirety -- The rules regarding devise and descent of transfer restricted homestead property do not apply to property owned as tenants by the entirety. This is because at the death of one spouse, property owned as tenants by the entirety passes to the surviving spouse automatically, outside of probate -- therefore, there is no devise or descent of the homestead property.

• Devise and Descent, Joint Tenants with Right of Survivorship -- The rules regarding devise and descent do not apply to transfer restricted homestead owned as joint tenants with right of survivorship, because, similar to property owned as tenants by the entirety, at death the property passes automatically to the other joint owners. Therefore, co-owners who want to preserve the transfer restricted homestead for their spouse or children should be cautious about owning property as joint tenants with right of survivorship....

• Devise and Descent, Tenants in Common -- When property is owned as tenants in common, the constitutional and statutory rules of devise and descent apply to transfer restricted homestead. Therefore, a co-owner is not free to devise his or her transfer restricted homestead when he or she has a surviving spouse or minor child. Instead, the co-owner's interest in the transfer restricted homestead property must pass to his or her surviving spouse and/or minor child(ren) as designated by law.

• Devise and Descent, Life Estates and Remainders -- The rules regarding devise and descent of transfer restricted homestead do not apply to life estates because life estates end at the death of the life tenant; thus, there is no interest for the life tenant to devise or pass along.

Like tenants by the entirety and joint tenants with right of survivorship, at death the interest passes automatically, and in the case of a life estate, to the remainderman.

As for the remainderman, the devise and descent rules do not apply because the remainderman, under current Florida law, do not have a present possessory interest necessary to receive the homestead protections.

Id. at 35-38 (footnotes omitted).

Notes and Questions to Consider:

1. The excerpt above opines that "co-owners who want to preserve the transfer restricted homestead for their spouse or children should be cautious about owning property as joint tenants with right of survivorship." Do you agree? Why or why not?

2. The excerpt reminds us that "the rules concerning alienation, devise, and descent only apply to a co-owner if the property is the co-owners' homestead pursuant to Fla. Const. art. X, §4 ('transfer restricted homestead')." Is the author referring to Florida Statutes § 732.401? It provides that a homestead jointly owned via "tenancy by the entireties" or via "joint tenancy with rights of survivorship" becomes solely owned by the surviving owner upon the co-owner's death, and does so free and clear of the deceased's debts and financial obligations. Or is the author referring to Florida Statutes § 731.201? It provides, in subsection 33, that "real property owned in tenancy by the entireties or in joint tenancy with rights of survivorship is not protected homestead."

F. Homestead Protects Proceeds from Home's Sale or Its Insurance Recovery

A Floridian may sell his homestead, and buy another, without losing his homestead protections. The proceeds from the sale are protected from levy or confiscation by creditors for a reasonable period of time. Likewise, the homesteader might suffer damage to her homestead for which she might receive an insurance recovery, and if so, those proceeds are protected from creditors. See *Orange Brevard Plumbing & Heating Co. v. La Croix*, 137 So. 2d 201, 203-04 (Fla. 1962). But what if the very creditor from whom the homesteader seeks protection is the person whose labor won the insurance recovery for the homesteader? Consider the holding of *Quiroga v. Citizens Prop. Ins. Corp.*, 34 So. 3d 101 (Fla. 3rd DCA 2010) (with the text, that is omitted from the footnote, now added to the opinion in brackets):

QUIROGA

V.

CITIZENS PROPERTY INSURANCE

Third District Court of Appeal of Florida, 2010

34 So. 3d 101

This is an appeal from an order denying the law firm of Katzman Garfinkel and Rosenbaum's motion to impress a charging lien on the homeowner's insurance proceeds for damages caused by two hurricanes. The Katzman law firm secured the proceeds for the benefit of its client and policy insured, Jesse Quiroga, in appreciation for which Quiroga not only terminated the law firm's contingent fee representation of him, but also sought to shield himself from any responsibility to compensate his counsel by claiming the insurance proceeds are exempt homestead property, not subject to attachment by means of a charging lien. See Art. X, § 4(a), Fla. Const. [Article X, section 4(a) reads as follows insofar as pertinent here:

> There shall be exempt from forced sale under process of any court, and no judgment, decree or execution shall be a lien thereon, except for the payment of taxes and assessments thereon, obligations contracted for

the purchase, improvement or repair thereof, or obligations contracted for house, field or other labor performed on the realty, the following property owned by a natural person:

(1) a homestead ...]

The parties do not dispute the hurricane-damaged property is constitutionally exempt homestead property. See *Cutler v. Cutler*, 994 So. 2d 341, 343 (Fla. 3d DCA 2008) ("To qualify for protection under Article X, section 4 of the Florida Constitution, a parcel of property must meet constitutionally defined size limitations and must be owned by a natural person who is a Florida resident who either makes or intends to make the property that person's residence."). In the event a homestead is damaged through fire, wind or flood, the proceeds of any insurance recovery are imbued with the same privilege. *Orange Brevard Plumbing & Heating Co. v. La Croix*, 137 So. 2d 201, 203-04 (Fla. 1962). Because Quiroga did not and, as a matter of public policy in this State, cannot through an unsecured agreement, such as the contingent fee agreement in this case, enter into an enforceable contract to divest himself from the exemptions afforded him through Article X, section 4(a), see *Chames v. DeMayo*, 972 So. 2d 850, 853 (Fla. 2007), this Court is compelled to affirm the order under review, the equities of the matter notwithstanding. See *Pub. Health Trust of Dade County v. Lopez*, 531 So. 2d 946, 951 (Fla. 1988) ("The homestead protection has never been based upon principles of equity.") (citing *Bigelow v. Dunphe*, 143 Fla. 603, 197 So. 328, 330 (1940)); *Pierrepont v. Humphreys (In re Newman's Estate),* 413 So. 2d 140, 142 (Fla. 5th DCA 1982) ("The homestead character of a piece of property ... arises and attaches from the mere existence of certain facts in combination in place and time.").

Affirmed.

Notes and Questions to Consider:

1. The facts of *Quiroga v. Citizens Property Insurance* involve a charging lien. As I wrote in my book FLORIDA ELEMENTS OF AN ACTION, "[a]

charging lien is an equitable remedy by which an attorney can have his fee for his litigation services secured to him in his client's judgment that was awarded in the litigation where his services were rendered." Patrick John McGinley, *Elements of the Prima Facie Case of a Charging Lien*, in FLORIDA ELEMENTS OF AN ACTION § 1601:1 (2017-2018 ed.). Noting that a charging lien is an equitable remedy, why did not the equities of the situation control the outcome of *Quiroga v. Citizens Property*?

2. Did you sense a hint of sarcasm in the *Quiroga* court noting that "[t]he Katzman law firm secured the proceeds for the benefit of its client and policy insured, Jesse Quiroga, in appreciation for which Quiroga not only terminated the law firm's contingent fee representation of him, but also sought to shield himself from any responsibility to compensate his counsel by claiming the insurance proceeds are exempt homestead property…"?

3. Would the outcome of *Quiroga* been different if the money to which the law firm was attempting to impose a charging lien had instead been the proceeds from the sale of the homestead? Consider this holding from *Orange Brevard Plumbing & Heating Co. v. La Croix*, 137 So. 2d 201 (Fla. 1962):

> [I]n recognition of the liberal interpretation of the homestead exemption to which this court is committed, we hold the proceeds of a voluntary sale of a homestead to be exempt from the claims of creditors just as the homestead itself is exempt if, and only if, the vendor shows, by a preponderance of the evidence an abiding good faith intention prior to and at the time of the sale of the homestead to reinvest the proceeds thereof in another homestead within a reasonable time. Moreover, only so much of the proceeds of the sale as are intended to be reinvested in another homestead may be exempt under this holding. Any surplus over and above that amount should be treated as general assets of the debtor. We further hold that in order to satisfy the requirements of the exemption the funds must not be commingled with other monies of the vendor but must be kept separate and apart and held for the sole purpose of acquiring another home. The proceeds of the sale are not exempt if they are not reinvested

> in another homestead in a reasonable time or if they are held for the general purposes of the vendor.
>
> The homestead exemption provision was not placed in our Constitution for the purpose of tying the owner thereof and his family to a particular home, once established, for the remaining period of their natural lives….

Id. at 206.

Chapter Twelve

Taxation and Finance

A. Taxation

Florida's Constitution considers the rights of taxpayers to be fundamental enough to warrant mentioning in the Declaration of Rights—the same preferred placement given to religious freedom, the freedom of speech and press, the right to assemble, the right to work, and the right to due process. Specifically, Article I of Florida's constitution reads:

> *SECTION 25. Taxpayer's Bill of Rights.*—By general law the legislature shall prescribe and adopt a Taxpayers' Bill of Rights that, in clear and concise language, sets forth taxpayers' rights and responsibilities and government's responsibilities to deal fairly with taxpayers under the laws of this state. This section shall be effective July 1, 1993.

Can Florida be called a "tax haven?" Famously, Florida is one of just a few U.S. states that do not impose a state income tax. Florida's constitution contains language restricting taxes and making new tax laws harder to enact. Article VII of Florida's Constitution requires a supermajority vote to impose, authorize, or raise state taxes or fees.

Florida's aversion to taxation does not end there. Article VII of Florida's constitution contains the following restrictions:

> *SECTION 5. Estate, inheritance and income taxes.*—
>
> (a) NATURAL PERSONS. No tax upon estates or inheritances or upon the income of natural persons who are residents or citizens of the state shall be levied by the state, or under its authority, in excess of the aggregate of amounts which may be allowed to be credited upon or deducted from any similar tax levied by the United States or any state.

(b) OTHERS. No tax upon the income of residents and citizens other than natural persons shall be levied by the state, or under its authority, in excess of 5% of net income, as defined by law, or at such greater rate as is authorized by a three-fifths (3/5) vote of the membership of each house of the legislature or as will provide for the state the maximum amount which may be allowed to be credited against income taxes levied by the United States and other states. There shall be exempt from taxation not less than five thousand dollars ($5,000) of the excess of net income subject to tax over the maximum amount allowed to be credited against income taxes levied by the United States and other states. . . .

Notes and Questions to Consider:

1. Florida's Legislature enacted the constitutionally-required Taxpayer's Bill of Rights in 1992. It enumerates 21 distinct rights, including:

> The right to available information and prompt, accurate responses to questions and requests for tax assistance;
>
> The right to request assistance from a taxpayers' rights advocate who may issue a stay order if a taxpayer has suffered or is about to suffer irreparable loss as a result of an action by the Florida Department of Revenue;
>
> The right to be represented or advised by counsel or other qualified representatives;
>
> The right to seek review, through formal or informal proceedings, of any adverse decisions;
>
> The right to have the taxpayer's tax information kept confidential unless otherwise specified by law;

> The right to an action at law within the limitations of Florida Statutes section 768.28, relating to sovereign immunity, to recover damages against the state or the Department of Revenue for injury caused by the wrongful or negligent act or omission of a department officer or employee; (see s. 768.28); and
>
> The right of the taxpayer or the department, as the prevailing party in a judicial or administrative action brought or maintained without the support of justiciable issues of fact or law, to recover all costs of the administrative or judicial action, including reasonable attorney's fees.

See Florida Statutes section 213.015.

2. Under Article VII of Florida's Constitution, the state lacks the power of ad valorem taxation, and ad valorem taxation is the only valid method of taxation possessed by local governments such as counties, cities, towns, villages, and districts. What is meant by "ad valorem?" Florida's supreme court, in *Smith v. Am. Airlines, Inc.*, 606 So. 2d 618, 621 n.2 (Fla. 1992), holds that "the term itself means '[a] tax imposed on the value of property.'" The Court notes that "[t]he more common ad valorem tax is that imposed by states, counties, and cities [is up]on real estate." *Id.* However, as noted by the Court, "the definition does not end there, but goes on to add that '[a]d valorem taxes, can, however, be imposed upon personal property.'" *Id.*

3. As to the ad valorem taxation of personal property, note that Florida's constitution at Article VII provides two important exemptions. "Twenty-five thousand dollars of the assessed value of property subject to tangible personal property tax shall be exempt from ad valorem taxation." *Id.* at sec. 3. "Motor vehicles, boats, airplanes, trailers, trailer coaches and mobile homes, as defined by law, shall be subject to a license tax for their operation in the amounts and for the purposes prescribed by law, but shall not be subject to ad valorem taxes." *Id.* at sec. 1.

4. Note that the means by which ad valorem taxation is computed is in "millage rates" which is often abbreviated as "mills." Millage "rates

shall be stated in terms of dollars and cents per thousand dollars of assessed property value." § 200.001, Fla. Stat. That means that one mill represents the amount of tax per every $1,000 of a property's assessed value. To convert millage rates to dollar rate amounts, divide each mill rate by 1,000. Then, multiply the result by the property's taxable value to compute the property tax.

5. Estate taxes are imposed by Florida's legislature upon a limited number of estates. It is avoided by the size of the estate, not by the drafting of the estate plan, because "[t]he estate tax is a tax on the privilege of transferring property at death and is charged on the entire estate of the deceased regardless of the manner of its distribution." 53 Fla. Jur 2d Taxation § 1865 (June 2019 update). One commentator summarizes the operation of Estate Tax Law of Florida, Florida Statutes chapter 198, as follows:

> The Florida estate tax is directly linked to the federal estate tax. Therefore, if no federal estate tax is due, then no Florida estate tax would be due. . . . [A] resident decedent is subject to Florida estate tax equal to the credit for state death taxes provided in Internal Revenue Code §2011, less any death taxes paid to another state. . . . [A] nonresident decedent is subject to the Florida estate tax on the pro rata share of the credit for state death taxes provided in IRC §2011, based upon the ratio of the taxable Florida property over the federal gross estate.
>
> Personal representatives may be called on to: 1) file Florida estate tax returns; 2) request refunds of Florida estate tax; 3) claim credits for prior transfers of tax in related estates; 4) comply with tax recapture provisions; 5) seek deferral of estate tax payment in certain circumstances; 6) receive release from estate tax liens on property; and 7) claim benefits of Florida generation-skipping transfer tax provisions. The personal representative of a decedent's estate is required to file an estate tax return with the Florida Department of Revenue (DOR) . . . contingent upon the value of the federal gross estate. If the value of the decedent's federal gross estate . . . is less than the decedent's remaining applicable exclusion amount, then the personal representative may . . . file an Affidavit

> of No Florida Estate Tax Due. . . . This affidavit should be filed in the county in which the decedent owned real estate.
>
> After the personal representative files the Florida estate tax return with the DOR, the DOR will require a copy of the Internal Revenue Service federal estate tax closing letter to determine the amount of the Florida estate tax due. The federal estate tax closing letter provides the credit for state death taxes and the amount of the credit for prior transfers.

Benjamin A. Jablow, *The Ins and Outs of the Florida Estate Tax*, FLA. B.J., January 2005, at 41.

6. Gross receipts taxes may be enacted by Florida's legislature despite Florida's constitution's restriction against personal income taxes. For example, "Florida imposes a gross receipts tax on utility and communications services." 53 Fla. Jur 2d Taxation § 1926 (June 2019 update). As another example, under Florida's "Insurance Code, insurers must pay to the Department of Revenue a tax on insurance premiums, premiums for title insurance, or assessments, including membership fees and policy fees and gross deposits received from subscribers to reciprocal or interinsurance agreements, and on annuity premiums or considerations received during the preceding calendar year." 53 Fla. Jur 2d Taxation § 1980 (June 2019 update). A gross receipts tax differs from a sales tax, which is imposed upon buyers, because a gross receipts tax is imposed upon sellers instead. Florida's supreme court, in interpreting Florida's constitution, holds that:

> No provision of the Constitution forbids the imposition of license or privilege taxes on the right to do business in the state and also on the gross receipts of such business. Both of these exactions are in the nature of license or privilege or occupational taxes. . . . By imposing a license tax as a condition precedent to the right to do intrastate business in the state, and also a tax upon the gross receipts of such business, the Legislature has not violated the Constitution or exceeded its powers; and it is not material whether the two taxes are imposed by one or by different statutes, enacted concurrently or at different times.

> The policy disclosed in the exactions made is not subject to judicial review.

Pullman Co. v. Knott, 69 So. 703, 704 (Fla. 1915). As to a state's authority to do so, considering the federal Constitution's Commerce Clause:

> Like other specific taxes, gross receipts taxes involving interstate commerce are subject to the U.S. Supreme Court's modern approach, under which the fact that a gross receipts tax reaches receipts from interstate commerce does not by itself invalidate the tax, which is valid as long as:
>
> (1) there is a substantial nexus between the taxed activity and the taxing state;
>
> (2) the tax is fairly apportioned to the taxing state in order to avoid multiple taxation of the receipts;
>
> (3) the tax does not discriminate against interstate commerce; and
>
> (4) the tax is fairly related to the services provided by the State imposing the tax.

50 Fla. Jur 2d Taxation § 248.

7. Excise taxes are within the taxing power of Florida's legislature. "An 'excise tax' is any tax that does not fall within the classification of a poll tax or a property tax and that embraces every form of burden not laid directly upon persons or property." 53 Fla. Jur 2d Taxation § 2017 (June 2019 update). Unlike sales taxes that apply to all items not exempted, excise taxes apply only to enumerated items. Whereas sales taxes are computed always as a percentage of the purchase price, excise taxes are computed either on a per-unit basis or as a percentage of the purchase price. For example, "a tax on the purchase of electricity, gas, water, and telephone service is an excise tax." *Id.* As another example, Florida's "doc stamp tax," codified at Florida Statutes chapter 201, taxes documents that transfer an interest in Florida real property such as deeds, and documents containing written obligations to

pay money such as promissory notes and mortgages. Such documents are unenforceable unless the doc stamp tax is paid. The tax is paid to the Clerk of Court when the document is recorded, or if unrecorded, is paid to the Florida Department of Revenue. Florida's counties may impose a surtax of their own on doc stamp taxes imposed upon deeds, except for single-family residences. See §§ 125.0167, 201.02, and 201.031, Fla. Stat. "The requirements as to uniformity and valuation do not ordinarily apply to excises. . . . [T]he only organic limitations upon the state are that due process, equal protection, and contract rights must be observed and that interstate commerce may not be burdened nor federal functions interfered with." 53 Fla. Jur 2d Taxation § 2019 (June 2019 update).

8. Sales and use taxes are imposed by Florida's legislature, plus a local option. Local option sales taxes are a surtax that increase Florida's sales tax on a regional basis, thereby making the sales tax rate vary throughout the state. In addition to the local option sales tax, other local option taxes permitted by Florida's legislature include discretionary sales surtaxes, fuel taxes, transient rental taxes, tourist development or impact taxes, convention development taxes, food and beverage taxes, and municipal resort taxes.

9. Does the state of Florida, its agencies, its counties, and its municipal corporations pay taxes to the state of Florida? Florida's supreme court holds that:

> [G]overnmentally owned property is generally excluded from taxation, through either immunity or exemption. An exemption presupposes an ability to tax, whereas an immunity implies the absence of that ability. See *Greater Orlando Aviation Auth. v. Crotty*, 775 So. 2d 978, 980 (Fla. 5th DCA 2000). The state and counties are immune from taxation. See *Canaveral Port Auth. v. Dep't of Revenue*, 690 So. 2d 1226, 1228 (Fla. 1996); *Park-N-Shop, Inc. v. Sparkman*, 99 So. 2d 571, 573 (Fla. 1957). Unlike counties, municipalities are not subdivisions of the state and are therefore subject to taxation absent an exemption. See *Greater Orlando Aviation Auth.*, 775 So.2d at 980.

> Article VII, section 3(a) of the Florida Constitution confers on property owned by municipalities an exemption from ad valorem taxation under certain circumstances. To qualify for the exemption in article VII, section 3(a), the property must be both owned by a municipality and used exclusively by the municipality for municipal or public purposes.

Florida Dept. of Revenue v. City of Gainesville, 918 So. 2d 250, 255 (Fla. 2005).

1. Power to Tax

"To impose, levy, and collect a tax is an exercise of the sovereign power" of a state. *Prevost v. Greneaux*, 60 U.S. 1, 3 (1856). States claim an inherent power to tax. As long ago as 1873, the Supreme Court of the United States held: "This power belongs in this country to the legislative sovereignty, State or National. In the case . . . [of state taxation, the] power must be derived from the legislature of the State. . . . [T]he State [can] delegated the power . . . by special statute or . . . vest the power in some other tribunal." *Heine v. Bd. of Levee Com'rs*, 86 U.S. 655, 661 (1873).

The Supreme Court of the United States recognized a state's broad power to tax, subject to certain restrictions, when it held:

> The power of taxation, however vast in its character and searching in its extent, is necessarily limited to subjects within the jurisdiction of the State. These subjects are persons, property, and business. Whatever form taxation may assume, whether as duties, imposts, excises, or licenses, it must relate to one of these subjects. It is not possible to conceive of any other, though as applied to them, the taxation may be exercised in a great variety of ways. It may touch property in every shape, in its natural condition, in its manufactured form, and in its various transmutations. And the amount of the taxation may be determined by the value of the property, or its use, or its capacity, or its productiveness. It may touch business in the almost infinite forms in which it is conducted, in professions, in commerce, in manufactures, and in transportation. Unless restrained

> by provisions of the Federal Constitution, the power of the State as to the mode, form, and extent of taxation is unlimited, where the subjects to which it applies are within her jurisdiction.

In re State Tax on Foreign-Held Bonds, 82 U.S. 300, 319 (1872).

Federal law imposes additional restrictions upon a state legislature's inherent power to tax. A state tax must be for a public purpose. *Citizens' Sav. & Loan Ass'n v. City of Topeka*, 87 U.S. 655 (1874). The Import-Export Clause of the U.S. Constitution prevents states from levying "any Imposts or Duties on Imports or Exports" and says that "[n]o Tax or Duty shall be laid on Articles exported from any State." Art. I, § 10, clause 2, U.S. Const.

Federal law also restricts a state's power to impose taxes extraterritorially. The so-called Dormant Commerce Clause, or Negative Commerce Clause, found by U.S. Supreme Court precedent to arise from Article I, Section 8, clause 3 of the U.S. Constitution, would mean that no state can impose any tax on interstate commerce unless that tax has a substantial nexus with the taxing state, is nondiscriminatory between in-state and out-of-state activity, is fairly apportioned to tax only the state's fair share of interstate activity, and is fairly related to services provided by the state, with the taxpayer enjoying state-provided services while in the state. *See generally Complete Auto Transit, Inc. v. Brady*, 430 U.S. 274 (1977). However, an out-of-state seller's physical presence in the taxing state is not necessary for the state to require the seller to collect and remit its sales tax. *S. Dakota v. Wayfair, Inc.*, 138 S. Ct. 2080 (2018) (overruling *Quill Corp. v. North Dakota By and Through Heitkamp*, 504 U.S. 298 (1992)).

Florida's constitution requires the state to raise "sufficient revenue to defray the expenses of the state for each fiscal period." Art. VII, § 1, Fla. Const. Of course, this does not empower the state to confiscate wealth, assets, or property without due process of law. *Green v. Frazier*, 253 U.S. 233, 234 (1920) ("The only ground of attack involving the validity of the [state's tax] which requires our consideration concerns the alleged deprivation of rights secured to the plaintiffs by the Fourteenth Amendment to the federal Constitution. It is contended that taxation under the laws in question has the effect of depriving plaintiffs of property without due process of law."). Indeed, Florida's constitution is clear: "No tax shall be levied except in pursuance of law." Art. VII, § 1, Fla. Const.

Florida's supreme court holds that Florida's legislature has an inherent power to tax as follows:

> As the Florida Constitution and the case law of this State evidence, the State, through the legislative branch of the government, possesses an inherent power to tax, and a municipality may exercise a taxing power only to the extent to which such power has been specifically granted to it by general law. See Fla. Constitution, Article VII, s 1(a); *Housing Authority of Plant City v. Kirk*, 231 So. 2d 522, (Fla. 1970); and *City of Miami Beach v. Lansburgh*, 218 So. 2d 519 (Fla. 3d DCA 1969). The right to determine the subjects of taxation and exemptions therefrom is within the [Florida] Legislature's prerogative in the exercise of its sovereign power. But this right is subject to the controlling constitutional limitations. *Cassady v. Consolidated Naval Stores, Inc.*, 119 So. 2d 35 (Fla. 1960). This Court has held in *City of Tampa et al. v. Birdsong*, [261 So. 2d 1 (Fla. 1972), that] municipalities may not impose a particular tax unless specifically authorized by general law to do so.

Belcher Oil Co. v. Dade County, 271 So. 2d 118, 122 (Fla. 1972). Stated somewhat differently, Florida's supreme court holds that "taxation by a city[, town, or village] must be expressly authorized either by the Florida Constitution or grant of the Florida Legislature." *State v. City of Port Orange*, 650 So. 2d 1, 3 (Fla. 1994). Florida's supreme court holds also that "the Florida Constitution authorizes municipalities to impose only ad valorem taxation 'except as provided by general law,' see art. VII, § 1(a), Fla. Const. . . " *City of Gainesville v. State*, 863 So. 2d 138, 143 n.3 (Fla. 2003).

When a local government is delegated the power to tax, what restrictions exist upon the use of that tax revenue? This issue was considered by Florida's attorney general in the following attorney general opinion number AGO 93-12.

FLORIDA ATTORNEY GENERAL ADVISORY OPINION

NUMBER: AGO 93-12

Date: February 9, 1993

Subject: Distribution of local option gas tax

To: Honorable J.E. Cooksey, Chairman, Jefferson County Board of County Commissioners . . .

[Question:]

> Must a county share local option gas tax levied pursuant to s. 336.025, F.S. (1992 Supp.), with an eligible municipality within the county, when the county is using such tax proceeds to fund infrastructure rather than transportation? . . .

In sum:

> A county eligible to levy a local option gas tax pursuant to s. 336.025, F.S. (1992 Supp.), must distribute the proceeds to eligible municipalities as directed therein, regardless of whether the funds are used for infrastructure.

[Analysis:]

Section 336.025, F.S. (1992 Supp.), allows counties to impose a local option gas tax upon every gallon of motor fuel and special fuel sold in a county and taxed under the provisions of Part I or Part II, Ch. 206, F.S. (1992 Supp.). Only those municipalities and counties eligible for participation in the distribution of moneys under Parts II and VI of Ch. 218, F.S., are eligible to receive moneys under this section. [Section 336.025(6), F.S. (1992 Supp.). Part II, Ch. 218, F.S., the Florida Revenue Sharing Act of 1972, allows those units of local government meeting the requirements in s. 218.23, F.S., to share in tax proceeds deposited in the revenue sharing trust funds created pursuant to the act. Part VI, Ch. 218, F.S., allows eligible county or municipal governments to receive a portion of the local government half-cent sales tax provided therein.]

A county may levy the tax by ordinance adopted by a majority vote of the governing body or approval by referendum. Under this procedure,

> "[t]he county may, prior to June 1, establish by interlocal agreement with one or more of the municipalities located therein, representing a majority of the population of the incorporated area within the county, a distribution formula for dividing the entire proceeds of the local option gas tax among the county government and all eligible municipalities within the county." (e.s.)

In the absence of an interlocal agreement, the county may, prior to June 10, adopt a resolution of intent to levy the tax. If no interlocal agreement or resolution is adopted, municipalities representing more than 50 percent of the county population may, prior to June 20, adopt uniform resolutions approving the local option tax, establishing the duration of the levy and the rate authorized, and setting the date for a countywide referendum on whether to impose the tax. In the event the tax is levied by county resolution or by uniform resolutions of the municipalities, the proceeds of the tax must be distributed "among the county government and eligible municipalities based on the transportation expenditures of each for the immediately preceding 5 fiscal years." Any newly incorporated municipality which is eligible for participation in the distribution of moneys under Parts II and VI, Ch. 218, F.S., located in a county levying the local option gas tax is also entitled to receive a share of the tax revenues.

The Legislature has made it clear, by the plain language of the statute, that proceeds from the local option gas tax are to be distributed among the county government and the eligible municipalities within the county. Where the Legislature has prescribed the manner in which a thing is to be done, it is, in effect, a prohibition against its being done in any other way.

Generally, local option gas tax proceeds received pursuant to s. 336.025, F.S. (1992 Supp.), may be used by the county and municipal governments only for transportation expenditures. However, s. 336.025(8), F.S. (1992 Supp.), provides that counties with a population of 50,000 or less on April 1, 1992, may use the tax proceeds to fund infrastructure projects, if consistent with the county's comprehensive plan and only after the local government, prior to the fiscal year in which the funds will be used, has held a duly noticed public hearing and adopted a resolution certifying that the local government has met all of the transportation needs identified in its comprehensive plan.

Thus, under the specified conditions, a county with a population of 50,000 or less may use the proceeds from the local option gas tax to fund infrastructure projects. There is nothing in the statute, however, indicating that a county using its gas tax proceeds for infrastructure purposes is entitled to all of the proceeds from the gas tax in the county, to the exclusion of the municipalities eligible to receive distributions pursuant to s. 336.025, F.S. (1992 Supp.). Absent such authority, it does not appear that Jefferson County may alter the distribution of proceeds from the local option gas tax to deprive eligible municipalities of their share of the tax proceeds.

Accordingly, a county eligible to levy a local option gas tax pursuant to s. 336.025, F.S. (1992 Supp.), must distribute the proceeds to eligible municipalities within the county as directed therein, regardless of whether the funds are used for transportation or infrastructure. . . .

Notes and Questions to Consider:

1. Florida's Attorney General's opinion quoted above interprets the statute where Florida's legislature gave Florida's local governments the option to levy a surtax (the "half-penny sales tax"). What gave Florida's legislature the right to require the revenue gained from that surtax to be distributed in the way described in the opinion?

2. Is it wise for a state legislature to impose tax and expenditure limitations upon local governments? Consider this commentator's analysis:

Empirical research on tax and expenditure limitations (TELs) has found several broad effects, although the effects vary considerably from state to state according to the terms of the specific restrictions.

Reduced Role of the Property Tax

TELs have contributed to the reduction in property taxes as a percentage of personal income and in the role of property taxes in funding local government. Nationwide (including the many states that did not adopt TELs), the property tax share of personal income dropped from 4.1% in 1978 to 3.2% in 1982, rebounded to 3.7% in 1992, and dropped modestly after that. . . .

Increased Role for Nontax Revenue Sources

TELs appear to have contributed to an increase in the role of assessments, fees (including development impact fees) and user and service charges in funding local governments. . . . Nationwide, by the early 1990s, fees and charges accounted for 14.6% of total local revenues and 23% of local own-source revenues. . . .

Shift in Power to the States

TELs imposed on local governments may have contributed to a shift in power to the states. The fiscal limits on local governments are typically more stringent than those imposed upon the states, and they have made local governments more dependent on state aid. . . .

Reduction in Local Revenue Growth

Even with the growth in intergovernmental aid, new taxes, and nontax local revenues, TELs appear to have reduced local revenue growth. . . . [F]or the most part, revenues in states with TELs have grown more slowly than in states without them. . . .

Richard Briffault, *State and Local Finance*, in G. Alan Tarr & Robert F. Williams, STATE CONSTITUTIONS FOR THE TWENTY-FIRST CENTURY, vol. 3, pp. 225–28 (State University of New York Press, 2006).

2. Nontax Revenue Sources

Florida's Supreme Court defines a "tax" as "an enforced burden imposed by sovereign right for the support of the government, the administration of law, and the exercise of various functions the sovereign is called on to perform." *State v. City of Port Orange*, 650 So. 2d 1, 3 (Fla. 1994).

Not every financial obligation imposed by a sovereign meets this definition of a "tax." Governmental entities that lack the power to tax may impose financial obligations that do not meet the definition of "tax," if that entity is granted such a power by a Florida Statute, or if that entity possesses Home Rule Powers. To be valid, these non-tax financial obligations must meet certain requirements, as illustrated by the case of *Morris v. City of Cape Coral*, 163 So. 3d 1174 (Fla. 2015) involving a Florida city's imposition of a special assessment upon city landowners for the cost of running the local fire department.

MORRIS

V.

CITY OF CAPE CORAL

Supreme Court of Florida, 2015

163 So. 3d 1174

This case arises from a final judgment validating the City of Cape Coral's special assessment to provide fire protection services. We have jurisdiction. See art. V, § 3(b)(2), Fla. Const. The City of Cape Coral ("City" or "Cape Coral") passed an ordinance levying a special assessment against all real property in the city, both developed and undeveloped. The assessment has two tiers—one for all property and a second that applies only to developed property. Scott Morris and other property owners (collectively referred to as either "Morris" or "Property Owners") appeal the validation, arguing that the two-tier methodology is arbitrary, [and] that the assessment violates existing law. . . . Because we find that Cape Coral properly exercised its authority to issue a special assessment to fund fire protection services and that the assessment does not violate existing law, we affirm the order of validation.

FACTS

In April 2013, Cape Coral authorized its city manager to hire Burton & Associates ("Burton") to prepare a study relating to a non-ad valorem assessment to fund the City's fire protection services. Burton presented its findings in a report dated June 10, 2013, which the City accepted. The report recommended a two-tier assessment, reasoning that all parcels in the city benefited from fire protection services and that developed property received an added benefit of protection from losses. Burton calculated the costs to maintain the facilities, equipment, and personnel necessary to provide fire protection services on a 24-hour-per-day, 365-days-per-year basis to all parcels in the city (exclusive of Emergency Medical Services costs). These costs represented seventy percent of the total fire protection services cost and were to be evenly distributed among all parcels. The costs for fuel, equipment maintenance, actual response to a fire, and other related operations were associated with protection from loss of structures.

At a June 10, 2013, public meeting, the City read and approved an Assessment Ordinance, which was again read and approved at the July 15, 2013, meeting. The City also passed a Note Ordinance at the same meeting. Thereafter, the Initial Assessment Resolution was adopted on July 29, 2013, and the Final Assessment Resolution was adopted on August 26, 2013. On August 28, 2013, the City filed its complaint to validate the debt under Chapter 75, Florida Statutes. The trial court issued an Order to Show Cause on September 11, 2013, which provided the time and date of the hearing. The Order to Show Cause was published in the local newspaper twenty days prior to the hearing and again the following week.

The trial court held the Show Cause hearing on October 7, 2013. Eight property owners appeared in opposition to the special assessment. The hearing was initially scheduled to last an hour, with each party given three minutes to present its argument. The trial court realized this was insufficient time and extended the hearing for two additional days. . . .

On December 11, 2013, the trial court entered its final judgment of validation. The judgment found, in pertinent part:

> (1) that the City of Cape Coral has the legal authority to issue the bond and assess properties within its jurisdiction as requested, (2) that the intended purpose of the bond is legal, to wit, it shall provide a continuation or provision of fire safety related service for all affected parcels, and (3) that the issuance of the bond and its related process comply with all essential elements and requirements of law, including reasonable apportionment.

[Four] property owners[] filed a Notice of Appeal with this Court on February 18, 2014.

STANDARD OF REVIEW

This Court's scope of review is limited to: (1) whether the municipality has the authority to issue the assessment; (2) whether the purpose of the assessment is legal; and (3) whether the assessment complies with the requirements of the law. See *City of Winter Springs v. State*, 776 So. 2d 255, 257 (Fla. 2001) (citations omitted).

"[A] valid special assessment must meet two requirements: (1) the property assessed must derive a special benefit from the service provided; and (2) the assessment must be fairly and reasonably apportioned according to the benefits received." *Sarasota Cnty. v. Sarasota Church of Christ*, 667 So. 2d 180, 183 (Fla. 1995) (citing *City of Boca Raton v. State*, 595 So. 2d 25, 30 (Fla. 1992)). "These two prongs both constitute questions of fact for a legislative body rather than the judiciary." *Id.* at 183. The standard to be applied to both prongs is that the legislative findings should be upheld unless the determination is arbitrary. *Id.* at 184. "Even an unpopular decision, when made correctly, must be upheld." *Winter Springs*, 776 So. 2d at 261.

ANALYSIS

. . . The authority to issue special assessments under a municipality's home rule powers was addressed by this Court in *Boca Raton*. In *Boca Raton*, after providing a history of home rule authority, we determined that

> a municipality may now exercise any governmental, corporate, or proprietary power for a municipal purpose except when expressly prohibited by law, and a municipality may legislate on any subject matter on which the legislature may act [with exceptions]. . . . Therefore, it would appear that the City of Boca Raton can levy its special assessment unless it is expressly prohibited. . . .

Boca Raton, 595 So. 2d at 28. . . . Accordingly, . . . there is no question that the City had the legal authority to levy the special assessment.

Further, we have previously upheld the validity of special assessments to fund fire protection services. See, e.g., *Lake Cnty. v. Water Oak Mgmt. Corp.*, 695 So. 2d 667 (Fla. 1997); *S. Trail Fire Control Dist., Sarasota Cnty. v. State*, 273 So. 2d 380 (Fla. 1973); *Fire Dist. No. 1 of Polk Cnty. v. Jenkins*, 221 So. 2d 740 (Fla. 1969).

The Property Owners allege that the benefit from the fire protection services is a general one, and not a specific benefit. To support their argument, the Property Owners rely on our decision in *St. Lucie County—Fort Pierce Fire Prevention & Control District v. Higgs*, 141 So. 2d 744 (Fla. 1962), for their contention that assessments levied on property for maintenance and operation of fire prevention services constitutes a tax. See *Higgs*, 141 So. 2d at 746. In *Higgs*, this Court agreed with the circuit court's finding that a particular assessment to fund fire services was invalid because "no parcel of land was specially or peculiarly benefited in proportion to its value. . . ." *Id.*

However, in 1997, we held that solid waste disposal and fire protection services funded by a special assessment did provide a special benefit. *Water Oak Mgmt.*, 695 So. 2d at 668. Therein, the Fifth District Court of Appeal found Lake County's assessment invalid under this Court's decision in *Higgs* because everyone in the county had access to fire protection services and so was not a special benefit. We found that the Fifth District had misconstrued our decision in *Higgs*, stating:

> In evaluating whether a special benefit is conferred to property by the services for which the assessment is imposed, the test is not whether the services confer a "unique" benefit or are different in type or degree from the benefit provided to the community as a whole; rather, the test is whether there is a "logical relationship" between the services provided and the benefit to real property.

Water Oak Mgmt., 695 So. 2d at 669 (citing *Whisnant v. Stringfellow*, 50 So. 2d 885 (Fla. 1951) (footnote omitted); *Crowder v. Phillips*, 1 So. 2d 629 (1941)). Noting our decision in *Fire District No. 1*, we found that "fire protection services do, at a minimum, specially benefit real property by providing for lower insurance premiums and enhancing the value of the property. Thus, there is a 'logical relationship' between the services provided and the benefit to real property." *Water Oak Mgmt.*, 695 So. 2d at 669. We then clarified that our decision in *Higgs* turned not on the benefit prong, but on the apportionment prong. *Id.* at 670.

In this case, Cape Coral has established that the assessed property receives a special benefit. In the Assessment Ordinance, the City made the following statement:

> *Legislative Determinations of Special Benefit:*
>
> It is hereby ascertained and declared that the Fire Protection services, facilities, and programs provide a special benefit to property because Fire Protection services possess a logical relationship to the use and enjoyment of property by: (1) protecting the value and integrity of the improvements, structures, and unimproved land through the provision

> of available Fire Protection services; (2) protecting the life and safety of intended occupants in the use and enjoyment of property; (3) lowering the cost of fire insurance by the presence of a professional and comprehensive Fire Protection program within the City and limiting the potential financial liability for uninsured or underinsured properties; and (4) containing and extinguishing the spread of fire incidents occurring on property, including but not limited to unimproved property, with the potential to spread and endanger the structures and occupants of property.

Likewise, the experts retained by Cape Coral determined that all parcels in the City received a special benefit from the City's fire protection services and facilities. In its report, Burton reasoned that the response-readiness of the fire department benefitted all parcels by raising property value and marketability, limiting liability by containing fire and preventing its spread to other parcels, ensuring immediate response, and heightening the use and enjoyment of all properties. These findings are similar to the reasons we accepted in *Water Oak Mgmt*. See *Water Oak Mgmt.*, 695 So. 2d at 669 ("[F]ire protection services do, at a minimum, specially benefit real property by providing for lower insurance premiums and enhancing the value of the property."). Thus, the facts of the present case lie squarely within the facts of *Water Oak Mgmt*. Only the methodology differs.

The Property Owners question the validity of Tier 1 and Tier 2 of the assessment. In short, the Property Owners argue that the assessment is not properly apportioned. We have instructed:

> To be legal, special assessments must be directly proportionate to the benefits to the property upon which they are levied and this may not be inferred from a situation where all property in a district is assessed for the benefit of the whole on the theory that individual parcels are peculiarly benefited in the ratio that the assessed value of each bears to the total value of all property in the district.

Higgs, 141 So. 2d at 746. In other words, the assessment cannot be in excess of the proportional benefits. *S. Trail Fire Control Dist.*, 273 So. 2d at 384.

And, the proportional benefits cannot be calculated by the ratio of the value of the assessed property against the value of all property. See *Water Oak Mgmt.*, 695 So. 2d at 670 (explaining that the decision in *Higgs* turned on whether the land was benefitted in proportion to its value, stating: "the assessment in that case was actually a tax because it had been wrongfully apportioned based on the assessed value of the properties rather than on the special benefits provided to the properties."). However, this Court has also held that "[t]he mere fact that some property is assessed on an area basis, and other property is assessed at a flat rate basis, does not in itself establish the invalidity of the special assessment." *S. Trail Fire Control Dist.*, 273 So. 2d at 384.

To this end, the Property Owners allege that Tier 1 of the assessment is invalid because it equally assesses all property and therefore is not proportional. The Property Owners further argue that Tier 2 of the assessment, being based on the value of any structures and improvements on a parcel, amounts to nothing more than a tax. In other words, the Property Owners allege that the City's chosen methodology is arbitrary and does not properly apportion the costs. We find that the City's methodology is not arbitrary. See *Sarasota Church of Christ*, 667 So. 2d at 184 ("[L]egislative determination as to the existence of special benefits and as to the apportionment of the costs of those benefits should be upheld unless the determination is arbitrary.").

In the present case, the City contracted for a study to determine the best method to apportion the costs of fire services. By adopting the approach recommended in the study, the City has attempted to apportion the costs based on both the general availability of fire protection services to everyone (Tier 1) and the additional benefit of improved property owners of protecting structures from damage (Tier 2). We have not previously addressed a bifurcated approach to fire service assessments. However, this sort of approach closely resembles the approach we approved in *Sarasota Church of Christ.*

In *Sarasota Church of Christ*, we considered the validity of special assessments against developed property for stormwater management services. There, undeveloped property was not assessed at all, residential property was assessed at a flat rate per number of individual dwelling units on the property, and non-residential property was assessed based on a formula. Specifically, "[t]his method for apportionment focuse[d] on the projected stormwater discharge from developed parcels based on the amount of 'horizontal impervious area' assumed for each parcel and divide[d] the contributions based on varying property usage." This Court held that "this method of apportioning the costs of the stormwater services is not arbitrary and bears a reasonable relationship to the benefits received by the individual developed properties. . . ." *Sarasota Church of Christ*, 667 So. 2d at 186.

The Tier 2 formula for improved properties is akin to the formula in *Sarasota Church of Christ* for determining the assessment against commercial property. Like that of *Sarasota County*, the City's methodology reasonably relates to the additional benefits received by improved properties. The formula contemplates that each improved parcel benefits differently because the cost to replace the respective structure differs. The use of the property appraiser's structure value is reasonable because the property appraiser is statutorily required to use a replacement cost to determine this value. See § 193.011(5), Fla. Stat. (2014). We find that this is a reasonable approach to apportionment and not arbitrary.

As we have stated, "[t]he manner of the assessment is immaterial and may vary within the district, as long as the amount of the assessment for each tract is not in excess of the proportional benefits as compared to other assessments on other tracts." *Boca Raton*, 595 So. 2d at 31 (quoting *S. Trail Fire Control Dist.*, 273 So. 2d at 384). In fact, we have acknowledged:

> No system of appraising benefits or assessing costs has yet been devised that is not open to some criticism. None have attained the ideal position of exact equality, but, if assessing boards would bear in mind that benefits actually accruing to the property improved in addition to those received by the community at large must control both as to the benefits prorated and the limit of assessments for cost of improvement, the system employed would be as near the ideal as it is humanly possible to make it.

Id. (quoting *City of Ft. Myers v. State*, 117 So. 97, 104 (Fla. 1928)). The methodology at issue here was found by the trial court to be "valid, non-arbitrary and considered established insofar as the [opposing parties] failed to present any competent, persuasive evidence to dispute or call into reasonable question [the court's] findings and determinations." A review of the record supports the trial court's determination. . . .

Likewise, the Property Owners have failed to establish that they were denied procedural due process. The Property Owners have not alleged that the City failed to provide notice or denied the Property Owners a meaningful opportunity to be heard. In addition to the validation hearing, the City publicly discussed the special assessment at four public meetings, for which notice was provided. At the validation hearing, the trial court extended the time for the Property Owners to voice their concerns. Based on the foregoing, the Property Owners have not established that they were denied procedural due process. . . .

CONCLUSION

For the foregoing reasons, we affirm the final judgment of validation.

Notes and Questions to Consider:

1. What is a special assessment, and why would a municipal corporation impose one? Commentators explain that:

> Cities impose special assessments to generate revenue to pay for services or capital improvements. These special assessments are estimated by assessing a charge on properties that receive a special benefit from those services or improvements. Special assessments and ad valorem property taxes are similar—for example, payment is mandatory and they are both levied on real property—but they are not the same. The central distinction is that "special assessments must confer a specific benefit upon the land burdened by the assessment," while property taxes do not.

> . . . In other words, property taxes may be levied to finance general government expenses, without regard to how the taxes benefit any particular property; however, with special assessments, there must be a connection between the assessed properties and the government expenses financed by the assessment revenue.
>
> . . . A special assessment is validly imposed . . . if it meets a two-prong test established by caselaw. Under the "special benefit" prong, all of the assessed parcels must receive a special benefit from the improvements or services to be financed by the special assessment revenues. Under the "fair apportionment" prong, the cost of the improvements or services "'"must be fairly and reasonably apportioned"'" among the parcels receiving the special benefit. . . . The question is whether the amount assessed for each property is reasonably proportional to the benefit the property receives.
>
> . . . A city's legislative determinations of fair apportionment are presumptively valid, and courts must review them under a highly deferential standard. A court cannot disturb a city's legislative determination unless it is arbitrary.

Susan Churuti, Chris Roe, Ellie Neiberger, Tyler Egbert & Zach Lombardo, *The Line between Special Assessments and Ad Valorem Taxes:* Morris v. City of Cape Coral, 45 STETSON L. REV. 471, 472–74 (2016).

2. What satisfies the first prong of the two-prong test for the validity of a special assessment, the "special benefit" prong? It is satisfied when "that portion of the community which is required to bear it [must] receive[] some special or peculiar benefit in the enhancement of value of the property against which it is imposed as a result of the improvement made with the proceeds of the special assessment. It is limited to the property benefited, is not governed by uniformity, and may be determined legislatively or judicially." *Klemm v. Davenport*, 129 So. 904, 907 (Fla. 1930). Stated somewhat differently, "the property of the taxpayer [must be] deemed by the legislative authority to be benefited over and beyond the general benefit to the community, and it is imposed and collected as an equivalent for that benefit and to

pay for the improvement in whole or in part. . . . The purpose for which such assessment is imposed must, of course, be public in its nature as distinguished from one designed solely for private benefit." *Atl. Coast Line R. Co. v. City of Lakeland*, 115 So. 669, 683–84 (Fla. 1927).

3. What satisfies the second prong of the two-prong test for validity of a special assessment, the "fair apportionment" prong? *See St. Lucie County-Fort Pierce Fire Prevention & Control Dist. v. Higgs*, 141 So. 2d 744, 746 (Fla. 1962) ("To be legal, special assessments must be directly proportionate to the benefits to the property upon which they are levied and this may not be inferred from a situation where all property in a district is assessed for the benefit of the whole on the theory that individual parcels are peculiarly benefited in the ratio that the assessed value of each bears to the total value of all property in the district.")

4. In *Morris v. City of Cape Coral*, the city lacked the power to tax its residents for fire services. Yet the city created a financial liability for all property owners (Tier 1) and additional liability for owners of developed property (Tier 2) to pay for fire services and labeled it all as a "special assessment." Florida's supreme court held that neither Tier 1 nor Tier 2 met the definition of a "tax," and that both tiers met the legal requirements for a "special assessment." Is this just a matter of semantics? Florida's supreme court holds that the "power of a municipality to tax should not be broadened by semantics. . . " *State v. City of Port Orange*, 650 So. 2d 1, 3 (Fla. 1994). Therefore, a financial liability that meets the definition of a "tax" cannot be levied just by labeling it as a special assessment. "[I]n Florida's Constitution, the voters have placed a limit on ad valorem millage available to municipalities, art. VII, § 9, Fla. Const.; made homesteads exempt from taxation up to minimum limits, art. VII, § 9, Fla. Const.; and exempted from levy those homesteads specifically delineated in article X, section 4 of the Florida Constitution. These constitutional provisions cannot be circumvented by creativity." *Id.* at 4.

5. Why can a Florida governmental entity forbidden to impose a tax still be able to impose a special assessment? In the 1950s, Florida's su-

preme court held that "obligations secured solely by special assessments do not come within the prohibition of Article IX, Section 6 of [Florida's] Constitution, since, historically, a pledge of special assessments has never been considered to be a 'pledge of the taxing power.'" *City of Orlando v. State*, 67 So. 2d 673, 674 (Fla. 1953). Fifty years later, Florida's supreme court held again that "[s]pecial assessments are not taxes because they confer a special benefit on the land burdened by the assessment." *City of Gainesville v. State*, 863 So. 2d 138, 143 n.3 (Fla. 2003).

6. Sovereign immunity protects Florida from liability to counties, municipal corporations, and districts who might enact a special assessment. Therefore, neither the state of Florida, nor its state agencies, may be liable for a special assessment unless a law passed by Florida's legislature permits it. *City of Gainesville v. State*, 863 So. 2d 138, 143 n.3 (Fla. 2003).

7. In lieu of a special assessment, another funding method used by Florida's governmental entities who lack the power to tax is a user fee. Examples include utility fees for sewer or electric, park pavilion rental fees, permits, licenses, and the like. "User fees are charges based upon the proprietary right of the governing body permitting the use of the instrumentality involved. Such fees share common traits that distinguish them from taxes: they are charged in exchange for a particular governmental service which benefits the party paying the fee in a manner not shared by other members of society, . . . and they are paid by choice, in that the party paying the fee has the option of not utilizing the governmental service and thereby avoiding the charge." *City of Gainesville v. State*, 863 So. 2d 138, 143 n.3 (Fla. 2003). Therefore, a financial obligation meets the definition of a "user fee" if it is an avoidable charge, paid voluntarily, in return for use of a thing or service provided by the governmental entity. To be valid, user fees must meet the following requirements. The fee must bear a rational relationship to the per capita cost of the thing or service. The fee must be used by the governing body toward its expense in owning, maintaining, or providing the thing or service. Home Rule Powers, whether granted by the state constitution or the state legislature, are sufficient authority for imposing user fees. If the governmental entity has

Home Rule Powers, then an enabling statute from Florida's legislature is not a necessary prerequisite to charging user fees. *See id.*

3. Just Valuation

Article VII, Section 4 of Florida's constitution requires that ad valorem taxation be calculated by multiplying the millage rate by the "just valuation" of the property. Florida's supreme court holds that "[t]he 'just valuation' at which property must be assessed under the Constitution . . . is synonymous with fair market value, i.e., the amount a purchaser willing but not obliged to buy would pay to a seller who is willing but not obliged to sell." *S. Bell Tel. & Tel. Co. v. Dade County*, 275 So. 2d 4, 8 (Fla. 1973).

What are the guiding principles for Florida's calculation of the "just valuation" of property for ad valorem taxation? Consider the case of *Straughn v. GAC Properties, Inc.*, 360 So. 2d 385, 386–87 (Fla. 1978) involving a property owner whose undeveloped parcel of land lies partially in one Florida county and partially in another.

STRAUGHN

V.

GAC PROPERTIES, INC.

Supreme Court of Florida, 1978

360 So. 2d 385

The narrow question presented in this case is whether . . . to compel equalization of ad valorem tax valuations where real property situated in one county is assessed on the basis of a higher value than that assigned to allegedly identical property located in another county.

GAC Properties owns a large tract of undeveloped land on both sides of the Osceola-Polk County line. The Polk County tax appraiser valued that portion of the property in his jurisdiction for 1975 at $300 per lot, while the Osceola County appraiser valued the lands in his domain at $560 per lot. GAC

Properties sued[, alleging] . . . that the discrepancy violates the "just valuation" requirement of Article VII, Section 4, Florida Constitution. . . .

. . . [We held in previous decisions that] inter-county assessment uniformity is not required by the Constitution, and that variations even between adjacent counties are not a basis for lowering tax assessments which are neither greater than 100% of fair market value nor unequally or improperly determined in relation to other properties within the same county. These principles flow from the constitutional directive that Florida's counties each have their own tax appraiser. . . . [Florida's L]egislature has in recent years endeavored to equalize real property tax assessments among the counties by developing statewide valuation standards, . . . [but] the ability of the legislature to harmonize tax assessments throughout the state[:]

> must remain conditioned by the Constitution's directive that a class of county officers are assigned the primary responsibility to perform assessment functions. At best the legislative goal can be achieved only incrementally through cooperative efforts of the assessors and the Department, and by the development of procedures which will accommodate the responsibilities of both.

[*Spooner v. Askew*, 345 So. 2d 1055, 1059–60 (Fla. 1976).]

We decline to hold, merely on the basis of an allegation that different values have been assigned to adjacent properties of like character in different counties, that a taxpayer can claim a violation of the "just valuation" requirement [of Florida's constitution] . . . .

Notes and Questions to Consider:

1. *Straughn v. GAC Properties* involved just a single parcel of land which happened to lie in two separate counties. One county said it was worth $300, and the other, $500. How did it arise that this one parcel would be assigned two different values using the same applicable law?

2. The opinion references the constitutional requirement that each county have its own property appraiser. Indeed, Florida's constitution provides: "There shall be elected by the electors of each county, for terms of four years, . . . a tax collector, [and] a property appraiser. . . ." Art. VIII, § 1, Fla. Const. How did the property appraiser's status as a constitutional officer impact the outcome of *Straughn v. GAC Properties*?

3. Why did the court not find a violation of the "just valuation" requirement when two different values were assigned to the one parcel, and the one owner paid different taxes to the two counties? Consider the fact that at least one noted treatise opines: "The mandate of just valuation for property taxation has as one of its goals the uniformity of treatment of taxpayers." 51A Fla. Jur 2d Taxation § 943 (June 2019 update).

4. The opinion also references a "recent" attempt by Florida's legislature to equalize real property tax assessments. After *Straughn v. GAC Properties*, how could such a goal ever be achieved?

4. "Save Our Homes" Amendment Supplements the Common Homestead Tax Exemption

Florida's common homestead tax exemption, it is not self-executing. Instead, Florida homesteaders must apply for the homestead tax exemption in a timely and proper manner. *See Zingale v. Powell*, 885 So. 2d 277, 285 (Fla. 2004).

Another benefit accruing to homesteaders who successfully apply for Florida's homestead tax exemption is the benefit of an amendment to Florida's constitution known as Save Our Homes. Florida's supreme court notes that "article VII, section 4(c) of the Florida Constitution, known as the 'Save Our Homes' amendment, . . . limits the annual change in property tax assessments on homestead exempt property to three percent of the previous assessment or the change in the Consumer Price Index, whichever is less." *Zingale v. Powell*, 885 So. 2d 277, 279 (Fla. 2004). Stated somewhat differently, Save Our Homes limits the annual increase of the homesteader's property tax to a certain percentage of last year's property tax bill. A subsequent amendment to Florida's constitution makes this tax savings "portable" so that moving from one tax-qualified homestead to another tax-qualified homestead results in bringing the benefits of that prior tax cap to the new homestead. If the former residence is retained not sold, it may qualify for a nonhomestead cap on annual increases. For the homesteader who is a longtime resident, these tax savings can be substantial.

What is required to maintain these ongoing tax benefits? Consider the case of *Orange County Prop. Appraiser v. Sommers*, 84 So. 3d 1277 (Fla. 5th DCA 2012).

ORANGE COUNTY PROPERTY APPRAISER

V.

SOMMERS

Fifth District Court of Appeal of Florida, 2012

84 So. 3d 1277

This case of first impression compels us to consider what the innocent looking phrase, "placed on the tax roll," means with respect to the ten per cent cap on increases in the assessment of continuously owned nonhomestead residential real property that previously enjoyed the status of homestead property. The phrase is found in section 193.1554(3), Florida Statutes (2010). The trial court concluded that the phrase meant that the homestead value of continuously owned residential property remained in place even after the property no longer bore a homestead classification, and that the assessment on the property could not be increased by more than the ten per cent limit found in section 193.1554(3). The appellants, Orange County Property Appraiser and Orange County Tax Collector, appeal the final judgment finding that the 2009 assessed value of the residential property owned by the appellees, Bernard D. Sommers and Arlene P. Sommers, was incorrect. We conclude that the trial court misinterpreted the statute and reverse.

The facts are neither complicated, nor contested. Mr. and Mrs. Sommers owned a home in Maitland, Florida, from 1960 to 2010. They continuously resided in that house from the date of purchase until they moved to a different residence in November 2008. Although they were not living in the home, they still owned it until January 2010, at which time they sold it. It is uncontested that the house was not homestead from the day Mr. and Mrs. Sommers moved out in 2008, to the day it was sold in 2010.

In 2008, the property enjoyed the homestead exemption because it was the Sommers' residence on January 1st of that year. The Property Appraiser assessed the home in 2008 in compliance with the "Save Our Homes" assessment cap contained in Article VII, Subsection 4(d) of the Florida Constitution, and implemented in section 193.155(1), Florida Statutes (2010). The assessment cap on the Sommers' property, assessed as homestead, was three per cent. After applying the homestead exemption with the Save Our Homes cap, the Property Appraiser assessed the taxable value of the Sommers' home for that year at $134,060.

In 2009, because Mr. and Mrs. Sommers no longer lived in the home, the property became a "nonhomestead residential" property for ad valorem tax purposes. The Property Appraiser assessed the Sommers' home as of January 1, 2009, using the just value or fair market value standard, at $279,955. Compared to the taxable value of the homestead in 2008 of $134,060, the assessment in 2009, was an increase in the taxable value of the home of $145,895, or 108.1%.

Mr. and Mrs. Sommers disputed the 2009 assessment and filed a petition with the Orange County Value Adjustment Board ("VAB"), seeking relief. They paid their taxes in full, but under protest. At the VAB hearing before a special magistrate, the Sommers argued that because the Property Appraiser had increased the assessment of their now nonhomestead residential property by an amount in excess of ten per cent of the previous-year assessment, the Appraiser had violated the ten per cent cap imposed on assessment increases for that classification of property under newly adopted Subsection 4(g) of Article VII of the Florida Constitution and section 193.1554, Florida Statutes.

The Property Appraiser countered that he properly assessed the Sommers' nonhomestead residential property at its just value for 2009 and that only in 2010 would the Sommers' property be subject to the ten per cent cap on assessment increases pursuant to section 193.1554.

. . . The section of the Florida Constitution governing the valuation of real property for ad valorem tax purposes and a number of statutes concerning the same matter must be spread upon the table in order to understand the arguments of the parties. We begin with the constitution.

The Florida Constitution mandates the just valuation of all property for ad valorem tax purposes. Art. VII, § 4, Fla. Const.; *Bystrom v. Whitman*, 488 So. 2d 520, 521 (Fla. 1986). General law provides, concomitantly, that all real property shall be assessed according to its just value on January 1 of each year. See § 192.042(1), Fla. Stat. Homestead property is treated somewhat differently in that it is benefitted by a number of tax breaks after it is justly valued. See, e.g., § 196.031, Fla. Stat. (2010). In the event of a termination of homestead status, however, real property must be assessed as provided by general law. Art. VII, § 4(d)(6).

Article VII, Section 4(g), of the Florida Constitution considers the subject of nonhomestead residential property. It provides:

> (g) For all levies other than school district levies, assessments of residential real property, as defined by general law, which contains nine units or fewer and *which is not subject to the assessment limitations set forth in subsections (a) through (d) [including the homestead exemption*] shall change only as provided in this subsection.
>
> (1) Assessments subject to this subsection shall be changed annually on the date of assessment provided by law; *but those changes in assessments shall not exceed ten percent (10%) of the assessment for the prior year.*

We have added emphasis to certain provisions of this passage because it is informative with regard to the codification by the legislature of its requirements. Section 4(g) essentially defines nonhomestead residential property as being residential real property of fewer than nine units which is not accorded homestead treatment for real property tax purposes. That is to say, in order to be classified as nonhomestead residential property and to receive the benefit of the ten per cent tax increase limitation, a parcel of real estate cannot at the same time be subject to the homestead exemption.

Section 193.1554, Florida Statutes, which implements these constitutional requirements, provides in pertinent part:

> (1) As used in this section, the term "nonhomestead residential property" means residential real property that contains nine or fewer dwelling units, including vacant property zoned and platted for residential use, *and that does not receive the exemption under [Florida Statutes section] 196.031* (the homestead exemption).
>
> (2) For all levies other than school district levies, nonhomestead residential property shall be assessed at just value as of January 1, 2008. Property placed on the tax roll after January 1, 2008, shall be assessed at just value as of January 1 of the year in which the property is placed on the tax roll.
>
> (3) Beginning in 2009, or *the year following the year the property is placed on the tax roll*, whichever is later, the property shall be reassessed annually on January 1. *Any change resulting from such reassessment may not exceed 10 percent of the assessed value of the property for the prior year.*
>
> (4) If the assessed value of the property as calculated under subsection (3) exceeds the just value, the assessed value of the property shall be lowered to the just value of the property.

(Emphasis added).

In accordance with the constitution, the statute also underscores that nonhomestead residential real property is a parcel that has nine or fewer units and which does not already enjoy a homestead exemption. Thus, if a property is homestead property, it cannot by definition also enjoy the ten per cent limitation for nonhomestead property. The conflict in the present case, however, stems from the words "placed on the tax roll" found in subsection (3). It says that nonhomestead residential property is subject to the ten per cent increase limitation beginning in the "year following the year the property is placed on the tax roll."

More specifically, the issue before us is whether the ten per cent cap applies to residential property that changes its classification from homestead to nonhomestead, but does not change ownership. Orange County argues that Mr. and Mrs. Sommers cannot enjoy the Save Our Homes cap on their property once it was no longer their homestead. Thus, according to Orange County, once the house became a nonhomestead property, the assessor was required to assess the house at its just or fair market value. Only in subsequent years would it be the beneficiary of the ten per cent cap. Otherwise, the property which is currently not entitled to the Save Our Homes discount, would inherently benefit from that discount if the 2008 homestead value of the house was utilized as the base value, so long as it continued to be owned by Mr. and Mrs. Sommers.

The Sommerses argue to the contrary that section 193.1554(3), Florida Statutes, which governs nonhomestead residential property, does not allow an assessment that exceeds ten per cent of the assessed value for the property for the prior year. They insist that their house has been on the tax roll since 1960, albeit as a homestead property, and that the simple change in the classification of the property does not put it on the tax roll anew. That is, the Sommers say their property was "placed on the tax roll" in 1960, not in 2008.

While we certainly understand the position adopted by Mr. and Mrs. Sommers, we conclude that the legislature did not intend a single piece of residential property to be entitled to both the homestead exemption and tax cap and the ten per cent nonhomestead tax cap at the same time. Article VII, Section 4(g) and section 193.1554(2) simply do not contemplate a single parcel receiving the benefit of both exemptions at the same time. The appellants are, therefore, correct that once the property changes classification from homestead to nonhomestead, it must then be revalued at its fair market value for ad valorem tax purposes before it can receive the benefit of the ten percent limitation in future tax years.

The architecture of the ad valorem tax structure within Florida confirms this conclusion. When real property first becomes classified as homestead, it is "assessed at just value as of January 1st of the year following the establishment of the homestead. . . ." See Art. VII, § 4(d)(4), Fla. Const. Analogously, when lands classified as agricultural are diverted to nonagricultural use, or are no longer used for agriculture, or are rezoned to a nonagricultural use at the request of the owner, those lands must also be reclassified and reassessed at just value accordingly. See § 193.461(4)(a), Fla. Stat. (2010). In similar fashion, nonhomestead residential property is also required to be assessed at just value on January 1st of the year following a change of ownership or control. See § 193.1554(5), Fla. Stat. (2010). The pattern is clear. . . .

Accordingly, the judgment is reversed and remanded for action consistent with this opinion.

REVERSED and REMANDED.

Notes and Questions to Consider:

1. In *Orange County Property Appraiser v. Sommers*, the court notes that the taxpayers asserted that their tax was improperly assessed at too high an amount. Then the taxpayers paid the tax anyway "under protest," and thereafter, initiated formal proceedings challenging the amount of the tax. Why did the taxpayers pay the tax despite believing it to be illegal? Consider this section of Article VII of Florida's constitution:

> *SECTION 13. Relief from illegal taxes.*—Until payment of all taxes which have been legally assessed upon the property of the same owner, no court shall grant relief from the payment of any tax that may be illegal or illegally assessed.

2. The taxpayers' claim was based upon the Save Our Homes Amendment, found in Article VII, Section 4, of Florida's constitution. It caps annual increases of common homestead property tax as follows: "changes in assessments shall not exceed the lower of the following: (a). Three percent (3%) of the assessment for the prior year. (b). The percent change in the Consumer Price Index . . . as initially reported by the United States Department of Labor, Bureau of Labor Statistics." What do you believe motivated Florida's electors to enact this amendment to Florida's constitution?

3. Regarding common homestead tax property that becomes nonhomestead and the effect upon the common homestead tax exemption, Florida's constitution states: "In the event of a termination of homestead status, the property shall be assessed as provided by general law." Art. VII, sec. 4, Fla. Const. Why not leave the common homestead tax exemption in place despite the termination of the homestead status?

4. Regarding the effect of home improvements upon the common homestead tax exemption, Florida's constitution states: "Changes, additions, reductions, or improvements to homestead property shall be assessed as provided for by general law; provided, however, after the adjustment for any change, addition, reduction, or improvement, the property shall be assessed as provided in this subsection." Art. VII, sec. 4, Fla. Const. It also provides:

> A county may, in the manner prescribed by general law, provide for a reduction in the assessed value of homestead property to the extent of any increase in the assessed value of that property which results from the construction or reconstruction of the property for the purpose of providing living quarters for one or more natural or adoptive grandparents or parents of the owner of the property or of the owner's spouse if at least one of the grandparents or parents for whom the living quarters are provided is 62 years of age or older. Such a reduction may not exceed the lesser of the following:
>
> (1) The increase in assessed value resulting from construction or reconstruction of the property.

(2) Twenty percent of the total assessed value of the property as improved.

Art. VII, sec. 4, Fla. Const.

5. Florida's constitution contains other homestead and nonhomestead tax benefits reducing ad valorem taxation in Article VII, Section 4, subsections (d) through (h); and Article VII, Section 6, subsections (a) through (h). Many address specific groups of people. For example, consider the following subsections of Article VII, Section 6:

SECTION 6. Homestead exemptions.—

. . .(c) By general law and subject to conditions specified therein, the Legislature may provide to renters, who are permanent residents, ad valorem tax relief on all ad valorem tax levies. Such ad valorem tax relief shall be in the form and amount established by general law.

(d) The legislature may, by general law, allow counties or municipalities, for the purpose of their respective tax levies and subject to the provisions of general law, to grant either or both of the following additional homestead tax exemptions:

(1) An exemption not exceeding fifty thousand dollars to a person who has the legal or equitable title to real estate and maintains thereon the permanent residence of the owner, who has attained age sixty-five, and whose household income, as defined by general law, does not exceed twenty thousand dollars; or

(2) An exemption equal to the assessed value of the property to a person who has the legal or equitable title to real estate with a just value less than two hundred and fifty thousand dollars, as determined in the first tax year that the owner applies and is eligible for the exemption, and who has maintained thereon the permanent residence of the owner for not less than twenty-five years, who has attained age sixty-five, and whose household income does not exceed the income limitation prescribed in paragraph (1).

The general law must allow counties and municipalities to grant these additional exemptions, within the limits prescribed in this subsection, by ordinance adopted in the manner prescribed by general law, and must provide for the periodic adjustment of the income limitation prescribed in this subsection for changes in the cost of living.

(e) Each veteran who is age 65 or older who is partially or totally permanently disabled shall receive a discount from the amount of the ad valorem tax otherwise owed on homestead property the veteran owns and resides in if the disability was combat related and the veteran was honorably discharged upon separation from military service. The discount shall be in a percentage equal to the percentage of the veteran's permanent, service-connected disability as determined by the United States Department of Veterans Affairs. To qualify for the discount granted by this subsection, an applicant must submit to the county property appraiser, by March 1, an official letter from the United States Department of Veterans Affairs stating the percentage of the veteran's service-connected disability and such evidence that reasonably identifies the disability as combat related and a copy of the veteran's honorable discharge. If the property appraiser denies the request for a discount, the appraiser must notify the applicant in writing of the reasons for the denial, and the veteran may reapply. The Legislature may, by general law, waive the annual application requirement in subsequent years. This subsection is self-executing and does not require implementing legislation.

(f) By general law and subject to conditions and limitations specified therein, the Legislature may provide ad valorem tax relief equal to the total amount or a portion of the ad valorem tax otherwise owed on homestead property to:

(1) The surviving spouse of a veteran who died from service-connected causes while on active duty as a member of the United States Armed Forces.

(2) The surviving spouse of a first responder who died in the line of duty.

(3) A first responder who is totally and permanently disabled as a result of an injury or injuries sustained in the line of duty. Causal connection between a disability and service in the line of duty shall not be presumed but must be determined as provided by general law. For purposes of this paragraph, the term "disability" does not include a chronic condition or chronic disease, unless the injury sustained in the line of duty was the sole cause of the chronic condition or chronic disease.

As used in this subsection and as further defined by general law, the term "first responder" means a law enforcement officer, a correctional officer, a firefighter, an emergency medical technician, or a paramedic, and the term "in the line of duty" means arising out of and in the actual performance of duty required by employment as a first responder.

B. Finance

Florida's constitution, at Article VII, Sections 10 through 19, imposes restrictions on Florida's ability to incur debt, pledge credit, or finance projects. State constitutions typically include such restrictions, even though the U.S. Constitution does not. As one commentator noted:

> Nearly all state constitutions give considerable attention to questions of state and local public finance. The typical state constitution devotes at least 2 articles to state and local taxation, borrowing, and spending. They limit the purposes for which states and localities can spend or lend their funds, and they expressly address specific spending techniques. Nearly all states also impose significant substantive or procedural restrictions or both on state and local borrowing, and on state and local taxation. Some constitutions limit expenditure levels as well.
>
> This state constitutional focus on governmental finance differs sharply from the federal Constitution's relative indifference to public finance. The Constitution simply authorizes Congress "to lay and col-

lect taxes, duties, imposts, and excises to pay the debts and provide for the common defense and the general welfare of the United States" and "to borrow money on the credit of the United States." Beyond those brief statements, the Constitution imposes two minor procedural constraints on federal spending and taxation: All bills for raising revenue must originate in the House of Representatives, and no money may be drawn from the Treasury "but in consequences of appropriations made by law; and a regular statement and account of the receipts and expenditures of all public money shall be published from time to time." There are also a handful of substantive constitutional constraints on federal taxation: "All duties, imposts, and excises shall be uniform throughout the United States." Taxes and duties on exports are barred; so, too, direct or capitation taxes are barred unless apportioned among the states according to population. The apportionment requirement, however, was modified by the 16th Amendment to authorize federal taxation on incomes without regard to apportionment. There are no constitutional limits on borrowing at all.

Where the federal Constitution primarily empowers Congress to raise and spend money, the state constitutions operate to limit state and local government financial support for private sector activities, and to protect state and local taxpayers from the burdens of state and local debt and taxation. In effect, they constitutionalize both the separation of the public from the private sector and the norm of financially limited government.

Or at least they would if they were honored according to their apparent terms. But one of the most striking aspects of the state constitutional law of state and local finance is the enormous gap between the written provisions of state constitutions and actual practice. The public purpose requirements that ostensibly prevent state and local spending, lending, and borrowing in aid of private endeavors are largely dead letters. The substantive and procedural debt limitations have, to a significant degree, been invaded by a host of financial instruments that the courts have held to be beyond the scope of these

> rules. The constitutional constraints on state and local taxation have been more effective, but their impact, too, has been cushioned by judicial determinations that certain revenue raising devices are not taxes subject to limitation. Moreover, courts have held that many special-purpose governments are beyond the scope of the constitutional tax and debt limits. As a result, these limits have contributed to the [excessively complicated] structure of state and local governance. . . .

Richard Briffault, *State and Local Finance*, in G. Alan Tarr & Robert F. Williams, STATE CONSTITUTIONS FOR THE TWENTY-FIRST CENTURY, vol. 3, pp. 211–12 (State University of New York Press, 2006).

It is with this background that we examine Florida's Constitution's Article VII, its restrictions upon pledging credit, and its requirements for state and local bonds.

1. Permissible Purposes for Pledging Credit

Florida's Constitution restricts Florida's state and local governments from pledging credit in Article VII, which, in relevant part, provides:

> *SECTION 10. Pledging credit.*—Neither the state nor any county, school district, municipality, special district, or agency of any of them, shall become a joint owner with, or stockholder of, or give, lend or use its taxing power or credit to aid any corporation, association, partnership or person; but this shall not prohibit laws authorizing:
>
> (a) the investment of public trust funds;
>
> (b) the investment of other public funds in obligations of, or insured by, the United States or any of its instrumentalities;
>
> (c) the issuance and sale by any county, municipality, special district or other local governmental body of (1) revenue bonds to finance or refinance the cost of capital projects for airports or port facilities, or (2) revenue bonds to finance or refinance the cost of capital

projects for industrial or manufacturing plants to the extent that the interest thereon is exempt from income taxes under the then existing laws of the United States, when, in either case, the revenue bonds are payable solely from revenue derived from the sale, operation or leasing of the projects. If any project so financed, or any part thereof, is occupied or operated by any private corporation, association, partnership or person pursuant to contract or lease with the issuing body, the property interest created by such contract or lease shall be subject to taxation to the same extent as other privately owned property.

(d) a municipality, county, special district, or agency of any of them, being a joint owner of, giving, or lending or using its taxing power or credit for the joint ownership, construction and operation of electrical energy generating or transmission facilities with any corporation, association, partnership or person.

What restrictions upon government financing result from these clauses in Florida's constitution? The answer to that question is well-illustrated by the following case of *N. Palm Beach County Water Control Dist. v. State*, 604 So. 2d 440, 447 (Fla. 1992) where the dissent took issue with Florida's supreme court's approval of the public financing of a private country club's multi-million dollar "Caribbean island" landscaping and the public financing of the guard gates erected to prevent the public from enjoying the country club's landscaping.

NORTHERN PALM BEACH COUNTY WATER CONTROL DISTRICT

V.

STATE OF FLORIDA

Supreme Court of Florida, 1992

604 So. 2d 440

This is an appeal from a final judgment which declined to validate water control and improvement bonds proposed to be issued by the Northern

Palm Beach Water Control District (District). We have jurisdiction pursuant to article V, section 3(b)(2) of the Florida Constitution, and chapter 75, Florida Statutes (1989).

The District is a drainage district organized and existing under [the] Laws of Florida. . . . The District sought validation of water control and improvement bonds to finance on-site road improvements in . . . the JDM Country Club[. It] is being developed by Hansen-Florida II, Inc., and will include single family residences, multifamily housing, park areas, and three golf courses.

The . . . improvements, which are the subject of this appeal, include interior or on-site road improvements such as paving, striping, signs, landscaping, irrigation, bridges, an overpass, culverts, street lighting, security gatehouses, and a secondary drainage system consisting of storm drain pipes, inlets, manholes and surface drainage. . . .

In December 1989, the Board of Supervisors of the District adopted a general bond resolution which authorized the issuance of Water Control and Improvement Bonds . . . in a principal amount not to exceed $16,312,500. The bond resolution provided that the bonds "shall not be general obligations or indebtedness" of the District, but instead are "special obligations payable solely" from, and secured by, a first lien and pledge of the proceeds of the drainage tax levied on the lands in [the JDM Country Club]. In March 1990, the Board of Supervisors adopted a resolution levying a $42,625,000 drainage tax on the lands in [the JDM Country Club]. . . . The amount levied consisted of an initial assessment of $18,125,000, plus the $24,500,000 interest estimated to accrue on the bonds.

After the bond validation hearing, the circuit court entered a final judgment which declined to validate the bonds because "[t]he intended use of the proceeds of this bond issue serves no valid public purpose." . . .

The scope of judicial inquiry in bond validation proceedings is limited to the following issues: 1) determining if the public body has the authority to issue the bonds; 2) determining if the purpose of the obligation is legal;

and 3) ensuring that the bond issuance complies with the requirements of law. *Taylor v. Lee County*, 498 So.2d 424 (Fla. 1986). Only two questions are presented for our consideration here: 1) whether the revenue bond proceeds will be used for a valid public purpose, and 2) whether the District has complied with the requirements of its enabling legislation in issuing the bonds.

As to the first issue, the State contends that these bonds violate article VII, section 10 of the Florida Constitution, which prohibits the District from using its taxing power or pledging public credit to aid private enterprise, and that no valid public purpose can be served by financing the construction of roadways within a private development where public access will be limited by security gatehouses. The District asserts that in enacting chapters 59–994 and 89–462 the legislature found a public purpose in designating roads for the exclusive use and benefit of a unit of development and its residents.

Article VII, section 10 of the Florida Constitution prohibits the state and its subdivisions, including special districts such as this water control district, from using its taxing power or pledging public credit to aid any private person or entity. However, if the project falls within one of the four subsections of article VII, section 10, then no constitutional prohibition is involved. *See Linscott v. Orange County Indus. Dev. Auth.*, 443 So. 2d 97 (Fla. 1983). The on-site road improvements planned for [the JDM Country Club] do not fall within these four subsections. Thus, in order to determine if the bonds run afoul of the constitution, we must first determine whether the District's taxing power or pledge of credit is involved. If either is involved, then the improvements must serve a paramount public purpose. *See Orange County Indus. Dev. Auth. v. State*, 427 So. 2d 174 (Fla. 1983). However, if we conclude that neither is involved, then the paramount public purpose test is not applicable and "it is enough to show only that a public purpose is served." *Linscott*, 443 So.2d at 101. . . .

As to the public purposes actually served by these bonds, we note that the roadway improvements at issue will provide access to the water management facilities and aid in the development of the reclaimed lands. However, the fact that public access to the roads will be limited raises a question of whether the stated public purposes are only incidental to a primary private purpose, the development of [the JDM Country Club] by Hansen-Florida II, Inc. "A broad, general public purpose . . . will not constitutionally sustain a project that in terms of direct, actual use, is purely a private enterprise." *Orange County*, 427 So. 2d at 179. In *Orange County*, the Court found that the expansion of a television station's broadcast facilities did not serve a paramount public purpose even though the public would receive a number of benefits from the proposed expansion. However, the Court also noted that the presence of public ownership would be a significant factor in a finding of public purpose. *Id.*

In this case, the District will retain ownership of the roadways in question. This public ownership coupled with the legislative declaration of public purpose contained in the District's enabling legislation leads us to the conclusion that the on-site road improvements serve a public purpose. Thus, the proposed water control and improvement bonds are not prohibited by article VII, section 10 of the Florida Constitution. . . .

Accordingly, we reverse the final judgment and remand with directions that the bond issue be approved.

It is so ordered.

OVERTON, BARKETT, GRIMES and HARDING, JJ., concur.

SHAW, C.J., dissents with an opinion, in which KOGAN, J., concurs.

McDONALD, J., dissents.

SHAW, C.J., dissenting.

The majority opinion trips lightly over the matter of how public financing of the construction and beautification of a private country club roadway serves a valid public purpose within the purview of article VII, section 10, Florida Constitution. I would affirm the trial court's judgment invalidating the bonds.

I. FACTS

A. *Private Country Club*

The Northern Palm Beach Water Control District ("District"), a public drainage district of the State of Florida, proposes to issue $16,312,500 in government revenue bonds to pay for the construction and maintenance of approximately 24,000 feet of roadway within Unit of Development No. 31, otherwise known as the JDM Country Club ("Club"), a planned 1,313-acre private golf and tennis club. The District's Board of Supervisors ("Board") adopted a formal Water Management Plan ("Plan") for the Club, which provides in part:

> The Unit 31 site, known as JDM Country Club, is being developed as a Planned Community District under the procedures and requirements of the City of Palm Beach Gardens Code of Ordinances. The development will include [2,384 single family dwelling units], park areas and three golf courses.

The homes within the Club will occupy prime residential sites abutting, or lying in close proximity to, the fairways and greens of the three golf courses and, according to Paul Urschalitz, the District's security expert, will vary in price from a quarter-million to over a million dollars apiece:

> Q. Would you anticipate looking at the type homes—did you have a chance to get an idea of what type of homes they're going to put in there?
>
> A. Yes.
>
> Q. What type of price range homes did you look at?
>
> A. I think they're listed in this document, two hundred and fifty thousand to over a million. . . .

In addition to the roadway itself, the District will pay for extensive roadway improvements within the Club. Tracy Bennett, the District's engineer, testified:

> The onsite roadway improvements include paving of the roadways, the striping, the signage, landscaping with the roadways, irrigation to maintain the landscaping and sodding, bridges, an overpass, culverts, street lighting, security gatehouses, and secondary drainage system consisting of storm drainage pipes, inlets, manholes and surface drainage.

B. *"Caribbean Island" Motif*

The District's Plan calls for extensive roadside landscaping paid for by the District to enhance the private Club's "Caribbean Island" theme[:]

> Extensive landscaping within the onsite roadway rights-of-way system is planned. . . . The overall theme of the development is to provide a Caribbean Island effect. Strong emphasis in the roadway planting will be on various palm species 20 to 30 feet high with a full-canopied backdrop, accented with dwarf palms and a wide variety of blooming groundcover plants. The remaining open areas will be sodded. The most intensive landscaping treatment is the median, followed by right-of-way adjacent to a development parcel, then right-of-way adjacent to lake open areas. . . .

According to the Plan, the initial cost to the District of this garden-like landscaping is vast. The Plan states . . . [that] the District, a public entity, will pay nearly six million dollars in initial roadside landscaping costs—more than the cost of the entire roadway itself—to promote the private Club's "Caribbean Island" motif. This amounts to almost *one and one-half million dollars of landscaping per mile of proposed roadway* for the private Club.

C. *Security Gatehouses*

In addition to the "Caribbean Island" landscaping and other improvements noted above, the District will also pay for the construction and maintenance of three gatehouses to be staffed by security personnel to block all public access to the private Club. The District's official Plan provides:

> In addition, the Board of Supervisors has the power to provide, control ingress and egress, and maintain roads for the exclusive use and benefit of a Unit of Development and its landowners, residents and invitees.
>
> The onsite roadway system [is] planned for the exclusive use and benefit of [the Club] and its landowners, residents, and invitees. . . .

Peter Pimental, executive director of the District, testified as follows:

> A. Want me to explain? What we proposed to do is construct these gatehouses as Mr. Bennett testified and with those gatehouses would be the security people who would control the ingress and egress to the project and those people or persons who have reason to be inside would be allowed inside the project. Those that have no purpose or no reason to be there, will not be permitted to just wander through the project.
>
> Q. How would you define "reason to be there?"
>
> A. There would be service directed, service oriented persons, residents, invitees, guests, police, fire, emergency service, all of those would have access to the project.
>
> Q. So if I was out on a Sunday afternoon driving around, just wanted to ride through the District, I would be restricted under your rules?
>
> A. Yes.
>
> Q. So it is not open to the public at all?
>
> A. Perhaps not. . . .

Thus, all on-site improvements within the Club—including the landscaping and roadway itself—that are paid for by the public District will be closed to the general public.

D. *Financing*

To pay for the District's proposed on-site improvements within the Club, the Board adopted a general bond resolution that authorizes issuance of Water Control and Improvement Bonds in a principal amount not to exceed $16,312,500. The resolution provides that the bonds shall not be general obligations or indebtedness of the District, but shall instead be special obligations payable solely from, and secured by, a first lien and pledge of the proceeds of a drainage tax levied on the lands of the Club. The Board subsequently adopted a resolution levying a $42,625,000 drainage tax on the lands of the Club in proportion to the benefits to be derived from the construction of the improvements. The tax, which consists of an initial assessment of $18,125,000 plus $24,500,000 interest expected to accrue on the bonds, will be paid solely by the landowners within the Club. The landowners will thus ultimately foot the bill for the District's proposed roadway improvements within the Club.

The bonds will be issued in the denomination of $5,000, or multiples thereof, will mature within 30 years, and significantly, will pay interest periodically (twice a year) from the District to bondholders at a rate to be determined later. In paying this interest, the Board covenants that it will comply with specific requirements of the federal tax code concerning the tax status of certain government bonds. These provisions, which are designed to stimulate funding for public projects, specify that interest payments by state and local governments to their investors may be tax-exempt for the investors. The Board's bond resolution states:

> Section 4.08. *Compliance with Tax Requirements.* The Issuer hereby covenants and agrees, for the benefit of the Owners from time to time of the Bonds, to comply with the requirements applicable to it contained in Section 103 and Part IV of Subchapter B of Chapter 1 of the

Code and to the extent necessary to preserve the exclusion of interest on the Bonds from gross income for federal income tax purposes.

Because the District's interest payments to bondholders will be tax-exempt for the holders, the bonds will be readily marketable even though the District may offer the bonds at an interest rate substantially below that of privately-issued, taxable securities. This reduced interest rate will minimize the District's financial obligations to bondholders and the resulting tax obligations of the Club's landowners.

II. THE APPLICABLE LAW

In *Taylor v. Lee County*, 498 So. 2d 424, 425 (Fla. 1986), Justice McDonald explained the nature of this Court's inquiry in bond validation proceedings:

> The scope of judicial inquiry in bond validation proceedings is limited. Specifically, courts should: 1) determine if a public body has the authority to issue the subject bonds; 2) determine if the purpose of the obligation is legal; and 3) ensure that the authorization of the obligations complies with the requirements of law.

In the present case, we are concerned primarily with whether the purpose of the District's bonds is legal.

Article VII, section 10, Florida Constitution, bars governments within Florida from using their taxing power or credit to aid private corporations or persons:

> *SECTION 10. Pledging credit.*—Neither the state nor any county, school district, municipality, special district, or agency of any of them, shall become a joint owner with, or stockholder of, or give, lend or use its taxing power or credit to aid any corporation, association, partnership or person. . . .

The purpose of section 10 is to prevent state government from using its vast resources to monopolize, or otherwise "destroy," a segment of private enterprise, and also "to protect public funds and resources from being exploited in assisting or promoting private ventures when the public would be at most only incidentally benefited." *Bannon v. Port of Palm Beach Dist.*, 246 So. 2d 737, 741 (Fla. 1971). To pass constitutional muster, a government bond issue must serve a truly public purpose, i.e., it must bestow a benefit on society exceeding that which is normally attendant to any successful business venture. . . .

III. CONCLUSION

Simply designating a project "public" by legislative fiat does not necessarily make it so, especially where uncontroverted facts attest otherwise. A quote from Lewis Carroll makes the point:

> "I don't know what you mean by 'glory,'" Alice said.
>
> Humpty Dumpty smiled contemptuously. "Of course you don't—till I tell you. I meant 'there's a nice knock-down argument for you!'"
>
> "But 'glory' doesn't mean 'a nice knock-down argument,'" Alice objected.
>
> "When I use a word," Humpty Dumpty said, in rather a scornful tone, "it means just what I choose it to mean—neither more nor less."
>
> "The question is," said Alice, "whether you can make words mean so many different things."
>
> "The question is," said Humpty Dumpty, "which is to be master—that's all."

Lewis Carroll, *Through the Looking Glass* 113 (Dial Books for Young Readers, NAL Penguin, Inc. 1988) (1872). Under our constitutional system of government in Florida, courts, not legislators or water control districts, are the ultimate "masters" of the constitutional meaning of such terms as "public purpose" in judicial proceedings.

While a restricted roadway may serve a valid public purpose under certain circumstances, I conclude that no reasonable and sufficient public purpose is served by issuance of government bonds to finance the construction and landscaping of roadways within the private JDM Country Club. The extraordinarily expensive roadside landscaping to enhance the "Caribbean Island" motif of the private residences and golf courses within the Club would serve virtually no reasonable public purpose even if the Club were to be open to the general public. The fact that security gatehouses will be erected for the sole purpose of barring the public from the premises renders any alleged benefit to the public from the landscaping or roadway moot.

It is perfectly clear to me that the District's bond project serves a simple, very private, purpose. It allows the owners of the proposed 2,384 residences within the Club to capitalize on a massive tax-break, intended for public projects, in financing the construction of a luxurious environment for their own private use. The undertaking smacks of state-sponsored, economic apartheid. I can conceive of few more private projects.

Rather than relying on . . . this Court's own examination of a cold record, I would place great weight on the reasoned judgment of the respected trial judge, for he alone had the opportunity to personally observe—on both direct and cross-examination—the demeanor of many of the Club's main functionaries, and he is far more familiar with the local circumstances surrounding this issue. Sufficient competent evidence supports his ruling.

I would affirm the trial court's judgment invalidating the bonds.

Notes and Questions to Consider:

1. Many of the facts of *N. Palm Beach County Water Control Dist. v. State* are missing from the majority's decision and appear only in the dissent. Why would the majority have omitted these facts?

2. The majority opinion cites to prior precedent in *Linscott v. Orange County Indus. Dev. Auth.*, 443 So. 2d 97 (Fla. 1983) to identify the

legal standard for applying Article VII, Section 10's prohibition upon the state and its subdivisions, including special districts such as this water control district, from using its taxing power or pledging public credit to aid any private person or entity. Under *Linscott*, first we determine if the project falls within one of these four enumerated of Article VII, Section 10, for which no constitutional prohibition applies: (a) the investment of public trust funds; (b) the investment of other public funds in obligations of, or insured by, the United States or any of its instrumentalities; (c) revenue bonds to finance or refinance the cost of capital projects for airports or port facilities, or for industrial or manufacturing plants to the extent that the interest thereon is exempt from income taxes under the then existing laws of the United States; or (d) the joint ownership, construction, and operation of electrical energy generating or transmission facilities. Second, we determine if the taxing power or pledge of credit is involved. If so, then the thing the bonds finance must serve a paramount public purpose. If not, then "it is enough to show only that a public purpose is served." *Linscott*, 443 So.2d at 101.

2. Types and Purposes of State and Municipal Bonds

States, counties, municipal corporations, and state-created districts borrow money by issuing a debt instrument called a municipal bond. *See, e.g.*, chapter 215, Fla. Stat. Municipal bonds are popular among certain investors who are eligible for their exemption from certain federal income tax liabilities. Municipal bonds were often popular before the Great Recession, and still somewhat popular thereafter, because "the municipal bond market has traditionally been viewed as a relatively safe market where credit risk was not a primary concern. . . ." Ming-Jie Wang, *Credit Default Swaps on Municipal Bonds: A Double-Edged Sword?*, 35 Yale J. on Reg. 301, 302 (2018). One commentator provides this primer on municipal bonds and how they work:

> Governmental entities, like states, cities, and counties, issue municipal bonds, or debt securities, to provide funding for capital projects and day-to-day obligations. Essentially, a bond provides a loan to a municipality, and the municipality must pay the principal on

that loan when it matures (and interest until it does so). Municipal bonds differ from corporate bonds because they usually involve less risk of default, are exempt from federal income tax, and in the case of default, are more likely to be repaid.

Three types of municipal bonds exist: general obligation bonds, revenue bonds, and short-term debt securities. General obligation bonds are backed by the issuer's “full faith and credit,” meaning the issuer can tax residents to provide revenue for repayment of the bonds. Revenue bonds are used to fund specific projects. Unlike general obligation bonds, the specific project's revenue repays the revenue bonds' obligations. Conduit bonds are a special form of revenue bonds, and municipalities issue them on behalf of a third party. As its name indicates, short-term debt securities mature quickly, within thirteen months. These securities provide funds for the gap in “time when expenses occur and when [other] revenues become available.” General obligation bonds and revenue bonds, however, remain the most common.

Issuers and underwriters are the players involved in the municipal bond process. The issuer—the governmental entity—sells the bonds to the underwriter. Neither the SEC [meaning the United States Securities and Exchange Commission] nor the Municipal Securities Rulemaking Board (MSRB) can require municipal bond issuers to file any document in connection with a bond offering. An underwriter functions as the municipal bond dealer by purchasing the municipal bonds from the issuer and selling them to investors. Thus, the underwriter serves as the middleman between the issuer and investors. . . .

Despite the municipal bond market's size and necessity, the federal regulatory scheme is limited compared to other U.S. capital markets. The [U.S.] Securities Act of 1933 (Securities Act) and the Securities Exchange Act of 1934 (Exchange Act) exempt municipal bonds from regulation. . . . Nevertheless, antifraud provisions of Section 17(a) of the Securities Act and Section 10(b) of the Exchange

> Act apply to municipal bonds . . . [to] prevent[] fraud and manipulation in securities' offerings, . . . [and to] prohibit[] fraud and manipulation in the secondary market.

Charlotte W. Rhodes, *Living in a Material World: Defining "Materiality" in the Municipal Bond Market and Rule 15c2-12*, 72 WASH. & LEE L. REV. 1989, 1994–97 (2015).

As the commentator notes, federal regulation of municipal bonds is limited insofar as federal law regulates municipal bonds only indirectly. For example, federal law "prohibits the SEC or the MSRB from requiring municipal issuers to file disclosures before municipal offerings." *Id.* (citing 15 U.S.C. § 78o-4(d)(1)-(2) (2012)).

So it may be surprising that state regulation of municipal bonds has relatively recent origins, according to these commentators:

> In the early years of the Republic, state constitutions did not impose restrictions on the use of long term debt to fund governmental activities as the state level. This constitutional silence was primarily due to the fact that the power of state government to borrow freely was widely accepted. Moreover, governmental borrowing was primarily limited to short term debt and war financing. This changed in 1817 when the state of New York financed the construction of the Erie canal. Revenues from the operation of the canal swiftly exceeded debt service costs. Buoyed by this success, other states commenced construction of other internal improvements. State borrowing grew dramatically.
>
> From 1837 through 1840, the American economy experienced a deep depression. In 1840, many of the state public improvement projects ceased construction due to economic setbacks. As a result, the states felt the dual wrath of declining revenues occasioned by the depression and unrelenting debt service requirements. Consequently, many states found themselves with non-income producing, partially funded projects, with the obligation to fully repay the outstanding in-

debtedness. From 1841 to 1842, nine separate states, including Florida, Illinois, Indiana, Michigan and Pennsylvania, were unable to resist the economic pressures and defaulted on their bonds. For example, the state of Mississippi alone defaulted on $7,000,000 worth of state bonds in 1841. The state continued to repudiate the bonds, and in 1875 the Mississippi Constitution was amended to include a specific provision prohibiting the state from repaying any of these bonds. *See* Mississippi Constitution of 1875, Article XII, Section 5.

These developments fueled a popular movement for revenue reform at the state level. As a result of the relative success of this movement, most state constitutions currently contain some restrictions on the issuance of state debt. . . .

Thomas C. Marks, Jr. and John F. Cooper, STATE CONSTITUTIONAL LAW IN A NUTSHELL 245–46 (2003).

Florida's constitution, at Article VII, contains the following restrictions upon government bonds:

SECTION 11. State bonds; revenue bonds.—

(a) State bonds pledging the full faith and credit of the state may be issued only to finance or refinance the cost of state fixed capital outlay projects authorized by law, and purposes incidental thereto, upon approval by a vote of the electors; provided state bonds issued pursuant to this subsection may be refunded without a vote of the electors at a lower net average interest cost rate. The total outstanding principal of state bonds issued pursuant to this subsection shall never exceed fifty percent of the total tax revenues of the state for the two preceding fiscal years, excluding any tax revenues held in trust under the provisions of this constitution.

(b) Moneys sufficient to pay debt service on state bonds as the same becomes due shall be appropriated by law.

(c) Any state bonds pledging the full faith and credit of the state issued under this section or any other section of this constitution may be combined for the purposes of sale.

(d) Revenue bonds may be issued by the state or its agencies without a vote of the electors to finance or refinance the cost of state fixed capital outlay projects authorized by law, and purposes incidental thereto, and shall be payable solely from funds derived directly from sources other than state tax revenues.

(e) Bonds pledging all or part of a dedicated state tax revenue may be issued by the state in the manner provided by general law to finance or refinance the acquisition and improvement of land, water areas, and related property interests and resources for the purposes of conservation, outdoor recreation, water resource development, restoration of natural systems, and historic preservation.

(f) Each project, building, or facility to be financed or refinanced with revenue bonds issued under this section shall first be approved by the Legislature by an act relating to appropriations or by general law.

SECTION 12. Local bonds.—Counties, school districts, municipalities, special districts and local governmental bodies with taxing powers may issue bonds, certificates of indebtedness or any form of tax anticipation certificates, payable from ad valorem taxation and maturing more than twelve months after issuance only:

(a) to finance or refinance capital projects authorized by law and only when approved by vote of the electors who are owners of freeholds therein not wholly exempt from taxation; or

(b) to refund outstanding bonds and interest and redemption premium thereon at a lower net average interest cost rate.

SECTION 14. Bonds for pollution control and abatement and other water facilities.—

(a) When authorized by law, state bonds pledging the full faith and credit of the state may be issued without an election to finance the construction of air and water pollution control and abatement and solid waste disposal facilities and other water facilities authorized by general law (herein referred to as "facilities") to be operated by any municipality, county, district or authority, or any agency thereof (herein referred to as "local governmental agencies"), or by any agency of the State of Florida. Such bonds shall be secured by a pledge of and shall be payable primarily from all or any part of revenues to be derived from operation of such facilities, special assessments, rentals to be received under lease-purchase agreements herein provided for, any other revenues that may be legally available for such purpose, including revenues from other facilities, or any combination thereof (herein collectively referred to as "pledged revenues"), and shall be additionally secured by the full faith and credit of the State of Florida.

(b) No such bonds shall be issued unless a state fiscal agency, created by law, has made a determination that in no state fiscal year will the debt service requirements of the bonds proposed to be issued and all other bonds secured by the pledged revenues exceed seventy-five per cent of the pledged revenues.

(c) The state may lease any of such facilities to any local governmental agency, under lease-purchase agreements for such periods and under such other terms and conditions as may be mutually agreed upon. The local governmental agencies may pledge the revenues derived from such leased facilities or any other available funds for the payment of rentals thereunder; and, in addition, the full faith and credit and taxing power of such local governmental agencies may be pledged for the payment of such rentals without any election of freeholder electors or qualified electors.

(d) The state may also issue such bonds for the purpose of loaning money to local governmental agencies, for the construction of such facilities to be owned or operated by any of such local governmental agencies. Such loans shall bear interest at not more than one-half of one per cent per annum greater than the last preceding issue of state bonds pursuant to this section, shall be secured by the pledged revenues, and may be additionally secured by the full faith and credit of the local governmental agencies.

(e) The total outstanding principal of state bonds issued pursuant to this section 14 shall never exceed fifty per cent of the total tax revenues of the state for the two preceding fiscal years.

SECTION 15. Revenue bonds for scholarship loans.—

(a) When authorized by law, revenue bonds may be issued to establish a fund to make loans to students determined eligible as prescribed by law and who have been admitted to attend any public or private institutions of higher learning, junior colleges, health related training institutions, or vocational training centers, which are recognized or accredited under terms and conditions prescribed by law. Revenue bonds issued pursuant to this section shall be secured by a pledge of and shall be payable primarily from payments of interest, principal, and handling charges to such fund from the recipients of the loans and, if authorized by law, may be additionally secured by student fees and by any other moneys in such fund. There shall be established from the proceeds of each issue of revenue bonds a reserve account in an amount equal to and sufficient to pay the greatest amount of principal, interest, and handling charges to become due on such issue in any ensuing state fiscal year.

(b) Interest moneys in the fund established pursuant to this section, not required in any fiscal year for payment of debt service on then outstanding revenue bonds or for maintenance of the reserve account, may be used for educational loans to students determined to be eligible therefor in the manner provided by law, or for such other related purposes as may be provided by law.

SECTION 16. Bonds for housing and related facilities.—

(a) When authorized by law, revenue bonds may be issued without an election to finance or refinance housing and related facilities in Florida, herein referred to as "facilities."

(b) The bonds shall be secured by a pledge of and shall be payable primarily from all or any part of revenues to be derived from the financing, operation or sale of such facilities, mortgage or loan payments, and any other revenues or assets that may be legally available for such purposes derived from sources other than ad valorem taxation, including revenues from other facilities, or any combination thereof, herein collectively referred to as "pledged revenues," provided that in no event shall the full faith and credit of the state be pledged to secure such revenue bonds.

(c) No bonds shall be issued unless a state fiscal agency, created by law, has made a determination that in no state fiscal year will the debt service requirements of the bonds proposed to be issued and all other bonds secured by the same pledged revenues exceed the pledged revenues available for payment of such debt service requirements, as defined by law.

SECTION 17. Bonds for acquiring transportation right-of-way or for constructing bridges.—

(a) When authorized by law, state bonds pledging the full faith and credit of the state may be issued, without a vote of the electors, to finance or refinance the cost of acquiring real property or the rights to real property for state roads as defined by law, or to finance or refinance the cost of state bridge construction, and purposes incidental to such property acquisition or state bridge construction.

(b) Bonds issued under this section shall be secured by a pledge of and shall be payable primarily from motor fuel or special fuel taxes, except those defined in Section 9(c) of Article XII, as provided by law, and shall additionally be secured by the full faith and credit of the state.

(c) No bonds shall be issued under this section unless a state fiscal agency, created by law, has made a determination that in no state fiscal year will the debt service requirements of the bonds proposed to be issued and all other bonds secured by the same pledged revenues exceed ninety percent of the pledged revenues available for payment of such debt service requirements, as defined by law. For the purposes of this subsection, the term "pledged revenues" means all revenues pledged to the payment of debt service, excluding any pledge of the full faith and credit of the state.

Notes and Questions to Consider:

1. Note that Florida's constitution refers to several types of bonds without defining them. Florida's legislature provides the following definitions in Florida Statutes chapter 215:

> (1). "General obligation bonds," which are obligations secured by the full faith and credit of a governmental unit or payable from the proceeds of ad valorem taxes of a governmental unit.
>
> (2). "Revenue bonds," which are obligations of a governmental unit issued to pay the cost of a self-liquidating project or improvements thereof, or combination of one or more projects or improvements thereof, and payable from the earnings of such project and any other special funds authorized to be pledged as additional security therefor, except for bonds issued to finance projects under part II [the Florida Industrial Development Financing Act], part III [Industrial Development Authorities], or part V [Housing Finance Authorities] of chapter 159 or health facilities under part III of chapter 154.
>
> (3). "Bond anticipation notes," which are notes issued by a governmental unit in anticipation of the issuance of general obligation or revenue bonds.
>
> (4). "Limited revenue bonds," which are obligations issued by a governmental unit to pay the cost of a project or improvement thereof, or combination of one or more projects or improvements thereof, and payable from funds of a governmental unit, exclusive of ad valorem taxes, special assessments, or earnings from such projects or improvements.
>
> (5). "Special assessment bonds," which are bonds that provide for capital improvements and are paid in whole or in part by levying and collecting special assessments on the abutting, adjoining, contiguous, or other specially benefited property.

§ 215.84, Fla. Stat. (2019).

2. General obligation bonds are backed by the "full faith and credit" of the issuing entity. Revenue bonds are not. Which type of bond would be preferable to the risk-averse investor? Which might be preferable to the investor seeking a higher yield?

3. For what purposes can the state issue a general obligation bond? Consider, for example, Article VII, Section 11 of Florida's constitution (stating that "[s]tate bonds pledging the full faith and credit of the state may be issued only to finance or refinance the cost of state fixed capital outlay projects authorized by law, and purposes incidental thereto. . .").

4. When does Florida's legislature need the approval of Florida's electors in order to issue a general obligation bond? Consider Florida's constitution at Article VII in Section 11 where it provides that "[s]tate bonds pledging the full faith and credit of the state may be issued only . . . upon approval by a vote of the electors; provided state bonds issued pursuant to this subsection may be refunded without a vote of the electors at a lower net average interest cost rate."

5. For what purposes can counties, school districts, municipalities, special districts, and local governmental bodies with taxing powers issue long-term bonds (meaning bonds maturing more than 12 months after issuance) payable from ad valorem taxation? Consider Article VII, Section 12 (restricting such bonds to these purposes: (a) to finance or refinance capital projects authorized by law and only when approved by vote of the electors who are owners of freeholds therein not wholly exempt from taxation; or (b) to refund outstanding bonds and interest and redemption premium thereon at a lower net average interest cost rate).

Chapter Thirteen

Criminal Justice and Procedure

A. Basic Rights of a Criminal Defendant

Article I, section 16(a) of Florida's Constitution provides, in relevant part, that:

> In all criminal prosecutions the accused shall, upon demand, be informed of the nature and cause of the accusation, and shall be furnished a copy of the charges, and shall have the right to have compulsory process for witnesses, to confront at trial adverse witnesses, to be heard in person, by counsel or both, and to have a speedy and public trial by impartial jury in the county where the crime was committed. If the county is not known, the indictment or information may charge venue in two or more counties conjunctively and proof that the crime was committed in that area shall be sufficient; but before pleading the accused may elect in which of those counties the trial will take place. Venue for prosecution of crimes committed beyond the boundaries of the state shall be fixed by law.

B. Freedom from Imprisonment Due to Financial Debt

Case law precedent finds that this right arises both under the Constitution of the United States and also appears in the text of the Constitution of the State of Florida. *Del Valle v. State*, 80 So. 3d 999 (Fla. 2011) holds:

> The Equal Protection and Due Process Clauses of the United States Constitution ensure that an indigent probationer is not incarcerated based solely upon inability to pay a monetary obligation. *See Bearden v. Georgia,* 461 U.S. 660, 664 (1983); U.S. Const. amends. V, XIV. Further, the Florida Constitution contains its own due process clause that parallels

> the language of the Fourteenth Amendment and states that "[n]o person shall be deprived of life, liberty or property without due process of law." Art. I, § 9, Fla. Const. The Florida Constitution contains a separate and specific provision that ensures that "[n]o person shall be imprisoned for debt, except in cases of fraud." Art. I, § 11, Fla. Const.

Id. at 1005. It is noteworthy, however, that *Del Valle v. State* finds imprisonment for an unpaid debt could be proper under certain facts involving restitution for crimes. Specifically, it holds that a probationer can be imprisoned for failing to pay a financial obligation such as a court-ordered restitution but only after a trial court enquires into the probationer's ability to pay and finds by the greater weight of the evidence that the ability exists but the probationer is willfully disobeying the requirement to pay. Any requirement that a probationer prove his inability to pay by the heightened standard of clear and convincing evidence is unconstitutional per *Del Valle v. State*, 80 So. 3d 999 (Fla. 2011).

Although *Del Valle v. State* disapproves of *Gonzales v. State*, *Guardado v. State* and *Martin v. State*, it is also consistent with prior case law precedent of both the Supreme Court of Florida and the Supreme Court of the United States. For example, *State ex rel. Lanz v. Dowling*, 110 So. 522 (1926), holds that Article I Section 11 of the Florida Constitution's "prohibition against imprisonment for debt protects against imprisonment of a person found in contempt for failure to pay a money judgment but does not prohibit imprisonment for failure to pay fines or penalties…." Talbot D'Alemberte, THE FLORIDA STATE CONSTITUTION 33 (Oxford University Press 2011).

C. Trial By Jury

The Constitution of the State of Florida discusses a Floridian's right to jury in the following paragraphs (emphasis added):

> **Section 11. Prohibited special laws.—**
>
> (a) There shall be no special law or general law of local application pertaining to: . . . (5) **petit juries, including compensation of jurors**, except establishment of jury commissions; . . .
>
> **Section 15. Prosecution for crime; offenses committed by children.—**

(a) No person shall be tried for capital crime without presentment or indictment by a **grand jury**, or for other felony without such presentment or indictment or an information under oath filed by the prosecuting officer of the court, except persons on active duty in the militia when tried by courts martial.

(b) When authorized by law, a child as therein defined may be charged with a violation of law as an act of delinquency instead of crime and tried without a jury or other requirements applicable to criminal cases. Any child so charged shall, upon demand made as provided by law before a trial in a juvenile proceeding, be tried in an appropriate court as an adult. A child found delinquent shall be disciplined as provided by law.

Section 16. Rights of accused and of victims.—

(a) In all criminal prosecutions the accused shall, upon demand, be informed of the nature and cause of the accusation, and shall be furnished a copy of the charges, and shall have the right to have compulsory process for witnesses, to confront at trial adverse witnesses, to be heard in person, by counsel or both, and to have a speedy and public **trial by impartial jury** in the county where the crime was committed. If the county is not known, the indictment or information may charge venue in two or more counties conjunctively and proof that the crime was committed in that area shall be sufficient; but before pleading the accused may elect in which of those counties the trial will take place. Venue for prosecution of crimes committed beyond the boundaries of the state shall be fixed by law.

(b) Victims of crime or their lawful representatives, including the next of kin of homicide victims, are entitled to the right to be informed, to be present, and to be heard when relevant, at all crucial stages of criminal proceedings, to the extent that these rights do not interfere with the constitutional rights of the accused. . . .

Section 22. Trial by jury.— The right of trial by jury shall be secure to all and remain inviolate. The qualifications and the number of jurors, not fewer than six, shall be fixed by law.

The concept of a jury is not new. Indeed, at least one legal commentator can trace its history to "15 centuries before Christ." Such is the language used in the following educational and entertaining article from the April 1961 edition of the Texas Law Review.

THE JURY

By Jack Pope

39 Tex. L. Rev. 426

... Independently, coincidentally, and rather frequently the notion of popular and representative assistance in the administration of justice has appeared in the affairs of many nations. Something inherent in man and his sense of justice has inclined him toward the idea that qualified citizens should have an active part in matters which we now can more distinctly classify as investigating committees, administrative bodies, or even the measuring of justice in gross. Indistinct yearning for popular participation in the affairs of justice have brooded over the spirits of many people, but only once did the idea survive the onslaughts of the centuries and develop historical continuity. The struggle for survival by the institution we call the jury is truly the epic of our law.

From Antiquity to Magna Carta

Fifteen centuries before Christ, Moses selected one man from each of the tribes of Israel which were encamped in the wilderness of Paran and sent them to spy out the land of Canaan. He charged them to inspect the land and its people, whether they be strong or weak, few or many; whether the land be good or bad, fat or lean, wooded or not; in what cities the people dwell, and whether they live in tents or in strongholds. Forty days later, the twelve returned with a divided opinion. Ten favored retreat; Caleb and Joshua voted for conquest. The twelve spies could hardly be called a jury, but certainly they possessed rudimentary characteristics of a jury. For example, they were selected by the public authority from the neighborhood, they were charged with respect to the limits of their duty, there were twelve of them, they were permitted to weigh the facts by free debate and deliberation, and they made a return of their divided decision to the public power.

Eleven hundred years later, Socrates was condemned to death by a Greek jury, called a dicast. Five hundred and one jurors served in that famous trial, and Plato in his *Apology* tells us that a change of thirty votes would have resulted in his acquittal. With such a large number of jurors one might suppose that anyone who happened to be in the public square would be eligible to serve, but this is not so. Qualifications among the Athenians were significant, for only citizens and property holders could serve. Each year six thousand citizens were selected by lot, and these were divided into groups of five hundred. Certain cases required a dicast of only two hundred Athenians, but more important cases required as many as two thousand. When a case came on for trial, the dicast that would hear the trial was selected by lot in order to avoid possible bribery. The decisions of the dicast were final. The trial of cases by great popular assemblies was a characteristic of the age of Pericles, and in 451 B.C. he enacted laws under which jurors received pay for their service. The jurors were put upon oath to give a verdict according to their honest opinions. The peculiar size of the Athenian juries defeated the development of the idea of deliberation, and Greek law failed to discern the difference between judicial and legislative matters as well as matters of law and those of fact, but their modes of proof were rather enlightened.

Rome contributed much to law generally and to the system of proofs but added very little to the idea of trial by jury. Trials were before magistrates who originally were possessed of *imperium*, a power similar to that of a military commander-in-chief. But early in the days of the republic, as a check upon this power, the citizens of Rome could appeal to the *populus Romanus*. Two centuries before Christ, citizens outside of Rome were accorded citizenship with the right of appeal. Even soldiers were later granted the right to appeal to the popular assembly. This right of appeal was a source of freedom to the people, but, in the days of the Empire, these popular trials succumbed to the great powers of imperial officials. Rome achieved a clearer distinction between justice and politics and also public and private wrongs. It also discovered the administrative value of an inquest as a means to investigate and seek out criminals.

Along the eastern Mediterranean the Sanhedrin exercised authority over both spiritual and temporal matters, functioning as the highest judicial body of the Jews. Its origin may be traced to the time of Jehoshaphat. There were seventy-one members consisting of the chief priests, the scribes or lawyers, and the elders. The elders were the heads of families and were the representatives of the laity. The Sanhedrin heard, deliberated and passed judgment on matters of law and of fact until it was swept away in 70 A.D. by the destruction of Jerusalem by Titus.

Thirteen centuries after Christ, Alfonso the Learned, published *Las Siete Partidas*. We again find the jury foreshadowed, but it made little progress and contributed no new ideas. A body of twelve men summoned by the king or his representative would select sea captains below the rank of Admiral, and also alfa queques, who were the appointed officials to negotiate for the ransom of captives.

The jury, Forsyth tells us, arose "silently and gradually out of the usages of a state of society which has forever passed away." He says that trial by jury "does not owe its existence to any positive law: it is not the creature of an Act of Parliament establishing the form and defining the functions of the new tribunal." . . .

Characteristics of the Jury Emerge

. . . Of what purpose is a jury if judges may usurp their functions? Judges were now experts in the law, and they were also the ones who managed, supervised, charged, and corrected the juries. Judges possessed the power to grant new trials, to fine, and to imprison. It was not until the seventeenth century that the jury, within its sphere of duties, won its independence from overbearing judges. The problem came into focus during the famous trial of William Penn for conducting a Quaker meeting. Penn and another were charged with unlawful assembly. The judge, bent on compelling a conviction, kept an English jury confined for three days without food or water. Chief Justice Vaughan, in the famous Bushell's Case of 1670 freed the jurors and explained that there was no use for a jury if it may be controlled by the notions of the judge. By this landmark decision, jurors were emancipated from judges on fact decisions. One of the great but little discussed checks and balances of our governmental system is this separation of functions of judge and jury over law and fact.

The great characteristics of the jury were isolated and understood by the time of Blackstone. Mingled with praise and criticism, the *Commentaries* give us a complete picture of the eighteenth century jury. The trial was presided over by a judge who was under oath and subject to uniform law. Jurors were selected from the county in which the cause arose and where the jurors lived, the summoning officer was under oath, and the parties were afforded ample notice so they might investigate the qualifications of the jurors. The whole array could be challenged in case of partiality by the selecting officers or the intermeddling of either party. Jurors were selected from the array at random from slips of paper on which the names of jurors were written, and jurors could be challenged for causes which are remarkably familiar. Proofs to the jury were by witnesses' testimony tendered upon oath in open court, and witnesses were sworn not only to tell the truth, but all of it. Objections to the evidence were publicly ruled upon by the judge, and errors in ruling were preserved by bills of exception. The judge charged the jury who then withdrew for private deliberation and confinement until they returned a unanimous verdict. Special issues were frequently used. Blackstone expressed displeasure with several practices of his time which were barbaric. The judge could still deprive jurors of food, water, heat, light and rest in order to coerce a unanimous verdict. If the judge needed to depart before a verdict was received, he would place the jurors in a cart and drive them around the circuit with him. Thus Blackstone described that institution which "ever will be looked upon as the glory of the English law."

The Jury Comes to America

. . . All of the states were using juries of varying forms prior to the Declaration of Independence. Several states, following the Declaration, assured their own freedoms by including Bills of Rights in their constitutions. The Articles of Confederation asserted no authority over individuals, but the congress in its approval of the Northwest Ordinance, agreed with the territory to protect certain fundamental rights including the right to trial by jury. Drafted by September 1787, ratified by March 1789, the Constitution was soon amended by the Bill of Rights as promised. The body of the Constitution did not overlook that institution which had protected Americans from the Stuart judges. It specifically provided for a jury in trials of crimes. There was no constitutional provision for a civil jury. Hamilton forcefully argued that juries in civil actions were not abolished simply because there was no specific provision for them, but the issue was resolved in the Seventh Amendment with a provision for civil juries.

The right to a jury is enthroned in three of the Amendments to the Constitution. In the case of capital or otherwise infamous crimes, the Fifth Amendment provides that no person need answer a charge unless on a presentment or indictment of a Grand Jury. It was a long road from the Prankish inquest to the Bill of Rights. By the Sixth Amendment, citizens are afforded a trial which is public, speedy and before an impartial jury where the crime was committed. The trial is by proofs of witnesses and the accused may have compulsory process and an attorney. In a single sentence is pressed the fruit of a struggle for human rights which spans the centuries. The Seventh Amendment assures citizens of trials in civil suits at common law which involve as much as twenty dollars and denies a judge the power to decide matters of pure fact.

The centuries have poured content and meaning into the simple word, "jury," that was incorporated into the Constitution. Concepts that once were confused, by the time of the constitutional fathers, were isolated, separated and defined. No single feature make a jury; it takes all of them. Assembled under the term, "jury," are these received ideas: (1) Citizens may participate in the administration of justice. (2) The administration of justice is a specialized branch of government. (3) There is a difference between an accusing and a trial jury. (4) Jurors are selected by the public authority, (5) and perform their services under the sanction of an oath. (6) They must possess certain qualifications and be from the vicinity of the dispute, (7) and their qualifications may be challenged by the litigants. (8) Some persons are entitled to an exemption [from jury service]. (9) Historically, twelve persons composed a jury. (10) Jurors are not witnesses or investigators, but (11) evidence must be presented before them in open court. (12) The judge may instruct and charge the jury (13) before they withdraw to deliberate (14) in private. (15) The jury's function is to decide the facts—not the law, and (16) in that sphere, it is independent of the judge. (17) The jury may return a special verdict, but (18) verdicts must be unanimous, and (19) returned in open court. (20) Judges may exercise corrective control over juries in cases of misconduct on corruption.

Conclusion

One may wonder how the jury survived at all. . . .

Tested against almost all known obstacles and filtered by the centuries, the jury is now workable and acceptable to judges, to the public, the jury itself, and a feasible body of law. It is one of the most durable and stubborn of all human institutions. The clans and tribes where it originated have dissolved into unrecorded history and are long forgotten. Kingdoms and world empires arose and vanished, but the jury held on. It outlasted oppression, intrigue and absolutism at many hands. It survived civil wars, revolutions and conquests. One by one, many practices appeared to challenge the jury's right of survival—compurgation, ordeal, trial by battle, inquisition, torture, witchcraft, sorcery, the Star Chamber. They are gone, but the jury tenaciously held on. Dialects were absorbed into languages and tongues which once lived and are now dead. The jury endured. . . .

. . . The jury did not cross the channel to the continent, but it was transplanted to America. It has withstood every ordeal of the ages; it has been tested in the battles of freedom, and free peoples of the world are today its strongest compurgators.

This story of people's interest and participation in the administration of justice through a system of trial by jury is truly the epic of our law.

Notes and Questions to Consider:

1. Author Jack Pope, when discussing the characteristics of a jury, discussed the famous trial of William Penn (of the family from whom the U.S. state of Pennsylvania takes its name). To what extent is the method of compelling a conviction used by the trial judge in William Penn’s case still available to trial judges today?

2. Just before the conclusion of the excerpt, author Jack Pope enumerates 20 ideas that constitute the notion of a fair jury system. Are all of those 20 ideas embodied in the Constitution of the State of Florida? Are all of them in use in Florida today?

3. As we can see from Jack Pope's article, a jury often consisted of 12 jurors. Yet Florida provides for less. The Supreme Court of the United States addressed this situation in *Williams v. Florida*, 399 U.S. 78 (1970):

WILLIAMS

V.

FLORIDA

Supreme Court of the United States, 1970

399 U.S. 78, 90 S.Ct. 1893, 26 L.Ed.2d 446

Mr. Justice White delivered the opinion of the Court.

Prior to his trial for robbery in the State of Florida, petitioner . . . filed a pretrial motion to impanel a 12-man jury instead of the six-man jury provided by Florida law in all but capital cases. That motion too was denied. Petitioner was convicted as charged and was sentenced to life imprisonment. …[P]etitioner claims that his Fifth and Sixth Amendment rights had been violated. We granted certiorari.. . .

In *Duncan v. Louisiana*, 391 U.S. 145 (1968), we held that the Fourteenth Amendment guarantees a right to trial by jury in all criminal cases that—were they to be tried in a federal court—would come within the Sixth Amendment's guarantee. Petitioner's trial for robbery on July 3, 1968, clearly falls within the scope of that holding. See *Baldwin v. New York*, 399 U.S. 66 (1970); *DeStefano v. Woods*, 392 U.S. 631 (1968). The question in this case then is whether the constitutional guarantee of a trial by 'jury' necessarily requires trial by exactly 12 persons, rather than some lesser number—in this case six. We hold that the 12-man panel is not a necessary ingredient of 'trial by jury,' and that respondent's refusal to impanel more than the six members provided for by Florida law did not violate petitioner's Sixth Amendment rights as applied to the States through the Fourteenth.

We had occasion in *Duncan v. Louisiana*, supra, to review briefly the oft-told history of the development of trial by jury in criminal cases. That history revealed a long tradition attaching great importance to the concept of relying on a body of one's peers to determine guilt or innocence as a safeguard against arbitrary law enforcement. That same history, however, affords little insight into the considerations that gradually led the size of that body to be generally fixed at 12. Some have suggested that the number 12 was fixed upon simply because that was the number of the presentment jury from the hundred, from which the petit jury developed. Other, less circular but more fanciful reasons for the number 12 have been given, 'but they were all brought forward after the number was fixed,' and rest on little more than mystical or superstitious insights into the significance of '12.' Lord Coke's explanation that the 'number of twelve is much respected in holy writ, as 12 apostles, 12 stones, 12 tribes, etc.,' is typical. In short, while sometime in the 14th century the size of the jury at common law came to be fixed generally at 12, that particular feature of the jury system appears to have been a historical accident, unrelated to the great purposes which gave rise to the jury in the first place. The question before us is whether this accidental feature of the jury has been immutably codified into our Constitution.

This Court's earlier decisions have assumed an affirmative answer to this question. The leading case so construing the Sixth Amendment is *Thompson v. Utah*, 170 U.S. 343 (1898). There the defendant had been tried and convicted by a 12-man jury for a crime committed in the Territory of Utah. A new trial was granted, but by that time Utah had been admitted as a State. The defendant's new trial proceeded under Utah's Constitution, providing for a jury of only eight members. This Court reversed the resulting conviction, holding that Utah's constitutional provision was an ex post facto law as applied to the defendant. In reaching its conclusion, the Court announced that the Sixth Amendment was applicable to the defendant's trial when Utah was a Territory, and that the jury referred to in the Amendment was a jury 'constituted, as it was at common law, of twelve persons, neither more nor less.' *Id.* at 349. Arbuably unnecessary for the result, this announcement was supported simply by referring to the Magna Carta, and by quoting passages from treatises which noted—what has already been seen—

that at common law the jury did indeed consist of 12. Noticeably absent was any discussion of the essential step in the argument: namely, that every feature of the jury as it existed at common law—whether incidental or essential to that institution—was necessarily included in the Constitution wherever that document referred to a 'jury.' Subsequent decisions have reaffirmed the announcement in Thompson often in dictum and usually by relying—where there was any discussion of the issue at all—solely on the fact that the common-law jury consisted of 12. . . .

While 'the intent of the Framers' is often an elusive quarry, the relevant constitutional history casts considerable doubt on the easy assumption in our past decisions that if a given feature existed in a jury at common law in 1789, then it was necessarily preserved in the Constitution. Provisions for jury trial were first placed in the Constitution in Article III's provision that '(t)he Trial of all Crimes * * * shall be by Jury; and such Trial shall be held in the State where the said Crimes shall have been committed.' The 'very scanty history (of this provision) in the records of the Constitutional Convention' sheds little light either way on the intended correlation between Article III's 'jury' and the features of the jury at common law. Indeed, pending and after the adoption of the Constitution, fears were expressed that Article III's provision failed to preserve the common-law right to be tried by a 'jury of the vicinage.' That concern, as well as the concern to preserve the right to jury in civil as well as criminal cases, furnished part of the impetus for introducing amendments to the Constitution that ultimately resulted in the jury trial provisions of the Sixth and Seventh Amendments. As introduced by James Madison in the House, the Amendment relating to jury trial in criminal cases would have provided that:

> The trial of all crimes * * * shall be by an impartial jury of freeholders of the vicinage, with the requisite of unanimity for conviction, of the right of challenge, and other accustomed requisites. * * *

The Amendment passed the House in substantially this form, but after more than a week of debate in the Senate it returned to the House considerably altered. While records of the actual debates that occurred in the Senate are not available, a letter from Madison to Edmund Pendleton on September 14, 1789, indicates that one of the Senate's major objections was to the 'vicinage' requirement in the House version. A conference committee was appointed. As reported in a second letter by Madison on September 23, 1789, the Senate remained opposed to the vicinage requirement, partly because in its view the then-pending judiciary bill—which was debated at the same time as the Amendments—adequately preserved the common-law vicinage feature, making it unnecessary to freeze that requirement into the Constitution. 'The Senate,' wrote Madison:

> are * * * inflexible in opposing a definition of the locality of Juries. The vicinage they contend is either too vague or too strict a term; too vague if depending on limits to be fixed by the pleasure of the law, too strict if limited to the county. It was proposed to insert after the word Juries, 'with the accustomed requisites,' leaving the definition to be construed according to the judgment of professional men. Even this could not be obtained. * * * The Senate suppose, also, that the provision for vicinage in the Judiciary bill will sufficiently quiet the fears which called for an amendment on this point.

The version that finally emerged from the Committee was the version that ultimately became the Sixth Amendment, ensuring an accused:

> the right to a speedy and public trial, by an impartial jury of the State and district wherein the crime shall have been committed, which district shall have been previously ascertained by law * * *

Gone were the provisions spelling out such common-law features of the jury as 'unanimity,' or 'the accustomed requisites.' And the 'vicinage' requirement itself had been replaced by wording that reflected a compromise between broad and narrow definitions of that term, and that left Congress the power to determine the actual size of the 'vicinage' by its creation of judicial districts.

Three significant features may be observed in this sketch of the background of the Constitution's jury trial provisions. First, even though the vicinage requirement was as much a feature of the common-law jury as was the 12-man requirement, the mere reference to 'trial by jury' in Article III was not interpreted to include that feature. Indeed, as the subsequent debates over the Amendments indicate, disagreement arose over whether the feature should be included at all in its common-law sense, resulting in the compromise described above. Second, provisions that would have explicitly tied the 'jury' concept to the 'accustomed requisites' of the time were eliminated. Such action is concededly open to the explanation that the 'accustomed requisites' were thought to be already included in the concept of a 'jury.' But that explanation is no more plausible than the contrary one: that the deletion had some substantive effect. Indeed, given the clear expectation that a substantive change would be [affected] by the inclusion or deletion of an explicit 'vicinage' requirement, the latter explanation is, if anything, the more plausible. Finally, contemporary legislative and constitutional provisions indicate that where Congress wanted to leave no doubt that it was incorporating existing common-law features of the jury system, it knew how to use express language to that effect. Thus, the Judiciary bill, signed by the President on the same day that the House and Senate finally agreed on the form of the Amendments to be submitted to the States, provided in certain cases for the narrower 'vicinage' requirements that the House had wanted to include in the Amendments. And the Seventh Amendment, providing for jury trial in civil cases, explicitly added that 'no fact tried by a jury, shall be otherwise re-examined in any Court of the United States, than according to the rules of the common law.'

We do not pretend to be able to divine precisely what the word 'jury' imported to the Framers, the First Congress, or the States in 1789. It may well be that the usual expectation was that the jury would consist of 12, and that hence, the most likely conclusion to be drawn is simply that little thought was actually given to the specific question we face today. But there is absolutely no indication in 'the intent of the Framers' of an explicit decision to equate the constitutional and common-law characteristics of the jury. Nothing in this history suggests, then, that we do violence to the letter of the Constitution by turning to other than purely historical considerations to determine which features of the jury system, as it existed at common law, were preserved in the Constitution. The relevant inquiry, as we see it, must be the function that the particular feature performs and its relation to the purposes of the jury trial. Measured by this standard, the 12-man requirement cannot be regarded as an indispensable component of the Sixth Amendment.

The purpose of the jury trial, as we noted in Duncan, is to prevent oppression by the Government. 'Providing an accused with the right to be tried by a jury of his peers gave him an inestimable safeguard against the corrupt or overzealous prosecutor and against the compliant, biased, or eccentric judge.' *Duncan*, 391 U.S. at 156. Given this purpose, the essential feature of a jury obviously lies in the interposition between the accused and his accuser of the commonsense judgment of a group of laymen, and in the community participation and shared responsibility that results from that group's determination of guilt or innocence. The performance of this role is not a function of the particular number of the body that makes up the jury. To be sure, the number should probably be large enough to promote group deliberation, free from outside attempts at intimidation, and to provide a fair possibility for obtaining a representative cross-section of the community. But we find little reason to think that these goals are in any meaningful sense less likely to be achieved when the jury numbers six, than when it numbers 12—particularly if the requirement of unanimity is retained. And, certainly the reliability of the jury as a factfinder hardly seems likely to be a function of its size.

It might be suggested that the 12-man jury gives a defendant a greater advantage since he has more 'chances' of finding a juror who will insist on acquittal and thus prevent conviction. But the advantage might just as easily belong to the State, which also needs only one juror out of twelve insisting on guilt to prevent acquittal. What few experiments have occurred—usually in the civil area—indicate that there is no discernible difference between the results reached by the two different-sized juries. In short, neither currently available evidence nor theory suggests that the 12-man jury is necessarily more advantageous to the defendant than a jury composed of fewer members.

Similarly, while in theory the number of viewpoints represented on a randomly selected jury ought to increase as the size of the jury increases, in practice the difference between the 12-man and the six-man jury in terms of the cross-section of the community represented seems likely to be negligible. Even the 12-man jury cannot insure representation of every distinct voice in the community, particularly given the use of the peremptory challenge. As long as arbitrary exclusions of a particular class from the jury rolls are forbidden, see, e.g., *Carter v. Jury Commission*, 396 U.S. 320, 329-30 (1970), the concern that the cross-section will be significantly diminished if the jury is decreased in size from 12 to six seems an unrealistic one.

We conclude, in short, as we began: the fact that the jury at common law was composed of precisely 12 is a historical accident, unnecessary to effect the purposes of the jury system and wholly without significance 'except to mystics.' *Duncan*, 391 U.S. at 182 (Harlan, J., dissenting). To read the Sixth Amendment as forever codifying a feature so incidental to the real purpose of the Amendment is to ascribe a blind formalism to the Framers which would require considerably more evidence than we have been able to discover in the history and language of the Constitution or in the reasoning of our past decisions. We do not mean to intimate that legislatures can never have good reasons for concluding that the 12-man jury is preferable to the smaller jury, or that such conclusions—reflected in the provisions of most States and in our federal system—are in any sense unwise. Legislatures may well have their own views about the relative value of the larger and smaller juries, and may conclude that, wholly apart from the jury's primary function, it is desirable to spread the collective responsibility for the determination of guilt among the larger group. In capital cases, for example, it appears that no State provides for less than 12 jurors—a fact that suggests implicit recognition of the value of the larger body as a means of legitimating society's decision to impose the death penalty. Our holding does no more than leave these considerations to Congress and the States, unrestrained by an interpretation of the Sixth Amendment that would forever dictate the precise number that can constitute a jury. Consistent with this holding, we conclude that petitioner's Sixth Amendment rights, as applied to the States through the Fourteenth Amendment, were not violated by Florida's decision to provide a six-man rather than a 12-man jury. The judgment of the Florida District Court of Appeal is

Affirmed.

D. Searches, Seizures and Probable Cause

Florida's Constitution discusses a Floridian's right to be free from certain searches and seizures when it provides the following in Article I:

> **SECTION 12. Searches and seizures.**—The right of the people to be secure in their persons, houses, papers and effects against unreasonable searches and seizures, and against the unreasonable interception of private communications by any means, shall not be violated. No warrant shall be issued except upon probable cause, supported by affidavit, particularly describing the place or places to be searched, the person or persons, thing or things to be seized, the communication to be intercepted, and the nature of evidence to be obtained. This right shall be construed in conformity with the 4th Amendment to the United States Constitution, as interpreted by the United States Supreme Court. Articles or information obtained in violation of this right shall not be admissible in evidence if such articles or information would be inadmissible under decisions of the United States Supreme Court construing the 4th Amendment to the United States Constitution.

WILLIAMS

V.

STATE OF FLORIDA

Fifth District Court of Appeal of Florida, 2004

869 So. 2d 750

Joerg F. Jaeger of Jaeger & Blankner, Orlando, for Appellant.

Charles J. Crist, Jr., Attorney General, Tallahassee, and Rebecca Rock McGuigan, Assistant Attorney General, Daytona Beach, for Appellee.

SAWAYA, C.J.

Zarek L. Williams appeals the judgment and sentences entered in accordance with a jury verdict finding him guilty of trafficking in 400 grams or more of cocaine, possession of a firearm in the commission of a felony, carrying a concealed firearm, and possession of drug paraphernalia. Williams argues that because the charges stem from an unreasonably prolonged traffic stop, the trial court erred in denying his motions to suppress. Specifically, Williams raises two issues that have merit: 1) the initial stop exceeded the time necessary to write the citation; and 2) Williams was illegally detained after he was issued the citation. We agree and reverse.

While on routine patrol, the arresting officer stopped Williams at 7:38 p.m. for a window tint violation and an obscured tag. A minute-and-a-half later, the officer requested back-up. Four minutes after the stop, the officer requested a drug dog, which arrived at 8:13 p.m. Ten minutes after the stop, the officer ran Williams' date of birth through the teletype and immediately received a response that no warrants were outstanding for Williams. Thirty-five minutes after the stop, the officer issued Williams a citation for the window tint violation. The record reveals that the citation the officer issued to Williams had been partially filled out before the stop even took place. After Williams was handed the citation and his driver's license, he was asked to step to the median so the drug dog could sweep the car. The dog alerted and Williams was arrested.

Williams claims that he was detained far longer than necessary for the officer to issue the citation and, therefore, the search of his vehicle via the drug dog was improper. Williams notes that there is no evidence that the officer had any basis for suspecting criminal activity when he stopped Williams or when issuing the citation to him. Therefore, Williams claims the trial court erred in denying his motion to suppress. We agree. An individual who is stopped for the commission of a traffic infraction may be subjected to a canine search of the exterior of the vehicle so long as it is done within the time required to issue a citation. *Eldridge v. State*, 817 So. 2d 884 (Fla. 5th DCA 2002); *Maxwell v. State*, 785 So. 2d 1277 (Fla. 5th DCA 2001) (citing *Cresswell v. State*, 564 So. 2d 480 (Fla. 1990)); *Welch v. State*, 741 So. 2d 1268 (Fla. 5th DCA 1999). In *Eldridge*, we further explained that the time to issue a citation "should last no longer than is necessary to write the citation and, when necessary, to make the license, tag, insurance and registration checks as long as that information can be obtained within a reasonable period of time." 817 So. 2d at 887 (citations omitted).

In the instant case, it took thirty-five minutes for the officer to obtain the necessary information and write the citation. We conclude, based on the facts and circumstances of this case, that this time far exceeded that which was necessary to issue the citation to Williams. Because Williams was illegally detained at the time the canine search began, the search was improper, and the drugs, paraphernalia and firearm were illegally seized and therefore inadmissible in evidence. *Eldridge; Maxwell.* Hence, the trial court erred in denying the motion to suppress.

Moreover, we cannot ignore the fact that the officer actually had completed the citation and handed it to Williams before the drug dog performed the search of the vehicle. Even if it was reasonable to take thirty-five minutes to obtain the necessary information and issue the citation, the stop had ended before Williams was directed to step to the median, citation in hand, so the dog could proceed with the search. Because the stop had ended before the drug search by the dog began and because the officer had no basis for suspecting criminal activity, the continued detention of Williams was illegal. Accordingly, we reverse the order denying the motion to suppress and remand with directions to discharge Williams.

REVERSED AND REMANDED.

ORFINGER and MONACO, JJ., concur.

[1] The officer admitted that when he approached the car, he could clearly see the temporary tag. Williams, therefore, argues that reversal is warranted based on *State v. Diaz*, 850 So. 2d 435 (Fla. 2003), cert. denied, 540 U.S. 1075 (2003), which clarified the law relative to what a law enforcement officer may do after stopping a vehicle for an apparent temporary tag violation. In Diaz, the officer stopped the vehicle because he could not read the temporary tag. As he approached the vehicle after it was stopped, he could clearly read the tag and found nothing improper. Because the officer did not have any other reason to stop or detain the driver, the court held that the deputy

could do no more than explain the reason for the stop to the driver and that any further detention or interrogation of the driver was improper. Williams' reliance on Diaz is misplaced because the record clearly establishes that the officer also stopped Williams for the window tint violation.

[2] The officer testified at the suppression hearing that he is a "slow writer" and in order to expedite the process of issuing citations, he fills in portions of a number of citations ahead of time. Specifically, he fills in the year, the county, the city and signs the citations. The "county traffic court" information was pre-stamped on the citation. The only information that the officer had to fill out at the time of the stop was the information obtained from Williams' driver's license and the VIN from the car. The officer testified that filling out this information on the citation took thirty-five minutes.

Notes and Questions to Consider:

1. Perhaps a routine traffic stop is more like a brief stop under *Terry v. Ohio*, 392 U.S. 1 (1968), than an arrest. Why was it relevant that the initial stop exceeded the time necessary to write the automobile citation? How did this implicate a constitutional right of the driver?

2. Was this 2004 decision of a Florida state court a harbinger of a future ruling of the Supreme Court of the United States? Eleven years later, the U.S. Supreme Court decided *Rodriguez v. United States*, 135 S. Ct. 1609, 191 L. Ed. 2d 492 (2015). There, a policeman finished issuing the citation to the driver but then delayed the occupants of the vehicle for another seven to eight minutes to do a walk around with a canine. The Federal Court of Appeals held this to be a *de minimis* infringement on liberty that did not violate any constitutional rights. The U.S. Supreme Court reversed, holding that "a police stop exceeding the time needed to handle the matter for which the stop was made violates the Constitution's shield against unreasonable seizures. A seizure justified only by a police-observed traffic violation, therefore, 'become[s] unlawful if it is prolonged beyond the time reasonably required to complete th[e] mission' of issuing a ticket for the violation." 135 S. Ct. at 1612 (citing *Illinois v. Caballes*, 543 U.S. 405 (2005)).

3. What if the officer's work issuing the citation is completed, or reasonably should be completed, but then the officer develops a reasonable suspicion about this driver about another matter?

TOBIN

v.

STATE

First District Court of Appeal of Florida, 2014

146 So. 3d 159

MARSTILLER, J.

We have for review the trial court's denial of Appellant's dispositive motion to suppress evidence he was driving with a suspended or revoked license, which led the court to find Appellant in violation of community control. Because the deputy sheriff who stopped Appellant's vehicle lacked the reasonable, articulable suspicion of criminal activity necessary to justify what the court determined—and the State conceded—was an investigatory stop, we conclude the court erred in denying the motion to suppress.

Appellant was on two years' community control, followed by two years' probation, for committing battery on a law enforcement officer and resisting an officer with violence. On the night in question, the Okaloosa County Sheriff's Office received two anonymous calls complaining of a disturbance at a particular residence or business located at the end of a privately-maintained road. The Sheriff's Office had received complaints in the past about disturbances at the property; some complaints were founded, some were not. The first anonymous call that night indicated firearms may be involved. When deputies investigated, they found no disturbance. Sometime later, a second call came in reporting a disturbance at the property, this time alleging someone on the property was overheard shouting "Shoot me now!" Two deputies responded, each in his own cruiser. The first deputy to arrive saw a vehicle leaving the property as he approached, and radioed to the second deputy, who was nearer to the intersection of the private road and the public street, to stop the vehicle. The second deputy, seeing the vehicle coming directly toward him, activated the blue lights on his cruiser, causing the then-unknown driver to stop his vehicle "beak to beak" with the cruiser. When Appellant began to get out of the vehicle, the deputy directed him to stay put. The deputy testified at the suppression hearing he did so because of concerns, based on the anonymous call, that a firearm may be present. Upon approaching the vehicle, however, the deputy recognized Appellant, knew he was on community control, and knew his driver's license was suspended. At that point, he arrested Appellant for driving with a suspended license. The deputy also smelled alcohol on Appellant's breath and found a cup containing an alcoholic beverage in the passenger or back seat of Appellant's vehicle.

The State later filed an affidavit of violation of community control based on the new law violation and failure to abstain from using alcohol. Upon denying Appellant's motion to suppress, the trial court found only the new law violation proven, revoked Appellant's community control on that basis, and entered judgment sentencing him to 36 months in prison.

It is well settled that, to effect a constitutionally-permissible investigatory stop, a law enforcement officer must have a well-founded, articulable suspicion that the person stopped has committed, is committing, or is about to commit a crime. § 901.151, Fla. Stat. (2012), *Terry v. Ohio,* 392 U.S. 1 (1968); *Popple v. State,* 626 So. 2d 185, 186 (Fla. 1993); *Berry v. State,* 86 So. 3d 595, 598 (Fla. 1st DCA 2012). "Mere suspicion is not enough to support a [*Terry*] stop." *Popple,* 626 So. 2d at 186.

The parties assert that whether the deputy who stopped Appellant's vehicle had the requisite well-founded suspicion of criminal activity turns on how the anonymous calls are characterized. *See State v. Maynard,* 783 So. 2d 226, 228, (Fla. 2001). Appellant argues the calls were merely anonymous tips that, absent additional information obtained by the deputies, were not sufficiently reliable to justify the detention that occurred here. The State counters that the callers can be reasonably characterized as citizen informants whose calls are presumed reliable and generally are sufficient to support an investigatory detention without further corroboration.

"Reasonable suspicion ... is dependent upon both the content of information possessed by police and its degree of reliability. Both factors—quantity and quality—are considered in the 'totality of circumstances—the whole picture,' that must be taken into account when evaluating whether there is reasonable suspicion." *Alabama v. White,* 496 U.S. 325, 330 (1990) (quoting *United States v. Cortez,* 449 U.S. 411, 417). " 'In analyzing whether third-party information can provide the requisite reasonable suspicion, courts have looked to the reliability of the informant as well as the reliability of the information provided.' " *Berry,* 86 So. 3d at 598 (quoting *D.P. v. State,* 65 So. 3d 123, 127 (Fla. 3d DCA 2011)). The less reliable the tip, the more independent corroboration will be required to establish reasonable suspicion. *White,* 496 U.S. at 330, 110 S.Ct. 2412. On the "spectrum of reliability," an anonymous tip has "relatively low" reliability. *Berry,* 86 So. 3d at 598; *see also State v. DeLuca,* 40 So. 3d 120, 124 (Fla. 1st DCA 2010). This is because "an anonymous tip alone seldom demonstrates the informant's basis of knowledge or veracity as ordinary citizens generally do not provide extensive recitations of the basis of their everyday observations and given that the veracity of persons supplying [such] tips" cannot be determined. *White,* 496 U.S. at 329. Thus, "[a]n anonymous tip requires that the information be 'sufficiently corroborated' by the officer to constitute reasonable suspicion[.]" *Berry,* 86 So. 3d at 598 (citing *State v. Evans,* 692 So. 2d 216, 218 (Fla. 4th DCA 1997)). A citizen informant, on the other hand, is presumed highly reliable because his or her "motivation in reporting illegality is the promotion of justice and public safety," and because the informant gives his or her name to police and "can be held accountable for the accuracy of the information given." *DeLuca,* 40 So. 3d at 124. Therefore, "[a] tip from a citizen informant is sufficient by itself to provide law enforcement with reasonable suspicion to conduct a *Terry* stop." *Berry,* 86 So. 3d at 599 (citing *State v. Maynard,* 783 So. 2d 226, 228 (Fla. 2001)).

Applying these principles to the facts in the instant case, we conclude the deputy who stopped Appellant's car did not have a well-founded suspicion of criminal activity needed to effect a lawful *Terry* stop. The disturbance calls that sent the deputies to the property on the night question were anonymous tips bereft of any details indicating the information given was reliable. Indeed, the first call proved to be unfounded after deputies investigated. The second call, alleging someone was overheard yelling "Shoot me now," still did not provide any specific, articulable facts indicating that Appellant (or any other identifiable person, for that matter) was engaged in criminal activity. Thus, even if, as the State argues, we could characterize the callers as citizen informants, there still was insufficient information given to support a reasonable, articulable suspicion that a crime had been, or was being, committed. *See Florida v. J.L.,* 529 U.S. 266 (2000) (holding anonymous tip claiming person was carrying a gun insufficient, without more, to justify stop and frisk of the person); *Baptiste v. State,* 995 So. 2d 285 (Fla. 2008) (holding anonymous 911 call describing person and alleging person had waved firearm in public not sufficiently reliable to provide reasonable suspicion for investigative stop of person matching the description).

Because the anonymous calls provided neither the quantity nor the quality of information necessary to create reasonable suspicion, the deputies needed additional, independently-obtained information. They had none, for they had not yet begun to investigate the alleged disturbance when Appellant's car was stopped. Nor did they observe any behavior by Appellant to generate reasonable suspicion he was or had been engaged in criminal activity involving a firearm. Compare *Hudson v. State,* 41 So. 3d 948 (Fla. 2d DCA 2010) (finding reasonable suspicion where officers received anonymous call that a man was burglarizing cars in stadium parking lot, and observed person matching "vague description" carrying two duffel bags and hurriedly walking away from stadium) and *J.H. v. State,* 106 So. 3d 1001 (Fla. 3d DCA 2013) (finding no reasonable suspicion where officer responded to scene of fight reported by anonymous caller and observed no fight, but saw and stopped a youth matching description who was merely sweating and out of breath and appeared nervous).

If the second deputy's action could be characterized as attempting a consensual encounter with Appellant, see generally *Popple,* 626 So. 2d at 186, we could affirm the trial court's denial of Appellant's motion to suppress. But the deputy effected the stop of Appellant's car by activating the blue lights on his cruiser, positioning the cruiser on the road such that Appellant had to stop directly opposite, and ordering Appellant to remain in the car when he attempted to step out. "Although there is no litmus-paper test for distinguishing a consensual encounter from a seizure, a significant identifying characteristic of a consensual encounter is that the officer cannot hinder or restrict the person's freedom to leave or freedom to refuse to answer inquiries[.]" *Id.* at 187. On the other hand, "a person is seized if, under the circumstances, a reasonable person would conclude that he or she is not free to end the encounter and depart." *Id.* at 188. What occurred in this case was a seizure—an investigatory stop for which a reasonable, articulable suspicion of criminal activity *by Appellant* was required. Because the anonymous calls failed to provide deputies with the requisite level of suspicion, the stop of Appellant's car was unlawful, and the trial court should have granted the motion to suppress. Accordingly, we reverse the order of revocation of community control and the subsequent judgment and sentence, and direct the trial court to reinstate Appellant's community control.

REVERSED and REMANDED with directions. . . .

Notes and Questions to Consider:

1. What is the court's rationale for concluding that "someone was overheard yelling 'Shoot me now'" does not yield a reasonable suspicion of criminal activity?

2. Would the court's logic hold true if that same yell had been heard inside a crowded theatre? What about if outside in an open, vacant field?

STATE

V.

TEAMER

Supreme Court of Florida, 2014

151 So. 3d 421

QUINCE, J.

This case is before the Court for review of the decision of the First District Court of Appeal in *Teamer v. State,* 108 So. 3d 664 (Fla. 1st DCA 2013).1 The district court certified that its decision is in direct conflict with the decision of the Fourth District Court of Appeal in *Aders v. State,* 67 So. 3d 368 (Fla. 4th DCA 2011). We have jurisdiction. *See* art. V, § 3(b)(4), Fla. Const. As we explain, we approve the First District's decision and disapprove that of the Fourth District.

FACTS AND PROCEDURAL HISTORY

On June 22, 2010, an Escambia County Deputy Sheriff observed Kerrick Teamer driving a *bright green* Chevrolet. *Teamer,* 108 So. 3d at 665. After noticing the car, the deputy continued on his patrol, driving into one of the neighborhoods in that area. Upon traveling back to where he had first seen Teamer, the deputy again observed Teamer driving the same car. The deputy then "ran" the number from Teamer's license plate through the Florida Department of Highway Safety and Motor Vehicles (DHSMV) database, as is customary for him while on patrol, and learned that the vehicle was registered as a *blue* Chevrolet. *Id.* The database did not return any information regarding the model of the vehicle. Based only on the color inconsistency, the deputy pulled the car over to conduct a traffic stop.

"Upon interviewing the occupants, the deputy learned that the vehicle had recently been painted, thus explaining the inconsistency." *Id.* However, during the stop, the deputy noticed a strong odor of marijuana emanating from the car and decided to conduct a search of the vehicle, Teamer, and the other passenger. *Id.* "Marijuana and crack cocaine were recovered from the vehicle, and about $1,100 in cash was recovered from [Teamer]. [He] was charged with trafficking in cocaine (between 28–200 grams), possession of marijuana (less than 20 grams), and possession of drug paraphernalia" (scales). *Id.*

On October 4, 2010, Teamer filed a motion to suppress the results of the stop as products of an unlawful, warrantless search. At the hearing on the motion to suppress, the deputy acknowledged that, in his training and experience, he had encountered individuals who would switch license plates and he could not verify a vehicle's identification number without pulling over the vehicle. *Id.* On cross-examination, the deputy acknowledged that the car was not reported stolen, he had not observed any other traffic violations or suspicious or furtive behavior, he was not "aware of any reports of stolen vehicles or swapped plates in the area," and "the only thing that was out of the ordinary was the inconsistency of the vehicle color from the registration." *Id.*

The trial court denied the motion to suppress, explaining that the rationale for the denial was that the deputy "had a legal right to conduct an investigatory stop when a registration search of the automobile license tag reflected a different color than the observed color of the vehicle." The trial court found that the deputy made the investigatory stop "because the registration was not consistent with the color of the vehicle" and that since "the vehicle was legally stopped for investigative purposes," the odor of marijuana that the officer smelled during the stop gave him probable cause to conduct a search. After a jury trial, Teamer was convicted on all three counts as charged in the information. The trial judge sentenced him to six years on count one and time served on the other two counts.

Teamer appealed, and the First District reversed the trial court's denial of Teamer's motion to suppress, certifying conflict with the Fourth District in *Aders. Id.* at 670. The First District acknowledged "that any discrepancy between a vehicle's plates and the registration may legitimately raise a concern that the vehicle is stolen or the plates were swapped from another vehicle," but found that such concern must be weighed "against a citizen's right under the Fourth Amendment to travel on the roads free from governmental intrusions." *Id.* at 667. The district court cited several cases demonstrating that color discrepancy is typically one of *several* factors constituting reasonable suspicion. *Id.* at 668. The First District then cited two non-binding cases for the principle that a color discrepancy alone does not provide reasonable suspicion for a stop. *Id.* at 668–69. Relying on those cases and other "somewhat analogous cases involving investigations of 'temporary tags,'" the district court ruled that a color discrepancy alone did not warrant an investigatory stop. *Id.* at 669–70. The court found that under the converse ruling, "every person who changes the color of [his or her] vehicle is continually subject to an investigatory stop so long as the color inconsistency persists." *Id.* at 670. The First District stated that it was "hesitant to license an investigatory stop" under such circumstances. *Id.*

ANALYSIS

In reviewing a trial court's ruling on a motion to suppress, the trial court's determinations of historical facts are reversed only if not supported by competent, substantial evidence. *Connor v. State,* 803 So. 2d 598, 608 (Fla. 2001). However, the application of the law to those facts is subject to de novo review. *Id.* Further, this Court is required to construe Florida's constitutional right against unreasonable searches and seizures "in conformity with the [Fourth] Amendment to the United States Constitution, as interpreted by the United States Supreme Court." Art. I, § 12, Fla. Const.; *Bernie v. State,* 524 So. 2d 988, 990–91 (Fla. 1988) ("[W]e are bound to follow the interpretations of the United States Supreme Court with relation to the [F]ourth [A]mendment....").

The United States Supreme Court has "held that the police can stop and briefly detain a person for investigative purposes if the officer has a reasonable suspicion supported by articulable facts that criminal activity 'may be afoot,' even if the officer lacks probable cause." *United States v. Sokolow,* 490 U.S. 1, 7 (1989) (quoting *Terry v. Ohio,* 392 U.S. 1, 30 (1968)); *Popple v. State,* 626 So. 2d 185, 186 (Fla. 1993) ("[A] police officer may reasonably detain a citizen temporarily if the officer has a reasonable suspicion that a person has committed, is committing, or is about to commit a crime." (citing § 901.151, Fla. Stat. (1991))). However, a "police officer must be able to point to specific and articulable facts which, taken together with rational inferences from those facts, reasonably warrant" an investigatory stop. *Terry,*

392 U.S. at 21. The Supreme Court has described reasonable suspicion as "a particularized and objective basis for suspecting the particular person stopped of criminal activity." *United States v. Cortez,* 449 U.S. 411, 417 (1981). This standard requires "something more than an 'inchoate and unparticularized suspicion or hunch.' " *Sokolow,* 490 U.S. at 7 (quoting *Terry,* 392 U.S. at 27) (internal quotation marks omitted).

"Reasonableness, of course, depends 'on a balance between the public interest and the individual's right to personal security free from arbitrary interference by law officers.' " *Pennsylvania v. Mimms,* 434 U.S. 106, 109 (1977) (quoting *United States v. Brignoni–Ponce,* 422 U.S. 873, 878 (1975)); *State v. Diaz,* 850 So. 2d 435, 439 (Fla. 2003) ("The real test is one of reasonableness, which involves balancing the interests of the State with those of the motorist."). "When a search or seizure is conducted without a warrant, the government bears the burden of demonstrating that the search or seizure was reasonable." *Hilton v. State,* 961 So. 2d 284, 296 (Fla. 2007) (citing *United States v. Johnson,* 63 F.3d 242, 245 (3d Cir.1995) ("As a general rule, the burden of proof is on the defendant who seeks to suppress evidence. However, once the defendant has established a basis for his motion, *i.e.,* the search or seizure was conducted without a warrant, the burden shifts to the government to show that the search or seizure was reasonable." (citation omitted))).

Reasonable suspicion must also be assessed based on "the totality of the circumstances—the whole picture," *Cortez,* 449 U.S. at 417; *United States v. Arvizu,* 534 U.S. 266, 277 (2002), and "from the standpoint of an objectively reasonable police officer," *Ornelas v. United States,* 517 U.S. 690, 696 (1996); *Arvizu,* 534 U.S. at 277. Thus, a police officer may draw inferences based on his own experience. *Ornelas,* 517 U.S. at 700; *Cortez,* 449 U.S. at 418 ("[A] trained officer draws inferences and makes deductions—inferences and deductions that might well elude an untrained person."). However, "the officer's subjective intentions are not involved in the determination of reasonableness." *Hilton,* 961 So. 2d at 294; *Whren v. United States,* 517 U.S. 806, 813 (1996) (recognizing the rejection of "any argument that the constitutional reasonableness of traffic stops depends on the actual motivations of the individual officers involved").

"[I]nnocent behavior will frequently provide the basis" for reasonable suspicion. *Sokolow,* 490 U.S. at 10; *see also Illinois v. Wardlow,* 528 U.S. 119, 125 (2000) (acknowledging this fact and recognizing that an officer can detain an individual to resolve an ambiguity regarding suspicious yet lawful or innocent conduct). "[T]he relevant inquiry is not whether particular conduct is innocent or guilty, but the degree of suspicion that attaches to particular types of noncriminal acts." *Sokolow,* 490 U.S. at 10 (internal quotation marks omitted). In the instant case, the State concedes that "the failure to update a vehicle registration to reflect a new color is not in specific violation of a Florida law." Thus, what degree of suspicion attaches to this noncriminal act?

To warrant an investigatory stop, the law requires not just a mere suspicion of criminal activity, but a reasonable, well-founded one. *Popple,* 626 So. 2d at 186 ("[A]n investigatory stop requires a well-founded, articulable suspicion of criminal activity."). In *Terry,* the stop was found appropriate because the officer "had observed [three men] go [t]hrough a series of acts, each of them perhaps innocent in itself, but which taken together warranted further investigation." *Terry,* 392 U.S. at 22. The U.S. Supreme Court described the scenario as follows:

> There is nothing unusual in two men standing together on a street corner, perhaps waiting for someone. Nor is there anything suspicious about people in such circumstances strolling up and down the street, singly or in pairs. Store windows, moreover, are made to be looked in. But the story is quite different where, as here, two men hover about a street corner for an extended period of time, at the end of which it becomes apparent that they are not waiting for anyone or anything; where these men pace alternately along an identical route, pausing to stare in the same store window roughly 24 times; where each completion of this route is followed immediately by a conference between the two men on the corner; where they are joined in one of these conferences by a third man who leaves swiftly; and where the two men finally follow the third and rejoin him a couple of blocks away.

Id. at 22–23. The Supreme Court found that "[i]t would have been poor police work indeed for an officer of 30 years' experience in the detection of thievery from stores in this same neighborhood to have failed to investigate this behavior further." *Id.* at 23. Thus each seemingly innocent activity in *Terry* had a cumulative effect of providing an officer with a reasonable suspicion.

Conversely, in *State v. Johnson,* 561 So. 2d 1139, 1142 (Fla. 1990), this Court rejected an officer's use of a self-created drug courier profile because "Florida law does not permit a profile based on factors that are little more than mundane or unremarkable descriptions of everyday law-abiding activities." We noted that a drug courier profile in a Supreme Court case was upheld "precisely because it described *unusual* conduct that set the defendant apart from other travelers and that strongly suggested concealed criminal conduct." *Id.* We invalidated the profile used in *Johnson* because "there was nothing at all unusual or out of the ordinary about the conduct that" fit within the profile. *Id.* at 1142–43. In so holding, we stated that individuals fitting within the officer's profile "simply cannot be described as an inherently 'suspicious' bunch." *Id.* at 1143. The innocent factors within the profile failed to create a reasonable suspicion.

Turning to the instant case, the sole basis here for the investigatory stop is an observation of one completely noncriminal factor, not several incidents of innocent activity combining under a totality of the circumstances to arouse a reasonable suspicion—as was the case in *Terry.* The discrepancy between the vehicle registration and the color the deputy observed does present an ambiguous situation, and the Supreme Court has recognized that an officer can detain an individual to resolve an ambiguity regarding suspicious yet lawful or innocent conduct. *Wardlow,* 528 U.S. at 125. However, the suspicion still must be a reasonable one. *Popple,* 626 So. 2d at 186 ("Mere suspicion is not enough to support a stop."). In this case, there simply are not enough facts to demonstrate reasonableness. Like the factors in *Johnson,* the color discrepancy here is not "inherently suspicious" or "unusual" enough or so "out of the ordinary" as to provide an officer with a reasonable suspicion of criminal activity, especially given the fact that it is not against the law in Florida to change the color of your vehicle without notifying the DHSMV.

The law allows officers to draw rational inferences, but to find reasonable suspicion based on this single noncriminal factor would be to license investigatory stops on nothing more than an officer's hunch. Doing so would be akin to finding reasonable suspicion for an officer to stop an individual for walking in a sparsely occupied area after midnight simply because that officer testified that, in his experience, people who walk in such areas after midnight tend to commit robberies. Without more, this one fact may provide a "mere suspicion," but it does not rise to the level of a reasonable suspicion. Neither does the sole innocent factor here—a color discrepancy—rise to such level. The deputy may have had a suspicion, but it was not a reasonable or well-founded one, especially given the fact that the driver of the vehicle was not engaged in any suspicious activity. Moreover, "the government provided no evidence to tip the scales from a mere hunch to something even approaching reasonable and articulable suspicion, despite attempting to justify a detention based on one observed incident of completely innocent behavior in a non-suspicious context." *United States v. Uribe,* 709 F.3d 646, 652 (7th Cir.2013).

Reasonableness also "depends 'on a balance between the public interest and the individual's right to personal security free from arbitrary interference by law officers.' " *Mimms,* 434 U.S. at 109 (quoting *Brignoni–Ponce,* 422 U.S. at 878); *Diaz,* 850 So. 2d at 439 ("The real test is one of reasonableness, which involves balancing the interests of the State with those of the motorist."). In order to determine reasonableness, courts "must balance the nature and quality of the intrusion on the individual's Fourth Amendment interests against the importance of the governmental interests alleged to justify the intrusion." *United States v. Place,* 462 U.S. 696, 703 (1983); *Delaware v. Prouse,* 440 U.S. 648, 654 (1979) ("[T]he permissibility of a particular law enforcement practice is judged by balancing its intrusion on the individual's Fourth Amendment interests against its promotion of legitimate governmental interests."). Thus we must balance the nature and quality of the intrusion required to stop an individual and investigate a color discrepancy against the government's interest in finding stolen vehicles or enforcing vehicle registration laws.

In *Brignoni–Ponce,* the Supreme Court invalidated a roving patrol stop by Border Patrol agents near a closed checkpoint operation at the Mexican border. 422 U.S. at 886. In stopping the vehicle, the agents had relied on a single factor—"the apparent Mexican ancestry of the occupants." *Id.* at 885–86. As part of balancing the public interest with the motorist's rights, the Supreme Court outlined as the governmental interest preventing illegal aliens from entering this country. *Id.* at 878–80. However, despite the importance of that interest, the "modest" intrusion of a brief stop, and the absence of practical alternatives for policing the border, the Court found that the apparent Mexican heritage of the occupants did not provide reasonable suspicion for a stop. *Id.* at 881, 886. The Court stated, "The likelihood that any given person of Mexican ancestry is an alien is high enough to make Mexican appearance a relevant factor, but standing alone it does not justify stopping all Mexican–Americans to ask if they are aliens." *Id.* at 886–87; *cf. United States v. Martinez–Fuerte,* 428 U.S. 543, 557–59 (1976) (upholding stops for brief questioning at fixed checkpoints even with no reasonable suspicion of illegal aliens because although the need for such stops is as great as that in *Brignoni–Ponce,* a checkpoint stop is much less intrusive since "the generating of concern or even fright on the part of lawful travelers is appreciably less").

Similarly, in *Prouse,* the Supreme Court invalidated a random vehicle stop by roving patrol officers *solely* to confirm a driver's compliance with licensure and registration requirements. 440 U.S. at 659. The Court described the intrusion on the motorist's interests as follows:

> We cannot assume that the physical and psychological intrusion visited upon the occupants of a vehicle by a random stop to check documents is of any less moment than that occasioned by a stop by border agents on roving patrol. Both of these stops generally entail law enforcement officers signaling a moving automobile to pull over to the side of the roadway, by means of a possibly unsettling show of authority. Both interfere with freedom of movement, are inconvenient, and consume time. Both may create substantial anxiety. For Fourth Amendment purposes, we also see insufficient resemblance between sporadic and random stops of individual vehicles making their way through city traffic and those stops occa-

> sioned by roadblocks where all vehicles are brought to a halt or to a near halt, and all are subjected to a show of the police power of the community. At traffic checkpoints the motorist can see that other vehicles are being stopped, he can see visible signs of the officers' authority, and he is much less likely to be frightened or annoyed by the intrusion.

Id. at 657 (internal quotation marks omitted). The Court balanced that intrusion with the state's interests in apprehending stolen vehicles—which the Court characterized as indistinguishable from a "general interest in crime control"—and promoting roadway safety. *Id.* at 658–59. The Supreme Court held that given the alternative mechanisms available for enforcing traffic and vehicle safety regulations—the foremost of which being to act only upon observed violations—the incremental contribution to highway safety of the random stops in that case did not justify their intrusion on Fourth Amendment rights. *Id.* at 659.

The intrusion involved in the instant case is similar to that described in *Prouse,* especially considering that anyone who chooses to paint his or her vehicle a different color could be pulled over by law enforcement every time he or she drives it. *Prouse,* 440 U.S. at 662–63 ("Were the individual subject to unfettered governmental intrusion every time he entered an automobile, the security guaranteed by the Fourth Amendment would be seriously circumscribed."). Furthermore, the governmental interest here is not nearly as strong as that in *Brignoni–Ponce* of developing "effective measures to prevent the illegal entry of aliens at the Mexican border," 422 U.S. at 878–79, but is more like that in *Prouse*—"ensuring that ... licensing, registration, and vehicle inspection requirements are being observed," 440 U.S. at 658. In fact, the Supreme Court described part of the interest at stake here—the apprehension of stolen vehicles—as indistinguishable "from the general interest in crime control." *Id.* at 659 n. 18.

Even more relevant is the Supreme Court's finding in *Brignoni–Ponce* that a single factor—the apparent Mexican ancestry of the vehicle's occupants—was not enough to furnish a reasonable suspicion that the occupants were illegal aliens. 422 U.S. at 885–86. Likewise, the likelihood that a color discrepancy such as that at issue here indicates a stolen vehicle *may* be high enough to make it a relevant factor, but standing alone, it does not justify initiating a stop to determine if the law has been violated. The deputy here needed more indicia of a violation to distinguish between an illegal transfer of license plates, for example, and a legal decision to paint one's vehicle. Conducting an investigatory stop based on a color discrepancy only when that discrepancy exists *in conjunction with* additional factors indicating potential criminal activity still protects the government's interests, while also preserving a motorist's right of freedom from arbitrary interference by law enforcement. We find that the governmental interest in this case is outweighed by Teamer's constitutional rights, and the investigatory stop was not warranted.

"Under the exclusionary rule announced by the United States Supreme Court, 'the Fourth Amendment bar[s] the use of evidence secured through an illegal search and seizure.' " *Hilton,* 961 So. 2d at 293 (alteration in original) (quoting *Mapp v. Ohio,* 367 U.S. 643, 648 (1961) (holding that the federal exclusionary rule applies to the states as well)). "Whether the exclusionary sanction is appropriately imposed in a particular case ... is 'an issue separate from the question whether the Fourth Amendment rights of the party seeking to invoke the rule were violated by police conduct.' " *United States v. Leon,* 468 U.S. 897, 906 (1984) (quoting *Illinois v. Gates,* 462 U.S. 213, 223 (1983)).

The primary rationale behind the exclusionary rule is to deter law enforcement from violating constitutional rights. *Terry,* 392 U.S. at 12; *see also United States v. Calandra,* 414 U.S. 338, 348 (1974) ("[T]he rule is a judicially created remedy designed to safeguard Fourth Amendment rights generally through its deterrent effect."). The instant case is not one in which the exclusionary rule "is powerless to deter invasions of constitutionally guaranteed rights [because] the police either have no interest in prosecuting or are willing to forgo successful prosecution in the interest of serving some other goal." *Terry,* 392 U.S. at 14. Applying the exclusionary rule here would have the required deterrent effect. *See, e.g., Prouse,* 440 U.S. at 651, 663 (affirming the trial court's judgment granting the defendant's motion to suppress).

Further, the State has not demonstrated that any exceptions apply. *Brown v. Illinois,* 422 U.S. 590, 604 (1975) (discussing whether to apply an exception to the exclusionary rule and stating that "the burden of showing admissibility rests, of course, on the prosecution"). The State argues a variation of the good faith exception to the exclusionary rule. This exception was first found to apply whenever a law enforcement officer conducts a search while relying, in good faith, upon a defective search warrant. *Leon,* 468 U.S. at 922; *Massachusetts v. Sheppard,* 468 U.S. 981, 987–89 (1984). Over time, however, the Supreme Court extended this exception to other factual scenarios, including searches where police acted in objectively reasonable reliance on binding judicial precedent. *Davis v. United States,* 131 S.Ct. 2419, 2428 (2011). However, the rule of *Davis* has no application to the present case because the *Aders* decision was issued on July 27, 2011—more than one year *after* the stop of Teamer's vehicle. Thus *Aders* was not binding precedent on which the deputy could have relied.

Despite this fact, the State argues that the good faith exception should still apply because the deputy here "arrived at a conclusion shared by non-binding courts in other jurisdictions, and later shared by the Fourth District" in *Aders.* However, there are also nonbinding courts in other jurisdictions that have arrived at the exact opposite conclusion. *United States v. Uribe,* No. 2:10–cr–17–JMS–CMM, 2011 WL 4538407 (S.D.Ind. Sept. 28, 2011); *Commonwealth v. Mason,* 78 Va. Cir. 474 (Cir.Ct.2009), *aff'd,* No. 1956–09–2, 2010 WL 768721 (Va.Ct.App. Mar. 9, 2010). We are satisfied that the exclusionary rule will have an appropriate deterrent effect in this case and that none of the exceptions to the rule apply.

CONCLUSION

Based on the foregoing, we disapprove the decision of the Fourth District in *Aders v. State,* 67 So. 3d 368 (Fla. 4th DCA 2011), and approve the First District's decision in *Teamer v. State,* 108 So. 3d 664 (Fla. 1st DCA 2013), reversing the trial court's judgment and sentence and ordering that Teamer be discharged.

It is so ordered.

LABARGA, C.J., and PARIENTE, LEWIS, and PERRY, JJ., concur.

CANADY, J., dissents with an opinion in which POLSTON, J., concurs.

CANADY, J., dissenting.

Because I conclude that the traffic stop of Kerrick Van Teamer's vehicle was based on a reasonable suspicion of criminal activity and that the trial court therefore correctly denied the motion to suppress, I dissent from the majority's approval of the First District Court of Appeal's decision reversing Teamer's judgment and sentence and ordering that he be discharged. I would quash the decision of the First District on review and approve the decision of the Fourth District in *Aders v. State,* 67 So. 3d 368 (Fla. 4th DCA 2011).

I.

"The Fourth Amendment permits brief investigative stops—such as the traffic stop in this case—when a law enforcement officer has 'a particularized and objective basis for suspecting the particular person stopped of criminal activity.' " *Navarette v. California,* 134 S.Ct. 1683, 1687 (2014) (quoting *United States v. Cortez,* 449 U.S. 411, 417–18 (1981)). This rule is rooted in *Terry v. Ohio,* 392 U.S. 1 (1968), where "the [Supreme] Court implicitly acknowledged the authority of the police to make a *forcible stop* of a person when the officer has reasonable, articulable suspicion that the person has been, is, or is about to be engaged in criminal activity." *United States v. Place,* 462 U.S. 696, 702 (1983).

The *Terry* rule recognizes that "[t]he Fourth Amendment requires 'some minimal level of objective justification' for making the stop." *United States v. Sokolow,* 490 U.S. 1, 7 (1989) (quoting *Immigration & Naturalization Serv. v. Delgado,* 466 U.S. 210, 217 (1984)). Reasonable suspicion thus requires "something more than an 'inchoate and unparticularized suspicion or "hunch." ' " *Sokolow,* 490 U.S. at 7 (quoting *Terry,* 392 U.S. at 27). "A determination that reasonable suspicion exists, however, need not rule out the possibility of innocent conduct." *United States v. Arvizu,*534 U.S. 266, 277 (2002). In permitting detentions based on reasonable suspicion, "*Terry* accepts the risk that officers may stop innocent people." *Illinois v. Wardlow,* 528 U.S. 119, 126 (2000). But when a stop lacks an objective basis, "the risk of arbitrary and abusive police practices exceeds tolerable limits." *Brown v.*

Texas, 443 U.S. 47, 52 (1979). Courts making "reasonable-suspicion determinations ... must look at the 'totality of the circumstances' of each case." *Arvizu,* 534 U.S. at 273.

The rule authorizing stops based on reasonable suspicion—which embodies an "exception to the probable-cause requirement"—rests on the Supreme Court's "balancing of the competing interests to determine the reasonableness of the type of seizure involved within the meaning of 'the Fourth Amendment's general proscription against unreasonable searches and seizures.' " *Place,* 462 U.S. at 703 (quoting *Terry,* 392 U.S. at 20). This balancing process involves weighing "the nature and quality of the intrusion on the individual's Fourth Amendment interests against the importance of the governmental interests alleged to justify the intrusion." *Id.* "A central concern in balancing these competing considerations in a variety of settings has been to assure that an individual's reasonable expectation of privacy is not subject to arbitrary invasions solely at the unfettered discretion of officers in the field." *Brown,* 443 U.S. at 51. The Supreme Court's categorical authorization of brief investigative detentions based on a reasonable suspicion of criminal activity flows from the conclusion that "[w]hen the nature and extent of the detention are minimally intrusive of the individual's Fourth Amendment interests, the opposing law enforcement interests can support a seizure based on less than probable cause." *Place,* 462 U.S. at 703.

II.

Here, the officer's suspicion was aroused by the discrepancy between the color of the vehicle driven by Teamer and the color that was indicated in the registration information for the vehicle associated with the license tag on Teamer's vehicle. Because of this discrepancy, a reasonable officer could suspect that the license tag may have been illegally transferred from the vehicle to which it was assigned. Although the color discrepancy was not necessarily indicative of illegality, it constituted "a particularized and objective basis for suspecting the particular person stopped of criminal activity." *Navarette,* 134 S.Ct. at 1687 (quoting *Cortez,* 449 U.S. at 417–18). The color discrepancy was "something more than an 'inchoate and unparticularized suspicion or "hunch." ' " *Sokolow,* 490 U.S. at 7 (quoting *Terry,* 392 U.S. at

27, 88 S.Ct. 1868). I would therefore conclude that the officer had the "minimal level of objective justification" necessary to conduct a stop for the purpose of further investigating the discrepancy. *Sokolow,* 490 U.S. at 7(quoting *Delgado,* 466 U.S. at 217).

"It is not uncommon for members of the same court to disagree as to whether the proper threshold for reasonable suspicion has been reached." William E. Ringel, *Searches & Seizures Arrests & Confessions* § 11:12 (Westlaw database updated March 2014). On the issue presented by this case, different courts have disagreed regarding whether the color discrepancy was sufficient to establish reasonable suspicion. Compare *Aders,* 67 So. 3d at 371 (holding that "[a] color discrepancy is enough to create a reasonable suspicion in the mind of a law enforcement officer of the violation of ... criminal law"); *United States v. Uribe,* 709 F.3d 646 (7th Cir.2013) (same); *Andrews v. State,* 289 Ga.App. 679, 658 S.E.2d 126 (2008) (same); *Smith v. State,* 713 N.E.2d 338 (Ind.Ct.App.1999) (same); with *Van Teamer,* 108 So. 3d 664 (Fla. 1st DCA 2013) (holding that color discrepancy alone does not warrant an investigatory stop); *United States v. Uribe,* 2011 WL 4538407 (S.D.Ind. Sept. 28, 2011) (same); *Commonwealth v. Mason,* 2010 WL 768721 (Va.Ct.App. Mar. 9, 2010) (same). Different views on this question are no doubt influenced by divergent judgments regarding the likelihood that the color discrepancy had an innocent explanation—namely, the repainting of the vehicle after it was registered—and was not indicative of illegality. The courts in fact have no empirical basis for reaching a conclusion about that likelihood. But a stop predicated on such a color discrepancy unquestionably falls outside the category of "arbitrary invasions solely at the unfettered discretion of officers in the field." *Brown,* 443 U.S. at 51. A stop in such circumstances cannot fairly be called an "arbitrary and abusive" police practice. *Id.* at 52.

The crux of the majority's decision in this case is its conclusion that finding "reasonable suspicion based on this single noncriminal factor would be to license investigatory stops on nothing more than an officer's hunch." Majority op. at 428. This conclusion suggests a categorical rule that is not consistent with the framework established in the Supreme Court's Fourth Amendment jurisprudence. Although the totality of the circumstances must be taken into account in every case, that does not mean that an officer's reliance on a "single noncriminal factor"—such as the vehicle color discrepancy here—is the equivalent of a "hunch." The majority is wholly unjustified in categorizing an undeniably objective factor as a hunch. The majority's "effort to refine and elaborate the requirements of 'reasonable suspicion' in this case creates unnecessary difficulty in dealing with one of the relatively simple concepts embodied in the Fourth Amendment." *Sokolow,* 490 U.S. at 7–8.

The two cases on which the majority places primary reliance do not support the majority's line of analysis. In *United States v. Brignoni–Ponce,* 422 U.S. 873, 876 (1975), the Supreme Court considered "whether a roving patrol may stop a vehicle in an area near the border and question its occupants when the only ground for suspicion is that the occupants appear to be of Mexican ancestry." The Supreme Court concluded that "Mexican appearance" "standing alone ... does not justify stopping all Mexican–Americans to ask if they are aliens." *Id.* at 887. The Supreme Court's rejection of stops based purely on ethnic classification does not support the conclusion that all stops where the officer relies on "a single noncriminal factor" are unconstitutional. Nor does *Delaware v. Prouse,* 440 U.S. 648, 655 (1979), where the Supreme Court rejected Delaware's argument "that patrol officers be subject to no constraints in deciding which automobiles shall be stopped for a license and registration check because the State's interest in discretionary spot checks as a means of ensuring the safety of its roadways outweighs the resulting intrusion on the privacy and security of the persons detained." *Prouse* thus does not address the issue of reasonable suspicion, and it sheds no light on whether reasonable suspicion existed in the case on review here.

III.

The officer's stop of Teamer did not transgress the requirements of the Fourth Amendment. The decision of the First District should be quashed, and Teamer's conviction and sentence should remain undisturbed.

POLSTON, J., concurs.

E. Searches, Seizures, and *Navarette v. California*

The protection against government search and seizure in Florida's Constitution states that this "right shall be construed in conformity with the 4th Amendment to the United States Constitution, as interpreted by the United States Supreme Court." Art. I, sec. 12, Fla. Const.

So this provision of the state constitution must be interpreted in light of *Navarette v. California*, 134 S. Ct. 1683, 188 L. Ed. 2d 680 (2014):

NAVARETTE

V.

CALIFORNIA

Supreme Court of the United States, 2014

134 S. Ct. 1683, 188 L. Ed. 2d 680

Justice Thomas delivered the opinion of the Court.

After a 911 caller reported that a vehicle had run her off the road, a police officer located the vehicle she identified during the call and executed a traffic stop. We hold that the stop complied with the Fourth Amendment because, under the totality of the circumstances, the officer had reasonable suspicion that the driver was intoxicated.

I

On August 23, 2008, a Mendocino County 911 dispatch team for the California Highway Patrol (CHP) received a call from another CHP dispatcher in neighboring Humboldt County. The Humboldt County dispatcher relayed a tip from a 911 caller, which the Mendocino County team recorded as follows: " 'Showing southbound Highway 1 at mile marker 88, Silver Ford 150 pickup. Plate of 8–David–94925. Ran the reporting party off the roadway and was last seen approximately five [minutes] ago.' " App. 36a. The Mendocino County team then broadcast that information to CHP officers at 3:47 p.m.

A CHP officer heading northbound toward the reported vehicle responded to the broadcast. At 4:00 p.m., the officer passed the truck near mile marker 69. At about 4:05 p.m., after making a U-turn, he pulled the truck over. A second officer, who had separately responded to the broadcast, also arrived on the scene. As the two officers approached the truck, they smelled marijuana. A search of the truck bed revealed 30 pounds of marijuana. The officers arrested the driver, petitioner Lorenzo Prado Navarette, and the passenger, petitioner José Prado Navarette.

Petitioners moved to suppress the evidence, arguing that the traffic stop violated the Fourth Amendment because the officer lacked reasonable suspicion of criminal activity. Both the magistrate who presided over the suppression hearing and the Superior Court disagreed. Petitioners pleaded guilty to transporting marijuana and were sentenced to 90 days in jail plus three years of probation.

The California Court of Appeal affirmed, concluding that the officer had reasonable suspicion to conduct an investigative stop. The court reasoned that the content of the tip indicated that it came from an eyewitness victim of reckless driving, and that the officer's corroboration of the truck's description, location, and direction established that the tip was reliable enough to justify a traffic stop. Finally, the court concluded that the caller reported driving that was sufficiently dangerous to merit an investigative stop without waiting for the officer to observe additional reckless driving himself. The California Supreme Court denied review. We granted certiorari, and now affirm.

II

The Fourth Amendment permits brief investigative stops—such as the traffic stop in this case—when a law enforcement officer has "a particularized and objective basis for suspecting the particular person stopped of criminal activity." *United States v. Cortez,* 449 U.S. 411, 417–418 (1981); see also *Terry v. Ohio,* 392 U.S. 1, 21–22 (1968). The "reasonable suspicion" necessary to justify such a stop "is dependent upon both the content of information possessed by police and its degree of reliability." *Alabama v. White,* 496 U.S. 325, 330 (1990). The standard takes into account "the totality of the circumstances—the whole picture." *Cortez, supra,* at 417. Although a mere "hunch" does not create reasonable suspicion, *Terry, supra,* at 27, the level of suspicion the standard requires is "considerably less than proof of wrongdoing by a preponderance of the evidence," and "obviously less" than is necessary for probable cause, *United States v. Sokolow,* 490 U.S. 1, 7 (1989).

A

These principles apply with full force to investigative stops based on information from anonymous tips. We have firmly rejected the argument "that reasonable cause for a[n investigative stop] can only be based on the officer's personal observation, rather than on information supplied by another person." *Adams v. Williams,* 407 U.S. 143, 147 (1972). Of course, "an anonymous tip *alone* seldom demonstrates the informant's basis of knowledge or veracity." *White,* 496 U.S. at 329 (emphasis added). That is because "ordinary citizens generally do not provide extensive recitations of the basis of their everyday observations," and an anonymous tipster's veracity is "'by hypothesis largely unknown, and unknowable.'" *Ibid.* But under appropriate circumstances, an anonymous tip can demonstrate "sufficient indicia of reliability to provide reasonable suspicion to make [an] investigatory stop." *Id.* at 327.

Our decisions in *Alabama v. White,* 496 U.S. 325 (1990), and *Florida v. J.L.,* 529 U.S. 266 (2000), are useful guides. In *White,* an anonymous tipster told the police that a woman would drive from a particular apartment building to a particular motel in a brown Plymouth station wagon with a broken right tail light. The tipster further asserted that the woman would be transporting cocaine. 496 U.S. at 327. After confirming the innocent details, officers stopped the station wagon as it neared the motel and found cocaine in the vehicle. *Id.* at 331. We held that the officers' corroboration of certain details made the anonymous tip sufficiently reliable to create reasonable suspicion of criminal activity. By accurately predicting future behavior, the tipster demonstrated "a special familiarity with respondent's affairs," which in turn implied that the tipster had "access to reliable information about that individual's illegal activities." *Id.* at 332. We also recognized that an informant who is proved to tell the truth about some things is more likely to tell the truth about other things, "including the claim that the object of the tip is engaged in criminal activity." *Id.* at 331 (citing *Illinois v. Gates,* 462 U.S. 213, 244 (1983)).

In *J.L.,* by contrast, we determined that no reasonable suspicion arose from a bare-bones tip that a young black male in a plaid shirt standing at a bus stop was carrying a gun. 529 U.S. at 268. The tipster did not explain how he knew about the gun, nor did he suggest that he had any special familiarity with the young man's affairs. *Id.* at 271. As a result, police had no basis for believing "that the tipster ha[d] knowledge of concealed criminal activity." *Id.* at 272. Furthermore, the tip included no predictions of future behavior that could be corroborated to assess the tipster's credibility. *Id.* at 271. We accordingly concluded that the tip was insufficiently reliable to justify a stop and frisk.

B

The initial question in this case is whether the 911 call was sufficiently reliable to credit the allegation that petitioners' truck "ran the [caller] off the roadway." Even assuming for present purposes that the 911 call was anonymous, we conclude that the call bore adequate indicia of reliability for the officer to credit the caller's account. The officer was therefore justified in proceeding from the premise that the truck had, in fact, caused the caller's car to be dangerously diverted from the highway.

By reporting that she had been run off the road by a specific vehicle—a silver Ford F–150 pickup, license plate 8D94925—the caller necessarily claimed eyewitness knowledge of the alleged dangerous driving. That basis of knowledge lends significant support to the tip's reliability. See *Gates, supra,* at 234 ("[An informant's] explicit and detailed description of alleged wrongdoing, along with a statement that the event was observed firsthand, entitles his tip to greater weight than might otherwise be the case"); *Spinelli v. United States,* 393 U.S. 410, 416 (1969) (a tip of illegal gambling is less reliable when "it is not alleged that the informant personally observed [the defendant] at work or that he had ever placed a bet with him"). This is in contrast to *J.L.,* where the tip provided no basis for concluding that the tipster had actually seen the gun. 529 U.S. at 271. Even in *White,* where we upheld the stop, there was scant evidence that the tipster had actually observed cocaine in the station wagon. We called *White* a "close case" because "[k]nowledge about a person's future movements indicates some familiarity with that person's affairs, but having such knowledge does not necessarily imply that the informant knows, in particular, whether that person is carrying hidden contraband." 529 U.S. at 271. A driver's claim that another vehicle ran her off the road, however, necessarily implies that the informant knows the other car was driven dangerously.

There is also reason to think that the 911 caller in this case was telling the truth. Police confirmed the truck's location near mile marker 69 (roughly 19 highway miles south of the location reported in the 911 call) at 4:00 p.m. (roughly 18 minutes after the 911 call). That timeline of events suggests that the caller reported the incident soon after she was run off the road. That sort of contemporaneous report has long been treated as especially reliable. In evidence law, we generally credit the proposition that statements about an event and made soon after perceiving that event are especially trustworthy because "substantial contemporaneity of event and statement negate the likelihood of deliberate or conscious misrepresentation." *Advisory Committee's Notes on Fed. Rule Evid. 803(1)*, 28 U.S.C.App., p. 371 (describing the rationale for the hearsay exception for "present sense impression[s]"). A similar rationale applies to a "statement relating to a startling event"—such as getting run off the road—"made while the declarant was under the stress of excitement that it caused." Fed. Rule Evid. 803(2) (hearsay exception for "excited utterances"). Unsurprisingly, 911 calls that would otherwise be inadmissible hearsay have often been admitted on those grounds. See D. Binder, HEARSAY HANDBOOK § 8.1, pp. 257–259 (4th ed. 2013–2014) (citing cases admitting 911 calls as present sense impressions); *id.* § 9.1 at 274–275 (911 calls admitted as excited utterances). There was no indication that the tip in *J L.* (or even in *White*) was contemporaneous with the observation of criminal activity or made under the stress of excitement caused by a startling event, but those considerations weigh in favor of the caller's veracity here.

Another indicator of veracity is the caller's use of the 911 emergency system. See Brief for Respondent 40–41, 44; Brief for United States as *Amicus Curiae* 16–18. A 911 call has some features that allow for identifying and tracing callers, and thus provide some safeguards against making false reports with immunity. See *J.L., supra,* at 276, 120 S.Ct. 1375 (KENNEDY, J., concurring). As this case illustrates, 911 calls can be recorded, which provides victims with an opportunity to identify the false tipster's voice and subject him to prosecution, see, *e.g.,* Cal.Penal Code Ann. § 653x (West 2010) (makes "telephon[ing] the 911 emergency line with the intent to annoy or harass" punishable by imprisonment and fine); see also § 148.3 (2014 West Cum. Supp.) (prohibits falsely reporting "that an 'emergency' exists"); § 148.5 (prohibits falsely reporting "that a felony or misdemeanor has been committed"). The 911 system also permits law enforcement to verify important information about the caller. In 1998, the Federal Communications Commission (FCC) began to require cellular carriers to relay the caller's phone number to 911 dispatchers. 47 CFR § 20.18(d)(1) (2013) (FCC's "Phase I enhanced 911 services" requirements). Beginning in 2001, carriers have been required to identify the caller's geographic location with increasing specificity. §§ 20.18(e)-(h) ("Phase II enhanced 911 service" requirements). And although callers may ordinarily block call recipients from obtaining their identifying information, FCC regulations exempt 911 calls from that privilege. §§ 64.1601(b), (d)(4)(ii) ("911 emergency services" exemption from rule that, when a caller so requests, "a carrier may not reveal that caller's number or name"). None of this is to suggest that tips in 911 calls are *per se* reliable. Given the foregoing technological and regulatory developments, however, a reasonable officer could conclude that a false tipster would think twice before using such a system. The caller's use of the 911 system is therefore one of the relevant circumstances that, taken together, justified the officer's reliance on the information reported in the 911 call.

C

Even a reliable tip will justify an investigative stop only if it creates reasonable suspicion that "criminal activity may be afoot." *Terry,* 392 U.S. at 30. We must therefore determine whether the 911 caller's report of being run off the roadway created reasonable suspicion of an ongoing crime such as drunk driving as opposed to an isolated episode of past recklessness. See *Cortez,* 449 U.S. at 417 ("An investigatory stop must be justified by some objective manifestation that the person stopped is, or is about to be, engaged in criminal activity"). We conclude that the behavior alleged by the 911 caller, "viewed from the standpoint of an objectively reasonable police officer, amount[s] to reasonable suspicion" of drunk driving. *Ornelas v. United States,* 517 U.S. 690, 696 (1996). The stop was therefore proper.

Reasonable suspicion depends on "the factual and practical considerations of everyday life on which reasonable and prudent men, not legal technicians, act." *Id.,* at 695. Under that common sense approach, we can appropriately recognize certain driving behaviors as sound indicia of drunk driving. See, *e.g., People v. Wells,* 38 Cal.4th 1078, 1081, 136 P.3d 810, 811 (2006) ("weaving all over the roadway"); *State v. Prendergast,* 103 Hawai'i 451, 452–453, 83 P.3d 714, 715–716 (2004) ("cross[ing] over the center line" on a highway and "almost caus[ing] several head-on collisions"); *State v. Golotta,* 178 N.J. 205, 209, 837 A.2d 359, 361 (2003) (driving "all over the road" and "weaving back and forth"); *State v. Walshire,* 634 N.W.2d 625, 626 (Iowa 2001) ("driving in the median"). Indeed, the accumulated experience of thousands of officers suggests that these sorts of erratic behaviors are strongly correlated with drunk driving. See Nat. Highway Traffic Safety Admin., THE VISUAL DETECTION OF DWI MOTORISTS 4–5 (Mar. 2010), online at http://nhtsa. gov/staticfiles/nti/pdf/808677.pdf (as visited Apr. 18, 2014, and available in Clerk of Court's case file). Of course, not all traffic infractions imply intoxication. Unconfirmed reports of driving without a seatbelt or slightly over the speed limit, for example, are so tenuously connected to drunk driving that a stop on those grounds alone would be constitutionally suspect. But a reliable tip alleging the dangerous behaviors discussed above generally would justify a traffic stop on suspicion of drunk driving.

The 911 caller in this case reported more than a minor traffic infraction and more than a conclusory allegation of drunk or reckless driving. Instead, she alleged a specific and dangerous result of the driver's conduct: running another car off the highway. That conduct bears too great a resemblance to paradigmatic manifestations of drunk driving to be dismissed as an isolated example of recklessness. Running another vehicle off the road suggests lane-positioning problems, decreased vigilance, impaired judgment, or some combination of those recognized drunk driving cues. See Visual Detection of DWI Motorists 4–5. And the experience of many officers suggests that a driver who almost strikes a vehicle or another object—the exact scenario that ordinarily causes "running [another vehicle] off the roadway"—is likely intoxicated. See *id.* at 5, 8. As a result, we cannot say that the officer acted unreasonably under these circumstances in stopping a driver whose alleged conduct was a significant indicator of drunk driving.

Petitioners' attempts to second-guess the officer's reasonable suspicion of drunk driving are unavailing. It is true that the reported behavior might also be explained by, for example, a driver responding to "an unruly child or other distraction." Brief for Petitioners 21. But we have consistently recognized that reasonable suspicion "need not rule out the possibility of innocent conduct." *United States v. Arvizu,* 534 U.S. 266, 277 (2002).

Nor did the absence of additional suspicious conduct, after the vehicle was first spotted by an officer, dispel the reasonable suspicion of drunk driving. Brief for Petitioners 23–24. It is hardly surprising that the appearance of a marked police car would inspire more careful driving for a time. Cf. *Arvizu, supra,* at 275 ("[s]lowing down after spotting a law enforcement vehicle" does not dispel reasonable suspicion of criminal activity). Extended observation of an allegedly drunk driver might eventually dispel a reasonable suspicion of intoxication, but the 5–minute period in this case hardly sufficed in that regard. Of course, an officer who already has such a reasonable suspicion need not surveil a vehicle at length in order to personally observe suspicious driving. See *Adams v. Williams,* 407 U.S. at 147 (repudiating the argument that "reasonable cause for a[n investigative stop] can only be based on the officer's personal observation"). Once reasonable suspicion of drunk driving arises, "[t]he reasonableness of the officer's decision to stop a suspect does not turn on the availability of less intrusive investigatory techniques." *Sokolow,* 490 U.S. at 11. This would be a particularly inappropriate context to depart from that settled rule, because allowing a drunk driver a second chance for dangerous conduct could have disastrous consequences.

III

Like *White,* this is a "close case." 496 U.S. at 332. As in that case, the indicia of the 911 caller's reliability here are stronger than those in *J.L.,* where we held that a bare-bones tip was unreliable. 529 U.S. at 271. Although the indicia present here are different from those we found sufficient in *White,* there is more than one way to demonstrate "a particularized and objective basis for suspecting the particular person stopped of criminal activity." *Cortez,* 449 U.S. at 417–418. Under the totality of the circumstances, we find the indicia of reliability in this case sufficient to provide the officer with reasonable suspicion that the driver of the reported vehicle had run another vehicle off the road. That made it reasonable under the circumstances for the officer to execute a traffic stop. We accordingly affirm.

It is so ordered.

Justice SCALIA, with whom Justice GINSBURG, Justice SOTOMAYOR, and Justice KAGAN join, dissenting.

The California Court of Appeal in this case relied on jurisprudence from the California Supreme Court (adopted as well by other courts) to the effect that "an anonymous and uncorroborated tip regarding a possibly intoxicated highway driver" provides without more the reasonable suspicion necessary to justify a stop. *People v. Wells,* 38 Cal.4th 1078, 1082, 136 P.3d 810, 812 (2006). See also, *e.g., United States v. Wheat,* 278 F.3d 722, 729–730 (C.A.8 2001); *State v. Walshire,* 634 N.W.2d 625, 626–627, 630 (Iowa 2001). Today's opinion does not explicitly adopt such a departure from our normal Fourth Amendment requirement that anonymous tips must be corroborated; it purports to adhere to our prior cases, such as *Florida v. J.L.*, 529 U.S. 266 (2000), and *Alabama v. White,* 496 U.S. 325 (1990). Be not deceived.

Law enforcement agencies follow closely our judgments on matters such as this, and they will identify at once our new rule: So long as the caller identifies where the car is, anonymous claims of a single instance of possibly careless or reckless driving, called in to 911, will support a traffic stop. This is not my concept, and I am sure would not be the Framers', of a people secure from unreasonable searches and seizures. I would reverse the judgment of the Court of Appeal of California.

I

The California Highway Patrol in this case knew nothing about the tipster on whose word—and that alone—they seized Lorenzo and José Prado

Navarette. They did not know her name. They did not know her phone number or address. They did not even know where she called from (she may have dialed in from a neighboring county, App. 33a–34a).

The tipster said the truck had "[run her] off the roadway," *id.,* at 36a, but the police had no reason to credit that charge and many reasons to doubt it, beginning with the peculiar fact that the accusation was anonymous. "[E]liminating accountability ... is ordinarily the very purpose of anonymity." *McIntyre v. Ohio Elections Comm'n,* 514 U.S. 334, 385, 115 S.Ct. 1511, 131 L.Ed.2d 426 (1995) (SCALIA, J., dissenting). The unnamed tipster "can lie with impunity," *J. L., supra,* at 275, 120 S.Ct. 1375 (KENNEDY, J., concurring). Anonymity is especially suspicious with respect to the call that is the subject of the present case. When does a victim complain to the police about an arguably criminal act (running the victim off the road) without giving his identity, so that he can accuse and testify when the culprit is caught?

The question before us, the Court agrees, *ante,* at 1690 – 1691, is whether the "content of information possessed by police and its degree of reliability," *White,* 496 U.S. at 330, gave the officers reasonable suspicion that the driver of the truck (Lorenzo) was committing an ongoing crime. When the only source of the government's information is an informant's tip, we ask whether the tip bears sufficient " 'indicia of reliability,' " *id.* at 328, to establish "a particularized and objective basis for suspecting the particular person stopped of criminal activity," *United States v. Cortez,* 449 U.S. 411, 417–418 (1981).

The most extreme case, before this one, in which an anonymous tip was found to meet this standard was *White, supra.* There the reliability of the tip was established by the fact that it predicted the target's behavior in the finest detail—a detail that could be known only by someone familiar with the target's business: She would, the tipster said, leave a particular apartment building, get into a brown Plymouth station wagon with a broken right tail light, and drive immediately to a particular motel. *Id.* at 327. Very few persons would have such intimate knowledge, and hence knowledge of the unobservable fact that the woman was carrying unlawful drugs was plausible. *Id.,* at 332. Here the Court makes a big deal of the fact that the tipster was dead right about the fact that a silver Ford F–150 truck (license plate 8D94925) was traveling south on Highway 1 somewhere near mile marker 88. But everyone in the world who saw the car would have that knowledge, and anyone who wanted the car stopped would have to provide that information. Unlike the situation in *White,* that generally available knowledge in no way makes it plausible that the tipster saw the car run someone off the road.

The Court says, *ante,* at 1689, that "[b]y reporting that she had been run off the road by a specific vehicle ... the caller necessarily claimed eyewitness knowledge." So what? The issue is not how she claimed to know, but whether what she claimed to know was true. The claim to "eyewitness knowledge" of being run off the road supports *not at all* its veracity; nor does the amazing, mystifying prediction (so far short of what existed in *White*) that the petitioners' truck *would be heading south on Highway 1.*

The Court finds "reason to think" that the informant "was telling the truth" in the fact that police observation confirmed that the truck had been driving near the spot at which, and at the approximate time at which, the tipster alleged she had been run off the road. *Ante,* at 1689. According to the Court, the statement therefore qualifies as a " 'present sense impression' " or " 'excited utterance,' " kinds of hearsay that the law deems categorically admissible given their low likelihood of reflecting " 'deliberate or conscious misrepresentation.' " *Ibid.* (quoting Advisory Committee's Notes on Fed. Rule Evid. 803(1), 28 U.S.C.App., p. 371). So, the Court says, we can fairly suppose that the accusation was true.

No, we cannot. To begin with, it is questionable whether either the "present sense impression" or the "excited utterance" exception to the hearsay rule applies here. The classic "present sense impression" is the recounting of an event that is occurring before the declarant's eyes, as the declarant is speaking ("I am watching the Hindenburg explode!"). See 2 K. Broun, McCormick on Evidence 362 (7th ed. 2013) (hereinafter McCormick). And the classic "excited utterance" is a statement elicited, almost involuntarily, by the shock of what the declarant is immediately witnessing ("My God, those people will be killed!"). See *id.* at 368–369. It is the immediacy that gives the statement some credibility; the declarant has not had time to dissemble or embellish. There is no such immediacy here. The declarant had time to observe the license number of the offending vehicle, 8D94925 (a difficult task if she was forced off the road and the vehicle was speeding away), to bring her car to a halt, to copy down the observed license number (presumably), and (if she was using her own cell phone) to dial a call to the police from the stopped car. Plenty of time to dissemble or embellish.

Moreover, even assuming that less than true immediacy will suffice for these hearsay exceptions to apply, the tipster's statement would run into additional barriers to admissibility and acceptance. According to the very Advisory Committee's Notes from which the Court quotes, cases addressing an unidentified declarant's present sense impression "indicate hesitancy in upholding the statement alone as sufficient" proof of the reported event. 28 U.S.C.App., at 371; see also 7 M. Graham, HANDBOOK OF FEDERAL EVIDENCE 19–20 (7th ed.2012). For excited utterances as well, the "knotty theoretical" question of statement-alone admissibility persists—seemingly even when the declarant is known. 2 McCormick 368. "Some courts ... have taken the position that an excited utterance is admissible only if other proof is presented which supports a finding of fact that the exciting event did occur. The issue has not yet been resolved under the Federal Rules." *Id.* at 367–368 (footnote omitted). It is even unsettled whether excited utterances of an unknown declarant are *ever* admissible. A leading treatise reports that "the courts have been reluctant to admit such statements, principally because of uncertainty that foundational requirements, including the impact of the event on the declarant, have been satisfied." *Id.* at 372. In sum, it is unlikely that the law of evidence would deem the mystery caller in this case "especially trustworthy," *ante,* at 1689.

Finally, and least tenably, the Court says that another "indicator of veracity" is the anonymous tipster's mere "use of the 911 emergency system," *ante,* at 1689. Because, you see, recent "technological and regulatory developments" suggest that the identities of unnamed 911 callers are increasingly less likely to remain unknown. *Ibid.* Indeed, the systems are able to identify "the caller's geographic location with increasing specificity." *Ibid. Amici* disagree with this, see Brief for National Association of Criminal Defense Lawyers et al. 8–12, and the present case surely suggests that *amici* are right—

since we know neither the identity of the tipster nor even the county from which the call was made. But assuming the Court is right about the ease of identifying 911 callers, it proves absolutely nothing in the present case unless the anonymous caller was *aware* of that fact. "It is the tipster's *belief* in anonymity, not its *reality,* that will control his behavior." *Id.* at 10 (emphasis added). There is no reason to believe that your average anonymous 911 tipster is aware that 911 callers are readily identifiable.

II

All that has been said up to now assumes that the anonymous caller made, at least in effect, an accusation of drunken driving. But in fact she did not. She said that the petitioners' truck " '[r]an [me] off the roadway.' " App. 36a. That neither asserts that the driver was drunk nor even raises the *likelihood* that the driver was drunk. The most it conveys is that the truck did some apparently non-typical thing that forced the tipster off the roadway, whether partly or fully, temporarily or permanently. Who really knows what (if anything) happened? The truck might have swerved to avoid an animal, a pothole, or a jaywalking pedestrian.

But let us assume the worst of the many possibilities: that it was a careless, reckless, or even intentional maneuver that forced the tipster off the road. Lorenzo might have been distracted by his use of a hands-free cell phone, see Strayer, Drews, & Crouch, A Comparison of the Cell Phone Driver and the Drunk Driver, 48 Human Factors 381, 388 (2006), or distracted by an intense sports argument with Jose, see D. Strayer et al., AAA FOUNDATION FOR TRAFFIC SAFETY, MEASURING COGNITIVE DISTRACTION IN THE AUTOMOBILE 28 (June 2013), online at https://www.aaafoundation.org/sites/default/files/MeasuringCognitiveDistractions.pdf as visited Apr. 17, 2014, and available in Clerk of Court's case file). Or, indeed, he might have intentionally forced the tipster off the road because of some personal animus, or hostility to her "Make Love, Not War" bumper sticker. I fail to see how reasonable suspicion of a *discrete instance* of irregular or hazardous driving generates a reasonable suspicion of *ongoing intoxicated driving*. What proportion of the hundreds of thousands—perhaps millions—of careless, reckless, or intentional traffic violations committed each day is attributable to drunken drivers? I say 0.1 percent. I have no basis for that except my own guesswork. But unless the Court has some basis in reality to believe that the proportion is many orders of magnitude above that—say 1 in 10 or at least 1 in 20—it has no grounds for its unsupported assertion that the tipster's report in this case gave rise to a *reasonable suspicion* of drunken driving.

Bear in mind that that is the only basis for the stop that has been asserted in this litigation.3 The stop required suspicion of an ongoing crime, not merely suspicion of having run someone off the road earlier. And driving while being a careless or reckless person, unlike driving while being a drunk person, is not an ongoing crime. In other words, in order to stop the petitioners the officers here not only had to assume without basis the accuracy of the anonymous accusation but also had to posit an unlikely reason (drunkenness) for the accused behavior.

In sum, at the moment the police spotted the truck, it was more than merely "*possib[le]*" that the petitioners were not committing an ongoing traffic crime. *United States v. Arvizu,* 534 U.S. 266, 277 (2002) (emphasis added). It was overwhelmingly likely that they were not.

III

It gets worse. Not only, it turns out, did the police have no good reason *at first* to believe that Lorenzo was driving drunk, they had very good reason *at last* to know that he was not. The Court concludes that the tip, plus confirmation of the truck's location, produced reasonable suspicion that the truck not only had been *but still was* barreling dangerously and drunkenly down Highway 1. *Ante,* at 1690 – 1692. In fact, alas, it was not, and the officers knew it. They followed the truck for five minutes, presumably to see if it was being operated recklessly. And *that* was good police work. While the anonymous tip was not enough to support a stop for drunken driving under *Terry v. Ohio,* 392 U.S. 1 (1968), it was surely enough to counsel observation of the truck to see if it was driven by a drunken driver. But the pesky little detail left out of the Court's reasonable-suspicion equation is that, for the five minutes that the truck was being followed (five minutes is a *long* time), Lorenzo's driving was irreproachable. Had the officers witnessed the petitioners violate a single traffic law, they would have had cause to stop the truck, *Whren v.*

United States, 517 U.S. 806, 810 (1996), and this case would not be before us. And not only was the driving *irreproachable,* but the State offers no evidence to suggest that the petitioners even did anything *suspicious,* such as suddenly slowing down, pulling off to the side of the road, or turning somewhere to see whether they were being followed. Cf. *Arvizu, supra,* at 270–271 (concluding that an officer's suspicion of criminality was enhanced when the driver, upon seeing that he was being followed, "slowed dramatically," "appeared stiff," and "seemed to be trying to pretend" that the patrol car was not there). Consequently, the tip's suggestion of ongoing drunken driving (if it could be deemed to suggest that) not only went uncorroborated; it was affirmatively undermined.

A hypothetical variation on the facts of this case illustrates the point. Suppose an anonymous tipster reports that, while following near mile marker 88 a silver Ford F–150, license plate 8D949925, traveling southbound on Highway 1, she saw in the truck's open cab several five-foot-tall stacks of what was unmistakably baled cannabis. Two minutes later, a highway patrolman spots the truck exactly where the tip suggested it would be, begins following it, but sees nothing in the truck's cab. It is not enough to say that the officer's observation merely failed to corroborate the tipster's accusation. It is more precise to say that the officer's observation *discredited* the informant's accusation: The crime was supposedly occurring (and would continue to occur) in plain view, but the police saw nothing. Similarly, here, the crime supposedly suggested by the tip was ongoing intoxicated driving, the hallmarks of which are many, readily identifiable, and difficult to conceal. That the officers witnessed nary a minor traffic violation nor any other "sound indici [um] of drunk driving," *ante,* at 1690, strongly suggests that the suspected crime was *not* occurring after all. The tip's implication of continuing criminality, already weak, grew even weaker.

Resisting this line of reasoning, the Court curiously asserts that, since drunk drivers who see marked squad cars in their rearview mirrors may evade detection simply by driving "more careful[ly]," the "absence of additional suspicious conduct" is "hardly surprising" and thus largely irrelevant. *Ante,* at 1691 – 1692. Whether a drunk driver drives drunkenly, the Court seems to think, is up to him. That is not how I understand the influence of alcohol. I subscribe to the more traditional view that the dangers of intoxicated driving are the intoxicant's impairing effects on the body—effects that no mere act of the will can resist. See, *e.g.*, A. Dasgupta, THE SCIENCE OF DRINKING: HOW ALCOHOL AFFECTS YOUR BODY AND MIND 39 (explaining that the physiological effect of a blood alcohol content between 0.08 and 0.109, for example, is "sever[e] impair[ment]" of "[b]alance, speech, hearing, and reaction time," as well as one's general "ability to drive a motor vehicle"). Consistent with this view, I take it as a fundamental premise of our intoxicated-driving laws that a driver soused enough to swerve once can be expected to swerve again—and soon. If he does not, and if the only evidence of his first episode of irregular driving is a mere inference from an uncorroborated, vague, and nameless tip, then the Fourth Amendment requires that he be left alone.

* * *

The Court's opinion serves up a freedom-destroying cocktail consisting of two parts patent falsity: (1) that anonymous 911 reports of traffic violations are reliable so long as they correctly identify a car and its location, and (2) that a single instance of careless or reckless driving necessarily supports a reasonable suspicion of drunkenness. All the malevolent 911 caller need do is assert a traffic violation, and the targeted car will be stopped, forcibly if necessary, by the police. If the driver turns out not to be drunk (which will almost always be the case), the caller need fear no consequences, even if 911 knows his identity. After all, he never alleged drunkenness, but merely called in a traffic violation—and on that point his word is as good as his victim's.

Drunken driving is a serious matter, but so is the loss of our freedom to come and go as we please without police interference. To prevent and detect murder we do not allow searches without probable cause or targeted *Terry* stops without reasonable suspicion. We should not do so for drunken driving either. After today's opinion all of us on the road, and not just drug dealers, are at risk of having our freedom of movement curtailed on suspicion of drunkenness, based upon a phone tip, true or false, of a single instance of careless driving. I respectfully dissent.

Notes and Questions to Consider:

1. When, if ever, must an anonymous tip be corroborated before law enforcement may act upon it?

2. The late Justice Scalia is renowned for his writing skills. To what extent does Justice Scalia's dissent reflect the power of the written word?

3. Imagine two policemen observe an orange car full of Floridians and desire to stop and search the car, but after the two policemen consult one another, they cannot conjure a legally sufficient reason to do so. The first policeman, believing the ends justify the means, leaves the presence of the second policeman and makes an anonymous 911 call like the one described in the case above. The second policeman, unaware of the actions of the first, is informed about the anonymous 911 call and based upon it stops and searches the orange car full of Floridians. Assuming the first policeman never takes responsibility for the 911 call, how can the rights of these Floridians be vindicated?

4. In the hypothetical above, what difference would it make if the anonymous 911 call described behavior that was not illegal but that the second policeman mistakenly believed to be illegal? Consider *Heinen v. North Carolina*, 135 S.Ct. 530, 190 L.Ed.2d 475 (2014):

HEIEN

V.

NORTH CAROLINA

Supreme Court of the United States, 2014

135 S.Ct. 530, 190 L.Ed.2d 475

Chief Justice Roberts delivered the opinion of the Court.

The Fourth Amendment prohibits "unreasonable searches and seizures." Under this standard, a search or seizure may be permissible even though the justification for the action includes a reasonable factual mistake. An officer might, for example, stop a motorist for traveling alone in a high-occupancy vehicle lane, only to discover upon approaching the car that two children are slumped over asleep in the back seat. The driver has not violated the law, but neither has the officer violated the Fourth Amendment.

But what if the police officer's reasonable mistake is not one of fact but of law? In this case, an officer stopped a vehicle because one of its two brake lights was out, but a court later determined that a single working brake light was all the law required. The question presented is whether such a mistake of law can nonetheless give rise to the reasonable suspicion necessary to uphold the seizure under the Fourth Amendment. We hold that it can. Because the officer's mistake about the brake-light law was reasonable, the stop in this case was lawful under the Fourth Amendment.

I

On the morning of April 29, 2009, Sergeant Matt Darisse of the Surry County Sheriff's Department sat in his patrol car near Dobson, North Carolina, observing northbound traffic on Interstate 77. Shortly before 8 a.m., a Ford Escort passed by. Darisse thought the driver looked "very stiff and nervous," so he pulled onto the interstate and began following the Escort. A few miles down the road, the Escort braked as it approached a slower vehicle, but only the left brake light came on. Noting the faulty right brake light, Darisse activated his vehicle's lights and pulled the Escort over. App. 4–7, 15–16.

Two men were in the car: Maynor Javier Vasquez sat behind the wheel, and petitioner Nicholas Brady Heien lay across the rear seat. Sergeant Darisse explained to Vasquez that as long as his license and registration checked out, he would receive only a warning ticket for the broken brake light. A records check revealed no problems with the documents, and Darisse gave Vasquez the warning ticket. But Darisse had become suspicious during the course of the stop—Vasquez appeared nervous, Heien remained lying down the entire time, and the two gave inconsistent answers about their destination. Darisse asked Vasquez if he would be willing to answer some questions. Vasquez assented, and Darisse asked whether the men were transporting various types of contraband. Told no, Darisse asked whether he could search the Escort. Vasquez said he had no objection, but told Darisse he should ask Heien, because Heien owned the car. Heien gave his consent, and Darisse, aided by a fellow officer who had since arrived, began a thorough search of the vehicle. In the side compartment of a duffle bag, Darisse found a sandwich bag containing cocaine. The officers arrested both men. 366 N.C. 271, 272–273, 737 S.E.2d 351, 352–353 (2012); App. 5–6, 25, 37.

The State charged Heien with attempted trafficking in cocaine. Heien moved to suppress the evidence seized from the car, contending that the stop and search had violated the Fourth Amendment of the United States Constitution. After a hearing at which both officers testified and the State played a video recording of the stop, the trial court denied the suppression motion, concluding that the faulty brake light had given Sergeant Darisse reasonable suspicion to initiate the stop, and that Heien's subsequent consent to the search was valid. Heien pleaded guilty but reserved his right to appeal the suppression decision. App. 1, 7–10, 12, 29, 43–44.

The North Carolina Court of Appeals reversed. 214 N.C.App. 515, 714 S.E.2d 827 (2011). The initial stop was not valid, the court held, because driving with only one working brake light was not actually a violation of North Carolina law. The relevant provision of the vehicle code provides that a car must be

> "equipped with a stop lamp on the rear of the vehicle. The stop lamp shall display a red or amber light visible from a distance of not less than 100 feet to the rear in normal sunlight, and shall be actuated upon application of the service (foot) brake. The stop lamp may be incorporated into a unit with one or more other rear lamps." N.C. Gen.Stat. Ann. § 20–129(g) (2007).

Focusing on the statute's references to "a stop lamp" and "[t]he stop lamp" in the singular, the court concluded that a vehicle is required to have only one working brake light—which Heien's vehicle indisputably did. The justification for the stop was therefore "objectively unreasonable," and the stop violated the Fourth Amendment. 214 N.C.App., at 518–522, 714 S.E.2d, at 829–831.

The State appealed, and the North Carolina Supreme Court reversed. 366 N.C. 271, 737 S.E.2d 351. Noting that the State had chosen not to seek review of the Court of Appeals' interpretation of the vehicle code, the North Carolina Supreme Court assumed for purposes of its decision that the faulty brake light was not a violation. *Id.,* at 275, 737 S.E.2d, at 354. But the court concluded that, for several reasons, Sergeant Darisse could have reasonably, even if mistakenly, read the vehicle code to require that both brake lights be in good working order. Most notably, a nearby code provision requires that "all originally equipped rear lamps" be functional. *Id.,* at 282–283, 737 S.E.2d, at 358–359 (quoting N.C. Gen.Stat. Ann. § 20–129(d)). Because Sergeant Darisse's mistaken understanding of the vehicle code was reasonable, the stop was valid. "An officer may make a mistake, including a mistake of law, yet still act reasonably under the circumstances.... [W]hen an officer acts reasonably under the circumstances, he is not violating the Fourth Amendment." *Id.,* at 279, 737 S.E.2d, at 356.

The North Carolina Supreme Court remanded to the Court of Appeals to address Heien's other arguments for suppression (which are not at issue here). *Id.,* at 283, 737 S.E.2d, at 359. The Court of Appeals rejected those arguments and affirmed the trial court's denial of his motion to suppress. [*See*] 741 S.E.2d 1 (2013). The North Carolina Supreme Court affirmed in turn. 367 N.C. 163, 749 S.E.2d 278 (2013). We granted certiorari. 134 S.Ct. 1872, 188 L.Ed.2d 910 (2014).

II

The Fourth Amendment [to the United States Constitution] provides:

> "The right of the people to be secure in their persons, houses, papers, and effects, against unreasonable searches and seizures, shall not be violated, and no Warrants shall issue, but upon probable cause, supported by Oath or affirmation, and particularly describing the place to be searched, and the persons or things to be seized."

A traffic stop for a suspected violation of law is a "seizure" of the occupants of the vehicle and therefore must be conducted in accordance with the Fourth Amendment. *Brendlin v. California,* 551 U.S. 249, 255–259, 127 S.Ct. 2400, 168 L.Ed.2d 132 (2007). All parties agree that to justify this type of seizure, officers need only "reasonable suspicion"—that is, "a particularized and objective basis for suspecting the particular person stopped" of breaking the law. *Prado Navarette v. California,* 134 S.Ct. 1683, 1687–88, 188 L.Ed.2d 680 (2014) (internal quotation marks omitted). The question here is whether reasonable suspicion can rest on a mistaken understanding of the scope of a legal prohibition. We hold that it can.

As the text indicates and we have repeatedly affirmed, "the ultimate touchstone of the Fourth Amendment is 'reasonableness.' "*Riley v. California,* 134 S.Ct. 2473, 2482, 189 L.Ed.2d 430 (2014) (some internal quotation marks omitted). To be reasonable is not to be perfect, and so the Fourth Amendment allows for some mistakes on the part of government officials, giving them "fair leeway for enforcing the law in the community's protection." *Brinegar v. United States,* 338 U.S. 160, 176, 69 S.Ct. 1302, 93 L.Ed. 1879 (1949). We have recognized that searches and seizures based on mistakes of fact can be reasonable. The warrantless search of a home, for instance, is reasonable if undertaken with the consent of a resident, and remains lawful when officers obtain the consent of someone who reasonably appears to be but is not in fact a resident. See *Illinois v. Rodriguez,* 497 U.S. 177, 183–186, 110 S.Ct. 2793, 111 L.Ed.2d 148 (1990). By the same token, if officers with probable cause to arrest a suspect mistakenly arrest an individual matching the suspect's description, neither the seizure nor an accompanying search of the arrestee would be unlawful. See *Hill v. California,* 401 U.S. 797, 802–805, 91 S.Ct. 1106, 28 L.Ed.2d 484 (1971). The limit is that "the mistakes must be those of reasonable men." *Brinegar, supra,* at 176, 69 S.Ct. 1302.

But reasonable men make mistakes of law, too, and such mistakes are no less compatible with the concept of reasonable suspicion. Reasonable suspicion arises from the combination of an officer's understanding of the facts and his understanding of the relevant law. The officer may be reasonably mistaken on either ground. Whether the facts turn out to be not what was thought, or the law turns out to be not what was thought, the result is the same: the facts are outside the scope of the law. There is no reason, under the text of the Fourth Amendment or our precedents, why this same result should be acceptable when reached by way of a reasonable mistake of fact, but not when reached by way of a similarly reasonable mistake of law.

The dissent counters that our cases discussing probable cause and reasonable suspicion, most notably *Ornelas v. United States,* 517 U.S. 690, 696–697, 116 S.Ct. 1657, 134 L.Ed.2d 911 (1996), have contained "scarcely a peep" about mistakes of law. *Post,* at 542 – 543 (opinion of Sotomayor, J.). It would have been surprising, of course, if they had, since none of those cases involved a mistake of law.

Although such recent cases did not address mistakes of law, older precedents did. In fact, cases dating back two centuries support treating legal and factual errors alike in this context. Customs statutes enacted by Congress not long after the founding authorized courts to issue certificates indemnifying customs officers against damages suits premised on unlawful seizures. See, *e.g.,* Act of Mar. 2, 1799, ch. 22, § 89, 1 Stat. 695–696. Courts were to issue such certificates on a showing that the officer had "reasonable cause"—a synonym for "probable cause"—for the challenged seizure. *Ibid.*; see *Stacey v. Emery,* 97 U.S. 642, 646, 24 L.Ed. 1035 (1878); *United States v. Riddle,* 5 Cranch 311, 3 L.Ed. 110 (1809). In *United States v. Riddle,* a customs officer seized goods on the ground that the English shipper had violated the customs laws by preparing an invoice that undervalued the merchandise, even though the American consignee declared the true value to the customs collector. Chief Justice Marshall held that there had been no violation of the customs law because, whatever the shipper's intention, the consignee had not actually attempted to defraud the Government. Nevertheless, because "the construction of the law was liable to some question," he affirmed the issuance of a certificate of probable cause: "A doubt as to the true construction of the *law* is as reasonable a cause for seizure as a doubt respecting the fact." *Id.,* at 313.

This holding—that reasonable mistakes of law, like those of fact, would justify certificates of probable cause—was reiterated in a number of 19th-century decisions. See, *e.g., The Friendship,* 9 F.Cas. 825, 826 (No. 5,125) (C.C.D.Mass.1812) (Story, J.); *United States v. The Reindeer,* 27 F.Cas. 758, 768 (No. 16,145) (C.C.D.R.I.1848); *United States v. The Recorder,* 27 F.Cas. 723 (No. 16,130) (C.C.S.D.N.Y.1849). By the Civil War, there had been "numerous cases in which [a] captured vessel was in no fault, and had not, under a true construction of the law, presented even ground of suspicion, and yet the captor was exonerated because he acted under an honest mistake of the law." *The La Manche,* 14 F.Cas. 965, 972 (No. 8,004) (D.Mass.1863).

Riddle and its progeny are not directly on point. Chief Justice Marshall was not construing the Fourth Amendment, and a certificate of probable cause functioned much like a modern-day finding of qualified immunity, which depends on an inquiry distinct from whether an officer has committed a constitutional violation. See, *e.g., Carroll v. Carman, ante,* at 7, 135 S.Ct. 348, 352 (2014) (*per curiam*). But Chief Justice Marshall was nevertheless explaining the concept of probable cause, which, he noted elsewhere, "in all cases of seizure, has a fixed and well known meaning. It imports a seizure made under circumstances which warrant suspicion." *Locke v. United States,* 7 Cranch 339, 348, 3 L.Ed. 364 (1813). We have said the phrase "probable cause" bore this "fixed and well known meaning" in the Fourth Amendment, see *Brinegar, supra,* at 175, and n. 14, 69 S.Ct. 1302, and *Riddle* illustrates that it encompassed suspicion based on reasonable mistakes of both fact and law. No decision of this Court in the two centuries since has undermined that understanding.

The contrary conclusion would be hard to reconcile with a much more recent precedent. In *Michigan v. DeFillippo,* 443 U.S. 31, 99 S.Ct. 2627, 61 L.Ed.2d 343 (1979), we addressed the validity of an arrest made under a criminal law later declared unconstitutional. A Detroit ordinance that authorized police officers to stop and question individuals suspected of criminal activity also made it an offense for such an individual "to refuse to identify himself and produce evidence of his identity." *Id.,* at 33, 99 S.Ct. 2627. Detroit police officers sent to investigate a report of public intoxication arrested Gary DeFillippo after he failed to identify himself. A search incident to arrest uncovered drugs, and DeFillippo was charged with possession of a controlled substance. The Michigan Court of Appeals ordered the suppression of the drugs, concluding that the identification ordinance was unconstitutionally vague and that DeFillippo's arrest was therefore invalid. *Id.,* at 34–35, 99 S.Ct. 2627.

Accepting the unconstitutionality of the ordinance as a given, we nonetheless reversed. At the time the officers arrested DeFillippo, we explained, "there was no controlling precedent that this ordinance was or was not constitutional, and hence the conduct observed violated a presumptively valid ordinance." *Id.,* at 37, 99 S.Ct. 2627. Acknowledging that the outcome might have been different had the ordinance been "grossly and flagrantly unconstitutional," we concluded that under the circumstances "there was abundant probable cause to satisfy the constitutional prerequisite for an arrest." *Id.,* at 37–38, 99 S.Ct. 2627.

The officers were wrong in concluding that DeFillippo was guilty of a criminal offense when he declined to identify himself. That a court only *later* declared the ordinance unconstitutional does not change the fact that DeFillippo's conduct was lawful when the officers observed it. See *Danforth v. Minnesota,* 552 U.S. 264, 271, 128 S.Ct. 1029, 169 L.Ed.2d 859 (2008). But the officers' assumption that the law was valid was reasonable, and their observations gave them "abundant probable cause" to arrest DeFillippo. 443 U.S., at 37, 99 S.Ct. 2627. Although DeFillippo could not be prosecuted under the identification ordinance, the search that turned up the drugs was constitutional.

Heien struggles to recast *DeFillippo* as a case solely about the exclusionary rule, not the Fourth Amendment itself. In his view, the officers' mistake of law resulted in a violation the Fourth Amendment, but suppression of the drugs was not the proper remedy. We did say in a footnote that suppression of the evidence found on DeFillippo would serve none of the purposes of the exclusionary rule. See *id.,* at 38, n. 3, 99 S.Ct. 2627. But that literally marginal discussion does not displace our express holding that the arrest was constitutionally valid because the officers had probable cause. See *id.,* at 40, 99 S.Ct. 2627. Nor, contrary to Heien's suggestion, did either *United States v. Leon,* 468 U.S. 897, 104 S.Ct. 3405, 82 L.Ed.2d 677 (1984), or *Illinois v. Gates,* 462 U.S. 213, 103 S.Ct. 2317, 76 L.Ed.2d 527 (1983), somehow erase that holding and transform *DeFillippo* into an exclusionary rule decision. See Brief for Petitioner 28–29. In *Leon,* we said *DeFillippo* paid "attention to the purposes underlying the exclusionary rule," but we also clarified that it did "not involv[e] the scope of the rule itself." 468 U.S., at 911–912, 104 S.Ct.

3405. As for *Gates,* only Justice White's separate opinion (joined by no other Justice) discussed *DeFillippo,* and it acknowledged that "*DeFillippo* did not modify the exclusionary rule itself" but instead "upheld the validity of an arrest." 462 U.S., at 256, n. 12, 103 S.Ct. 2317 (opinion concurring in judgment).

Heien is correct that in a number of decisions we have looked to the reasonableness of an officer's legal error in the course of considering the appropriate remedy for a constitutional violation, instead of whether there was a violation at all. See, *e.g., Davis v. United States,* 131 S.Ct. 2419, 2429–30, 180 L.Ed.2d 285 (2011) (exclusionary rule); *Illinois v. Krull,* 480 U.S. 340, 359–360, 107 S.Ct. 1160, 94 L.Ed.2d 364 (1987) (exclusionary rule); *Wilson v. Layne,* 526 U.S. 603, 615, 119 S.Ct. 1692, 143 L.Ed.2d 818 (1999) (qualified immunity); *Anderson v. Creighton,* 483 U.S. 635, 641, 107 S.Ct. 3034, 97 L.Ed.2d 523 (1987) (qualified immunity). In those cases, however, we had already found or assumed a Fourth Amendment violation. An officer's mistaken view that the conduct at issue did *not* give rise to such a violation—no matter how reasonable—could not change that ultimate conclusion. See Brief for Respondent 29–31; Brief for United States as *Amicus Curiae* 30, n. 3. Any consideration of the reasonableness of an officer's mistake was therefore limited to the separate matter of remedy.

Here, by contrast, the mistake of law relates to the antecedent question of whether it was reasonable for an officer to suspect that the defendant's conduct was illegal. If so, there was no violation of the Fourth Amendment in the first place. None of the cases Heien or the dissent cites precludes a court from considering a reasonable mistake of law in addressing that question. Cf. *Herring v. United States,* 555 U.S. 135, 139, 129 S.Ct. 695, 172 L.Ed.2d 496 (2009) (assuming a Fourth Amendment violation while rejecting application of the exclusionary rule, but noting that "[w]hen a probable-cause determination was based on reasonable but mistaken assumptions, the person subjected to a search or seizure has not necessarily been the victim of a constitutional violation").

Heien also contends that the reasons the Fourth Amendment allows some errors of fact do not extend to errors of law. Officers in the field must make factual assessments on the fly, Heien notes, and so deserve a margin of error. In Heien's view, no such margin is appropriate for questions of law: The statute here either requires one working brake light or two, and the answer does not turn on anything "an officer might suddenly confront in the field." Brief for Petitioner 21. But Heien's point does not consider the reality that an officer may "suddenly confront" a situation in the field as to which the application of a statute is unclear—however clear it may later become. A law prohibiting "vehicles" in the park either covers Segways or not, see A. Scalia & B. Garner, Reading Law: The Interpretation of Legal Texts 36–38 (2012), but an officer will nevertheless have to make a quick decision on the law the first time one whizzes by.

Contrary to the suggestion of Heien and *amici,* our decision does not discourage officers from learning the law. The Fourth Amendment tolerates only *reasonable* mistakes, and those mistakes—whether of fact or of law—must be *objectively* reasonable. We do not examine the subjective understanding of the particular officer involved. Cf. *Whren v. United States,* 517 U.S. 806, 813, 116 S.Ct. 1769, 135 L.Ed.2d 89 (1996). And the inquiry is not as forgiving as the one employed in the distinct context of deciding whether an officer is entitled to qualified immunity for a constitutional or statutory violation. Thus, an officer can gain no Fourth Amendment advantage through a sloppy study of the laws he is duty-bound to enforce.

Finally, Heien and *amici* point to the well-known maxim, "Ignorance of the law is no excuse," and contend that it is fundamentally unfair to let police officers get away with mistakes of law when the citizenry is accorded no such leeway. Though this argument has a certain rhetorical appeal, it misconceives the implication of the maxim. The true symmetry is this: Just as an individual generally cannot escape criminal liability based on a mistaken understanding of the law, so too the government cannot impose criminal liability based on a mistaken understanding of the law. If the law required two working brake lights, Heien could not escape a ticket by claiming he reasonably thought he needed only one; if the law required only one, Sergeant Darisse could not issue a valid ticket by claiming he reasonably thought drivers needed two. But just because mistakes of law cannot justify either the imposition or the avoidance of criminal liability, it does not follow that they cannot justify an investigatory stop. And Heien is not appealing a brake-light ticket; he is appealing a cocaine-trafficking conviction as to which there is no asserted mistake of fact or law.

III

Here we have little difficulty concluding that the officer's error of law was reasonable. Although the North Carolina statute at issue refers to "*a* stop lamp," suggesting the need for only a single working brake light, it also provides that "[t]he stop lamp may be incorporated into a unit with one or more *other* rear lamps." N.C. Gen.Stat. Ann. § 20–129(g) (emphasis added). The use of "other" suggests to the everyday reader of English that a "stop lamp" is a type of "rear lamp." And another subsection of the same provision requires that vehicles "have all originally equipped rear lamps or the equivalent in good working order," § 20–129(d), arguably indicating that if a vehicle has multiple "stop lamp[s]," all must be functional.

The North Carolina Court of Appeals concluded that the "rear lamps" discussed in subsection (d) do not include brake lights, but, given the "other," it would at least have been reasonable to think they did. Both the majority and the dissent in the North Carolina Supreme Court so concluded, and we agree. See 366 N.C., at 282–283, 737 S.E.2d, at 358–359; *id.,* at 283, 737 S.E.2d, at 359 (Hudson, J., dissenting) (calling the Court of Appeals' decision "surprising"). This "stop lamp" provision, moreover, had never been previously construed by North Carolina's appellate courts. See *id.,* at 283, 737 S.E.2d, at 359 (majority opinion). It was thus objectively reasonable for an officer in Sergeant Darisse's position to think that Heien's faulty right brake light was a violation of North Carolina law. And because the mistake of law was reasonable, there was reasonable suspicion justifying the stop.

The judgment of the Supreme Court of North Carolina is

Affirmed.

Justice KAGAN, with whom Justice GINSBURG joins, concurring.

I concur in full in the Court's opinion, which explains why certain mistakes of law can support the reasonable suspicion needed to stop a vehicle under the Fourth Amendment. In doing so, the Court correctly emphasizes that the "Fourth Amendment tolerates only ... *objectively* reasonable" mistakes of law. *Ante,* at 539. And the Court makes clear that the inquiry into whether an officer's mistake of law counts as objectively reasonable "is not as forgiving as the one employed in the distinct context of deciding whether an officer is entitled to qualified immunity." *Ibid.* I write separately to elaborate briefly on those important limitations.

First, an officer's "subjective understanding" is irrelevant: As the Court notes, "[w]e do not examine" it at all. *Ibid.* That means the government cannot defend an officer's mistaken legal interpretation on the ground that the officer was unaware of or untrained in the law. And it means that, contrary to the dissenting opinion in the court below, an officer's reliance on "an incorrect memo or training program from the police department" makes no difference to the analysis. 366 N.C. 271, 284, 737 S.E.2d 351, 360 (2012) (Hudson, J., dissenting). Those considerations pertain to the officer's subjective understanding of the law and thus cannot help to justify a seizure.

Second, the inquiry the Court permits today is more demanding than the one courts undertake before awarding qualified immunity. See Tr. of Oral Arg. 51 (Solicitor General stating that the two tests "require essentially the opposite" showings); Brief for Respondent 31–32 (making a similar point). Our modern qualified immunity doctrine protects "all but the plainly incompetent or those who knowingly violate the law." *Ashcroft v. al–Kidd,* 131 S.Ct. 2074, 2085, 179 L.Ed.2d 1149 (2011) (quoting *Malley v. Briggs,* 475 U.S. 335, 341, 106 S.Ct. 1092, 89 L.Ed.2d 271 (1986)). By contrast, Justice Story's opinion in *The Friendship,* 9 F.Cas. 825, 826 (No. 5,125)(C.C.D.Mass.1812) (cited *ante,* at 537), suggests the appropriate standard for deciding when a legal error can support a seizure: when an officer takes a reasonable view of a "vexata questio" on which different judges "h[o]ld opposite opinions." See Brief for United States as *Amicus Curiae* 26 (invoking that language). Or to make the same point without the Latin, the test is satisfied when the law at issue is "so doubtful in construction" that a reasonable judge could agree with the officer's view. *The Friendship,* 9 F.Cas., at 826.

A court tasked with deciding whether an officer's mistake of law can support a seizure thus faces a straightforward question of statutory construction. If the statute is genuinely ambiguous, such that overturning the officer's judgment requires hard interpretive work, then the officer has made a reasonable mistake. But if not, not. As the Solicitor General made the point at oral argument, the statute must pose a "really difficult" or "very hard question of statutory interpretation." Tr. of Oral Arg. 50. And indeed, both North Carolina and the Solicitor General agreed that such cases will be "exceedingly rare." Brief for Respondent 17; Tr. of Oral Arg. 48.

The Court's analysis of Sergeant Darisse's interpretation of the North Carolina law at issue here appropriately reflects these principles. As the Court explains, see *ante,* at 540, the statute requires every car on the highway to have "a stop lamp," in the singular. N.C. Gen.Stat. Ann. § 20–129(g) (2007). But the statute goes on to state that a stop lamp (or, in more modern terminology, brake light) "may be incorporated into a unit with one or more *other* rear lamps," suggesting that a stop lamp itself qualifies as a rear lamp. *Ibid.* (emphasis added). And the statute further mandates that every car have "*all* originally equipped rear lamps ... in good working order." § 20–129(d) (emphasis added). The North Carolina Court of Appeals dealt with the statute's conflicting signals in one way (deciding that a brake light is *not* a rear lamp, and so only one needs to work); but a court could easily take the officer's view (deciding that a brake light *is*a rear lamp, and if a car comes equipped with more than one, as modern cars do, all must be in working order). The critical point is that the statute poses a quite difficult question of interpretation, and Sergeant Darisse's judgment, although overturned, had much to recommend it. I therefore agree with the Court that the traffic stop he conducted did not violate the Fourth Amendment.

Justice SOTOMAYOR, dissenting.

The Court is, of course, correct that "the ultimate touchstone of the Fourth Amendment is 'reasonableness.'" *Riley v. California,* 134 S.Ct. 2473, 2482 (2014). But this broad statement simply sets the standard a court is to apply when it conducts its inquiry into whether the Fourth Amendment has been violated. It does not define the categories of inputs that courts are to consider when assessing the reasonableness of a search or seizure, each of which must be independently justified. What this case requires us to decide is whether a police officer's understanding of the law is an input into the reasonableness inquiry, or whether this inquiry instead takes the law as a given and assesses an officer's understanding of the facts against a fixed legal yardstick.

I would hold that determining whether a search or seizure is reasonable requires evaluating an officer's understanding of the facts against the actual state of the law. I would accordingly reverse the judgment of the North Carolina Supreme Court, and I respectfully dissent from the Court's contrary holding….

…[W]hen we have talked about the leeway that officers have in making probable-cause determinations, we have focused on their assessments of facts. See, *e.g., Terry v. Ohio,* 392 U.S. 1, 21–22 (1968) (framing the question as whether the "facts" give rise to reasonable suspicion). We have conceded that an arresting officer's state of mind does not factor into the probable-cause inquiry, "except for *the facts* that he knows." *Devenpeck v. Alford,* 543 U.S. 146, 153 (2004) (emphasis added). And we have said that, to satisfy the reasonableness requirement, "what is generally demanded of the many *factual determinations* that must regularly be made by agents of the government ... is not that they always be correct, but that they always be reasonable." *Illinois v. Rodriguez,* 497 U.S. 177, 185 (1990) (emphasis added). There is scarcely a peep in these cases to suggest that an officer's understanding or conception of anything other than the facts is relevant.

This framing of the reasonableness inquiry has not only been focused on officers' understanding of the facts, it has been justified in large part based on the recognition that officers are generally in a superior position, relative to courts, to evaluate those facts and their significance as they unfold. In other words, the leeway we afford officers' factual assessments is rooted not only in our recognition that police officers operating in the field have to make quick decisions, see *id.,* at 186, 110 S.Ct. 2793, but also in our understanding that police officers have the expertise to "dra[w] inferences and mak[e] deductions ... that might well elude an untrained person." *United States v. Cor-*

tez, 449 U.S. 411, 418 (1981). When officers evaluate unfolding circumstances, they deploy that expertise to draw "conclusions about human behavior" much in the way that "jurors [do] *as factfinders.*" *Ibid.* (emphasis added).

The same cannot be said about legal exegesis. After all, the meaning of the law is not probabilistic in the same way that factual determinations are. Rather, "the notion that the law is definite and knowable" sits at the foundation of our legal system. *Cheek v. United States,* 498 U.S. 192, 199 (1991). And it is courts, not officers, that are in the best position to interpret the laws....

... Traffic stops like those at issue here can be "annoying, frightening, and perhaps humiliating." *Terry,* 392 U.S. at 25; see *Delaware v. Prouse,* 440 U.S. 648, 657 (1979). We have nevertheless held that an officer's subjective motivations do not render a traffic stop unlawful. *Whren v. United States,* 517 U.S. 806 (1996). But we assumed in *Whren* that when an officer acts on pretext, at least that pretext would be the violation of an actual law. See *id.,* at 810 (discussing the three provisions of the District of Columbia traffic code that the parties accepted the officer had probable cause to believe had been violated). Giving officers license to effect seizures so long as they can attach to their reasonable view of the facts some reasonable legal interpretation (or misinterpretation) that suggests a law has been violated significantly expands this authority. Cf. *Barlow v. United States,* 7 Pet. 404, 411, 8 L.Ed. 728 (1833) (Story, J.) ("There is scarcely any law which does not admit of some ingenious doubt"). One wonders how a citizen seeking to be law-abiding and to structure his or her behavior to avoid these invasive, frightening, and humiliating encounters could do so.

In addition to these human consequences—including those for communities and for their relationships with the police—permitting mistakes of law to justify seizures has the perverse effect of preventing or delaying the clarification of the law. Under such an approach, courts need not interpret statutory language but can instead simply decide whether an officer's interpretation was reasonable. Indeed, had this very case arisen after the North Carolina Supreme Court announced its rule, the North Carolina Court of Appeals would not have had the occasion to interpret the statute at issue. Similarly, courts in the Eighth Circuit, which has been the only Circuit to include police mistakes of law in the reasonableness inquiry, have observed that they need not decide interpretive questions under their approach. See,*e.g., United States v. Rodriguez–Lopez,* 444 F.3d 1020, 1022–1023 (C.A.8 2006). This result is bad for citizens, who need to know their rights and responsibilities, and it is bad for police, who would benefit from clearer direction. Cf. *Camreta v. Greene,* 131 S.Ct. 2020, 2031–32 (2011) (recognizing the importance of clarifying the law).

Of course, if the law enforcement system could not function without permitting mistakes of law to justify seizures, one could at least argue that permitting as much is a necessary evil. But I have not seen any persuasive argument that law enforcement will be unduly hampered by a rule that precludes consideration of mistakes of law in the reasonableness inquiry. After all, there is no indication that excluding an officer's mistake of law from the reasonableness inquiry has created a problem for law enforcement in the overwhelming number of Circuits which have adopted that approach. If an officer makes a stop in good faith but it turns out that, as in this case, the officer was wrong about what the law proscribed or required, I know of no penalty that the officer would suffer. See 366 N.C. 271, 286–288, 737 S.E.2d 351, 361–362 (2012) (Hudson, J., dissenting) (observing that "officers (rightfully) face no punishment for a stop based on a mistake of law"). Moreover, such an officer would likely have a defense to any civil suit on the basis of qualified immunity. See *Ashcroft v. al–Kidd,* 131 S.Ct. 2074, 2085 (2011) ("Qualified immunity gives government officials breathing room to make reasonable but mistaken judgments about open legal questions").

Nor will it often be the case that any evidence that may be seized during the stop will be suppressed, thanks to the exception to the exclusionary rule for good-faith police errors. See, *e.g., Davis v. United States*, 131 S.Ct. 2419, 2427–28 (2011). It is true that, unlike most States, North Carolina does not provide a good-faith exception as a matter of state law, see *State v. Carter,* 322 N.C. 709, 721–724, 370 S.E.2d 553, 560–562 (1988), but North Carolina recognizes that it may solve any remedial problems it may perceive on its own, see *id.,* at 724, 370 S.E.2d, at 562; N.C. Gen.Stat. Ann. § 15A–974 (2013) (statutory good-faith exception). More fundamentally, that is a remedial concern, and the protections offered by the Fourth Amendment are not meant to yield to accommodate remedial concerns. Our jurisprudence draws a sharp "analytica[l] distinct[ion]" between the existence of a Fourth Amendment violation and the remedy for that violation. *Davis,* 131 S.Ct., at 2431.

In short, there is nothing in our case law requiring us to hold that a reasonable mistake of law can justify a seizure under the Fourth Amendment, and quite a bit suggesting just the opposite. I also see nothing to be gained from such a holding, and much to be lost.

III

In reaching the contrary conclusion, the Court makes both serious legal and practical errors. On the legal side, the Court barely addresses *Ornelas* and the other cases that frame the reasonableness inquiry around factual determinations. Instead, in support of its conclusion that reasonable suspicion "arises from the *combination* of an officer's understanding of the facts *and* his understanding of the relevant law," *ante,* at 536 (emphasis added), the Court first reaches to founding-era customs statutes and cases applying those statutes. It concedes, however, that these cases are "not directly on point" because they say nothing about the scope of the Fourth Amendment and are instead equivalents of our modern-day qualified immunity jurisprudence for civil damages. *Ante,* at 537.

The only link in the tenuous chain the Court constructs between those cases and this one that has anything to say about the Fourth Amendment is *Brinegar v. United States,* 338 U.S. 160 (1949). See *ante,* at 537 – 538. But all that our opinion in *Brinegar* actually says is that probable cause exists where " 'the facts and circumstances within [the officers'] knowledge and of which they had reasonably trustworthy information [are] sufficient in themselves to warrant a man of reasonable caution in the belief that' an offense has been or is being committed." 338 U.S. at 175–176 (quoting *Carroll v. United States,* 267 U.S. 132, 162 (1925)). It thus states the uncontroversial proposition that the probable-cause inquiry looks to the reasonableness of an officer's understanding of the facts. Indeed, *Brinegar* is an odd case for the Court to rely on given that, like the cases I discussed above, it subsequently emphasizes that "the mistakes must be those of reasonable men, acting on *facts* leading sensibly to their conclusions of probability." 338 U.S. at 176 (emphasis added). Again, reasonable understandings of the facts, not reasonable understandings of what the law says....

...To my mind, the more administrable approach—and the one more consistent with our precedents and principles—would be to hold that an officer's mistake of law, no matter how reasonable, cannot support the individualized suspicion necessary to justify a seizure under the Fourth Amendment. I respectfully dissent.

Notes and Questions to Consider:

1. How many times can the same officer make the same mistake of law and it still constitute a reasonable mistake sufficient to support the individualized suspicion necessary to justify a seizure?

2. When can a citizen make a reasonable mistake of law yet still avoid the adverse consequences that arise?

3. C an a series of innocent acts, none of which is sufficient by itself to support an individualized suspicion necessary to support a search, together add up to an individualized suspicion?

F. Pretrial Release and Detention

Article I, Section 14 of Florida's Constitution provides:

> *Pretrial release and detention.*—Unless charged with a capital offense or an offense punishable by life imprisonment and the proof of guilt is evident or the presumption is great, every person charged with a crime or violation of municipal or county ordinance shall be entitled to pretrial release on reasonable conditions. If no conditions of release can reasonably protect the community from risk of physical harm to persons, assure the presence of the accused at trial, or assure the integrity of the judicial process, the accused may be detained.

G. Prosecution of Offenses Committed by Children

Article I, Section 15 of Florida's Constitution provides:

Prosecution for crime; offenses committed by children.—

(a) No person shall be tried for capital crime without presentment or indictment by a grand jury, or for other felony without such presentment or indictment or an information under oath filed by the prosecuting officer of the court, except persons on active duty in the militia when tried by courts martial.

(b) When authorized by law, a child as therein defined may be charged with a violation of law as an act of delinquency instead of crime and tried without a jury or other requirements applicable to criminal cases. Any child so charged shall, upon demand made as provided by law before a trial in a juvenile proceeding, be tried in an appropriate court as an adult. A child found delinquent shall be disciplined as provided by law.

H. Rights of Accused and of Victims

Article I, Section 16 of Florida's Constitution provides:

Rights of accused and of victims.—

(a) In all criminal prosecutions the accused shall, upon demand, be informed of the nature and cause of the accusation, and shall be furnished a copy of the charges, and shall have the right to have compulsory process for witnesses, to confront at trial adverse witnesses, to be heard in person, by counsel or both, and to have a speedy and public trial by impartial jury in the county where the crime was committed. If the county is not known, the indictment or information may charge venue in two or more counties conjunctively and proof that the crime was committed in that area shall be sufficient; but before pleading the accused may elect in which of those counties the trial will take place.

Venue for prosecution of crimes committed beyond the boundaries of the state shall be fixed by law.

(b) To preserve and protect the right of crime victims to achieve justice, ensure a meaningful role throughout the criminal and juvenile justice systems for crime victims, and ensure that crime victims' rights and interests are respected and protected by law in a manner no less vigorous than protections afforded to criminal defendants and juvenile delinquents, every victim is entitled to the following rights, beginning at the time of his or her victimization:

(1) The right to due process and to be treated with fairness and respect for the victim's dignity.

(2) The right to be free from intimidation, harassment, and abuse.

(3) The right, within the judicial process, to be reasonably protected from the accused and any person acting on behalf of the accused. However, nothing contained herein is intended to create a special relationship between the crime victim and any law enforcement agency or office absent a special relationship or duty as defined by Florida law.

(4) The right to have the safety and welfare of the victim and the victim's family considered when setting bail, including setting pretrial release conditions that protect the safety and welfare of the victim and the victim's family.

(5) The right to prevent the disclosure of information or records that could be used to locate or harass the victim or the victim's family, or which could disclose confidential or privileged information of the victim.

(6) A victim shall have the following specific rights upon request:

a. The right to reasonable, accurate, and timely notice of, and to be present at, all public proceedings involving the criminal conduct, including, but not limited to, trial, plea, sentencing, or adjudication, even if the victim will be a witness at the proceeding, notwithstanding any rule to the contrary. A victim shall also be provided reasonable, accurate, and timely notice of any release or escape of the defendant or delinquent, and any proceeding during which a right of the victim is implicated.

b. The right to be heard in any public proceeding involving pretrial or other release from any form of legal constraint, plea, sentencing, adjudication, or parole, and any proceeding during which a right of the victim is implicated.

c. The right to confer with the prosecuting attorney concerning any plea agreements, participation in pretrial diversion programs, release, restitution, sentencing, or any other disposition of the case.

d. The right to provide information regarding the impact of the offender's conduct on the victim and the victim's family to the individual responsible for conducting any presentence investigation or compiling any presentence investigation report, and to have any such information considered in any sentencing recommendations submitted to the court.

e. The right to receive a copy of any presentence report, and any other report or record relevant to the exercise of a victim's right, except for such portions made confidential or exempt by law.

f. The right to be informed of the conviction, sentence, adjudication, place and time of incarceration, or other disposition of the convicted offender, any scheduled release date of the offender, and the release of or the escape of the offender from custody.

g. The right to be informed of all postconviction processes and procedures, to participate in such processes and procedures, to provide information to the release authority to be considered before any release decision is made, and to be notified of any release decision regarding the offender. The parole or early release authority shall extend the right to be heard to any person harmed by the offender.

h. The right to be informed of clemency and expungement procedures, to provide information to the governor, the court, any clemency board, and other authority in these procedures, and to have that information considered before a clemency or expungement decision is made; and to be notified of such decision in advance of any release of the offender.

(7) The rights of the victim, as provided in subparagraph (6)a., subparagraph (6)b., or subparagraph (6)c., that apply to any first appearance proceeding are satisfied by a reasonable attempt by the appropriate agency to notify the victim and convey the victim's views to the court.

(8) The right to the prompt return of the victim's property when no longer needed as evidence in the case.

(9) The right to full and timely restitution in every case and from each convicted offender for all losses suffered, both directly and indirectly, by the victim as a result of the criminal conduct.

(10) The right to proceedings free from unreasonable delay, and to a prompt and final conclusion of the case and any related postjudgment proceedings.

a. The state attorney may file a good faith demand for a speedy trial and the trial court shall hold a calendar call, with notice, within fifteen days of the filing demand, to schedule a trial to commence on a date at least five days but no more than sixty days after the date of the calendar call unless the trial judge enters an order with specific findings of fact justifying a trial date more than sixty days after the calendar call.

b. All state-level appeals and collateral attacks on any judgment must be complete within two years from the date of appeal in non-capital cases and within five years from the date of appeal in capital cases, unless a court enters an order with specific findings as to why the court was unable to comply with this subparagraph and the circumstances causing the delay. Each year, the chief judge of any district court of appeal or the chief justice of the supreme court shall report on a case-by-case basis to the speaker of the house of representatives and the president of the senate all cases where the court entered an order regarding inability to comply with this subparagraph. The legislature may enact legislation to implement this subparagraph.

(11) The right to be informed of these rights, and to be informed that victims can seek the advice of an attorney with respect to their rights. This information shall be made available to the general public and provided to all crime victims in the form of a card or by other means intended to effectively advise the victim of their rights under this section.

(c) The victim, the retained attorney of the victim, a lawful representative of the victim, or the office of the state attorney upon request of the victim, may assert and seek enforcement of the rights enumerated in this section and any other right afforded to a victim by law in any trial or appellate court, or before any other authority with jurisdiction over the case, as a matter of right. The court or other authority with jurisdiction shall act promptly on such a request, affording a remedy by due course of law for the violation of any right. The reasons for any decision regarding the disposition of a victim's right shall be clearly stated on the record.

(d) The granting of the rights enumerated in this section to victims may not be construed to deny or impair any other rights possessed by victims. The provisions of this section apply throughout criminal and juvenile justice processes, are self-executing, and do not require implementing legislation. This section may not be construed to create any cause of action for damages against the state or a political subdivision of the state, or any officer, employee, or agent of the state or its political subdivisions.

(e) As used in this section, a "victim" is a person who suffers direct or threatened physical, psychological, or financial harm as a result of the commission or attempted commission of a crime or delinquent act or against whom the crime or delinquent act is committed. The term "victim" includes the victim's lawful representative, the parent or guardian of a minor, or the next of kin of a homicide victim, except upon a showing that the interest of such individual would be in actual or potential conflict with the interests of the victim. The term "victim" does not include the accused. The terms "crime" and "criminal" include delinquent acts and conduct.

I. Excessive Punishments

Article I, Section 17 of Florida's Constitution provides, in relevant part:

Excessive punishments.—Excessive fines, cruel and unusual punishment, attainder, forfeiture of estate, indefinite imprisonment, and unreasonable detention of witnesses are forbidden. . . .The prohibition against cruel or unusual punishment, and the prohibition against cruel and unusual punishment, shall be construed in conformity with decisions of the United States Supreme Court which interpret the prohibition against cruel and unusual punishment provided in the Eighth Amendment to the United States Constitution. . . . Methods of execution may be designated by the legislature, and a change in any method of execution may be applied retroactively. A sentence of death shall not be reduced on the basis that a method of execution is invalid....

Chapter Fourteen

Amending Florida's Constitution

A. Different than Amending the U.S. Constitution

"Unlike the Federal Constitution, Florida's Constitution is constantly being amended." *Amending the Constitution*, 18 Nova L. Rev. 1487 (1994). "The Florida Constitution has more methods of amendment than any other state constitution." P.K. Jameson & Marsha Hoscak, *Citizen Initiatives in Florida: An Analysis of Florida's Constitutional Initiative Process, Issues, and Alternatives*, 23 Fla. St. U. L.Rev. 417, 424 (1995).

To learn how to amend an American constitution, we look to the plain language of the constitution itself. Like the federal Constitution, the Constitution of the State of Florida may be amended by following the terms and conditions that are stated in the text of the constitution. But the terms and conditions of amending the federal and the Florida Constitution are quite different.

To amend the U.S. Constitution, Article V of that document states:

> The Congress, whenever two thirds of both houses shall deem it necessary, shall propose amendments to this Constitution, or, on the application of the legislatures of two thirds of the several states, shall call a convention for proposing amendments, which, in either case, shall be valid to all intents and purposes, as part of this Constitution, when ratified by the legislatures of three fourths of the several states, or by conventions in three fourths thereof, as the one or the other mode of ratification may be proposed by the Congress; provided that no amendment which may be made prior to the year one thousand eight hundred and eight shall in any manner affect the first and fourth clauses in the ninth section of the first article; and that no state, without its consent, shall be deprived of its equal suffrage in the Senate.

Art. V, U.S. Const.

By comparison, the terms and conditions for amending Florida's Constitution appear in Article XI where it is not Florida's counties but Florida's citizenry who decide the fate of amendments to Florida's Constitution. As you will see in this chapter, Article XI of Florida's Constitution offers five sources of proposed constitutional amendments. The success or failure of any proposal, regardless of its source, depends upon a vote of the people of the State of Florida.

The January 1996 edition of Columbia Law Review contained the article by Henry Paul Monaghan, *We the People(s), Original Understanding, and Constitutional Amendment*, 96 Colum. L. Rev. 121 (1996) that considered, in part, the role of the people in amending the federal Constitution.

WE THE PEOPLE(S), ORIGINAL UNDERSTANDING, AND CONSTITUTIONAL AMENDMENT

Henry Paul Monaghan

96 Colum. L. Rev. 121

> Given current interest in the relationship between state and national power, it is important to examine…the amendment process outlined in Article V in some detail. Article V clearly demonstrates that, in requiring supermajorities to amend the Constitution and in entrenching state equality in the Senate, the original Constitution not only envisaged the continued existence of the states as vital parts of the new constitutional order, but also excluded the people from any direct role in constitution-making.
>
> *Article V*
>
> The place to begin, of course, is with the text of Article V itself. The constitutional text clearly shows that the states were given the key role in approving amendments to the charter of the national government. The supermajority requirement further reinforces the distinctly undemocratic features of the Constitution.

> Article V was designed to permit a very small number of states (currently thirteen) containing but a fraction of the total national population to block constitutional change. Constitutional amendments require both initiation and approval by large supermajorities of Congress ("two thirds of both Houses") and of the states ("three fourths of the several States"). Amendments also require an interaction between Congress and the several states. There is no role in the amending process for a national "We the People of the United States." Even after all that, "no State, without its Consent, shall be deprived of equal Suffrage in the Senate."
>
> Federalist No. 39 has long been understood to provide the canonical explanation for Article V's strongly state-centered (and countermajoritarian) process. In a famous passage, Madison states that:
>
>> [The Constitution] is neither wholly national nor wholly federal. Were it wholly national, the supreme and ultimate authority would reside in the majority of the people of the Union; and this authority would be competent at all times, like that of a majority of every national society to alter or abolish its established government.... In requiring more than a majority, and particularly in computing the proportion by States, not by citizens, it departs from the national and advances towards the federal character.
>
> In Federalist No. 43, Madison adds that Article V's amendment mechanism "guards...against that extreme facility, which would render the Constitution too mutable."
>
> Article V has been almost universally understood to be the exclusive method for amending the Constitution.

Id. at 125–27.

Putting aside the issue of why Article V of the federal Constitution reads as it does, history suggests that Article V's language has not "render[ed] the Constitution too mutable." In the more than 230 years since the U.S. Constitution was approved on September 17, 1787 by the majority of the delegates to the Constitutional Convention, the Constitution had only 27 amendments.

State constitutions do not share the characteristic of a lack of mutability. Nor do state constitutions further a goal, if any, of excluding the people from amending the constitution. To the contrary, state constitutions have been criticized for the ease and frequency of amendments.

Notes and Questions to Consider:

1. You represent a client who does not like a part of Florida's Constitution. What can you do about that?

2. Would society benefit from allowing the U.S. Constitution to be amended with the relative ease and frequency of Florida's Constitution?

B. Five Methods of Proposing Amendments

Five methods exist for proposing amendments to Florida's Constitution. In the next 5 subsections of this chapter, we discuss each in turn. Each method results in a proposal. Each proposal is put before Florida's electorate. So regardless of the origin of the proposal, all amendments are made by a vote of the people of the State of Florida – if Florida's courts allow such a vote. The penultimate section of this chapter discusses the requirements for the vote, and as discussed in the final subsection of this chapter, grounds exist for Florida courts to strike a proposal from the ballot.

1. Proposal by Florida's Legislature

"State legislatures typically have a role in amending state constitutions, and Florida is no exception. According to Article XI Section 1 of the Florida Constitution, the Florida Legislature may propose an amendment to the Florida Constitution via a joint resolution agreed to by three-fifths of the membership of each house of the legislature." Patrick John McGinley, FLORIDA MUNICIPAL LAW AND PRACTICE § 1:4 (2017-2018 ed.). The relevant language appears in Florida's Constitution in its Article XI where is says:

> *SECTION 1. Proposal by legislature.*—Amendment of a section or revision of one or more articles, or the whole, of this constitution may be

proposed by joint resolution agreed to by three-fifths of the membership of each house of the legislature. The full text of the joint resolution and the vote of each member voting shall be entered on the journal of each house.

2. Constitutional Revision Commission

Florida's Constitutional Revision Commission, or CRC, is a:

> means by which a proposed amendment may arise [that] is rather unique to Florida.... Once every 20 years, a 37-member revision commission is created as required by Florida's Constitution for the purpose of reviewing Florida's Constitution and proposing changes for voter consideration. The 37 members consist of the Florida Attorney General, three members appointed by the Chief Judge of the Supreme Court of Florida, nine members each by the Florida Senate President and Speaker of the House of Representatives, and the remaining 15 members (including the chairman) by Florida's Governor. The Commission typically meets for approximately one year to perform its research and possibly recommend changes. The commission's final recommendations are transmitted to the Florida Secretary of State to be included in the November ballot for voting by the franchised citizens of Florida. The last comprehensive review of Florida's Constitution occurred in 2017.

Patrick John McGinley, FLORIDA MUNICIPAL LAW AND PRACTICE § 1:4 (2017-2018 ed.). The CRC's operative language appears in Florida's Constitution in Article XI which reads:

> *SECTION 2. Revision commission.—*
>
> (a) Within thirty days before the convening of the 2017 regular session of the legislature, and each twentieth year thereafter, there shall be established a constitution revision commission composed of the following thirty-seven members:
>
> (1) the attorney general of the state;
>
> (2) fifteen members selected by the governor;
>
> (3) nine members selected by the speaker of the house of represent-

atives and nine members selected by the president of the senate; and

(4) three members selected by the chief justice of the supreme court of Florida with the advice of the justices.

(b) The governor shall designate one member of the commission as its chair. Vacancies in the membership of the commission shall be filled in the same manner as the original appointments.

(c) Each constitution revision commission shall convene at the call of its chair, adopt its rules of procedure, examine the constitution of the state, hold public hearings, and, not later than one hundred eighty days prior to the next general election, file with the custodian of state records its proposal, if any, of a revision of this constitution or any part of it.

3. Initiative by the People

The 1968 enactment of Florida's Constitution provided citizens with the right to propose amendments to the constitution by initiative. This means that "[r]esidents of Florida have a specific right that citizens of many other states do not have. They have the power to amend their state constitution by gathering a set number of signatures on petitions calling for an amendment to be placed on a statewide ballot for ratification." Jim Smith, *So You Want to Amend the Florida Constitution? A Guide to Initiative Petitions*, 18 Nova L. Rev. 1509. 1510 (1994).

Note that Floridians are the direct origin of these proposed constitutional amendments, and no involvement is required of Florida's executive, legislative, or judicial branches, no involvement by any state agency or administrative law entity, and no involvement by any county, city, town, village law-making body. This makes a citizen initiative different from a referendum. "Earlier Florida Constitutions provided for a referendum to amend or revise the constitution. A referendum is first proposed by the Legislature and then decided by the voters at a general election. Initiatives, by contrast, originate with the people and do not require legislative approval." *Id.*

The operative language appears in Article XI of Florida's Constitution and reads:

> *SECTION 3. Initiative.*—The power to propose the revision or amendment of any portion or portions of this constitution by initiative is reserved to the people, provided that, any such revision or amendment, except for those limiting the power of government to raise revenue, shall embrace but one subject and matter directly connected therewith. It may be invoked by filing with the custodian of state records a petition containing a copy of the proposed revision or amendment, signed by a number of electors in each of one half of the congressional districts of the state, and of the state as a whole, equal to eight percent of the votes cast in each of such districts respectively and in the state as a whole in the last preceding election in which presidential electors were chosen.

The *Nova Law Review* published the following step-by-step guide to amending Florida's Constitution by initiative. It was written by a former Florida Attorney General and Secretary of State:

> 1. Contact the Department of State's Division of Elections and request a free packet of information. You will receive a packet which includes the 1994 initiative petition information, a handbook for committees, all pertinent laws and rules, and necessary forms for filing as a political committee. [Also, this information is available on the Division's website.]
>
> 2. Sponsors must register as a political committee with the Division of Elections, before circulating a petition. The division will furnish the sponsors with all necessary information on how to form a committee and the duties of a committee. Committees are advised to begin work at least four years before the election in order to have sufficient time to gather the necessary signatures and deal with any legal challenges that might arise. However, some committees have made ballot position in less than two years.
>
> 3. Sponsors must submit the text of the proposed amendment to the Secretary of State for review. The Secretary approves the form of the petition, but not its legal sufficiency. The form will be checked for completeness, for the correct number of words in the ballot title (fifteen or less) and in the summary (seventy-five or less), and for correct

> size and format of the petition. Once approved, the petition can be circulated to obtain signatures of registered voters.
>
> 4. When at least ten percent of the required number of signatures from one-quarter of the congressional districts is collected, the Secretary of State shall submit the petition language to the Attorney General, who will then forward the petition to the Supreme Court of Florida for an advisory opinion on whether the text conforms to the requirements of article XI, section 3 of the Florida Constitution. The court will also determine if the ballot title and summary of the amendment comply with section 101.161 of the Florida Statutes.
>
> 5. Sponsors must deliver the petitions to the supervisors of elections in order for the signatures to be verified, a process that can take several weeks or longer if the supervisor's staff is extremely busy. Verification will usually take less time if signature cards are submitted as they are collected and the final group is submitted several months before the deadline. Once certified as having obtained the necessary number and distribution of signatures of registered voters, certification is sent to the Division of Elections by the supervisor of elections. The actual petitions are retained by the supervisor of elections. Any initiative which receives the required number of signatures no later than ninety-one days prior to the general election will appear on the ballot, unless successfully challenged in court.

Id. at 1512-13.

Notes and Questions to Consider:

1. What are the advantages and disadvantage to amending state constitutions by citizen initiatives. Consider this comment from FLORIDA MUNICIPAL LAW AND PRACTICE:

> From one point a view, this is the purest form of direct democracy in state lawmaking. From another point of view, this is the reason why state constitutions are so long and mundane. For example, thanks to a

> voter initiative, the Constitution of the State of Florida grants constitutional rights to pregnant pigs in Article X Section 21.

Patrick John McGinley, Florida Municipal Law and Practice § 1:4 (2017-2018 ed.).

2. Florida Municipal Law and Practice summarizes the voter initiative process as follows:

> Voter initiatives occur in Florida when the custodian of state records receives a petition containing a copy of the proposed revision or amendment, signed by a number of electors in each of one half of the congressional districts of the state, and of the state as a whole, equal to 8% of the votes cast in each of such districts respectively and in the state as a whole in the last preceding election in which presidential electors were chosen. These specific numbers and percentages are mandated by Article XI Section 3 of the Florida Constitution.

Id. Are these requirements unduly burdensome?

4. Constitutional Convention

One way of "amending a state's constitution is to do away with the existing constitution and start over. Like most states, Florida refers to this as the calling of a constitutional convention." Patrick John McGinley, Florida Municipal Law and Practice § 1:4 (2017-2018 ed.). The procedure may be summarized as follows:

> Article XI Section 3 of the Florida Constitution requires the following actions and deadlines. A Constitutional Convention convenes if Florida's voters file, with the custodian of the state records, a petition containing a declaration that a constitutional convention is desired, signed by a number of electors in each of one half of the congressional districts of the state, and of the state as a whole, equal to fifteen per cent of the votes cast in each such district respectively and in the state as a whole in the last preceding election of presidential electors. At the next general election held more than ninety days after the filing of such petition there shall be submitted to the electors of the state the question: "Shall a constitutional convention be held?" If a majority

> voting on the question votes in the affirmative, at the next succeeding general election there shall be elected from each representative district a member of a constitutional convention. On the twenty-first day following that election, the convention shall sit at the capital, elect officers, adopt rules of procedure, judge the election of its membership, and fix a time and place for its future meetings. Not later than ninety days before the next succeeding general election, the convention shall cause to be filed with the custodian of state records any revision of this constitution proposed by it.

Id. at § 1:4. The full text of the relevant section of Florida's Constitution provides:

SECTION 4. Constitutional convention.—

(a) The power to call a convention to consider a revision of the entire constitution is reserved to the people. It may be invoked by filing with the custodian of state records a petition, containing a declaration that a constitutional convention is desired, signed by a number of electors in each of one half of the congressional districts of the state, and of the state as a whole, equal to fifteen per cent of the votes cast in each such district respectively and in the state as a whole in the last preceding election of presidential electors.

(b) At the next general election held more than ninety days after the filing of such petition there shall be submitted to the electors of the state the question: "Shall a constitutional convention be held?" If a majority voting on the question votes in the affirmative, at the next succeeding general election there shall be elected from each representative district a member of a constitutional convention. On the twenty-first day following that election, the convention shall sit at the capital, elect officers, adopt rules of procedure, judge the election of its membership, and fix a time and place for its future meetings. Not later than ninety days before the next succeeding general election, the convention shall cause to be filed with the custodian of state records any revision of this constitution proposed by it.

5. Taxation and Budget Reform Commission

Article VII of Florida's Constitution creates a Taxation and Budget Reform Commission that is scheduled to convene once every twenty years to consider making proposals for amending Florida's Constitution. The operative language reads:

SECTION 6. Taxation and budget reform commission.—

(a) Beginning in 2007 and each twentieth year thereafter, there shall be established a taxation and budget reform commission composed of the following members:

(1) eleven members selected by the governor, none of whom shall be a member of the legislature at the time of appointment.

(2) seven members selected by the speaker of the house of representatives and seven members selected by the president of the senate, none of whom shall be a member of the legislature at the time of appointment.

(3) four non-voting ex officio members, all of whom shall be members of the legislature at the time of appointment. Two of these members, one of whom shall be a member of the minority party in the house of representatives, shall be selected by the speaker of the house of representatives, and two of these members, one of whom shall be a member of the minority party in the senate, shall be selected by the president of the senate.

(b) Vacancies in the membership of the commission shall be filled in the same manner as the original appointments.

(c) At its initial meeting, the members of the commission shall elect a member who is not a member of the legislature to serve as chair and the commission shall adopt its rules of procedure. Thereafter, the commission shall convene at the call of the chair. An affirmative vote of two thirds of the full commission shall be necessary for any revision of this constitution or any part of it to be proposed by the commission.

(d) The commission shall examine the state budgetary process, the revenue needs and expenditure processes of the state, the appropriateness of the tax structure of the state, and governmental productivity and efficiency; review policy as it relates to the ability of state and local government to tax and adequately fund governmental operations and capital facilities required to meet the state's needs during the next twenty year period; determine methods favored by the citizens of the state to fund the needs of the state, including alternative methods for raising sufficient revenues for the needs of the state; determine measures that could be instituted to effectively gather funds from existing tax sources; examine constitutional limitations on taxation and expenditures at the state and local level; and review the state's comprehensive planning, budgeting and needs assessment processes to determine whether the resulting information adequately supports a strategic decisionmaking process.

(e) The commission shall hold public hearings as it deems necessary to carry out its responsibilities under this section. The commission shall issue a report of the results of the review carried out, and propose to the legislature any recommended statutory changes related to the taxation or budgetary laws of the state. Not later than one hundred eighty days prior to the general election in the second year following the year in which the commission is established, the commission shall file with the custodian of state records its proposal, if any, of a revision of this constitution or any part of it dealing with taxation or the state budgetary process.

C. Voting on Proposed Amendments

Although proposals for amendments can arise using any of the five methods, proposals become amendments only from one source: the people. Ultimately, the decision as to whether the proposal will become an amendment to Florida's Constitution is a decision made directly by the Floridians who vote on that amendment. As Florida's Supreme Court acknowledged:

> A[] thing we should keep in mind is that we are dealing with a constitutional democracy in which sovereignty resides in the people. It is their Constitution that we are construing. They have a right to change, abrogate or modify it in any manner they see fit so long as they keep within the confines of the Federal Constitution.

Gray v. Golden, 89 So. 2d 785, 790 (Fla. 1956).

Article VI of Florida's Constitution contains two sections relevant to the vote of the people:

> *SECTION 5. Amendment or revision election.—*
>
> (a) A proposed amendment to or revision of this constitution, or any part of it, shall be submitted to the electors at the next general election held more than ninety days after the joint resolution or report of revision commission, constitutional convention or taxation and budget reform commission proposing it is filed with the custodian of state records, unless, pursuant to law enacted by the affirmative vote of three-fourths of the membership of each house of the legislature and limited to a single amendment or revision, it is submitted at an earlier special election held more than ninety days after such filing.
>
> (b) A proposed amendment or revision of this constitution, or any part of it, by initiative shall be submitted to the electors at the general election provided the initiative petition is filed with the custodian of state records no later than February 1 of the year in which the general election is held.
>
> (c) The legislature shall provide by general law, prior to the holding of an election pursuant to this section, for the provision of a statement to the public regarding the probable financial impact of any amendment proposed by initiative pursuant to section 3.
>
> (d) Once in the tenth week, and once in the sixth week immediately preceding the week in which the election is held, the proposed amendment or revision, with notice of the date of election at which it will be submitted to the electors, shall be published in one newspaper of general circulation in each county in which a newspaper is published.

(e) Unless otherwise specifically provided for elsewhere in this constitution, if the proposed amendment or revision is approved by vote of at least sixty percent of the electors voting on the measure, it shall be effective as an amendment to or revision of the constitution of the state on the first Tuesday after the first Monday in January following the election, or on such other date as may be specified in the amendment or revision.

. . .

SECTION 7. Tax or fee limitation.—Notwithstanding Article X, Section 12(d) of this constitution, no new State tax or fee shall be imposed on or after November 8, 1994 by any amendment to this constitution unless the proposed amendment is approved by not fewer than two-thirds of the voters voting in the election in which such proposed amendment is considered. For purposes of this section, the phrase "new State tax or fee" shall mean any tax or fee which would produce revenue subject to lump sum or other appropriation by the Legislature, either for the State general revenue fund or any trust fund, which tax or fee is not in effect on November 7, 1994 including without limitation such taxes and fees as are the subject of proposed constitutional amendments appearing on the ballot on November 8, 1994. This section shall apply to proposed constitutional amendments relating to State taxes or fees which appear on the November 8, 1994 ballot, or later ballots, and any such proposed amendment which fails to gain the two-thirds vote required hereby shall be null, void and without effect.

D. Judicial Review of Proposed Amendments and Ballot Summaries

Florida Statutes chapter 101 contains the enabling acts for the voting requirements in Article V Sections 5 and 7 of Florida's Constitution. These enabling acts contain various requirements for the amendments that appear on the ballot. The enabling acts state that the full text of the amendment does not appear. Instead, a ballot summary appears, and it is restricted to a maximum length. The summary is preceded by a ballot title, which also has a maximum length. The summary is followed by a question that the voter can answer with "yes" or "no." The question must be phrased so that a "yes" vote indicates approval of the proposal.

One means by which Florida's Supreme Court can review such ballots prior to election day is as follows. Article IV, Section 4 of Florida's Constitution provides that Florida's "attorney general shall, as directed by general law, request the opinion of the justices of the supreme court as to the validity of any initiative petition circulated pursuant to Section 3 of Article XI." Section 4 also provides that Florida's Supreme Court "[J]ustices shall, subject to their rules of procedure, permit interested persons to be heard on the questions presented and shall render their written opinion no later than April 1 of the year in which the initiative is to be submitted to the voters pursuant to Section 5 of Article XI."

A recent example of such judicial review is *Detzner v. Anstead*, 256 So. 3d 820 (Fla. 2018):

DETZNER

V.

ANSTEAD

Supreme Court of Florida, 2018

256 So. 3d 820

Secretary of State Ken Detzner seeks review of the judgment of the Circuit Court for the Second Judicial Circuit … which … ordered that ballot titles and summaries of three proposed amendments to the Florida Constitution ("Amendment 7," "Amendment 9," and "Amendment 11") be stricken from the November 2018 general election ballot. The First District Court of Appeal certified the order as presenting a question of great public importance requiring immediate resolution by this Court. We have jurisdiction. *See* art. V, § 3(b)(5), Fla. Const. As explained below, we reverse the judgment of the circuit court….

…[T]he circuit court was incorrect in finding any deficiency in the proposals or ballot summaries on the merits.

The circuit court found the ballot language of Amendments 7, 9, and

11 to be defective because each of those amendments bundled together separate and unrelated proposals. The court held that such bundling violates section 101.161(1), Florida Statutes, and potentially deprives voters of their First Amendment right to vote on independent proposals. We rejected similar arguments regarding "bundling" in *County of Volusia v. Detzner*, 253 So. 3d 507 (Fla. 2018), and reject the circuit court's contrary conclusions in this case. Unlike proposed amendments that originate through initiative petitions, amendments proposed by the CRC are not bound by the single-subject rule limiting amendments to one subject. *Charter Review Comm'n of Orange Cty. v. Scott*, 647 So. 2d 835, 836-37 (Fla. 1994). The CRC's proposed amendments, may, and often do, combine several subjects "because [the CRC's] process embodies adequate safeguards to protect against logrolling and deception." *Id.* at 837. CRC revisions containing bundled proposals have previously been placed on the ballot by the Secretary. Moreover, the Florida Constitution expressly authorizes bundling, as it gives the CRC authority to revise the entire constitution or any part of it. *See* art. XI, § 2(c), Fla. Const. The power to amend the whole constitution in one proposal necessarily includes the lesser power to amend parts of the constitution in one proposal....

The circuit court also addressed Appellees' First Amendment argument and determined that the bundling of proposals prevents voters from voting yes or no "without potentially being deprived of their First Amendment constitutional right to cast a meaningful vote on each independent and unrelated proposal." *Anstead*, No. 2018-CA-1925, slip op. at 5. However, neither Appellees nor the circuit court supply any analysis in support of the bald assertion of a potential constitutional violation. Appellees merely assert that they have a right to vote for a proposition without voting against an unrelated proposition, a novel theory with no apparent support in the law. Because Appellees have not demonstrated the violation of any First Amendment right, we conclude that the circuit court erred to the extent that it found that the bundling of amendments implicates the First Amendment.

Finally, the circuit court also concluded that Amendment 11's ballot language was defective because it would mislead voters by failing to inform them of the effect and consequences of their vote. We disagree with this conclusion as well. The summary accurately describes the effect of Amendment

11's approval—the removal of discriminatory language in the constitution regarding real property rights. The amendment would delete the state's alien land law, a short provision authorizing the Legislature to regulate or prohibit the ownership, inheritance, disposition, or possession of real property by aliens ineligible for citizenship as an exception to constitutional language providing that all "natural persons" have "inalienable rights" to "acquire, possess and protect property." The summary states that the amendment would "[r]emove[ ] discriminatory language related to real property rights." This is an accurate description of what the proposed amendment will do, consistent with the requirement that ballot language accurately represent the main legal effect and ramifications of a proposed amendment. *See Armstrong*, 773 So. 2d at 12; *Wadhams v. Bd. of Cty. Comm'rs*, 567 So. 2d 414, 417-18 (Fla. 1990). In other words, the summary clearly communicates what it is that voters are being asked to approve or reject, and Florida law does not require that it do more than that. *See Evans v. Firestone*, 457 So. 2d 1351, 1355 (Fla. 1984) (explaining that the ballot summary should tell the voter "the legal effect of the amendment, and no more"); *see also Askew v. Firestone*, 421 So. 2d 151, 155 (Fla. 1982) (stating that the ballot summary must "advise the voter sufficiently to enable him intelligently to cast his ballot"...)); *cf. Fla. Educ. Ass'n v. Fla. Dep't of State*, 48 So. 3d 694, 702 (Fla. 2010) (upholding proposed amendment and concluding that it was not misleading where the ballot summary did not disclose the amendment's specific financial impact on class size funding).

For the foregoing reasons, we hold that the circuit court erred in granting the petition for writ of quo warranto because the standard for obtaining relief was not met. We further hold the proposed amendments are not defective for bundling independent and unrelated measures. Finally, we hold the ballot language of Amendment 11 does not mislead voters with respect to the amendment's legal effect. Accordingly, we reverse the decision of the circuit court and order that Amendments 7, 9, and 11 appear on the ballot for the November 2018 general election. No motion for rehearing will be allowed, and the mandate shall issue immediately.

It is so ordered.

CANADY, C.J., and POLSTON, LABARGA, and LAWSON, JJ., concur.

PARIENTE, J., concurs in result with an opinion, in which LEWIS and QUINCE, JJ., concur.

PARIENTE, J., concurring in result.

Voters beware! When amending our Florida Constitution, voters should not be forced to vote "yes" on a proposal they disfavor in order to also vote "yes" on a proposal they support because of how the Constitution Revision Commission (CRC) has unilaterally decided to bundle multiple, independent and unrelated proposals.... I write separately to emphasize the obvious dangers of logrolling—combining popular and unpopular proposals into a single proposal—even by the CRC.

I also respectfully disagree that the process that occurred with this CRC provided "adequate safeguards to protect against logrolling." Majority op. at 823.... Logrolling occurs when proposals that are attractive to one group of voters are intentionally combined with proposals that may be unpopular to the same group of voters in order to secure approval of the unpopular proposal. *Advisory Op. to the Att'y Gen.—Save Our Everglades*, 636 So. 2d 1336, 1339 (Fla. 1994). Logrolling can also be used to mask a controversial or unpopular proposal because it is more difficult to accurately explain multiple, independent and unrelated proposals in a single ballot title and 75-word summary. *Advisory Op. to the Att'y Gen. re Right of Citizens to Choose Health Care Providers*, 705 So. 2d 563, 566 (Fla. 1998). For these reasons, I would conclude that the CRC improperly bundled multiple, independent and unrelated proposals.

The per curiam opinion's justification for allowing the CRC to employ this type of bundling is that the CRC's process embodies "adequate safeguards to protect against logrolling and deception." Majority op. at 823.... However, as CRC Commissioner Roberto Martinez, one of this Court's three appointees, explained, the safeguards envisioned by the per curiam opinion do not exist. First, the CRC's legal staff provided no guidance with respect to the bundling....

Second, the CRC's public hearings also provide no additional safeguards with respect to the bundling because the Style and Drafting Committee bundled the proposals after the CRC concluded its public hearings....

The more complex an amendment is and the more independent and unrelated the proposals are, the more difficult it will be for voters to ascertain its true purpose and effect on Election Day. Rather than being able to vote up or down on each individual proposal based on its merits, voters will be forced to weigh the costs and benefits of each group of proposals.

For example, the ballot summary for Amendment 7 states:

> *Grants mandatory payment of death benefits and waiver of certain educational expenses to qualifying survivors of certain first responders and military members who die performing official duties. Requires supermajority votes by university trustees and state university system board of governors to raise or impose all legislatively authorized fees if law requires approval by those bodies. Establishes existing state college system as constitutional entity; provides governance structure.*

This amendment bundles together (1) a proposal to require university boards of trustees and the university board of governors to approve any proposal or action to raise, impose, or authorize any fee by a designated minimum number of members; (2) a proposal to create a single state college system comprised of all public community and state colleges; and (3) a proposal to provide death benefits for survivors of first responders and military members. It would seem self-evident that death benefits for survivors of first responders and military members, however laudable, is completely unrelated to amendments dealing with the university system, which may be controversial.

Additionally, Amendment 9 bundles together a proposal to prohibit drilling for exploration or extraction of oil or natural gas in certain lands beneath all state waters with a proposal to prohibit the use of vapor-generating electronic devices in enclosed indoor workspaces—two independent and unrelated subjects about which voters may feel strongly. However, the bundled amendment requires voters to either agree with both proposals or reject both.

While both proposals deal in an attenuated manner with improving the environment, they do so in totally different and unrelated ways.

Bundling multiple, independent and unrelated proposals in this way makes the task of voting significantly more difficult for Florida's citizens, requiring them to decide—in addition to weighing the independent merits of each proposal—whether voting in favor of one proposal they approve of is worth also approving a proposal they do not favor. Voters should not be required to exercise their all-important authority to amend the constitution under these restrictions.

As I explained in relation to another CRC proposed amendment challenged before this Court:

> [T]he manner in which Revision 8 was bundled … added to the misleading nature of the amendment by explaining term limits and civic literacy before the ambiguous and cursory explanation of the change to the operation and establishment of free public schools…. [V]oters would have been presented with "two ... proposals that are popular and easily understood" before getting to the "vague but significant proposal" [about public schools]. [A]s a result of the bundling, voters who really wanted term limits and civic literacy would be forced "to give up control of [their] local schools."

Detzner v. League of Women Voters, 256 So. 3d 803 (Fla. 2018) (Pariente, J., concurring)….

The bottom line is that the ultimate authority to amend the constitution rests with the voters in this State. By bundling multiple, independent and unrelated proposals, combining "popular" amendments with controversial amendments on the ballot, the CRC makes it more difficult for voters to intelligently exercise their right to vote. Indeed, in some cases, bundling prohibits voters from exercising this right altogether because it forces them to reject proposals they would otherwise approve because they disapprove of another unrelated controversial proposal….

LEWIS and QUINCE, JJ., concur.

Notes and Questions to Consider:

1. The dissent laments the majority's decision because, in the dissent's opinion, the majority does not honor the fact that "the ultimate authority to amend the constitution rests with the voters in this State." But is the dissent correct? If the voters can overcome the burdens imposed in getting a proposed amendment into the hands of the Secretary of State, only to have that amendment removed from the ballot by Florida's Supreme Court, then is it not more accurate to say that Florida's Supreme Court is the ultimate authority?

2. Does Florida's Supreme Court have sufficient safeguards and rules to follow to assure that it is not arbitrary or subjective in its decision as to what proposals make the ballot?

Chapter Fifteen

Due Process of Law

A. Substantive and Procedural Due Process

Like the federal Constitution, the Constitution of the State of Florida provides for both substantive due process and procedural due process. "The Florida case law in these areas is generally similar to that developed by the federal courts in interpreting similar language of the U.S. Constitution." Talbot D'Alemberte, THE FLORIDA STATE CONSTITUTION 32 (Oxford University Press 2011). This excerpt from the 1991 decision of the Supreme Court of the State of Florida in *Department of Law Enforcement v. Real Property*, 588 So. 2d 957 (Fla. 1991) reminds us of what we learned in our studies of the U.S. Constitutional:

The Due Process Requirement

> The basic due process guarantee of the Florida Constitution provides that: "[n]o person shall be deprived of life, liberty or property without due process of law." Article I, section 9, Florida Constitution. Substantive due process under the Florida Constitution protects the full panoply of individual rights from unwarranted encroachment by the government. To ascertain whether the encroachment can be justified, courts have considered the propriety of the state's purpose, the nature of the party being subjected to state action, the substance of that individual's right being infringed upon, the nexus between the means chosen by the state and the goal it intended to achieve, whether less restrictive alternatives were available, and whether individuals are ultimately being treated in a fundamentally unfair manner in derogation of their substitute rights....
>
> Procedural due process serves as a vehicle to ensure fair treatment through the proper administration of justice where substantive rights are at issue. Procedural due process under the Florida Constitution:

> guarantees to every citizen the right to have that course of legal procedure which has been established in our judicial system for the protection and enforcement of private rights. It contemplates that the defendant shall be given fair notice . . . and afforded a real opportunity to be heard . . . before judgment is rendered against him.
>
> While the doctrines of substantive and procedural due process play distinct roles in the judicial process, they frequently overlap. Hence, many cases do not expressly stated the distinction between procedural and substitute of due process.

Id. at 980.

So as summarized above, substantive due process and procedural due process as provided by Florida's Constitution are the same rights as provided by the U.S. Constitution.

But with that truth having been acknowledged, perhaps the argument could be made that the right of due process of law under Florida's Constitution slightly exceeds that granted by the U.S. Constitution at least insofar as Florida Constitutional jurisprudence makes much ado about rejecting as unconstitutional any civil law of the Florida Legislature that establishes a factual presumption that may not be rebutted by contrary factual evidence. "An irrebuttable presumption removes an element that must be proved once the State has proved the predicate fact or facts giving rise to the presumption. The fact finder, however, is not free to reject the presumption. Thus, once it is presented, the defendant may not attempt to rebut the connection between the proven and the presumed facts." *Ibarrondo v. State*, 1 So. 3d 226, 233 (Fla. 5th DCA 2008).

B. Conclusive or Irrebuttable Presumptions

It is important to understand the difference between a presumption and an inference. As former Chief Judge and current Judge of Florida's Fifth District Court of Appeal, Thomas D. Sawaya explains:

> When dealing with presumptions in the law, the courts have a tendency to blur the distinctions between presumptions and inferences. Although the lines of demarcation between the two are not always clear, important

> differences do exist. An inference is a deduction of fact that the factfinder may logically draw from another group of facts that are found to exist from the evidence or are otherwise established in the proceedings. The most important difference between a presumption and an inference relates to how each is considered by the jury. When the basic fact giving rise to a presumption is established and there is no evidence to contradict the presumption, the presumed fact must be found to exist by the jury. When an inference is established, the jury may, in its discretion, completely disregard it even though there is no evidence to contradict or rebut it. Thus an inference is always permissive while a presumption is mandatory in that it requires the jury to find that the presumed fact follows the proven fact unless evidence is presented to contradict or rebut the existence of the presumed fact.
>
> The power to establish evidentiary presumptions is vested solely in the courts and the legislature. Thus, absent specific statutory or constitutional authority, an administrative agency may not promulgate rules or regulations that establish presumptions because they are not a branch of the judiciary or the legislature. In order for a statutory presumption to be valid, there must be a rational connection between the ultimate fact that is presumed and there must be a right to rebut it in a fair manner.

Thomas D. Sawaya, PERSONAL INJURY & WRONGFUL DEATH ACTIONS § 24:7 (Thomson Reuters 2015-2016 ed.).

Once a statute is properly identified as a presumption, it may be tested as to whether it is unconstitutional under the due process of law requirements in Florida's Constitution. "The test for the constitutionality of statutory presumptions is twofold. First, there must be a rational connection between the fact proved and the ultimate fact presumed …. Second, there must be a right to rebut in a fair manner." *Straughn v. K & K Land Management, Inc.,* 326 So. 2d 421, 424 (Fla. 1976).

When the second element is not met, then Florida case law refers to that presumption as either a "conclusive presumption" or an "irrebuttable presumption." Such a presumption is invalid as violating the right to due process of law as enshrined in the Constitution of the State of Florida, even when that presumption applies solely to civil actions.

"Presumptions in criminal proceedings are treated much differently than in civil proceedings primarily because of the constitutional guarantees that are afforded an individual accused of a crime that do not apply to litigants in civil proceedings." Thomas D. Sawaya, PERSONAL INJURY & WRONGFUL DEATH ACTIONS § 24:7 (2015-2016 ed.). Perhaps for this reason, conclusive or irrebuttable presumptions in **criminal** law statutes routinely are found to violate the federal Constitution. See *Tot v. United States*, 319 U.S. 463, 466 (1943); *United States v. Gainey*, 380 U.S. 63, 66 (1965). On rare occasions, conclusive or irrebuttable presumptions in **civil** law statutes can be found to violate the federal Constitution. See *Lindsley v. Natural Carbonic Gas Co.*, 220 U.S. 61 (1911); *Mobile, Jackson & Kansas City R. Co. v. Turnipseed*, 219 U.S. 35 (1910).

Where Florida Constitutional Law jurisprudence arguably expands upon that federal Constitutional right is in *always* finding conclusive or irrebuttable presumptions in ***civil*** law statutes to violate the due process rights enshrined in the Florida Constitution. As explained by Professor Charles W. Ehrhardt:

> Frequently judges and lawyers refer to a presumption as a conclusive or irrebuttable presumption. If facts X and Y are proven, fact A must be found to be true. Most of these so-called conclusive presumptions are not true presumptions but are rules of law. For example, when two persons die simultaneously, each is presumed by statute to have survived the other for the purpose of title and devolution of property.
>
> In Florida, it is frequently unconstitutional to legislatively create a true irrebuttable presumption. For example, a statutory presumption that the value of livestock killed by a railroad was the value of the animals as established in an affidavit by the owner or some other person acquainted with the stock was invalid. Although statutory language is sometimes used which apparently creates a conclusive presumption, it will pass muster if it is interpreted so that it can be rebutted in a fair manner.

> The [Florida Evidence] Code does not make any provision for conclusive presumptions since most are not valid in Florida. Although some rules of law are called conclusive presumptions from time to time, they are not properly included in a codification of the law of evidence since they are rules of substantive law in the particular area in which they exist.

Charles W. Ehrhardt, EHRHARDT'S FLORIDA EVIDENCE § 301.3 (Thomson Reuters 2015 ed.).

Regarding case law precedent striking civil law statutory presumptions as violating the Florida Constitution's due process clause, examples exist in the decisions of the Supreme Court of the State of Florida. *See, e.g.*, *Straughn v. K & K Land Management, Inc.,* 326 So. 2d 421 (Fla. 1976); *Bass v. General Development Corp.,* 374 So. 2d 479 (Fla. 1979). For our purposes, we turn first to this 1996 decision of the First District Court of Appeal of Florida in *Hall v. Recchi America, Inc.*, 671 So. 2d 197 (Fla. 1st DCA 1996), aff'd, 692 So. 2d 153 (Fla. 1997).

HALL

V.

RECCHI AMERICA INC.

First District Court of Appeal of Florida, 1996

671 So. 2d 197

Appellant, Astley Hall, appeals an order of the judge of compensation claims (JCC) denying his workers' compensation claim solely on the basis that he had a positive drug test shortly after his accident at the employer's drug-free workplace. The JCC based the denial of benefits upon the conclusive presumption of section 440.09(3), Florida Statutes (1991), that an injury in a drug-free workplace to an employee who has positive confirmation of a drug shall be presumed to have been occasioned primarily by the intoxication of the employee. The JCC did not find, however, that marijuana ingestion by appellant primarily caused the injury. Because section 440.09(3), Florida

Statutes (1991), establishes an irrebuttable or conclusive presumption which violates the constitutional right to due process, we reverse. . . .

On the morning of Thursday, June 13, 1991, three weeks after commencing work, the claimant and a co-worker were doing concrete form work. . . .[T]he claimant's co-worker tripped over a steel form work and jabbed the screed into the back of the claimant's head. . . . After his supervisor appeared on the scene, the claimant was taken to the Workers' Compensation Medical Center. The claimant provided a urine sample for drug testing within 30 minutes of arriving at the Workers' Compensation Medical Center. . . . The test result was two percent above the 100 nanogram per milliliter positive cut-off for marijuana metabolites. A confirmatory gas chromatography/mass spectrography analysis showed [this first test result was accurate]. . . . The claimant admitted he had smoked marijuana five days earlier . . . .Dr. Jay Poupko, who holds a Ph.D. in pharmacology and is a member of the University of Miami School of Medicine, . . . testified that the 78 nanograms per milliliter of inactive metabolite found in the claimant's urine was entirely consistent with the claimant having smoked marijuana five days before the accident as the claimant claimed. He explained that a person who smokes marijuana remains impaired for only four to six hours after ingestion of the drug. Based upon Dr. Poupko's testimony, the JCC found it probable that the claimant was not, at the time of the injury, impaired from marijuana ingestion.

In denying all benefits, the JCC concluded, "the Legislature intended to deny workers' compensation benefits to any employee who chooses to engage in drug use where their employer has implemented a drug-free workplace." In this appeal, the claimant maintains that the workers' compensation drug-free workplace statutes facially violate the Federal and Florida Constitutions by encouraging indiscriminate, suspicionless searches. He further argues that the irrebuttable presumption of causation provided in section 440.09(3), which results in forfeiture of workers' compensation benefits, violates due process and equal protection.

We hold that section 440.09(3), Florida Statutes (1991), establishes an irrebuttable or conclusive presumption which violates the constitutional right to due process. Section 440.09(3), provides, in pertinent part:

> No compensation shall be payable if the injury was occasioned primarily by the intoxication of the employee ... If there was at the time of the injury 0.10 percent or more by weight of alcohol in the employee's blood, or if the employee has a positive confirmation of a drug as defined in this act, it shall be presumed that the injury was occasioned primarily by the intoxication of, or by the influence of the drug upon, the employee. In the absence of a drug-free workplace program, this presumption may be rebutted by clear and convincing evidence that the intoxication or influence of the drug did not contribute to the injury ...

Under the plain language of this statute, the presumption that the injury was occasioned primarily by the intoxication or influence of drugs is rebuttable when there is no drug-free workplace program in place, and is irrebuttable when such a program has been properly instituted. A presumption is conclusive if a party is not given a reasonable opportunity to disprove either the predicate fact or the ultimate fact presumed. *City of Coral Gables v. Brasher,* 120 So. 2d 5, 9 (Fla. 1960); *Chandler v. Department of Health & Rehabilitative Servs.,* 593 So. 2d 1183 (Fla. 1st DCA 1992). In this instance it is the ultimate fact, that the injury was primarily occasioned by intoxication or the influence of drugs, that the claimant is being foreclosed from disproving.

The constitutionality of a conclusive presumption under the due process clause is measured by determining (1) whether the concern of the legislature was reasonably aroused by the possibility of an abuse which it legitimately desired to avoid; (2) whether there was a reasonable basis for a conclusion that the statute would protect against its occurrence; and (3) whether the expense and other difficulties of individual determinations justify the inherent imprecision of a conclusive presumption. *Markham v. Fogg,* 458 So. 2d 1122, 1125 (Fla. 1984); *Bass v. General Dev. Corp.,* 374 So. 2d 479, 484 (Fla. 1979).

As to the first prong of the due process test, the concern of the legislature regarding drug use in the workplace is reasonable. Section 440.101, Florida Statutes (1991), provides that "[i]t is the intent of the Legislature to promote drug-free workplaces in order that employers in the state be afforded the opportunity to maximize their levels of productivity, enhance their competitive positions in the marketplace, and reach their desired levels of success without experiencing the costs, delays, and tragedies associated with work-related accidents resulting from drug abuse by employees." As to the second prong of the due process test, there is a reasonable basis to conclude that the statute would deter drug use in the workplace. Section 440.101 provides that it is "the intent of the Legislature that drug abuse be discouraged and that employees who choose to engage in drug abuse face the risk of unemployment and the forfeiture of workers' compensation benefits."

The conclusive presumption contained in section 440.09(3) fails, however, to satisfy the third prong of the due process test. Because of the high potential for inaccuracy of the conclusive presumption set forth in section 440.09(3), and the feasibility of individualized determinations, fact finding on an individualized basis must be required to afford the employee due process. The conclusive presumption that "it shall be presumed that the injury was occasioned primarily by the intoxication of, or by the influence of the drug upon, the employee" if the employee has a positive confirmation of a drug as defined in section 440.102, may be erroneous. A positive confirmation of a drug at the time of the industrial injury does not conclusively establish that the industrial accident was causally related to the intoxication of, or the influence of the drug upon, the employee. The lack of a causal relationship between a positive drug test and the industrial accident is readily apparent in the present case because the uncontradicted testimony established that the industrial accident was not the fault of the claimant, but rather resulted from a co-worker tripping and jabbing him in the back of the head with a screed that he and the co-worker were carrying.

Additionally, the imprecision of the presumption of intoxication or influence of a drug upon the employee when urine testing is employed was established in the present case through the testimony of Dr. Poupko, a pharmacologist. Dr. Poupko testified that urine testing is inherently incapable of determining whether the active drug was present in an individual at the precise time of the injury. Rather, urine testing measures drug metabolites, which implies nothing about the presence of the active drug in the blood at the relevant time. In the case of marijuana, the drug used by the claimant, Dr. Poupko testified that urine testing measures an inactive metabolite, which has no effect on the nervous system. Dr. Poupko testified that the concentration of inactive metabolite found in the claimant's urine was entirely consistent with his having smoked marijuana five days before the industrial accident, as contended by the claimant. Dr. Poupko explained that an individual who smokes marijuana remains impaired for only four to six hours following ingestion of the marijuana. The JCC relied upon Dr. Poupko's testimony in concluding that it was probable that the claimant was *not* impaired from the ingestion of marijuana at the time of the industrial accident. Nevertheless, because section 440.09(3) creates an irrebuttable presumption that the industrial injury was occasioned primarily by the intoxication of, or by the influence of the drug upon, the employee when the employee has a positive confirmation of a drug as defined in section 440.102, the JCC concluded that the claimant's claim was not compensable. These findings and conclusions clearly support our conclusion that the presumption contained in section 440.09(3) must be rebuttable to survive due process analysis.

Because section 440.09(3) fails to allow rebuttal of the presumption that the industrial accident was causally related to the intoxication or influence of a drug upon the employee if the employer has a drug-free workplace program in effect, the conclusive presumption set forth in section 440.09(3) results in a denial of due process. The unconstitutionality of that one presumption, however, does not render all of the workers' compensation drug-free workplace provisions defective. In determining whether parts of a statute are severable from the remainder of the law, the court must look to the relationship between the unconstitutional provisions and the overall legislative intent. The court must then evaluate whether the remaining provisions of the statute continue to accomplish that intent. *See Eastern Air Lines, Inc. v. Department of Revenue,* 455 So. 2d 311, 317 (Fla. 1984), *appeal dismissed mem.,* 474 U.S. 892 (1985). The workers' compensation drug-free workplace statutes are designed to accomplish twin goals: discouraging drug abuse and maximizing industrial productivity by eliminating "the costs, delays, and tragedies associated with work-related accidents resulting from drug abuse by employees." § 440.101, Fla. Stat. (1991). The remaining provisions of this statute will serve those goals even if the irrebuttable presumption is excised. For example, an employer instituting a drug-free workplace must provide education and notice which should discourage drug abuse. It is also clear that requiring a causal nexus between the drug abuse and the work-related accident will do nothing to detract from the legislative goal of eliminating such accidents attributable to such cause. We therefore hold that section 440.09(3) is severable from the remainder of the law.

Accordingly, the order of the JCC is reversed and remanded for further proceedings using the constitutionally legitimate rebuttable presumption.

Kahn, Judge, concurring.

I agree completely with the analysis and conclusion reached by Judge Davis. I would also note that the result in this case is completely consistent with my understanding of Florida's workers' compensation system.

A basic premise of workers' compensation law in Florida, as in other places, has always been to release society of the expenses of injuries caused by industry in favor of a program under which industry would bear such costs. *Whitehead v. Keene Roofing Co.,* 43 So. 2d 464 (Fla. 1949). The purpose of our [Florida Workers' Compensation] Act is "to provide for employers a liability that is limited and determinative, and to employees a remedy that is both expeditious and independent of proof of fault." *Florida Erection Services, Inc. v. McDonald,* 395 So. 2d 203, 209 (Fla. 1st DCA 1981). The legislation now at hand abrogates these long-accepted understandings, at least in a class of cases, including Mr. Hall's. Despite the apparent fact that Hall's injury was caused completely by risks normally attendant to the construction industry, he would be left without any remedy under the Workers' Compensation Act. Thus, the limited statutory provision we invalidate today was itself at odds with a central premise of compensation law. Moreover, it directly contravenes the intent of our legislature recently set out in the 1993 revisions to the workers' compensation law: "[W]orkers' compensation cases shall be decided on their merits." § 440.015, Florida Statutes (1994 Supp.).

Notes and Questions to Consider:

1. It appears the Florida Legislature may have pursued two permissible goals with the legislation at issue in *Hall v. Recci America*: to provide an expeditious remedy for those injured at work, and to discourage drug use at the workplace. So why was the statutory presumption arising from a positive drug test a violation of the Constitution of the State of Florida?

2. What was the remedy for this violation of state constitutional law? When else would that remedy apply?

3. Did the court apply procedural due process, or substantive due process, in striking down the presumption at issue in *Hall v. Recci America*? Does it matter?

4. How could the statute at issue advanced the goal of a drug free workplace, and created consequences for a positive drug test showing controlled substances, without running afoul of the constitutional prohibition against conclusive or "irrebuttable" presumptions?

5. How persuasive is Judge Kahn's dissent? To what extent does Judge Kahn do a better job of applying the canons of construction in reaching his interpretation of the statute?

6. The issue of conclusive or "irrebuttable" presumptions as addressed in *Hall v. Recci America* was also one of the topics of the Florida's Supreme Court holding in *Castellanos v. Next Door Co.*, 192 So. 3d 431 (Fla. 2016) where the court struck down a mandatory fee schedule in a fee-shifting statute.

Chapter Sixteen

Access to Courts

A. Creating a Right to a Remedy

Article I, section 21, of the Constitution of the State of Florida provides in its Declaration of Rights that:

> The courts shall be open to every person for redress of any injury, and justice shall be administered without sale, denial or delay.

Like in our analysis of previous rights from Florida's Declaration of Rights, it could be said that this may be an example of Florida Constitutional Law jurisprudence expanding upon the rights embodied in the federal Constitution insofar as it affords Floridians rights in civil cases that the federal Constitution typically restricts in whole or in part to criminal cases. Of course, be it via a writ of habeas corpus or via the right to a prison law library, those facing punishment under a criminal statute have a right to access to the courts under the First, Fifth, and Fifteenth Amendments to the United States Constitution. See, e.g., *Lewis v. Casey*, 518 U.S. 343 (1996); *Bounds v. Smith*, 430 U.S. 817 (1977); *Johnson v. Avery*, 383 U.S. 483 (1969); *Ex parte Hull*, 312 U.S. 546 (1941).

Yet Article I Section 21 of Florida's Constitution enshrines a right to access to courts that is fully applicable to civil cases. As Professor D'Alemberte explains:

> [Article I] Section 21 [of Florida's Constitution] is a free-standing right-of-access-to-courts provision that has no explicitly stated companion in the federal Constitution. This section, derived from a provision in the Magna Carta, requires that courts be open and that justice be available without impediments.
>
> This right has been held to limit the state's legislative power to abolish rights to redress of grievances existing at common law when the constitution was adopted unless there is a reasonable alternative provided or

> unless there is some overpowering public necessity (*Kluger v. White*, 1973). This provision has been cited when the Florida Supreme Court has declared unconstitutional such legislation as the imposition of no-fault insurance for property loss without providing an alternative. Section 21 has been the basis for deciding that financial preconditions for maintaining actions or asserting defenses are invalid, except for the normal filing fee for a solvent litigant (*G.B.B. Investments v. Hinterkopf*, 1977). The access-to-courts language has not prevented changes in the statutes of limitations or the imposition of a demand for retraction prior to filing a libel action.

Talbot D'Alemberte, THE FLORIDA STATE CONSTITUTION 29 (Oxford University Press 2011).

Stated somewhat differently, Article I Section 21 of the Florida Constitution provides a limitation upon the Florida Legislature's power to abolish causes of action that existed prior to the enactment of the 1968 Constitution of the State of Florida. That limitation is that the Legislature must provide a "reasonable alternative" to the abolished cause of action unless there is an "overpowering public necessity" not to do so. Such is the holding of *Kluger v. White,* 281 So. 2d 1 (Fla. 1973), which despite its age remains the leading Florida opinion on the topic, and which has frequently appeared on the Florida Bar Exam.

KLUGER

V.

WHITE

Supreme Court of Florida, 1973

281 So. 2d 1

This is an appeal from an order of dismissal entered for defendants and against plaintiff in this property damage action by the Dade County Circuit Court, specifically passing upon the constitutionality of Fla. Stat. section 627.738. We have jurisdiction pursuant to Fla. Const., art. V, s 3(b)(1).

The cause of action arose from an automobile collision between a car owned by appellant, and driven by her son, and one owned by appellee, and driven by another person. The amended complaint filed by appellant alleged that the driver of appellee's car was negligent and had been formally charged with failure to yield the right of way; that there were no personal injuries; that there were damages to appellant's car to the extent of $774.95; and that the fair market value of the car was $250.00.

Appellant was insured with appellee, Manchester Insurance and Indemnity Company, but the policy did not provide for 'basic or full' property damage coverage. Appellant alleged that the Manchester agent had not specifically explained to her the possible results of failing to include property damage coverage.

Fla. Stat. section 627.738 provides, in effect, that the traditional right of action in tort for property damage arising from an automobile accident is abolished, and one must look to property damage with one's own insurer, unless the plaintiff is one who (1) has chosen not to purchase property damage insurance, and (2) has suffered property damage in excess of $550.00.

The appellant falls into that class of accident victims with no recourse against any person or insurer for loss caused by the fault of another, taking her allegations as true. She did not choose to purchase either 'full or basic coverage for accidental property damage' to her automobile, and her damages were the fair market value of her automobile since repair costs cannot be recovered where they exceed the fair market value of the automobile before the collision.

Appellant has raised numerous constitutional challenges to Fla. Stat. section 627.738. We find, as explained below, that Florida Statutes section 627.738 fails to comply with a reasonable interpretation of Fla. Const., art. I, sec. 21, which reads as follows:

> The courts shall be open to every person for redress of any injury, and justice shall be administered without sale, denial or delay.'

This Court has never before specifically spoken to the issue of whether or not the constitutional guarantee of a 'redress of any injury' (Fla. Const., art. I, sec. 21) bars the statutory abolition of an existing remedy without providing an alternative protection to the injured party.

Corpus Juris Secundum provides:

> A constitutional provision insuring a certain remedy for all injuries or wrongs does not command continuation of a specific statutory remedy. However, in a jurisdiction wherein the constitutional guaranty applies to the legislature as well as to the judiciary, . . . it has been held that the guaranty precludes the repeal of a statute allowing a remedy where the statute was in force at the time of the adoption of the Constitution. Furthermore, . . . the guaranty also prevents, in some jurisdictions, the total abolition of a common-law remedy.'

16A C.J.S. Constitutional Law sec. 710, pp. 1218-1219.

This Court has held that the Declaration of Rights of the Constitution of the State of Florida does apply to State government and to the Legislature. *Spafford v. Brevard County*, 92 Fla. 617, 110 So. 451 (1926). The right to a cause of action in tort for negligent causation of damage to an automobile in a collision was recognized by statute prior to the adoption of the 1968 Constitution of the State of Florida, as evidenced by the fact that Fla. Stat. section 627.738, the statute under attack, specifically exempts owners and drivers of automobiles from tort liability for such damages. In addition, the cause of action for damage to property by force or violence -- *trespass Vi et armis* -- was one of the earliest causes of action recognized at English Common Law.

It is essential, therefore, that this Court consider whether or not the Legislature is, in fact, empowered to abolish a common law and statutory right of action without providing an adequate alternative.

Upon careful consideration of the requirements of society, and the ever-evolving character of the law, we cannot adopt a complete prohibition against such legislative change. Nor can we adopt a view which would allow the Legislature to destroy a traditional and long-standing cause of action upon mere legislative whim, or when an alternative approach is available.

We hold, therefore, that where a right of access to the courts for redress for a particular injury has been provided by statutory law predating the adoption of the Declaration of Rights of the Constitution of the State of Florida, or where such right has become a part of the common law of the State . . . the Legislature is without power to abolish such a right without providing a reasonable alternative to protect the rights of the people of the State to redress for injuries, unless the Legislature can show an overpowering public necessity for the abolishment of such right, and no alternative method of meeting such public necessity can be shown.

It is urged that this Court has previously approved action by the Legislature which violated the rule which we have laid down. We disagree.

In *McMillan v. Nelson*, 149 Fla. 334, 5 So. 2d 867 (1942), this Court approved the so-called 'Guest Statute' which merely changed the degree of negligence necessary for a passenger in an automobile to maintain a tort action against the driver. It did not abolish the right to sue, and does not come under the rule which we have promulgated.

Workmen's compensation abolished the right to sue one's employer in tort for a job-related injury, but provided adequate, sufficient, and even preferable safeguards for an employee who is injured on the job, thus satisfying one of the exceptions to the rule against abolition of the right to redress for an injury.

The Legislature in 1945 enacted Fla. Stat. Chapter 771, which abolishes the rights of action to sue for damages for alienation of affections, criminal conversation, seduction or breach of promise. This Court upheld the validity of the chapter in *Rotwein v. Gersten*, 160 Fla. 736, 36 So. 2d 419 (1948). The Court opined:

> The causes of action proscribed by the act under review were a part of the common law and have long been a part of the law of the country. They have no doubt served a good purpose, but When they become an instrument of extortion and blackmail, the legislature has the power to, and may, limit or abolish them.' (Emphasis supplied)

Id. at 421.

Thus, in abolishing the right of action for alienation of affections, etc., the Legislature showed the public necessity required for the total abolition of a right to sue.

The Legislature has not presented such a case in relation to the abolition of the right to sue an automotive tortfeasor for property damage. Nor has alternative protection for the victim of the accident been provided, as evidenced by the facts here before the Court.

Had the Legislature chosen to require that appellant be insured against property damage loss -- as is, in effect, required by Fla. Stat. section 627.733 with respect to other possible damages -- the issues would be different. A reasonable alternative to an action in tort would have been provided and the issue would have been whether or not the requirement of insurance for all motorists was reasonable. That issue is not before us.

Retaining the right of action for damages over $550.00 (Fla. Stat. section 627.738(5)) does not correct the constitutional infirmity….

Accordingly, the decision of the trial court holding Fla. Stat. section 627.738 to be constitutional and denying appellant a cause of action against appellee is reversed, and the cause is remanded for further proceedings not inconsistent herewith.

It is so ordered.

B. Allowing for the Creation of an Alternative but Adequate Remedy

Article I, section 21 of the Constitution of the State of Florida provides a right of access to courts, but that right is not absolute. *Kluger v. White,* 281 So. 2d 1 (Fla. 1973) is the seminal Florida case interpreting Article I Section 21 of the Florida Constitution and its limitation upon the Florida Legislature's power to abolish causes of action that existed prior to the enactment of the 1968 Constitution of the State of Florida. Identical language does not appear in the federal Constitution. But many other U.S. state constitutions contain language similar to Florida's Article I Section 21.

Thirty-nine states have such "open courts" or "remedies" clauses in their state constitutions. David Schuman, *The Right to a Remedy*, 65 Temp. L. Rev. 1197, 1201 & n.25 (1992). A commentator notes the following:

> Historically, these provisions were intended as constitutional safeguards of an individual's right to a legal remedy. More than state equivalents of the federal Due Process Clause, these remedy provisions have resulted in a myriad of interpretations by state courts. Plaintiffs generally use state remedy provisions to challenge statutes restricting or eliminating previously established causes of action. In the last few decades, for example, injured parties have used state remedy provisions to challenge tort reform legislation, such as workers' compensation acts and statutory caps on medical malpractice damages. With continued tort reform, this diverse area of state constitutional law promises to generate further debate and attention.

Shannon M. Roesler, *The Kansas Remedy by Due Course of Law Provision: Defining A Right to A Remedy*, 47 U. Kan. L. Rev. 655 (1999).

Other commentators agree that a state constitution's "access to courts" clause "is often at the epicenter of the current battle between businesses and the plaintiffs' bar over legislative tort reform, as well as the historic power struggle between legislatures and courts." Jonathan M. Hoffman, *Questions Before Answers: The Ongoing Search to Understand the Origins of the Open Courts Clause*, 32 Rutgers L.J. 1005 (2001).

Indeed, here in Florida, the seemingly unceasing accusation that the Florida Workers' Compensation Law is unconstitutional is often a battle fought under Florida's Article I Section 21 "Access to Courts" Clause, as I once wrote in an earlier edition of my book FLORIDA WORKERS' COMPENSATION:

> Historically, state workers' compensation acts as a whole have been held to be constitutional, and Florida's Chapter 440 is no exception. Replacing or abolishing the common law right of action and all its uncertainties with the certainty of the receipt of compensation benefits, however limited, is the historical justification. Because the purpose of the

Florida Workers' Compensation Law is to provide efficient delivery of disability and medical benefits to the injured employee at a reasonable cost to the employer, the Florida Supreme Court ruled that the Workers' Compensation Law is not arbitrary or discriminatory and that its benefits are constitutionally adequate. Certain subsections of the Act, however, have been found unconstitutional. For example, the irrebuttable presumption that an employee of a drug free workplace's injury was caused by the drugs present in his drug test was stricken by Florida's Supreme Court as unconstitutional. As another example, Fla. Stat. §§ 440.34 and 440.105(3)(c), as applied to a claimant defending against a motion to tax costs filed against him by his employer after an unsuccessful workers' compensation claim, infringes upon the claimant's constitutional rights under the First Amendment of the Constitution to the extent that it prohibits him from retaining counsel to defend the motion to tax costs against him. . . .

The proper level of judicial scrutiny in workers' compensation cases involving equal protection and due process challenges is the rational basis test. Probably due to this low standard of review, equal protection challenges based on disparate benefits historically fail. . . . "Access to courts" arguments also historically fail. A statute does not violate "access to courts" if it passes the *Kluger* test. The 1973 decision of the Florida Supreme Court in *Kluger v. White* holds that "where a right of access to the courts for redress for a particular injury has been provided by statutory law predating the adoption of the Declaration of Rights of the Constitution of the State of Florida, or where such right has become a part of the common law of the State pursuant to Fla. Stat. § 2.01, the Legislature is without power to abolish such a right without providing a reasonable alternative to protect the rights of the people of the State to redress for injuries, unless the Legislature can show an overpowering public necessity for the abolishment of such right, and no alternative method of meeting such public necessity can be shown." As an example of the first situation, the 1973 *Kluger* court named the Florida's Workers' Compensation Law because it had "abolished the right to sue one's employer in tort for a job-related injury, but provided adequate, sufficient, and even preferable safeguards for an employee who is injured on the job, thus satisfying one of the exceptions to the rule against abolition of the right to redress for an injury." Despite Chapter 440 serving as one of the original examples in 1973 of a statute that does not violate the "access to courts," Chapter 440 continued to be challenged as an unconstitutional violation of "access to courts" throughout the subsequent four decades, but never with success. In one case, Florida's Supreme Court held that a reduction in benefits in the workers' compensation statute did not unconstitutionally deny access to the courts. Florida's First District Court of Appeal found no merit in the claimant's constitutional challenges to the specificity requirements of pleadings as codified at Fla. Stat. §§ 440.192(2)(i) and 440.45(3) on grounds of impediments to access to courts in violation of due process. The claimant had omitted information from his petition that identified the justification for the medical treatment he sought. In another case, the First District found Fla. Stat. § 440.15(3)(a) 3., which provides for impairment benefits to be paid weekly at a rate of 50% of the employee's average weekly temporary total disability benefit, does not violate the claimant's right of access to the courts, because the Act provides injured workers with full medical care and benefits for disability and permanent impairment regardless of fault without delay and uncertainty of tort litigation. As another example, the First District held in 2012 that Fla. Stat. section 440.15(1), providing that the duration of the payment of Permanent Total Disability benefits could not exceed five years if the accident occurred after a claimant reached the age of 70, did not violate a claimant's constitutional right of access to courts because Chapter 440 provided for a reasonable alternative for the redress of the claimant's injuries. Then in 2013, a violation of access to courts was found as applied to workers whose temporary total disability endured longer than the 104-week maximum by a three-judge panel of Florida's First District Court of Appeal, only for that decision to be withdrawn later that year with an *en banc* decision rejecting that constitutional argument. So ultimately, all accusations of "access to courts" violations by the Florida Workers' Compensation Law have been rejected.

Patrick John McGinley, FLORIDA WORKERS' COMPENSATION § 28:3 (Thomson Reuters 2015 ed.).

One might fairly conclude that it is a high burden to prove a law to be unconstitutional under Florida's Article I Section 21 "Access to Courts" Clause. Consider, for example, the Supreme Court of Florida's decision in *Anderson v. Gannett Co*., 994 So. 2d 1048 (Fla. 2008) and its rationale as to why the Florida Supreme Court's apparent abrogation of a previously-used common law cause of action did not violate Florida's right of Access to Courts:

ANDERSON

V.

GANNETT COMPANY

Supreme Court of Florida, 2008.

994 So. 2d 1048

This case is before the Court for review of the decision of the First District Court of Appeal in *Gannett Co. v. Anderson,* 947 So. 2d 1 (Fla. 1st DCA 2006). In its decision, the district court ruled upon the following question, which the court certified to be of great public importance:

> Is an action for invasion of privacy based on the false light theory governed by the two-year statute of limitations that applies to defamation claims or by the four-year statute that applies to unspecified tort claims?

Id. at 11. The First District concluded that the two-year statute of limitations for defamation applied to false light, reversed the judgment for the plaintiff on the false light cause of action, and certified conflict with *Heekin v. CBS Broadcasting, Inc.,* 789 So. 2d 355 (Fla. 2d DCA 2001), which held that false light invasion of privacy was governed by the four-year statute of limitations for unspecified torts. We have jurisdiction. *See* art. V, § 3(b)(4), Fla. Const.

Although the First District questioned the validity of false light, the certified question is predicated upon the existence of such a cause of action. At the time of its decision, the First District did not have benefit of our decision in Jews for Jesus v. Rapp, 997 So. 2d 1098 (Fla. 2008), in which we addressed the following question certified by the Fourth District:

> Does Florida recognize the tort of false light invasion of privacy, and if so, are the elements of the tort set forth in section 652E of Restatement (Second) of Torts?

Id. at 1100. We answered the question in the negative, concluding that Florida does not recognize the tort of false light "because the benefit of recognizing the tort, which only offers a distinct remedy in relatively few unique situations, is outweighed by the danger in unreasonably impeding constitutionally protected speech." *Id.* at 1114.

Because we declined to recognize the tort of false light, our analysis of the applicable statute of limitations in this case is unnecessary and moot. However, Anderson received a jury verdict based on false light and asserted in his amicus brief in *Rapp* that we cannot retroactively abolish the cause of action. *Cf. Warren v. State Farm Mut. Auto. Ins. Co.,* 899 So. 2d 1090, 1097 (Fla. 2005)(stating that a statute is unconstitutional if it abolishes a cause of action that was provided for at common law without providing a reasonable alternative, absent an "overpowering public necessity," quoting *Kluger v. White,* 281 So. 2d 1, 4 (Fla. 1973)); *Village of El Portal v. City of Miami Shores,* 362 So. 2d 275, 277 (Fla. 1978) (holding that retrospective statutes are unconstitutional "in those cases wherein *vested rights* are adversely affected or destroyed or when a new obligation or duty is created or imposed") (quoting *McCord v. Smith,* 43 So. 2d 704, 709 (Fla. 1950)). Although we acknowledged in *Rapp* that this Court had previously referred to false light as one of the four common law invasion of privacy torts, we also stated that "none of these cases actually involved a claim of false light and we have never discussed any of the competing policy concerns." *Rapp,* 997 So. 2d at 1103.

We therefore determined in *Rapp* that the issue of whether false light actually existed in Florida was one of first impression because the tort never existed at common law and any of our statements concerning false light in previous cases were dicta. Unlike cases where a previously recognized common law cause of action was abolished by the Legislature, see *Kluger* and its progeny, *Rapp* involved the refusal to recognize a cause of action that never existed at common law. Accordingly, our decision in *Rapp* did not retroactively abolish a cause of action for false light, but rather concluded that false light should not be recognized as a common law tort.

Because we decided false light was not a viable cause of action in this state, it is not necessary for us to resolve the issue of what would be the applicable statute of limitations and whether any exceptions would apply if the defamation and false light causes of action arose from the same set of facts. We thus decline to answer the certified question. We approve the result of the First District's decision in *Anderson,* but not the reasoning to the extent it recognized that a cause of action for false light existed. Because *Heekin* also assumed the existence of a cause of action and discussed the elements, we disapprove of the Second District's decision in *Heekin* on that basis.

It is so ordered.

C. Can an Amendment to a "Reasonable Alternative" Become a "Tipping Point" that Transforms a Previously "Reasonable Alternative" into an Unreasonable One?

In *Kluger v. White,* the Supreme Court of Florida cited Florida's Workers' Compensation Law as its example of an "adequate alternative" to the access to court. But in 2016, a new generation of Florida Supreme Court justices applied the holding of *Kluger v. White* to find an amendment to Florida's Workers' Compensation Law to be a violation of the access to courts under the Florida Constitution.

A potential cessation of payments of temporary "indemnity" (a type of wage-substitution benefits), combined with a potential delay on the start of permanent "indemnity," created a potential "gap" where injured workers were unpaid for a potentially indefinite period. This prompted the Florida Supreme Court to hold that "there must eventually come a 'tipping point,' where the diminution of benefits becomes so significant as to constitute a *de-*

nial of benefits—thus creating a constitutional violation." *Westphal v. City of St. Petersburg*, 194 So. 3d 311 (Fla. 2016). That opinion appears below.

Westphal

v.

City of St. Petersburg

Supreme Court of Florida, 2016

194 So. 3d 311

In this case, we consider the constitutionality of section 440.15(2)(a), Florida Statutes (2009)—part of the state's workers' compensation law—which cuts off disability benefits after 104 weeks to a worker who is totally disabled and incapable of working but who has not yet reached maximum medical improvement. We conclude that this portion of the worker's compensation statute is unconstitutional under article I, section 21, of the Florida Constitution, as a denial of the right of access to courts, because it deprives an injured worker of disability benefits under these circumstances for an indefinite amount of time—thereby creating a system of redress that no longer functions as a reasonable alternative to tort litigation.

. . .[W]e conclude that section 440.15(2)(a) of the workers' compensation law is plainly written and therefore does not permit this Court to resort to rules of statutory construction. *See Knowles v. Beverly Enters.-Fla., Inc.,* 898 So. 2d 1, 5 (Fla. 2004). Instead, we must give the statute its plain and obvious meaning, which provides that "[o]nce the employee reaches the maximum number of weeks allowed [104 weeks], or the employee reaches the date of maximum medical improvement, whichever occurs earlier, temporary disability benefits shall cease …".

… Applying the statute's plain meaning, we conclude that the 104–week limitation on temporary total disability benefits results in a statutory gap in benefits, in violation of the constitutional right of access to courts. . . .

… [F]or injured workers like Westphal who are not yet legally entitled to assert a claim for permanent total disability benefits at the conclusion of 104 weeks of temporary total disability benefits, the workers' compensation law lacks adequate and sufficient safeguards and cannot be said to continue functioning as a "system of compensation without contest" that stands as a reasonable alternative to tort litigation.... [T]he seminal case on the meaning of the Florida Constitution's access to courts provision, *Kluger v. White,* 281 So. 2d 1 (Fla. 1973), specifically discussed the test for determining the constitutionality of the workers' compensation statutory scheme under the access to courts provision, article I, section 21, of the Florida Constitution. The constitutional yardstick ... determining whether an access-to-courts violation occurred as a result of changes made to the workers' compensation statutory scheme, is whether the scheme continues to provide "adequate, sufficient, and even preferable safeguards for an employee who is injured on the job." *Kluger,* 281 So. 2d at 4.

Accordingly, we hold that the statute as written by the Legislature is unconstitutional....

I. FACTS AND PROCEDURAL HISTORY

In December 2009, Bradley Westphal, then a fifty-three-year-old firefighter in St. Petersburg, Florida, suffered a severe lower back injury caused by lifting heavy furniture in the course of fighting a fire. As a result of the lower back injury, Westphal experienced extreme pain and loss of feeling in his left leg below the knee and required multiple surgical procedures, including an eventual spinal fusion....

At the expiration of temporary total disability benefits, Westphal was still incapable of working or obtaining employment, based on the advice of his doctors and the vocational experts that examined him. In an attempt to replace his pre-injury wages of approximately $1,500 per week that he was losing because of his injuries, Westphal filed a petition for benefits, claiming either further temporary disability or permanent total disability pursuant to section 440.15(1), Florida Statutes (2009)....

The Judge of Compensation Claims (JCC) . . . denied Westphal's claim. . . . Thus, Westphal fell into the statutory gap—still totally disabled at the cessation of temporary total disability benefits, but not yet entitled to permanent total disability benefits. . . . He was, in essence, completely cut off from disability benefits for an indefinite amount of time, unless and until he could claim entitlement to permanent total disability benefits at some future date and, even then, without any ability to recover disability benefits for his time in the statutory gap.

II. ANALYSIS

. . . [W]e are forced to confront the constitutional issue of whether the statute, as applied to Westphal and other similarly situated severely injured workers, is unconstitutional. Concluding that the statute, as applied, violates the access to courts provision of the Florida Constitution, we conclude by considering the appropriate remedy.

A. Section 440.15, Florida Statutes

Section 440.15, Florida Statutes (2009), governs the payment of disability benefits to injured workers. As of the 1968 adoption of the Florida Constitution, . . . section 440.15(2) provided for the payment of temporary total disability benefits for a duration not to exceed 350 weeks. § 440.15(2), Fla. Stat. (1968)....

In 1990, the Legislature reduced the duration of temporary total disability benefits from 350 weeks to 260 weeks. § 440.15(2), Fla. Stat. (1990). Then, just four years later, and as part of an extensive statutory overhaul, the Legislature further reduced the duration of temporary total disability benefits from 260 weeks to 104 weeks. § 440.15(2)(a), Fla. Stat. (1994)....

As the First District recognized ... "[t]he statutory scheme in section 440.15 works seamlessly when the injured employee reaches [maximum medical improvement] prior to the expiration of the 104 weeks of temporary disability benefits." *Id.* But where "the employee is not at [maximum medical improvement] at the expiration of the 104 weeks, there is the potential for a 'gap' in disability benefits because [temporary total disability] benefits cease by operation of law after 104 weeks and entitlement to [permanent total disability] benefits is generally not ripe until the employee reaches [maximum medical improvement]." *Id.*

. . . It is clear from the statute that the Legislature intended to limit the duration of temporary total disability benefits to a maximum of 104 weeks. It is further clear that the Legislature intended to limit the class of individuals who are entitled to permanent total disability benefits to those with catastrophic injuries and those who are able to demonstrate a permanent inability to engage in even sedentary employment within a fifty-mile radius of their home. In other words, these provisions "create a gap in disability benefits for those injured workers who are totally disabled upon the expiration of temporary disability benefits but fail to prove prospectively that total disability will exist after the date of [maximum medical improvement]."

Because we hold that the statute is clear in creating a statutory gap in benefits, and thus not susceptible to the rules of statutory construction, we turn to Westphal's constitutional challenge—that the statute as plainly written results in a denial of access to courts.

B. Denial of Access to Courts

Article I, section 21, of the Florida Constitution, part of our state constitutional "Declaration of Rights" since 1968, guarantees every person access to the courts and ensures the administration of justice without denial or delay: "The courts shall be open to every person for redress of any injury, and *justice shall be administered without sale, denial or delay.*" Art. I, § 21, Fla. Const. (emphasis added). This important state constitutional right has been construed liberally in order to "guarantee broad accessibility to the courts for resolving disputes." . . .In *Kluger,* this Court explained the meaning of the access to courts provision and the necessary showing for demonstrating a constitutional violation based on access to courts:

> [W]here a right of access to the courts for redress for a particular injury has been provided by statutory law predating the adoption of the Declaration of Rights of the Constitution of the State of Florida, or where such right has become a part of the common law of the State pursuant to Fla. Stat. § 2.01, F.S.A., the Legislature is without power to abolish such a right without providing a reasonable alternative to protect the rights of the people of the State to redress for injuries, unless the Legislature can

> show an overpowering public necessity for the abolishment of such right, and no alternative method of meeting such public necessity can be shown.

281 So. 2d at 4.

Prior to 1968, when the access to courts provision was adopted, the Legislature had already abolished the common-law tort remedy for injured workers and enacted a workers' compensation law "as administrative legislation to be simple, expeditious, and inexpensive so that the injured employee, his family, or society generally, would be relieved of the economic stress resulting from work-connected injuries, and place the burden on the industry which caused the injury." *Lee Eng'g & Constr. Co. v. Fellows,* 209 So. 2d 454, 456 (Fla. 1968). The workers' compensation law "abolishes the right to sue one's employer and substitutes the right to receive benefits under the compensation scheme." *Sasso v. Ram Prop. Mgmt.,* 452 So. 2d 932, 933 (Fla. 1984).

Nevertheless, the fact that workers' compensation was created prior to 1968 as a non-judicial statutory scheme of no fault benefits intended to provide full medical care and wage-loss payments does not mean that changes to the workers' compensation law to reduce or eliminate benefits are immune from a constitutional attack based on access to courts. In fact, this Court in *Kluger* specifically discussed the alternative remedy of workers' compensation, explaining that "[w]orkmen's compensation abolished the right to sue one's employer in tort for a job-related injury, *but provided adequate, sufficient, and even preferable safeguards for an employee who is injured on the job,* thus satisfying one of the exceptions to the rule against abolition of the right to redress for an injury." *Kluger,* 281 So. 2d at 4 (emphasis added). In other words, as *Kluger* held, workers' compensation constitutes a "reasonable alternative" to tort litigation—and therefore does not violate the access to courts provision—so long as it provides adequate and sufficient safeguards for the injured employee. *Id.* . . .

Therefore, although this Court has rejected constitutional challenges to the workers' compensation law in the past, our precedent clearly establishes that, when confronted with a constitutional challenge based on access to courts, we must determine whether the law "remains a reasonable alternative to tort litigation." *Acton v. Fort Lauderdale Hosp.,* 440 So. 2d 1282, 1284 (Fla. 1983). . . .

The 104–week limitation on temporary total disability benefits and the statutory gap must therefore be viewed through the analytical paradigm of *Kluger,* asking whether the workers' compensation law continues to provide adequate and sufficient safeguards for the injured worker and thus constitutes a constitutional, reasonable alternative to tort litigation. *Kluger,* 281 So. 2d at 4. The "reasonable alternative" test is then the linchpin and measuring stick, and this Court has undoubtedly upheld as constitutional many limitations on workers' compensation benefits as benefits have progressively been reduced over the years and the statutory scheme changed to the detriment of the injured worker.

But, there must eventually come a "tipping point," where the diminution of benefits becomes so significant as to constitute a denial of benefits—thus creating a constitutional violation. [Emphasis added.] We accordingly must review what has occurred to the workers' compensation system … in order to determine whether we have now reached that constitutional "tipping point."

As applied to Westphal, the current workers' compensation statutory scheme does not just reduce the amount of benefits he would receive … but in fact completely cuts off his ability to receive any disability benefits at all. It does so even though there is no dispute that Westphal remained a severely injured and disabled firefighter under active treatment by doctors the City selected for him.… In other words, even though doctors chosen by the City had performed multiple surgical procedures culminating in a five-level spinal fusion, because those same doctors did not render an opinion that Westphal had reached [his Maximum Medical Improvement,] Westphal without disability benefits for an indefinite amount of time while he was still totally disabled and incapable of working.

In comparing the rights of a worker such as Westphal injured on the job today with those of a worker injured in 1968, the extent of the changes in the workers' compensation system is dramatic. A worker injured in 1968 was entitled to receive temporary total disability benefits for up to 350 weeks. *See* § 440.15(2), Fla. Stat. (1968). In 1990, the Legislature reduced the availability of temporary total disability benefits from 350 to 260 weeks—a 25.7% reduction of two years. *See* ch. 90–201, § 20, Laws of Fla. Then, in 1993, the Legislature again reduced the availability of temporary total disability benefits, this time from 260 weeks to 104 weeks—a 60% reduction .*See* ch. 93–415, § 20, Laws of Fla. This means that an injured worker such as Westphal is now eligible to receive only 104 weeks of temporary total disability benefits—a massive 70% reduction when compared to the temporary total disability benefits available in 1968.

It is uncontroverted that decreasing substantially the period of payments from 350 weeks to 104 weeks, standing alone, results in a dramatic reduction from almost seven years of disability benefits down to two years. Whereas almost seven years or even five years post-accident should be a reasonable period for an injured worker to achieve maximum medical improvement, clearly two years is not for the most severely injured of workers, like Westphal, who might be in need of multiple surgical interventions.

Currently, at the conclusion of the 104–week limit, temporary total disability benefits cease, regardless of the condition of the injured worker. Therefore, rather than receive "full medical care and wage-loss payments" for a continuing disability, as the workers' compensation law was intended, an injured worker's full medical care and wage-loss payments are eliminated after 104 weeks if the worker falls into the statutory gap. This is true even if the worker remains incapable of working for an indefinite period of time, based on the advice of the employer-selected doctors.

. . .We have now reached that point at which "the claimant's cause of action has been effectively eliminated"—the constitutional "tipping point" of which [prior case law precedent] forewarned. [emphasis added]

We conclude that the 104–week limitation on temporary total disability benefits, as applied to a worker like Westphal, who falls into the statutory gap at the conclusion of those benefits, does not provide a "reasonable alternative" to tort litigation. Under the current statute, workers such as Westphal are denied their constitutional right of access to the courts....

Thus, under the access to courts analysis articulated in *Kluger,* the only way to avoid a holding of unconstitutionality under these circumstances would be to demonstrate an overwhelming public necessity to justify the Legislature's elimination of temporary total disability benefits after 104 weeks for our most injured workers. *See Kluger,* 281 So. 2d at 4. We conclude that this showing has not been made. The statute is unconstitutional as applied....

III. CONCLUSION

For all the reasons explained in this opinion, we hold section 440.15(2)(a), Florida Statutes (2009), unconstitutional as applied to Westphal and all others similarly situated, as a denial of access to courts under article I, section 21, of the Florida Constitution. . . . Accordingly, we quash the First District's en banc decision in *Westphal* and remand this case to the First District for further proceedings consistent with this opinion.

LaBarga, Chief Justice, and Quince, and Perry, Justices, concur.

Justice Lewis concurs in result with an opinion....

Justice Canady, dissenting:

. . . I would reject Westphal's argument that the statutory limitation on the period of eligibility for temporary total disability benefits violates the right of access to courts provided for in article I, section 21 of the Florida Constitution.

In the foundational case of *Kluger v. White,* 281 So. 2d 1, 4 (Fla. 1973) (emphasis added), we set forth the test for determining whether an access-to-courts violation has occurred:

> [W]here a right of access to the courts for redress for a particular injury has been provided by statutory law predating the adoption of the Declaration of Rights of the [1968] Constitution of the State of Florida, or where such right has become a part of the common law of the State pursuant to [section 2.01, Florida Statutes], the Legislature is without power to *abolish such a right* without providing a reasonable alternative to protect the rights of the people of the State to redress for injuries, unless the Legislature can show an overpowering public necessity for the abolishment of such right, and no alternative method of meeting such public necessity can be shown.

The threshold question in evaluating an access-to-courts claim therefore is whether the Legislature has abolished a right of redress that was in existence when the access to courts provision was incorporated into the 1968 Constitution.

Here, the challenged statutory provision restructures an existing right of redress. It does not abolish that right. The State argues persuasively that "today's workers' compensation system allowed Westphal substantially greater temporary total disability benefits than any 1968 statutory right provided" and that "[t]he amendment limiting temporary total disability benefits to 104 weeks, therefore, did not 'abolish' any pre-existing right." State's Answer Brief at 14. Westphal does not dispute the State's assertion that the aggregate compensation paid to him for temporary total disability benefits substantially exceeded the aggregate compensation for such benefits that would have been available under the pre–1968 law, even when the pre–1968 benefits are adjusted for inflation. Instead, he contends that "[t]his case is about weeks, not about dollars." Petitioner's Reply Brief at 9. But the decision to substantially increase weekly compensation for temporary total disability and to reduce the number of weeks that such benefits are paid is a trade-off that is a matter of policy within the province of the Legislature. The Legislature—rather than this Court—has the institutional competence and authority to make such policy judgments.

We have long recognized that the Legislature should be afforded latitude in the structuring of remedies both outside the worker's compensation context … and within the workers compensation context…. We should do likewise here and reject Westphal's access-to-courts challenge.

Justice Polston Concurs.

Chapter Seventeen

Privacy

A. Different Origins: Federal versus State

The text of the U.S. Constitution does not enumerate a right of privacy. But of course, case law precedent of the Supreme Court of the United States found one. The World War I era case of *Meyer v. Nebraska*, 262 U.S. 390 (1923) overturned school teacher Robert T. Meyer's criminal conviction for teaching the German language to his students. In so doing, the Supreme Court of the United States cited the Fourteenth Amendment to the U.S. Constitution and held:

> While this court has not attempted to define with exactness the liberty thus guaranteed, the term has received much consideration and some of the included things have been definitely stated. Without doubt, it denotes not merely freedom from bodily restraint but also the right of the individual to contract, to engage in any of the common occupations of life, to acquire useful knowledge, to marry, establish a home and bring up children, to worship God according to the dictates of his own conscience, and generally to enjoy those privileges long recognized at common law as essential to the orderly pursuit of happiness by free men. . . .The established doctrine is that this liberty may not be interfered with, under the guise of protecting the public interest, by legislative action which is arbitrary or without reasonable relation to some purpose within the competency of the state to effect. Determination by the Legislature of what constitutes proper exercise of police power is not final or conclusive but is subject to supervision by the courts.

262 U.S. at 399.

This 1923 decision implies but does not find a right to privacy, and does so under the right of "substantive due process" arising from the Fourteenth Amendment to the U.S. Constitution. But contemporaneously with this opinion, justices of the U.S. Supreme Court were citing to parts of the U.S. Constitution other than the Fourteenth Amendment as the source of a right to privacy. For example, in the 1928 decision of *Olmstead v. United States*, 277 U.S. 438 (1928), Justice Brandeis, dissenting, wrote:

> The protection guaranteed by the amendments [to the U.S. Constitution] is much broader in scope. The makers of our Constitution undertook to secure conditions favorable to the pursuit of happiness. They recognized the significance of man's spiritual nature, of his feelings and of his intellect. They knew that only a part of the pain, pleasure and satisfactions of life are to be found in material things. They sought to protect Americans in their beliefs, their thoughts, their emotions and their sensations. They conferred, as against the government, the right to be let alone--the most comprehensive of rights and the right most valued by civilized men. To protect, that right, every unjustifiable intrusion by the government upon the privacy of the individual, whatever the means employed, must be deemed a violation of the Fourth Amendment. And the use, as evidence in a criminal proceeding, of facts ascertained by such intrusion must be deemed a violation of the Fifth.

277 U.S. at 478 (Brandeis, J., dissenting).

But as time progressed, the U.S. Supreme Court did not confine itself to the Fourth, Fifth, or Fifteenth Amendment as the alleged source of a federal constitutional right to privacy. In the 1960's, the implication of a right of privacy arising from the First Amendment to the U.S. Constitution "reemerged under the Warren Court to protect personal liberties of speech, association, religion, and privacy." Kathleen M. Sullivan, *Unconstitutional Conditions*, 102 Harv. L. Rev. 1417 (1989). From this era came the U.S. Supreme Court's decision regarding a right to privacy called *Griswold v. Connecticut*, 381 U.S. 479 (1965). Two members of the Connecticut branch of Planned Parenthood opened a clinic with the goal of getting themselves arrested and convicted of violating Connecticut's law against birth control. In overturning the conviction, the Supreme Court of the United States held:

> In *NAACP v. State of Alabama*, 357 U.S. 449, 462, 78 S.Ct. 1163, 1172, we protected the 'freedom to associate and privacy in one's asso-

ciations,' noting that freedom of association was a peripheral First Amendment right. Disclosure of membership lists of a constitutionally valid association, we held, was invalid 'as entailing the likelihood of a substantial restraint upon the exercise by petitioner's members of their right to freedom of association.' *Ibid.* In other words, the First Amendment has a penumbra where privacy is protected from governmental intrusion. . . .

The right of 'association,' like the right of belief (*West Virginia State Board of Education v. Barnette*, 319 U.S. 624, 63 S.Ct. 1178), is more than the right to attend a meeting; it includes the right to express one's attitudes or philosophies by membership in a group or by affiliation with it or by other lawful means. Association in that context is a form of expression of opinion; and while it is not expressly included in the First Amendment its existence is necessary in making the express guarantees fully meaningful.

The foregoing cases suggest that specific guarantees in the Bill of Rights have penumbras, formed by emanations from those guarantees that help give them life and substance. See *Poe v. Ullman*, 367 U.S. 497, 516-522, 81 S.Ct. 1752, 6 L.Ed.2d 989 (1961) (dissenting opinion). Various guarantees create zones of privacy. The right of association contained in the penumbra of the First Amendment is one, as we have seen. The Third Amendment in its prohibition against the quartering of soldiers 'in any house' in time of peace without the consent of the owner is another facet of that privacy. The Fourth Amendment explicitly affirms the 'right of the people to be secure in their persons, houses, papers, and effects, against unreasonable searches and seizures.' The Fifth Amendment in its Self-Incrimination Clause enables the citizen to create a zone of privacy which government may not force him to surrender to his detriment. The Ninth Amendment provides: 'The enumeration in the Constitution, of certain rights, shall not be construed to deny or disparage others retained by the people.'

The Fourth and Fifth Amendments were described in *Boyd v. United States*, 116 U.S. 616, 630, 6 S.Ct. 524, 532, 29 L.Ed. 746, as protection

> against all governmental invasions 'of the sanctity of a man's home and the privacies of life.' We recently referred in *Mapp v. Ohio*, 367 U.S. 643, 656, 81 S.Ct. 1684, 1692, 6 L.Ed.2d 1081, to the Fourth Amendment as creating a 'right to privacy, no less important than any other right carefully and particularly reserved to the people.' See Beaney, *The Constitutional Right to Privacy*, 1962 Sup.Ct.Rev. 212; Griswold, *The Right to be Let Alone*, 55 Nw.U.L.Rev. 216 (1960).
>
> We have had many controversies over these penumbral rights of 'privacy and repose.' . . . These cases bear witness that the right of privacy which presses for recognition here is a legitimate one.

381 U.S. at 483-84.

This quoted rationale from *Griswold v. Connecticut* shows that, unlike Meyer v. Nebraska which implied a right to privacy arising from the Fourteenth Amendment to the U.S. Constitution, *Griswold v. Connecticut* found a right to privacy in *penumbras, formed by emanations* from the First Amendment (per the majority opinion) and Ninth Amendment (per a concurring opinion) to the U.S. Constitution.

Yet by 1973, the majority of the justices of the Supreme Court of the United States cited the Fourteenth Amendment, and not the First Amendment, as the source of this unwritten Right to Privacy that U.S. Supreme Court case law developed out of the penumbras and emanations of the Bill of Rights of the U.S. Constitution. Specifically, in *Roe v. Wade*, 410 U.S. 113 (1973), the appellant argued to the Supreme Court of the United States:

> that the Texas statutes were unconstitutionally vague and that they abridged her right of personal privacy, protected by the First, Fourth, Fifth, Ninth, and Fourteenth Amendments. . . The principal thrust of appellant's attack on the Texas statutes is that they improperly invade a right, said to be possessed by the pregnant woman, to choose to terminate her pregnancy. Appellant would discover this right in the concept of personal 'liberty' embodied in the Fourteenth Amendment's Due Process Clause; or in personal marital, familial, and sexual privacy said to be protected by the Bill of Rights or its penumbras, see *Griswold v. Connecticut*, 381 U.S. 479 (1965);. . . or among those rights reserved to the

> people by the Ninth Amendment, *Griswold v. Connecticut*, 381 U.S. at 486 (Goldberg, J., concurring).

410 U.S. at 120 & 129. In response, the U.S. Supreme Court held:

> The Constitution [of the United States] does not explicitly mention any right of privacy. In a line of decisions, however, going back perhaps as far as [1891] . . . the Court has recognized that a right of personal privacy, or a guarantee of certain areas or zones of privacy, does exist under the Constitution. In varying contexts, the Court or individual Justices have, indeed, found at least the roots of that right in the First Amendment, . . . in the Fourth and Fifth Amendments, . . . in the penumbras of the Bill of Rights, *Griswold v. Connecticut*, 381 U.S., at 484-485; in the Ninth Amendment, *id.* at 486 (Goldberg, J., concurring); or in the concept of liberty guaranteed by the first section of the Fourteenth Amendment, see *Meyer v. Nebraska*, 262 U.S. 390, 399 (1923). These decisions make it clear that only personal rights that can be deemed 'fundamental' or 'implicit in the concept of ordered liberty,' . . . are included in this guarantee of personal privacy. They also make it clear that the right has some extension to activities relating to marriage, . . . procreation, . . . contraception, . . . family relationships, . . . and child rearing and education, ...
>
> This right of privacy, whether it be founded in the Fourteenth Amendment's concept of personal liberty and restrictions upon state action, as we feel it is, or, as the District Court determined, in the Ninth Amendment's reservation of rights to the people, is broad enough to encompass a woman's decision whether or not to terminate her pregnancy.

410 U.S. at 153. Thus, the Supreme Court of the United States both acknowledged that the U.S. "Constitution does not explicitly mention any right of privacy" but that nevertheless a federal right to privacy exists and is "founded in the Fourteenth Amendment's concept of personal liberty and restrictions upon state action." *Id.*

By comparison, the Constitution of the State of Florida contains language enumerating an explicit right to privacy. Specifically, Article I, Section 23, of Florida's Constitution states:

> Every natural person has the right to be let alone and free from governmental intrusion into the person's private life except as otherwise provided herein. This section shall not be construed to limit the public's right of access to public records and meetings as provided by law.

Professor D'Alemberte analyzes this section as it was enacted in 1980 and before it was amended in 1998:

> The final section of [Article I of the Florida Constitution] is the free-standing right of privacy contained in section 23. It guarantees the right of every natural person "to be let alone" except as otherwise provided in the constitution, and it specifically states that it "shall not be construed to limit the public's right of access to public records and meetings as provided by law." The language originated with the 1978 Constitution Revision Commission. When the wide-ranging proposals of that commission met defeat in 1978, this provision was taken up separately by the legislature in 1980 and passed by the electorate. Although it was opposed by most media organizations in the state on the grounds that it might interfere with the broad concepts of open government in Florida, this section actually protects open government principles by expressly negating privacy claims posed against open government (see *Forsberg v. Housing Authority of City of Miami Beach*, 1984).
>
> Questions about the right to be free from government inquiry into the realms of private conduct are separated from the right of the public to have access to information once collected. Thus, it is conceivable that a person would have a cause of action under this section to prevent the collection of private information by the government, but, once collected, the information would be available to the public.
>
> The Florida right of privacy provision has been used to prevent disclosure of the names of blood donors who were suspected of transmitting the AIDS virus (*South Florida Blood Service v. Rasmussen*, 1985), but the court declined to find the disclosure of medical records of an ap-

plicant to the bar to be violative of the privacy protection (*Florida Board of Bar Examiners, Re: Applicant*, 1983). The courts have also declined to find a privacy interest in limiting investigations by criminal authorities (*In re Getty*, 1983).

A special problem with section 23 concerns its relationship to section 12 and the subject of search and seizure. Section 12 [of the Florida Constitution] contains the curious language that appears to tie the judicial construction of the Florida Constitution to the decisions of the Fourth Amendment [to the federal Constitution] even though the federal Constitution does not have the same language as section 12. Moreover, since the federal Constitution has no explicit right to privacy, the state constitution is a bit more complex in this area. The [Florida Supreme C]ourt's approach to the problem is articulated in *Winfield v. Division of Pari-Mutuel Wagering, Department of Business Regulation* (1985), which held that although banking records were generally entitled to the protections of privacy under the Florida Constitution, the state investigation of pari-mutuel operations was a sufficiently compelling state interest to permit the subpoena of bank records and that the state's method of investigating (through the use of a subpoena) was the least intrusive method of investigation. This approach to the problem of privacy has allowed the state to employ "pen registers," which record the telephone number to which a telephone is connected but not the actual telephone conversation (*Shaktman v. State*, 1989).

The Supreme Court [of the State of Florida] has relied on the state right of privacy in upholding a person's right to refuse medical treatment against the contention that the parent of the minor children would be, in effect, abandoning those children by refusing the necessary treatment (*Public Health Trust v. Wons*, 1989).

The most significant case decided under this section is *In re T.W.* (1989), which declared unconstitutional a Florida statute requiring the consent of parents or a court order before a pregnant minor could have an abortion. The Florida Supreme Court held that the state's right of privacy protected the right of pregnant women, including minors, and that

> the right to choose an abortion was that of the woman, at least for the first trimester of her pregnancy.
>
> The decision in the abortion rights context, read with the decisions relating to the right to refuse medical treatment, indicates that the Florida courts will protect from state interference those highly personal decisions that go to the core of individual privacy.

Talbot D'Alemberte, THE FLORIDA STATE CONSTITUTION 39-40 (Oxford University Press 2011).

B. Enforcing Florida's Right of Privacy

Note that Professor D'Alemberte opines in 2011 that "it is conceivable that a person would have a cause of action under this section to prevent the collection of private information by the government." *Id.* at 39. Time has proven this opinion correct. As explained in FLORIDA ELEMENTS OF AN ACTION:

> Section 23, Article I of the Constitution of the State of Florida [and its] right to privacy... "embraces more privacy interests, and extends more protection to the individual in those interests, than does the federal Constitution." The elements of an action in Florida for a violation of this right to privacy are:
>
> (1) State action;
>
> and
>
> (2) A legitimate expectation of privacy;
>
> and
>
> (3) Infringement upon that expectation of privacy by the state action;
>
> and
>
> (4) Such infringement cannot be shown [by the government] to both:
>
> > (a) protect a compelling state interest and
> >
> > (b) achieve that protection in the least-intrusive manner possible.

> The right of privacy "was not intended to provide an absolute guarantee against all governmental intrusion into the private life of an individual." However, Florida's Supreme Court has held that "although there is no catalogue in our constitutional provision as to those matters encompassed by the term privacy, it seems apparent to us that personal finances are among those private matters kept secret by most people." . . .
>
> The Florida right to privacy has been found to protect the privacy rights of citizens from the unreasonable interception of communications. Similarly, "the constitutional right of privacy undoubtedly expresses a policy that compelled disclosure through discovery be limited to that which is necessary for a court to determine contested issues"....

Patrick John McGinley, FLORIDA ELEMENTS OF AN ACTION § 1502:1 (2017 ed.) (footnotes omitted).

C. Privacy as a Fundamental Right

Note

In the following case of *Winfield v Division of Pari-Mutual Wagering*, 477 So. 2d 544 (Fla. 1985) – a case that from time to time appears on the Florida Bar Exam – the Supreme Court of the State of Florida identified the right of privacy as a fundamental right entitled to heightened protection under Florida's Constitution.

WINFIELD

V.

DIVISION OF PARI-MUTUEL WAGERING,

DEPARTMENT OF BUSINESS REGULATION

Supreme Court of Florida, 1985

477 So. 2d 544

This cause is before us for review of two questions certified by the Fourth District Court of Appeal to be of great public importance.... We have jurisdiction. Art. V, § 3(b)(4), Fla. Const.

The Department of Business Regulation and the Division of Pari-Mutuel Wagering, respondents, issued subpoenas duces tecum to various banking institutions to obtain banking records of the accounts of Nigel Winfield and Malcolm Winfield, petitioners. Respondents gave no notice of the subpoenas to petitioners and asked the banks not to inform petitioners of the investigation.

Petitioners filed for declaratory and injunctive relief against the subpoenas duces tecum alleging that the subpoenas were facially invalid, that they violated petitioners' constitutional right to privacy and due process, and that maintenance of the records as public records in the respondent's files constituted an additional violation of their constitutional right to privacy. The circuit court found that respondents had probable cause to institute the investigation, and that it had acted within its authority. The court nevertheless granted petitioners relief on the grounds that their constitutional privacy rights would be violated if the subpoenaed records became public records in the hands of respondents pursuant to chapter 119, Florida Statutes. The court thereupon confirmed a previous interlocutory order in effect restraining respondents from inspecting, copying or using the records or the information contained in them, and directing that the records be maintained under court seal. Appeal was taken to the district court which ruled in favor of respondents and certified the following questions to this Court as being of great public importance:

I. Does article I, section 23 of the Florida Constitution prevent the Division of Pari-Mutuel Wagering from subpoenaing a Florida citizen's bank records without notice?

II. Does the subpoenaing of *all* of a citizen's bank records under the facts of this case constitute an impermissible and unbridled exercise of legislative power?

443 So. 2d at 457. We answer both questions in the negative and approve the decision of the district court.

The concept of privacy or right to be let alone is deeply rooted in our heritage and is founded upon historical notions and federal constitutional expressions of ordered liberty. Justice Brandeis, sometimes called the father of the idea of privacy, recognized this fundamental right of privacy when he wrote:

> The makers of our Constitution undertook to secure conditions favorable to the pursuit of happiness. They recognized the significance of man's spiritual nature, of his feelings and of his intellect.... They sought to protect Americans in their beliefs, their thoughts, their emotions and their sensations. They conferred, as against the Government, the right to be let alone-the most comprehensive of rights and the right most valued by civilized men.

Olmstead v. United States, 277 U.S. 438, 478 (1928) (Brandeis, J., dissenting).

The United States Supreme Court has fashioned a right of privacy which protects the decision-making or autonomy zone of privacy interests of the individual. The Court's decisions include matters concerning marriage, procreation, contraception, family relationships and child rearing, and education. *Roe v. Wade,* 410 U.S. 113, 152-53 (1973). Other privacy interests enunciated by the Court in *Nixon v. Administrator of General Services*, 433 U.S. 425 (1977), and *Whalen v. Roe*, 429 U.S. 589 (1976), involve one's interest in avoiding the public disclosure of personal matters. However, *Nixon, Whalen,* and those cases involving the autonomy zone of privacy are not directly applicable to the case at bar.

In formulating privacy interests, the Supreme Court has given much of the responsibility to the individual states. *Katz v. United States,*389 U.S. 347, 350-51, 88 S.Ct. 507, 511, 19 L.Ed.2d 576 (1967). Thus, on November 4, 1980, the voters of Florida approved article I, section 23, thereby adding a new privacy provision to the Florida Constitution. Article I, section 23 provides:

> *Right of privacy.* - Every natural person has the right to be let alone and free from governmental intrusion into his private life except as otherwise

provided herein. This section shall not be construed to limit the public's right of access to public records and meetings as provided by law.

Heretofore, we have not enunciated the appropriate standard of review in assessing a claim of unconstitutional governmental intrusion into one's privacy rights under article I, section 23. Since the privacy section as adopted contains no textual standard of review, it is important for us to identify an explicit standard to be applied in order to give proper force and effect to the amendment. The right of privacy is a fundamental right which we believe demands the compelling state interest standard. This test shifts the burden of proof to the state to justify an intrusion on privacy. The burden can be met by demonstrating that the challenged regulation serves a compelling state interest and accomplishes its goal using the least intrusive means.

Although we choose a strong standard to review a claim under article I, section 23, "this constitutional provision was not intended to provide an absolute guarantee against all governmental intrusion into the private life of an individual." *Florida Board of Bar Examiners Re: Applicant*, 443 So. 2d 71, 74 (Fla. 1983). The right of privacy does not confer a complete immunity from governmental regulation and will yield to compelling governmental interests.

However, before the right of privacy is attached and the delineated standard applied, a reasonable expectation of privacy must exist. Thus, implicit within the question of whether article I, section 23 of the Florida Constitution prevents the Division of Pari-Mutuel Wagering from subpoenaing a Florida citizen's bank records without notice, is the threshold question of whether the law recognizes an individual's legitimate expectation of privacy in financial institution records.

The United States Supreme Court addressed the threshold question in *United States v. Miller*, 425 U.S. 435 (1976), where it held that bank records, subpoenaed by the government without notice to a depositor under investigation, did not fall within a protected zone of privacy and were not "private papers" protected by the Fourth Amendment. *Id.* at 440. In reaching its conclusion, the Court further noted that there is no legitimate "expectation of privacy" in the contents of original checks and deposit slips in the possession of a bank. *Id.* at 442. However, as previously noted, the United States Supreme Court has also made it absolutely clear that the states, not the federal government, are responsible for the protection of personal privacy: "the protection of a person's general right to privacy-his right to be let alone by other people-is, like the protection of his property and of his very life, left largely to the law of the individual States." *Katz v. United States*, 389 U.S. 347, 350-51 (1967). This Court accepted that responsibility of protecting the privacy interests of Florida citizens when we stated that "the citizens of Florida, through their state constitution, may provide themselves with more protection from governmental intrusion than that afforded by the United States Constitution." *State v. Sarmiento,* 397 So. 2d 643, 645 (1981).

The citizens of Florida opted for more protection from governmental intrusion when they approved article I, section 23, of the Florida Constitution. This amendment is an independent, freestanding constitutional provision which declares the fundamental right to privacy. Article I, section 23, was intentionally phrased in strong terms. The drafters of the amendment rejected the use of the words "unreasonable" or "unwarranted" before the phrase "governmental intrusion" in order to make the privacy right as strong as possible. Since the people of this state exercised their prerogative and enacted an amendment to the Florida Constitution which expressly and succinctly provides for a strong right of privacy not found in the United States Constitution, it can only be concluded that the right is much broader in scope than that of the Federal Constitution.

This is a case of first impression in the state of Florida; therefore, it is within the discretion of this Court to decide the limitations and latitude afforded article I, section 23. We believe that the amendment should be interpreted in accordance with the intent of its drafters. Thus, we find that the law in the state of Florida recognizes an individual's legitimate expectation of privacy in financial institution records. However, we further find that the state's interest in conducting effective investigations in the pari-mutuel industry is a compelling state interest and that the least intrusive means was employed to achieve that interest. We also note that pre-disclosure notification by a bank to its customers should not be and is not mandated by article I, section 23. Thus, we hold that article I, section 23, of the Florida Constitution does not prevent the Division of Pari-Mutuel wagering from subpoenaing a Florida citizen's bank records without notice.

Concerning the second certified question, we believe that the information sought by the government was essential to its inquiry. To ensure that it has all of the information necessary for a complete investigation, the agency rather than the bank or depositor must calculate what is and what is not relevant. The subpoenas in question were reasonably calculated to obtain information relevant to a state investigation. There is nothing in the record to support a contrary finding. Thus, we hold that the subpoenaing of all of a citizen's bank records under the facts of this case does not constitute an impermissible and unbridled exercise of legislative power.

It is so ordered. . . .

D. Limits Upon Florida's Right of Privacy

The following case of *City of North Miami v. Kurtz*, 653 So. 2d 1025 (Fla. 1995) is an illustration of the limits that the Supreme Court of the State of Florida places upon the right of privacy enumerated in Florida's Constitution. After the full text of the case, we discuss a student case comment from the Florida Law Review criticizing the case.

CITY OF NORTH MIAMI

V.

KURTZ

Supreme Court of Florida, 1995.

653 So. 2d 1025

We have for review … the following question as one of great public importance:

Does Article I, Section 23 of the Florida Constitution Prohibit a Municipality from Requiring Job Applicants to Refrain from Using Tobacco or Tobacco Products for One Year Before Applying For, and As a Condition For Being Considered For Employment, Even Where the Use of To-

bacco Is Not Related to the Job Function in the Position Sought By the Applicant?

This question involves the issue of whether applicants seeking government employment have a reasonable expectation of privacy under article I, section 23, as to their smoking habits.... We have jurisdiction. Art. I, § 3(b)(4), Fla. Const. For the reasons expressed, we answer the certified question in the negative, finding that Florida's constitutional privacy provision does not afford Arlene Kurtz, the job applicant in this case, protection under the circumstances presented.

The record establishes the following unrefuted facts. To reduce costs and to increase productivity, the City of North Miami adopted an employment policy designed to reduce the number of employees who smoke tobacco. In accordance with that policy decision, the City issued Administrative Regulation 1–46, which requires all job applicants to sign an affidavit stating that they have not used tobacco or tobacco products for at least one year immediately preceding their application for employment. The intent of the regulation is to gradually reduce the number of smokers in the City's work force by means of natural attrition. Consequently, the regulation only applies to job applicants and does not affect current employees. Once an applicant has been hired, the applicant is free to start or resume smoking at any time. Evidence in the record, however, reflects that a high percentage of smokers who have adhered to the one year cessation requirement are unlikely to resume smoking.

Additional evidence submitted by the City indicates that each smoking employee costs the City as much as $4,611 per year in 1981 dollars over what it incurs for non-smoking employees. The City is a self-insurer and its taxpayers pay for 100% of its employees' medical expenses. In enacting the regulation, the City made a policy decision to reduce costs and increase productivity by eventually eliminating a substantial number of smokers from its work force. Evidence presented to the trial court indicated that the regulation would accomplish these goals.

The respondent in this case, Arlene Kurtz, applied for a clerk-typist position with the City. When she was interviewed for the position, she was informed of Regulation 1–46. She told the interviewer that she was a smoker and could not truthfully sign an affidavit to comply with the regulation. The interviewer then informed Kurtz that she would not be considered for employment until she was smoke-free for one year. Thereafter, Kurtz filed this action seeking to enjoin enforcement of the regulation and asking for a declaratory judgment finding the regulation to be unconstitutional.

In ruling on a motion for summary judgment, the trial judge recognized that Kurtz has a fundamental right of privacy under article I, section 23, of the Florida Constitution. The trial judge noted that Kurtz had presented the issue in the narrow context of whether she has a right to smoke in her own home. While he agreed that such a right existed, he concluded that the true issue to be decided was whether the City, as a governmental entity, could regulate smoking through employment. Because he found that there is no expectation of privacy in employment and that the regulation did not violate any provision of either the Florida or the federal constitutions, summary judgment was granted in favor of the City.

The Third District Court of Appeal reversed. The district court first determined that Kurtz' privacy rights are involved when the City requires her to refrain from smoking for a year prior to being considered to employment. The district court then found that, although the City does have an interest in saving taxpayers money by decreasing insurance costs and increasing productivity, such interest is insufficient to outweigh the intrusion into Kurtz' right of privacy and has no relevance to the performance of the duties involved with a clerk-typist. Consequently, the district court concluded that the regulation violated Kurtz's privacy rights under article I, section 23, of the Florida Constitution. We disagree.

Florida's constitutional privacy provision, which is contained in article I, section 23, provides as follows:

> *Right of privacy.*—Every natural person has the right to be let alone and free from governmental intrusion into his private life except as otherwise provided herein. This section shall not be construed to limit the public's right of access to public records and meetings as provided by law.

This right to privacy protects Florida's citizens from the government's uninvited observation of or interference in those areas that fall within the ambit of the zone of privacy afforded under this provision. *Shaktman v. State*, 553 So. 2d 148 (Fla. 1989). Unlike the implicit privacy right of the federal constitution, Florida's privacy provision is, in and of itself, a fundamental one that, once implicated, demands evaluation under a compelling state interest standard. *Winfield v. Division of Pari–Mutuel Wagering*, 477 So. 2d 544 (Fla. 1985). The federal privacy provision, on the other hand, extends only to such fundamental interests as marriage, procreation, contraception, family relationships, and the rearing and educating of children. *Carey v. Population Serv. Int'l*, 431 U.S. 678 (1977).

Although Florida's privacy right provides greater protection than the federal constitution, it was not intended to be a guarantee against all intrusion into the life of an individual. *Florida Bd. of Bar Examiners re Applicant*, 443 So. 2d 71 (Fla. 1983). First, the privacy provision applies only to government action, and the right provided under that provision is circumscribed and limited by the circumstances in which it is asserted. *Id.* Further, "[d]etermining 'whether an *individual* has a legitimate expectation of privacy in any given case must be made by considering all the circumstances, especially objective manifestations of that expectation.' " *Stall v. State*, 570 So. 2d 257, 260 (Fla. 1990) (alteration in original). Thus, to determine whether Kurtz, as a job applicant, is entitled to protection under article I, section 23, we must first determine whether a governmental entity is intruding into an aspect of Kurtz's life in which she as a "legitimate expectation of privacy." If we find in the affirmative, we must then look to whether a compelling interest exists to justify that intrusion and, if so, whether the least intrusive means is being used to accomplish the goal.

In this case, we find that the City's action does not intrude into an aspect of Kurtz' life in which she has a legitimate expectation of privacy. In today's society, smokers are constantly required to reveal whether they smoke. When individuals are seated in a restaurant, they are asked whether they want a table in a smoking or non-smoking section. When individuals rent hotel or motel rooms, they are asked if they smoke so that management may ensure that certain rooms remain free from the smell of smoke odors. Likewise, when individuals rent cars, they are asked if they smoke so that rental agencies can make proper accommodations to maintain vehicles for non-smokers. Further, employers generally provide smoke-free areas for non-smokers, and employees are often prohibited from smoking in certain areas. Given that individuals must reveal whether they smoke in almost every aspect of life in today's society, we conclude that individuals have no reasonable expectation of privacy in the disclosure of that information when applying for a government job and, consequently, that Florida's right of privacy is not implicated under these unique circumstances.

In reaching the conclusion that the right to privacy is not implicated in this case, however, we emphasize that our holding is limited to the narrow issue presented. Notably, we are not addressing the issue of whether an applicant, once hired, could be compelled by a government agency to stop smoking. Equally as important, neither are we holding today that a governmental entity can ask any type of information it chooses of prospective job applicants.

Having determined that Kurtz has no legitimate expectation of privacy in revealing that she is a smoker under the Florida constitution, we turn now to her claim that the regulation violates her rights under the federal constitution. As noted, the federal constitution's implicit privacy provision extends only to such fundamental interests as marriage, procreation, contraception, family relationships, and the rearing and educating of children. *Carey.* Clearly, the "right to smoke" is not included within the penumbra of fundamental rights protected under that provision. *Grusendorf v. City of Oklahoma City*, 816 F.2d 539 (10th Cir.1987) (the act of smoking a cigarette does not rise to the level of a fundamental right). Moreover, even if we were to find that some protected interest under the federal constitution were implicated so as to require a rational basis for the regulation we would still find the regulation to be constitutional. *Kelley v. Johnson*, 425 U.S. 238 (1976) (when assuming a liberty interest exists in an employment regulation, regulation must be reviewed under a rational basis test). As acknowledged by the district court, the City has a legitimate interest in attempting to reduce health insurance costs and to increase productivity. On these facts, the City's policy cannot be deemed so irrational that it may be branded arbitrary. *Kelley.* In fact, under the special circumstances supported by the record in this case, we would find that the City has established a compelling interest to support implementation of the regulation. As previously indicated, the record reflects that each smoking employee costs the City as much as $4,611 per year in 1981 dollars over what it incurs for non-smoking employees; that, of smokers who have adhered to the one year cessation requirement, a high percentage are unlikely to resume smoking; and that the City is a self-insurer who pays 100% of its employees' medical expenses. We find that the elimination of these costs, when considered in combination with the other special circumstances of this case, validates a compelling interest in the City's policy of gradually eliminating smokers from its work force. We also find that the City is using the least intrusive means in accomplishing this compelling interest because the regulation does not prevent current employees from smoking, it does not affect the present health care benefits of employees, and it gradually reduces the number of smokers through attrition. Thus, we find the regulation to be constitutional under both the federal and Florida constitutions.

For the reasons expressed, we answer the question in the negative, finding that Florida's constitutional privacy provision does not afford the applicant, Arlene Kurtz, protection because she has no reasonable expectation of privacy under the circumstances of this case. Accordingly, we quash the district court's decision, and we remand this case with directions that the district court of appeal affirm the trial court judgment.

It is so ordered.

Justice Kogan, dissenting:

As the majority itself notes, job applicants are free to return to tobacco use once hired. I believe this concession reveals the anti-smoking policy to be rather more of a speculative pretense than a rational governmental policy. Therefore, I would find it unconstitutional under the right of due process. See *Department of Law Enforcement v. Real Property*, 588 So. 2d 957 (Fla. 1991).

The privacy issue is more troublesome, to my mind. There is a "slippery-slope" problem here because, if governmental employers can inquire too extensively into off-job-site behavior, a point eventually will be reached at which the right of privacy under article I, section 23 clearly will be breached. An obvious example would be an inquiry into the lawful sexual behavior of job applicants in an effort to identify those with the "most desirable" lifestyles. Such an effort easily could become the pretext for a constitutional violation. The time has not yet fully passed, for example, when women job applicants have been questioned about their plans for procreation in an effort to eliminate those who may be absent on family leave. I cannot conceive that such an act is anything other than a violation of the right of privacy when done by a governmental unit.

Health-based concerns like those expressed by the City also present a definite slippery slope to the courts. The time is fast approaching, for example, when human beings can be genetically tested so thoroughly that susceptibility to particular diseases can be identified years in advance. To my mind, any governmental effort to identify those who might eventually suffer from cancer or heart disease, for instance, itself is a violation of bodily integrity guaranteed by article I, section 23. Moreover, I cannot help but note that any such effort comes perilously close to the discredited practice of eugenics.

The use of tobacco products is more troubling, however. While legal, tobacco use nevertheless is an activity increasingly regulated by the law. If the federal government, for instance, chose to regulate tobacco as a controlled substance, I have no trouble saying that this act alone does not undermine anyone's privacy right. However, regulation is not the issue here because tobacco use today remains legal. The sole question is whether the government may inquire into off-job-site behavior that is legal, however unhealthy it might be. In light of the inherently poor fit between the governmental objective and the ends actually achieved, I am more inclined to agree with the district court that the right of privacy has been violated here. I might reach a different result if the objective were better served by the means chosen.

Notes and Questions to Consider:

1. To what extent does *City of North Miami v. Kurtz* acknowledge a greater right to privacy than found under the federal constitution?

2. If the Supreme Court of the United States issued a new decision, disagreeing with its own prior precedent, and finding that there never was a right to privacy under the federal Constitution, then would a right to privacy still exist in Florida? If so, to what extent would its existence change?

3. In a Florida Law Review comment written by Joseph Beatty that is titled IS THE EXPECTATION OF PRIVACY UNDER THE FLORIDA CONSTITUTION BROADER IN SCOPE THAN IT IS UNDER THE FEDERAL CONSTITUTION? *CITY OF NORTH MIAMI V. KURTZ*, 653 SO. 2D 1025 (FLA. 1995), 47 Fla. L. Rev. 287 (April 1995), the author opines:

> After *Kurtz*, however, it is apparent that the state constitutional right of privacy in Florida extends protection no greater in scope than the minimum federal guarantee. Even if the Florida Constitution had contained no express right of privacy, the Florida Supreme Court could not have narrowed any further the scope of the privacy protection extended to Floridians.

Do you agree with this opinion? If so, how do you explain the right to financial privacy found under Florida's Constitution in *Winfield v. Div. of Pari-Mutuel Wagering*, 477 So. 2d 544 (Fla. 1983) but not yet found under the U.S. Constitution?

www.ingramcontent.com/pod-product-compliance
Lightning Source LLC
Chambersburg PA
CBHW060752300126
38837CB00005B/328
* 9 7 8 1 5 1 3 6 5 9 0 8 4 *